DECKER'S

PATTERNS OF
EXPOSITION 15

DECKER'S

PATTERNS OF
EXPOSITION 15

Randall E. Decker

Robert A. Schwegler
University of Rhode Island

 LONGMAN

An imprint of Addison Wesley Longman, Inc.

New York • Reading, Massachusetts • Menlo Park, California • Harlow, England
Don Mills, Ontario • Sydney • Mexico City • Madrid • Amsterdam

Executive Editor: Anne Elizabeth Smith
Developmental Editor: Lynn Walterick
Supplements Editor: Donna Campion
Text Design and Project Management: Interactive Composition Corporation
Cover Designer: Mary McDonnell
Cover Illustration: Warren Linn Copyright
Art Studio: Interactive Composition Corporation
Full-Service Production Manager: Eric Jorgensen
Manufacturing Manager: Hilda Koparanian
Electronic Page Makeup: Interactive Composition Corporation
Printer and Binder: RR Donnelley & Sons Company
Cover Printer: Coral Graphic Services, Inc.

Library of Congress Cataloging-in-Publication Data

Decker's patterns of exposition 15 / [edited by] Randall E. Decker,
    Robert A Schwegler.
        p.   cm.
    Includes bibliographical references.
    ISBN 0–321–01218–6 (pb)
    1. College readers. 2. Exposition (Rhetoric) 3. English language—
Rhetoric. I. Decker, Randall E. II. Schwegler, Robert A.
PE1417.P395   1997   97-2028
                                                          CIP

ISBN 0–321–01218–6

345678910—DOH—009998

Contents

Thematic Contents /xv

Essay Pairs /xix

To the Instructor /xxiii

Acknowledgments /xxvii

1   Ways of Writing /1

2   Becoming a Critical Reader /43

Brent Staples, *Just Walk on By* /59

3   Illustrating Ideas by Use of *Example* /67

Sample Paragraph: Lowell Ponte, "What's Wrong with our Weather"

Andy Rooney, *In and of Ourselves We Trust* /71
This columnist decides that stopping for red lights is part of a contract Americans have with each other—and we trust each other to honor the contract.

William F. Buckley, Jr., *Why Don't We Complain* /75
The dean of conservative writers believes that we've become so numb to mistakes and injustices that we no longer have the spunk to complain about anything and that this apathy could have grave consequences.

Barbara Ehrenreich, *What I've Learned from Men* /83
Acting like a man means speaking up for your rights, says
this feminist, and it is a way of behaving that women can
learn from men. As an example, she tells of a time when
she acted in a manner that was too ladylike.

Issues and Ideas: **Discovering and Constructing Identities**

Antonya Nelson, *Fear of Flying* /90
When the tornado hit, it crushed the family station wagon
and terrified the occupants. For some of the family members, the event is still important.

Mary Karr, *Dysfunctional Nation* /94
Don't think everyone else's family life is calmer than the
chaos in your home, warns this writer. On a book tour she
met people who overcame family backgrounds even more
dysfunctional than her own.

Alan Buczynski, *Iron Bonding* /98
Do men share feelings? Of course, says this ironworker,
but they do it through stories and other indirect tactics.

4 Analyzing a Subject by *Classification* /103

Sample Paragraph: "Talking 'Bout Their Generation"

Judith Viorst, *What, Me? Showing Off?* /108
Though we may be reluctant to admit it, we all show off,
and we do it in many different ways.

Judith Stone, *Personal Beast* /116
Looking for a pet? Why settle for a dog or cat when you
can have a pot-bellied pig, a llama, or a ferret?

Issues and Ideas: **Images of Ourselves and Others**

Renee Tajima, *Lotus Blossoms Don't Bleed: Images of Asian
American Women* /126
The Asian American women in Hollywood movies do not
bear much resemblance to real people. And the roles they
play are sometimes absurd and insulting.

Brenda Peterson, *Life Is a Musical* /136
Feeling down? You might want to follow this writer's
lead by creating tapes of music that help shut out "the
noisy yak and call of the outside world."

5 Explaining by means of *Comparison and Contrast* /145

Sample Paragraph: Robert Jastrow, *The Enchanted Loom*

Mark Twain, *Two Ways of Seeing a River* /150
What happens when you start looking at a thing of
beauty in terms of its use?

Bruce Catton, *Grant and Lee: A Study in Contrasts* /154
A famous historian identifies these two great Civil War
generals as the embodiments of the passing and rising
orders.

Phillip Lopate, *A Nonsmoker with a Smoker* /160
Many things pass through the mind of the nonsmoking
member of a couple: anger, regret, concern, and even
some surprising fantasies.

Issues and Ideas: **Gender and Other Differences**

Scott Russell Sanders, *The Men We Carry in Our Minds* /167
Memories of men whose lives were hard and short makes
it hard for this author to understand why women might
envy men.

Marianna De Marco Torgovnick, *On Being White, Female, and Born in Bensonhurst* /173
The differences within the neighborhood serve to unite;
differences with other neighborhoods and neighbors often
serve to divide.

Alice Walker, *Am I Blue?* /188
This well-known author entertains the possibility that we
are not as different from animals as we think, and she
looks at the way a horse named Blue displayed feelings
we are accustomed to thinking of as particularly "human."

6   Using *Analogy* as an Expository Device /197

Sample Paragraph: James Trefil, *The Dark Side of the Universe*

Loren C. Eiseley, *The Brown Wasps* /201
>In a reflective mood, this distinguished anthropologist-philosopher-author makes an analogical comparison between homeless old men in a railroad station and brown wasps waiting to die, still clinging to the old abandoned nest.

Patricia Raybon, *Letting in Light* /210
>Washing windows may seem an insignificant task for an educated person, but this journalist argues that the work helps us understand ourselves and lets light into our spirits.

Issues and Ideas: **Discovering Patterns in Behavior and Relationships**

Tom Wolfe, *O Rotten Gotham—Sliding Down into the Behavioral Sink* /216
>Our leading New Journalist says that New York City drives people crazy—and you can observe the same effects of overcrowding in a jammed cage of rats.

Barbara Kingsolver, *High Tide in Tucson* /225
>When a hermit crab brought home to Tucson starts obeying the tidal patterns of a far-away ocean, the author decides that it is time to reflect how far away she has moved from her original home.

7   Explaining through *Process Analysis* /241

Sample Paragraph: Ira Flatow, "Storm Surge"

Joe Buhler and Ron Graham, *Give Juggling a Hand!* /245
>It's not as hard to become a juggler as you might think, and juggling is certainly a lot of fun.

Ann Faraday, *Unmasking Your Dream Images* /250
>Many of us would like to know what our dreams mean. This author describes one way to interpret them and says that we are the people best equipped to understand our own dreams.

Mike Rose, *Writing Around Rules* /257
Speaking directly to students, this writer and teacher of writing talks about rules that can make writing difficult and then offers ways to work around them.

Issues and Ideas: **Advertising and Appearances—Shaping Realities**

James B. Twitchell, *We Build Excitement* /268
You already live in the world advertising created. Here's how it works.

Jessica Mitford, *To Dispel Fears of Live Burial* /278
A contemporary muckraker parts "the formaldehyde curtain" for a hair-raising look into an undertaker's parlor.

Jean E. Kilbourne, *Beauty . . . And the Beast of Advertising* /286
Advertising images bombard us every day. How do we respond to them?

8 Analyzing *Cause-and-Effect* Relationships /293

Sample Paragraph: Nelson George, *The Death of Rhythm and Blues*

Susan Perry and Jim Dawson, *What's Your Best Time of Day?* /298
When is the best time to study for an exam? To relax with friends? This intriguing essay talks about the when and the why of the cycles that govern our lives and behavior.

Linda Hasselstrom, *A Peaceful Women Explains Why She Carries a Pistol* /303
This writer and rancher explains that for a woman in a hostile world, carrying a gun may be a good way to even the odds and prevent violence.

Cullen Murphy, *Hello, Darkness* /310
Tired? No wonder. Everyone else is too. This writer explains why we are all getting less sleep.

Issues and Ideas: **Work, Success, and Failure**

William Severini Kowinski, *Kids in the Mall: Growing Up Controlled* /317
What do the malls teach teenagers? All sorts of lessons, few of them very useful and some of them perhaps even harmful.

Peter Hillary, *Everest Is Mighty, We are Fragile* /324
If we try to prevent people from undertaking dangerous challenges like climbing mountains, we will be banishing something very important to all of us, says this mountaineer.

Randall Rothenberg, *What makes Sammy Walk?* /330
In a time when most everyone is worried about getting and keeping a job, why are some people trying to work less and itching to stop working altogether?

9 Using *Definition* to Help Explain /345

Sample Paragraph: Linton Robinson, "Marathoning with Maps"

Roger Welsch, *Gypsies* /349
What is there to admire in a group of people who have made thievery into a fine art? Plenty, or at least that is what this writer and anthropologist believes, and he offers some reasons.

John Berendt, *The Hoax* /357
A hoax is a lot more than a simple prank, says this well-known author. It has wit and style.

Stephen L. Carter, *The Insufficiency of Honesty* /361
What we need a lot more than honesty is integrity, says this writer and law professor.

Issues and Ideas: **Redefining Relationships and Identities**

Michael Dorris, *Father's Day* /370
Can someone other than a father be a father?

Kesaya Noda, *Growing Up Asian in America* /375
Finding an identity as an Asian, an Asian American, and an Asian-American woman was a difficult but essential task of self-definition for this author.

Veronica Chambers, *Mother's Day* /385
When your identity changes, does your mother's change
too? What about your relationship with her?

10 Explaining with the Help of *Description* /393

Sample Paragraph: Donald Hall, *Seasons at Eagle Pond*

Sharon Curtin, *Aging in the Land of the Young* /398
All of us, says a former nurse, are so afraid of aging that
we treat old people as personal insults and threats to our
society.

George Simpson, *The War Room at Bellevue* /403
The author takes us through one unforgettable evening in
the emergency room of a huge city hospital. But, says the
head nurse, the succession of crises was "about normal . . .
no big deal."

Issues and Ideas: **Place and Person**

Joyce Maynard, *The Yellow Door House* /412
Visits to the house where she grew up give this writer a
chance to reflect on her parents' lives, her own life, and
the lives of her children.

Luis J. Rodríguez, *The Ice Cream Truck* /418
What does life in an impoverished barrio look like from
the inside? This writer, a former gang member, provides a
glimpse.

E. B. White, *Once More to the Lake* /424
A visit with his son to the lake where he spent summer
vacations as a boy gives this famous essayist a kind of
double vision that mingles memories of the past with
scenes from the present.

11 Using *Narration* as an Expository Technique /435

Sample Paragraph: Edwin Mickleburgh, *Beyond the Frozen Sea:
Visions of Antarctica*

Martin Gansberg, 38 *Who Saw Murder Didn't Call the Police* /439
Years after the fact, the murder of Kitty Genovese is still a harrowing tale of urban apathy.

Chang-rae Lee, *Uncle Chul Gets Rich* /445
No matter how hard he tried or how successful he became, Uncle Chul could never seem to earn his sister-in-law's approval.

Issues and Ideas: **Telling Stories about Ourselves and Our Values**

George Orwell, *A Hanging* /453
The well-known essayist and author of *1984* writes of an experience in Burma and makes a subtle but biting commentary on both colonialism and capital punishment.

Rita Williams, *The Quality of Mercy* /460
Crime is not a black and white issue for the African-American writer who shares her first-hand experience as a victim facing young and potentially violent criminals.

Garrett Hongo, *Kubota* /466
Kubota told him to remember, and the writer remembers not only Kubota but also his story, along with that of other Japanese Americans during World War II.

12 Reasoning by Use of *Induction and Deduction* /481

Sample Paragraphs: Daniel Cohen, "Cooking Off for Fame and Fortune"
Lois G. Forer, *A Chilling Effect*

Barbara Ehrenreich, *Star Dreck* /487
What is really important for this country is the serious study of stars—the kind that appear on the covers of magazines, on television, and on movie screens.

Patricia Kean, *Blowing Up the Tracks* /492
Our school systems have long taken for granted that students learn best when they are segregated by ability. Yet

as this writer points out, those teachers and schools that have been willing to break the mold find that mixed classrooms are often the most successful.

Issues and Ideas: Digital Realities

Maia Szalavitz, *A Virtual Life* /502
When you stay at home working on the computer all day long, life on the screen can become real life.

Nicholas Negroponte, *Place Without Space* /506
In the world of computers we can be in one place while our bodies are somewhere else.

13 Using Patterns for *Argument* /511

Sample Paragraph: "Grime and Punishment"

Issues and Ideas: Current and Classic Controversies

Christopher B. Daly, *How the Lawyers Stole Winter* /520
Argument Through Comparison and Contrast
When we try to make everything safe and prevent accidents, we also take away responsibility for our own safety and the opportunity to develop good judgment.

Richard Lynn, *Why Johnny Can't Read, but Yoshio Can* /525
Argument Through Comparison and Contrast
How good are our schools compared to those of Japan? Not very good, says this writer, and he proposes ways to improve them, including solutions that may raise the hackles of some readers.

Alan Hirsch, *Don't Blame the Jury* /533
Argument Through Example
We complain about the verdicts, but often it is the judges and the lawyers, not the juries, that are to blame.

Barbara Lawrence, *Four-Letter Words Can Hurt You* /542
Argument Through Definition
Dirty words have a history of violent meanings. This history, not narrow-minded sexual hang-ups, is what makes the words harmful and offensive.

John Davidson, *Menace to Society* /547
Argument Through Cause and Effect
Can children's cartoons be a major cause of agressive and
violent behavior? That's what this writer believes, and he
offers evidence to support his case.

Martin Luther King, Jr., *Letter from Birmingham Jail* /555
Complex Argument
The martyred civil rights leader explains in this now-clas-
sic letter just why he is in Birmingham, and justifies the
activities that led to his jailing.

Further Readings /575

Margaret Atwood, *Pornography* /576
We are naive if we think that all pornography appeals to
sexual fantasies, points out this well-known novelist.
Some pornography contains scenes of cruelty that even
people concerned about freedom of expression are likely
to find repulsive and dangerous.

Bill McKibben, *Late Afternoon* /583
Time on television and time on a mountainside in the late
afternoon are dissimilar in so many ways that the two
might as well be in different dimensions.

Leslie Marmon Silko, *Yellow Woman and a Beauty of the
Spirit* /590
Beauty is a matter of the individual's spirit, not physical
appearance, says the author, who points out that spiritual
beauty is central to the Laguna Pueblo way to life.

A Guide to Terms /599

Thematic Contents

Men and Women

Barbara Ehrenreich, What I've Learned from Men, 82
Alan Buczynski, Iron Bonding, 97
Scott Russell Sanders, The Men We Carry in Our Minds, 167
Linda Hasselstrom, A Peaceful Woman Explains Why She Carries
    a Pistol, 303
Michael Dorris, Father's Day, 370
Kesaya Noda, Growing Up Asian in America, 375
Barbara Lawrence, Four-Letter Words Can Hurt You, 542
Margaret Atwood, Pornography, 576

Work

Alan Buczynski, Iron Bonding, 97
Mark Twain, Two Ways of Seeing a River, 150
Patricia Raybon, Letting in Light, 210
Tom Wolfe, O Rotten Gotham—Sliding Down into the Behavioral
    Sink, 216
Jessica Mitford, To Dispel Fears of Live Burial, 278
Randall Rothenberg, What Makes Sammy Walk?, 330
Sharon Curtin, Aging in the Land of the Young, 398
Luis J. Rodriguez, The Ice Cream Truck, 418
Barbara Ehrenreich, Star Dreck, 487

Culture and Customs

Andy Rooney, In and of Ourselves We Trust, 70
Judith Stone, Personal Beast, 116
Renee Tajima, Lotus Blossoms Don't Bleed: Images of Asian
    American Women, 126
Brenda Peterson, Life Is a Musical, 136

Marianna de Marco Torgovnick, On Being White, Female, and
    Born in Bensonhurst, 173
Barbara Kingsolver, High Tide in Tucson, 225
Cullen Murphy, Hello, Darkness, 310
Roger Welsch, Gypsies, 349
John Berendt, The Hoax, 357
Kesaya Noda, Growing Up Asian in America, 375
Richard Lynn, Why Johnny Can't Read, but Yoshio Can, 525

Politics and Leaders

Brenda Peterson, Life Is a Musical, 136
Bruce Catton, Grant and Lee: A Study in Contrasts, 154
George Orwell, A Hanging, 453
Martin Luther King, Jr., Letter from Birmingham Jail, 555

Personality and Behavior

Brent Staples, Just Walk on By, 59
Mary Karr, Dysfunctional Nation, 93
Judith Viorst, What, Me? Showing Off?, 108
Judith Stone, Personal Beast, 116
Brenda Peterson, Life Is a Musical, 136
Phillip Lopate, A Nonsmoker with a Smoker, 160
Scott Russell Sanders, The Men We Carry in Our Minds, 167
Alice Walker, Am I Blue?, 188
Loren C. Eiseley, The Brown Wasps, 201
Patricia Raybon, Letting in Light, 210
Tom Wolfe, O Rotten Gotham—Sliding Down into the Behavioral
    Sink, 216
Ann Faraday, Unmasking Your Dream Images, 250
Susan Perry and Jim Dawson, What's Your Best Time of Day, 298
Peter Hillary, Everest Is Mighty, We are Fragile, 324
Kesaya Noda, Growing Up Asian in America, 375
Veronica Chambers, Mother's Day, 385

Nature and the Environment

Antonya Nelson, Fear of Flying, 89
Mark Twain, Two Ways of Seeing a River, 150
Alice Walker, Am I Blue?, 188
Barbara Kingsolver, High Tide in Tucson, 225
Cullen Murphy, Hello, Darkness, 310

Peter Hillary, Everest Is Mighty, We are Fragile, 324
Bill McKibben, Late Afternoon, 583

Morals, Crime, and Punishment

Judith Viorst, What, Me? Showing Off?, 108
Alice Walker, Am I Blue?, 188
Stephen L. Carter, The Insufficiency of Honesty, 361
Sharon Curtin, Aging in the Land of the Young, 398
Luis J. Rodriguez, The Ice Cream Truck, 418
Martin Gansberg, 38 Who Saw Murder Didn't Call the Police, 439
Rita Williams, The Quality of Mercy, 460
Martin Luther King, Jr., Letter from Birmingham Jail, 555
Margaret Atwood, Pornography, 576

Growing Up/Getting Old

Antonya Nelson, Fear of Flying, 89
Loren C. Eiseley, The Brown Wasps, 201
Scott Russell Sanders, The Men We Carry in Our Minds, 167
William Severini Kowinski, Kids in the Mall: Growing Up
    Controlled, 317
Kesaya Noda, Growing Up Asian in America, 375
Sharon Curtin, Aging in the Land of the Young, 398
Joyce Maynard, The Yellow Door House, 12
E.B. White, Once More to the Lake, 424

Differences

Brent Staples, Just Walk on By, 59
Barbara Kingsolver, High Tide in Tucson, 225
William Severini Kowinski, Kids in the Mall: Growing Up
    Controlled, 317
Roger Welsch, Gypsies, 349
George Simpson, The War Room at Bellevue, 403

Families and Children

Antonya Nelson, Fear of Flying, 89
Mary Karr, Dysfunctional Nation, 93
Judith Viorst, What, Me? Showing Off?, 108
Patricia Raybon, Letting in Light, 210
William Severini Kowinski, Kids in the Mall: Growing Up
    Controlled, 317

Michael Dorris, Father's Day, 370
Veronica Chambers, Mother's Day, 385
Joyce Maynard, The Yellow Door House, 412
Chang-rae Lee, Uncle Chul Gets Rich, 445
Garret Hongo, Kubota, 466

Society and Social Change

Andy Rooney, In and of Ourselves We Trust, 70
William F. Buckley, Jr., Why Don't We Complain?, 74
Barbara Ehrenreich, What I've Learned from Men, 82
Phillip Lopate, A Nonsmoker with a Smoker, 160
Linda Hasselstrom, A Peaceful Woman Explains Why She Carries
     a Pistol, 303
Rita Williams, The Quality of Mercy, 460
Garret Hongo, Kubota, 466
Patricia Kean, Blowing Up the Tracks, 492
Nicholas Negroponte, Place without Space, 506
Richard Lynn, Why Johnny Can't Read, but Yoshio Can, 525
Margaret Atwood, Pornography, 576

Media

Renee Tajima, Lotus Blossoms Don't Bleed; Images of Asian
     American Women, 126
James B. Twitchell, We Build Excitement, 268
Jean E. Kilbourne, Beauty . . . and the Beast of Advertising, 286
Maia Szalavitz, A Virtual Life, 502

Essay Pairs

Among the selections in *Patterns of Exposition* 15 are a number of essay pairs whose similarities in topic or theme and contrasts in perspective or style offer interesting insights. These relationships show that the strategies a writer chooses can affect the way readers come to view the subject matter of an essay. The following list identifies some sets of essays that are particularly well suited for study and discussion; there are, of course, many other interesting and revealing ways of pairing the selections in the text.

A few of the pairs illustrate different ways of using the same pattern, such as example or definition. In other sets, the patterns offer contrasting strategies for expression or alternate ways of viewing a subject.

Andy Rooney, In and of Ourselves We Trust, 70
Peter Hillary, Everest Is Mighty, We Are Fragile, 324

William F. Buckley, Jr., Why Don't We Complain?, 74
Barbara Ehrenreich, What I've Learned from Men, 82

Mary Karr, Dysfunctional Nation, 93
Michael Dorris, Father's Day, 370

Alan Buczynski, Iron Bonding, 97
Brenda Peterson, Life Is a Musical, 136

Judith Stone, Personal Beast, 116
Alice Walker, Am I Blue?, 188

Renee Tajima, Lotus Blossoms Don't Bleed: Images of Asian American Women, 126
Marianna de Marco Torgovnick, On Being White, Female and Born in Bensonhurst, 173

Mark Twain, Two Ways of Looking at a River, 150
E.B. White, Once More to the Lake, 424

Bruce Catton, Grant and Lee: A Study in Contrasts, 154
Barbara Ehrenreich, Star Dreck, 487

Scott Russell Sanders, The Men We Carry in Our Minds, 167
Michael Dorris, Father's Day, 370

Alice Walker, Am I Blue?, 188
Barbara Kingsolver, High Tide in Tucson, 225

Loren C. Eiseley, The Brown Wasps, 201
Sharon Curtin, Aging in the Land of the Young, 398

Tom Wolfe, O Rotten Gotham—Sliding Down into the Behavioral
    Sink, 216
George Simpson, The War Room at Bellvue, 403

Patricia Raybon, Letting in Light, 210
William Severini Kowinski, Kids in the Mall: Growing Up Con-
    trolled, 317

James B. Twitchell, We Build Excitement, 268
Barbara Ehrenreich, Star Dreck, 487

Jean E. Kilbourne, Beauty . . . and the Beast of Advertising, 286
Renee Tajima, Lotus Blossoms Don't Bleed: Images of Asian Amer-
    ican Women, 126

Susan Perry and Jim Dawson, What's Your Best Times of Day, 298
Cullen Murphy, Hello, Darkness, 310

Randall Rothenberg, What Makes Sammy Walk?, 330
Chang-rae Lee, Uncle Chul Gets Rich, 445

Joyce Maynard, The Yellow Door House, 412
Jean E. Kilbourne, Beauty . . . and the Beast of Advertising, 286

Kesaya Noda, Growing Up Asian in America, 375
Luis Rodriquez, The Ice Cream Truck, 418

George Simpson, The War Room at Bellevue, 403
Luis J. Rodriguez, The Ice Cream Truck, 418

Martin Gansberg, 38 Who Saw Murder Didn't Call the Police, 439
Rita Williams, The Quality of Mercy, 460

Sharon Curtin, Aging in the Land of the Young, 398
Garnet Hongo, Kubota, 466

Maia Szalavitz, A Virtual Life, 502
Bill McKibben, Late Afternoon, 583

Patricia Kean, Blowing Up the Tracks, 492
Richard Lynn, Why Johnny Can't Read, but Yoshio Can, 525

Christopher B. Daly, How the Lawyers Stole Winter, 520
Alan Hirsch, Don't Blame the Jury, 533

Barbara Lawrence, Four-Letter Words Can Hurt You, 542
Margaret Atwood, Pornography, 576

John Davidson, Menace to Society, 547
Luis J. Rodriquez, The Ice Cream Truck, 418

To the Instructor

Instructors familiar with *Patterns of Exposition* will recognize in this edition the same overall design, basic principles, and apparatus that have been so successful in previous editions. They, and new users as well, will notice how the focus on patterns of exposition and argument and on essays illustrating these strategies have been supplemented and extended to demonstrate the ways rhetorical patterns enable writers and readers to explore, understand, and take a stand on questions of culture, identity, and value in college communities, in the workplace, and in society at large.

As in previous editions, each section begins with a brief discussion of the roles a particular pattern of exposition (or argument) can play for writers and readers, a discussion that concludes with an annotated example of the pattern at work in a paragraph and with an example of its use in a paragraph by a professional writer. The first few essay selections that follow these sample paragraphs illustrate some of the many roles the pattern can play in organizing thought and expression within an essay or by working with other rhetorical patterns to create an organized, purposeful, effective exposition (or argument).

Each chapter concludes with a cluster of essays focusing on "Issues and Ideas" of contemporary and (we hope) enduring significance. Our primary goal in creating these clusters has not been simply to encourage students to think and write about the specific themes and issues, but to help students develop an awareness of rhetorical strategies as a critical tool for understanding differing perspectives and to demonstrate the variety of purposes a strategy can serve. It is precisely the broad similarity in subject matter and strategy among the essays in a cluster that serves to highlight for students the important differences and the varied models for expression the selections provide.

New to this edition, too, are the questions and activities labeled "Read to Write" appearing at the end of each selection. The first activity in each "Read to Write" section encourages students to use a particular selection as a springboard for discovering topics and ideas for their own writing. The second activity highlights specific writing strategies within the sample essay and suggests ways students can use this strategy to prompt their own thinking for an essay or to organize and develop their own writing. The third activity helps students view the sample essay as a broad model for their own work—a model which they are encouraged to alter and develop in a fashion appropriate to their own perspectives and purposes. These activities provide practice linking reading to writing—one of the primary focuses of the book as a whole. The "Writing Suggestions" at the end of each section, a feature retained from earlier editions, offer further avenues for students to follow from reading into writing.

To place even greater emphasis on the links between reading and writing, we have expanded our treatment of reading into a full section titled "Becoming a Critical Reader." At the same time, we have given fuller treatment to the writing process in the book's opening section, "Ways of Writing." These extended, detailed, and practical discussions reflect not only the desire of the book's adopters for extended treatment of the writing and reading processes but also our belief that practical advice followed by actual writing and reading practice is the best way for students to increase their sophistication as writers and readers. Instead of extended theoretical discussions that are so much the fashion, therefore, we offer students an overview of the main elements of the writing process accompanied by concrete strategies, specific suggestions, and concise illustrations. Likewise, we introduce critical reading not as a theoretical or academic pursuit but as a practice—a necessary part of every effective writer's work and an educated and aware person's outlook. Our emphasis in discussing critical reading is again on the process itself as well as particular techniques and focused illustrations.

In choosing new essays and retaining those from previous editions, we have looked first for selections that are well-written and insightful and that reward careful (re-)reading and then for selections that can serve as useful models for thought, organization, and expression. We have also drawn on suggestions from the text's instructor-users and have reviewed the responses of students. Although obviously we are unable to comply with all requests, we have seriously considered and fully appreciated all of them, and we have incorporated many suggestions into this new edition. We have responded, as well, to requests for added essays in some of the most heavily used sections of the book.

The wealth of excellent and recent nonfiction writing reflecting the perspective of many different cultural and social groups has made it possible for us to choose selections reflecting the intellectual ferment and challenge of our times. In drawing on this diversity, we have not tried to represent every identity in an unimaginative and rigid fashion but have instead tried to use it to create an exciting mixture of perspectives and backgrounds designed to encourage varied, engaged responses from students.

Because so many instructors find it useful, we continue to retain the table of contents listing pairs of essays. Each pair provides contrasts (or similarities) in theme, approach, and style that are worth study. The essay pairs can form the focus of class discussion or writing assignments.

The "Further Readings" section provides contemporary selections to provoke discussion. The pieces also suggest some intriguing forms and goals that essays can pursue in the hands of skilled and daring writers. The essays in this section can be used on their own or with the other sections of the book.

Throughout *Patterns of Exposition 15* we have tried, as always, to make possible the convenient use of all materials in whatever ways instructors think best for their own classes. With a few exceptions, only complete essays or freestanding units of larger works have been included. With their inevitable overlap of patterns, they are more complicated than excerpts illustrating single principles, but they are also more realistic examples of exposition and more useful for other classroom purposes. Versatility has been an important criterion in choosing materials.

Thirty-six of the selections best liked in previous editions have been retained. Twenty-five selections are new, and all but a few of these are anthologized for the first time.

The arrangement of essays is but one of the many workable orders; instructors can easily develop another if they so desire. The Thematic Contents and the table of Essay Pairs also suggest a variety of arrangements.

We have tried to vary the study questions—and undoubtedly have included far more than any one teacher will want—from the purely objective to those calling for some serious self-examination by students. (The Instructor's Manual supplements these materials.)

"A Guide to Terms," at the end of the book, briefly discusses matters from *Abstract* to *Unity* and refers whenever possible to the essays themselves for illustrations. Its location is designed to permit unity and easy access, but there are cross-references to it in the study questions following each selection.

In all respects—size, content, arrangement, format—we have tried to keep *Patterns of Exposition 15* uncluttered and easy to use.

Acknowledgments

We would like to thank Nancy Newman Schwegler for sharing with us her knowledge of contemporary nonfiction and helping us identify essays that explore current issues and cultural perspectives.

The second editor wishes to thank Brian Schwegler for his advice on current treatments of identity formation, both social and cultural; Tara Schwegler for heightening his awareness of social change; Christopher Schwegler for his smiles; and Nancy Newman Schwegler for her love and support.

The continued success of *Patterns of Exposition* is due to a great extent to the many students and instructors who respond to questionnaires and offer helpful suggestions, making the job of revision easier. Our special thanks go to five reviewers:

- Helen Marie Casey, Fisher College at Framingham
- P. J. Colbert, Marshalltown Community College
- Richard Courage, Westchester Community College
- Barbara J. Martin, University of Massachusetts at Dartmouth
- Brian Monahan, North Rockland Central School System

Randall E. Decker
Robert A. Schwegler

1

Ways of Writing

Good writing is just as much a matter of habits as of imagination and skill with words. By "habits," we mean techniques of active writing and reading—like freewriting, keeping a writer's (or reader's) journal, or using questions to guide revising such strategies in order. You can learn and practice to maximize your ability to think and express yourself. Admittedly, only a few people have the potential to be exceptional writers. You can become an effective, confident writer, however, by developing strategies for exploring experience and ideas, for drawing on your reading and understanding your own readers, and for shaping words and insights through careful drafting and revising.

Developing strategies for effective writing often means overcoming myths about composing and getting rid of composing behaviors that make it harder for you to write well. Here is what several students have to say about writing.

KIM: I used to think that topics for an essay just "came" to writers through inspiration, so I would wait and wait for a good idea or a thesis or whatever to come to me. I used to get really frustrated and worry about being able to write 'cause I could never get started. I would end up at the last minute writing really short papers that didn't say anything.

Finally, I started keeping a writer's journal and doing things like freewriting, brainstorming, and listing. Pretty soon I began writing better papers with a lot less hassle.

KIESHA: I like to do things at the last minute, and this works pretty well for me most times. In sports, especially, I like to improvise and be spontaneous. This spontaneity used to work well for me in writing, especially with creative projects. But when my friends started telling me that I needed to have a plan and my teachers started complaining that my writing was "all over the place" and "lacked a clear purpose or organization," I decided I was in trouble. I haven't gotten better at planning my life—my best friend still calls me "clueless"—but I've developed some habits like clustering, using planning questions, and creating generalization-and-support plans that help me plan my writing.

NEAL: I like to do things my own way, to be an individual. The hardest thing for me to do is to change a word or sentence I have written when I think it says exactly what I mean or what I feel. This attitude can get in my way at times, I admit. When a teacher or a friend had trouble understanding a paper of mine, I used to try convincing them the trouble was with the way they were reading it, not with what I had written.

To overcome this problem, I made a list of things I can do to help me imagine how others might view my writing. This helps me see my work from the outside, and to recognize changes I need to make if I want to get my point across. I've even got my own set of questions for readers. I use it when I ask friends and classmates to help me discover what parts of a paper need revising.

TRAN: When I read a book for class, I make lots of notes because I want to remember as much as I can for a test. I used to do this kind of note-taking when I was writing a paper, but my instructors complained that I ended up repeating what my sources said without adding any ideas of my own. This was really frustrating because no matter how hard I worked, my papers kept getting the same comment.

I'm a pretty disciplined person, so what I needed was a set of things I could plan on doing to turn my reading into good writing. I've learned to keep response journals for my ideas and for reactions to what I read, not just for the author's ideas. I also record things I like about how an author writes so I can do the same kinds of things in my own papers.

Each of these people faced a writing problem and developed concrete strategies for overcoming it. Kim stopped viewing composing as a matter of mysterious inspiration and started relying on her writer's journal and brainstorming. Kiesha learned to depend less on improvisation and more on self-conscious planning. Neal started turning to readers for advice and developed ways to keep their needs in mind. Tran began building on his reading instead of simply reproducing it. In short, each person developed composing and reading strategies that made him or her a better writer (and reader). The rest of this chapter offers you a detailed tour through the composing process and introduces you to strategies like those above and many more that may help you become an effective writer.

WAYS OF WRITING

Good writers know that the composing process needs to be more than a jumble of activities that somehow string loosely related ideas and information into a finished essay or report. They know that effective writing is a thoughtful process that generally moves from the discovery of ideas and information through the planning and drafting of an essay to revising and polishing—all with the help of specific composing strategies. They also know that there is no single formula for all writing tasks or audiences, and that the movement from discovering through planning, drafting, revising, and polishing should be a flexible sequence that allows you, for example, to discover new ideas as you draft or to alter an essay's plan as you revise.

Finally, effective writers know that all the decisions they make, from initial choice of topic to final choice of wording, should involve an awareness of the demands of their particular writing task and subject, the needs of their audience, and their purposes for writing. In the pages that follow, we offer you concrete, detailed advice on the writing process with suggestions for keeping audience and purpose in mind as you compose.

We have arranged our advice in the following sections according to the steps you are most likely to follow as you compose an essay or report.

Getting Started: Active Writing
                        Keeping a Journal

Discovering: Freewriting, Focused Freewriting, and Looping
                    Brainstorming and Listing
                    Listing and Detailing
                    Developing a Focus through Questioning
Planning: Clustering and Diagramming
                    Using Questions to Organize
                    Planning Visually
                    Creating a Discovery Draft
                    Outlining
                    Identifying a Purpose and Deciding on a Thesis
Drafting
Revising: Reading for Revision
                    Questioning Reading
                    Peer Response
Editing and Final Revision

Getting Started

Much writing begins with an assignment, at work or at school, or with an opportunity, a call for submissions to a local newspaper, for example. You need not wait for an assignment or opportunity to begin writing, however. By being an active writer and by keeping a writer's journal, you can be ready to respond to situations that call for writing—or even to write at any time for your own purposes.

Active Writing

Active writing is not a way of communicating. It is a way of reaching out, exploring, and discovering. Active writing starts from what you know and leads to questions and new ideas. It prompts you to observe people, places, events, and concepts, and it encourages you to move towards fresh solutions and to redefine issues. Active writing leads you to think about how the world *might be* rather than how it *is*.

If writing for you means putting ideas on paper in proper order and expressing them in formal language, then you are not used to doing active writing. Active writing is often messy and fragmentary. It may contain the beginnings of thoughts, but not their conclusions. It is close to thinking—at least thinking in its most inquisitive and imaginative form. While it is often an important first step in communicating with others because it enables you to understand your own thoughts and feelings, active writing is often hard for others to read and follow.

You can undertake active writing at almost any time and place: on scraps of paper at lunch, in the margins of books, as part of the early drafts of papers, or even in your head as you run, bike, or swim (remembering your thoughts to be jotted down later). Yet the best place for active writing that eventually leads to formal essays, reports, and articles is a journal. An **academic journal** is a place (often a notebook or a computer file) in which you jot down ideas and discoveries, try out different perspectives on a topic, prepare rough drafts of paragraphs or essays, and note responses to reading or observations. Journals are not diaries: journals are starting places for public writing while diaries are places to record and keep your private observations.

Here are some of the differences between a formal paper or essay and active writing in a journal:

Journal (Active Writing)	Essay
Explores, tests, imagines, learns—uses writing to do something new	Communicates ideas, information, opinions, and conclusions
Forgets about readers	Keeps readers in mind
In progress; ready to be used or perhaps ignored, but not evaluated	A finished product that readers can evaluate
Loosely structured, if at all; contains fresh and surprising detail; raises questions without necessarily providing answers	Organized and developed in appropriate detail with an eye towards adequate explanation and support
Often rough, with idiosyncratic expressions and a casual attitude towards spelling, grammar, and usage	Polished and correct

This passage from Scott Giglio's journal, made in response to an article in his local newspaper, illustrates some of the ways active writing can provide an imaginative start for the essay-writing process while at the same time being hard for anyone but the author to read.

Article in PrJo 6/10/96 "Hispanics losing ground in strong economy" hadn't thought about this. Why? I figured unemployment was down etc. and that most people were either doing well or things getting better for them so what abt. Hispanics? Article claims—uh, where is it—Census Bureau claims Hispanic families income down 5.1% rest up 2.7 (can get rest of stats from article if impt. cut it out of paper) Ok Ok why happening and why important is this something to argue about or can I use it as part of paper on how people just seem to be same but lead diff. lives?? A campaign issue or do people vote on personality rather than how things are going?

Keeping a Journal

A journal can take any form you find comfortable: pad, notebook, computer file, even loose sheets of paper. Whatever form you choose, make sure you keep the journal easily accessible so you can use active writing to explore your observations, your reading, your insights and feelings as well as ideas and opinions others offer to you.

Having a specific time to write (and maybe even a specific place) can be a good idea because active writing becomes more helpful the more you practice it. Sometimes maintaining a journal can seem like drudgery, so you may want to write for only a few minutes. But writing *regularly* is the key to an effective journal and to developing the habits of active, productive thinking that go along with active writing.

Don't restrict your journal to your composition or English course. Use it as part of your work in chemistry, economics, psychology, and art history. Practice active writing outside academic settings, too. Reflect on and solve problems in your work or daily life.

Here are some strategies for active writing that work especially well in journal entries.

• Translate. When you encounter challenging ideas or interesting information through reading, lectures, or discussion, translate it into your own terms. This process will aid your understanding and help you identify unresolved issues and problems that require further thinking. As you translate, moreover, you will probably begin to speculate about the meaning and consequences of the ideas and information. Record your speculations for later use, perhaps as the subject of another journal entry or in a formal essay. Translation not only helps you make concepts and details your own, it puts them into language you may later decide to use for your readers.

- Generate. Use a journal entry as a place to begin generating topics, ideas, details, even phrases for some formal writing you are going to be working on. Simply let your mind run freely, letting each idea suggest the next or discovering their connections. Or generate by employing one of the techniques also useful for discovering ideas and details about a particular subject: Brainstorming, Listing, and Freewriting (see pages 9–13).

- Extend. Consider an idea you have encountered in reading or discussion. Speculate about its consequences. Apply it to different situations. Question its usefulness or validity. Compare it to similar ideas or to sharply differing ones. In short, extend the idea with your own words and insights until it becomes something you can draw on later as you prepare a formal essay.

- Relate. Think about a concept or issue in terms of your own experience. Consider how it might alter your outlook or way of behaving. Use it to interpret events or emotions. Apply it to problems you find intriguing.

- Take issue. React to someone else's opinion or conclusion. Endorse it or argue with it. Be blunt, even impolite in your reaction; don't worry, you won't offend anyone, but you will discover the intensity of your own feelings and beliefs. You may even find yourself making a commitment to an idea or proposition that you will later wish to share with readers.

- Get down to work. If you have been avoiding the due date for an essay or report, explore your reasons for delaying. You may uncover problems, misconceptions, or a need for further information—all of which have prevented you from getting down to work. You may come face to face with fears and uncertainties that you need to deal with so that you can get on with your writing. You may even discover some important things you want to say in an essay.

- Explore confusions. Does something in your coursework confuse or irritate you? Has a topic that came up in a casual conversation continued to puzzle or intrigue you? Do you need to "vent" a bit about a challenging or confusing problem? Doing these things in a journal entry can lead to ideas or topics worth following up in later writing.

Your journal writing will be most effective if you follow these tips. **Be personal:** Use "I" in your entries both as a way of drawing out your own insights and reactions and as a way of avoiding complicated, formal sentences. **Be conversational:** In a journal entry you talk to yourself, so feel free to use informal language, even slang, that may not be appropriate for a formal essay. Informal language can help you feel freer to explore unfamiliar perspectives and to make your responses honest and direct. **Use shortcuts:** Help your writing capture thoughts quickly by using abbreviations or your personal shorthand expressions; don't worry about niceties like underlining and complicated punctuation. Look up the spelling of words later on, if you need to. **Experiment:** Try out unusual ideas or unusual and inventive forms of expression. In playing with words and ideas, you may discover something worth sharing.

If you intend to make your journal a place where more formal writing has its beginning, three further tips should prove useful. **Think about what might be:** List the kinds of papers you might want to write, speculate about solutions to problems, or think about puzzling phenomena that you wish you could understand. **Think about what you want to happen:** Consider the ways you want readers to feel as they read what you have written or the ways you hope they will act or react after finishing your essay. **Make action notes:** Jot down kinds of writing you plan to do, things you will need to read, and research or observations you are planning to undertake.

Discovering

However your composing process for an essay begins—with active writing in a journal, in response to an assignment, or with a cluster of information and ideas you wish to explore—you will soon be involved in two more or less simultaneous activities: discovering and planning.

Discovering focuses on the content of an essay, the information and ideas you are going to share with readers. **Planning** pays attention to the organization and purpose of your writing. Working on the content of an essay at the same time you create its organization is not as tricky as it may sound. The tasks often go hand in hand. Frequently, an essay's pattern seems to evolve naturally as a writer works with ideas and details, or a particular pattern of explanation suggests information worth including in an essay or a perspective worth sharing with readers. For the sake of simplicity, however, we have separated our discussions of discovering and planning. The

Discovering section offers you a variety of strategies for developing the topic and content of your writing. The *Planning* section offers strategies for deciding on a plan of organization.

Freewriting, Focused Freewriting, and Looping

One good way to identify a topic for your writing or to explore and develop a topic is to use **freewriting.** In freewriting, you let a pen (or keyboard) follow your mind as it runs freely over subjects that interest you—until you hit upon a topic (or several topics) that you might wish to pursue further. Freewriting can also capture remembered events, feelings, ideas, and details and may stimulate the beginnings of a plan for an essay incorporating them. To freewrite, jot down (or type) all the thoughts that come to your mind until the details and ideas begin to take the shape of a topic (a focus for your writing) or until a possible direction for your writing begins to emerge. You needn't worry about spelling, grammar, or complete sentences as you freewrite. Instead, focus on exploring ideas and details.

Focused freewriting is a slightly different process. It helps you develop insights, details, opinions, and examples. In focused freewriting, you begin with an idea or topic for writing, then write down all the associated insights, information, concepts, examples, or questions you can bring to mind, without worrying about the particular order in which they occur to you. Focused freewriting can help you recognize what you know, what you want to say or share about a topic, and what you need to learn more about.

In her composition class, Sarah Lake was asked to write about a community of some sort, taking the perspective of an outsider trying to understand how the community works and what kinds of relationships people in the community form. She decided to visit her college's fitness center to learn something about the people who spend a lot of time there. Here is part of the focused freewriting she did as a way of reflecting on what she learned during her several visits to the fitness center.

I've been transmitted into an episode of "Captain Cave Man" I'm afraid that at any moment one of the wt. lifters will club a female and take her back to his cave or better yet his training room.
!Men———Weightlifting!
Why do they find it necessary?

- the cave man look
- the way a man should be
- society today vs. tomorrow
- manliness vs. the sensitive man

Notice how Sarah's freewriting started out in sentence form then turned into phrases arranged in a list as she became more and more focused on ideas and a topic that seemed promising.

Often, focused freewriting can help you develop a purpose or thesis for writing. If you have a particular assertion in mind, you can use it to begin your focused freewriting, to explore ways to present the assertion to readers, to consider supporting details and arguments, or to speculate on the ways readers are likely to respond.

As she continued freewriting about her visits to the fitness center, Sarah Lake began to develop an assertion about why men were exercising, and then she turned her attention to women, eventually producing another assertion along with some possible supporting evidence.

The bigger, stronger, the better they are (some men think), the more women may find them attractive (!?) What kind of women? What about women?
We are embarrassed by our size and often can't explain why. As I grow older I see more and more women with these ideas, esp. in a college setting. Women in the fitness center seem to have a balance scale in their heads. As their weight increases they feel less attractive and when their weight decreases they feel more attractive. Society's commercial image displays a goddess, a woman of perfection in form and in weight. Many women may not fit the commercial standards.

You can also focus on an assertion that appears in the course of a freewrite. This is what Sarah started doing in her focused freewrite. One good way to do this is to tell yourself (on screen or paper) to change directions and start focusing: "Wait. That sounds like an assertion I'd like to develop into a paper. *Focus on it now!*"

The technique known as **looping** takes you a step closer to the actual drafting of a paper. Looping means going back to your freewriting to pick out ideas, details, or assertions worth extra attention and then freewriting further on one or more of them. Using several cycles of looping can take you a long way towards developing a content, purpose, and plan for an essay.

Here is how Sarah Lake returned to the subject of commercial influences on women's concerns about weight and body image.

commercial image

What a woman should be. . .

   —thin, beautiful by whose standards

   —working mom, wife

   —provider

Where do we get the images

   —"Baywatch"

   —magazines

   —TV

   —posters

   —movies

Brainstorming and Listing

If you are beginning to work on an essay but have only a broad subject in mind, **brainstorming** and **listing** can be a good strategy. Brainstorming and listing can also be helpful when a writing assignment gives you a general direction but leaves you free to decide on the specific topic and purpose for your writing.

To **brainstorm,** let your mind run freely over possible topics for writing, leaping from one cluster of ideas, information, and experience to another. With pen in hand or at a keyboard, note whatever details, intriguing concepts, or fresh and interesting perspectives occur to you. From time to time, look over your brainstorming to identify clusters of related ideas and information. Every time you recognize such clusters, begin **listing** by giving each cluster a name and putting it on a list of possible subjects. When your list is finished, you may wish to circle the subjects you find most promising or think your readers would find most interesting. You can also brainstorm and list in response to your reading, as a result of talking with others, listening to a speaker, or watching a television program.

When he was asked to prepare an essay offering a generality and explaining it through examples, Bernie Stevens opened a file entitled "Possibles" on his computer and created the following list.

> I could write about. . .
>
> High School—pretty dull
> College?
> Sports—college
> Typical college sports
> College fans
> Students vs. alums
> Money and college sports
> Lacrosse
> Less familiar college sports
>> Lacrosse again
>> Field hockey (h.s. too)
>> Golf—do college players end up as pros—have the pros gone to college?
>> Hockey (good to watch—fans)
>> Figure skating (college sport?)
>> Swimming
> What it's like to be on a college team

After taking his list this far, Bernie took a break and decided to focus on the subjects that seemed to interest him most and that seemed the most likely candidates for development in an essay that would interest readers by introducing them to new experiences and perspectives.

You can extend brainstorming by **focusing** on one or more subjects from your original list and generating a further list of associated subjects. When you have finished creating the extended list, circle the subjects you consider the most promising.

Bernie Stevens presented his initial brainstorming list to his peer group in writing class, and the discussion that followed helped him extend the list in the following ways.

Possible Subjects	Extended
Less familiar college sports	Field events—hammer, javelin, triple jump
	Woodsman (and women!)—axes, sawing
	Volleyball (pretty familiar)
	Sailing
Golf	Competitive team golfing
	Golfing as a sport rather than recreation
	Division I competition (how good)
	College players and pros (how many start in college; how many attended college)
What's it like to be on a college team	Athletic teams—social and psychological
	Athletes in college—different from other students (are they students?)
	College athletes in big-time sports
	College athletes in lesser-known sports
	Time and energy demands of college sports
	Personal experience as student athlete—what I have experienced and what I know from other people's experiences

Listing and Detailing

Often, the difference between successful and unsuccessful writing lies in the amount of detail each presents to readers. Successful essays, reports, and position papers generally provide readers with concrete details to help recreate an experience, sufficient information to create understanding, and specific support for a thesis. The further you go in the process of writing a paper, the more attention you will have to pay to organization, to the wording of sentences, and to the structure of paragraphs—and the less attention you will have available for developing new ideas and discovering details and information, though you certainly can and should pay attention to these matters as you draft and revise your writing.

By developing ideas and information early in the writing process, you not only give an essay substance but also enable the organization you choose to grow from an in-depth understanding of your topic—an understanding you wish to share with readers through detailed paragraphs of explanation and support. A detailing list can be a very helpful way of exploring and developing your topic.

To create a **detailing list,** start by writing down personal impressions, ideas, observations, and generalizations about a topic. Under each impression or generalization list the specific details or experiences that led to it or that provide the kind of explanation and support readers will need in order to understand and agree with your perspective. On the left side of your list, label each kind of entry (general statement or impression, general detail, or specific detail), and on the right side write any questions that might spring to readers' minds and that can be answered through details.

Detailing lists can be general enough to cover entire essays or parts of essays. Or, lists can focus on smaller elements, as in the detailing Andy Chang used to help revise a paragraph.

General Focus	**Careers**	
Personal	Different careers=	} Just how different?
Idea	Different rewards	} Significant differences?
Detail	Father and aunt run small business—entrepreneurs	
Detail	Devote most time making business succeed—little time for family	} Aren't other jobs demanding?
Detail	Great risks—possibility for big success, money, and personal satisfaction	

Detail	{	Uncle and grandfather work for corporations— more time for family, though have to travel a lot	}	Still somewhat similar; are other jobs even more different?

Detail — Good money, more security—though office politics and downsizing cause tension, stress

Detail — Mom works for county government—regular hours allow involvement in family life

Detail — { Security; job doesn't dominate life; able to spend time developing rewarding personal relationships (but money could be a worry) } — But isn't the work rewarding too?

Detail — Mom considers helping people receive government services a personally rewarding job

Developing a Focus Through Questioning

Once you have a topic in mind, you can begin envisioning how to develop it into an essay. Many writers use groups of questions to identify aspects of a subject likely to interest readers, to develop perspectives and insights worth sharing, or to clarify their purposes for writing. Questions can also suggest possible designs for an essay.

The **journalist's questions—who, what, where, when, why** and **how**—help you with expository writing by identifying aspects of a topic about which your readers are likely to ask for detailed information. If you add the question, **why not,** to your list, you can use the questions to begin identifying support for your position in argumentative writing.

Focusing questions help you identify goals or main ideas for   39
your writing and may suggest general ways to divide a topic into
parts and organize an essay around key points. They may even
point towards a thesis around which you can build an essay (see
pages 27–28).

Here are some focusing questions that ask you to consider both
your perspective on a topic and your readers' likely responses.

- What parts of this subject or ways of looking at it interest me the
  most? Is the subject as a whole interesting or does some part of it
  or specific way of looking at it seem more intriguing?
- What aspect or perspective of the subject is most likely to interest
  readers?
- What would I most like to learn about this subject? Would readers like to learn the same thing?
- What feelings about the subject do I want to share with readers?
  What knowledge, opinions, or insights do I want to share?
- How is my perspective different from the ones readers will likely
  bring with them?
- What are two (three? four?) fresh, unusual, unsettling, or contro-
  versial insights I have to share? Why may some readers have
  trouble understanding or accepting them?

Pattern questions embody ways of thinking about a topic and
also ways of writing about it. They are related to the patterns of
exposition and argument presented in this text, and as a result, they
help you explore a topic and begin planning an essay at the same
time. They also ask you to consider readers' perspectives. (The sections in this text offer further suggestions for using the patterns to
plan an essay.)

Pattern questions	Section in text
What examples come to mind as I think about the subject, and why might they be worth exploring?	Section 3, "Example."
What groups or categories does the subject form, and what do these divisions reveal?	Section 4, "Classification."

What parts of the subject suggest interesting similarities or differences?	Section 5, "Comparison and Contrast."
Does the subject suggest any analogies? Would one of the analogies be worth exploring as the topic of an essay?	Section 6, "Analogy."
Is there some part of this subject that readers might want to know how to do or whose workings are interesting enough to deserve explanation?	Section 7, "Process Analysis."
Are there some events or phenomena whose causes might surprise or interest readers or whose likely effects are worth considering?	Section 8, "Cause and Effect."
What key terms or concepts are important enough to require clarification?	Section 9, "Definition."
Does the subject include any scenes or people whose meaning or significance might be revealed through a detailed portrait?	Section 10, "Description."
Are there any meaningful stories that the subject brings to mind?	Section 11, "Narration."
What aspects of the subject suggest specific conclusions? Do these conclusions suggest ways of viewing other parts of the subject?	Section 12, "Induction and Deduction."
What specific issues, opinions, disagreements, and possible actions are involved?	Section 13, "Argument."

Here is a topic list generated by Mary McCloskey as she used questions to focus her work on a writing assignment that asked her to discuss a topic in the area of sports and fitness.

Subject	Possible Topics
Women in Sports	People are trying to make women's sports more popular.
	More people watch men's sports.
	Are some kinds of sports traditionally for women or are there some in which women are more likely to excel?
	More professional men's sports.
	What are the possible consequences of Title IX for college sports?
	(What exactly is Title IX?)
	Men's sports are more popular. Why? How can this be changed?
	Women's sports are often more exciting. Is this true?
	How do people benefit from watching women's sports?
	Male spectators enjoy watching women's tennis because they learn things to use when they play.

Planning

Planning before you draft an essay does not mean deciding ahead of time the exact order in which you will present each detail or idea and the precise conclusions you will draw and support in each paragraph. For most writers, writing is itself a form of discovery. The very act of putting sentences and paragraphs together brings idea and information into often unanticipated relationships that create fresh perspectives worth sharing with readers.

But a lack of planning can be harmful to the quality of an essay or report and frustrating to you as the writer. If you begin writing without a plan, you are probably dooming yourself to false starts and long periods of inactivity when you try to decide what to say next— or whether to scrap the whole draft and start over. You are probably also creating unnecessary stress for yourself by taking on too many jobs at once: decisions about the overall direction of the essay, about the point to make next and those that come later, about the amount of detail for the paragraph you are composing, about the order of that detail, and about the words to choose for the sentence you are working on.

When the stress of so many decisions piles up and writers face too many questions without clear answers, most are overwhelmed and stop composing. This experience of being "blocked" is familiar to professionals and students alike, but there are ways to deal with it. Planning before you begin drafting will not always keep you from moments when the words won't come or from your essay seeming like a directionless journey, but it will help. At the very least, planning will help you divide your work into more manageable chunks.

How can you know when to begin planning? Sometimes your exploration of possible ideas and details will reveal a clear pattern or direction for your essay. Sometimes your freewriting, brainstorming, or questioning may guide you to the point or thesis around which you wish to build your essay. These are appropriate times to make use of one of the planning techniques described below. Another time to turn to the planning techniques is when you have piled up so many possible ideas, opinions, details, and chunks of information for your essay that you realize you need to start constructing the whole before you are overwhelmed by the raw materials.

There are two main kinds of planning techniques: those that help you identify patterns in the information and ideas you have been developing for an essay and those that help you construct an organizing scheme to follow as you write.

Clustering and Diagramming

Both clustering and diagramming (creating tree diagrams) are ways of creating conceptual maps that group ideas and help you see relationships.

In **clustering** you develop ideas related to a central topic and link the ideas with lines to display how they are associated. Clustering encourages the interconnection of ideas. You may begin by developing a single idea into several seemingly unconnected nodes, but on further reflection recognize some connections you hadn't yet considered.

Begin by writing a concept, idea, or topic in the center of a page, and circle it. Then randomly jot down associations with this central idea, circling them and connecting them with lines to the center, like the spokes of a wheel. As you continue to generate ideas around the central focus, think about the interconnections among subsidiary ideas, and draw lines to show those. After a few minutes, you will probably have something like the cluster below that Seveon Robertson used while working on an assignment that asked her to draw conclusions about her first two months as a college student.

You can also create clusters in cycles, each subsidiary idea becoming the central focus on a new page. You'll soon find that some clusters begin petering out once you've exhausted your fund of knowledge. Stand back and assess what you have. Is there enough to go on, without further consideration? If so, you may be ready to start some harder, more critical consideration of your paper's direction. If not, perhaps further strategies will open up additional ideas.

Tree diagrams resemble clusters, but their branches tend to be a little more linear, with few interconnections. Tree diagrams rely on the notion of subordination: each larger branch can lead to smaller and smaller branches. For this reason, tree diagramming can provide a useful way to visualize the components of your paper. You can even revise a tree diagram into a sort of preliminary outline (see pages 25–26) to use when deciding what to place in each paragraph of your paper.

Using Questions to Organize

Organizing questions help you see how the ideas, information, and arguments you wish to share lend themselves to a pattern of exposition or argument like those discussed and illustrated in this text. In the list below, we indicate the sections that correspond to each set of questions so that you can turn to the advice and examples in each section for further guidance.

Organizing Questions	**Chapter**
Have I gathered examples and illustrations that illustrate a generality? Can I use examples to help readers understand my topic and my conclusions? How can I best arrange examples to illustrate and support my thesis?	Section 3, "Example."
Into what categories do my information or my ideas fall? Does each category have different characteristics? What is the order of importance or interest among the categories? What arrangement of categories best explains or supports my conclusions?	Section 4, "Classification."

In what ways do these concepts, activities, outlooks, situations, or subjects differ, and in what ways are they the same? Which similarities or differences are worth special attention and in what order?	Section 5, "Comparison and Contrast."
What surprising similarities between my subject and another, seemingly very different subject, can I use to help illustrate or explain the issues, object, process, concept, or event I am writing about?	Section 6, "Analogy."
How does the subject work, or how can it be done? What arrangement will best clarify the steps, stages, or elements for readers? Can the explanation be organized to support my conclusions?	Section 7, "Process Analysis."
Why did it happen, and what is likely to happen in the future? How can the discussion of causes or effects be best organized in order to clarify their relationship?	Section 8, "Cause and Effect."
What is being defined, and what features characterize it and set it off from other things? What order of presentation will make the definition clear to readers? How can the definition be arranged to support or lead up to my conclusions?	Section 9, "Definition."
What are its features (physical, emotional, etc.), and does the arrangement of these elements in time and space suggest an organization for my explanation or presentation? What organization will best enable readers to understand the whole and the relationship of its parts?	Section 10, "Description."

What happened? To whom? When? Where? What is the best way to arrange the story to make a point?	Section 11, "Narration."
What generalization do the facts or events support? What further facts or events does the generalization help explain? In what order should the facts, events, and generalizations be presented in order to best illustrate the process of reasoning?	Section 12, "Induction and Deduction."
What is the proposition and what is the supporting evidence? Which patterns of argument (or combination of patterns) will present the supporting evidence in the most convincing fashion?	Section 13, "Argument."

Planning Visually
Putting ideas and information into a visual pattern such as a problem-solution grid or a generalization-and-support plan helps many writers envision possible arrangements for an essay. When you are writing expository papers that analyze or interpret a subject and that present your generalization (or thesis), you may want to create a generalization-and-support plan.

A **generalization-and-support plan** helps you arrange details and ideas so that they either lead up to a conclusion or follow and provide support for a generalization (thesis) presented near the beginning of an essay. To create such a plan, begin by listing facts and ideas about your subject. Then look over the items on the list and decide what principle or generalization sums up their meaning and significance, explains their consequences and importance for readers, or helps explain the "what" and "why" of new information or unfamiliar situations. Summarize different clusters of facts and ideas and write down the brief summaries in a sequence that either leads up to your conclusion (stated briefly) or that flows from your generalization (stated briefly) and supports it.

```
Generalization: Manufacturing children's toys is
a risky business
```

Support: Fashions in children's toys change quickly—sometimes several times within a year

Support: Toy manufacturers must make product decisions a year before the toys appear in stores, so they need to predict trends a year ahead

Support: Bringing a new toy to market can cost millions of dollars

Support: Most new toys are not successes; many make very little money

Support: There are many well-managed and imaginative companies competing for business in the toy market

A **problem-solution grid** helps you plan papers that argue for a particular approach to an issue or problem or for the advantages of one course of action over others. To create a problem-solution grid, start with a phrase or a sentence summarizing or illustrating the problem. Draw a box around this statement and add several vertical lines to boxes below, labeling these boxes as "solutions." In each of the secondary boxes put a word or phrase summarizing the solution. Then move downward to boxes that deal with further problems that the solutions themselves might create or that deal with further aspects of the main solution that need to be considered. (These later boxes offer you a chance to consider objections to your solution and to weigh the advantages of different solutions.)

Lack of Computer Facilities for Student Use at Freshwater State University		
Solution: Tuition Surcharge to Buy More Computers	Solution: User Fee Paid into New Facilities Fund	Solution: Lobby State Legislature for Funds
Objection: Tuition is High Already	Objection: Many Students Can't Afford User Fees	Problem: May Take a Long Time

Objection: Not All Students Use the Computer Facilities	Problem: Fees May Not Generate Enough Money	Problem: Legislature in a Budget- Cutting Mood

Creating a Discovery Draft

For some people, writing itself can be a way of discovering ideas, details, and possible arrangements. This strategy can be successful if it involves creation of a **zero draft** or **discovery draft,** but not if it means the painfully slow process of trying to create a detailed, well-organized first draft without adequate planning. Written at top speed and filled with partly developed thoughts and expressions—like freewriting (see pages 9–11)—a discovery draft gives you a chance to try out ideas and arrangements and to see a plan for a paper emerge as the writing goes along. Though it can take more time than other planning methods, a discovery draft can be useful. Often writers stop partway into a discovery draft as soon as they have a clear idea of where the paper is going. Then they move on to some other planning techniques or to creating a full first draft.

Outlining

Not all writers can envision a paper's content and its arrangement in the kind of detail necessary to create a formal outline with numerous sections and levels of subheadings. And even writers who can plan an essay in such detail often find themselves altering their plans during drafting and revision as they recognize new and better directions for their work. If your topic lends itself to a detailed outline, however, you may wish to prepare one as a planning strategy or utilize one later in the writing process as a revision technique (see pages 29–30).

On the other hand, many writers use informal outlines and purpose outlines to test possible plans for an essay, and you may wish to try these techniques. When you have in mind the various ideas and details you wish to present in an essay, create an **informal outline** arranging the ideas and details in groups (perhaps by clustering) and summarize each group in a heading. Then write down the headings in the order you wish to present them, putting the most important ideas and details under each.

An alternative technique is to create a **purpose outline** by stating the purpose or role each group of ideas and details will play in the essay. Then arrange the groups in the order that you think will best accomplish your overall purpose for writing. Here is Bippin Kumar's purpose outline for a paper exploring the reasons why college students may lose the motivation necessary to succeed at their studies.

1. Get readers' attention by mentioning the *bad habits* most of us have and that we may be able to correct on our own. (minor causes of the problem)

> lack of sleep
>
> disorganization
>
> distractions (television, etc.)

2. Show how we are often responsible because of the choices we make and explain that we need to make wiser choices. (more serious causes)

> sports and other extracurricular activities
>
> friends and socializing
>
> Greek life
>
> letting ourselves get frustrated and angry over daily hassles (bookstores, commuting)

3. Conclude with problems that we can't avoid and that may require special planning or counseling to overcome. (more serious causes)

> work
>
> financial stresses
>
> family demands or problems
>
> lack of necessary skills

Identifying a Purpose and Deciding on a Thesis

A successful essay has a clear purpose and a central theme (or thesis) that it conveys to readers and that ties together its parts. A purpose and theme (thesis) should begin to emerge during the planning process. If not, your attempts to complete a full draft of your essay are likely to be marked with confusion, misdirections, and restarts.

Your purpose or purposes for writing may change as you draft and revise, of course, but you should nonetheless make identifying a tentative purpose part of your planning process. Try writing yourself a note stating your potential topic along with possible goals for your writing (and, perhaps, anticipated reactions from readers). To remain flexible and open to new ideas, you might begin your statement with a phrase like "I'd like to . . ." or "I'm planning to . . ." For example;

> I'm planning to explain the reasons why many college students lose their motivation to work hard at their studies.
>
> —Bippin Kumar

> I'd like to tell what it felt like to be forced to leave my homeland, Haiti, so that my readers can understand why to leave something you love is to die a little.
>
> —Fredza Leger

Most likely, you will also alter, revise, or change the main point (theme or thesis) of your essay as you write, and such changes often make for a better essay. By the time your essay is complete, moreover, you will also have to decide whether to announce your main point directly to readers in a concise thesis statement (see below), to present it less directly in a series of statements in the body of the essay, or to imply it through the details and arrangement of the paper. No matter which strategy you choose, you should have a relatively clear idea of your main point (theme, thesis) before you begin drafting. Try stating your theme to yourself. You can do this in several ways:

- Start with a phrase like "I want my readers to understand . . ." or "The point of the whole essay is. . . "
- Make up a title that embodies your main idea.
- Send an imaginary note to your readers: "By the time you are finished with this essay, I hope you will see (or agree with me) that. . . "

If you want to share your knowledge of bicycling as a sport, for instance, you might try one or more of these strategies, as in the following examples.

1. The point of the whole essay is that people can choose what kind of bicycle riders they want to be—recreational, competitive, or cross-country.

2. What Kind of Bicycle Rider Do You Want to Be?

3. By the time you are finished with this essay, I hope you will be able to choose the kind of bicycle riding—recreational, competitive, or cross-country—that is best for you.

A **tentative thesis statement** can act as focus when you draft and as a reminder of your essay's main point (thesis). You can create a tentative thesis statement by summing up in a sentence or two your main point, the conclusion you plan to draw from the information and ideas you will present, or the proposition for which you plan to argue. You may eventually use a revised form of the tentative thesis statement in your completed essay as a way of announcing clearly to readers the main idea behind your writing.

For example, when Kin Chin was preparing a paper on different meanings of the phrase "recent immigrant," he used the following tentative thesis statement: "For some people, *recent immigrant* means a threat to their jobs or more strain on the resources of schools and social service agencies. For others it means fresh ideas and a broadening of our culture and outlook." In his final paper he used this thesis statement: "For some, *recent immigrant* means *cheap labor* or *higher taxes;* for others, it means *fresh ideas* and *a richer, more diverse culture.*"

Drafting

Drafting involves a good deal more than setting pen to paper or fingers to keyboard and letting the words flow according to your plan. It means paying attention to the way each section of an essay relates to the other sections and to the central theme. It means making sure you begin and end the essay in ways that are clear, helpful, and interesting to readers. And it means making sure each section and each paragraph present sufficient, detailed information so that readers can understand your subject and have reasons to agree with your explanations and conclusions.

Drafting does not mean getting everything right the first time. Such a goal is likely to prove both exhausting and impossible to achieve. A much better goal is to draft with the most important features of an essay in mind and to work quickly enough so that you have sufficient time to revise later and then pay attention to details.

As you draft, therefore, make sure that you introduce readers to your topic, indicate its importance, generate interest in it, and suggest the direction your essay will take. The essays in this collection can provide you with models of successful strategies for the beginnings of essays, and the *Introductions* entry in the "Guide to Terms"(at the back of the text) offers a detailed list of opening strategies. The "Guide" also provides advice about another important feature that should be a focus during drafting—your essay's conclusion.

Keep in mind the various sections you have planned for your essay, or keep at hand a copy of any planning strategies you have used, especially those that identify the planned parts of your essay, their general content, and their purposes.

As you write, include statements that alert readers to the various sections, along with transitions marking the movement from one section to the next (or from paragraph to paragraph). Make sure, too, that in making shifts in time, place, ideas, and content you do not confuse readers, but instead give them adequate indication of the shifts. Remember to provide readers with concrete, specific details and evidence that will give them the information they need about your topic, or the support necessary to make your explanations or arguments convincing.

Pay attention to the arrangement of your essay, especially to the patterns of exposition or argument you are employing. In any essay that classifies, for example, don't provide a detailed treatment of one category in the classification but skimpy treatment of the others—unless you have a special reason for doing so. Let your readers know, directly or indirectly, whatever pattern(s) you are employing. This will make them aware of your essay's design and will help to guide their attention to the key points you cover. Make every effort to stick to your main idea (perhaps using your tentative thesis statement as a guide—see page 28), and check to see that the parts of the essay are clearly related to and support the main idea. If you have trouble developing a section because you need more information, or because you can't express ideas as clearly as you want, make a note of the things that need to be done and then move on.

When you are finished drafting, you may wish to create a formal outline to help you understand what you have included (or

failed to include) in your draft and to check whether the arrangement of your essay is clear and reasonable. A formal outline can also
help you identify those elements of your work that need attention
during revision.

In a formal outline, you group the elements of an essay into different levels (I, II, III; A, B, C; 1, 2, 3; a, b, c, and so on) according to
their level of generality. You should develop your outline logically so
that, for example, each level of an outline has at least two elements.

In outlining her paper on contrasting images of cigarette smoking, for instance, Rachel Ritchie was able to check whether she was
providing a balanced and detailed treatment of the different portrayals of smokers and smoking.

I. Cigarette smoking used to be regarded as socially acceptable
and fashionable behavior.
   A. Movie heroes used smoking to display their confidence
   and sophistication.
      1. Handsome, virile men like Humphrey Bogart made
      cigarettes a part of their image.
      2. Glamorous leading ladies used cigarettes as elegant
      fashion accessories.
   B. Smoking was associated with social status and general
   well-being.
      1. . . .

II. Today, experience and research have given smoking a
deadly image.
   A. Many Americans die from cigarette smoking.
      1. In 1980, 485,000 Americans died from cigarette-related
      diseases.
      2. Recently, around 500,000 die each year (more than
      one-quarter of the deaths from all causes).
   B. . . .

Revising

When you shift your focus to revising, you pay special attention to
the success with which your draft essay embodies your intentions
and meets your readers' likely expectations. You examine the draft
to see if it does a good job presenting insights, reasoning, and
details. You look at the draft from a reader's perspective to see if the

discussions are clear and informative, the reasoning is logical, and the examples and supporting details are related to the central theme.

Reading for Revision

Revision starts with rereading—looking over your draft with a dual perspective: as an author and as a member of your potential audience. As you read for revision, keep track of the places that need more work and make note of the directions your rewriting might take. Most writers find it hard to read for revision directly from a computer screen, and they print a hard copy of their drafts for this purpose.

Whether you are working with a handwritten text, a typed copy, or a print from a word processor, you may find reading for revision most effective if you do it with a pencil or pen in hand to record your reactions and plans for revision.

Reading for revision can be even more effective when another writer does it for you (and you return the favor). Remember, collaborative readings of this sort are best done in a cooperative, rather than harshly critical atmosphere. Your job and that of your reader(s) is to identify strengths as well as weaknesses and to suggest (if possible) ways to turn weaknesses into strong points. (For more about collaborative revising and editing, see pages 37–38.)

Whether you are reading your own work or someone else's, you may find these symbols useful shortcuts for making marginal comments to guide revision.

Reader Response Symbols

?	Could you explain this a bit more? I can't really understand this.
Add?	I would like to know more about this. I think you could use more detail here.
Leave out?	This information or this passage may not be necessary. You have already said this.
Missing?	Did you leave something out? I think there is a gap in the information, explanation, or argument here.
Confusing?	I have trouble following this explanation/argument? The information here is presented in a confusing manner.

Reorganize?   I think this section (or paper) would be more effective if you presented it in a different order.

Interesting,   Your writing really works here. I like it.
Good,
Effective,
etc.

You may be tempted to revise as you read, and for sentences or paragraphs that need a quick fixup, this approach is often adequate. In most cases, however, your revisions need to go beyond tinkering with words and sentences if they are to lead to real improvement. You will need to pay attention to the overall focus, to the need for additional paragraphs presenting detailed evidence, and to the arrangement of the steps in an explanation or argument. To see the need for such large-scale changes you need to read the draft paying attention to the essay as a whole, something you cannot do if you stop frequently to rework the parts. In addition, it makes little sense to correct the flaws in a sentence if you realize a bit later on that the entire paragraph ought to be dropped.

Questioning Reading
One good way to read for revision is to prepare questions that will focus your attention as you read—questions appropriate for your topic, your purposes, your pattern(s) of exposition or argument, and your intended readers. You may wish to direct attention to those features you worked on while drafting (introductions, or transitions for example). You may wish to use questions that reflect the specific topic or purposes of your essay or that reflect the probable outlook of your intended readers. Make notes in the margins of your draft or on a separate sheet of paper (or computer file). Don't keep too many questions in mind as you read; instead, reread as many times as necessary, each time with a different set of questions. Following are some possible questions to help you evaluate your draft.

Questions for Revision
General
    Does my essay have a clear topic and focus?
    Does it stick to the topic and focus throughout?
    How have I signaled the topic and focus to readers?

Is the essay divided into parts? What are they?
Are the parts clearly identified for readers?

Thesis and theme
Does the essay have a thesis statement? Is it clearly stated?
Is the thesis statement in the best possible location?
Should the thesis statement be more (or less) specific?
Are all the different parts of the essay clearly related to the thesis statement or the central theme?
In what ways have I reminded readers of the thesis or theme in the course of the essay? Do I need to remind them more often or in other ways?

Introductions and conclusions
Does my introduction make the topic clear? Does it interest readers in what I will have to say?
Does my introduction give readers some indication of the arrangement of the essay and its purpose(s)?
Does the conclusion help tie together the main points of the essay or remind readers of the significance of the information and ideas I have presented?
Does my conclusion have a clear purpose or have I ended the essay without any clear strategy?

Information and ideas
Have I presented enough information and enough details so that readers will feel they have learned something worthwhile about the topic?
At what specific places would the essay be improved if I added more information?
What information can be cut because it is repetitive, uninteresting, or unrelated to the topic or theme of the essay?
Is my information fresh and worth sharing? Do I need to do more thinking or research so that the content of my essay is worth sharing?
Do the examples and details I present support my conclusions in a convincing way? Do I need to explain them more fully? Would more research or thinking enable me to offer better support?
Have I learned something new or worthwhile about my topic and communicated it to readers?

Sentences and paragraphs
>   Have I divided the essay into paragraphs that help readers
>   identify shifts in topic, stages in an explanation, steps in a
>   line of reasoning, key ideas, or important segments of
>   information?
>
>   Does each paragraph make its topic or purpose clear to readers?
>
>   Which short paragraphs need greater development through the
>   addition of details or explanations?
>
>   Which long paragraphs could be trimmed or divided?
>
>   Do the sentences reflect what I want to say? Which sentences
>   could be clearer?
>
>   Are the sentences varied in length? Do they provide appropri-
>   ate emphasis to key ideas?
>
>   Can I word the explanations or arguments more clearly?
>
>   Can I use more vivid and concrete language?
>
>   Would the paper benefit from more complicated or imaginative
>   language? From simpler, more direct wording?

Readers' perspective
>   In what ways are my readers likely to view this topic or argu-
>   ment? Have I taken their perspectives into account?
>
>   What do I want my readers to learn from this essay? What opin-
>   ion do I want them to share? What do I want them to do?
>
>   Have I considered what my readers are likely to know or
>   believe and how this will shape their response to my pur-
>   pose(s) for writing?

(The essays presented in this text and the questions that follow them
also suggest things you can ask yourself as you revise.)

Here is the draft of an essay Sarah Lake produced in response
to an assignment asking her to write about a community of some
sort, taking the perspective of an outsider trying to understand how
the community works and what kinds of relationships people in the
community form. The marginal comments on the paper are notes
she has addressed to the classmates (peer readers) who will be
responding to her paper with revision suggestions.

```
              Welcome to the Gym!
       As I stepped up to the door to the field
       house I saw myself in the reflection from
```

the door. I had chosen mesh shorts, a
white v-neck T-shirt, and tattered old
sneakers in hope to "fit in" with the
crowd. Luckily, I still possess the Ram
sticker on the back of my I.D. I was all
set. I was in. A cheery eyed student
asked for my I.D., and pointed me towards
the training room. So far, so good, I
thought. My only hopes were that the gym
was going to be a great place.

The smell was rather distinct; one part
sweat, one part machine oil, and one part
cleaner, or maybe it was the chlorine
coming from the pool. Surprisingly, it
was a rather welcoming smell. The kind of
smell that says "Come on in, have fun,
workout, sweat, be hot and sticky and
smelly, it's O.K." I liked what it had to
say, so I continued on, farther into the
training room. As I stepped inside to the
training room, heavy breathing and strenuous shouts of "One!, Two!, Three!" could
be heard. The shouting seemed common, and
went unnoticed by regulars. Weightlifters,
mostly men, would grunt, scream, moan,
and sometimes yell in agony as they tried
to lift weights two, three times the
weight they could handle. Their heads
turned a tomato red and looked as if they
were about to explode. Their veins, like
thick rope, popped through the skin on
their necks, arms, and legs. Due to the
fact that I'm not a weightlifter or a
man, I surely don't understand the meaning behind this behavior. It looked
rather painful and it wasn't very flatter-
ing to them, but it was entertaining.

I've tried to make this interesting. Is it?

This is the community I studied. Is my purpose clear?

I added a lot of detail. Does it work?

I squirmed my way through the machines,
and people, and found myself a spot on
one of the stair masters. I curiously
stared at the screen in front of me.
Blinking letters zoomed across the screen
reading enter your weight and then press
enter. Enter my weight? That's a lot to
ask of a girl. I thought about it, and
even considered lying to the machine, but
reality set in, I realized it was just a
machine. Why lie to a machine? I punched
in my weight, and continued to answer the
questions the screen produced.

As I started my workout, I began to
gaze around and inspect everyone's interaction with each other. "Rules of the
Gym" were listed on the wall and were
followed by everyone. Everyone respected
everyone and everything. On the other
hand rules for socializing weren't
posted, but underlying rules seemed to be
understood. Socializing while working out
or better yet, while in motion was not
encouraged. Talking only took place while
one was motionless or waiting for a
machine. It seemed as if it took so much
concentration to work out that no one
could even talk while doing so. I, on the
other hand, couldn't wait to talk when I
got finished. I felt like I had gone
through withdrawal. I needed some sort of
outlet to make the time go by and my
workout faster so I turned from people
behavior watching to people's attire
watching.

Gym attire was rather diverse. Some
wore the typical workout uniform, which

I think my punctuation and grammar got a bit out of control at times in this draft. Help!

Are my sentences clear?

consisted of tight spandex. It included
tops, tops over tops, bottoms, bottoms
over bottoms, etc., etc. Others wore outfits very similar to my own which was very
comforting. My favorite outfit (I'm being
sarcastic) was on a young woman, about
21, who turned more heads in twenty minutes than Cindy Crawford has in her whole
career. It consisted of, from top to bottom: a bright pink scrunchie (one of
those cloth elastics), a black headband,
a bright pink jog bra, black lycra span-

**Is this too
much detail?**

dex, covered by a workout g-string, also
bright pink in color. As I worked my eyes
down to her legs and then to her feet I
noticed she had boxing sneakers on. The
ones NIKE made in the eighties with the
high laces. Smashing, was the only word
to describe her ensemble.

Peer Response Before you revise (or in between successive drafts),
getting a look at your work through another's eyes can help you
spot strengths and weaknesses and identify steps you can take to
improve your essay. To do this, ask a person or a group of people to
read and comment on the strengths and weaknesses of your draft
essay. Ask them, too, to suggest ways the writing might be
improved. Their comments are most likely to be useful if you ask
them to respond to specific questions (like those in the list above, pp.
32–34) and to make concrete suggestions for improvement.

Here are some comments Tonya Williams and Dave Cisneros
made on Sarah Lake's essay.

Does this essay have a clear and interesting thesis statement or
generalization?

TONYA: I don't see any thesis statement. The assignment asked us to
make a generalization about the community. What is yours?

DAVE: In the planning materials you shared with us, you talked
about the reasons people were exercising. Could you add

a generalization about the motivations of people in this community?

Does this essay provide detailed examples that support or explain the essay's thesis statement or generalization?

TONYA: I like some of the pictures of gym life that you provide, but I don't see how they fit with any kind of generalization. The last example probably talks too much about clothes.

DAVE: I suggest cutting the last paragraph. It doesn't fit with the rest of the paper.

Are the sentences clear and effective? How might they be improved?

TONYA: A lot of the sentences begin with I, so the paper seems to focus on you rather than the community you are exploring.

DAVE: I like the way you write. I think your sentences are easy to read in general. At times, though, the paper seems a bit informal. I'm not sure whether the writing is too informal in style or whether you are focusing more on your personal feelings than on the kinds of observations and conclusions you are trying to explain.

Are there any places the grammar and spelling might be improved?

TONYA: I think you have some grammar problems, especially fragments and run-ons. I put a question mark next to these on the paper.

DAVE: I noticed a few spelling problems and other small errors. It tried to mark them, but I may have missed a few.

Editing and Final Revision

After you have carefully rewritten your essay at least one time and perhaps several, you can focus on editing and final revision. In creating your finished paper, pay special attention to matters such as the style and clarity of sentences and paragraphs as well as correctness in grammar and usage. Before you hand in your final draft, carefully correct any typographical errors along with any mistakes in spelling or expression that remain.

Here is the final version of Sarah Lake's paper, including some revision that she made during a last reading and some editing before she typed the final copy. In revising, Sarah took into account the comments of her classmates and those her instructor wrote on a copy of her draft. In addition, she went back to her planning document for ideas she left out of the draft, and she developed these ideas at some length in the revised version of the paper. The comments in the margin of the paper below have been added to highlight features of the essay.

Welcome to the Gym: A Community of Worriers

As I stepped up to the door of the field house, I saw my reflection in the glass, and I started worrying. I had chosen mesh shorts, a white v-neck T-shirt, and tattered old sneakers in hopes of fitting in with the community I planned to observe: people exercising for fitness inside the gym. I was worrying about how well I would fit in. After my visit, I realized I fit in quite well. Not only had I dressed appropriately, but I was also worried, and worrying about appearance seemed to be one trait everybody at the gym shared. *It seems to be the attribute that defines this community and ties its members together.*

Moves from personal experience to the conclusion that will be explored in the essay.

Thesis statement

As I stepped inside the training room I heard heavy breathing and strenuous shouts of "One! Two! Three!" Weightlifters, mostly men, were grunting, screaming, moaning, and yelling in agony as they tried to lift weights two, three times more than they could handle. Their heads turned tomato red, and they looked as if

Paragraph presents observations

they were about to explode. I'm neither a
man nor a weightlifter, and I had no idea
why they were trying to overexert themselves, or so it seemed to me.

Evidence   When I spoke with several of the
supports   weightlifters, they admitted that for
overall thesis many people who spend time lifting
weights, appearance is a primary concern.
They claimed that many male weightlifters
begin exercising because they feel infe-
rior about their physical appearance or
because they want to get that "He-man" or
"Caveman" look that they consider an
ideal for men. Though the men I talked to
said that they, personally, weren't that
anxious about the way they looked, they
also admitted that they felt that potential dates pay more attention to a man
who has "bulked up." I asked why they
felt it was important to have a muscular
and masculine appearance in today's society, especially when a lot of people
(women especially) talk about the need
Observations for men to be "sensitive." I was sur-
likely to   prised by the answers because they seemed
surprise and to reveal worry and insecurity—which was
intrigue   surprising coming from a group of very
reader   well muscled college men. The
weightlifters said they thought sensitivity was a good thing, and they claimed to
work towards it in their relationships.
They also said that sensitivity grows out
of self-confidence, and that for me self-
confidence often comes through physical
Transition to fitness and athletic ability.
second set of   Though the weightlifters seemed sin-
observations cere, as a woman I felt rather awed by

their appearance and kept waiting for one
of them to knock one of the female exer-
cisers over the head and drag her back to
his cave. This thought made me shift my
attention to the women, most of whom were
working on machines like Stair Masters,
stationary bicycles, or Nautilus. To
enter into the women's part of this community, I squirmed my way through the
machines and people, and I found a spot
on one of the Stair Masters. I stared
curiously at the screen in front of me.
Blinking letters zoomed across the screen
asking me to enter my weight. "Enter my
weight," I thought, "That's a lot to ask

Personal experience supports thesis

of a girl." I even thought about lying,
but then I got embarrassed about lying to
a machine. Later, when I shared this
worry with some of the women at the gym,
I realized they shared my apprehension

Observations act as evidence for thesis

and a lot of my other worries.
 Like the men, the women shared many
concerns about their appearance, espe
cially about their attractiveness and
about the relationship of appearance to
self-confidence. They spoke of how the
"Baywatch" girls are the ideals of appearance for women in our society, and of how
they felt a need to compete with the

Summarizes interviews

"Barbies" of this world, even though such
an appearance is unrealistic for the average woman. They also talked about having
a kind of balance scale in their heads.
As their weight increases, they feel less
attractive, and as their weight decreases,
they feel more attractive. They pointed
out how magazines, TV programs, and movies

seem to equate thinness with attractiveness and link attractiveness to self-confidence. Though they admitted that working
women with responsibilities as wives and
mothers might not have time or energy to
work out in a gym, they worried about how
their self-confidence might suffer if they
didn't have the opportunity to exercise to
control their weight.

    After my time on the Stair Master came
to an end and I had finished talking to
the members of the gym community, I left,
feeling as though I fit in. I was a wor-
rier and I had dressed like many of the
women. On my way out, however, I passed a
woman dressed in a daring pink and black

Conclusion outfit who began turning heads as soon as
echos main she walked in the door. I started worrying
point again, and I knew the people in the gym
were now worrying even more about their
looks.

2

Becoming a Critical Reader

You encounter **expository writing** every day in one of its many forms, including essays, magazine articles, reports, memos, newspaper reports, and nonfiction books. Expository writing brings you facts and insights—it helps writers and readers share experiences and build understanding.

You also encounter **argumentative writing** in many places: editorials and opinion essays, reports and proposals, policy statements and investigative reporting, and academic or professional writing. Argumentative writing focuses on differences and helps build agreement; it provides reasons for readers to agree with writers or at least come to an understanding of another's perspective.

Expository writing and argumentative writing often work together. Exposition can lead to persuasion as writers offer support for their explanations and conclusions. Argument frequently turns to exposition for the facts, statistics, examples, and explanations that are evidence for a line of reasoning.

CRITICAL READING

You are probably aware of the challenges exposition and argument pose to writers, but you may underestimate the importance of analyzing the *how* and *why* of an essay as you read. Or you may underestimate the need to question a writer's information and ideas and to imagine alternatives in content and expression. In short, you need to remind yourself of the need for critical reading and work on developing your analyzing, questioning, and responding skills.

An expository essay on a difficult topic—a scientific explanation, for example—obviously calls for careful reading, as does a complicated argument. But even an apparently straightforward explanation offers interpretations, information, and conclusions that call for the kind of analysis and evaluation an uncritical reader may fail to provide. A serious argument, too, even one on a familiar issue, calls for a reader willing to raise questions and attend to logic and evidence before deciding to share the writer's stance.

In addition, good expository (and argumentative) writing does more than present detailed, reliable information (or clear reasoning and support). It can transport you to unfamiliar places and enable you to share someone else's experiences. It can recreate an author's voice and feelings in rich, evocative detail. It can surprise you, helping alter the way you see and understand. It can move you to respond creatively (perhaps in writing of your own) or it can move you to informed, self-aware action. Goals like these call for the participation of a critical reader, the kind of reader Pete Hamill assumes for his "before" portrait of the Everglades—that is, *before* agriculture, dams, and cities began drawing precious water from the plants and animals of the region.

> Then, before dawn, at Naples, she turned onto the Tamiami Trail. And stopped talking.
>
> In memory, a lavender wash covered the world. We parked and stepped out of the car. I looked out at a flat, empty prairie, its monotony relieved by the occasional silhouettes of nameless trees against the black early-morning sky. "What is this?" I asked. "Where are we?"
>
> "Listen," she whispered.
>
> And I heard them, far off, almost imperceptible at first: thin, high, and then like the sound of a million whips cutting the air. They came over the edge of the horizon and then the sky was black with them. Birds. Thousands of them. Tens of thousands. Maybe a million. I shivered in fear and awe. The woman held my city-boy's hand. And then the vast dense flock was gone. The great molten ball of the sun oozed over the horizon.
>
> "We're in The Everglades," she said.
>
> Pete Hamill, "The Neverglades"

Critical reading involves **previewing, reading,** and **reviewing,** activities that you can undertake in a number of ways depending in part on the kind of essay, article, or book and in part on your reasons for reading. In the pages that follow, we offer practical suggestions for developing and enhancing these critical reading skills. We also show how they can become part of **reading to write,** an activity characteristic of accomplished writers and an approach to reading that the essays collected in this text and the accompanying questions are designed to help you develop.

Active Reading

All the activities we describe in this chapter are active reading strategies. This means that they involve some activity on your part— questioning the ideas and information in a text, jotting down ideas and responses, speculating about consequences of a concept, or making notes for an essay of your own, to mention just a few possibilities. Critical reading is active reading. At times, of course, you may wish to read simply to gather ideas and information from a text, not to interact with it. But even when you do, the habit of critical attention can come to your aid by prompting you to consider just how reliable the text's information is. It can lead you to ask if the manner in which ideas are being presented makes some questionable concepts seem more believable.

For writers, the habit of critical attention turns each act of reading into a source of ideas, details, and techniques that they can draw on and transform into their own work. For writers and people trying to develop their writing skills, therefore, reading is generally a process of reading to write, and it takes place with a pen, pencil, or keyboard close by or with an exceptionally sharp memory. Here are some of the ways active readers often store responses, questions, ideas, and techniques for further use:

- Reading journals
- Marginal notes
- Highlighting

Reading Journals

A **reading journal** is a notebook, folder, or computer file in which you keep your responses to reading: notes, questions, ideas, criticisms, and the like. Turning the fleeting ideas, questions, and responses that occur to you as you read into sentences in a journal helps you remember them, gives you a chance to consider them at greater length, and makes them available for later use, perhaps in an essay of your own.

Some people like to keep a journal beside them as they read so they can jot down ideas and responses as they occur during the reading process or write out their judgments and speculations as soon as they have finished an article or a section of a longer work. People who keep a journal at hand as they read also use it to make note of ideas and information from a text that they find particularly interesting and may wish to draw on later in their own writing. (Note: this technique works best if you record the specific source, that is, author; title; name, date, and place of publication; and page numbers.)

Other people reserve the journal for reactions and notetaking after they are finished reading on the grounds that too much writing can interfere with reading. Many of these people make marginal annotations as they read (see below) and later turn the annotations into journal entries. The particular approach you use should depend on your reading habits.

You can organize entries in a reading journal according to the particular selection, allotting a few pages to each article, chapter, or book, for example. Or you can organize the journal by categories, such as "Ideas and Questions for Further Writing," "Quotations and Information for Use in My 'Dangers of Dieting' Paper," or "Useful Strategies for Beginning an Essay." The particular organization you choose and the kinds of entries you make should reflect your purposes as a reader (and as a writer). Are you looking for strategies to help improve your writing? Then take note of the ways other writers begin and end a selection, the kinds of details they include, the ways they develop paragraphs, or any other strategies that need improvement in your own writing. Are you looking for topics and issues to address in your own papers? Then make a note of interesting or controversial topics and ideas that you come across as you read, particularly those that the writer does not treat in depth so that you have an opportunity to provide detailed treatment of the matter in your own writing.

Marginal Notes

Marginal notes are the scribbles, jottings, abbreviations, and other annotations you make in the margins of a book or magazine. Typically, you make such annotations when something you read prompts a strong response that you can record in brief form rather than in a more extended form, such as in a journal entry (see above).

You may wish to make a note of agreements of disagreements you have with the writer, of passages or techniques you admire, or of important ideas and information. In doing so, you are reading actively and critically, not passively accepting what the author has to say. Your marginal annotations are most likely to be of use to you as a writer when they indicate ways to turn the text or your responses to it into material for your own writing, as with the following marginal comments.

No! Putting attractive people in an ad is not necessarily a way of using sex to sell.

Add one more kind of horror flick—violence not shown. Sometimes even creepier. Use in my "How to Scare" paper.

Great detail. Her mom is really believable.

What abt. Mit's essay on embalming? Fit here?

Reasonable? More evidence?

cf—Wolfe, Raybon

Most margins leave you limited room for comments, so you will probably have to resort to some kind of shorthand, as a few of the examples above indicate. Since you will be the person reading the notes, use whatever system of abbreviations works best for you—as long as you can remember what the annotations meant when you return to the text.

Do not feel you need to restrict marginal comments to those that occur to you while you are reading. Many readers make a habit of pausing at breaks in a narrative or a line of reasoning to ask themselves what the writer's main point is so far or to formulate questions they would like to have answered. You can use marginal notes to summarize briefly your understanding of a text at a particular point or to record questions you hope the rest of the selection will answer. When you are finished with the entire selection, you can return to the annotations to assess (or re-assess) your understanding of the piece and to see which questions were answered or left unanswered. You might even wish to turn some of your marginal notes into more extensive journal entries (see above).

To make your marginal annotations as useful as possible, try to give some variety to your responses. Consider making these kind of comments: interpretations of what the author is trying to say, indications of passages you find confusing, questions you wish the author had answered, objections to the author's conclusions or counterarguments the writer fails to mention, brief restatements or summaries that make the point more clearly and concisely, and evaluations of the writer's conclusions or techniques of expression.

Highlighting

Highlighting is any technique that calls attention to a passage in a text. Using highlighting pens, underlining, arrows, circling—all these are ways of indicating that one section of a text is of special importance. You can highlight passages for various reasons: to help you remember information or concepts, to provide a way of locating phrases and sentences for later use, or to aid you in summarizing part or all of a selection by making note of the most important ideas and statements.

Try to decide on your purpose for highlighting ahead of time; otherwise, you may end up underlining or coloring passages for so many different reasons that your highlighting does not serve any purpose well and is hard to decipher when you return to the text later. In addition, if your highlighting serves several purposes, try using a different kind of marking for each: red highlighting or squiggly underlining for key ideas, for example, or yellow high-lighting and straight lines for passages you plan to quote in your paper.

TECHNIQUES FOR ACTIVE READING: PREVIEWING

People who write and edit for a living know how important it is to preview, or "read before you start reading." Newspapers use head-lines to tell you what to expect in an article; authors create titles; book writers and editors often provide brief summaries at the begin-ning of a chapter or in a table of contents, just as we do at the begin-ning of this text; and magazine editors often take key statements from an article and reprint them in large type within boxes where you can see them as you flip through an article prior to reading it.

What all these people know is that the knowledge and expecta-tions you bring to a piece of writing can determine how well you understand it and what you are able to draw from it. For example, reading an expository or argumentative essay without an idea of where it is going or what the author plans to do is like following a complicated set of directions without any idea of what you are building or where you are going. When you have some idea of an essay's overall plan and purpose, you can pay attention to and remember the facts and ideas you encounter along the way, and you can begin to evaluate their relevance as well as the way the author presents and develops information. Otherwise, you will need to spend your time figuring out where the essay is going and why, rather than on understanding what the essay is saying and how (or how well) ideas and information are being presented.

Likewise, when you already know something about a topic or issue, you can more readily understand and evaluate the complex information presented in an essay or the author's arguments in favor of a specific point of view. When you know little or nothing about a subject even a clearly and simply written discussion can be an overwhelming challenge.

Previewing is the process of bringing to mind what you already know about a subject before you begin to move sentence by sentence through an essay, and of developing reasonable expectations about the directions that the explanation or argument will take. It can also involve learning something new about the subject, the author, or the kind of writing. Two good ways to think about previewing are "reading before you read" and "reading in order to read." For example, if you know beforehand that William F. Buckley, Jr. writes from the perspective of the political right and Barbara Ehrenreich from the left, you can read their essays in this collection (pages 74–87) with a greater appreciation of the origins and consequences of the ideas they present. You also can let the essays "speak" to each other through your imagination in ways that can lead to a new perspective you develop in an essay of your own.

Look for Help from the Writer or Editor
Writers and editors recognize the importance of previewing, and they often provide you with considerable guidance. Titles are a good place to start. Some may be imaginative and intriguing and not particularly helpful. Others may tell you as much about a work's contents and organization as Don Aslett's *How Do I Clean the Moosehead? And 99 More Tough Questions about Housecleaning.*

Look at the table of contents in a book or collection of essays for detailed information about the contents and purpose of the work and perhaps even for a summary of chapters and selections. In the table of contents for this book, we offer brief summaries of the essays it contains. Here, for instance, are the entries for William F. Buckley, Jr. and Barbara Ehrenreich's essays.

Buckley:

The dean of conservative writers believes that we've become so numb to mistakes and injustices that we no longer have the spunk to complain about anything. And this apathy could have grave consequences.

Ehrenreich:

Acting like a man means speaking up for your rights, says this feminist, and it is a way of behaving that women can learn from men. As an example, she tells of a time when she acted in a manner that was too ladylike.

When an article or a book does not have a table of contents, skim through it looking for headings and subheadings that reveal the writer's plan and the topics being covered. If the editor highlights important passages, pay attention to them. Here are three passages from Randall Rothenberg's essay "What Makes Sammy Walk?" (pages 330–342) that the editor of the magazine in which it first appeared chose to reprint in large type in the middle of a page.

Less than 70 percent of U.S. men are now full-time year-round workers.

"You don't have a social life," Dave's daughter says, "and you don't do anything."

"I just put in a proposal to cut my hours to thirty-two a week and take a 20 percent pay cut," says a woman. "It's been accepted. I'm so happy."

These brief quotes help you begin reading with expectations about both the essay's subject and the author's attitude towards it.

Look at the Context

Pay attention to the kind of magazine, journal, or newspaper in which an essay appears. Some have a reputation for publishing articles with a particular point of view. Look for any statements of the periodical's editorial outlook; pay attention to the magazine's title and to the titles of the other articles it contains. The dust jacket of a book often provides a brief summary of its contents and perspective or quotations from reviewers that highlight its main points.

The date when a work was published can help you interpret and evaluate its facts and ideas. Any information you can gather from the book jacket or a "Writer's Profile" page in a magazine can also prove helpful.

In the headnotes to essays in this collection, we provide background information on the author and the selection that can help you in previewing. Here is one headnote from the text.

CULLEN MURPHY

CULLEN MURPHY grew up in Greenwich, Connecticut and attended school in both Greenwich and Dublin, Ireland. He received a B.A. from Amherst College in 1974 and soon after began working in the production department of *Change* magazine. In 1977, he was named editor of *The Wilson Quarterly*, and he has been managing editor of *The Atlantic Monthly* since 1985. In his parallel career, he has written the comic strip Prince Valiant since the middle 1970s (a comic strip which his father draws). Murphy is an essayist and nonfiction writer as well. His essays on different topics, many with a humorous or satirical view of contemporary society and behavior, have appeared in *The Atlantic Monthly* and other magazines, including *Harper's*. His first book, *Rubbish!* (with William Rathje), appeared in 1992, and a collection of his essays, *Just Curious*, was published in 1995.

A reader looking over this headnote might be prepared for an essay taking a critical and humorous look at contemporary habits or tastes and might expect writing that reflects the writer's wide range of interests. (Such expectations would be quite accurate, as the essay on pages 310–314 demonstrates.)

Sample and Predict
Skim the selection you are going to read looking for key terms or repeated phrases, names, or concepts. These can give you an idea of the topics and subtopics the writer presents, the order of presentation, and the conclusions the writer offers.

Sample some sentences (or even paragraphs) throughout the selection to discover what you can about its purpose and perspective. Look for charts and illustrations that highlight key elements of the text as well as passages in which the author summarizes the selection's ideas or reviews its organization.

Drawing on these various sources, try predicting what the selection is about, what its purpose is, and what conclusions the writer will offer. As you read, use your predictions to evaluate the essay's progress, but be ready to change your perspective if your predictions prove to be incorrect.

If in sampling an essay or a book you realize that you don't know enough about the subject to benefit from your reading, be ready to turn to an encyclopedia or a similar reference work for background information that will enable you to read in an informed, critical manner.

To help readers develop accurate predictions and expectations, editors often provide a brief introduction to an article, and writers often begin a report or position paper with a brief summary (or "abstract") of its content. Here is how a magazine editor introduced Veronica Chambers's essay "Mother's Day."

> When a daughter creates a life for herself that is completely different from her mother's, can love make a bridge? In this excerpt from her forthcoming memoir, *Mama's Girl*, Veronica Chambers says yes.

Based on this introduction, a reader can clearly expect an essay that draws contrasts between the experiences and outlooks of the author and her mother and that suggests ways of communicating and maintaining a relationship in spite of these differences.

At the beginning of each essay in this collection, we provide an introduction to help you develop predictions and expectations for what you are about to read. In our introduction to "Mother's Day," we try to give you an understanding of the topics it covers and also highlight the essay's pattern of organization (exposition) and its purpose.

> In this selection from her book *Mama's Girl*, published as an essay in *Glamour* magazine, Chambers uses a variety of expository patterns (comparison, example, narrative, cause-and-effect) to help you understand why her Mother's Day gift received such a cool reception. As she shifts through the differences between her perspective as an African American professional woman, a college-educated writer, and that of her mother, who struggled to raise her child on a maid's salary in the days when educational and occupational opportunities for African Americans were strictly limited, Chambers comes to a deeper appreciation of her mother's achievements.

TECHNIQUES FOR ACTIVE READING: READING AND UNDERSTANDING

When you read you need to pay attention to many things. Here is a short list of things to watch for:

- the different subjects covered and any interpretations or conclusions the writer offers. (Topic, Theme, and Thesis)

- the way the writer organizes the explanation or argument, especially any particular patterns of exposition or argument the writer employs. (See pages 21–23 for a brief summary of some patterns).
- the detail and effectiveness of the explanation; the examples and evidence the writer offers to support any conclusions, interpretations, or opinions; and the logic of the argument. (Development, Support, and Logic)
- any unanswered questions, confusing explanations, unsupported assertions, or illogical arguments that you encounter; any parts of the essay you find particularly effective or interesting.
- the words chosen by the writer; the arrangement and style of sentences; and the focus, organization, and detail of the paragraphs. (Diction, Syntax, and Style)
- any issues, questions, ideas, topics, or problems that you might wish to address further in writing of your own; any patterns or strategies you might like to employ in your own essays; and any elements of sentence or paragraph style you wish to adapt for your own purposes. (Reading to Write)

Of course, you cannot possibly pay attention to all these matters at the same time, nor do you need to do so. As you preview and as you read, decide which elements are most important for a particular essay and most related to your purposes for reading. Remember that as you review your reading (see pages 57–58), you can return to look at elements that escaped your focus on earlier readings. Remember, too, that for many essays, especially essays you are reading critically, one reading is seldom enough.

A Process for Reading

No single way of reading is best, yet some approaches are certainly more effective than others as ways of comprehending or producing creative responses that eventually take written form themselves. Instead of a lock-step system for reading, we offer the following suggestions you can employ according to the reading situation.

For the First Reading:

1. As you read for the first time, relax. Read the selection casually, as you would a magazine article, for whatever enjoyment or new ideas you get without straining. Do not stop to look up new

words unless the sentences in which they are used are meaningless until you do. Have a pen or pencil in hand and mark all words or passages you are doubtful about, and then go on.

Jot down spontaneous reactions to the essay in the margins, in a journal, or in a computer file. Disagreements and agreements are worth recording as are speculations of your own that the reading prompts. Do not allow yourself to be drawn too far away from the reading, but do capture the fleeting thoughts so that you can later call them to mind. (See pages 46–47 for further advice on annotating an essay and recording your responses.)

2. After the first reading, put the book down. For a few minutes think over what you have read. Don't spend too much time at this point figuring out exactly what the writer has to say. The memories, feelings, and opinions that come to mind at this stage are an important part of the reading process. They can be the basis for detailed comprehension or for your own writing. This is a good time for recording your responses to the reading in a journal (see pages 45–46) or discussing them with other readers.

3. Use the dictionary to help you understand words you have marked. Do not make the mistake of finding and trying to memorize the first or the shortest definition of a word. Instead, examine the various meanings and look for the word's uses as a noun, verb, and modifier. **Think** about them. Pronounce the word. Use it in a few sentences. Identify it with similar words you already know. Then see how the author has used it.

For the Second Reading:

4. Reread, the essay, pausing at times to think and **question** (see page 56). Underline important ideas; mark sentences or phrases that seem especially interesting, misleading, amusing, or well expressed. Pursue your own ideas, responses, objections, and speculations in marginal notes (see page 56) or a reading journal (see page 57).

5. Focus your reading on such elements as thesis, theme, topic, patterns of exposition or argument, development, support, logic, diction, syntax, and style (see pages 52–53).

6. Reread the essay in whole or part as many times as necessary to understand any passages you find especially challenging and to observe in detail any writing strategies, ideas, issues, or topics you might wish to employ in your own essays.

Reading Strategies

Here are some active reading strategies that can aid your understanding of an essay's meaning, your critical analysis of its strategies, and your ability to draw on it for your own writing.

Pause, Question, and Summarize

As you read, remember to pause to consider what you have read and what you expect to encounter next. You can pause at shifts from topic to topic (or subtopic to subtopic), steps in an explanation, or stages in a line of reasoning. Or you can pause whenever you feel a need to make sense of what you have been reading.

When you pause, ask yourself what topics and issues the writer has been covering and what conclusions or interpretations the essay offers. These questions may be helpful:

- What is the topic of this paragraph or passage? What does the author have to say about the topic?
- How are the ideas and details in this passage related to those in the prior section? The following section?
- What point of view or opinion is the writer offering in this passage? How is it related to the central theme or the thesis statement?

Think also of what you have learned from the reading and what you still want to know. Identify points or passages you find confusing and those that have been especially clear and effective.

Try to summarize what you have read so far and evaluate its effectiveness. Then try predicting what you will encounter in the rest of the essay. In predicting, you become more aware of the ways you have been reading and responding to an essay and you develop criteria to use in evaluating an essay's success.

Responding as You Read

As you read an essay to understand its ideas and information, you will often have a second stream of thoughts in your mind as well—one in which you carry on a dialogue with the author, commenting on or arguing with ideas, admiring passages, or raising questions about the topic. Whether this dialogue takes place in the foreground of your attention or remains a quiet rumbling in the background depends on the content and challenges posed by the essay, as well as your own attitudes. An essay that presents disquieting ideas or information is likely to bring responses, feelings, and questions into the foreground. On the other hand, an essay that is difficult to understand may lead you to keep your judgments and ideas in the background as you work on comprehension.

Capturing this fleeting dialogue is part of being a critical reader and it can be a rich source of ideas, purposes, and techniques for writing of your own.

Marginal notes. Use the margins of a text to record disagreements and agreements with what the author has to say or to hold short-hand references to memories and ideas that might be developed in essays of your own. Admittedly, making extensive marginal notes can sometimes interfere with the pleasure you take in reading an essay and learning about an intriguing topic. Keep your notes short and perhaps even develop a set of abbreviations to use in them. Try to develop a habit of stopping every page or two to see if there are any notes you wish to make.

Three Questions. In the margins of an essay or in a notebook that you keep to record your responses to reading, jot down brief answers to these questions, identifying each kind of answer by a letter corresponding to the type of question.

W (=*Why interesting?*) Why do I find this topic, passage, or example interesting?

D (=*Detail?*) Do the concrete details and the detailed explanations and arguments this author provides seem especially convincing?

M (=*More information?*) What more would I like to know about this topic? Are other readers likely to be interested in it as well?

Reading Journal. Keep a notebook of ideas, feelings, and experiences that come to mind either as you read or later as you reflect on your reading. These perceptions and responses can help you understand the content and technique of an essay and may develop into sources of ideas and strategies for essays of your own. Try to label journal entries according to the name of the essay. If possible, label the kinds of entries as well. Use headings that will be useful to you later, for example, "Idea," "My Opinions," or "Possible Topics."

Double-Entry Notebook. Draw a vertical line down the middle of the pages of your reading journal. On the left side of the page, make brief notes summarizing the content of what you read. On the right side, record questions that occur to you as you read. The questions can be trivial or serious. They may be about the author, about what is coming next in the selection, or about a subject related to the one under discussion.

The summaries in a double-entry journal aid your understanding and can be a source of information for your writing. The questions tell you about your reading process, provide insights into ideas and problems that concern you, and can be springboards for your essays.

TECHNIQUES FOR ACTIVE READING: REVIEWING

The questions you ask while reading, your pauses to summarize and understand, your marginal notes and journal entries—all these activities are part of the process of reviewing what you have read. But the most important reviewing process is that which occurs after you have given an essay or other piece of writing a careful, critical reading. We suggest the following framework for review, though we also encourage you to develop an approach which best suits your purposes for reading.

Focus your review on four areas: Meanings and Values, Expository (or Argumentative) Techniques, Diction and Vocabulary, and Reading to Write. When you focus on meanings and values, you look back at the different topics covered in a text and the writer's conclusions about them. You ask if the various topics are linked by a focus on a primary concern (or theme) and if the various conclusions or interpretations are unified by a single perspective in the form of a thesis or an argumentative proposition. You also consider the values and value judgments advanced in the essay.

When you focus on expository or argumentative techniques, you pay attention to overall patterns of organization and development (see pages 21–23), to opening and closing strategies, to paragraph and sentence techniques, to the use of detail and kinds of support—in short, to the many different strategies a writer employees, except for those dealing primarily with words and groups of words.

In focusing on diction and vocabulary, you look at the words an author has chosen, the patterns of word choice (or diction), the way the diction supports the writer's purposes, and any words you need to look up in order to understand the text.

Finally, when you focus on reading to write, you look at the ways you can use the essay as a springboard for your own writing. We suggest asking three kinds of questions, though our list is by no means exhaustive.

- What topics or issues have I encountered in this essay that I might develop further in my own writing?
- What specific techniques in this essay suggest an approach for an essay of my own or could be incorporated into my own writing?
- In what way could the author's approach in this essay be used for my own writing, either on a related topic or a different one?

We have arranged the review questions following each of the readings in this text into four categories: Meanings and Values, Expository (or Argumentative) Techniques, Diction and Vocabulary, and Reading to Write. The questions are intended to help you review each reading from a critical and analytical perspective, but you should also review each selection in ways that best suit your purposes for reading and your needs as a writer.

To observe the process of critical, analytical reading in action, read the essay below and the questions that follow. After each question we offer a sample response, but not with the intention of excluding other, equally valid ways of responding. As you read, make marginal notes reflecting any responses you have to the ideas and values expressed in the essay or to the techniques the writer employs. Make notes, too, about ways you think other writers might respond to the essay. (See pages 55–57 for advice on responding and making notes.) Pay attention as well to the biographical information and introductory comments at the beginning of the essay. As is the case with the other selections in the text, this material points out significant features of the essay and provides background information that can provide an appropriate context for understanding and analyzing the piece.

BRENT STAPLES

BRENT STAPLES was born in 1951 in Chester, Pennsylvania. He received his B.A. in 1973 from Widener University and his Ph.D. (in psychology) in 1982 from the University of Chicago. He is a member of *The New York Times* editorial board, writing on matters of culture and society. He was formerly a reporter for the *Chicago Sun Times* and an editor of *The New York Times Book Review*. Staples is the author of *Parallel Time* (1994), a memoir.

Just Walk on By

The power of examples to enable a reader to see through someone else's eyes is evident in this selection. Though many of the examples in the essay draw on a reader's sympathy, their main purpose appears to be explanatory; hence, the author accompanies them with detailed discussions. The result is a piece that is both enlightening and moving.

My first victim was a woman—white, well dressed, probably in her early twenties. I came upon her late one evening on a deserted street in Hyde Park, a relatively affluent neighborhood in an otherwise mean, impoverished section of Chicago. As I swung onto the avenue behind her, there seemed to be a discreet, uninflammatory distance between us. Not so. She cast back a worried glance. To her, the youngish black man—a broad six feet two inches with a beard and billowing hair, both hands shoved into the pockets of a bulky military jacket—seemed menacingly close. After a few more quick glimpses, she picked up her pace and was soon running in earnest. Within seconds she disappeared into a cross street.

That was more than a decade ago. I was 22 years old, a graduate student newly arrived at the University of Chicago. It was in the echo of that terrified woman's footfalls that I first began to know the unwieldy inheritance I'd come into—the ability to alter public space in ugly ways. It was clear that she thought herself the quarry of a mugger, a rapist, or worse. Suffering a bout of insomnia, however, I was stalking sleep, not defenseless wayfarers. As a softy who is scarcely able to take a knife to a raw chicken—let alone hold it to a

1

2

person's throat—I was surprised, embarrassed, and dismayed all at once. Her flight made me feel like an accomplice in tyranny. It also made it clear that I was indistinguishable from the muggers who occasionally seeped into the area from the surrounding ghetto. That first encounter, and those that followed, signified that a vast, unnerving gulf lay between nighttime pedestrians—particularly women—and me. And I soon gathered that being perceived as dangerous is a hazard in itself. I only needed to turn a corner into a dicey situation, or crowd some frightened, armed person in a foyer somewhere, or make an errant move after being pulled over by a policeman. Where fear and weapons meet—and they often do in urban America—there is always the possibility of death.

In the first year, my first away from my hometown, I was to   3
become thoroughly familiar with the language of fear. At dark, shadowy intersections in Chicago, I could cross in front of a car stopped at a traffic light and elicit the *thunk, thunk, thunk, thunk* of the driver—black, white, male, or female—hammering down the door locks. On less traveled streets after dark, I grew accustomed to but never comfortable with people who crossed to the other side of the street rather than pass me. Then there were the standard unpleasantries with police, doormen, bouncers, cab drivers, and others whose business it is to screen out troublesome individuals *before* there is any nastiness.

I moved to New York nearly two years ago and I have   4
remained an avid night walker. In central Manhattan, the near-constant crowd cover minimized tense one-on-one street encounters. Elsewhere—visiting friends in SoHo, where sidewalks are narrow and tightly spaced buildings shut out the sky—things can get very taut indeed.

Black men have a firm place in New York mugging literature.   5
Norman Podhoretz in his famed (or infamous) 1963 essay, "My Negro Problem—And Ours," recalls growing up in terror of black males; they "were tougher than we were, more ruthless," he writes—and as an adult on the Upper West Side of Manhattan, he continues, he cannot constrain his nervousness when he meets black men on certain streets. Similarly, a decade later, the essayist and novelist Edward Hoagland extols a New York where once "Negro bitterness bore down mainly on other Negroes." Where some see mere panhandlers, Hoagland sees "a mugger who is clearly screwing up his nerve to do more than just *ask* for money." But Hoagland

has "the New Yorker's quick-hunch posture for broken-field maneuvering," and the bad guy swerves away.

I often witness that "hunch posture," from women after dark on   6
the warrenlike streets of Brooklyn where I live. They seem to set their faces on neutral and, with their purse straps strung across their chests bandolier style, they forge ahead as though bracing themselves against being tackled. I understand, of course, that the danger they perceive is not a hallucination. Women are particularly vulnerable to street violence, and young black males are drastically overrepresented among the perpetrators of that violence. Yet these truths are no solace against the kind of alienation that comes of being ever the suspect, against being set apart, a fearsome entity with whom pedestrians avoid making eye contact.

It is not altogether clear to me how I reached the ripe old age of   7
22 without being conscious of the lethality nighttime pedestrians attributed to me. Perhaps it was because in Chester, Pennsylvania, the small, angry industrial town where I came of age in the 1960s, I was scarcely noticeable against a backdrop of gang warfare, street knifings, and murders. I grew up one of the good boys, had perhaps a half-dozen fist fights. In retrospect, my shyness of combat has clear sources.

Many things go into the making of a young thug. One of those   8
things is the consummation of the male romance with the power to intimidate. An infant discovers that random flailings send the baby bottle flying out of the crib and crashing to the floor. Delighted, the joyful babe repeats those motions again and again, seeking to duplicate the feat. Just so, I recall the points at which some of my boyhood friends were finally seduced by the perception of themselves as tough guys. When a mark cowered and surrendered his money without resistance, myth and reality merged—and paid off. It is, after all, only manly to embrace the power to frighten and intimidate. We, as men, are not supposed to give an inch of our lane on the highway; we are to seize the fighter's edge in work and in play and even in love; we are to be valiant in the face of hostile forces.

Unfortunately, poor and powerless young men seem to take   9
all this nonsense literally. As a boy, I saw countless tough guys locked away; I have since buried several. They were babies, really—a teenage cousin, a brother of 22, a childhood friend in his mid-twenties—all gone down in episodes of bravado played out in

the streets. I came to doubt the virtues of intimidation early on. I chose, perhaps even unconsciously, to remain a shadow—timid, but a survivor.

The fearsomeness mistakenly attributed to me in public places   10
often has a perilous flavor. The most frightening of these confusions occurred in the late 1970s and early 1980s when I worked as a journalist in Chicago. One day, rushing into the office of a magazine I was writing for with a deadline story in hand, I was mistaken for a burglar. The office manager called security and, with an ad hoc posse, pursued me through the labyrinthine halls, nearly to my editor's door. I had no way of proving who I was. I could only move briskly toward the company of someone who knew me.

Another time I was on assignment for a local paper and killing   11
time before an interview. I entered a jewelry store on the city's affluent Near North Side. The proprietor excused herself and returned with an enormous red Doberman pinscher straining at the end of a leash. She stood, the dog extended toward me, silent to my questions, her eyes bulging nearly out of her head. I took a cursory look around, nodded, and bade her good night. Relatively speaking, however, I never fared as badly as another black male journalist. He went to nearby Waukegan, Illinois, a couple of summers ago to work on a story about a murderer who was born there. Mistaking the reporter for the killer, police hauled him from his car at gunpoint and but for his press credentials would probably have tried to book him. Such episodes are not uncommon. Black men trade tales like this all the time.

In "My Negro Problem—And Ours," Podhoretz writes that the   12
hatred he feels for blacks makes itself known to him through a variety of avenues—one being his discomfort with that "special brand of paranoid touchiness" to which he says blacks are prone. No doubt he is speaking here of black men. In time, I learned to smother the rage I felt at so often being taken for a criminal. Not to do so would surely have led to madness—via that special "paranoid touchiness" that so annoyed Podhoretz at the time he wrote the essay.

I began to take precautions to make myself less threatening. I   13
move about with care, particularly late in the evening. I give a wide berth to nervous people on subway platforms during the wee hours, particularly when I have exchanged business clothes for jeans. If I happen to be entering a building behind some people who appear skittish, I may walk by, letting them clear the lobby before I return,

so as not to seem to be following them. I have been calm and extremely congenial on those rare occasions when I've been pulled over by the police.

And on late-evening constitutionals along streets less traveled   14 by, I employ what has proved to be an excellent tension-reducing measure: I whistle melodies from Beethoven and Vivaldi and the more popular classical composers. Even steely New Yorkers hunching toward nighttime destinations seem to relax, and occasionally they even join in the tune. Virtually everybody seems to sense that a mugger wouldn't be warbling bright, sunny selections from Vivaldi's *Four Seasons*. It is my equivalent of the cowbell that hikers wear when they know they are in bear country.

Meanings and Values

1. Identify the statement of the essay's central theme (thesis) that the author offers in paragraph 2, and then state it in your own words.
    The second sentence of paragraph 2 speaks of "the ability to alter public space in ugly ways" as an "unwieldy inheritance" passed on to African American males. Here is a possible statement of the theme (or thesis): One of the consequences of racism is that it causes young black males in general to be viewed as hostile and dangerous, and this inaccurate judgment distorts social relationships by creating unnecessary fear and hostility.

2. How is it likely that the author's "victim" (par. 1) viewed him? What does the author have to say about his personality and values in paragraphs 2, 7 and 9?
    The woman described in paragraph 1 probably regarded him as an unknown and menacing figure, potentially a rapist or mugger, and a source of threat and violence. Paragraphs 2, 7, and 9 focus on the author at age twenty-two. He was relatively young and innocent of the racial tensions of a major urban area, particularly of the way whites would view him. He is surprised that other people might regard him as a threat, having survived the violent neighborhood in which he grew up by avoiding the violence and by refusing to follow "tough guy" patterns of behavior. Indeed, he describes himself as one who continues to try to avoid violent behavior.

3. In what ways are the contrasting perspectives on the author given in
    the opening (par. 1) and in paragraphs 2, 7, and 9 related to the es-
    say's central theme (thesis)?
    The different perspectives help readers understand how the
    stereotyped view of young black males as victimizers can
    itself serve to victimize the many men who do not deserve to
    be viewed in this way. This contrast helps convey the main
    idea by highlighting the injustice of the stereotype and its
    negative consequences.

Expository Techniques

1. The writer presents examples of women affected by his presence or
    the presence of other young black males. Where in the essay does he
    present examples of other groups that are also affected, and what
    groups are they?
    In paragraph 3 he describes the effect on automobile drivers
    of all kinds ("black, white, male, or female"); in paragraph 5
    he describes the effect on white men; and in paragraph 11 he
    describes the effect on police.

2. Does the introduction of Podhoretz's comment about the "special
    brand of paranoid touchiness" (par.12) of blacks weaken or
    strengthen the essay? How? Characterize the author's response to
    the comment. Tell why it is appropriate that the paragraph quoting
    Podhoretz on "paranoid touchiness" comes after the two examples
    presented in paragraphs 10 and 11.
    The inclusion of the comment strengthens the essay in sev-
    eral ways. It shows that the writer is open-minded in that he
    is willing to consider an alternative view of the phenomenon
    and is also willing to present it to readers even though he
    disagrees with it. Open-mindedness and acknowledgment of
    other interpretations are two qualities that make it more
    likely that readers will accept the writer's analysis and
    explanation of the subject. Staples's response seems to be
    that Podhoretz is blaming the victim. Staples shows in the
    essay that the "touchiness" has clear causes and is by no
    means paranoid. The placement is appropriate because the
    preceding paragraphs help show that the touchiness is often
    justified, not a product of paranoia. The placement also helps
    suggest that Podhoretz's view is another example of the
    racism that victimizes black men.

3. What strategy for beginning an essay does Staples employ in this essay? (See "Guide to Terms": *Introductions.*) In what sense can the opening be considered ironic? (Guide: *Irony.*)

   He refers to "the writer's experience with the subject," and gives "a detailed account of that experience" (Guide: Introductions). It is ironic in the sense that in the first paragraph we (like the woman) believe the speaker/writer to be a rapist or mugger, when the opposite is actually true; he is, in fact, a victim of the stereotypes that reflect a kind of racism that is still part of our culture. The irony is an "irony of situation, in which there is a sharp contradiction between what is logically expected to happen and what does happen" (Guide: Irony).

4. The quotations in paragraph 5 contribute to the essay in what ways?

   They give an "outsider's" point of view to contrast with the author's "inside" point of view, broadening and deepening the quality of the explanation and suggesting some reasons people react as they do the author and to other young men in similar positions.

Diction and Vocabulary

1. The diction of this essay is often quite formal: for example, "The fearsomeness mistakenly attributed to men in public places often has a perilous flavor" (par. 10). Discuss the likely effect of such diction on the way readers view the author's character and values. (Guide: *Diction.*)

   The diction makes the author seem educated, upper class, and restrained—not the kind of person likely to commit street crimes.

2. Discuss how the author's choice of words in paragraph 11 (including the connotations and denotations) make the black men seem like victims and the other people seem like aggressors. (Guide: *Diction, Connotation/Denotation.*)

   The words used to describe the other people and their actions are active and denote violent action or carry suggestions of it ("returned with an enormous red Doberman pinscher straining at the end of a leash. . . her eyes bulging nearly out of her head"). The black men are portrayed as recipients of the actions which are either potentially or actually violent ("police hauled him from his car at gunpoint").

3. If you find any of the following words puzzling, look them up in a dictionary: quarry, unnerving, dicey (par. 2); taut (4); warrenlike, bandolier (6); lethality (7); consummation (8); perilous, *ad hoc* (10); cursory (11); constitutionals (14).

    quarry=something that is hunted; unnerving=unsettling; dicey=tense; taut=tense; warrenlike=similar to a mass of tunnels made by rabbits; bandolier=a belt containing cartridges and worn across the chest; lethality=capability to cause death; consummation=coming together or fulfillment; perilous=filled with danger; ad hoc=*for a specific purpose; cursory=hasty and superficial; constitutionals=walks taken for one's health*

Read to Write

1. Staples portrays himself as an outsider. Use the contrasting concepts of "outsiders" and "insiders" to explore some common social arrangements or phenomena and to come up with a topic (and perhaps a thesis) for your own writing.

2. Begin an essay of your own with a brief episode (either from your experience or from some other source) that suggests the rest of the essay will go in one direction (or take a particular point of view), then switch directions or point of view just as Staples does after the first paragraph of his essay.

3. Using Staples's essay as a model, prepare your own paper explaining what you have learned from your experiences as an "outsider" or your observations about the way our society creates and treats "outsiders."

3

Illustrating Ideas by Use of *Example*

The use of examples to illustrate an idea under discussion is the most common, and frequently the most efficient, pattern of exposition. It is a method we use almost instinctively; for instance, instead of talking in generalities about the qualities of a good city manager, we cite Harry Hibbons as an example. We may go further and illustrate Harry's virtues by a specific account of his handling of a crucial situation during the last power shortage or hurricane. In this way we put our abstract ideas into concrete form—a process that is always an aid to clarity. (As a matter of fact, with the "for instance" in this very paragraph, examples are employed to illustrate even the *use* of example.)

Lack of clear illustrations may leave readers with only a hazy conception of the points the writer has tried to make. Even worse, readers may try to supply examples from their own knowledge or experience, and these might do the job poorly or even lead them to an impression different from that intended by the author. Since writers are the ones trying to communicate, clarity is primarily their responsibility.

Not only do good examples put into clear form what otherwise might remain vague and abstract, but the writing also becomes more interesting, with a better chance of holding the reader's attention. With something specific to be visualized, a statement also becomes more convincing—but convincing within certain limitations. If we use the Volvo as an example of Swedish workmanship, the reader is probably aware that this car may not be entirely typical. Although isolated examples will not hold up well in logical argument, for ordinary purposes of explanation the Volvo example could make its point convincingly enough. In supporting an argument, however, we need either to choose an example that is clearly typical or to present several examples to show we have represented the situation fairly.

As in the selection and use of all materials for composition, of course, successful writers select and use examples cautiously, always keeping in mind the nature of their reader-audience and their own specific purpose for communicating. To be effective, each example must be pertinent, respecting the chief qualities of the generality it illustrates. Its function as an example must be either instantly obvious to the readers or fully enough developed so that they learn exactly what it illustrates, and how. Sometimes, however, illustration may be provided best by something other than a real-life example—a fictional anecdote, an analogy, or perhaps a parable that demonstrates the general idea. Here even greater care is needed to be sure these examples are both precise and clear.

Illustration is sometimes used alone as the basic means of development, but it also frequently assists other basic techniques, such as comparison and contrast. In either of its functions, authors may find their purpose best served by one well-developed example, possibly with full background information and descriptive details. But sometimes citing several shorter examples is best, particularly if the authors are attempting to show a trend or a prevalence. In more difficult explanations, of course, a careful combination of the two techniques—using both one well-developed example and several shorter examples—may be worth the extra time and effort required.

Whichever method is used, the writers are following at least one sound principle of writing: they are trying to make the general more specific, the abstract more concrete.

Sample Paragraph (Annotate)

The topic sentence—
what the paragraph is
about. Also the
generality in need of
specific examples.

Valley City and its suburbs have become so congested that people have begun moving to small towns two or more hours' drive away from the city center. In turn, these rapidly growing towns have begun experiencing growing pains and some strange contrasts. For instance, Palmville used to be a rural town with a dozen farms

Developed example.

inside the city limits and its own Department of Agriculture. Gradually the farms were sold and turned into tracts of one-family homes, shopping malls, and movie theaters. Now the head of the Department of Agriculture is repsonsible for two new pools, three golf courses (one under construction), and a physical fitness and nature trail— along with the three remaining farms.

Minor examples.

The McKetchie Family still operates its fresh fruit, vegetable, and egg stand on Route 20, only now the stand has a pizza restaurant on one side and the parking lot for the Palmville Mall on the other two sides. School enrollment has quadrupled over the past five years, and the Palmville Senior High (built in 1978) has temporary classrooms in trailers on the lawn in front of the main building.

Some *undeveloped examples* to show prevalence.

An old feed store, Abando's Groceteria, and Isaakson's Pharmacy are all that remain of the old downtown except for the City Hall. The elegant Victorian City Hall now has a towering steel and glass Civic Center on one side and the sprawling new headquarters for the Nedco Corporation on the other side.

Concluding example.

Figurative language. The simile emphasizes the "growing pains and strange contrasts" mentioned in the topic sentence.

The beautiful old building looks as out of place as a person who dressed for a formal dinner party and arrived to find a barbecue in progress around the backyard pool.

Sample Paragraph (Example)

Something strange is happening to our weather. And it didn't just begin last summer. During the past decade, the United States has seen three of the

coldest winters and four of the warmest
average years ever recorded, a string of
weather extremes that would occur by
chance less than once in 1000 years.
Elsewhere, weather has also run to
extremes—with the Soviet Union and
India experiencing their highest
temperatures. Last winter, snow fell on
the gondolas of Venice, the usually
sunny beaches of the French Riviera,
arid South Africa and even subtropical
Brazil.

Excerpted with permission from "What's Wrong With Our Weather" by Lowell
Ponte, *Reader's Digest*, November 1988. Copyright © 1988 by the Reader's Digest
Association, Inc.

ANDREW A. ROONEY was born in 1920 in Albany, New York. Drafted into the army while still a student at Colgate University, he served in the European theater of operations as a *Stars and Stripes* reporter. After the war Rooney began what has been a prolific and illustrious career as a writer-producer for various television networks—chiefly for CBS—and has won numerous awards, including the Writers Guild Award for Best Script of the Year (six times—more than any other writer in the history of the medium) and three National Academy Emmy awards. The author of a number of magazine articles in publications like *Esquire, Harper's,* and *Playboy,* Rooney is nonetheless probably most familiar for his regular appearances as a commentator on the television program "60 Minutes." Rooney also writes a syndicated column, which appears in more than 250 newspapers, and has lectured on documentary writing at various universities. His most recent books are *Pieces of My Mind* (1984), *Word for Word* (1986), *Not That you Asked . . .* (1989) *Sweet and Sour* (1992), and *My War* (1995). He now lives in Rowayton, Connecticut.

In and of Ourselves We Trust

"In and of Ourselves We Trust" was one of Rooney's syndicated columns. Rooney's piece uses one simple example to illustrate a generality. He draws from it a far-reaching set of conclusions: that we have a "contract" with each other to stop for red lights—and further, that our whole system of trust depends on everyone doing the right thing.

Last night I was driving from Harrisburg to Lewisburg, Pa., a distance of about 80 miles. It was late, I was late, and if anyone asked me how fast I was driving, I'd have to plead the Fifth Amendment to avoid self-incrimination. 1

At one point along an open highway, I came to a crossroads with a traffic light. I was alone on the road by now, but as I approached the light, it turned red, and I braked to a halt. I looked 2

left, right, and behind me. Nothing. Not a car, no suggestion of headlights, but there I sat, waiting for the light to change, the only human
being, for at least a mile in any direction.

I started wondering why I refused to run the light. I was not   3
afraid of being arrested, because there was obviously no cop anywhere around and there certainly would have been no danger in
going through it.

Much later that night, after I'd met with a group in Lewisburg   4
and had climbed into bed near midnight, the question of why I'd
stopped for that light came back to me. I think I stopped because it's
part of a contract we all have with each other. It's not only the law,
but it's an agreement we have, and we trust each other to honor it:
We don't go through red lights. Like most of us, I'm more apt to be
restrained from doing something bad by the social convention that
disapproves of it than by any law against it.

It's amazing that we ever trust each other to do the right thing,   5
isn't it? And we do, too. Trust is our first inclination. We have to
make a deliberate decision to mistrust someone or to be suspicious
or skeptical.

It's a darn good thing, too, because the whole structure of our   6
society depends on mutual trust, not distrust. This whole thing we
have going for us would fall apart if we didn't trust each other most
of the time. In Italy they have an awful time getting any money for
the government because many people just plain don't pay their
income tax. Here, the Internal Revenue Service makes some gestures
toward enforcing the law, but mostly they just have to trust that
we'll pay what we owe. There has often been talk of a tax revolt in
this country, most recently among unemployed auto workers in
Michigan, and our government pretty much admits that if there were
a widespread tax revolt here, they wouldn't be able to do any thing
about it.

We do what we say we'll do. We show up when we say we'll   7
show up.

I was so proud of myself for stopping for that red light. And   8
inasmuch as no one would ever have known what a good person I
was on the road from Harrisburg to Lewisburg, I had to tell someone.

Meanings and Values

1. Explain the concept of a "contract we all have with each other:" (par.
    4). How is the "agreement" achieved (par. 4)?

2. Why do you suppose exceeding the speed limit (par. 1) would not also be included in the "contract"? Or is there some other reason for Rooney's apparent inconsistency?

3. Explain the significance of the title of this selection.

Expository Techniques

1. What generality is exemplified by the solution to Rooney's red-light enigma? In this instance, what does the generality have to do with the central theme? (See "Guide to Terms": *Unity*.) Is there any disadvantage in this generality's location? Explain.

2. Does the example of the red light prove anything? Do you think it is a good example of what it illustrates? Is it typical?

3. What other uses of example do you find in the selection?

4. How effective do you consider Rooney's closing? Why? (Guide: *Closings*.)

5. What, if anything, do the brief examples in paragraph 6 add to this piece? (Guide: *Evaluation*.)

Diction and Vocabulary

1. Does it seem to you that the diction and vocabulary levels of this selection are appropriate for the purpose intended? Why or why not? (Guide: *Diction*.)

2. Could this be classified as a formal essay? Why or why not? (Guide: *Essay*.)

Read to Write

1. Read the following quotations from Rooney's essay, think about ways they might apply to familiar situations or experiences, and then develop a list of possible topics or issues you might address in writing.

   "Like most of us, I'm more apt to be restrained from doing something bad by the social convention that disapproves of it than by any law against it."
   "Trust is our first inclination. We have to make a deliberate decision to mistrust someone or to be suspicious or skeptical."
   ". . . the whole structure of our society depends on mutual trust, not distrust."

2. Rooney alters a familiar quotation for the title of his essay as a way of pointing to a generality. Make a list of quotations and sayings and

alter as many as you can so that they suggest generalities you might develop in an essay.

3. Choose an experience that revealed to you something about your personal characteristics, the traits of family or friends, or the "character" of a larger cultural or social group to which you belong. Using Rooney's essay as a model, use this experience as an example to illustrate a generality about your subject, and draw also on briefer examples in the course of your essay.

(NOTE: Suggestions for topics requiring development by use of EXAMPLE are on page 101 at the end of this section.)

WILLIAM F. BUCKLEY, JR.

WILLIAM F. BUCKLEY, Jr., was born in 1925 in New York, where he now lives. He graduated from Yale University and holds honorary degrees from a number of universities, including Seton Hall, Syracuse University, Notre Dame, and Lafayette College. He was editor in chief of *National Review* from 1955 to 1990. In addition, he has been a syndicated columnist since 1962, and host of public television's "Firing Line" since 1966. Generally considered one of the most articulate conservative writers, Buckley has published in various general circulation magazines and has received numerous honors and awards. He lectures widely and is the author of many novels and nonfiction books, among them *God and Man at Yale: The Superstitions of "Academic Freedom"* (1951), *Saving the Queen* (1976), *Stained Glass* (1978), *Marco Polo, If You Can* (1982), *Atlantic High* (1982), *Overdrive: A Personal Documentary* (1983), *The Story of Henri Tod* (1984), *The Tall Ships* (1986), *Mongoose R.I.P.* (1988), *On the Firing Line: The Public Life of Our Public Figures* (1989), *Happy Days Were Here again* (1993), *Brothers No More* (1996), **and** *McCarthy and His Enemies* (1995).

Why Don't We Complain?

First published in *Esquire*, "Why Don't We Complain?" is a good illustration of the grace and wit that characterize most of Buckley's writing. For students of composition, it can also provide another demonstration of the use of varied examples—some well developed, others scarcely at all—to make a single generality more specific. And the generality itself, as we can see toward the end, is of considerably broader significance than it appears at first.

It was the very last coach and the only empty seat on the entire train, 1
so there was no turning back. The problem was to breathe. Outside, the temperature was below freezing. Inside the railroad car the temperature must have been about 85 degrees. I took off my overcoat, and few minutes later my jacket, and noticed that the car was flecked with the white shirts of the passengers. I soon found my hand mov-

ing to loosen my tie. From one end of the car to the other, as we rattled through Westchester County, we sweated; but we did not moan.

I watched the train conductor appear at the head of the car.   2
"Tickets, all tickets, please!" In a more virile age, I thought, the passengers would seize the conductor and strap him down on a seat over the radiator to share the fate of his patrons. He shuffled down the aisle, picking up tickets, punching commutation cards. *No one addressed a word to him.* He approached my seat, and I drew a deep breath of resolution. "Conductor," I began with a considerable edge to my voice. . . . Instantly the doleful eyes of my seatmate turned tiredly from his newspaper to fix me with a resentful stare: what question could be so important as to justify my sibilant intrusion into his stupor? I was shaken by those eyes. I am incapable of making a discreet fuss, so I mumbled a question about what time were we due in Stamford (I didn't even ask whether it would be before or after dehydration could be expected to set in), got my reply, and went back to my newspaper and to wiping my brow.

The conductor had nonchalantly walked down the gauntlet of   3
eighty sweating American freemen, and not one of them had asked him to explain why the passengers in that car had been consigned to suffer. There is nothing to be done when the temperature *outdoors* is 85 degrees, and indoors the air conditioner has broken down; obviously when that happens there is nothing to do, except perhaps curse the day that one was born. But when the temperature outdoors is below freezing, it takes a positive act of will on somebody's part to set the temperature *indoors* at 85. Somewhere a valve was turned too far, a furnace overstocked, a thermostat maladjusted: something that could easily be remedied by turning off the heat and allowing the great outdoors to come indoors. All this is so obvious. What is not obvious is what has happened to the American people.

It isn't just the commuters, whom we have come to visualize as   4
a supine breed who have got on to the trick of suspending their sensory faculties twice a day while they submit to the creeping dissolution of the railroad industry. It isn't just they who have given up trying to rectify irrational vexations. It is the American people everywhere.

A few weeks ago at a large movie theater I turned to my wife   5
and said, "The picture is out of focus." "Be quiet," she answered. I obeyed. But a few minutes later I raised the point again, with mounting impatience. "It will be all right in a minute," she said apprehensively. (She would rather lose her eyesight than be around

when I make one of my infrequent scenes.) I waited. It was *just* out of focus—not glaringly out, but out. My vision is 20–20, and I assume that is the vision, adjusted, of most people in the movie house. So, after hectoring my wife throughout the first reel, I finally prevailed upon her to admit that it *was* off, and very annoying. We then settled down, coming to rest on the presumption that: (a) someone connected with the management of the theater must soon notice the blur and make the correction; or (b) that someone seated near the rear of the house would make the complaint in behalf of those of us up front; or (c) that—any minute now—the entire house would explode into catcalls and foot stamping, calling dramatic attention to the irksome distortion.

What happened was nothing. The movie ended, as it had begun, *just* out of focus, and as we trooped out, we stretched our faces in a variety of contortions to accustom the eye to the shock of normal focus.   6

I think it is safe to say that everybody suffered on that occasion. And I think it is safe to assume that everyone was expecting someone else to take the initiative in going back to speak to the manager. And it is probably true even that if we had supposed the movie would run right through the blurred image, someone surely would have summoned up the purposive indignation to get up out of his seat and file his complaint.   7

But notice that no one did. And the reason no one did is because we are all increasingly anxious in America to be unobtrusive, we are reluctant to make our voices heard, hesitant about claiming our rights; we are afraid that our cause is unjust, or that if it is not unjust, that it is ambiguous; or if not even that, that it is too trivial to justify the horrors of a confrontation with Authority; we still sit in an oven or endure a racking headache before undertaking a head-on, I'm-here-to-tell-you complaint. That tendency to passive compliance, to a heedless endurance, is something to keep one's eyes on—in sharp focus.   8

I myself can occasionally summon the courage to complain, but I cannot, as I have intimated, complain softly. My own instinct is so strong to let the thing ride, to forget about it—to expect that someone will take the matter up, when the grievance is collective, in my behalf—that it is only when the provocation is at a very special key, whose vibrations touch simultaneously a complexus of nerves, allergies, and passions, that I catch fire and find the reserves of courage and assertiveness to speak up. When that happens, I get   9 quite carried away. My blood gets hot, my brow wet, I become unbearably and unconscionably sarcastic and bellicose; I am girded for a total showdown.

Why should that be? Why could not I (or anyone else) on that   10
railroad coach have said simply to the conductor, "Sir"—I take that back: that sounds sarcastic—"Conductor, would you be good enough to turn down the heat? I am extremely hot. In fact, I tend to get hot every time the temperature reaches 85 degr—" Strike that last sentence. Just end it with the simple statement that you are extremely hot, and let the conductor infer the cause.

Every New Year's Eve I resolve to do something about the   11
Milquetoast in me and vow to speak up, calmly, for my rights, and for the betterment of our society, on every appropriate occasion. Entering last New Year's Eve, I was fortified in my resolve because that morning at breakfast I had had to ask the waitress three times for a glass of milk. She finally brought it—after I had finished my eggs, which is when I don't want it any more. I did not have the manliness to order her to take the milk back, but settled instead for a cowardly sulk, and ostentatiously refused to drink the milk— though I later paid for it—rather than state plainly to the hostess, as I should have, why I had not drunk it, and would not pay for it.

So by the time the New Year ushered out the Old, riding in on   12
my morning's indignation and stimulated by the gastric juices of resolution that flow so faithfully on New Year's Eve, I rendered my vow. Henceforward I would conquer my shyness, my despicable disposition to supineness. I would speak out like a man against the unnecessary annoyances of our time.

Forty-eight hours later, I was standing in line at the ski repair   13
store in Pico Peak, Vermont. All I needed, to get on with my skiing, was the loan, for one minute, of a small screwdriver, to tighten a loose binding. Behind the counter in the workshop were two men. One was industriously engaged in servicing the complicated requirements of a young lady at the head of the line, and obviously he would be tied up for quite a while. The other—"Jiggs," his work-mate called him—was a middle-aged man, who sat in a chair puff-ing a pipe, exchanging small talk with his working partner. My pulse began its telltale acceleration. The minutes ticked on. I stared at the idle shopkeeper, hoping to shame him into action, but he was impervious to my telepathic reproof and continued his small talk with his friend, brazenly insensitive to the nervous demands of six good men who were raring to ski.

Suddenly my New Year's Eve resolution struck me. It was now   14
or never. I broke from my place in line and marched to the counter.
I was going to control myself. I dug my nails into my palms. My
effort was only partially successful:

"If you are not too busy," I said icily, "would you mind hand-   15
ing me a screwdriver?"

Work stopped and everyone turned his eyes on me, and I expe-   16
rienced that mortification I always feel when I am the center of centripetal shafts of curiosity, resentment, perplexity.

But the worst was yet to come. "I am sorry, sir," said Jiggs def-   17
erentially, moving the pipe from his mouth. "I am not supposed to
move. I have just had a heart attack." That was the signal for a great
whirring noise that descended from heaven. We looked, stricken,
out the window, and it appeared as though a cyclone had suddenly
focused on the snowy courtyard between the shop and the ski lift.
Suddenly a gigantic army helicopter materialized, and hovered
down to a landing. Two men jumped out of the plane carrying a
stretcher, tore into the ski shop, and lifted the shopkeeper onto the
stretcher. Jiggs bade his companion good-by, was whisked out the
door, into the plane, up to the heavens, down—we learned—to a
nearby army hospital. I looked up manfully—into a score of man-
eating eyes. I put the experience down as a reversal.

As I write this, on an airplane, I have run out of paper and   18
need to reach into my briefcase under my legs for more. I cannot
do this until my empty lunch tray is removed from my lap. I
arrested the stewardess as she passed empty-handed down the
aisle on the way to the kitchen to fetch the lunch trays for the passengers up forward who haven't been served yet. "Would you
please take my tray?" "Just a *moment*, sir!" she said, and marched
on sternly. Shall I tell her that since she is headed for the kitchen
anyway, it could not delay the feeding of the other passengers by
more than two seconds necessary to stash away my empty tray? Or
remind her that not fifteen minutes ago she spoke unctuously into
the loudspeaker the words undoubtedly devised by the airline's
highly paid public relations counselor: "If there is anything I or
Miss French can do for you to make your trip more enjoyable,
please let us—" I have run out of paper.

I think the observable reluctance of the majority of Americans to   19
assert themselves in minor matters is related to our increased sense
of helplessness in an age of technology and centralized political and
economic power. For generations, Americans who were too hot, or

too cold, got up and did something about it. Now we call the plumber, or the electrician, or the furnace man. The habit of looking after our own needs obviously had something to do with the assertiveness that characterized the American family familiar to readers of American literature. With the technification of life goes our direct responsibility for our material environment, and we are conditioned to adopt a position of helplessness not only as regards the broken air conditioner, but as regards the overheated train. It takes an expert to fix the former, but not the latter; yet these distinctions, as we withdraw into helplessness, tend to fade away.

Our notorious political apathy is a related phenomenon. Every   20
year, whether the Republican or the Democratic Party is in office, more and more power drains away from the individual to feed vast reservoirs in far-off places; and we have less and less say about the shape of events which shape our future. From this alienation of personal power comes the sense of resignation with which we accept the political dispensations of a powerful government whose hold upon us continues to increase.

An editor of a national weekly news magazine told me a few   21
years ago that as few as a dozen letters of protest against an editorial stance of his magazine was enough to convene a plenipotentiary meeting of the board of editors to review policy. "So few people complain, or make their voices heard," he explained to me, "that we assume a dozen letters represent the inarticulated views of thousands of readers." In the past ten years, he said, the volume of mail has noticeably decreased, even though the circulation of his magazine has risen.

When our voices are finally mute, when we have finally sup-   22
pressed the natural instinct to complain, whether the vexation is trivial or grave, we shall have become automatons, incapable of feeling. When Premier Khrushchev first came to this country late in 1959, he was primed, we are informed, to experience the bitter resentment of the American people against his tyranny, against his persecutions, against the movement which is responsible for the great number of American deaths in Korea, for billions in taxes every year, and for life everlasting on the brink of disaster; but Khrushchev was pleasantly surprised, and reported back to the Russian people that he had been met with overwhelming cordiality (read: apathy), except, to be sure, for "a few fascists who followed me around with their wretched posters, and should be horsewhipped."

I may be crazy, but I say there would have been lots more   23
posters in a society where train temperatures in the dead of winter
are not allowed to climb to 85 degrees without complaint.

Meanings and Values

1. Restate completely what you believe to be the meaning of the last sen-
    tence of paragraph 8. How close does Buckley's sentence, or your ver-
    sion of it, come to stating the central theme of the selection? (See
    "Guide to Terms": *Unity*.)

2. Why do you think the author said to "strike that last sentence" of the
    quoted matter in paragraph 10?

3. Explain the connection between anti-Kruschev posters and complain-
    ing about the heat in a train (par. 23).

Expository Techniques

1. What generality do Buckley's examples illustrate? (You may use his
    words or your own.)

2. Does the use of examples seem to you the best way for the writer to
    have developed his theme? If not, what might have been a better
    way?

3. Which of the standard methods of introduction does the first para-
    graph demonstrate? How successful is its use? (Guide: *Introductions;
    Evaluation.*)

4. What seems to be the purpose, or purposes, of paragraphs 4 and 12?

5. Why do you think the Kruschev example is kept until last? (Guide:
    Emphasis.)

Diction and Vocabulary

1. Explain the allusion to Milquetoast in paragraph 11. (Guide: *Figures of
    Speech.*)

2. Explain the meaning (in par. 22) of Kruschev's being "met with over-
    whelming cordiality (read: apathy)."

3. To what extent, if at all, were you annoyed by Buckley's liberal use of
    "dictionary-type" words? Is the use of such terms a matter of personal
    style alone or does it serve other purposes? What might those other
    purposes be?

4. Use a dictionary as needed to understand the meanings of the follow-
    ing words: virile, doleful, sibilant, discreet (par. 2); gauntlet,
    consigned (3); supine, faculties, dissolution, rectify (4); hectoring (5);

purposive (7); unobtrusive, ambiguous (8); provocation, complexus, unconscionably, bellicose, girded (9); infer (10); ostentatiously (11); impervious, reproof (13); centripetal (16); deferentially (17); unctuously (18); technification (19); apathy, phenomenon, dispensations (20); stance, plenipotentiary, inarticulated (21); automatons (22).

Read to Write

1. Buckley builds his essay around sets of contrasting ideas and behaviors, including apathy/involvement and servility/independence. Discussions of public, personal, or political behavior are often constructed around similar pairs. To identify topics for your own writing, look for paired terms and then search for behaviors that illustrate them. (Hint: begin with a single term such as passivity or commitment, identify the opposing term, and then think of ways the two terms highlight kinds of behavior typical of our public, personal, or political lives.)

2. Buckley uses examples from his own experience, including some in which he pokes fun at himself or criticizes his own behavior. Try building an essay around similar examples in which you look critically at your actions as a way of illustrating a generality.

3. Follow Buckley's lead in using a series of examples to explain a generality about ways we commonly behave and to suggest what we might do to "improve" our behavior.

(NOTE: Suggestions for topics requiring development by use of EXAMPLE are on page 101 at the end of this section.)

BARBARA EHRENREICH received a B.A. from Reed College and a
Ph.D. from Rockefeller University in biology. She has been
active in the women's movement and other movements for social
change and she has taught women's issues at several universi-
ties, including New York University and the State University of
New York—Old Westbury. She is a Fellow of the Institute for
Policy Studies in Washington, D.C., and is active in the Democratic Socialists of America. A prolific author, Ehrenreich has
published articles in a wide range of magazines, among them
Esquire, the *Atlantic, Vogue, New Republic*, the *Wall Street Journal,
TV Guide, Ms., The New York Times Magazine, Social Policy*, and *The
Nation*. Her books include *For Her Own Good: 150 Years of the
Experts' Advice to Women* (with Deirdre English) (1978); *The Hearts
of Men: American Dreams and the Flight from Commitment* (1983); *Fear
of Falling: The Inner Life of the Middle Class* (1989); *The Worst Years of
Our Lives: Irreverent Notes from a Decade of Greed* (1990); and *The
Snarling Citizen: Essays* (1995).

What I've Learned from Men

The theme and strategies of this essay (first published in *Ms.*) are
similar in some striking ways to those of Buckley's piece. Nonetheless, the essays' perspectives are clearly different, reflecting the
social and political outlooks of their authors. Yet Ehrenreich, like
Buckley, provides numerous illustrations of the skillful use of
examples in support of a generality. In addition, she demonstrates
the role of examples in definition as she contrasts "lady" with
"woman."

For many years I believed that women had only one thing to learn   1
from men: how to get the attention of a waiter by some means short
of kicking over the table and shrieking. Never in my life have I gotten the attention of a waiter, unless it was an off-duty waiter whose
car I'd accidentally scraped in a parking lot somewhere. Men, however, can summon a maître d' just by thinking the word "coffee,"

and this is a power women would be well advised to study. What else would we possibly want to learn from them? How to interrupt someone in mid-sentence as if you were performing an act of conversational euthanasia? How to drop a pair of socks three feet from an open hamper and keep right on walking? How to make those weird guttural gargling sounds in the bathroom?

But now, at mid-life, I am willing to admit that there are some real   2 and useful things to learn from men. Not from all men—in fact, we may have the most to learn from some of the men we like the least. This realization does not mean that my feminist principles have gone soft with age: what I think women could learn from men is how to get *tough*. After more than a decade of consciousness-raising, assertiveness training, and hand-to-hand combat in the battle of the sexes, we're still too ladylike. Let me try that again—we're just too *damn* ladylike.

Here is an example from my own experience, a story that I   3 blush to recount. A few years ago, at an international conference held in an exotic and luxurious setting, a prestigious professor invited me to his room for what he said would be an intellectual discussion on matters of theoretical importance. So far, so good. I showed up promptly. But only minutes into the conversation—held in all-too-adjacent chairs—it emerged that he was interested in something more substantial than a meeting of minds. I was disgusted, but not enough to overcome 30-odd years of programming in ladylikeness. Every time his comments took a lecherous turn, I chattered distractingly; every time his hand found its way to my knee, I returned it as if it were something he had misplaced. This went on for an unconscionable period (as much as 20 minutes); then there was a minor scuffle, a dash for the door, and I was out—with nothing violated but my self-esteem. I, a full-grown feminist, conversant with such matters as rape crisis counseling and sexual harassment at the workplace, had behaved like a ninny—or, as I now understand it, like a lady.

The essence of ladylikeness is a persistent servility masked as   4 "niceness." For example, we (women) tend to assume that it is our responsibility to keep everything "nice" even when the person we are with is rude, aggressive, or emotionally AWOL. (In the above example, I was so busy taking responsibility for preserving the veneer of "niceness" that I almost forgot to take responsibility for myself.) In conversations with men, we do almost all the work: sociologists have observed that in male-female social interactions it's the woman who throws out leading questions and verbal encouragements ("So how did you *feel* about that?" and so on) while the man, typically, says "Hmmmm." Wherever we go, we're perpetually smiling—the on-cue smile, like the now-outmoded curtsy, being one of our culture's little rituals of submission. We're trained to feel embarrassed if we're praised, but if we see a criticism coming at us from miles down the road, we rush to acknowledge it. And when we're feeling aggressive or angry or resentful, we just tighten up our smiles or turn them into rueful little moues. In short, we spend a great deal of time acting like wimps.

For contrast, think of the macho stars we love to watch. Think,   5 for example, of Mel Gibson facing down punk marauders in "The Road Warrior". . . John Travolta swaggering his way through the early scenes of "Saturday Night Fever". . . or Marlon Brando shrugging off the local law in "The Wild One." Would they simper their way through tight spots? Chatter aimlessly to keep the conversation going? Get all clutched up whenever they think they might—just might—have hurt someone's feelings? No, of course not, and therein, I think, lies their fascination for us.

The attraction of the "tough guy" is that he has—or at least   6 seems to have—what most of us lack, and that is an aura of power and control. In an article, feminist psychiatrist Jean Baker Miller writes that "a woman's using self-determined power for herself is equivalent to selfishness [and] destructiveness"—an equation that makes us want to avoid even the appearance of power. Miller cites cases of women who get depressed just when they're on the verge of success—and of women who do succeed and then bury their achievement in self-deprecation. As an example, she describes one company's periodic meetings to recognize outstanding salespeople: when a woman is asked to say a few words about her achievement, she tends to say something like, "Well, I really don't know how it happened. I guess I was just lucky this time." In contrast, the men will cheerfully own up to the hard work, intelligence, and so on, to which they owe their success. By putting herself down, a woman avoids feeling brazenly powerful and potentially "selfish"; she also does the traditional lady's work of trying to make everyone else feel better ("She's not really so smart, after all, just lucky").

So we might as well get a little tougher. And a good place to   7 start is by cutting back on the small acts of deference that we've been programmed to perform since girlhood. Like unnecessary smiling. For many women—waitresses, flight attendants, receptionists— smiling is an occupational requirement, but there's no reason for anyone to go around grinning when she's not being paid for it. I'd suggest that we save our off-duty smiles for when we truly feel like sharing them, and if you're not sure what to do with your face in the meantime, study Clint Eastwood's expressions—both of them.

Along the same lines, I think women should stop taking respon-   8 sibility for every human interaction we engage in. In a social encounter with a woman, the average man can go 25 minutes saying nothing more than "You don't say?" "Izzat so?" and, of course, "Hmmmm." Why should we do all the work? By taking so much responsibility for making conversations go well, we act as if we had much more at stake in the encounter than the other party—and that gives him (or her) the power advantage. Every now and then, we deserve to get more out of a conversation than we put into it: I'd suggest not offering information you'd rather not share ("I'm really terrified that my sales plan won't work") and not, out of sheer politeness, soliciting information you don't really want ("Wherever did you get that lovely tie?"). There will be pauses, but they don't have to be awkward for *you.*

It is true that some, perhaps most, men will interpret any   9 decrease in female deference as a deliberate act of hostility. Omit the free smiles and perky conversation-boosters and someone is bound to ask, "Well, what's come over *you* today?" For most of us, the first impulse is to stare at our feet and make vague references to a terminally ill aunt in Atlanta, but we should have as much right to be taciturn as the average (male) taxi driver. If you're taking a vacation from smiles and small talk and some fellow is moved to inquire about what's "bothering" you, just stare back levelly and say, the international debt crisis, the arms race, or the death of God.

There are all kinds of ways to toughen up—and potentially   10 move up—at work, and I leave the details to the purveyors of assertiveness training. But Jean Baker Miller's study underscores a fundamental principle that anyone can master on her own. We can stop acting less capable than we actually are. For example, in the matter of taking credit when credit is due, there's a key difference between saying "I was just lucky" and saying "I had a plan and it worked." If you take the credit you deserve, you're letting people know that you were confident you'd succeed all along, and that you fully intend to do so again.

Finally, we may be able to learn something from men about   11 what to do with anger. As a general rule, women get irritated: men get *mad*. We make tight little smiles of ladylike exasperation; they pound on desks and roar. I wouldn't recommend emulating the full basso profundo male tantrum, but women do need ways of expressing justified anger clearly, colorfully, and, when necessary, crudely. If you're not just irritated, but *pissed off*, it might help to say so.

I, for example, have rerun the scene with the prestigious profes-   12
sor many times in my mind. And in my mind, I play it like Bogart. I start by moving my chair over to where I can look the professor full in the face. I let him do the chattering, and when it becomes evident that he has nothing serious to say, I lean back and cross my arms, just to let him know that he's wasting my time. I do not smile, neither do I nod encouragement. Nor, of course, do I respond to his blandishments with apologetic shrugs and blushes. Then, at the first flicker of lechery, I stand up and announce coolly, "All right, I've had enough of this crap." Then I walk out—slowly, deliberately, confidently. Just like a man.

Or—now that I think of it—just like a woman.   13

Meanings and Values

1. How are most women likely to respond to the opening paragraph? How are most men likely to respond? Why?

2. Define the psychological and moral problem that women face in grasping and exercising power (outlined in paragraph 6). Does the explanation of the problem and its causes offered by Ehrenreich seem reasonable to you? Be ready to explain your answer and to cite examples from your experience, if possible.

3. Is the main purpose of this essay expository or argumentative? If you have read the Buckley piece earlier in this section, you may wish to compare his aim in writing with Ehrenreich's. (See "Guide to Terms": *Purpose; Argument*.)

Expository Techniques

1. Why do you think the author chose to wait until paragraph 2 to state the essay's thesis? (Guide: *Unity*.)

2. Besides paragraph 3, which other parts of the essay discuss the definition of "lady" and "woman"? Discuss how the writer links paragraphs within the essay through repetition of these terms.

3. Examine the use of contrasting pairs of quotations in paragraphs 4, 8, and 10, and be ready to explain how the author uses them to make generalities more forceful or convincing.

4. If you have read Buckley's "Why Don't We Complain?", compare the strategies Ehrenreich and Buckley use to open and conclude their essays. (Guide: *Introductions; Closings.*)

Diction and Vocabulary

1. List the connotations that "lady" is likely to have for most readers and compare them with the connotations the word acquires in the course of this selection. (Guide: *Connotation/Denotation.*)

2. Identify the contrasts in diction in paragraph 11, and indicate the ways in which parallelism adds emphasis to them. (Guide: *Parallel Structure.*)

3. The following words may be unfamiliar to many readers. Use your dictionary, if necessary, to discover their meanings: maître d', guttural (par. 1); adjacent, lecherous, unconscionable, conversant (3); servility, veneer (4); simper (5); self-deprecation, brazenly (6); deference (7); taciturn (9); basso profundo (11); blandishments (12).

Read to Write

1. Make a list of the social and political values Ehrenreich seems to endorse in this essay and those she criticizes. From your list select three values (or issues) that particularly interest you and write down examples and ideas associated with each that you could develop into an essay.

2. The opening words of Ehrenreich's title "What I've Learned from . . ." suggest an approach you can use for other essays. Begin by thinking of people who are very different from you, situations that are not part of your regular life, or exotic customs and ideas. Then imagine how you might act in different ways if you learned something from such an unfamiliar source, or think of examples from your experience whose meaning changes when you view them from an unfamiliar perspective.

3. Drawing on Ehrenreich's strategies in "What I've Learned from Men," construct an essay in which you use examples to provide explanations and advice to some other group of people: men, schoolteachers, auto mechanics, lawyers, TV reporters—or any other group that might benefit from a fresh look at its behavior.

(NOTE: Suggestions for topics requiring development by use of EXAMPLE are on page 101 at the end of this section.)

Issues and Ideas:

Discovering and Constructing Identities

Discovering who we are—exploring the attitudes, feelings, and ways of behaving that make us individuals—is an ongoing job for most people. Personal identity is a favorite topic for writers, too, because it plays an important role in determining what we believe and how we act.

Though they may agree on its importance, writers are just as likely to disagree about the meaning of "identity," or its causes and consequences. For some, identity is an individual matter, the product of our unique experiences and personal outlooks; for others, it is part of the "character" we share with people who are shaped by similar social and cultural forces. Likewise, writers often disagree about the extent to which we are responsible for shaping (or reshaping) our own identities.

The first three essays in this section (by Andy Rooney, William F. Buckley, Jr., and Barbara Ehrenreich) alert readers to some of the perspectives that shape our lives, often without our being fully aware of their presence. The three essays that follow offer generalities and examples that focus more specifically on the various ways we discover, construct, and struggle with our personal and social selves.

ANTONYA NELSON was born in Wichita, Kansas and attended both the University of Kansas (B.A.) and the University of Arizona (M.F.A.). She now lives in New Mexico and teaches English at New Mexico State University. Nelson has published short fiction in a number of magazines, including *Esquire,* the *New Yorker, Redbook,* and *North American Review.* Her published collections of short stories include *The Expendables* (1990) (winner of the Flannery O'Connor Award for Short Fiction), *In the Land of Men* (1992), and *Family Terrorists* (1994). Her stories have been reprinted in several collections of the best contemporary short fiction, and she has received numerous grants and awards for her work. Her most recent book is a novel, *Talking in Bed* (1996).

Fear of Flying

In this essay, first published in the *New York Times Magazine,* Nelson uses examples drawn from her family's experiences and from movies to share her perspective on the way events can shape identity. She suggests that while the two are probably linked, their relationship is not always as direct as we might suppose.

When I was 5 years old, a tornado lifted my family from our suburban 1
neighborhood, in our Ford station wagon, and turned us onto our collective back like a bug. Then, strangely enough, the tornado lifted our car once more, and righted us. Flatter, yes, but restored to our wheels, bodies more or less intact. Inside the car were: my father, my mother— eight months pregnant with what would soon be my sister —two of my brothers, a family friend and I. My brother David and I were in what we called the "way back," the two facing seats in the rear of the car that folded down to create cargo space, up to accommodate children.

It was 1965: we lived in Wichita, Kan. We'd been out to dinner, 2
a rare occasion in my family, when the storm began. Candles were lighted at the Ramada Inn when the lights went out; I was allowed a Shirley Temple, also rare. The mood was festive. There was neither

a tornado watch nor warning in effect. As we drove home, lightning struck, one thick bolt still imprinted in my memory, sizzling across a field.

My father remembers electric lines suddenly snapping at the   3
pavement, whipped by the wind from their poles. My older brother saw a roof fly off a house. It was dark dusk, the peculiar green of tornado weather, not unlike that sickly black-and-white pallor Dorothy Gale lives under before she lands among the Munchkins. My father steered us into a parking lot, where, amid all the unoccupied cars, ours alone was singled out by the storm.

Out the way-back window my 3-year-old brother flew. He cried   4
for our mother, who, by some maternal miracle, had made her hugely pregnant way over two sets of seats to spread her arms, winglike, above us. The glass she took left a series of scars like small slugs crawling from wrists to shoulders, What must she have thought when my brother disappeared? What must he have thought, out there on the asphalt with a drinking straw driven into his cheek?

We fled our wrecked car to someone else's. In that car we   5
waited, my mother bleeding on the back seat, my older brother furiously sounding the horn, my younger brother sobbing, me needing so badly to urinate I thought I'd wet myself. That's what I remember of the arrival of the ambulance, at last, of the photographer who took my picture as I was loaded into its chamber, of the ride to the hospital, of the gurney trip to our room, of the arrival of my terrified grandparents: fierce pressure on my bladder, embarrassment of bursting.

We survived. My father's shoulder was injured, my mother had   6
her stitches. The baby was fine, born five weeks later at the same hospital. Now there's a Dillon's Food Store where we were lifted, smashed down, lifted once more; my father prefers its selection to Safeway's. Whenever I'm back home in Wichita, I enter that parking lot without a lot of internal fanfare.

Which is not to say that my tornado hasn't left a memory. It just   7
isn't the Hollywood version of memory, à la Helen Hunt in "Twister": tornado did her wrong, she kicks tornado tail. In my experience, memory is indirect, and fear is lodged bodily. Probably that isn't odd at all; it just isn't a cinematic equation. The members of my family who were in that Ford station wagon are one and all afraid of flying. My parents and older brother simply won't do it; my parents drive west a few times a year, and every Christmas my brother Bill drives home from California to Kansas just to avoid the

skies. My brother's a psychologist and has actually spent a considerable amount of energy assuring his clients that flying is safer than driving. He's perfectly happy entrusting the airlines with his wife and daughter. But not himself. My younger brother and I fly, grudgingly. For myself, it's never the purported dangerous times that frighten me. Takeoff and landing are nothing when compared with the long hurtle from point A to point B, the tremble and shudder of a vehicle in the air, with me inside it.

My little sister, the one in utero, says she sort of enjoys flying. 8 The other older brother, the one who was too cool back in 1965 to dine out with his family, isn't bothered by airplanes, either.

But among the rest of us is a shared fear, one based on an act of 9 God that didn't kill us but that probably spun us in another direction. Who knows who any of us would be without that fateful whirl? Would my family feel the strong urge to convene, at least twice a year, without it?

Humankind prevails in "Twister." Helen Hunt's quest is satis- 10 fied, 100 percent. For the rest of us, however, deep in the body's odd strongbox a mysterious tempest or two still must govern, and we may count ourselves lucky to predict a harmless shower, let alone a deadly funnel.

Meanings and Values

1. What generalities about the shared identity of her family does Nelson offer in paragraph 9? To what extent do the examples in the essay support what she has to say about the traits the family members share?

2. Do you think Nelson believes there is a direct link between the events described in paragraphs 1–5 and specific behaviors in the later lives of the participants? If so, how do you account for the examples she offers in paragraph 6? If not, state in your own words what generalities Nelson offers about the tornado's consequences for the family members.

Expository Techniques

1. Why does the writer wait until paragraph 7 to present generalities about the identities developed (and shared) by the members of her family? Why would the essay be more (or less) effective if the generalities were presented near the beginning? (See "Guide to Terms": *Evaluation*.)

2. What purpose does the example of Helen Hunt and the movie *Twister* serve in the essay? To what other movie does the writer allude, and why is it appropriate? (Guide: *Purpose; Figures of Speech.*)

3. Nelson's choice of details makes many of her examples particularly vivid and memorable. Which details in paragraphs 3, 4, and 5 are especially effective, and why? Are they specific and concrete, or are there other reasons for their success? (Guide: *Concrete/Abstract; Specific/General.*)

Diction and Vocabulary

1. To describe extraordinary events and emotions, Nelson uses a number of similes. Identify the similes in paragraphs 1 and 4 and tell what they add to the examples being presented. (Guide: *Figures of Speech.*)

2. Why do you think the writer chose the Latin phrase *in utero* (par. 8) rather than a more easily understood English equivalent?

3. If you do not know the meaning of any of the following words, look them up in a dictionary: pallor (par. 3); gurney (5); cinematic (7).

Read to Write

1. When we try explaining our preferences, values, or personalities to people, we often rely on examples of events that, we believe, helped shape our identities. Sift through your memories looking for formative events in your life, make note of them, and then decide what generalities about you these events might illustrate and explain.

2. "Fear of Flying" opens with an extended, vivid example before offering some general statements about the writer and her family. Use a similar strategy to begin an essay in which you generalize about particular kinds of behavior.

3. Using "Fear of Flying" as a model, provide examples of shared experiences to illustrate and explain identities of people in your family or some other social or cultural group to which you belong.

(NOTE: Suggestions for topics requiring development by use of EXAMPLE are on page 101 at the end of this section.)

MARY KARR

MARY KARR's highly-praised memoir of her Texas childhood and unusual family, *The Liar's Club,* was first published in 1995. It won a PEN Prize and is frequently cited as among the best of the many moving and insightful accounts of growing up that have appeared in recent years. Karr, who teaches creative writing at Syracuse University, has also published several volumes of poetry: *Abacus* (1987) and *The Devil's Tour* (1993).

Dysfunctional Nation

To make the point that her dysfunctional family was far from unique, Karr draws examples from the many stories of other families she heard on a tour to promote her memoir. She suggests, in addition, that growing up in such a setting may not prevent a person from achieving a healthy identity and sense of self as an adult.

When I set out on a book tour to promote the memoir about my less-than-perfect Texas clan, I did so with soul-sucking dread. Surely we'd be held up as grotesques, my beloveds and I. Instead, I shoved into bookstores where sometimes hundreds of people stood claiming to identify with my story, which fact stunned me.   1

For one thing, my artist mother had been married seven times, twice to my Texas oil-worker daddy, who was Nos. 5 and 7. Both of my parents drank hard enough to hit some jackpots. Both were well armed. (The tile man who came to redo my mother's kitchen last spring pried more than one .22 slug from the wall.)   2

Yet in towns across this country I sat at various bookstore tables till near closing and heard people posit that reading about my tribe brought not slack-jawed horror, but recognition. Maybe these peoples' family lives differed from mine in terms of surface pyrotechnics—houses set afire and fortunes squandered. But the feelings didn't. After eight weeks of travel, I ginned up this working definition for a dysfunctional family: any family with more than one person in it.   3

Even the most perfect-looking clan seemed to suffer a rough patch. "I'm from one of these Donna Reed households you always   4 wanted to belong to," said the elegant woman in Chicago. But her doctor daddy got saddled with a wicked malpractice suit, a few more martinis than usual got poured from his silver shaker every night. Rumor was he took up with his nurse.

What happened? "We worked it out. It passed." But not before   5 his Cadillac plowed over her bicycle one drunken night and her mother threatened divorce. Like me, she'd lain awake listening to her parents storm around in the masks of monsters and felt the metaphorical foundations of her house tremble, hopeless to prop it all up.

Not all folks reported such rough times as mere blips on the   6 family time line. In fact, I met dozens of people from way more chaotic households than mine. One guy's drug-dealer parents allegedly dragged him across several borders with bags of heroin taped under his Doctor Denton sleeper. Another woman had, at age 5, watched her alcoholic mother stick her head in a noose and step off a kitchen stool while the girl fought to shield her toddler brother's eyes. Surely many don't survive such childhoods intact (or they don't go to book signings because they're too busy being serial killers). But the myth that such a childhood condemns you to a life curled up in the back ward of a mental institution dissolved for me. On the surface, people seemed to have got over their troubled upbringings.

The female therapist in a Portland bookstore talked specifically   7 about the power of narrative in her life. She'd been raised by a chronic schizophrenic. On a given day, her school clothes were selected by God himself talking to her mother through scalp implants. The girl got good at worming her way into the homes of neighbors and any halfway decent teacher. In college, she fought depression with counseling she continued for nearly 10 years.

At 50, happily married, she wore a Burberry raincoat and toted   8 a briefcase of fine leather. She showed no visible signs of trauma. The real miracle? She was in fairly close touch with her mother, whose psychosis had diminished with new medications.

In part, this woman claimed to have survived through stories.   9 Traditional therapy, of course, starts with retelling family dramas. Talk about it, in the old wisdom, and the hurt eventually recedes. From narratives about her childhood, a self eventually emerged. Her tendency otherwise would have been to lop herself off from her own past, to make a false self for navigating the world. But false selves rarely withstand the real blows life delivers, Hence, her need for stories, her own and other peoples'.

In our longing for some assurance that we're behaving O.K.   10
inside fairly isolated families, personal experience has assumed
some new power. Just as the novel form once took up experiences of
urban, industrialized society that weren't being handled in epic
poems or epistles, so memoir—with its single, intensely personal
voice—wrestles subjects in a way readers of late find compelling.
The good ones I've read confirm my experience in a flawed family.
They reassure the same way belonging to a community reassures.

My bookstore chats did the same. On the road, I came to believe   11
that our families are working, albeit in new forms. People go on
birthing babies and burying dead and loving those with whom
they've shared deeply wretched patches of history. We do this partly
by telling stories, in voices that seek neither to deny family struggles
nor to make demons of our beloveds.

Meanings and Values

1. What conclusion about families does Karr offer in paragraph 3? What
   examples does she provide to illustrate and support this generality?

2. Does Karr believe our identities and well being are primarily determined by our family backgrounds? If so, where in the essay does she
   make this point? If not, what else does she believe shapes who we are?

Expository Techniques

1. Explain how the statement, "On the surface, people seemed to have
   got over their troubled upbringings" (par. 6), serves both to separate
   the two halves of the essay and to link them (see "Guide to Terms":
   Transition.) In what ways does the second half of the essay answer
   questions suggested by the statement?

2. In what specific ways does the example in the second half of the essay
   (pars. 7–9) and the way it is presented differ from the examples in the
   first half? How much space does the writer devote to presenting the
   later example and how much to commenting on and interpreting it?

3. What strategy does the writer employ to conclude the essay? (Guide:
   Closings.)

Diction and Vocabulary

1. Karr uses a number of vivid phrases in the course of the essay: "soul-
   sucking dread" (par. 1); "drank hard enough to hit some jackpots" (2),
   "in the masks of monsters" and "the metaphorical foundations of her

house" (5). Tell what each of these phrases means and what it contributes to the essay's effectiveness.

2. If you do not know the meaning of any of the following words, look them up in a dictionary: memoir, grotesques (par. 1); pyrotechnics, squandered, ginned, dysfunctional (3); trauma, psychosis (8); epistles (10); albeit (11).

Read to Write

1. Karr's essay touches on a variety of subjects, including storytelling, alcoholism, and family relationships. Make a list of all the subjects she mentions, and then choose two that you find most interesting. Then for each subject, make a list of topics or issues you might wish to explore in an essay of your own.

2. Karr begins her essay by describing a situation that surprised her by turning out to be the opposite of what she expected. Use this strategy to begin an essay of your own, and then go on to explore what you learned through the experience (just as Karr docs).

3. Using "Dysfunctional Nation" as a model, discuss situations, relationships, or social forces that make it hard for people to establish healthy identities and explore some of the ways people overcome, or fail to overcome, these difficulties.

(NOTE: Suggestions for topics requiring development by use of EXAMPLE are on page 101 at the end of this section.)

ALAN BUCZYNSKI is a construction worker and a writer who lives in the Detroit area.

Iron Bonding

Newspaper columns, magazine articles, and everyday conversations are often filled with generalities about the different ways men and women behave. This essay looks at the emotional life of men, offering a working person's perspective rather than that of the intellectuals and professional people often associated with the "men's movement." The essay first appeared in *The New York Times Magazine*.

"I just don't get it." We were up on the iron, about 120 feet, waiting 1 for the gang below to swing up another beam. Sweat from under Ron's hard hat dripped on the beam we were sitting on and evaporated immediately, like water thrown on a sauna stove. We were talking about the "men's movement" and "wildman weekends."

"I mean," he continued, "if they want to get dirty and sweat and 2 cuss and pound on things, why don't they just get *real* jobs and get paid for it?" Below, the crane growled, the next piece lifting skyward.

I replied: "Nah, Ron, that isn't the point. They don't want to 3 sweat every day, just sometimes."

He said: "Man, if you only sweat when you want to, I don't call 4 that real sweatin."

Although my degree is in English, I am an ironworker by trade; 5 my girlfriend, Patti, is a graduate student in English literature. Like a tennis ball volleyed by two players with distinctly different styles, I am bounced between blue-collar maulers and precise academicians. My conversations range from fishing to Foucault, derricks to deconstruction. There is very little overlap, but when it does occur it is generally the academics who are curious about the working life.

Patti and I were at a dinner party. The question of communica- 6 tion between men had arisen. Becky, the host, is a persistent interrogator: "What do you and Ron talk about?"

I said, "Well, we talk about work, drinking, ah, women." 7
Becky asked, "Do you guys ever say, 'I love you' to each other?" 8
This smelled mightily of Robert Bly and the men's movement.
I replied: "Certainly. All the time." 9
I am still dissatisfied with this answer. Not because it was a lie, 10
but because it was perceived as one.

The notion prevails that men's emotional communication skills 11
are less advanced than that of chimpanzees, that we can no more
communicate with one another than can earthworms.

Ironworkers as a group may well validate this theory. We are not 12
a very articulate bunch. Most of us have only a basic education. Construction sites are extremely noisy, and much of our communication
takes place via hand signals. There is little premium placed on words
that don't stem from our own jargon. Conversations can be blunt.

Bly's approach, of adapting a fable for instruction, may instinc- 13
tively mimic the way men communicate. Ironworkers are otherwise
very direct, yet when emotional issues arise we speak to one another
in allegory and parable. One of my co-workers, Cliff, is a good storyteller, with an understated delivery: "The old man got home one
night, drunk, real messed up and got to roughhousing with the cat.
Old Smoke, well she laid into him, scratched him good. Out comes
the shotgun. The old man loads up, chases Smoke into the front yard
and blam! Off goes the gun. My Mom and my sisters and me we're
all screamin'. Smoke comes walkin' in the side door. Seems the old
man blew away the wrong cat, the neighbor's Siamese. Red lights
were flashin' against the house, fur was splattered all over the lawn,
the cops cuffed my old man and he's hollerin' and man, I'll tell you,
I was cryin'."

Now, we didn't all get up from our beers and go over and hug 14
him. This was a story, not therapy. Cliff is amiable, but tough, more
inclined to solving any perceived injustices with his fists than verbal
banter, but I don't need to see him cry to know that he can. He has
before, and he can tell a story about it without shame, without any
disclaimers about being "just a kid," and that's enough for me.

Ron and I have worked together for nine years and are as close 15
as 29 is to 30. We have worked through heat and cold and seen each
other injured in the stupidest of accidents. One February we were
working inside a plant, erecting steel with a little crane; it was near
the end of the day, and I was tired. I hooked onto a piece and, while
still holding the load cable, signaled the operator "up." My thumb
was promptly sucked into the sheave of the crane. I screamed, and

the operator came down on the load, releasing my thumb. It hurt. A
lot. Water started leaking from my eyes. The gang gathered around
while Ron tugged gently at my work glove, everyone curious
whether my thumb would come off with the glove or stay on my
hand.

"O.K., man, relax, just relax," Ron said. "See if you can move it."   16
Ron held my hand. The thumb had a neat crease right down the center, lengthwise. All the capillaries on one side had burst and were
turning remarkable colors. My new thumbnail was on back order
and would arrive in about five months. I wiggled the thumb, an
eighth of an inch, a quarter, a half.

"You're O.K., man, it's still yours and it ain't broke. Let's go   17
back to work."

Afterwards, in the bar, while I wrapped my hand around a cold   18
beer to keep the swelling and pain down, Ron hoisted his bottle in a
toast: "That," he said, "was the best scream I ever heard, real authen-
tic, like you were in actual pain, like you were really *scared*."

If this wasn't exactly Wind in His Hair howling eternal friend-   19
ship for Dances With Wolves, I still understood what Ron was saying. It's more like a 7-year-old boy putting a frog down the back of
a little girl's dress because he has a crush on her. It's a backward way
of showing affection, of saying "I love you," but it's the only way we
know. We should have outgrown it, and hordes of men are now
paying thousands of dollars to sweat and stink and pound and
grieve together to try and do just that. Maybe it works, maybe it
doesn't. But no matter how cryptic, how Byzantine, how weird and
weary the way it travels, the message still manages to get through.

Meanings and Values

1. According to the writer, how do men communicate with each other
   on emotional matters?

2. Buczynski concludes that "no matter how cryptic, how Byzantine,
   how weird and weary the way it travels, the message still manages to
   get through" (par. 19). Does he convince you that this generality is
   well-founded? Why or why not?

Expository Techniques

1. Identify those places in the essay where the generality being illustrated is stated more or less directly. Would presenting the generality

as a thesis statement in the opening paragraphs make the essay more effective? (See "Guide to Terms": *Thesis; Evaluation*.)

2. What strategy does the writer use in paragraphs 1–10 to open the essay? (Guide: *Introduction*.)

3. Identify the main examples Buczynski uses and then discuss the effectiveness of each. (Guide: *Evaluation*.)

Diction and Vocabulary

1. Discuss how the simile in the third sentence of the opening paragraph, "like water thrown on a sauna stove," heightens the contrast between iron workers and people involved in the "men's movement." (Guide: *Figures of Speech*.)

2. Explain how the word choice in paragraph 5 emphasizes contrasts between academics and blue-collar workers. (Guide: *Diction; Emphasis*.)

3. If you do not know the meaning of any of the following words, look them up in a dictionary: maulers (par. 5); interrogator (6); articulate (12); allegory, parable (13); disclaimers (14).

Read to Write

1. Think of the roles of stories, especially allegories or parables, in communicating emotion within your family or some other community to which you belong. Make a list of the roles stories play. Decide which, if any, might be a good subject for an expository essay.

2. Begin an essay of your own the way Buczynski does: with an extended example that raises some important questions about the way people communicate, or that provides contradictory explanations of the way people commonly relate to each other.

3. Using "Iron Bonding" as a model, use example to explain the communication strategies of a particular group of people with which you are familiar.

(NOTE: Suggestions for topics requiring development by use of EXAMPLE follow.

Writing Suggestions for Section 3
Example

Use one of the following statements or another suggested by them as your central theme. Develop it into a unified composition, using examples from history, current events, or personal experience to illustrate your ideas. Be sure to have your reader-audience clearly in mind, as well as your specific purpose for the communication.

1. Successful businesses keep employees at their highest level of competence.

2. In an age of working mothers, fathers spend considerable time and effort helping raise the children.

3. Family life can create considerable stress.

4. Laws holding parents responsible for their children's crimes would (or would not) result in serious injustices.

5. Letting people decide for themselves which laws to obey and which to ignore would result in anarchy.

6. Many people find horror movies entertaining.

7. Service professions are often personally rewarding.

8. Religion in the United States is not dying.

9. Democracy is not always the best form of government.

10. A successful career is worth the sacrifices it requires.

11. "An ounce of prevention is worth a pound of cure."

12. The general quality of television commercials may be improving (or deteriorating).

13. An expensive car can be a poor investment.

14. "Some books are to be tasted; others swallowed; and some few to be chewed and digested." (Francis Bacon, English scientist-author, 1561–1626).

15. Most people are superstitious in one way or another.

16. Relationships within the family are much more important than relationships outside the family.

4

Analyzing a Subject by *Classification*

People naturally like to sort and classify things. The untidiest urchin, moving into a new dresser of his own, will put his handkerchiefs together, socks and underwear in separate stacks, and perhaps his toads and snails (temporarily) into a drawer of their own. He may classify animals as those with legs, those with wings, and those with neither. As he gets older, he finds that schoolteachers have ways of classifying *him*, not only into a reading group but, periodically, into an "A" or "F" category, or somewhere in between. On errands to the grocery store, he discovers the macaroni in the same department as the spaghetti, the pork chops somewhere near the ham. In reading the local newspaper, he observes that its staff has done some classifying for him, putting most of the comics together and seldom mixing sports stories with the news of bridal showers. Eventually he finds courses neatly classified in the college catalogue, and he knows enough not to look for biology courses under "Social Science." (Examples again—used to illustrate a "prevalence.")

Our main interest in classification here is its use as a structural pattern for explanatory writing. Many subjects about which either students or graduates may need to write will remain a hodgepodge of facts and opinions unless they can find some system of analyzing the material, dividing the subject into categories, and classifying individual elements into those categories. Here we have the distinction usually made between the rhetorical terms *division* and *classification*—for example, dividing "meat" into pork, beef, mutton, and fowl, then classifying ham and pork chops into the category of "pork." But this distinction is one we need scarcely pause for here; once the need for analysis is recognized, the dividing and classifying become inevitable companions and result in the single scheme of "classification" itself, as we have been discussing it. The original division into parts merely sets up the system that, if well chosen, best serves our purpose.

Obviously, no single system of classification is best for all purposes. Our untidy urchin may at some point classify girls according to athletic prowess, then later by size or shape or hair color. (At the same time, of course, the girls may be placing him into one or more categories.) Other people may need entirely different systems of classification: the music instructor classifies girls as sopranos, altos, contraltos; the psychologist, according to their behavior patterns; the sociologist, according to their ethnic origins.

Whatever the purpose, for the more formal uses of classification ("formal," that is, to the extent of most academic and on-the-job writing), we should be careful to use a logical system that is complete and that follows a consistent principle throughout. It would not be logical to divide Protestantism into the categories of Methodist, Baptist, and Lutheran, because the system would be incomplete and misleading. But in classifying Protestants attending some special conference—a different matter entirely—such a limited system might be both complete and logical. In any case, the writer must be careful that classes do not overlap: to classify the persons at the conference as Methodists, Baptists, Lutherans, and clergy would be illogical, because some are undoubtedly both Lutheran, for instance, and clergy.

In dividing and classifying, we are really using the basic process of outlining. Moreover, if we are dealing with classifiable *ideas*, the resulting pattern *is* our outline, which has been our aim all along— a basic organizational plan.

This process of classification frequently does, in fact, organize much less tangible things than the examples mentioned. We might wish to find some orderly basis for discussing the South's post–Civil War problems. Division might give us three primary categories of information: economic, political, and social. But for a full-scale consideration of these, the major divisions themselves may be subdivided for still more orderly explanation: the economic information may be further divided into agriculture and industry. Now it is possible to isolate and clarify such strictly industrial matters as shortage of investment capital, disrupted transportation systems, and lack of power development.

Any plan like this seems almost absurdly obvious, of course— *after* the planning is done. It appears less obvious, however, to inexperienced writers who are dealing with a jumble of information they must explain to someone else. This is when they should be aware of the patterns at their disposal, and one of the most useful of these, alone or combined with others, is classification.

Sample Paragraph (Annotated)

Background suggesting the topic of the paragraph.

> Palmville is not a planned town that sprang full-blown from an architect's drawing board. After all, the town has been around since 1880, and for its first ninety years it grew more or less by chance. In 1980, however, M&T Realty developed a building plan that has been followed informally by most of the other major developers.

Topic announcing the division into four categories.

> As a result, the town now has four main neighborhoods, each characterized by a different kind of housing, and each using the name originally assigned by M&T's urban planner.

Classification, with each category containing a presentation of characteristics.

> Brooktown is a neighborhood of modest starter homes, each with three bedrooms, 1½ baths, a small dining area, and a one-car garage. The plain occupied by the homes is bisected by Talley's Creek (now running mostly in culverts), and is the dustiest area in town, at least by general reputation. The houses in Kingston Hills are a bit more costly. Some have three bedrooms, some four, but all have dens, dining rooms, two-car garages, and yards big enough for an in-ground pool or an elaborate patio. The streets in Brooktown and Kingston Hills are straight, but those in Paddock Estates curve gracefully around the three-acre lots of custom-built homes. Buyers get to choose from eight basic plans ranging from sprawling ranches, to oversized capes, to French Colonial chateaus. Each basic plan must be

modified inside and out both to suit the homeowner's taste and to make sure that each house appears different enough to justify the ad for the development: "Unique Executive Homes on three-acre lots." In contrast, Village Green, the center of the original village, offers charming restored Victorian homes and cottages mixed with modern reproductions of homes from the same period. The homes (or the styles) may be old, but the prices are contemporary, and almost as high as for the luxury homes in Paddock Estates.

Sample Paragraph (Classification)

Rock and roll is old enough now to have its generations. Some of you reading this may be part of the first (those who grew up in the fifties on Elvis and Chuck Berry), or the second (fans of the British Invasion and the Motown sound), or even the third generation (kids in the seventies for whom the members of Led Zeppelin were *eminences grises* and the Beatles were Paul McCartney's *old* band). But no matter what wave you rode in on, the chances are pretty good that your parents didn't listen to rock, that they in fact detested it and regarded everything you listened to with the utmost disdain. I can still recall my mother's reaction to the first 45 I ever bought with my own money, the Rolling Stones' "Paint it Black," with "Stupid Girl" on the flip side. Staring in outrage at the photograph that adorned the sleeve—

> Mick, Keith, and the boys in their foppish, Edwardian finest—she finally exclaimed, "I suppose *that's* how you want to look!"

From "Talking 'Bout Their Generation," *Parenting Magazine* (September 1988). Reprinted by permission.

JUDITH VIORST

JUDITH VIORST was born in Newark, New Jersey, and attended
Rutgers University. Formerly a contributing editor of *Redbook*
magazine, for which she wrote a monthly column, she has also
been a newspaper columnist, and in 1970 she received an Emmy
award for her contributions to a CBS television special. She has
written numerous fiction and nonfiction books for children,
including *Alexander and the Terrible, Horrible, No Good, Very Bad
Day* (1982). Among her various books of verse and prose for
adults are *It's Hard to Be Hip Over Thirty and Other Tragedies of Married Life* (1968) (a collection of poems), *Yes, Married: A Saga of Love
and Complaint* (1972) (prose pieces), and, more recently, *If I Were in
Charge of the World and Other Worries* (1981), *Love and Guilt and the
Meaning of Life* (1984), *Necessary Losses* (1986), and *Murdering Mr.
Monti* (1995) (a novel).

What, Me? Showing Off?

In "What, Me? Showing Off?" first published in *Redbook*, Viorst
uses classification to explore a behavior that most of us notice readily enough in other people but may be reluctant to acknowledge in
our own actions—showing off. Though its tone is breezy and it
contains frequent touches of humor, this essay is carefully organized and serious in purpose. Besides classification, Viorst makes
good use of examples, definition, brief narratives, and even a short
dramatic episode.

We're at the Biedermans' annual blast, and over at the far end of the   1
living room an intense young woman with blazing eyes and a throb-
bing voice is decrying poverty, war, injustice and human suffering.
Indeed, she expresses such anguish at the anguish of mankind that
attention quickly shifts from the moral issues she is expounding to
how very, very, very deeply she cares about them.

She's showing off.   2

Down at the other end of the room an insistently scholarly fel-   3
low has just used *angst, hubris,* Kierkegaard and *epistemology* in the

same sentence. Meanwhile our resident expert in wine meditatively
sips, then pushes away, a glass of unacceptable Beaujolais.

They're showing off. 4

And then there's us, complaining about how tired we are today 5
because we went to work, rushed back to see our son's school play,
shopped at the market and hurried home in order to cook gourmet,
and then needlepointed another dining-room chair.

And what we also are doing is showing off. 6

Indeed everyone, I would like to propose, has some sort of need 7
to show off. No one's completely immune. Not you. And not I. And
although we've been taught that it's bad to boast, that it's trashy to
toot our own horn, that nice people don't strut their stuff, seek attention or name-drop, there are times when showing off may be for-
givable and maybe even acceptable.

But first let's take a look at showing off that *is* obnoxious, that's 8
not acceptable, that's never nice. Like showoffs motivated by a fierce,
I'm-gonna-blow-you-away competitiveness. And like narcissistic
showoffs who are willing to do anything to be—and stay—the center of attention.

Competitive showoffs want to be the best of every bunch. Com- 9
petitive showoffs must outshine all others. Whatever is being discussed, they have more—expertise or money or even aggravation—
and better—periodontists or children or marriages or recipes for
pesto—and deeper—love of animals or concern for human suffering
or orgasms. Competitive showoffs are people who reside in a permanent state of sibling rivalry, insisting on playing Hertz to everyone else's Avis.

(You're finishing a story, for instance, about the sweet little card 10
that your five-year-old recently made for your birthday when the
CSO interrupts to relate how her daughter not only made her a
sweet little card, but also brought her breakfast in bed and saved her
allowance for months and months in order to buy her—obviously
much more beloved—mother a beautiful scarf for her birthday.
Grrr.)

Narcissistic showoffs, however, don't bother to compete 11
because they don't even notice there's anyone there to compete with.
They talk nonstop, they brag, they dance, they sometimes quote
Homer in Greek, and they'll even go stand on their head if attention
should flag. Narcissistic showoffs want to be the star while everyone
else is the audience. And yes, they are often adorable and charming
and amusing—but only until around the age of six.

(I've actually seen an NSO get up and leave the room when the conversation shifted from his accomplishments. "What's the matter?" I asked when I found him standing on the terrace, brooding darkly. "Oh, I don't know," he replied, "but all of a sudden the talk started getting so superficial." *Aagh!*) 12

Another group of showoffs—much more sympathetic types—are showoffs who are basically insecure. And while there is no easy way to distinguish the insecure from the narcissists and competitors, you may figure out which are which by whether you have the urge to reassure or to strangle them. 13

Insecure showoffs show off because, as one close friend explained, "How will they know that I'm good unless I tell them about it?" And whatever the message—I'm smart, I'm a fine human being, I'm this incredibly passionate lover—showoffs have many different techniques for telling about it. 14

Take smart, for example. 15

A person can show off explicitly by using flashy words, like the hubris-Kierkegaard fellow I mentioned before. 16

Or a person can show off implicitly, by saying not a word and just wearing a low-cut dress with her Phi Beta Kappa key gleaming softly in the cleavage. 17

A person can show off satirically, by mocking showing off: "My name is Bill Sawyer," one young man announces to every new acquaintance, "and I'm bright bright bright bright bright." 18

Or a person can show off complainingly: "I'm sorry my daughter takes after me. Men are just so frightened of smart women." 19

Another way showoffs show off about smart is to drop a Very Smart Name—if this brain is my friend, goes the message, I must be a brain too. And indeed, a popular showing-off ploy—whether you're showing off smartness or anything else—is to name-drop a glittery name in the hope of acquiring some gilt by association. 20

The theory seems to be that Presidents, movie stars, Walter Cronkite and Princess Di could be friends, if they chose, with anyone in the world, and that if these luminaries have selected plain old Stanley Stone to be friends with, Stanley Stone must be one hell of a guy. (Needless to say, old Stanley Stone might also be a very dreary fellow, but if Walt and Di don't mind him, why should I?) 21

Though no one that I know hangs out with Presidents and movie stars, they do (I too!) sometimes drop famous names. 22

As in: "I go to John Travolta's dermatologist." 23

Or: "I own the exact same sweater that Jackie Onassis wore in a newspaper photograph last week." 24

Or: "My uncle once repaired a roof for Sandra Day O'Connor." 25
Or: "My cousin's neighbor's sister-in-law has a child who is 26
Robert Redford's son's best friend."

We're claiming we've got gilt—though by a very indirect asso- 27
ciation. And I think that when we do, we're showing off.

Sometimes showoffs ask for cheers to which they're not enti- 28
tled. Sometimes showoffs earn the praise they seek. And sometimes folks achieve great things and nonetheless do not show off
about it.

Now *that's* impressive. 29

Indeed, when we discover that the quiet mother of four with 30
whom we've been talking intimately all evening has recently been
elected to the state senate—*and she never even mentioned it!*—we are
filled with admiration, with astonishment, with awe.

What self-restraint! 31

For we know damn well—*I* certainly know—that if we'd been 32
that lucky lady, we'd have worked our triumph into the conversation. As a matter of fact, I'll lay my cards right on the table and confess that the first time some poems of mine were published, I not
only worked my triumph into every conversation for months and
months, but I also called almost every human being I'd ever known
to proclaim the glad tidings both local and long distance. Furthermore—let me really confess—if a stranger happened to stop me on
the street and all he wanted to know was the time or directions, I
tried to detain him long enough to enlighten him with the news that
the person to whom he was speaking was a Real Live Genuine Hon-
est-to-God Published Poet.

Fortunately for everyone, I eventually—it took me awhile— 33
calmed down.

Now, I don't intend to defend myself—I was showing off, I was 34
bragging and I wasn't the slightest bit shy or self-restrained, but a
golden, glowing, glorious thing had happened in my life and I had
an overwhelming need to exult. Exulting, however (as I intend to
argue farther on), may be a permissible form of showing off.

Exulting is what my child does when he comes home with an *A* 35
on his history paper ("Julius Caesar was 50," it began, "and his good
looks was pretty much demolished") and wants to read me the
entire masterpiece while I murmur appreciative comments at frequent intervals.

Exulting is what my husband does when he cooks me one of his 36
cheese-and-scallion omelets and practically does a tap dance as he
carries it from the kitchen stove to the table, setting it before me with

the purely objective assessment that this may be the greatest omelet ever created.

Exulting is what my mother did when she took her first grand-   37
son to visit all her friends, and announced as she walked into the room, "Is he gorgeous? Is that a gorgeous baby? Is that the most gorgeous baby you ever saw?"

And exulting is what that mother of four would have done if   38
she'd smiled and said, "Don't call me 'Marge' any more. Call me 'Senator.'"

Exulting is shamelessly shouting our talents or triumphs to the   39
world. It's saying: I'm taking a bow and I'd like to hear clapping. And I think if we don't overdo it (stopping strangers to say you've been published is overdoing it), and I think if we know when to quit ("Enough about me. Let's talk about you. So what do you think about me?" does not count as quitting), and I think if we don't get addicted (i.e., crave a praise-fix for every poem or *A* or omelet), and I think if we're able to walk off the stage (and clap and cheer while others take their bows), then I think we're allowed, from time to time, to exult.

Though showing off can range from very gross to very subtle,   40
and though the point of showing off is sometimes nasty, sometimes needy, sometimes nice, showoffs always run the risk of being thought immodest, of being harshly viewed as . . . well . . . showoffs. And so for folks who want applause without relinquishing their sense of modesty, the trick is keeping quiet and allowing someone else to show off *for* you.

And I've seen a lot of marriages where wives show off for hus-   41
bands and where husbands, in return, show off for wives. Where Joan, for instance, mentions Dick's promotion and his running time in the marathon. And where Dick, for instance, mentions all the paintings Joanie sold at her last art show. And where both of them lean back with self-effacing shrugs and smiles and never once show off about themselves.

Friends also may show off for friends, and parents for their   42
children, though letting parents toot our horns is risky. Consider, for example, this sad tale of Elliott, who was a fearless and feisty public-interest lawyer:

"My son," his proud mother explained to his friends, "has   43
always been independent." (Her son blushed modestly.)

"My son," his proud mother continued, "was the kind of person   44
who always knew his own mind." (Her son blushed modestly.)

"My son," his proud mother went on, "was never afraid. He   45
never kowtowed to those in authority." (Her son blushed modestly.)

"My son," his proud mother concluded, "was so independent   46
and stubborn and unafraid of authority that we couldn't get him
toilet-trained—he wet his pants till he was past four." (Her son ...)

But showing off is always a risk, whether we do it ourselves or   47
whether somebody else is doing it for us. And perhaps we ought to
consider the words Lord Chesterfield wrote to his sons: "Modesty is
the only sure bait when you angle for praise."

And yes, of course he's right, we know he's right, he must be   48
right. But sometimes it's so hard to be restrained. For no matter what
we do, we always have a lapse or two. So let's try to forgive each
other for showing off.

Meanings and Values

1. Name the categories into which Viorst divides showoffs (and non-
    showoffs). Which of the categories does Viorst divide into subcate-
    gories? What are the subcategories? Where, if anywhere, do the cate-
    gories in this essay overlap? If the categories overlap, is the result
    confusing and misleading, or is some overlap inevitable in any classi-
    fication that attempts to explain human behavior?

2. According to the examples in paragraphs 36 and 37, exulting may
    sometimes mean exaggerating or stretching the truth. Do you agree
    with Viorst that exulting should be permissible even if it means inflat-
    ing one's accomplishments? Be ready to defend your answer.

3. What does Viorst imply about the personalities of narcissistic
    showoffs when she says, "they are often adorable and charming
    and amusing—but only until around the age of six" (par. 11)? What
    message is the woman with the Phi Beta Kappa key conveying (par.
    17)?

Expository Techniques

1. In what order are the categories arranged? Worst to best? Most forgiv-
    able to least forgivable? Some other order? Where and how is this
    arrangement announced to the reader?

2. The introduction to this essay is relatively long (pars. 1–8). What
    does Viorst do to get readers interested in the subject? Where in the
    introduction does she announce the central theme (thesis)? Where
    else in the essay does she speak directly about it? Where in the intro-
    duction does she indicate the plan of organization? (See "Guide to
    Terms": *Introductions*.)

3. At several places in the essay Viorst comments on its organization and summarizes the categories. Identify these places.

4. For some of the categories the discussion consists of a general defini- tion followed by examples. Which discussions follow this arrange- ment? Describe briefly the organization of the remaining discussions.

5. Identify a section of the essay where Viorst uses parallel paragraphs and discuss their effect. Do the same with parallel sentences and par- allel sentence parts. (Guide: *Parallel Structure.*)

Diction and Vocabulary

1. What words or kinds of words does Viorst repeat frequently in the course of the essay? What purposes does the repetition serve?

2. To what does the phrase "gilt by association" allude? (Guide: *Figures of Speech.*) Identify as many as you can of the direct references and allusions to people, ideas, or events in the following paragraphs: pars. 3, 9, 11, 21, and 23–26. What purposes do these references serve?

3. How is irony (understatement) used in paragraph 36? (Guide: *Irony.*) How is exaggeration used in paragraph 32?

4. Viorst uses some devices that in many essays would seem excessively informal or careless: unusual or made-up words ("*Grrr,*" par. 10; "*Aagh,*" 12); informal phrases ("strut their stuff," 7); exclamation points; and parentheses surrounding an entire paragraph, among other things. In what ways do such devices contribute to the humor of the essay?; to its overall tone? (Guide: *Style/Tone.*)

5. If you are unfamiliar with any of the following words, consult your dictionary as necessary: decrying, expounding (par. 1); *angst, hubris, epistemology* (3); narcissistic (8); periodontists, sibling (9); brooding (12); cleavage (17); dermatologist (23); enlighten (32); exult (34); ap- preciative (35); assessment (36); shamelessly, crave (39); gross, im- modest, relinquishing (40); feisty (42); kowtowed (45).

Read to Write

1. Showing off is not the only irritating (but understandable) behavior you are likely to encounter every day. Start by making a list in the morning of all irritating behaviors that come to mind. Then spend the rest of the day on the lookout for others. In the evening, use your ob- servations to expand the list, then look it over and circle those that might make a good topic for an essay classifying typical kinds of be- havior.

2. Viorst makes herself and her family part of the essay by including her own (and their) behaviors in the classification. Use a similar strategy in an essay of your own.

3. Follow Viorst's lead and use a social event of some sort for an essay of your own classifying human behavior. Use the guests or participants as representatives (examples) of the different categories, just as Viorst does.

(NOTE: Suggestions for topics requiring development by use of CLASSIFICATION are on pages 143–144 at the end of this section.)

JUDITH STONE has been a regular contributor to a number of magazines, including *Discover*. Her writings have been collected in *Light Matters: Essays in Science from Gravity to Levity* **(1991)**. As the title suggests, Stone writes about science and scientific matters with both wit and detailed knowledge.

Personal Beast

From the play of words in its title through the rest of its many puns and humorous images, this essay looks critically and understandingly at our often exaggerated and absurd affection for pets—and the status they can confer on their owners. The essay first appeared as a column in *Discover* magazine.

For the past several millennia, dogs have pretty much had the Man's 1
Best Friend market cornered. Lately, however, thanks to a sort of demographic Darwinism, several strong contenders for the title are nipping at the heels of the chosen species.

The dog emerged as protopet in Mesopotamia, where our 2
nomadic ancestors first began living in villages about 12,000 to 14,000 years ago. (And if you think it's hard to paper-train a puppy, imagine having to use stone tablets.)

"Domestication was an urban event," explains Alan Beck, 3
Ph.D., Director of the University of Pennsylvania's Center for the Interaction of Animals and Society. "The garbage generated by these new high-density human communities probably attracted wolf packs; villagers may have bred the pups into pets with the idea of making peace with the pack. These domesticated creatures could bark a warning when nondomestic animals came around, and also help with trash control. And perhaps one of the earliest reasons for breeding pets was for companionship; the desire to nurture is part of human culture." (Those days, when Hector was a pup, probably marked the first time in history that a human being uttered the words, "Aw, Ma, can't I keep it?")

Now a new kind of urbanization is creating a new kind of pet. 4
People are choosing animals that better fit a busier life and a smaller
dwelling. Is there room for Fido in Mondo Condo, a world of two-
income families with less time but more discretionary income? Folks
want pets that are small and independent, pets that offer them a way
to announce their individuality in a crowded, standardized world.
Miniaturization, convenience, chic—the pet of the nineties has many
of the same fine qualities as an under-the-counter microwave or a
car phone. Here, hot off the Ark Nouveau, are the exotic animals that
busy Americans simply must have.

Some of you may be seeking a companion that's low-mainte- 5
nance, affectionate, cute (though swaybacked and paunchy), and
perfectly content curled up in front of the TV, pigging out on junk
food. (Yeah, yeah, I know—you're already married to it. You're a
scream, honestly.) I mean the Vietnamese pot-bellied pig, the
nation's top-selling Asian import. A black, beagle-sized porker that's
also called a Chinese house pig, it looks like a cross between a hog,
a honey bear, and a hand puppet.

"If you can keep a poodle, you can keep one of these pigs," says 6
Fredericka Wagner, co-owner, with husband Bob, of Flying W
Farms in Piketon, Ohio, which sends more of the little piggies to
market than anyone in the country. "They're very appealing. Full
grown, they weigh up to 45 or 50 pounds and stand about 12 to 13
inches high. They graze instead of root. Ordinary pigs have a long,
straight snout; this one has a short, pushed-in, wrinkly nose. Its little ears stick straight up like a bat's and it has a straight tail that it
wags like a dog's. It barks, too, and it can learn tricks—to come when
it's called, sit up and beg, or roll over and play dead hog instead of
dead dog." And it's easier to housebreak than a cat, Wagner says.
Her three little pigs, Choo-Choo, Matilda, and Hamlet; like to sit
around with the family and watch movies on TV (presumably
Porky's I through *III*), and they enjoy supplementing their diet of
Purina Pig Chow with candy, brownies, peanuts, and potato chips.

When the pigs arrived two years ago from Vietnam (by way of 7
Sweden and Canada, after three years of red tape), the Wagners
already ran a midget menagerie, selling impossibly cute 18-inch
miniature sheep (perfect for baby sweaters, easy to count for insom-
niacs), pygmy goats, miniature donkeys, and championship miniature Arabian horses. (Apparently there are no bonsai bovines, or the
Wagners would have them.) "Miniature horses are bred down from
larger horses—anything from huge Belgian draft horses to Shetland

ponies—a process that can take a century," Wagner says. "In our experience, to reduce a horse from 48 inches to 34 inches takes six generations—about twenty years. You can do it in only three generations if you have a 30-inch stallion, but you'd have to dig a hole to put the mare in."

Wagner first heard about the pigs from a friend in California;   8
reportedly they'd been imported by Vietnam veterans who recalled the friendly critters from their tours of duty. Though Wagner was instantly attracted to them, she wasn't sure she'd get the business off the ground. But the swine flew. "We can't keep up with the demand," she says. "In the first eighteen months we sold a hundred pigs." Wagner is boarish on pot-bellied pigs as an investment. "Not even the stock market will pay you back as fast as these pigs will. I've had several retired people buy them to supplement their income. They breed at six months [the pigs, not the retirees] and it takes three weeks, three months, and three days for them to have babies. By the time your gilt is a year old—a gilt is a pregnant sow— she's given you her first litter of pigs and you have your investment back three times over." Since you can only have gilt by association, those who want to breed pigs must buy an unrelated pair for $2,500. "We expect that to go up to $3,000, because the demand is so great," says Wagner, in hog heaven. "We've sold them to everyone from poets to princes—we shipped some overseas to a Saudi Arabian prince. Stephanie Zimbalist, the actress, has one."

Stephanie Zimbalist! A recommendation, indeed. But what   9
about having the same pet as *Michael Jackson*? For part of his personal zoo (boa, deer, chimp/valet, glove, and, nearly, the Elephant Man), Jackson has chosen a taller order of hip creature, the llama. His is one of about 15,000 in the country. "But in years to come, we'll see more and more of them in the average home," says Florence Dicks, owner of the Llonesome Llama Ranch in Sumner, Washington. "They're great hiking companions, their wool is increasingly in demand, and they make wonderful pets. They've been part of domestic life in South America for centuries. I think of them as one of life's necessities."

Dicks, who runs Llama Lluvs Unlltd., the world's only Llama-   10
gram delivery service, notes that the recent lifting of a government ban on imports will increase the llama population; most American-born llamas are descended from a single herd owned by William Randolph Hearst.

"They're very gentle," Dicks says. "Many of my fifteen llamas 11
lived in the house for their first year. They're easier to house-train
than a cat." (You know how all weird meat is described as "sort of
like chicken"? Apparently all weird pets are easier to housebreak
than a cat.) Dicks explains, in more detail than necessary, that llamas
are what's called communal voiders—a great name for a rock band.
Spread some llama droppings where you want them to go, and, in
the comradely way of communal voiders everywhere, they will use
that spot forever after. "We've shared our bathroom with llamas for
five years, and they've never had an accident," Dicks says. Okay,
they squeeze the toothpaste from the top, but nobody's perfect.

"I train my llamas to hum—that's the noise they make—when 12
they want to go outside," Dicks reports. "They communicate by tone
variance. If they're relaxed, there's a musical quality to the hum. If
they're stressed, you can hear the anxiety. I have a llama who hums
with a rising inflection when he's curious."

Full-grown llamas can stand over six feet tall and weigh up to 13
500 pounds. A male costs between $1,500 and $15,000. (And at a
recent auction, a male said to have outstanding stud qualities—he
always sends a thank-you note—fetched $100,000). A gelded male
will set you back $700 or $800, a female about $8,000. The only bad
thing about llamas, Dicks says, is that you have to clip their toenails
every three or four months. Which doesn't sound like a big deal if
you're already sharing a bathroom.

But more and more of us have life-styles and living spaces—to 14
use a pair of expressions even more nauseating than the word *pus*—
that can't accommodate a dog, let alone a llama. I know I barely have
room in my apartment for a pet peeve. Hence the proliferation
among city dwellers of ferrets, dwarf rabbits, and birds. According
to the American Veterinary Medical Association, birds are the fastest
growing pet category. Their numbers increased 24 percent between
1983 and 1987, from 10.3 million to 12.8 million. Talking birds, like
Amazon parrots, are especially sought after, reports veterinarian
Katherine Quesenberry, head of the exotic pet service of the Animal
Medical Center of New York. (And I guess if you crossed these South
American birds with llamas, you'd get Fernando Llamas six-foot
communal voiders that squawk, "You look *mah*velous." Cheep gag.)

The ferret, a more personable cousin of the weasel, has been 15
bred in captivity for a century, mostly for lab research. But its popularity as a pet has steadily risen over the last decade. Says Tina Ellenbogen, a Seattle veterinarian and information services director for

the Delta Society, a national organization dedicated to the study of human-animal bonding, "People become attached to ferrets because they have a lot of personality. They're small, clean, and amusing." (It's sometimes hard to tell when people are talking about ferrets and when they're talking about Dudley Moore.) You can walk them on a harness or let them play on a ferrets wheel. They're easily litter-trained, says Ellenbogen—easier than a cat, I imagine—and statisti-cally less likely to bite than a dog is. Males are unpleasant if you don't remove their stink glands, and females are sexually insatiable until you have them fixed, but hey.

Maybe you're a person who doesn't understand all the sound   16
and furry over mammals. Maybe you'd rather see something in cold blood.

The reptile of the hour is the African Old World chameleon.   17
"Having one is like owning a dinosaur!" says Gary Bagnall, head of California Zoological Supplies, one of the five largest reptile distrib-utors in the country. "They look truly prehistoric. Their eyes move independently and they have 10-inch tongues with stickum at the end for catching insects. The base color is green, but they can blend into their surroundings by changing to yellow, orange, white, black, brown, and sometimes blue." The 6- to 10-inch chameleons start at $35; a foot-long variety, called Miller's chameleon, goes for $1,000. "We get only about four of them a year," Bagnall says. "There's a waiting list."

The nation's most sought-after amphibian, according to Bagnall,   18
is the poison arrow frog, a tiny (less than an inch long), jewel-like native of South America that comes in orange and black, yellow and black, or blue. The really great thing about the poison arrow frog is that if you boil up about fifty of them, you get enough of the toxin they secrete to brew a dandy blowdart dip guaranteed to make hunt-ing small jungle mammals a breeze.

Alive, the frogs, which cost from $35 to $200, require a lot of   19
attention, Bagnall warns. "They can't take extremes in temperature or dryness, and their diet is restricted to very small insects. In fact, you have to raise fruit flies for them." Most of us don't have time to raise fruit flies for our families, let alone for a pet. But, paradoxically, though exotic pet owners are getting busier, they're also getting savvier and more dedicated.

"The whole pet industry has changed," says Bagnall. "Exotic   20
pet owners can't afford to be ignorant, because they're paying more." Making a fatal mistake with a $3,500 miniature ram and ewe

is a whole different thing from accidentally offing a twenty-five-cent baby turtle. (I'd like to take this opportunity to make a public confession. I'm sorry, Shelly. I was only seven, and I didn't know that painting your back with nail polish would kill you. Forgive me, too, for digging you up two weeks after the funeral, but I was curious to see if the rumors I'd heard about deterioration were true. You didn't disappoint.) Continues Bagnall, "I can't speak for birds and mammals, but the prices of even standard, bread-and-butter reptiles—boas, garter snakes, pythons—have tripled over the last three years because of government regulation of imports." But the high prices seem to add to the mystique, he says. "Reptiles attract people who want something not everybody has. Also, if you're allergic to fur, they're a nice alternative." (And probably a certain percentage of newly minted MBAs are even now saying to their mentors, "Rep *ties*? I thought you said 'invest in some rep*tiles!*'") Bagnall adds that poison arrow frogs and Old World chameleons are especially popular now because they've only recently appeared in zoos. "And if a reptile shows up in a movie, its popularity increases tenfold, like the Burmese python in *Raiders of the Lost Ark.*"

Yes, it's a cachet as cachet can world. Perhaps all human progress   21
stems from the tension between two basic drives: to have just what everyone else has and to have what no one has. Covet your neighbor's ass? Get yourself a miniature one and watch him mewl with envy. But be careful: Once an odd animal enters the main-stream, those on the cutting edge of the pet thing have to push for a new personal beast. "Pygmy goats used to be really rare," Fredericka Wagner says with a sigh. "Now everyone has them." (Haven't you noticed that the first question you're asked at the best restaurants these days is "May I check your goat?")

The proliferation of peculiar pets may necessitate a revamping   22
of terminology, says veterinarian Quesenberry. "The term *exotics* is no longer valid. We're talking about animals that haven't historically been domesticated, but they're not wild anymore, either, because they're being bred in captivity and exposed to humans from an early age. Somebody has suggested using the term *special species* for these animals, and reserving the term *exotics* for the zoo stuff."

If you're not ready to pay big bucks for little pigs, you'll be   23
happy to know that the classic exotic pet, the simple yet eloquent sea monkey, retails for just $3.99. Remember sea monkeys? When some of us were kids, during what scientists call the Late Cleaver-Brady Epoch, sea monkeys were advertised in the backs of magazines, usu-

ally between the Mark Eden Bust Developer and the Can You Draw This Elf School of Art. A smiling, bikini-clad creature with the head of a monkey and the body of a seahorse promised the requisite hours of fun for kids from eight to—if I recall the stats correctly—eighty. Remember your disappointment when the "monkeys" turned out to be brine shrimp, so infinitesimal that they could only be clearly seen with the enclosed magnifying glass? Remember how not one of them wore a bathing suit? Well, for the same low price, a new generation of kids can learn a powerful lesson about the true nature of existence (sometimes when you expect a bikini-clad aquatic primate, you get a bunch of stupid, skinny-dipping germs). And sea monkeys are easier to house-train than cats.

Meanings and Values

1. In your own words, tell what Stone considers the main qualities of the pet of the 90s. Explain the differences she sees between contemporary pets (and owners) and those of the past.

2. Identify the categories Stone presents in this essay. Are there any subcategories? If so, what are they? Do any of the categories overlap? If so, is the overlap confusing?

3. If you believe this essay has a serious purpose, tell what it is.

Expository Techniques

1. Can the second sentence in this essay be considered a thesis statement? If so, why? (See "Guide to Terms": *Thesis.*) Are there any other sentences that might be considered additional thesis statements or repetitions and developments of the second sentence? Identify any such sentences and discuss their role in the essay.

2. Why does the author choose to begin the essay by discussing dogs? Would the essay have been more effective had she begun with a discussion of cats or of some other familiar kind of pet? (Guide: *Evaluation.*)

3. Discuss the role of the comments within the parentheses in paragraph 20. Explain the ways these comments are similar to or different from other parenthetical comments in the essay.

Diction and Vocabulary

1. What does "Mondo Condo" (par. 4) mean, and for what purpose does the writer use the phrase?

2. Identify the source of each of the following allusions, and discuss what each means: Hector (par. 3); Ark Nouveau (4); swine flew (8); in cold blood (16). (Guide: *Figures of Speech.*)

3. How does the word choice in the last sentence of paragraph 5 emphasize the meaning and create a pattern of sound? (Guide: *Emphasis; Diction.*)

4. If you do not know the meaning of some of the following words, look them up in the dictionary; nomadic (par. 2); discretionary (4); voiders (11); variance (12); gelded (13); insatiable (15); cachet (21).

Read to Write

1. Pets are a kind of possession, though a pretty independent kind. Plants are possessions, too, if they are house or garden plants. Indeed, all kinds of things can be possessions. Consider writing about the different kinds of possessions people have and the different relationships people have with these possessions. The more unusual the possessions and the more varied the relationships, the more interesting and insightful your essay is likely to be.

2. Make an essay of your own grow from Stone's by coming up with some other kinds of pets that might be included in Stone's classification, or subdivide a single category of pets, such as cats, to create a classification that will introduce readers to unfamiliar members of the larger category.

3. Taking Stone's essay as a model, classify the contemporary versions of some activity or object (like pet owning and pets) that has been around in different forms for a long time. Following Stone's lead, show how the modern versions reflect changes in attitude and fashion.

(NOTE: Suggestions for topics requiring development by use of CLASSIFICATION are on page 143–144 at the end of this section.)

Issues and Ideas:

Images of Ourselves and Others

Every day on television, in films, in magazine articles, through songs, and in countless other places we encounter images of people like us and also images of people whose lives are unfamiliar to us except as we encounter them through these images. Because images have the power to shape perceptions, relationships, and values, we need to recognize they can sometimes represent accurately and yet sometimes simplify and distort.

But what is an image? This is an easy question to answer for visual media like films, television, advertisements, and posters. It is a representation of a person's actions, attitudes, character traits, and relationships. The image can represent the person as an individual or as a typical member of a group. When the image is constructed simply from the traits of a group (often negative traits) we can refer to it as a stereotype. Negative (and often hurtful) stereotypes are quite familiar: the bimbo, the less-than-intelligent "jock," the absent-minded professor, or the violent gang member.

People frequently share traits with other members of a group, of course, but a stereotype erases individual differences. When all we know about a group comes from stereotypic images, especially negative ones, we need to be aware of the limitations of our understanding and look for more accurate images. Renee Tajima's goal in "Lotus Blossoms Don't Bleed: Images of Asian American Women" is in part to alert us to the need for more realistic images and to the unfortunate effects of inaccurate ones, both of individuals and of the society at large.

The images we receive through music, literature, and other forms of reading can be a bit harder to describe. In representing relationships, feelings, and values, these media present us with definitions of appropriate (or inappropriate) behavior and attitudes. These, in turn, can shape our perceptions, self-understanding, values, and relationships. Many of the images we receive through music can be positive and useful, as Brenda Peterson points out in "Life Is a Musical." Renee Tajima also emphasizes the role of positive, realisitic images in her discussion of recent films by independent directors.

Images are not simply given to us by others. We can create them as well, especially in this age of recorders, cameras, and computers. Brenda Peterson's discussion of the way her family uses music to create and maintain its identity and the ways she integrates collections of songs into her own life are particularly interesting illustrations of how we can create images of ourselves (and others)—images that may act as creative responses to those thrust upon us every day.

RENEE E. TAJIMA is a filmmaker and writer. She produced a documentary for public television entitled "Adopted Son: The Death of Vincent Chin." Currently she is associated editor of *The Independent Film and Video Monthly* as well as a freelance writer. With Christine Choy she runs the Film News Now Foundation. Formerly editor of *Bridge: Asian American Perspectives,* Tajima has also edited *Journey Across Three Continents: Black and African Films, Asian American Film and Video,* and *Reel Change: Guide to Social Issue Media* (2d ed.).

Lotus Blossoms Don't Bleed: Images of Asian American Women

Categories are an important tool for thinking, but unless created with care, they can become unrepresentative stereotypes. Tajima's essay reminds us of the need to be aware of how the categories presented by film and television can shape our perceptions. And she demonstrates how restrictive and harmful stereotypes can be. The classification system here is somewhat complex, consisting of two different kinds of characters, "Lotus Blossoms" and "Dragon Ladies," that appear in several different types of movie roles.

In recent years the media have undergone spectacular technical innovations. But whereas form has leaped toward the year 2000, it seems that content still straddles the turn of the last century. A reigning example of the industry's stagnation is its portrayal of Asian women. And the only real signs of life are stirring far away from Hollywood in the cutting rooms owned and operated by Asian America's independent producers. 1

The commercial media are, in general, populated by stereotyped characterizations that range in complexity, accuracy, and per- 2 sistence over time. There is the hooker with a heart of gold and the steely tough yet honorable mobster. Most of these characters are white, and may be as one-dimensional as Conan the Barbarian or as complex as R. P. McMurphy in *One Flew Over the Cuckoo's Nest.*

Images of Asian women, however, have remained consistently   3
simplistic and inaccurate during the sixty years of largely forgettable screen appearances. There are two basic types: the Lotus Blossom Baby (a.k.a. China Doll, Geisha Girl, shy Polynesian beauty), and the Dragon Lady (Fu Manchu's various female relations, prostitutes, devious madames). There is little in between, although experts may differ as to whether Suzie Wong belongs to the race-blind "hooker with a heart of gold" category, or deserves one all of her own.

Asian women in American cinema are interchangeable in   4
appearance and name, and are joined together by the common language of non-language—that is, uninterpretable chattering, pidgin English, giggling, or silence. They may be specifically identified by nationality—particularly in war films—but that's where screen accuracy ends. The dozens of populations of Asian and Pacific Island groups are lumped into one homogeneous mass of Mama-sans.

Passive Love Interests

Asian women in film are, for the most part, passive figures who exist   5
to serve men, especially as love interests for white men (Lotus Blossoms) or as partners in crime with men of their own kind (Dragon Ladies). One of the first Dragon Lady types was played by Anna May Wong. In the 1924 spectacular *Thief of Bagdad* she uses treachery to help an evil Mongol prince attempt to win the Princess of Bagdad from Douglas Fairbanks.

The Lotus Blossom Baby, a sexual-romantic object, has been the   6
prominent type throughout the years. These "Oriental flowers" are utterly feminine, delicate, and welcome respites from their often loud, independent American counterparts. Many of them are the spoils of the last three wars fought in Asia. One recent television example is Sergeant Klinger's Korean wife in the short-lived series "AfterMash."

In the real world, this view of Asian women has spawned an   7
entire marriage industry. Today the Filipino wife is particularly in vogue for American men who order Asian brides from picture catalogues, just as you might buy an imported cheese slicer from Spiegel's. (I moderated a community program on Asian American

women recently. A rather bewildered young saleswoman showed
up with a stack of brochuers to promote the Cherry Blossom companion service, or some such enterprise.) Behind the brisk sales of
Asian mail-order brides is a growing number of American men who
are seeking old-fashioned, compliant wives, women they feel are no
longer available in the United States.

Feudal Asian customs do not change for the made-for-movie   8
women. Picture brides, geisha girls, concubines, and hara-kari are all
mixed together and reintroduced into any number of settings. Take
for example these two versions of Asian and American cultural
exchange:

1. It's Toko Riki on Japan's Okinawa Island during the late   9
1940s in the film *Teahouse of the August Moon.* American occupation
forces nice guy Captain Fisby (Glenn Ford) gets a visit from Japanese yenta Sakini (Marlon Brando).

Enter Brando: "Hey Boss, I Sonoda has a present for you."   10
Enter the gift: Japanese actress Machiko Kyo as a geisha, giggling.   11
Ford: "Who's she?"   12
Brando: "Souvenir. . . introducing Lotus Blossom geisha girl   13
first class."
Ford protests the gift. Kyo giggles.   14
Brando sneaks away with a smile: "Goodnight, Boss." Kyo,   15
chattering away in Japanese, tries to pamper a bewildered Ford who
holds up an instructive finger to her and repeats slowly, "Me . . . me
. . . no." Kyo looks confused.

2. It's San Francisco, circa 1981, in the television series "The   16
Incredible Hulk." Nice guy David Banner (Bill Bixby a.k.a. The
Hulk) gets a present from Chinese yenta Hyung (Beulah Quo).

Enter Quo: "David, I have something for you."   17
Enter Irene Sun as Tam, a Chinese refugee, bowing her head   18
shyly.
Quo: "The Floating Lotus Company hopes you will be very   19
happy. This is Tam, your mail-order bride."
Bixby protests the gift. Sun, speaking only Chinese, tries to   20
pamper a bewildered Bixby who repeats slowly in an instructive
tone, "you . . . must . . . go!" Sun looks confused.

Illicit Interracial Love

On film Asian women are often assigned the role of expendability in   21
situations of illicit Asian-white love. In these cases the most expedi-

ent way of resolving the problems of miscegenation has been to get rid of the Asian partner. Thus, some numbers of hyphenated (made-for-television, wartime, wives-away-from-home) Asian women have expired for the convenience of their home-bound soldier lovers. More progressive-minded GI's of the Vietnam era have returned to Vietnam years later to search for the offspring of these love matches.

In 1985 the General Foods Gold Showcase proudly presented a 22 post-Vietnam version of the wilting Lotus Blossom on network television. "A forgotten passion, a child he never knew.... All his tomorrows forever changed by *The Lady from Yesterday*." He is Vietnam vet Craig Weston (Wayne Rogers), official father of two, and husband to Janet (Bonnie Bedelia). She is Lien Van Huyen (Tina Chen), whom Weston hasn't seen since the fall of Saigon. She brings the child, the unexpected consequence of that wartime love match, to the United States. But Janet doesn't lose her husband, she gains a son. As *New York Times* critic John J. O'Connor points out, Lien has "the good manners to be suffering from a fatal disease that will conveniently remove her from the scene."

The geographic parallel to the objectification of Asian women is 23 the rendering of Asia as only a big set for the white leading actors. What would "Shogun" be without Richard Chamberlain? The most notable exception is the 1937 movie version of Pearl Buck's novel *The Good Earth*. The story is about Chinese in China and depicted with some complexity and emotion. Nevertheless the lead parts played by Louise Rainer and Paul Muni follow the pattern of choosing white stars for Asian roles, a problem which continues to plague Asian actors.

One film that stands out as an exception because it was cast 24 with Asian people for Asian characters is *Flower Drum Song* (1961), set in San Francisco's Chinatown. Unfortunately the film did little more than temporarily take a number of talented Asian American actresses and actors off the unemployment lines. It also gave birth for a while to a new generation of stereotypes—gum-chewing Little Leaguers, enterprising businessmen, and all-American tomboys—variations on the then new model minority myth. *Flower Drum Song* hinted that the assimilated, hyphenated Asian American might be much more successful in American society than the Japanese of the 1940s and the Chinese and Koreans of the 1950s, granted they keep to the task of being white American first.

The women of *Flower Drum Song* maintain their earlier image 25 with few modernizations. Miyoshi Umeki is still a picture bride.

And in *Suzie Wong* actress Nancy Kwan is a hipper, Americanized version of the Hong Kong bar girl without the pidgin English. But updated clothes and setting do not change the essence of these images.

In 1985 director Michael Cimino cloned Suzie Wong to TV news   26
anchor Connie Chung and created another anchor, Tracy Tzu (Ariane), in the disastrous exploitation film *Year of the Dragon*. In it Tzu is ostensibly the only positive Asian American character in a film that vilifies the people of New York's Chinatown. The Tzu character is a success in spite of her ethnicity. Just as she would rather eat Italian than Chinese, she'd rather sleep with white men than Chinese men. (She is ultimately raped by three "Chinese boys.") Neither does she bat an eye at the barrage of racial slurs fired off by her lover, lead Stanley White, the Vietnam vet and New York City cop played by Mickey Rourke.

At the outset Tzu is the picture of professionalism and sophisti-   27
cation, engaged in classic screen love/hate banter with White. The turning point comes early in the picture when their flirtatious sparring in a Chinese restaurant is interrupted by a gangland slaughter. While White pursues the culprits, Tzu totters on her high heels into a phone booth where she cowers, sobbing, until White comes to the rescue.

The standard of beauty for Asian women that is set in the   28
movies deserves mention. Caucasian women are often used for Asian roles, which contributes to a case of aesthetic imperialism for Asian women. When Asian actresses are chosen they invariably have large eyes, high cheekbones, and other Caucasian-like characteristics when they appear on the silver screen. As Judy Chu of the University of California, Los Angeles, has pointed out, much of Anna May Wong's appeal was due to her Western looks. Chu unearthed this passage from the June 1924 *Photoplay* which refers to actress Wong, but sounds a lot like a description of Eurasian model/actress Ariane: "Her deep brown eyes, while the slant is not pronounced, are typically oriental. But her Manchu mother has given her a height and poise of figure that Chinese maidens seldom have."

Invisibility

There is yet another important and pervasive characteristic of Asian   29
women on the screen, invisibility. The number of roles in the Oriental

flower and Dragon Lady categories have been few, and generally only supporting parts. But otherwise Asian women are absent. Asian women do not appear in films as union organizers, or divorced mothers fighting for the custody of their children, or fading movie stars, or spunky trial lawyers, or farm women fighting bank foreclosures; Asian women are not portrayed as ordinary people.

Then there is the kind of invisibility that occurs when individ-   30
ual personalities and separate identities become indistinguishable from one another. Some memorable Asian masses are the islanders fleeing exploding volcanoes in *Krakatoa: East of Java* (1969) and the Vietnamese villagers fleeing Coppola's airborne weaponry in various scenes from *Apocalypse Now* (1979). Asian women populate these hordes or have groupings of their own, usually in some type of harem situation. In *Cry for Happy* (1961), Glenn Ford is cast as an American GI who stumbles into what turns out to be the best little geisha house in Japan.

Network television has given Asian women even more oppor-   31
tunities to paper the walls, so to speak. They are background characters in "Hawaii 5-0," "Magnum PI," and other series that transverse the Pacific. I've seen a cheongsam-clad maid in the soap "One Life to Live," and assorted Chinatown types surface whenever the cops and robbers shows revive scripts about the Chinatown Tong wars.

The most stunning exceptions to television's abuse of Asian   32
images is the phenomenon of news anchors: Connie Chung (CBS) and Sasha Foo (CNN) have national spots, and Tritia Toyota (Los Angeles), Wendy Tokuda (San Francisco), Kaity Tong (New York), Sandra Yep (Sacramento), and others are reporters in large cities. All of them cover hard news, long the province of middle-aged white men with authoritative voices. Toyota and Yep have been able to parlay their positions so that there is more coverage of Asian American stories at their stations. Because of their presence on screen— and ironically, perhaps because of the celebrity status of today's newscasters—these anchors wield much power in rectifying Asian women's intellectual integrity in the media. (One hopes *Year of the Dragon's* Tracy Tzu hasn't canceled their positive effect.)

Undoubtedly the influence of these visible reporters is fortified   33
by the existence of highly organized Asian American journalists. The West Coast-based Asian American Journalists Association has lobbied for affirmative action in the print and broadcast media. In film and video, the same types of political initiatives have spurred a new

movement of independently produced works made by and about
Asian Americans.

Small Gems from Independents

The independent film movement emerged during the 1960s as an alter-   34
native to the Hollywood mill. In a broad sense it has had little direct
impact in reversing the distorted images of Asian women, although
some gems have been produced. . . . But now Asian American inde-
pendents, many of whom are women, have consciously set out to bury
sixty years of Lotus Blossoms who do not bleed and Mama-sans who
do not struggle. These women filmmakers—most of whom began their
careers only since the 1970s—often draw from deeply personal perspectives in their work: Virginia Hashii's *Jenny* portrays a young
Japanese American girl who explores her own Nikkei heritage for the
first time; Christine Choy's *From Spikes to Spindles* (1976) documents
the lives of women in New York's Chinatown; Felcia Lowe's *China:
Land of My Father* (1979) is a film diary of the filmmaker's own first
reunion with her grandmother in China; Renee Cho's *The New Wife*
(1978) dramatizes the arrival of an immigrant bride to America; and
Lana Pih Jokel's *Chiang Ching: A Dance Journey* traces the life of dancer-
actress-teacher Chiang. All these films were produced during the
1970s and together account for only a little more than two hours of
screen time. Most are first works with the same rough-edged quality
that characterized early Asian American film efforts.

Women producers have maintained a strong presence during   35
the 1980s, although their work does not always focus on women's
issues. . . . Also in this decade veteran filmmakers Emiko Omori and
Christine Choy have produced their first dramatic efforts. Omori's
The Departure is the story of a Japanese girl who must give up her
beloved traditional dolls in pre-World War II California. . . . In *Fei
Tien: Goddess in Flight,* Choy tries to adapt a nonlinear cinematic structure to Genny Lim's play *Pigeons*, which explores the relationship
between a Chinese American yuppie and a Chinatown "bird lady."

Perhaps the strongest work made thus far has been directed by   36
a male filmmaker, Arthur Dong. *Sewing Woman* is a small, but beautifully crafted portrait of Dong's mother, Zem Ping. It chronicles her
life from war-torn China to San Francisco's garment factories. Other
films and tapes by Asian men include Michael Uno's *Emi* (1978), a
portrait of the Japanese American writer and former concentration
camp internee Emi Tonooka; the Yonemoto brothers' neonarrative

Green Card, a soap-style saga of a Japanese immigrant artist seeking truth, love, and permanent residency in Southern California; and Steve Okazaki's *Survivors,* a documentary focusing on the women survivors of the atomic blasts over Hiroshima and Nagasaki. All these filmmakers are American-born Japanese. *Orientations,* by Asian Canadian Richard Fung, is the first work I've seen that provides an in-depth look at the Asian gay community, and it devotes a good amount of time to Asian Canadian lesbians.

Our Own Image

These film and videomakers, women and men, face a challenge far   37
beyond creating entertainment and art. Several generations of Asian women have been raised with racist and sexist celluloid images. The models for passivity and servility in these films and television programs fit neatly into the myths imposed on us, and contrast sharply with the more liberating ideals of independence and activism. Generations of other Americans have also grown up with these images. And their acceptance of the dehumanization implicit in the stereotypes of expendability and invisibility is frightening.

Old images of Asian women in the mainstream media will likely remain stagnant for a while. After sixty years, there have been few signs of progress. However, there is hope because of the growing number of filmmakers emerging from our own communities. Wayne Wang in 1985 completed *Dim Sum,* a beautifully crafted feature film about the relationship between a mother and daughter in San Francisco's Chinatown. *Dim Sum,* released through a commercial distributor, could be the first truly sensitive film portrayal of Asian American women to reach a substantial national audience. In quality and numbers, Asian American filmmakers may soon constitute a critical mass out of which we will see a body of work that gives us a new image, our own image.

Meanings and Values

1. What are the two main images of Asian women in Hollywood films (par. 3)? What are the three main roles Asian women have played in Hollywood films? (Note: See paragraphs 5, 21, and 29.)

2. How do the roles Asian women play in recent independent productions differ from those generally created for them in Hollywood productions?

3. How would you characterize the *overall* tone of this essay? (See "Guide to Terms": *Style/Tone.*) Identify any sections of the essay where the tone varies noticeably. Point out any passages in the essay that offer clear instances of irony, especially sarcasm or understatement. (Guide: *Irony.*)

Expository Techniques

1. Does Tajima offer a clear definition of each category? If not, how might the categories be introduced and defined more clearly?

2. Are the categories in this essay distinct or is there some overlapping? If the categories overlap, does the author acknowledge this? Where?

3. Would this essay be more effective if it had fewer examples? A greater number? Explain. (Guide: *Evaluation.*) Evaluate the examples in the following paragraphs for clarity and effectiveness: 8–20, 22, and 26–27.

4. Discuss whether the examples of work by independent filmmakers provide convincing evidence that these films go beyond the stereotypes.

Diction and Vocabulary

1. The names used to identify many of the standard character types are clichés. Point out the clichés used in this way in paragraphs 2 and 3.

2. Explain the meaning of the following terms: "cutting rooms" (par. 1); "Mama-sans" (4); "a cheongsam-clad maid" (31).

3. If you do not know the meanings of some of the following words, look them up in a dictionary: simplistic (par. 3); homogeneous (4); Mongol (5); compliant (7); yenta (9); objectification (23); vilifies (26); pervasive (29).

Read to Write

1. Films and television programs frequently follow stereotypes in their treatment of various ethnic and social groups (such as African Americans or people in their twenties) or in the representation of groups united by beliefs or behaviors (religious conservatives or athletes, for example). List groups of people you often encounter that are represented by stereotypical characters on film or television, and choose one or more of these representations to discuss in an essay of your own. Consider classifying the ways a particular group is treated, or arrange the different groups into categories based on the way they are represented.

2. As Tajima's essay shows, immigrant groups are often subject to negative stereotyping. Draw on your own experience and knowledge for examples of this practice, or do research on immigrant groups that are now considered part of the mainstream but were once treated as outsiders.

3. Using Tajima's essay as a model, classify films or some other sort of media (television programs, newspapers, magazines, popular songs, advertisements) according to the treatment they give to groups of people, to ideas (especially political viewpoints and value systems) or to fashion (or other customs and behaviors).

(NOTE: Suggestions for topics requiring development by use of CLASSIFICATION are on pages 143–144 at the end of this section.)

BRENDA PETERSON, a novelist and essayist, was born in 1950 on a forest ranger station in the Sierra Nevada Mountains. As a child she lived in many different places, especially in the Southeast. Currently, she lives in Seattle. Peterson received a B.A. in 1972 from the University of California-Davis. From 1972 to 1976 she worked as an editorial assistant at *The New Yorker* magazine. She has taught creative writing at Arizona State University and now works as an environmental writer. Her novels include *River of Light* (1978), *Becoming the Enemy* (1988), and *Duck and Cover* (1991). Her essays have been collected in *Living by Water: Essays on Life, Land and Spirit* (1990), *Nature and Other Mothers* (1992), and *Sister Stories: Taking the Journey Together* (1996).

Life Is a Musical

In this essay, Peterson offers several closely related classifications as a way of exploring the ways music can (and ought to) enrich and heal our emotional lives. This essay was first published in *Nature and Other Mothers*.

When the day is too gray, when the typewriter is too loud, after a lovers' quarrel, when a sister calls with another family horror story, when the phone never stops and those unanswered messages blink on my machine like angry, red eyes—I tune out my life and turn up the music. Not my favorite public radio station but my own personal frequency—I have my own soul's station. It is somewhere on the dial between Mozart's *Magic Flute,* the gospel-stomping tiger growl of Miss Aretha Franklin, Motown's deep dance 'n' strut, and the singing story of Broadway musicals.   1

    Whether it's Katie Webster's Swamp Boogie Queen singing "Try a Little Tenderness," or a South American samba, whether it's the Persuasions crooning "Let It Be" or that throbbing baritone solo "Other Pleasures" from *Aspects of Love,* my musical solace is so complete it surrounds me in a mellifluous bubble like a placenta of   2 sound. To paraphrase the visionary Stevie Wonder, I have learned to survive by making sound tracks in my own particular key of life.

For years now I've made what I call "tapes against terror" to   3 hide me away from the noisy yak and call of the outside world. These homemade productions are dubbed Mermaid Music; sometimes I send them to friends for birthdays and feel the pleasure of playing personal disc jockey to accompany their lives too. Among my siblings, we now exchange music tapes instead of letters. It is particularly gratifying to hear my nieces and nephews singing along to my tapes, as another generation inherits our family frequency.

I trace making my musical escapes to a childhood of moving   4 around. As we packed the cardboard boxes with our every belonging—sometimes we hadn't even bothered to unpack our dresses from those convenient hanging garment containers provided by the last moving company—the singing began. From every corner of the emptying house, we'd hear the harmonies: my father a walking bass as he heaved-ho in the basement; my mother's soprano sometimes shrill and sharp as the breaking glass in the kitchen; my little brother between pure falsetto and a tenor so perfect we knew he'd stopped packing his room simply to sing; my sisters and I weaving between soprano and first and second alto from our bedrooms as we traded and swapped possessions for our next life. At last gathered in the clean, white space that was once our house, we'd hold hands and sing "Auld Lang Syne." Piling into the station wagon, with the cat in a wooden box with slats for air holes, Mother would shift into a rousing hymn, "We'll Leave It All Behind," or sometimes, if she was mutinously happy to hightail it out of some small "burg" as she called them, she'd lead us into "Shuffle Off to Buffalo," substituting wherever we were moving for the last word. "Chattanooga Choo Choo" and "California, Here We Come" were her standard favorites for leave-taking. If, as we drove past our schools and our friends' houses for the last time, the harmonies in the backseat faltered, Mother might remind us that choirs of angels never stayed long in one place singing because the whole world needed music. Father might suggest some slower songs, as long as they weren't sad.

In all the shifting landscapes and faces of my childhood, what   5 stays the same is the music. First, there was my mother's music, which seems now to have entered effortlessly into her children's minds as if we were tiny tape recorders: the mild, sweetly suave Mills Brothers, Mitch Miller's upbeat swing, the close sibling harmonies of the Andrews Sisters, and always the church music, the heartfelt Sunday singing, which is the only thing I ever miss since leaving that tight fellowship of Southern Baptist believers.

Ever since I can remember—certainly I have flashes of being bounced around in the floating dark of my mother's womb as she tap-danced on the church organ pedals, sang at the top of her voice, and boogied across the keys—there has been this music. It is the only counterpoint to, the only salvation from a sermon that paralyzes the soul into submitting to a jealous God. From the beginning, music was an alternative to that hellfire terror. I can still hear it: a preacher's voice, first a boom, then a purr that raises into a hiss and howl to summon that holy hurricane of fire and brimstone. But after enduring the scourge of sins, there came the choir. Cooing and shushing, mercy at last fell upon those of us left on an Earth that this God had long ago abandoned. Listening to the full-bodied harmonies, I could close my eyes and heretically wonder, Wasn't Heaven still here? 6

Yessss, hallelujah, still here . . . Hush, can't you hear? the choir murmured like so many mammies' lullabies. Then silence as a small woman stepped forward, her rapt vibrato shimmering like humid heat lightning right before rain. Or a baritone dropping his woes and his dulcet voice low as a cello, caressing a whole congregation. If we were blessed that Sunday, there might be a shorter sermon and a "songfest" with harmonies we could hear in our heads, syncopating, counterpointing in a lovely braid of bright sound that beckoned us. *Sing now, brothers and sisters.* And we were many voices making one song. The fundamental fear was gone; weren't we already angels in Heaven? 7

Now that I am forty and have been what my family pityingly refers to as "settled-down" for ten years, now that I am so far backslid from the fellowship of the Southern Baptist believers, now that I no longer even make top ten on my mother's prayer list, now that the terror of Hell has been replaced by the terror of living, I still find myself calling upon my homemade choirs to accompany me in my car, to surround my study or kitchen and sing back the demons of daily life. Sometimes I've even caught myself slipping another tape against terror into the stereo and singing a distracted riff of my mother's favorite, "We'll Leave It All Behind." 8

During the recent holy war between the United States and Iraq, with the apocalyptic rhetoric about "Satan" and "infidels" eerily reminiscent of southern revivals—Mermaid Music was working 9 long hours to meet my own and my friends' wartime demands. To offset NPR's daily interviews with military experts commenting on the allied video-war air strikes with the zealous aplomb of sportscasters, I'd surrender to the tender tenor of Aaron Neville singing "With God on Our Side" or "Will the Circle Be Unbroken?" As I drove along freeways where phosphorescent orange bumper stickers shouted USA KICKS BUTT! or OPERATION DESERT STORM, as if it were a souvenir banner of a hot vacation spot, I wondered that there was no music for the Gulf War. Where were the songs like "My Buddy" or "It's a Long Way to Tipperary"?

    During the last days of the war, I relied upon Bach's Violin Concerto in D Minor, the fierce longing of Jacqueline DePres's cello, Fauré's Requiem and, as always, Mozart. On a particularly bad day, between the Pentagon press conferences—men with pointers, target maps, smart-bomb videos, and a doublespeak war doggerel that called bombing "servicing a target"—I made a beeline to my public library and checked out every musical from *Oklahoma* to *Miss Saigon*. I made a tape entitled "Life Is a Musical" and divided it into three sections: (1) Love Found in Strange Places, (2) Love Lost Everywhere, and (3) Love Returns. It was astonishing how songs from vastly different time periods and places segued together. My favorite storyline riff is "Empty Chairs at Empty Tables," from *Les Misérables* to "The American Dream" from *Miss Saigon* to "Carefully Taught" from *South Pacific* to "Don't Cry for Me, Argentina," from *Evita* to "Bring Him Home" from *Les Misérables*. When I sent copies out to a select group of musicals-loving friends, it was as if we were all together at a candlelight mass or cross-continent communion, trying to imagine a war where no bombs fell. 10

    Playing my own tapes against terror is a way to document and summon back the necessities that mothered them. For example, "My Funny Valentine," with its Billie Holiday/Sarah Vaughan/Ella Fitzgerald/Alberta Hunter blues and ebullience is still a favorite, long after that lover has gone. Upon hearing that an old friend had bone cancer, I made him a tape called "Music to Heal By," which included the Delta Rhythm Boys' version of "Dry Bones." My friend wrote to say it was the first time he'd laughed in a long time. Now he's making his own tapes. After a writer friend of mine drank herself to death, I felt so bereft—since, after all, we'd planned to retire to the Black Hole Nursing Home for Wayward Writers together— that I made a tape called "The Ten Commandments of Love, or Southern Baptists Beware!" It's every song I ever slow-danced to or 11 memorized in the sweaty backseat of a borrowed car as my date and I broke Sunday school rules on Saturday night. Declared by my siblings and southern pals to have gone into "metal" (their word for platinum or gold), it includes Etta James's soaring "At Last," Sam Cooke's silky "Wonderful World," and a steamy duet of "634–5789" with Robert Cray and Tina Turner. It's a great tape for getting in the mood.

Since ancient times, the Chinese have believed that certain   12
sounds can balance and heal. In acupressure, for example, each organ has a sound. Listening to a healthy heart, an astute healer can hear laughter or, if there is disease, wind. The gallbladder shouts; the stomach speaks in a singsong, sometimes overly sympathetic voice; and the kidney, ever the perfectionist, groans. Sighs can be a sign of liver ailments, and the pitch of a person's voice can tell a story of that body's health just as well as a tongue. In some Taoist practices to enhance longevity, re-creating the sounds of certain organs can strengthen and tone them. For example, the *whuuuh whuuuh* sound of the kidney can revitalize the adrenals, fortifying the immune system. If one cannot take time to sing in the key of every organ, I'd suggest Chinese wind chimes like the ones that grace my back porch. When a strong salt wind blows off the beach, my chimes, which are perfectly pitched to a five-element Chinese scale, play an impromptu arpeggio—a momentary transport to some monastic garden, a Shangri-la of sound. Scientific studies report that the actual sound of nature resonates at the level of eight hertz; by comparison, a refrigerator reverberates at eighty hertz. Is it any wonder some of us need to return to a musical womb to retreat from such technological onslaughts to our nervous systems?

In fact, our time in the womb is not at all quiet; it is a noisy sym-   13
phony of voices, lower-tract rumbles, whirrings like waterfalls, and white noise. One of my friends found that if she played a tape of the roar of her sturdy Kirby vacuum cleaner, the sound immediately put her boisterous newborn twins to sleep. I have another friend whose entire house is wall-to-wall egg cartons, which absorb sound as well as enhance his audiophilic tendencies. I've visited houses that sound like living inside an aquarium, where pleasant underwater burbles from elaborate tropical fish tanks drown out the world. I've also entered homes where cuckoo clocks, grandfather chimes, and deep gongs count the hours so that I felt I was inside a ticking time bomb. Consciously or unconsciously we all make sound tracks to underscore our lives.

Mermaid Music has allowed me to enter a reverie of song, a   14
backstage "smaller-than-life" sojourn away from all the stresses.
Right now I'm at work on two dance tapes for a summer roll-up-
the-rug party. Entitled "Bop till You Drop" and "Bad Girls," the
tapes defy all hearers not to kick up their heels with such all-time
hits as "Heat Wave" and "I Heard It Through the Grapevine," as
well as the ever-popular "R-E-S-P-E-C-T." Of course, I've had
request for sequels and am at work on "Life Is a Musical II" divided
into (1) "Falling," (2) "Feeling," and (3) "Forever Ruined/Recov-
ery." It flows from "People Will Say We're in Love" to "Happy
Talk" to "Just You Wait, Henry Higgins!"

My siblings say I should sell my tapes against terror on late-   15
night TV in the company of such classics as Veg-O-Matics and "Elvis
Lives" medleys. The idea fills me with horror. After all, there are
copyright violations cops who come like revenuers in the dark of the
night to bust local moonshiners and music makers. I'd rather stay
strictly small-time and nonprofit, like that long-ago lullaby service I
had in college, a trio of nannies against nightmares. But if anyone
out there in music land is making his or her own tapes against terror, I'd be open to an exchange. After all, it's better than bombs
through the mail or collecting baseball cards.

So tune in, and maybe we'll find ourselves on the same fre-   16
quency. On this lifelong Freeway of Love, I just want to be an Earth
Angel with my Magic Flute. Because after all, Everybody Plays the
Fool and Ain't Nobody's Business If I Do.

Meanings and Values

1. In a paragraph of your own, summarize what this essay has to say
   about music, human emotions, and the relationship between them.

2. What subject or subjects is Peterson classifying in this essay?

3. Explain what the writer means by the phrase "my soul's station"
   (par. 11).

Expository Techniques

1. Which paragraph announces the purpose and theme of the essay?
   (See "Guide to Terms": *Purpose; Unity.*) Can this essay be said to have
   a thesis statement? If so, where is it? (Guide: *Thesis.*)

2. What pattern other than classification does the writer employ in paragraph 4? (Hint: see Section 8.)

3. What different subjects does Peterson classify in this essay? How, if at all, does the writer keep these different classifications from overlapping in a confusing manner? Would this essay be more effective if the writer had concentrated on only one or two of the classifications? Explain. (Guide: *Evaluation.*)

4. What is the function of the clauses that open the first sentence in the essay? (Guide: *Syntax; Introductions.*)

Diction and Vocabulary

1. Identify the extended comparison in paragraph 12 and explain its relation to the central theme of the essay. (Guide: *Figures of Speech; Unity.*)

2. Identify those paragraphs in the essay that begin with transition words indicating that they will further develop the topic or ideas of the preceding paragraph. Discuss whether the transition words serve effectively to link paragraphs and ideas within the essay. (Guide: *Transition.*)

3. If you do not know the meaning of some of the following words, look them up in the dictionary: solace, mellifluous, placenta (par. 2); falsetto (4); suave (5); heretically (6); dulcet (7); riff (8); eerily, zealous, aplomb (9); segued (10); ebullience (11); astute (12); audiophilic (13).

Read to Write

1. Peterson links music to states of mind and emotional moods. Think about other things that people link with moods and mental states, such as landscapes, clothing, artwork, and certain kinds of activity. Consider exploring these links in an essay, perhaps analyzing the categories into which they fall.

2. Peterson provides detailed discussions of the effects of music and of experiences she and other people associate with music. Provide similar explanations in your own discussion of music or of some other activity or art form you choose to write about.

3. Drawing strategies from Peterson's essay, prepare an essay of your own classifying tastes in music, art, movies, sports, another art form, or another activity. If you can, explain why differences in people's tastes in art or preferences for certain activities can be explained on the basis of differences in character, background, or some other factor.

(NOTE: Suggestions for topics requiring development by use of CLASSIFICATION follow.)

Writing Suggestions for Section 4
Classification

Use division and classification (into at least three categories) as your basic method of analyzing one of the following subjects from an interesting point of view. (Your instructor may have good reason to place limitations on your choice of subject.) Narrow the topic as necessary to enable you to do a thorough job.

1. College students.
2. College teachers.
3. Athletes.
4. Coaches.
5. Salespeople.
6. Hunters (or fishers).
7. Parents.
8. Drug users.
9. Police officers.
10. Summer (or part-time) jobs.
11. Sailing vessels.
12. Game show hosts.
13. Friends.
14. Careers.
15. Horses (or other animals).
16. Television programs.
17. Motivations for study.
18. Methods of studying for exams.
19. Lies.
20. Selling techniques.
21. Tastes in clothes.
22. Contemporary music or films.
23. Love.
24. Ways to spend money.

25. Attitudes toward life.
26. Fast foods (or junk foods).
27. Smokers.
28. Investments.
29. Actors.
30. Books or magazines.

5

Explaining by Means of *Comparison* and *Contrast*

One of the first expository methods we used as children was *comparison*, noticing similarities of objects, qualities, and actions, or *contrast*, noticing their differences. We compared the color of the new puppies with that of their mother, contrasted our father's height with our own. Then the process became more complicated. Now we employ it frequently in college essay examinations or term papers when we compare or contrast forms of government, reproductive systems of animals, or ethical philosophies of humans. Later, in the business or professional world, we may prepare important reports based on comparison and contrast—between kinds of equipment for purchase, the personnel policies of different departments, or precedents in legal matters. Nearly all people use the process, though they may not be aware of this, many times a day—in choosing a head of lettuce, in deciding what to wear to school, in selecting a house, or a friend, or a religion.

In the more formal scholastic and professional uses of comparison and contrast, however, an ordered plan is needed to avoid having a mere list of characteristics or a frustrating jumble of similarities and differences. If authors want to avoid communication blocks that will prevent their "getting through" to their readers, they will observe a few basic principles of selection and development. These principles apply mostly to comparisons between two subjects only; if three or more subjects are to be considered, they should be grouped to make the discussion easy to follow.

A *logical* comparison or contrast can be made only between subject of the same general type. (Analogy, a special form of comparison used for another purpose, is discussed in the next section.) For example, contrasting a pine and a maple could be useful or meaningful, but little would be gained, except exercise in sentence construction, by contrasting the pine and the pansy.

Of course, logical but informal comparisons that are merely incidental to the basic structure, and hence follow no special pattern, may be made in any writing. Several of the preceding selections make limited use of comparison and contrast; Viorst does some contrasting of types of showoffs, and Judith Stone uses some comparison between the long history of dogs as pets and today's more fashionable pets. But once committed to a formal, full-scale analysis by comparison and contrast, the careful writer ordinarily gives the subjects similar treatment. Points used for one should also be used for the other, and usually in the same order. All pertinent points should be explored—pertinent, that is, to the purpose of the comparison.

The purpose and the complexity of materials will usually suggest their arrangement and use. Sometimes the purpose is merely to point out *what* the likenesses and differences are, sometimes it is to show the *superiority* of one thing over another—or possibly to convince the reader of the superiority, as this is also a technique of argumentation. The purpose may be to explain the *unfamiliar* (wedding customs in Ethiopia) by comparing it to the *familiar* (wedding customs in Kansas). Or it may be to explain or emphasize some other type of *central idea*, as in most of the essays in this section.

One of the two basic methods of comparison is to present all the information on the two subjects, one at a time, and to summarize by combining their most important similarities and differences. This method may be desirable if there are few points to compare, or if the individual points are less important than the overall picture they present. Therefore, this procedure might be a satisfactory means of showing the relative difficulty of two college courses or of comparing two viewpoints concerning an automobile accident. (Of course, as in all other matters of expository arrangement, the last subject discussed is in the most emphatic position.)

However, if there are several points of comparison to be considered, or if the points are of individual importance, alternation of the material would be a better arrangement. Hence, in a detailed comparison of Oak Valley and Elm Hill hospitals, we might compare their sizes, locations, surgical facilities, staffs, and so on, always in the same order. To tell all about Oak Valley and then all about Elm Hill would create a serious communication block, requiring readers constantly to call on their memory of what was cited earlier or to turn back to the first group of facts again and again in order to make the meaningful comparisons that the author should have made for them.

Often the subject matter or the purpose itself will suggest a more casual treatment, or some combination or variation of the two basic methods. We might present the complete information on the first subject, then summarize it point by point within the complete information on the second. In other circumstances it may be desirable simply to set up the thesis of likeness or difference, and then to explain a *process* that demonstrates this thesis. And although expository comparisons and contrasts are frequently handled together, it is sometimes best to present all similarities first, then all differences—or vice versa, depending on the emphasis desired. In argument, the arrangement we choose is that which best demonstrates the superiority of one thing (or plan of action) over another. This may mean a point-by-point contrast or the presentation of a weaker alternative before a stronger one.

In any basic use of comparison (conveniently, the term is most often used in a general sense to cover both comparison and contrast), the important thing is to have a plan that suits the purpose and material thoughtfully worked out in advance.

Sample Paragraph (Annotated)

Similarity announced. Though differences are not mentioned, the word "Parents" points towards "children" and suggests that the next generation may have a different perspective.

A *contrast* that serves to emphasize how similar are the outlooks of the parents.

Parents who moved from Valley City to Palmville generally have one thing in common: they agree there is little reason to make the long drive back to the metropolis, except, perhaps, to commute to work, for special shopping, or to hear a big star in concert. The talk at neighborhood gatherings, at youth baseball games, and in the aisles at Kwik Shop often revolves around how good it is to live in Palmville and how happy everyone is to have left Valley City. A few voices can even be heard claiming that the two new malls, the industries moving to Caton Industrial Park, and new groups like the Palmville Community Symphony mean "there just aren't good reasons to go to Valley City

Contrast announced (Note use of transition: "In contrast")	anymore." In contrast, most of the town's children have their eyes set on Valley City as a distant Oz with I–104 as the Yellow Brick Road. To most it means
Point-by-point presentation of similarities in outlook that also offers point-by-point differences from the parents. The kids' own slogan used as vivid example. Final comparision (similarity).	entertainment in the form of mammoth rock shows; shopping at W.P. Sowerby's Department Store or the three-tier Okono Mall; and days on the beach watching glamorous people and being seen, too. To many it means opportunity in the form of large universities, jobs with major corporations, or careers in advertising and fashion. And to a few it means escape: "Anywhere but Palmville." Both parents and children share a desire to strike out on their own, the first group to get away from Valley City, the second group to return.

Sample Paragraph (Comparison/Contrast)

Large computers have some essential attributes of an intelligent brain: they have large memories, and they have gates whose connections can be modified by experience. However, the thinking of these computers tends to be narrow. The richness of human thought depends to a considerable degree on the enormous number of wires, or nerve fibers, coming into each gate in the human brain. A gate in a computer has two, or three, or at most four wires entering on one side, and one wire coming out the other side. In the brain of an animal, the gates may have thousands of wires entering one side, instead of two or three. In the human brain, a gate may have as many as 100,000 wires entering it. Each wire comes from another gate or nerve cell. This means that every gate in the human brain is connected to as many as 100,000 other gates in other parts of the brain. During the process or thinking innumerable gates open and close throughout the brain. When one of these gates "decides" to open, the decision is the result of a complicated assessment involving inputs from thousands of other gates. This circumstance explains much of the difference between human thinking and computer thinking.

MARK TWAIN was the pen name of Samuel Clemens (1835–1910). He was born in Missouri and became the first author of importance to emerge from "beyond the Mississippi." Although best known for bringing humor, realism, and Western local color to American fiction, Mark Twain wanted to be remembered as a philosopher and social critic. Still widely read, in most languages and in all parts of the world, are his numerous short stories (his "tall tales," in particular), autobiographical accounts, and novels, especially *Adventures of Huckleberry Finn* (1884). Ernest Hemingway called the last "the best book we've had," an appraisal with which many critics agree.

Two Ways of Seeing a River

"Two Ways of Seeing a River" (editors' title) is from Mark Twain's "Old Times on the Mississippi," which was later expanded and published in book form as *Life on the Mississippi* (1883). It is autobiographical. The prose of this selection is vivid, as is all of Mark Twain's writing, but considerably more reflective in tone than most.

Now when I had mastered the language of this water and had 1 come to know every trifling feature that bordered the great river as familiarly as I knew the letters of the alphabet, I had made a valuable acquisition. But I had lost something, too. I had lost something which could never be restored to me while I lived. All the grace, the beauty, the poetry, had gone out of the majestic river! I still kept in mind a certain wonderful sunset which I witnessed when steamboating was new to me. A broad expanse of the river was turned to blood; in the middle distance the red hue brightened into gold, through which a solitary log came floating, black and conspicuous; in one place a long, slanting mark lay sparkling upon the water; in another the surface was broken by boiling, tumbling rings that were as many-tinted as an opal; where the ruddy flush was faintest was a smooth spot that was covered with graceful circles and radiating lines, ever so delicately traced; the shore on our left was densely wooded, and the somber shadow that fell from this forest was broken in one place by a long, ruffled trail that shone like silver; and high above the forest wall a clean-stemmed dead tree waved a single leafy bough that glowed like a flame in the unobstructed splendor that was flowing from the sun. There were graceful curves, reflected images, woody heights, soft distances, and over the whole scene, far and near, the dissolving lights drifted steadily, enriching it every passing moment with new marvels of coloring.

I stood like one bewitched. I drank it in, in a speechless rapture. 2
The world was new to me and I had never seen anything like this at home. But as I have said, a day came when I began to cease from noting the glories and the charms which the moon and the sun and the twilight wrought upon the river's face; another day came when I ceased altogether to note them. Then, if that sunset scene had been repeated, I should have looked upon it without rapture and should have commented upon it inwardly after this fashion: "This sun means that we are going to have wind tomorrow; that floating log means that the river is rising, small thanks to it; that slanting mark on the water refers to a bluff reef which is going to kill somebody's steamboat one of these nights, if it keeps on stretching out like that; those tumbling 'boils' show a dissolving bar and a changing channel there; the lines and circles in the slick water over yonder are a warning that that troublesome place is shoaling up dangerously; that silver streak in the shadow of the forest is the 'break' from a new snag and he has located himself in the very best place he could have found to fish for steamboats; that tall dead tree, with a single living branch, is not going to last long, and then how is a body ever going to get through this blind place at night without the friendly old landmark?"

No, the romance and beauty were all gone from the river. All 3
the value any feature of it had for me now was the amount of usefulness it could furnish toward compassing the safe piloting of a steamboat. Since those days, I have pitied doctors from my heart. What does the lovely flush in a beauty's cheek mean to a doctor but a "break" that ripples above some deadly disease? Are not all her visible charms sown thick with what are to him the signs and symbols of hidden decay? Does he ever see her beauty at all, or doesn't he simply view her professionally and comment upon her unwholesome condition all to himself? And doesn't he sometimes wonder whether he has gained most or lost most by learning his trade?

Meanings and Values

1. What is the point of view in paragraph 1? (See "Guide to Terms": *Point of View.*) Where, and how, does it change in paragraph 2? Why is the shift important to the author's contrast?

2. Show how the noticeable change of tone between paragraphs 1 and 2 is related to the change in point of view. (Guide: *Style/Tone.*) Specifically, what changes in style accompany the shift in tone and attitude? How effectively do they all relate to the central theme itself? (Remember that such effects seldom just "happen"; the writer *makes* them happen.)

3. Is the first paragraph primarily objective or subjective? (Guide: *Objective/Subjective.* How about the latter part of paragraph 2? Are your answers related to point of view? Is so, how?

4. Do you think the last sentence refers only to doctors? Why, or why not?

Expository Techniques

1. Where do you find a second comparison or contrast? Which is it? Is the comparison/contrast made within itself, with something external, or both? Explain.

2. Is the second comparison/contrast closely enough related to the major contrast to justify its use? Why, or why not?

3. In developing the numerous points of the major contrast, would an alternating, point-to-point system have been better? Why, or why not? Show how the author uses organization within the groups to assist in the overall contrast.

4. What is the most noteworthy feature of syntax in paragraphs 1 and 2? (Guide: *Syntax.*) How effectively does it perform the function intended?

5. What is gained by the apparently deliberate decision to use rhetorical questions only toward the end? (Guide: *Rhetorical Questions.*)

Diction and Vocabulary

1. Why would the colloquialism in the last sentence of paragraph 2 have been inappropriate in the first paragraph? (Guide: *Colloquial Expressions.*)

2. Compare the quality of metaphors in the quotation of paragraph 2 with the quality of those preceding it. (Guide: *Figures of Speech.*) Is the difference justified? Why, or why not?

Read to Write

1. We spend much of our lives preparing for work, working, and thinking about work. As Twain's essay points out, moreover, work shapes the way we perceive things and respond to them. Work can therefore be an excellent source of writing topics that are interesting to both writers and readers.

    Add five more questions about work to the following list, and then use it to help generate possible topics for an essay: How do specific kinds of work shape perceptions and values? Are people's outlooks likely to vary according to the kinds of jobs they hold (or want to hold)? How do my work habits, preferences, or experiences set me apart from others (or bring me closer)?

2. In opening and closing this selection, Twain speaks of having both gained and lost some things as his perspective changes. Designing an essay to convey a sense of both loss and gain (the one dependent on the other) can lead you and your readers to a deeper understanding of a subject. Consider employing this strategy as you write; it works effectively not only with comparison and contrast but with other expository strategies as well.

3. The design of Twain's essay makes it a useful model for expository writing. To draw on Twain's work in your own writing, explore your subject from two quite different perspectives, varying the style and approach of each segment of your essay to reflect each perspective.

(NOTE: Suggestions for topics requiring development by use of COMPARISON and CONTRAST are on page 195, at the end of this section.)

BRUCE CATTON (1899–1978) was a Civil War specialist whose
early career included reporting for various newspapers. In 1954
he received both the Pulitzer Prize for historical work and the
National Book Award. He served as director of information for
the United States Department of Commerce and wrote many
books, including *Mr. Lincoln's Army* (1951), *Glory Road* (1952), *A
Stillness at Appomattox* (1953), *The Hallowed Ground* (1956), *America
Goes to War* (1958), *The Coming Fury* (1961), *Terrible Swift Sword*
(1963), *Never Call Retreat* (1966), *Waiting for the Morning Train: An
American Boyhood* (1972), and *Gettysburg: The Final Fury* (1974). For
five years, Catton edited *American Heritage.*

Grant and Lee: A Study in Contrasts

"Grant and Lee: A Study in Contrasts" was written as a chapter of
The American Story, a collection of essays by noted historians. In
this study, as in most of his other writing, Catton does more than
recount the facts of history: he shows the significance within them.
It is a carefully constructed essay, using contrast and comparison
as the entire framework for his explanation.

When Ulysses S. Grant and Robert E. Lee met in the parlor of a mod-   1
est house at Appomattox Court House, Virginia, on April 9, 1865, to
work out the terms for the surrender of Lee's Army of Northern Virginia, a great chapter in American life came to a close, and a great
new chapter began.

These men were bringing the Civil War to its virtual finish. To   2
be sure, other armies had yet to surrender, and for a few days the
fugitive Confederate government would struggle desperately and
vainly, trying to find some way to go on living now that its chief
support was gone. But in effect it was all over when Grant and Lee
signed the papers. And the little room where they wrote out the
terms was the scene of one of the most poignant, dramatic contrasts
in American history.

They were two strong men these oddly different generals, and   3
they represented the strengths of two conflicting currents that,
through them, had come into final collision.

Back of Robert E. Lee was the notion that the old aristocratic   4
concept might somehow survive and be dominant in American life.

Lee was tidewater Virginia, and in his background were family,   5
culture, and tradition . . . the age of chivalry transplanted to a New
World which was making its own legends and its own myths. He
embodied a way of life that had come down through the age of
knighthood and the English country squire. America was a land that
was beginning all over again, dedicated to nothing much more complicated than the rather hazy belief that all men had equal rights and
should have an equal chance in the world. In such a land Lee stood
for the feeling that it was somehow of advantage to human society
to have a pronounced inequality in the social structure. There
should be a leisure class, backed by ownership of land; in turn, society itself should be keyed to the land as the chief source of wealth
and influence. It would bring forth (according to this ideal) a class of
men with a strong sense of obligation to the community; men who
lived not to gain advantage for themselves, but to meet the solemn
obligations which had been laid on them by the very fact that they
were privileged. From them the country would get its leadership; to
them it could look for the higher values—of thought, of conduct, or
personal deportment—to give it strength and virtue.

Lee embodied the noblest element of this aristocratic ideal.   6
Through him, the landed nobility justified itself. For four years, the
Southern states had fought a desperate war to uphold the ideals for
which Lee stood. In the end, it almost seemed as if the Confederacy
fought for Lee; as if he himself was the Confederacy . . . the best thing
that the way of life for which the Confederacy stood could ever have
to offer. He had passed into legend before Appomattox. Thousands
of tired, underfed, poorly clothed Confederate soldiers, long since
past the simple enthusiasm of the early days of the struggle, somehow considered Lee the symbol of everything for which they had
been willing to die. But they could not quite put this feeling into
words. If the Lost Cause, sanctified by so much heroism and so many
deaths, had a living justification, its justification was General Lee.   7

Grant, the son of a tanner on the Western frontier, was everything Lee was not. He had come up the hard way and embodied
nothing in particular except the eternal toughness and sinewy fiber
of the men who grew up beyond the mountains. He was one of a

body of men who owed reverence and obeisance to no one, who were self-reliant to a fault, who cared hardly anything for the past but who had a sharp eye for the future.

These frontier men were the precise opposites of the tidewater   8
aristocrats. Back of them, in the great surge that had taken people over the Alleghenies and into the opening Western country, there was a deep, implicit dissatisfaction with a past that had settled into grooves. They stood for democracy, not from any reasoned conclusion about the proper ordering of human society, but simply because they had grown up in the middle of democracy and knew how it worked. Their society might have privileges, but they would be privileges each man had won for himself. Forms and patterns meant nothing. No man was born to anything, except perhaps to a chance to show how far he could rise. Life was competition.

Yet along with this feeling had come a deep sense of belonging   9
to a national community. The Westerner who developed a farm, opened a shop, or set up in business as a trader could hope to prosper only as his own community prospered—and his community ran from the Atlantic to the Pacific and from Canada down to Mexico. If the land was settled, with towns and highways and accessible markets, he could better himself. He saw his fate in terms of the nation's own destiny. As its horizons expanded, so did his. He had, in other words, an acute dollars-and-cents stake in the continued growth and development of his country.

And that, perhaps, is where the contrast between Grant and Lee   10
becomes most striking. The Virginia aristocrat, inevitably, saw himself in relation to his own region. He lived in a static society which could endure almost anything except change. Instinctively, his first loyalty would go to the locality in which that society existed. He would fight to the limit of endurance to defend it, because in defending it he was defending everything that gave his own life its deepest meaning.

The Westerner, on the other hand, would fight with an equal   11
tenacity for the broader concept of society. He fought so because everything he lived by was tied to growth, expansion, and a constantly widening horizon. What he lived by would survive or fall with the nation itself. He could not possibly stand by unmoved in the face of an attempt to destroy the Union. He would combat it with everything he had, because he could only see it as an effort to cut the ground out from under his feet.

So Grant and Lee were in complete contrast, representing two   12
diametrically opposed elements in American life. Grant was the

modern man emerging; beyond him, ready to come on the stage, was the great age of steel and machinery, of crowded cities and a restless burgeoning vitality. Lee might have ridden down from the old age of chivalry, lance in hand, silken banner fluttering over his head. Each man was the perfect champion of his cause, drawing both his strengths and his weaknesses from the people he led.

Yet it was not all contrast, after all. Different as they were—in 13 background, in personality, in underlying aspiration—these two great soldiers had much in common. Under everything else, they were marvelous fighters. Furthermore, their fighting qualities were really very much alike.

Each man had, to begin with, the great virtue of utter tenacity 14 and fidelity. Grant fought his way down the Mississippi Valley in spite of acute personal discouragement and profound military handicaps. Lee hung on in the trenches at Petersburg after hope itself had died. In each man there was an indomitable quality . . . the born fighter's refusal to give up as long as he can still remain on his feet and lift his two fists.

Daring and resourcefulness they had, too: the ability to think 15 faster and move faster than the enemy. These were the qualities which gave Lee the dazzling campaigns of Second Manassas and Chancellorsville and won Vicksburg for Grant.

Lastly, and perhaps greatest of all, there was the ability, at the 16 end, to turn quickly from war to peace once the fighting was over. Out of the way these two men behaved at Appomattox came the possibility of a peace of reconciliation. It was a possibility not wholly realized, in the years to come, but which did, in the end, help the two sections to become one nation again . . . after a war whose bitterness might have seemed to make such a reunion wholly impossible. No part of either man's life became him more than the part he played in their brief meeting in the McLean house at Appomattox. Their behavior there put all succeeding generations of Americans in their debt. Two great Americans, Grant and Lee—very different, yet under everything very much alike. Their encounter at Appomattox was one of the great moments of American history.

Meanings and Values

1. Clarify the assertions that through Lee "the landed nobility justified itself" and that "if the Lost Cause . . . had a living justification," it was General Lee (par. 6.) Why are these assertions pertinent to the central theme?

2. Does it seem reasonable that "thousands of tired, underfed, poorly clothed Confederate soldiers" (par. 6) had been willing to fight for the aristocratic system in which they would never have had even a chance to be aristocrats? Why or why not? Can you think of more likely reasons why they were willing to fight?

3. What countries of the world have recently been so torn by internal war and bitterness that reunion has seemed, or still seems, impossible? Do you see any basic differences between the trouble in those countries and that in America at the time of the Civil War?

4. The author calls Lee a symbol (par. 6). Was Grant also a symbol? If so, of what? (See "Guide to Terms": *Symbol.*) How would you classify this kind of symbolism?

Expository Techniques

1. Make an informal list of paragraph numbers from 3 to 16, and note by each number whether the paragraph is devoted primarily to Lee, to Grant, or to direct comparison or contrast of the two. This chart will show you Catton's basic pattern of development. (Notice, for instance, how the broad information of paragraphs 4–6 and 7–9 seems almost to "funnel" down through the narrower summaries in paragraphs 10 and 11 into paragraph 12, where the converging elements meet and the contrast is made specific.)

2. What new technique of development is started in paragraph 13?

3. What is gained, or lost, by using one sentence for paragraph 3? For paragraph 4?

4. How many paragraphs does the introduction comprise? How successfully does it fulfill the three basic requirements of a good introduction? (Guide: *Introductions.*)

5. Show how Catton has constructed the beginning of each paragraph so that there is a smooth transition from the one preceding it. (Guide: *Transition.*)

6. What seems to be the author's attitude toward Grant and Lee? Show how his tone reflects this attitude. (Guide: *Style/Tone.*)

Diction and Vocabulary

1. Why would a use of colloquialisms have been inconsistent with the tone of this writing?

2. List or mark all metaphors in paragraphs 1, 3, 5, 7–11, and 16. (Guide: *Figures of Speech.*) Comment on their general effectiveness.

3. If you are not already familiar with the following words, study their meanings as given in the dictionary and as used in this essay: virtual,

poignant (par. 2); concept (4); sinewy, obeisance (7); implicit (8); tenacity (11); diametrically, burgeoning (12); aspiration (13); fidelity, profound, indomitable (14); succeeding (16).

Read to Write

1. When do differences become conflicts? When do disagreements become so severe that people stop trying to resolve them or to find common ground? What happens to such conflicts in fully democratic societies? In less democratic societies? Identify some moral, social, economic, or political disagreements that have or might become conflicts.

    Focus on those differences you might explore in an expository essay about conflicts and explain why they are so difficult to resolve. Concentrate on explaining, not on arguing for one side or the other or on trying to persuade readers to adopt a particular solution.

2. One special achievement of Catton's "Grant and Lee: A Study in Contrasts" is its portrait of the two generals as embodiments of contrasting societies and cultures. Consider using this strategy in an essay offering a contrast between ideas, values, or cultures by means of a contrast between people who embody the differences. The strategy can be applied to a wide variety of subjects, not simply to public or political ones. You might use it to talk about different parenting strategies, for example, or about various religious beliefs or value systems.

3. Catton focuses on a dramatic moment in history and explains its long-range significance. Drawing on his approach, select some important moment in your life or some dramatic moment in history, and show its long-range significance. Remember that by focusing on the contrasting elements of the moment, as Catton does, you can also highlight important forces leading up to the moment and beyond it.

(NOTE: Suggestions for topics requiring development by means of COMPARISON and CONTRAST are on page 195 at the end of this section.)

PHILLIP LOPATE was born in 1943 in New York City. He attended
Columbia University and received a B.A. in 1964. He has taught
creative writing in the Teachers and Writers Collaborative program in New York City and is currently on the faculties of the
University of Houston and Columbia University. His publications include *The Eyes Don't Always Want to Stay Open* (1972) and
The Daily Round (1976) (poems); *Confessions of Summer* (1979),
Bachelorhood: Tales of the Metropolis (1981), and *The Rug Merchant*
(1988) (fiction); *Being with Children* (1975) (nonfiction); and *Against
Joie de Vivre: Personal Essays* (1989) and *Portrait of My Body* (1996)
(collections of essays). His essays have appeared in a variety of
publications, including *New Age Journal, Texas Monthly, The New
York Times Book Review, Columbia, House and Garden, Vogue, Esquire,*
and Interview.

A Nonsmoker with a Smoker

In this essay, which first appeared in *New Age Journal,* Lopate uses
comparison and contrast to explore his own ambiguous feelings
about smoking—and about his relationship with a smoker. In the
course of the essay, he touches on many aspects of the smoking/
nonsmoking conflict, yet he offers a personal perspective often lost
in the public controversy.

Last Saturday night my girlfriend, Helen, and I went to a dinner   1
party in the Houston suburbs. We did not know our hosts, but were
invited on account of Helen's chum Barry, whose birthday party it
was. We had barely stepped into the house and met the other guests,
seated on a U-shaped couch under an A-framed ceiling, when Helen
lit a cigarette. The hostess froze. "Uh, could you please not smoke in
here? If you have to, we'd appreciate your using the terrace. We're
both sort of allergic."

Helen smiled understandingly and moved toward the glass   2
doors leading to the backyard in a typically ladylike way, as though

merely wanting to get a better look at the garden. But I knew from that gracious "Southern" smile of hers that she was miffed.

As soon as Helen had stepped outside, the hostess explained 3 that they had just moved into this house, and that it had taken weeks to air out because of the previous owner's tenacious cigar smoke. A paradigmatically awkward conversation about tobacco ensued: like testifying sinners, two people came forward with confessions about kicking the nasty weed; our scientist-host cited a recent study of indoor air pollution levels; a woman lawyer brought up the latest California legislation protecting nonsmokers; a roly-poly real estate agent admitted that, though he had given up smokes, he still sat in the smoking section of airplanes because "you meet a more interesting type of person there"—a remark his wife did not find amusing. Helen's friend Barry gallantly joined her outside. I did not, as I should have; I felt paralyzed.

For one thing, I wasn't sure which side I was on. I have never 4 been a smoker. My parents both chain-smoked, so I grew up accustomed to cloudy interiors and ever since have been tolerant of other people's nicotine urges. To be perfectly honest, I'm not crazy about inhaling smoke, particularly when I've got a cold, but that irritating inconvenience pales beside the damage that would be done to my pluralistic worldview if I did not defend smokers' rights.

On the other hand, a part of me wished Helen *would* stop smok- 5 ing. That part seemed to get a satisfaction out of the group's "banishing" her: they were doing the dirty work of expressing my disapproval.

As soon as I realized this, I joined her in the garden. Presently a 6 second guest strolled out to share a forbidden toke, then a third. Our hostess ultimately had to collect the mutineers with an announcement that dinner was served.

At the table, Helen appeared to be having such a good time, jok- 7 ing with our hosts and everyone else, that I was unprepared for the change that came over her as soon as we were alone in the car afterward. "I will never go back to that house!" she declared. "Those people have no concept of manners or hospitality, humiliating me the moment I stepped in the door. And that phony line about 'sort of allergic'!" 8

Normally, Helen is forbearance personified. Say anything that touches her about smoking, however, and you touch the rawest of nerves. I remembered the last time I foolishly suggested that she "think seriously" about stopping. I had just read one of those newspaper articles about the increased possibility of heart attacks, lung cancer, and birth deformities among women smokers, and I was worried for her. My concern must have been maladroitly expressed, because she burst into tears.

"Can't we even talk about this without your getting so sensi-   9
tive?" I had asked.

"You don't understand. Nonsmokers never understand that it a   10
real addiction. I've tried quitting, and it was hell. Do you want me to go around for months mean and cranky outside and angry inside. You're right, I'm sensitive, because I'm threatened with having taken away from me the thing that gives me the most pleasure in life, day in, day out," she said. I shot her a look: careful, now. "Well, practically the most pleasure. You know what I mean." I didn't. But I knew enough to drop it.

I love Helen, and if she wants to smoke, knowing the risks   11
involved, that remains her choice. Besides, she wouldn't quit just because I wanted her to; she's not that docile, and that's part of what I love about her. Sometimes I wonder why I even keep thinking about her quitting. What's it to me personally? Certainly I feel protective of her health, but I also have selfish motives. I don't like the way her lips taste when she's smoked a lot. I associate her smoking with nervousness, and when she lights up several cigarettes in a row, I get jittery watching her. Crazy as this may sound, I also find myself becoming jealous of her cigarettes. Occasionally, when I go to her house and we're sitting on the couch together, if I see Helen eyeing the pack I make her kiss me first, so that my lips can engage hers (still fresh) before the competition's. It's almost as though there were another lover in the room—a lover who was around long before I entered the picture, and who pleases her in mysterious ways I cannot.

A lit cigarette puts a distance between us: it's like a weapon in   12
her hand, awakening in me a primitive fear of being burnt. The memory is not so primitive, actually. My father used to smoke absentmindedly, letting the ash grow like a caterpillar eating every leaf in its path, until gravity finally toppled it. Once, when I was about nine, my father and I were standing in line at a bakery, and he accidentally dropped a lit ash down my back. Ever since, I've inwardly winced and been on guard around these little waving torches, which epitomize to me the dangers of intimacy.

I've worked hard to understand from the outside the satisfac-   13
tion of smoking. I've even smoked "sympathetic" cigarettes, just to

see what the other person was experiencing. But it's not the same as being hooked. How can I really empathize with the frightened but stubborn look Helen gets in her eyes when, despite the fact we're a little late going somewhere, she turns to me in the car and says, "I need to buy a pack of cigarettes first"? I feel a wave of pity for her. We are both embarrassed by this forced recognition of her frailty— the "indignity," as she herself puts it, of being controlled by something outside her will.

I try to imagine myself in that position, but a certain smugness   14
keeps getting in the way (I don't have that problem and *am I glad*). We pay a price for our smugness. So often it flip-flops into envy: the outsiders wish to be included in the sufferings and highs of others, as if to say that only by relinquishing control and surrendering to some dangerous habit, some vice or dependency, would one be able to experience "real life."

Over the years I have become a sucker for cigarette romanti-   15
cism. Few Hollywood gestures move me as much as the one in *Now Voyager*, when Paul Henreid lights two cigarettes, one for himself, the other for Bette Davis: these form a beautiful fatalistic bridge between them, a complicitous understanding like the realization that their love is based on the inevitability of separation. I am all the more admiring of this worldly cigarette gallantry because its experiential basis escapes me.

The same sort of fascination occurs when I come across a liter-   16
ary description of nicotine addiction, like this passage in Mailer's *Tough Guys Don't Dance:* "Over and over again I gave them up, a hundred times over the years, but I always went back. For in my dreams, sooner or later, I struck a match, brought flame to the tip, then took in all my hunger for existence with the first puff. I felt impaled on desire itself—those fiends trapped in my chest and screaming for one drag."

"Impaled on desire itself"! Such writing evokes a longing in   17
me for the centering of self that tobacco seems to bestow on its faithful. Clearly, there is something attractive about having this umbilical relation to the universe—this curling pillar, this spiral staircase, this prayer of smoke that mediates between the smoker's inner substance and the alien ether. Inwardness of the nicotine trance, sad wisdom ("every pleasure has its price"), beauty of ritual, squandered health—all those romantic meanings we read into the famous photographic icons of fifties saints, Albert Camus or James Agee or James Dean or Carson McCullers puffing away, in a

sense they're true. Like all people who return from a brush with death, smokers have gained a certain power. They know their "coffin nails." With Helen, each cigarette is a measuring of the perishable, an enactment of her mortality, from filter to end-tip in fewer than five minutes. I could not stand to be reminded of my own death so often.

Meanings and Values

1. Tell why you think the writer made the title say *with* rather than *and*.

2. Does the writer's portrayal of the party (pars. 1–6) make Helen's anger (7) seem justified? Why or why not?

3. To what parts of this essay might smokers and nonsmokers react in different ways? How might their reactions differ? Be specific in answering this question.

4. What conclusion about smoking, if any, does the writer reach in the last paragraph of the essay?

Expository Techniques

1. The focus of the essay shifts at the end of paragraph 3. What role does the last sentence in the paragraph play, and in what way does the focus shift?

2. How would you characterize the tone and style in paragraph 1? In paragraph 3? (See "Guide to Terms": *Style/Tone*.) What contrast does the writer emphasize through the differences in tone and style?

3. To what extent does the focus of paragraphs 7–11 lie on the question of smoking versus not smoking, and to what extent does if focus on the relationship between the writer and Helen? Be ready to defend your answer with specific evidence from the text.

4. What is being compared in paragraph 11? How is this comparison related to the overall pattern of comparison in the essay?

5. In what ways do paragraphs 13 and 14 contrast with 15 and 16?

6. State in your own words the contrast the author makes in the last two sentences of the essay. Do these sentences make an effective conclusion? (Guide: *Closings; Evaluation*.)

Diction and Vocabulary

1. Identify the informal diction in paragraph 1 and the formal diction in paragraph 3. (Guide: *Diction*.) Why has the writer created these contrasts in diction? (Hint: see "Expository Techniques.")

2. Indentify the similes in paragraph 12, and tell what they suggest about the effect of smoking on personal relationships. (Guide: *Figures of Speech.*)

3. Explain how cigarettes act as symbols in paragraph 15. (Guide: *Symbol.*)

4. Identify the metaphors in paragraph 15. Discuss their meaning and their effect, both as individual metaphors and as a cluster. (Guide: *Figures of Speech.*)

5. If you do not know the meaning of some of the following words, look them up in a dictionary: tenacious, paradigmatically, ensued (par. 3); pluralistic (4); toke (6); forbearance, maladroitly (8); epitomize (12); fatalistic, complicitious (15).

Read to Write

1. Even familiar issues and controversies can be a source of new understanding for you and your readers when you take a personal approach to them and write with an expository purpose. Explore some potential subjects by asking questions like these: If smoking, wearing a fur coat, or some other activity or belief offends you, should you let the person doing the activity know about your feelings? What steps can you take to communicate your feelings without offending the other person? Should you worry about upsetting the other person?

2. Lopate takes a fresh approach to an issue by discussing it in terms of personal relationships rather than as either a public controversy or a personal choice. What habits, preferences, or activities other than smoking can cause difficulties in relationships? Prepare an expository essay looking at an issue or behavior in terms of its consequences for a relationship.

3. In his essay, Lopate views behaviors and attitudes not so much as matters of choice (things we choose to do or believe) but as outgrowths of our experiences, our personalities, and our interactions with others. Follow Lopate's approach and explore a pattern of behavior (perhaps one you do not entirely approve of) by looking at the motivations of someone who engages in it and (perhaps) by exploring your own reactions to the behavior.

(NOTE: Suggestions for topics requiring development by use of COMPARISON and CONTRAST are on page 195 at the end of this section.)

Issues and Ideas

Gender and Other Differences

Male and female. Black and white. Wealthy, less wealthy, and a lot less wealthy. We understand our world by differences. We also come to understand who and what we are by learning who and what we are not.

The use of simple differences—opposites or contrasts—as a way of understanding is so widespread that we may fail to notice its effects. While separating into opposites can help create an orderly picture of the world or a clear sense of belonging to one group or another, it can also oversimplify, distort, and lead to destructive conflict. As Marianna De Marco Torgovnick points out in "On Being White, Female, and Born in Bensonhurst," opposites may attract as well as differ, and we are all constructed of multiple differences and similarities of culture, gender, belief, and experience.

As an expository pattern, comparison and contrast parallels the identification of differences and similarities—one of our main tools of understanding. Both Torgovnick and Scott Russell Sanders ("The Men We Carry in Our Minds") make good use of the pattern to explore surprising similarities that complicate, or even call into question, differences that many readers may consider obvious and unchanging, in Sanders's case the differences between men and women. Neither Sanders nor Torgovnick attempt to deny differences, but both demonstrate that by focusing on a single kind of difference—gender or ethnicity, for example—we may distort rather than clarify.

Alice Walker goes one step further by presenting evidence that encourages readers to question the widespread and deeply held assumption that humans are different from animals. While this might at first seem a startling conclusion, Walker's careful exploration of similarities not only encourages readers to consider their kinship with animals, but also implies that we need to look again at the differences we use to structure our relationships with others—people and animals alike.

SCOTT RUSSELL SANDERS was born in 1945 in Memphis, Tennessee. He studied at Brown University (B.A., 1967) and Cambridge University (Ph.D., 1971). Since 1971, he has been teaching
in the English Department at Indiana University. Sanders has
published a wide variety of books, including a scholarly study of
the British novelist D. H. Lawrence; several children's books
including *Aurora Means Dawn* (1989) and *Bad Man Ballad* (1986);
and a collection of short stories, *Invisible Company* (1989). His
essays have appeared in a number of collections, among them,
The Paradise of Bombs (1987), *In Limestone Country* (1991), and
Writing From the Center (1995). In 1995, Sanders won the Lanna
Literary Award, thereby joining the ranks of some of the finest
essayists of recent decades.

The Men We Carry in Our Minds

In this essay, originally published in 1984 in the journal *Milkweed
Chronicle,* Sanders questions the assumption that differences come
in simple pairs: men and women, rich and poor, oppressed and
oppressor, and the like. In place of such oppositions, he offers a
more complex view of the differences that help construct each of
us. He also expresses a hope that these very differences might
develop into grounds for mutual understanding.

"This must be a hard time for women," I say to my friend Anneke.   1
"They have so many paths to choose from, and so many voices calling them."

"I think it's a lot harder for men," she replies.   2

"How do you figure that?"   3

"The women I know feel excited, innocent, like crusaders in a   4
just cause. The men I know are eaten up with guilt."

"Women feel such pressure to be everything, do everything," I   5
say. "Career, kids, art, politics. Have their babies and get back to the
office a week later. It's as if they're trying to overcome a million
years' worth of evolution in one lifetime."

"But we help one another. And we have this deep-down sense   6
that we're in the *right*—we've been held back, passed over, used—
while men feel they're in the wrong. Men are the ones who've been
discredited, who have to search their souls."

I search my soul. I discover guilt feelings aplenty—toward the   7
poor, the Vietnamese, Native Americans, the whales, an endless list
of debts. But toward women I feel something more confused, a snarl
of shame, envy, wary tenderness, and amazement. This muddle
troubles me. To hide my unease I say, "You're right, it's tough being
a man these days."

"Don't laugh," Anneke frowns at me. "I wouldn't be a man for   8
anything. It's much easier being the victim. All the victim has to do
is break free. The persecutor has to live with his past."

How deep is that past? I find myself wondering. How much of   9
an inheritance do I have to throw off?

When I was a boy growing up on the back roads of Tennessee   10
and Ohio, the men I knew labored with their bodies. They were marginal farmers, just scraping by, or welders, steelworkers, carpenters;
they swept floors, dug ditches, mined coal, or drove trucks, their
forearms ropy with muscle; they trained horses, stoked furnaces,
made tires, stood on assembly lines wrestling parts onto cars and
refrigerators. They got up before light, worked all day long whatever the weather, and when they came home at night they looked as
though somebody had been whipping them. In the evenings and on
weekends they worked on their own places, tilling gardens that
were lumpy with clay, fixing broken-down cars, hammering on
houses that were always too drafty, too leaky, too small.

The bodies of the men I knew were twisted and maimed in   11
ways visible and invisible. The nails of their hands were black and
split, the hands tattooed with scars. Some had lost fingers. Heavy
lifting had given many of them finicky backs and guts weak from
hernias. Racing against conveyor belts had given them ulcers. Their
ankles and knees ached from years of standing on concrete. Anyone
who had worked for long around machines was hard of hearing.
They squinted, and the skin of their faces was creased like the
leather of old work gloves. There were times, studying them, when
I dreaded growing up. Most of them coughed, from dust or cigarettes, and most of them drank cheap wine or whiskey, so their eyes
looked bloodshot and bruised. The fathers of my friends always
seemed older than the mothers. Men wore out sooner. Only women
lived into old age.

As a boy I also knew another sort of men, who did not sweat   12
and break down like mules. They were soldiers, and so far as I could
tell they scarcely worked at all. But when the shooting started, many
of them would die. This was what soldiers were *for*, just as a hammer was for driving nails.

Warriors and toilers: those seemed, in my boyhood vision, to be   13
the chief destinies for men. They weren't the only destinies, as I
learned from having a few male teachers, from reading books, and
from watching television. But the men on television—the politicians,
the astronauts, the generals, the savvy lawyers, the philosophical
doctors, the bosses who gave orders to both soldiers and laborers—
seemed as remote and unreal to me as the figures in Renaissance
tapestries. I could no more imagine growing up to become one of
these cool, potent creatures than I could imagine becoming a prince.

A nearer and more hopeful example was that of my father, who   14
had escaped from a red-dirt farm to a tire factory, and from the
assembly line to the front office. Eventually he dressed in a white
shirt and tie. He carried himself as if he had been born to work with
his mind. But his body, remembering the earlier years of slogging
work, began to give out on him in his fifties, and it quit on him
entirely before he turned 65.

A scholarship enabled me not only to attend college, a rare   15
enough feat in my circle, but even to study in a university meant
for the children of the rich. Here I met for the first time young men
who had assumed from birth that they would lead lives of comfort
and power. And for the first time I met women who told me that
men were guilty of having kept all the joys and privileges of the
earth for themselves. I was baffled. What privileges? What joys? I
thought about the maimed, dismal lives of most of the men back
home. What had they stolen from their wives and daughters? The
right to go five days a week, 12 months a year, for 30 to 40 years to
a steel mill or a coal mine? The right to drop bombs and die in war?
The right to feel every leak in the roof, every gap in the fence, every
cough in the engine as a wound they must mend? The right to feel,
when the layoff comes or the plant shuts down, not only afraid but
ashamed?

I was slow to understand the deep grievances of women. This   16
was because, as a boy, I had envied them. Before college, the only
people I had ever known who were interested in art or music or literature, the only ones who read books, the only ones who ever
seemed to enjoy a sense of ease and grace were the mothers and

daughters. Like the menfolk, they fretted about money, they scrimped and made do. But, when the pay stopped coming in, they were not the ones who had failed. Nor did they have to go to war, and that seemed to me a blessed fact. By comparison with the narrow, ironclad days of fathers, there was an expansiveness, I thought, in the days of mothers. They went to see neighbors, to shop in town, to run errands at school, at the library, at church. No doubt, had I looked harder at their lives, I would have envied them less. It was not my fate to become a woman, so it was easier for me to see the graces. I didn't see, then, what a prison a house could be, since houses seemed to me brighter, handsomer places than any factory. I did not realize—because such things were never spoken of—how often women suffered from men's bullying. Even then I could see how exhausting it was for a mother to cater all day to the needs of young children. But if I had been asked, as a boy, to choose between tending a baby and tending a machine, I think I would have chosen the baby. (Having now tended both, I know I would choose the baby.)

So I was baffled when the women at college accused me and my   17
sex of having cornered the world's pleasures. I think something like my bafflement has been felt by other boys (and by girls as well) who grew up in dirt-poor farm country, in mining country, in black ghettos, in Hispanic barrios, in the shadows of factories, in third World nations—any place where the fate of men is just as grim and bleak as the fate of women.

When the women I met at college thought about the joys and   18
privileges of men, they did not carry in their minds the sort of men I had known in my childhood. They thought of their fathers, who were bankers, physicians, architects, stockbrokers, the big wheels of the big cities. They were never laid off, never short of cash at month's end, never lined up for welfare. These fathers made decisions that mattered. They ran the world.

The daughters of such men wanted to share in this power, this   19
glory. So did I. They yearned for a say over their future, for jobs worthy of their abilities, for the right to live at peace, unmolested, whole. Yes, I thought, yes yes. The difference between me and these daughters was that they saw me, because of my sex, as destined from birth to become like their fathers, and therefore as an enemy to their desires. But I knew better. I wasn't an enemy, in fact or in feeling. I was an ally. If I had known, then, how to tell them so, would they have believed me? Would they now?

Meanings and Values

1. Identify the differences that Sanders discusses in this essay. Does he treat some as more important than others? If so, which ones? Why does he consider them more important?

2. How do you think readers are likely to react to Sanders's essay? Do you think that some groups of readers are likely to find his essay reasonably convincing and others less so? Which groups, and why?

3. To what extent does this essay have an expository purpose and to what extent is its purpose argumentative? Which purpose predominates? Be ready to defend your answer with references to the text. (See "Guide to Terms": *Argument; Purpose.*)

Expository Techniques

1. Does this essay have a thesis statement? If so, what is it? (Guide: *Thesis.*) If not, state the central theme in your own words.

2. What strategy does Sanders use to introduce this essay? (Guide: *Introductions.*) Do you consider the opening effective? Why or why not? (Guide: *Evaluation.*)

3. Explain the use of transition words to highlight contrasts and relationships among ideas in paragraph 16. (Guide: *Transition.*) Tell how Sanders uses parallelism in paragraphs 15 and 17 to emphasize ideas. (Guide: *Parallel Structure.*) How else does he create emphasis in these paragraphs?

4. Where in the essay does the writer use rhetorical questions, and for what reasons does he employ them? (Guide: *Rhetorical Questions.*)

Diction and Vocabulary

1. Tell how the diction in paragraphs 10 and 11 contributes to their overall effectiveness (Guide: *Diction.*)

2. How does the writer qualify his statements in paragraph 16? Why do you think he decided to qualify his ideas and generalizations in this part of the essay? (Guide: *Qualification.*)

Read to Write

1. The differences we notice among people are often an inheritance from the behaviors we observed as we were growing up and from the attitudes of parents and friends. As you consider possible topics for an essay, think about the attitudes you encountered when you

were a child. Were they consistent or contradictory? Have you accepted them or modified them? Does preserving such an inheritance help build continuity and community or is it way of holding up necessary progress?

2. Insights into the way people differ often arise in conversation— something the opening of "The Men We Carry in Our Minds" seems to acknowledge. Consider opening an essay of your own with part of a conversation (recollected or invented) that touches on ideas you wish to explain and explore.

3. Sanders begins with an "opposition" many people take for granted and modifies it by showing that it is not simple and does not apply to everyone in the same way. He also suggests that people who appear to be opposites may actually share many traits and attitudes. Using Sanders's essay as a model, challenge another set of differences that people routinely accept (perhaps distinctions of race, class, intelligence, or taste) in a way that shows they are neither simple nor universal.

(NOTE: Suggestions for topics requiring development by use of COMPARISON and CONTRAST are on page 195 at the end of this section.)

MARIANNA DE MARCO TORGOVNICK

MARIANNA DE MARCO TORGOVNICK grew up in the Bensonhurst
section of Brooklyn, an experience she recounts in detail in the
following essay, "On Being White, Female, and Born in Bensonhurst." She is currently a professor of English at Duke University and author of a much-praised scholarly book, *Gone Primitive:
Savage Intellects, Modern Lives* (1990) as well as numerous scholarly articles. Her essays on contemporary culture and media have
been collected in *Crossing Ocean Parkway: Readings by an Italian
American Daughter* (1994).

On Being White, Female, and Born in Bensonhurst

In this essay, first published in the *Partisan Review* in 1990, the
author explores the mixture of differences that created and defined
her identity as she was growing up—and the further differences
that have served both to distance her from, and to bind her to, the
community of her childhood. While showing how "difference" can
be essential to both community and personal identity, she also
shows how it can be a source of conflict and hatred.

The Mafia protects the neighborhood, our fathers say, with that   1
peculiar satisfied pride with which law-abiding Italian Americans
refer to the Mafia: the Mafia protects "the neighborhood" from "the
coloreds." In the fifties and sixties, I heard that information repeated,
in whispers, in neighborhood parks and in the yard at school in Bensonhurst. The same information probably passes today in the parks
(the word now "blacks," not "coloreds") but perhaps no longer in
the school yards. From buses each morning, from neighborhoods
outside Bensonhurst, spill children of all colors and backgrounds—
American black, West Indian black, Hispanic, and Asian. But the
blacks are the ones especially marked for notice. Bensonhurst is no
longer entirely protected from "the coloreds." But in a deeper sense,
at least for Italian Americans, Bensonhurst never changes.

Italian American life continues pretty much as I remember it.   2
Families with young children live side by side with older couples
whose children are long gone to the suburbs. Many of those families
live "down the block" from the previous generation or, sometimes
still, live together with parents or grandparents. When a young family leaves, as sometimes happens, for Long Island or New Jersey or
(very common now) Staten Island, another arrives, without any special effort being required, from Italy or from a poorer neighborhood
in New York. They fill the neat but anonymous houses along the
mostly tree-lined streets: two-, three-, or four-family houses for the
most part (this is a working-class area, and people need rents to pay
mortgages), with a few single-family or small apartment houses
tossed in at random. Tomato plants, fig trees, and plaster madonnas
often decorate small but well-tended yards that face out onto the
street; the grassy front lawn, like the grassy backyard, are relatively
uncommon.

Crisscrossing the neighborhood and marking out ethnic   3
zones—Italian, Irish, and Jewish, for the most part, though there are
some Asian Americans and some people (usually Protestants) called
simply Americans—are the great shopping streets: 86th Street,
Kings Highway, Bay Parkway, 20th Avenue, 18th Avenue, each
with its own distinctive character. On 86th Street, crowds bustle
along sidewalks lined with ample vegetable and fruit stands.
Women wheeling shopping carts or baby strollers check the fruit
carefully, piece by piece, and bargain with the dealer, cajoling for a
better price or letting him know that the vegetables, this time, aren't
up to snuff. A few blocks down, the fruit stands are gone and the
streets are lined by clothing and record shops, mobbed by teenagers.
Occasionally, the elevated train ("the El") rumbles overhead, a few
stops out of Coney Island on its way to "the city," a trip of around
one hour.

On summer nights, neighbors congregate on "stoops" that   4
during the day serve as play yards for children. Air-conditioning
exits everywhere in Bensonhurst, but people still sit outside in the
summer—to supervise children, to gossip, to stare at strangers.
"Buona sera," I say, or "Buona note," as I am ritually presented to
Sal and Lily and Louie: the neighbors, sitting on the stoop. "Gra-
zie," I say when they praise my children or my appearance. It's the
only time I use Italian, which I learned at high school, although my
parents (both first-generation Italian Americans, my father Sicilian,
my mother Calabrian) speak it at home, to each other, but never to

me or my brother. My accent is the Tuscan accent taught at school, not the southern Italian accents of my parents and the neighbors.

It's important to greet and please the neighbors; any break in 5 this decorum would seriously offend and aggrieve my parents. For the neighbors are second only to family in Bensonhurst and serve as stern arbiters of conduct. Does Lucy keep a clean house? Did Anna wear black long enough after her mother's death? Was the food good at Tony's wedding? The neighbors know and pass judgment. Any news of family scandal (my brother's divorces, for example) provokes from my mother the agonized words: "But what will I tell *people?*" I sometimes collaborate in devising a plausible script.

A large sign on the church I attended as a child for me sums up 6 the ethos of neighborhoods like Bensonhurst. The sign urges contributions to the church building fund with the message, in huge letters: "EACH YEAR THIS CHURCH SAVES THIS NEIGHBORHOOD ONE MILLION DOLLARS IN TAXES." Passing the church on the way from largely Jewish and middle-class Sheepshead Bay (where my husband grew up) to Bensonhurst, year after year, my husband and I look for the sign and laugh at the crass level of its pitch, its utter lack of attention to things spiritual. But we also understand *exactly* the values it represents.

In the summer of 1989, my parents were visiting me at my 7 house in Durham, North Carolina, from the apartment in Bensonhurst where they had lived since 1942, ever since the day they had wed: three small rooms, rent controlled, floor clean enough to eat off, every corner and crevice known and organized. My parents' longevity in a single apartment is unusual even for Bensonhurst, but not that unusual; many people live for decades in the same place or move within a ten-block radius. When I lived in this apartment, there were four rooms; one has since been ceded to a demanding "landlord," one of the various "landlords" who have haunted my parents' life and must always be appeased least the ultimate threat—removal from the rent-controlled apartment—be brought into play. That summer, during the time of their visit, on August 23rd (my younger daughter's birthday) a shocking, disturbing, news report issued from "the neighborhood": it had become another Howard Beach.

Three black men, walking casually through the streets at night, 8 were attacked by a much larger group of whites. One was shot dead, mistaken, as it turned out, for another black youth who was dating a white, although part-Hispanic, girl in the neighborhood. It all

made sense: the crudely protective men, expecting to see a black
arriving at the girl's house and overreacting; the rebellious girl dating the outsider boy; the black dead as a sacrifice to the feelings of
"the neighborhood."

I might have felt outrage, I might have felt guilt or shame, I   9
might have despised the people among whom I grew up: in a way I
felt all four emotions when I heard the news. I expect that there were
many people in Bensonhurst itself who felt the same rush of emotions. But mostly I felt that, given the setup, this was the only way
things could have happened. I detested the racial killing; but I also
understood it. Those streets, which should be public property,
belong to "the neighborhood." All the people sitting on the stoops
on August 23rd knew that as well as they knew their own names.
The black men walking through probably knew it too—though their
casual walk sought to deny the fact that, for the neighbors, even the
simple act of blacks walking through "the neighborhood" would be
seen as invasion.

Italian Americans in Bensonhurst are notable for their cohesive-   10
ness and provinciality; the slightest pressure turns those qualities
into prejudice and racism. Their cohesiveness is based on the stable
economic and ethical level that links generation to generation, keeping Italian Americans in Bensonhurst and the Italian American community alive as the Jewish American community of my youth is no
longer alive. (Its young people routinely moved to the suburbs or
beyond, and were never replaced, so that Jews in Bensonhurst today
are almost all very old people.) Their provinciality results from the
Italian Americans' devotion to jealous distinctions and discrimina-
tions. Jews are suspect but (the old Italian women admit) "they
make good husbands." The Irish are okay, fellow Catholics, but not
really "like us"; they make bad husbands because they drink and
gamble. Even Italians come in varieties by region (Sicilian, Calabrian, Neapolitan, very rarely any region further north), and by history in this country (the newly arrived and ridiculed "gaffoon"
versus the first or second generation).

Bensonhurst is a neighborhood dedicated to believing that its   11
values are the only values; it tends towards certain forms of inertia.
When my parents visit me in Durham, they routinely take chairs
from the kitchen and sit out on the lawn in front of the house, not
on the chairs on the back deck; then they complain that the streets
are too quiet. When they walk around my neighborhood and look
at the mailboxes, they report (these De Marcos descended from

Cozzitortos, who have friends named Travaglianti and Pelliccioni) that my neighbors have strange names. Prices at my local super-market are compared, in unbelievable detail, with prices on 86th Street. Any rearrangement of my kitchen since their last visit is reg-istered and criticized. Difference is not only unwelcome, it is unac-ceptable. One of the most characteristic things my mother ever said was in response to my plans for renovating my house in Durham. When she heard my plans, she looked around, crossed her arms, and said, "If it was me, I wouldn't change nothing." My father once asked me to level with him about a Jewish boyfriend, who lived in a different portion of the neighborhood, reacting to his Jewishness, but even more to the fact that he often wore Bermuda shorts: "Tell me something, Marianna. Is he a Communist?" Such are the stan-dards of normalcy and political thinking in Bensonhurst.

I often think that one important difference between Italian 12 American in neighborhoods like Bensonhurst and Italian Americans elsewhere is that the others moved on—to upstate New York, to Pennsylvania, to the Midwest. Though they often settled in commu-nities of fellow Italians, they moved on. Bensonhurst Italian Ameri-cans seem to have felt that one large move, over the ocean, was enough. Future moves could only be local: from the Lower East Side, say, to Brooklyn or from one part of Brooklyn to another. Benson-hurst was for many of these people the *summa* of expectations. If their America were to be drawn as a *New Yorker* cover, Manhattan would be tiny in proportion to Bensonhurst itself, and to its satel-lites, Staten Island, New Jersey, and Long Island.

"Oh, no," my father says when he hears the news about the 13 shooting. Though he still refers to blacks as "coloreds," he's not really a racist and is upset that this innocent youth was shot in his neighborhood. He has no trouble acknowledging the wrongness of the death. But then, like all the news accounts, he turns to the fact, repeated over and over, that the blacks had been on their way to look at a used car when they encountered the hostile mob of whites. The explanation is right before him but, "Yeah," he says, still shak-ing his head, "yeah, but what were they *doing* there. They didn't belong." The "they," it goes without saying, refers to the blacks.

[As I write this essay, I am teaching Robert Frost: "What had 14 that flower to do with being white / The wayside blue and innocent heal-all? / What brought the kindred spider to that height, / Then steered the white moth thither in the night? / What but design of darkness to appall?—/ If design govern in a thing so small." Thus

Frost in "Design" on a senseless killing and the ambiguity of causation and color symbolism. My father: "They didn't belong."]

Over the next few days, the TV news is even more disturbing.   15
Rows of screaming Italians, lining the streets, many of them looking
like my relatives. The young men wear under shirts and crosses dangle from their necks as they hurl curses. I focus especially on one
woman who resembles almost completely my mother: stocky but
not fat, mid-seventies but well preserved, full face showing only
minimal wrinkles, ample steel-gray hair neatly if rigidly coiffed in a
modified beehive hairdo left over from the sixties. She shakes her fist
at the camera, protesting the arrest of the Italian American youths in
the neighborhood and the incursion of more blacks into Bensonhurst, protesting the shooting. I look a little nervously at my mother
(the parent I resemble) but she has not even noticed the woman and
stares impassively at the television.

What has Bensonhurst to do with what I teach today and write?   16
Why did I need to write about this killing in Bensonhurst, but not in
the manner of a news account or a statistical sociological analysis?
Within days of hearing the news, I began to plan this essay, to tell
the world what I knew, though I stopped midway, worried that my
parents or their neighbors would hear about it. I sometimes think
that I looked around from my baby carriage and decided that someday, the sooner the better, I would get out of Bensonhurst. Now,
much to my surprise, Bensonhurst—the antipodes of the intellectual
life I sought, the least interesting of places—had become a
respectable intellectual topic. People would be willing to hear about
Bensonhurt—and all by the dubious virtue of a racial killing in the
streets.

The story as I would have to tell it would be to some extent a   17
class narrative: about the difference between working class and
upper middle class, dependence and a profession, Bensonhurst and
a posh suburb. But I need to make it clear that I do not imagine
myself as writing from a position of enormous self-satisfaction, or
even enormous distance. You can take the girl out of Bensonhurst
(that much is clear); but you may not be able to take Bensonhurst out
of the girl. Upward mobility is not the essence of the story, though it
is an important marker and symbol.

In Durham today, I live in a modern house, surrounded by an   18
acre of trees. When I sit on my back deck, on summer evenings, no
houses are visible through the trees. I have a guaranteed income,
teaching English at an excellent university, removed by my years of

education from the fundamental economic and social conditions of Bensonhurst. The one time my mother ever expressed pleasure at my work was when I got tenure—what my father called, with no irony intended, "ten years." "What does that mean?" my mother said when she heard the news. Then she reached back into her experiences as a garment worker, subject to seasonal "layoffs": "Does it mean they can't fire you just for nothing and can't lay you off?" When I said that was exactly what it means, she said, "Very good. Congratulations. *That's wonderful.*" I was free from the bosses and from the network of petty anxieties that had formed, in large part, her very existence. Of course, I wasn't really free of petty anxieties: would my salary increase keep pace with my colleagues', how would my office compare, would this essay be accepted for publication, am I happy? The line between these worries and my mother's is the line between the working class and the upper middle class.

But getting out of Bensonhurst never meant to me a big house, or nice clothes, or a large income. And it never meant feeling good about looking down on what I left behind or hiding my background. Getting out of Bensonhurst meant freedom—to experiment, to grow, to change. It also meant knowledge in some grand, abstract way. All the material possessions I have acquired, I acquired simply along the way—and for the first twelve years after I left Bensonhurst, I chose to acquire almost nothing at all. Now, as I write about "the neighborhood," I recognize that although I've come far in physical and material distance, the emotional distance is harder to gauge. Bensonhurst has everything to do with who I am and even with what I write. "We can never cease to be ourselves" (Conrad, *The Secret Agent*). Occasionally I get reminded of my roots, of their simultaneously choking and nutritive power. 19

Scene One: It's after a lecture at Duke, given by a visiting professor of German from a major university. The lecture was long and I'm tired but—bad luck—I had agreed to be one of the people having dinner with the lecturer afterwards. I settle into the table at the restaurant with my companions: this man, the head of the Comparative Literature program (also a professor of German), and a couple I like who teach French. The conversation is sluggish, as it often is when a stranger, in this case the visiting professor, has to be assimilated into a group. So I ask the visitor a question to personalize things: "How did you get interested in what you do? What made you become a professor of German?" The man gets going and begins 20

talking about how it was really unlikely that he, a nice Jewish boy
from Bensonhurst, would have chosen, in the mid-fifties, to study
German. Unlikely indeed.

I remember seeing *Judgment at Nuremberg* in a local movie the-   21
ater and having a woman in the row in back of me get hysterical
when some clips of a concentration camp were shown; "My God,"
she screamed in a European accent, "look at what they did. Murderers, MURDERERS!"—and she had to be supported out by her family. I couldn't see, in the dark, whether her arm bore the neatly
tattooed numbers that the arms of some of my classmates' parents
did—and that always affected me with a thrill of horror. This man is
about ten years older than I am; he had lived more directly through
those feelings, lived every day at home with those feelings. The first
chance he got he raced to study German. I myself have twice chosen
not to visit Germany—but I would understand an impulse to identify with the Other as a way of getting out of the neighborhood.

At the dinner, the memory about the movie pops into my mind   22
but I pick up instead on Bensonhurst—I'm also from there, but Italian American. Like a flash, he asks something I haven't been asked
in years: Where did I go to high school and (a more common question) what was my family name? I went to Lafayette High School, I
say, and my name was De Marco. Everything changes: his facial
expression, his posture, his accent, his voice. "Soo Dee Maw-ko," he
sez, "dun anything wrong at school today—got enny pink slips?
Wanna meet me later at the park or maybe bye the Baye?" When I
laugh, recognizing the stereotype that Italians get pink slips for mis-
conduct at school and the notorious chemistry between Italian
women and Jewish men, he says, back in his elegant voice: "My
God, for a minute I felt like I was turning into a werewolf."

It's odd that although I can remember almost nothing else about   23
this man—his face, his body type, even his name—I remember this
lapse into his "real self" with enormous vividness. I am especially
struck by how easily he was able to slip into the old, generic Brooklyn accent. I myself have no memory of ever speaking in that accent,
though I also have no memory of trying *not* to speak it, except for
teaching myself, carefully, to say "oil" rather than "earl."

But the surprises aren't over. The female French professor,   24
whom I have known for at least five years, reveals for the first time
that she is also from "the neighborhood," though she lived on the
other side of Kings Highway, went to a different, more elite high
school, and is Irish American. Three of six professors, sitting at an

"eclectic" vegetarian restaurant in Durham, all from Bensonhurst—
a neighborhood where (I swear) you couldn't get the *New York Times*
at any of the local stores.

Scene Two: In this scene, I still live in Bensonhurst. I'm waiting for   25
my parents to return from a conference at my school, where they've
been summoned to discuss my transition from elementary to junior
high school. I am already a full year younger than any of my classmates, having been "skipped" a grade, a not uncommon occurrence
for "gifted" youngsters. Now the school is worried about putting me
in an accelerated track through junior high, since that would make
me two years younger. A compromise is reached: I will be put in a
special program for "gifted" children, but one that takes three, not
two years. It sounds okay.

Three years later, another wait. My parents have gone to school   26
to make another decision. Lafayette High School has three tracks:
academic, for potentially college-bound kids; secretarial, mostly for
Italian American girls or girls with low aptitude scores; and voca-
tional, mostly for boys with the same attributes, ethnic or intellectual. (The high school is segregated de facto so none of the tracks is
as yet racially coded, though they are coded by ethnic group and
gender.) Although my scores are superb, the guidance counselor has
recommended the secretarial track; when I protested, the conference
with my parents was arranged. My mother's preference is clear: the
secretarial track—college is for boys; I will need to make a "good living" until I marry and have children. My father also prefers the secretarial track, but he wavers, half proud of my aberrantly high
scores, half worried. I press the attack, saying that if I were Jewish I
would have been placed, without question, in the academic track. I
tell him I have sneaked a peek at my files and know that my IQ is
genius level. I am allowed to insist on the change into the academic
track.

What I had done, and I was ashamed of it even then, was to play   27
upon my father's competitive feelings with Jews: his daughter could
and should be as good as theirs. In the bank where he was a mes-
senger and the insurance company where he worked in the mail
room, my father worked with Jews, who were almost always his
immediate supervisors. Several times, my father was offered the
supervisory job but turned it down, after long conversations with
my mother about the dangers of making a change, the difficulty of
giving orders to friends. After her work sewing dresses in a local

garment shop, after cooking dinner and washing the floor each night, my mother often did "piecework" making bows for a certain amount of money per bow; sometimes I would help her for fun, but it *wasn't* fun and I was free to stop while she continued for long, tedious hours to increase the family income. Once a week, her part-time boss, Dave, would come by to pick up the boxes of bows. Short, round, with his shirttails sloppily tucked into his pants and a cigar almost always dangling from his lips, Dave was a stereotypical Jew but also, my parents always said, a nice guy, a decent man. The first landlord I remember was Mrs. Rosenberg. My father was a sitting duck.

Years later, similar choices come up and I show the same   28
assertiveness I showed with my father, the same ability to deal for survival, but tinged with Bensonhurst caution. Where will I go to college? Not to Brooklyn College, the flagship of the city system—I know that, but don't press the invitations I have received to apply to prestigious schools outside of New York City. The choice comes down to two: Barnard, which gives me a full scholarship, minus five hundred dollars a year that all scholarship students are expected to contribute from summer earnings, or New York University, which offers me a thousand dollars above tuition. I waver. My parents stand firm: they are already losing money by letting me go to college; I owe it to the family to contribute the extra thousand plus my summer earnings. Besides, my mother adds, harping on a favorite theme, there are no boys at Barnard; at N.Y.U. I'm more likely to meet someone to marry. I go to N.Y.U., and marry in my senior year, but someone I didn't meet at college. I am secretly relieved, I think now (though at the time I thought I was just placating my parents' conventionality), to be out of the marriage sweepstakes.

The first boy who ever asked me for a date was Robert Zucker-   29
man, in eighth grade: tall and skinny to my average height and pre-teen chubbiness. I turned him down, thinking we would make a ridiculous couple. Day after day, I cast my eyes at stylish Juliano, the class cutup; day after day, I captivated Robert Zuckerman. Occa-sionally, one of my brother's Italian American friends would ask me out, and I would go, often to R.O.T.C. dances; my specialty was making political remarks so shocking that the guys rarely asked again. After a while, I recognized destiny: the Jewish man was a passport out of Bensonhurst. When I married, I of course did marry a Jewish man, who gave me my freedom, and, very important,

helped remove me from the expectations of Bensonhurst. Though raised in a largely Jewish section of Brooklyn, he had gone to college in Ohio and knew how important it was (as he put it) "to get past the Brooklyn Bridge"; we met on neutral ground, in Central Park, at a performance of Shakespeare. The Jewish-Italian marriage is a common enough catastrophe in Bensonhurst for my parents to have accepted, even welcomed my marriage—though my parents continued to treat my husband as an outsider for the first twenty years ("Now Mary Ann. Here's what's going on with you' brother. But don't tell you' husband").

Along the way, I make other choices, more fully marked by Bensonhurst cautiousness. I am attracted to journalism or the arts as careers, but the prospects for income seem iffy. I choose instead to imagine myself as a teacher. Only the availability of NDEA Fellowships when I graduate, with their generous terms, propels me from high school teaching (a thought I never much relished) to college teaching (which seems like a brave new world). Within college teaching, I choose offbeat specializations: the novel, interdisciplinary approaches (not something clear and clubby, like Milton or the eighteenth century). Eventually I write the book I like best about "primitive" Others as they figure within Western obsessions: my identification with "the Other," my sense of being "Other," surfaces at last. I avoid all mentoring structures for a long time, but accept aid when it comes to me on the basis of what I perceive to be merit. I'm still, deep down, Italian American Bensonhurst, though by this time I'm a lot of other things as well.

Scene Three: In the summer of 1988, a little more than a year before the shooting in Bensonhurst, my father woke up trembling and in what appeared to be a fit. Hospitalization revealed that he had a pocket of blood on his brain, a frequent consequence of falls for older people. About a year earlier, I had stayed home, heeding my father's suggestion that I remain with my children, when my aunt, my father's much-loved sister, died; only now does my mother tell me how much my father resented my missing the funeral. Now, confronted with what is described as "brain surgery," but turns out to be less dramatic than it sounds, I fly to New York immediately.

My brother drives three hours back and forth from New Jersey every day to drive my mother and me to the hospital, which is about fifteen minutes from my parents' apartment: he is being a fine Italian American son. Often, for the first time in years, we have long conversations alone. He is two years older than I am, a chemical engineer who has also left "the neighborhood," but has remained closer to its values, with a suburban, Republican inflection. He talks a lot about New York, saying that (except for neighborhoods like Bensonhurst) it's a "Third World city now." It's the summer of the Tawana Brawley incident, when Brawley accused white men of abducting her and smearing racial slurs on her body with her own excrement. My brother is filled with dislike for Al Sharpton and Brawley's other vocal supporters in the black community—not because they are black but because they are "troublemakers, stirring things up." The city is drenched in racial hatred that makes itself felt in the halls of the hospital: Italians and Jews in the beds and as doctors; blacks as nurses and orderlies.

This is the first time since I left New York in 1975 that I have vis-   33
ited Brooklyn without once getting into Manhattan. It's the first time I have spent several days alone with my mother, living in her apartment in Bensonhurst. My every move is scrutinized and commented on. I feel like I am going to go crazy.

Finally, it's clear that my father is going to be fine and I can go   34
home. My mother insists on accompanying me to the travel agent to get my ticket home, even though I really want to be alone. The agency (a Mafia front?) has no one who knows how to ticket me for the exotic destination of North Carolina and no computer for doing so. The one person who can perform this feat by hand is out. I have to kill time for an hour and suggest to my mother that she go home, to be there for my brother when he arrives from Jersey. We stop in a Pork Store, where I buy a stash of cheeses, sausages, and other delicacies unavailable in Durham. My mother walks home with the shopping bags, and I'm on my own.

More than anything I want a kind of sorbetto or "ice" I remem-   35
ber from growing up called "cremolata": almond-vanilla flavored, with large chunks of nuts. I pop into the local bakery (at an unlikely 11 A.M.) and ask for a cremolata, usually eaten after dinner. The woman—a younger version of my mother—refuses: they haven't made a fresh ice yet and what's left from the day before is too icy, no good. I explain that I'm about to get on a plane for North Carolina and want that ice, no good or not. But she has her standards and holds her ground, even though North Carolina has about the same status in her mind as Timbuktu and she knows I will be banished, perhaps forever, from the land of cremolata.

Then, while I'm taking a walk, enjoying my solitude, I have   36
another idea. Near my parents' house, there's a club for men from a
particular town or region in Italy: six or seven tables, some on the
sidewalk beneath a garish red, green, and white sign; no women
allowed or welcome unless they're with the men; and no women at
all during the day when the real business of the club—a game of
cards for old men who would be much quainter in Italy than they
are in Bensonhurst—is in progress. Still, I know that inside the club
would be coffee and a cremolata ice. I'm thirty-eight, well dressed,
very respectable looking; I know what I want. I also know I'm not
supposed to enter that club. I enter anyway, asking the teenage boy
behind the counter firmly, in my most professorial tones, for a cremolata ice. Dazzled, he complies immediately. The old men at the
card table have been staring at this scene, unable to place me,
exactly, though my facial type is familiar. Finally, a few old men's
hisses pierce the air. "Strega," I hear as I leave, "mala strega,"
"witch," or "brazen whore." I have been in Bensonhurst less than a
week but I have managed to reproduce, on my final day there for
this visit, the conditions of my youth. Knowing the rules, I have broken them. I shake hands with my discreetly rebellious past, still an
outsider walking through the neighborhood, marked and insulted—
though unlikely to be shot.

Meanings and Values

1. The opening paragraph mentions many of the differences the author
    discusses later in the essay. Which differences are mentioned? What
    other differences, if any, does the author introduce later?

2. In what ways does the author try to distance herself in paragraphs 4,
    6, 11, 13, and 17 from the attitudes and experiences of Bensonhurst?
    In what ways does she try to maintain a connection in paragraphs 15,
    16, 17, and 18?

3. Does the author believe that viewing the world according to the
    kinds of differences she discusses in the essay should be regarded as
    a positive behavior? A negative one? Or does she offer a different
    kind of judgment? Be ready to support your answer with evidence
    from the text.

Expository Techniques

1. What is the significance of the essay's title, and how is it related to
    the rest of the essay?

2.   Characterize the subject matter and purpose of each of the following sections of the essay: paragraphs 1–6, 7–14, 15–18, 19–23, 24–29. (See "Guide to Terms": *Purpose.*)

3.   What does "Scene One" (pars. 19–23) contribute to the effectiveness of the essay? Would the essay have been more effective without it? (Guide: *Evaluation.*)

4.   What strategies does the writer use to create a unity within "Scene Two" (pars. 24–29)? How does she unify this section with the rest of the essay? (Guide: *Unity.*)

5.   What does the author accomplish by concluding the essay with two paragraphs highlighting her rebelliousness and her position as an outsider (pars. 34–35)? What strategy for concluding an essay is represented by these paragraphs? (Guide: *Closings.*)

Diction and Vocabulary

1.   What strategies of diction and qualification does the author use in paragraphs 8, 9, 10, 13, and 32 to explain the actions and attitudes she recounts without seeming to endorse or condemn them as entirely racist? (Guide: *Diction; Qualification.*) Does she succeed in maintaining a neutral or even-handed perspective? If not, what point of view does she seem to take?

2.   What language does the author use to refer to various ethnic groups in paragraphs 1, 10, 22, 29, and 32? What does her choice of words reveal about her attitudes towards the groups and to ethnic differences in general?

3.   If you do not know the meaning of any of the following words, look them up in a dictionary: plausible (par. 5); ethos, crass (6); longevity, ceded (7); cohesiveness (10); *summa* (12); causation (14); antipodes (16); nutritive (19);

Read to Write

1.   To arrive at a topic for an essay of your own, consider how the physical or social patterns of the neighborhood(s) in which you grew up shaped your values and your ideas of important "differences." Do the same for family influences and experiences at school. Approach these potential topics from an expository perspective, looking for ways to explain the patterns and the "differences" they created, as well as the way these experiences shaped you and other people from the same background.

2. Torgovnick places three "Scenes" in the middle of her essay, using each to explore her topic from a different perspective. Construct an expository essay of your own using this technique to introduce varied perspectives or ideas.

3. What attitudes or views of difference that you disagree with have you encountered among family, friends, colleagues, or other people you like and respect? Using all or part of "On Being White, Female and Born in Bensonhurst" as a model, describe these disagreements and how you deal with them (or have trouble dealing with them).

ALICE WALKER

ALICE WALKER was born in Georgia in 1944, the youngest in a family of eight. Her parents were sharecroppers, and she attended rural schools as a child, going on eventually to attend Spelman College and Sarah Lawrence College, from which she graduated. She worked as an editor of *Ms.* magazine and taught at several colleges. At present she teaches at the University of California— Berkeley and lives in northern California. Her work as a poet, novelist, and essayist has been highly acclaimed, and one of her novels, *The Color Purple* (1982), received both a Pulitzer Prize and the American Book Award for fiction. Some of her other works are *Revolutionary Petunias and Other Poems* (1973) *Her Blue Body Everything We Know: Earthling Poems 1989–1990* (1991); *In Love and Trouble* (1973), short stories; *Meridian* (1976), *The Temple of My Familiar* (1989), and *Possessing the Secret of Joy* (1992), novels; and *In Search of Our Mothers' Gardens* (1983), *Living by the Word* (1988), and *The Same River Twice: Honoring the Difficult* (1996), essays.

Am I Blue?

Humans and horses might seem at first so different that any comparison would have to take the form of an analogy—a pairing of essentially unlike subjects whose limited similarities can be used for explanatory purposes (see Section 4). Walker's strategy in this essay from *Living by the Word* is just the opposite, however. She explains that despite their obvious differences, humans and animals are essentially alike, at least in important matters such as the capacity to love and to communicate.

"Ain't these tears in these eyes tellin' you?" 1

For about three years my companion and I rented a small house in 2 the country that stood on the edge of a large meadow that appeared to run from the end of our deck straight into the mountains. The mountains, however, were quite far away, and between us and them there was, in fact, a town. It was one of the many pleasant aspects of the house that you never really were aware of this.

It was a house of many windows, low, wide, nearly floor to ceil-   3
ing in the living room, which faced the meadow, and it was from one of these that I first saw our closest neighbor, a large white horse, cropping grass, flipping its mane, and ambling about—not over the entire meadow, which stretched well out of sight of the house, but over the five or so fenced-in acres that were next to the twenty-odd that we had rented. I soon learned that the horse, whose name was Blue, belonged to a man who lived in another town, but was boarded by our neighbors next door. Occasionally, one of the children, usually a stocky teenager, but sometimes a much younger girl or boy, could be seen riding Blue. They would appear in the meadow, climb up on his back, ride furiously for ten or fifteen minutes, then get off, slap Blue on the flanks, and not be seen again for a month or more.

There were many apple trees in our yard, and one by the fence   4
that Blue could almost reach. We were soon in the habit of feeding him apples, which he relished, especially because by the middle of summer the meadow grasses—so green and succulent since January—had dried out from lack of rain, and Blue stumbled about munching the dried stalks half-heartedly. Sometimes he would stand very still just by the apple tree, and when one of us came out he would whinny, snort loudly, or stamp the ground. This meant, of course: I want an apple.

It was quite wonderful to pick a few apples, or collect those that   5
had fallen to the ground overnight, and patiently hold them, one by one, up to his large, toothy mouth. I remained as thrilled as a child by his flexible dark lips, huge, cubelike teeth that crunched the apples, core and all, with such finality, and his high, broad-breasted *enormity;* beside which, I felt small indeed. When I was a child, I used to ride horses, and was especially friendly with one named Nan until the day I was riding and my brother deliberately spooked her and I was thrown, head first, against the trunk of a tree. When I came to, I was in bed and my mother was bending worriedly over me; we silently agreed that perhaps horseback riding was not the safest sport for me. Since then I have walked, and prefer walking to horseback riding—but I had forgotten the depth of feeling one could see in horses' eyes.

I was therefore unprepared for the expression in Blue's. Blue   6
was lonely. Blue was horribly lonely and bored. I was not shocked that this should be the case; five acres to tramp by yourself,

endlessly, even in the most beautiful of meadows—and his was—cannot provide many interesting events, and once rainy season turned to dry that was about it. No, I was shocked that I had forgotten that human animals and nonhuman animals can communicate quite well; if we are brought up around animals as children we take this for granted. By the time we are adults we no longer remember. However, the animals have not changed. They are in fact *completed* creations (at least they seem to be, so much more than we) who are not likely to change; it is their nature to express themselves. What else are they going to express? And they do. And, generally speaking, they are ignored.

After giving Blue the apples, I would wander back to the house,   7
aware that he was observing me. Were more apples not forthcoming then? Was that to be his sole entertainment for the day? My partner's small son had decided he wanted to learn how to piece a quilt; we worked in silence on our respective squares as I thought . . . .

Well, about slavery: about white children, who were raised by   8
black people, who knew their first all-accepting love from black women, and then, when they were twelve or so, were told they must "forget" the deep levels of communication between themselves and "mammy" that they knew. Later they would be able to relate quite calmly, "My old mammy was sold to another good family." "My old mammy was ____ ____." Fill in the blank. Many more years later a white woman would say: "I can't understand these Negroes, these blacks. What do they want? They're so different from us."

And about the Indians, considered to be "like animals" by the   9
"settlers" (a very benign euphemism for what they actually were), who did not understand their description as a compliment.

And about the thousands of American men who marry Japan-   10
ese, Korean, Filipina, and other non-English-speaking women and of how happy they report they are, *"blissfully,"* until their brides learn to speak English, at which point the marriages tend to fall apart. What then did the men see, when they looked into the eyes of the women they married, before they could speak English? Apparently only their own reflections.

I thought of society's impatience with the young. "Why are   11
they playing the music so loud?" Perhaps the children have listened to much of the music of oppressed people their parents danced to before they were born, with its passionate but soft cries for acceptance and love, and they have wondered why their parents failed to hear.

I do not know how long Blue had inhabited his five beautiful,   12
boring acres before we moved into our house; a year after we had
arrived—and had also traveled to other valleys, other cities, other
worlds—he was still there.

But then, in our second year at the house, something happened   13
in Blue's life. One morning, looking out the window at the fog that
lay like a ribbon over the meadow, I saw another horse, a brown one,
at the other end of Blue's field. Blue appeared to be afraid of it, and
for several days made no attempt to go near. We went away for a
week. When we returned, blue had decided to make friends and the
two horses ambled or galloped along together, and Blue did not
come nearly as often to the fence underneath the apple tree.

When he did, bringing his new friend with him, there was a dif-   14
ferent look in his eyes. A look of independence, of self-possession, of
inalienable *horse*ness. His friend eventually became pregnant. For
months and months there was, it seemed to me, a mutual feeling
between me and the horses of justice, of peace. I fed apples to them
both. The look in Blue's eyes was one of unabashed "this is *it*ness."

It did not, however, last forever. One day, after a visit to the city,   15
I went out to give Blue some apples. He stood waiting, or so I
thought, though not beneath the tree. When I shook the tree and
jumped back from the shower of apples, he made no move. I carried
some over to him. He managed to half-crunch one. The rest he let fall
to the ground. I dreaded looking into his eyes—because I had of
course noticed that Brown, his partner, had gone—but I did look. If
I had been born into slavery, and my partner had been sold or killed,
my eyes would have looked like that. The children next door
explained that Blue's partner had been "put with him" (the same
expression that old people used, I had noticed, when speaking of an
ancestor during slavery who had been impregnated by her owner)
so that they could mate and she conceive. Since that was accomplished, she had been taken back by her owner, who lived somewhere else.

Will she be back? I asked.   16
They didn't know.   17
Blue was like a crazed person. Blue *was*, to me, a crazed person.   18
He galloped furiously, as if he were being ridden, around and
around his five beautiful acres. He whinnied until he couldn't. He
tore at the ground with his hooves. He butted himself against his
single shade tree. He looked always and always toward the road
down which his partner had gone. And then, occasionally, when he

came up for apples, or I took apples to him, he looked at me. It was
a look so piercing, so full of grief, a look so *human*, I almost laughed
(I felt too sad to cry) to think there are people who do not know that
animals suffer. People like me who have forgotten, and daily forget,
all that animals try to tell us. "Everything you do to us will happen
to you; we are your teachers, as you are ours. We are one lesson" is
essentially it, I think. There are those who never once have even considered animals' rights: those who have been taught that animals
actually want to be used and abused by us, as small children "love"
to be frightened, or women "love" to be mutilated and raped. . . .
They are the great-grandchildren of those who honestly thought,
because someone taught them this: "Women can't think," And "niggers can't faint." But most disturbing of all, in Blue's large brown
eyes was a new look, more painful than the look of despair: the look
of disgust with human beings, with life; the look of hatred. And it
was odd what the look of hatred did. It gave him, for the first time,
the look of a beast. And what that meant was that he had put up a
barrier within to protect himself from further violence; all the apples
in the world wouldn't change that fact.

And so Blue remained, a beautiful part of our landscape, very   19
peaceful to look at from the window, white against the grass. Once
a friend came to visit and said, looking out on the soothing view:
"And it *would* have to be a white horse; the very image of freedom."
And I thought, yes, the animals are forced to become for us merely
"images" of what they once so beautifully expressed. And we are
used to drinking milk from containers showing "contented" cows,
whose real lives we want to hear nothing about, eating eggs and
drumsticks from "happy" hens, and munching hamburgers advertised by bulls of integrity who seem to command their fate.

As we talked of freedom and justice one day for all, we sat   20
down to steaks. I am eating misery, I thought, as I took the first bite.
And spit it out.

Meanings and Values

1.   In which paragraphs does Walker describe what she believes to be
     Blue's thoughts and feelings?

2.   According to Walker, in what ways is Blue similar to a human? In
     what ways is he different? To what other groups does the author
     compare Blue and his relationships with humans in paragraphs 8–11?

3. What thematic purposes are served by the following phrases:

   a. "human animals and nonhuman animals" (par. 6)

   b. "who did not understand their description as a compliment" (par. 9)

   c. "Am I Blue?" (title)

   d. "If I had been born into slavery, and my partner had been sold or killed, my eyes would have looked like that." (par. 15)

   e. "It gave him, for the first time, the look of a beast." (par. 18)

Expository Techniques

1. Why do you think Walker chose to wait until near the end of the essay (paragraph 18) for a detailed discussion of its theme? ("Guide to Terms": *Unity*.) To what extent does the placement of this discussion give the essay an expository rather than an argumentative purpose? (*Guide: Argument*.)

2. Discuss how the "'images'" presented in paragraph 19 can be regarded as ironic symbols. (Guide: *Symbol; Irony*.)

3. Describe the way Walker alters the tempo of the sentences and builds to a climax in the concluding paragraph of the essay. (Guide: *Closings*.)

4. Some readers might consider the ending effective. Others might consider it overly dramatic or distasteful. Explain which reaction you consider most appropriate. (Guide: *Evaluation*.)

Diction and Vocabulary

1. Describe the ways in which Walker uses syntax and figurative language (simile) for thematic purposes in this passage: "Blue was like a crazed person. Blue *was*, to me, a crazed person" (par. 18). (Guide: *Syntax; Figures of Speech*.)

2. In speaking of the "'settlers,'" Walker says that this term is "a very benign euphemism for what they actually were" (par. 9). What does she mean by this comment? What other terms might be applied to them (from Walker's point of view)? Why might she have chosen not to use such terms?

3. The title of this essay is taken from a song of the same name. In terms of the content of the essay, to what ideas or themes does it refer? Can it be considered a paradox? (Guide: *Paradox*.) The quotation from the song that opens the essay points to some of the ideas discussed in the essay. What are they?

Read to Write

1. Your responses to Walker's essay may be a source of potential topics
    for your own writing. Phrase your responses as questions like these:
    Is Walker correct in linking racism and disregard for the rights of an-
    imals, or is the connection farfetched? Should people adopt vegetari-
    anism for moral as well as health reasons?

2. Many writers other than Walker have used comparisons with ani-
    mals and animal behavior as a way of shedding light on human
    traits or of revealing human-like traits in animals. Some even go so
    far as to portray humans as animals or animals as humans. Draw on
    a comparison of humans and animals for all or part of an expository
    essay of your own.

3. Walker's essay moves from obvious differences to surprising simi-
    larities, getting there through careful observation and comparison of
    horses and humans. Apply this pattern to a topic of your own choos-
    ing, using it to express hidden similarities you have already noticed
    or to reveal similarities as you write.

(NOTE: Suggestions for topics requiring development by means of COMPARISON and
CONTRAST follow.)

Writing Suggestions for Section 5
Comparison and Contrast

Base your central theme on one of the following, and develop your composition primarily by use of comparison and/or contrast. Use examples liberally for clarity and concreteness, chosen always with your purpose and reader-audience in mind.

1. Two kinds of families.
2. The sea at two different times.
3. The innate qualities needed for success in two different careers.
4. The natural temperaments of two acquaintances.
5. Two musicians.
6. The teaching techniques of two instructors or former teachers.
7. Two methods of parental handling of teenage problems.
8. Two family attitudes toward the practice of religion.
9. Two "moods" of the same town at different times.
10. The personalities (or atmospheres) of two cities or towns of similar size.
11. Two politicians with different leadership styles.
12. Two people who approach problems in different ways.
13. Two different attitudes toward the same thing or activity: one "practical," the other romantic or aesthetic.
14. The beliefs and practices of two religions or denominations concerning one aspect of religion.
15. Two courses on the same subject: one in high school and one in college.
16. The differing styles of two players of some sport or game.
17. The hazards of frontier life and those of life today.
18. Two companies with very different styles or business philosophies.
19. Two recent movies or rock videos.
20. Two magazines focusing on similar subjects but directed at different audiences.
21. The "rewards" of two different kinds of jobs.
22. Two views of loyalty.

6

Using *Analogy* as an
Expository Device

Analogy is a special form of comparison that is used for a specific purpose: to explain something abstract or difficult to understand by showing its similarity to something concrete or easy to understand. A much less commonly used technique than logical comparison (and contrast), analogy is, nonetheless, a highly efficient means of explaining some difficult concepts or of giving added force to the explanations.

Logical comparison is made between two members of the same general class, usually assuming the same kind of interest in the subject matter of both. But in analogy we are really concerned only with the subject matter of one, using a second just to help explain the first. The two subjects, quite incomparable in most respects, are never of the same general class; if they are, we then have logical comparison, not analogy.

If the analogy is to be effective, the writer should be able to assume that the reader is familiar enough with the easier subject, or can quickly be made so, that it really helps explain the more difficult one. A common example is the explanation of the human circulatory system, which we may have trouble comprehending, by comparing the heart and arteries with a pump forcing water through the pipes of a plumbing system. This analogy has been carried further to liken the effect of cholesterol deposits on the inner walls of the arteries to that of mineral deposits that accumulate inside water pipes and eventually close them entirely. Although there is little logical similarity between a steel pipe and a human artery, the *analogical* similarity would be apparent to most readers—but the analogy might cause even greater confusion for anyone who did not know about pumps.

Distinguishing between analogy and metaphor is sometimes difficult. The difference is basically in their purpose: the function of a metaphor is merely to *describe,* to create a brief, vivid image for the reader; the function of analogy is primarily one of exposition, to *explain,* rather than to describe. In this sense, however, the function of a metaphor is actually to *suggest* an analogy: instead of showing the similarities of the heart and the pump, a metaphor might simply refer to "that faithful pump inside my chest," implying enough of a comparison to serve its purpose as description. (We can see here why some people refer to analogy as "extended" metaphor.) The analogist, when trying to explain the wide selection of college subjects and the need for balance in a course of study, could use the easily understood principle of a cafeteria, which serves Jell-O and lemon meringue pie as well as meat and potatoes. If his purpose had been only to create an image, to describe, he might have referred simply to the bewildering variety in "the cafeteria of college courses"—and that would have been a metaphor. (For still another example of the more conventional type of analogy, see the explanation of *Unity,* in the "Guide to Terms.")

But as useful as analogy can be in exposition, it is a difficult technique to use in logical argument. The two subjects of an analogy, although similar in one or more ways useful for illustration, may be basically too different for any reliable conclusions to be drawn from their similarity.

Sample Paragraph (Annotated)

Introduces the *analogy.*

Residents of Palmville have a saying: "Living here is like living in a fishbowl." It certainly does seem like everybody's business (personal or not) is open to view from all sides. When the result is gossip about people's personal lives, this characteristic of Palmville life is not very pleasant. But it does have good sides. When Jake Mollicone grew depressed because of business problems and tried to commit suicide, "nosey" neighbors were right there to save his life and help him recover, physically

Uses the analogy to explain events and relationships.

and mentally. When the Statler twins tried to make extra money by delivering less heating fuel than the bill showed, the rumor mill put the police on the case right away. In addition, a recent editorial in the *Palmville Gazette* suggested that extending the familiar "fishbowl" analogy might be a good idea for Palmville. The editorial pointed out that most fish tanks can be homes to a wide variety of colorful species and that the recent growth of Palmville has likewise brought together people of different backgrounds and qualities in an interesting and healthy mix. The editorial also reminded readers that when a fish tank becomes too crowded, it turns into a dirty, unhealthy environment—and the inhabitants often try to eat each other. "The lesson is clear," the paper concluded, "that while some growth is enriching and beneficial, too much expansion would be the wrong thing for life in our 'fishbowl.'"

Editorial extends the analogy. More a speculation or warning than an argument.

Sample Paragraph (Analogy)

If distant galaxies are really receding from the earth, and if more distant galaxies are receding faster than nearby ones, a remarkable picture of the universe emerges. Imagine that the galaxies were raisins scattered through a rising lump of bread dough. As the dough expanded, the raisins would be carried farther and farther apart from each other. If you were standing on one of the raisins, how would things look? You wouldn't feel any motion yourself, of course, just as you don't feel the

effects of the earth's motion around the
sun, but you would notice that your
nearest neighbor was moving away
from you. This motion would be due to
the fact that the dough between you and
your nearest neighbor would be
expanding, pushing the two of you
apart.

LOREN C. EISELEY

LOREN C. EISELEY (1907–1977) was professor of anthropology and
the history of science at the University of Pennsylvania, where
he also served as provost from 1959 to 1961. He was a Guggen-
heim Foundation Fellow and was in charge of anthropological
expeditions for various universities and for the Smithsonian
Institution. Eiseley, a respected naturalist and conservationist,
also served on many public service boards and commissions and
was awarded many honorary degrees and medals. Widely published in both scholarly and popular magazines, Eiseley also
wrote several books, including *The Immense Journey* (1957), *Dar-
win's Century* (1959), *The Firmament of Time* (1960), *The Unexpected
Universe* (1969), and *The Night Country* (1971).

The Brown Wasps

"The Brown Wasps" was selected from Eiseley's book *The Night
Country*. It is an essay with a simple theme, developed through a
rather intricate web of simple analogies. In reading this selection,
you will see why Eiseley was—and is—widely admired for his
lucid, almost poetic style, as well as for his sensitive, philosophical
approach to all living things.

There is a corner in the waiting room of one of the great Eastern sta-   1
tions where women never sit. It is always in the shadow and over-
hung by rows of lockers. It is, however, always frequented—not so
much by genuine travelers as by the dying. It is here that a certain
element of the abandoned poor seeks a refuge out of the weather,
clinging for a few hours longer to the city that has fathered them. In
a precisely similar manner I have seen, on a sunny day in midwinter,
a few old brown wasps creep slowly over an abandoned wasp nest
in a thicket. Numbed and forgetful and frost-blackened, the hum of
the spring hive still resounded faintly in their sodden tissues. Then
the temperature would fall and they would drop away into the white

oblivion of the snow. Here in the station it is in no way different save the city is busy in its snows. But the old ones cling to their seats as though these were symbolic and could not be given up. Now and then they sleep, their gray old heads resting with painful awkwardness on the backs of the benches.

Also they are not at rest. For an hour they may sleep in the gasping 2 exhaustion of the ill-nourished and aged who have to walk in the night. Then a policeman comes by on his round and nudges them upright.

"You can't sleep here," he growls. 3

A strange ritual then begins. An old man is difficult to waken. 4 After a muttered conversation the policeman presses a coin into his hand and passes fiercely along the benches prodding and gesturing toward the door. In his wake, like birds rising and settling behind the passage of a farmer through a cornfield, the men totter up, move a few paces and subside once more upon the benches.

One man, after a slight, apologetic lurch, does not move at all. 5 Tubercularly thin, he sleeps on steadily. The policeman does not look back. To him, too, this has become a ritual. He will not have to notice it again officially for another hour.

Once in a while one of the sleepers will not awaken. Like the 6 brown wasps, he will have had his wish to die in the great droning center of the hive rather than in some lonely room. It is not so bad here with the shuffle of footsteps and the knowledge that there are others who share the bad luck of the world. There are also the whistles and the sounds of everyone, everyone in the world, starting on journeys. Amidst so many journeys somebody is bound to come out all right. Somebody.

Maybe it was on a like thought that the brown wasps fell away 7 from the old paper nest in the thicket. You hold till the last, even if it is only to a public seat in a railroad station. You want your place in the hive more than you want a room or a place where the aged can be eased gently out of the way. It is the place that matters, the place at the heart of things. It is life that you want, that bruises your gray old head with the hard chairs; a man has a right to his place.

But sometimes the place is lost in the years behind us. Or 8 sometimes it is a thing of air, a kind of vaporous distortion above a heap of rubble. We cling to a time and place because without them man is lost, not only man but life. This is why the voices, real or unreal, which speak from the floating trumpets at spiritualist seances are so unnerving. They are voices out of nowhere whose only reality lies in their ability to stir the memory of a living person with some fragment of the past. Before the medium's cabinet both the dead and the living revolve endlessly about an episode, a place, an event that has already been engulfed by time.

This feeling runs deep in life; it brings stray cats running over 9 endless miles, and birds homing from the ends of the earth. It is as though all living creatures, and particularly the more intelligent, can survive only by fixing or transforming a bit of time into space or by securing a bit of space with its objects immortalized and made permanent in time. For example, I once saw, on a flower pot in my own living room, the efforts of a field mouse to build a remembered field. I have lived to see this episode repeated in a thousand guises, and since I have spent a large portion of my life in the shade of a nonexistent tree, I think I am entitled to speak for the field mouse.

One day as I cut across the field, which at that time extended on 10 one side of our suburban shopping center, I found a giant slug feeding from a runnel of pink ice cream in an abandoned Dixie cup. I could see his eyes telescope and protrude in a kind of dim, uncertain ecstasy as his dark body bunched and elongated in the curve of the cup. Then, as I stood there at the edge of the concrete, contemplating the slug, I began to realize it was like standing on a shore where a different type of life creeps up and fumbles tentatively among the rocks and sea wrack. It knows its place and will only creep so far until something changes. Little by little as I stood there, I began to see more of this shore that surrounds the place of man. I looked with sudden care and attention at things I had been running over thoughtlessly for years. I even waded out a short way into the grass and the wild-rose thickets to see more. A huge black-belted bee went droning by and there were some indistinct scurryings in the underbrush.

Then I came to a sign which informed me that this field was to 11 be the site of a new Wanamaker suburban store. Thousands of obscure lives were about to perish, the spores of puffballs would go smoking off to new fields, and the bodies of little white-footed mice would be crunched under the inexorable wheels of the bulldozers. Life disappears or modifies its appearances so fast that everything takes on an aspect of illusion—a momentary fizzing and boiling with smoke rings, like pouring dissident chemicals into a retort. Here man was advancing, but in a few years his plaster and bricks would be disappearing once more into the insatiable maw of the clover. Being of an archaeological cast of mind, I thought of this fact with an obscure sense of satisfaction and waded back through the rose thickets to the concrete parking lot. As I did so, a mouse scurried

ahead of me, frightened of my steps if not of that ominous Wanamaker sign. I saw him vanish in the general direction of my apartment
house, his little body quivering with fear in the great open sun on the
blazing concrete. Blinded and confused, he was running straight
away from his field. In another week scores would follow him.

I forgot the episode then and went home to the quiet of my liv-   12
ing room. It was not until a week later, letting myself into the apartment, that I realized I had a visitor. I am fond of plants and had
several ferns standing on the floor in pots to avoid the noon glare by
the south window.

As I snapped on the light and glanced carelessly around the   13
room, I saw a little heap of earth on the carpet and a scrabble of pebbles that had been kicked merrily over the edge of one of the flower
pots. To my astonishment I discovered a full-fledged burrow delv-
ing downward among the fern roots. I waited silently. The creature
who had made the burrow did not appear. I remembered the wild
field then, and the flight of the mice. No house mouse, no *Mus
domesticus,* had kicked up this little heap of earth or sought refuge
under a fern root in a flower pot. I thought of the desperate little
creature I had seen fleeing from the wild-rose thicket. Through intri-
cacies of pipes and attics, he, or one of his fellows, had climbed to
this high green solitary room. I could visualize what had occurred.
He had an image in his head, a world of seed pods and quiet, of
green sheltering leaves in the dim light among the weed stems. It
was the only world he knew and it was gone.

Somehow in his flight he had found his way to this room with   14
drawn shades where no one would come till nightfall. And here he
had smelled green leaves and run quickly up the flower pot to dab-
ble his paws in common earth. He had even struggled half the afternoon to carry his burrow deeper and had failed. I examined the hole,
but no whiskered twitching face appeared. He was gone. I gathered
up the earth and refilled the burrow. I did not expect to find traces
of him again.

Yet for three nights thereafter I came home to the darkened   15
room and my ferns to find the dirt kicked gaily about the rug and
the burrow reopened, though I was never able to catch the field
mouse within it. I dropped a little food about the mouth of the burrow, but it was never touched. I looked under beds or sat reading
with one ear cocked for rustling in the ferns. It was all in vain; I
never saw him. Probably he ended in a trap in some other tenant's
room.

But before he disappeared, I had come to look hopefully for his   16
evening burrow. About my ferns there had begun to linger the insubstantial vapor of an autumn field, the distilled essence, as it were, of
a mouse brain in exile from its home. It was a small dream, like our
dreams, carried a long and weary journey along pipes and through
spider webs, past holes over which loomed the shadows of waiting
cats, and finally, desperately, into this room where he had played in
the shuttered daylight for an hour among the green ferns on the
floor. Every day these invisible dreams pass us on the street, or rise
from beneath our feet, or look out upon us from beneath a bush.

Some years ago the old elevated railway in Philadelphia was   17
torn down and replaced by a subway system. This ancient El with its
barnlike stations containing nut-vending machines and scattered
food scraps had, for generations, been the favorite feeding ground of
flocks of pigeons, generally one flock to a station along the route of
the El. Hundreds of pigeons were dependent upon the system. They
flapped in and out of its stanchions and steel work or gathered in
watchful little audiences about the feet of anyone who rattled the
peanut-vending machines. They even watched people who jingled
change in their hands, and prospected for food under the feet of the
crowds who gathered between trains. Probably very few among the
waiting people who tossed a crumb to an eager pigeon realized that
this El was like a food-bearing river, and that the life which haunted
its banks was dependent upon the running of the trains with their
human freight.

I saw the river stop.   18

The time came when the underground tubes were ready; the   19
traffic was transferred to a realm unreachable by pigeons. It was like
a great river subsiding suddenly into desert sands. For a day, for two
days, pigeons continued to circle over the El or stand close to the red
vending machines. They were patient birds, and surely this great
river which had flowed through the lives of unnumbered generations was merely suffering from some momentary drought.

They listened for the familiar vibrations that had always her-   20
alded an approaching train; they flapped hopefully about the head
of an occasional workman walking along the steel runways. They
passed from one empty station to another, all the while growing
hungrier. Finally, they flew away.

I thought I had seen the last of them about the El, but there was   21
a revival and it provided a curious instance of the memory of living
things for a way of life or a locality that has long been cherished.

Some weeks after the El was abandoned, workmen began to tear it down. I went to work every morning by one particular station, and the time came when the demolition crews reached this spot. Acetylene torches showered passers-by with sparks, pneumatic drills hammered at the base of the structure, and a blind man who, like the pigeons, had clung with his cup to a stairway leading to the change booth, was forced to give up his place.

It was then, strangely, momentarily, one morning that I wit-   22
nessed the return of a little band of the familiar pigeons. I even recognized one or two members of the flock that had lived around this particular station before they were dispersed into the streets. They flew bravely in and out among the sparks and the hammers and the shouting workmen. They had returned—and they had returned because the hubbub of the wreckers had convinced them that the river was about to flow once more. For several hours they flapped in and out through the empty windows, nodding their heads and watching the fall of girders with attentive little eyes. By the following morning the station was reduced to some burned-off stanchions in the street. My bird friends had gone. It was plain, however, that they retained a memory for an insubstantial structure now compounded of air and time. Even the blind man clung to it. Someone had provided him with a chair, and he sat at the same corner staring sightlessly at an invisible stairway where, so far as he was concerned, the crowds were still ascending to the trains.

I have said my life has been passed in the shade of a nonexistent   23
tree, so that such sights do not offend me. Prematurely I am one of the brown wasps and I often sit with them in the great droning hive of the station, dreaming sometimes of a certain tree. It was planted sixty years ago by a boy with a bucket and a toy spade in a little Nebraska town. That boy was myself. It was a cottonwood sapling and the boy remembered it because of some words spoken by his father and because everyone died or moved away who was supposed to wait and grow old under its shade. The boy was passed from hand to hand, but the tree for some intangible reason had taken root in his mind. It was under its branches that he sheltered; it was from this tree that his memories, which are my memories, led a way into the world.

After sixty years the mood of the brown wasps grows heavier   24
upon one. During a long inward struggle I thought it would do me good to go and look upon that actual tree. I found a rational excuse in which to clothe this madness. I purchased a ticket and at the end

of two thousand miles I walked another mile to an address that was still the same. The house had not been altered.

I came close to the white picket fence and reluctantly, with great effort, looked down the long vista of the yard. There was nothing there to see. For sixty years that cottonwood had been growing in my mind. Season by season its seeds had been floating farther on the hot prairie winds. We had planted it lovingly there, my father and I, because he had a great hunger for soil and live things growing, and because none of these things had long been ours to protect. We had planted the little sapling and watered it faithfully, and I remembered that I had run out with my small bucket to drench its roots the day we moved away. And all the years since, it had been growing in my mind, a huge tree that somehow stood for my father and the love I bore him. I took a grasp on the picket fence and forced myself to look again.   25

A boy with the hard bird eye of youth pedaled a tricycle slowly up beside me.   26

"What'cha lookin' at?" he asked curiously.   27

"A tree," I said.   28

"What for?" he said.   29

"It isn't there," I said, to myself mostly, and began to walk away at a pace just slow enough not to seem to be running.   30

"What isn't there?" the boy asked. I didn't answer. It was obvious I was attached by a thread to a thing that had never been there, or certainly not for long. Something that had to be held in the air, or sustained in the mind, because it was part of my orientation in the universe and I could not survive without it. There was more than an animal's attachment to a place. There was something else, the attachment of the spirit to a grouping of events in time; it was part of our morality.   31

So I had come home at last, driven by a memory in the brain as surely as the field mouse who had delved long ago into my flower pot or the pigeons flying forever amidst the rattle of nut-vending machines. These, the burrow under the greenery in my living room and the red-bellied bowls of peanuts now hovering in midair in the minds of pigeons, were all part of an elusive world that existed nowhere and yet everywhere. I looked once at the real world about me while the persistent boy pedaled at my heels.   32

It was without meaning, though my feet took a remembered path. In sixty years the house and street had rotted out of my mind. But the tree, the tree that no longer was, that had perished in its first   33 season, bloomed on in my individual mind, unblemished as my father's words. "We'll plant a tree here, son, and we're not going to move any more. And when you're an old, old man you can sit under it and think how we planted it here, you and me, together."

I began to outpace the boy on the tricycle.   34

"Do you live here, Mister?" he shouted after me suspiciously. I   35 took a firm grasp on airy nothing—to be precise, on the bole of a great tree. "I do," I said. I spoke for myself, one field mouse, and several pigeons. We were all out of touch but somehow permanent. It was the world that had changed.

Meanings and Values

1. What was Eiseley's apparent purpose in writing this essay? How well did he achieve his purpose? (See "Guide to Terms": *Evaluation*.) ("Purpose" is the key word in this question: it is significant that this essay was written for inclusion in a book.)

2. Explain how the seats were "symbolic" to the old men (par. 1). (Guide: *Symbol*.)

3. Clarify the meaning, or meanings, of paragraph 8. What was it, precisely, that caused Eiseley's "obscure sense of satisfaction? (par. 11)? Why?

4. Where would you place this essay on an objective-to-subjective continuum? Why (Guide: *Objective/Subjective*.)

Expository Techniques

1. What three major analogies are linked in this essay? Do they all have the same analogical purpose? If not, what is their relationship?

2. The transition between paragraphs 7 and 8 is especially important. Why? (Guide: *Transition*.) How does Eiseley assure a smooth connection?

3. Is unity damaged by the introduction of the boy toward the end? (Guide: *Unity*.) Explain how it is damaged, or why you think Eiseley included him. (The fact that the child happened along in "real life" would not have justified including him here; the author *selects* his own details.)

4. Did you find it difficult to get at the essence of Eiseley's meanings— in other words, did you find the essay hard to read? If so, try to determine why. Could these difficulties have been avoided by the author without sacrificing quality or message? Do you think a more experienced reader would have had any difficulties?

Diction and Vocabulary

1. Explain why the diction and syntax, and the pace of the writing, would, or would not, be appropriate for most college papers. For most newspaper writing.

2. Demonstrate the meaning of the term *metaphor* using examples from this selection. (Guide: *Figures of Speech*.) The meaning of *simile*. The meaning of *personification*.

3. If you are not familiar with the meaning of any of the following words, consult your dictionary: sodden (par. 1); subside (4); vaporous (8); guises (9); runnel, wrack (10); inexorable, dissident, retort, insatiable, maw (11); dispersed (22).

Read to Write

1. Many sentences and longer passages in this essay are worth pondering both for what they have to say to readers and for the ideas and topics they suggest for further writing. Many of them also suggest analogies around which you might structure an essay. Reread the essay looking for passages of this sort and write down any that you consider particularly intriguing. You might start your list with these: "We cling to a time and place because without them man is lost, not only man but life" (par. 8) and "Life disappears or modifies its appearances so fast that everything takes on an aspect of illusion . . . " (11).

2. Eiseley pays considerable attention to animal behaviors in many of the analogies in this essay. Consider using a similar approach in your writing. Think of animal behaviors or natural events (storms, ocean tides, or plant cycles, for example) that both suggest a topic and provide analogies to include in your writing.

3. Follow Eiseley's approach in "The Brown Wasps" and prepare an essay that presents several related analogies in order to explore a topic in depth or look at it from differing perspectives.

(NOTE: Suggestions for topics requiring development by use of ANALOGY are on page 239, at the end of this section.)

PATRICIA RAYBON was born in 1949. She attended Ohio State University (B.A. 1971) and the University of Colorado (M.A. 1977). For a number of years she was a newspaper reporter, writer, and editor. Currently she is an associate professor at the University of Colorado School of Journalism and Mass Communication. Her work has been published in a wide variety of magazines and newspapers, including *The New York Times Magazine* and *USA Today*. Raybon's book, *My First White Friend: Confessions on Race, Love, and Forgiveness* appeared in 1996.

Letting in Light

The analogy around which this essay is built is a subtle but particularly effective one. To observe it at work, consider the following relationships as you read: washing windows *equals* women's work *equals* letting in light. By the end of the essay, Raybon may have changed your mind about activities that many people no longer consider particularly important or valuable. This essay first appeared in *The New York Times Magazine*.

The windows were a gift or maybe a bribe—or maybe a bonus—for 1
falling in love with such a dotty old house. The place was a wreck. A showoff, too. So it tried real hard to be more. But it lacked so much— good heat, stable floors, solid walls, enough space. A low interest rate.

But it had windows. More glass and bays and bows than people 2
on a budget had a right to expect. And in unlikely places—like the window inside a bedroom closet, its only view a strawberry patch planted by the children next door.

None of it made sense. So we bought the place. We saved up 3
and put some money down, then toasted the original builder—no doubt some brave and gentle carpenter, blessed with a flair for the grand gesture. A romantic with a T-square.

We were young then and struggling. Also, we are black. We 4
looked with irony and awe at the task now before us. But we did not faint.

The time had come to wash windows.   5

Yes, I do windows. Like an amateur and a dabbler, perhaps, but   6
the old-fashioned way—one pane at a time. It is the best way to pay
back something so plain for its clear and silent gifts—the light of
day, the glow of moon, hard rain, soft snow, dawn's early light.

The Romans called them *specularia*. They glazed their windows   7
with translucent marble and shells. And thus the ancients let some
light into their world.

In my own family, my maternal grandmother washed win-   8
dows—and floors and laundry and dishes and a lot of other things
that needed cleaning—while doing day work for a rich, stylish red-
head in her Southern hometown.

To feed her five children and keep them clothed and happy, to   9
help them walk proudly and go to church and sing hymns and have
some change in their pockets—and to warm and furnish the house
her dead husband had built and added onto with his own hands—
my grandmother went to work.

She and her third daughter, my mother, put on maids' uniforms   10
and cooked and sewed and served a family that employed my
grandmother until she was nearly 80. She called them Mister and
Missus—yes, ma'am and yes, sir—although she was by many years
their elder. They called her Laura. Her surname never crossed their
lips.

But her daughter, my mother, took her earnings from the cook-   11
ing and serving and window washing and clothes ironing and went
to college, forging a life with a young husband—my father—that
granted me, their daughter, a lifetime of relative comfort.

I owe these women everything.   12

They taught me hope and kindness and how to say thank you.   13

They taught me how to brew tea and pour it. They taught me   14
how to iron creases and whiten linen and cut hair ribbon on the bias
so it doesn't unravel. They taught me to carve fowl, make butter
molds and cook a good cream sauce. They taught me "women's
work" —secrets of home, they said, that now are looked on mostly
with disdain: how to sweep, dust, polish and wax. How to mow,
prune, scrub, scour and purify.

They taught me how to wash windows.   15

Not many women do anymore, of course. There's no time. Life   16
has us all on the run. It's easier to call a "window man," quicker to
pay and, in the bargain, forget about the secret that my mother and
her mother learned many years before they finally taught it to me:

Washing windows clears the cobwebs from the corners. It's   17
plain people's therapy, good for troubles and muddles and other
consternations. It's real work, I venture—honest work—and it's a
sound thing to pass on. Mother to daughter. Daughter to child.
Woman to woman.

This is heresy, of course. Teaching a girl to wash windows is   18
now an act of bravery—or else defiance. If she's black, it's an act of
denial, a gesture that dares history and heritage to make something
of it.

But when my youngest was 5 or 6, I tempted fate and ancestry   19
and I handed her a wooden bucket. Together we would wash the
outdoor panes. The moment sits in my mind:

She works a low row. I work the top. Silently we toil, soaping   20
and polishing, each at her own pace—the only sounds the squeak of
glass, some noisy birds, our own breathing.

Then, quietly at first, this little girl begins to hum. It's a non-   21
sense melody, created for the moment. Soft at first, soon it gets
louder. And louder. Then a recognizable tune emerges. Then she is
really singing. With every swish of the towel, she croons louder and
higher in her little-girl voice with her little-girl song. "This little light
of mine—I'm gonna let it shine! Oh, this little light of mine—I'm
gonna let it shine!" So, of course, I join in. And the two of us sere-
nade the glass and the sparrows and mostly each other. And too
soon our work is done.

"That was fun," she says. She is innocent, of course, and does   22
this work by choice, not by necessity. But she's not too young to look
at truth and understand it. And her heart, if not her arm, is resolute
and strong.

Those years have passed. And other houses and newer win-   23
dows—and other "women's jobs"—have moved through my life. I
have chopped and puréed and polished and glazed. Bleached and
folded and stirred. I have sung lullabies.

I have also marched and fought and prayed and taught and tes-   24
tified. Women's work covers many bases.

But the tradition of one simple chore remains. I do it without   25
apology.

Last week, I dipped the sponge into the pail and began the gen-   26
tle bath—easing off the trace of wintry snows, of dust storms and
dead, brown leaves, of too much sticky tape used to steady paper
pumpkins and Christmas lights and crepe-paper bows from holidays now past. While I worked, the little girl—now 12—found her

way to the bucket, proving that her will and her voice are still up to the task, but mostly, I believe, to have some fun.

We are out of step, the two of us. She may not even know it. But   27 we can carry a tune. The work is never done. The song is two-part harmony.

Meanings and Values

1. Why do windows make the house attractive (pars. 1–2)? What do they seem to symbolize in paragraphs 1–4? 26? (See "Guide to Terms": *Symbol*.) Do they take on symbolic meaning anywhere else in the essay? If so, what are these other meanings?

2. According to the essay, why might people view window washing as a negative, unnecessary, or demeaning act? Be specific in your answer and point to passages that support your conclusions. What positive reasons for washing windows does the author give? Be specific.

3. Where in the essay does the author equate washing windows with "women's work"?

4. Raybon points out that washing windows means letting in light. Are we to take the idea of letting in light simply and literally, or might it have deeper meanings? If it has deeper meanings, point to passages that suggest them, and summarize in your own words the ideas being conveyed.

Expository Techniques

1. How does Raybon call attention to a particular subject in the opening sentences of paragraphs 1 and 2? (Guide: *Emphasis*.)

2. Explain the role paragraph 5 plays as a transition. Is it effective? (Guide: *Transition; Evaluation*.)

3. Point out the parallel sentence structures in paragraphs 13–15 and tell what the writer achieves with this use of parallelism. (Guide: *Parallel Structure*.)

4. Identify the transitions in paragraphs 16 and 23 and discuss their function within the essay as a whole.

Diction and Vocabulary

1. To what extent should the phrase "clears the cobwebs from the corners" (par. 17) be taken literally? To what extent can it be regarded as a metaphor? Explain. (Guide: *Figures of Speech*.)

2. Explain how the phrase "A romantic with a T-Square" might be applied to the author, the "we" of paragraphs 3–4, and the house itself. Discuss how the phrase might be regarded as presenting a paradox. (Guide: *Paradox.*)

3. The song quoted in paragraph 21 is an allusion (Guide: *Figures of Speech.*) To what does it allude? What does the allusion suggest about the meaning of light for the writer?

4. Are we to take the last sentences of the essay literally as a statement about singing? If not, what figurative or metaphoric meaning might they carry? Explain. (Guide: *Figures of Speech.*)

Read to Write

1. Think about which kinds of work, or other activities, have traditionally been regarded as "women's work" and which have been regarded as "men's work." Next, freewrite about the connections traditionally made between gender and work (or some similar linking such as age and kind of work, or gender and leisure activities). If your freewriting does not suggest topics for an essay, try asking *Who? What? When? Where?* and *Why?* to probe the links. For example, you might ask, "Who thinks shopping for food is 'women's work'?" "Do people still believe this or are attitudes changing?" "Why have women traditionally been associated with food shopping, and why might this point of view be less common today?"

2. Raybon uses parent-child relationships and experiences for many examples and ideas in her essay and as an important way of viewing her subject. Consider using a similar tactic (and source) for an essay of your own. You might focus on positive ideas, habits, and values that are passed on from generation to generation, or on negative behaviors and attitudes learned from elders and "taught" to children.

3. As the basis for her analogy, Raybon uses an object (windows) that comes to symbolize and embody ideas and values in the essay. Use a similar strategy in an essay of your own by choosing an object or place, developing an analogy from it, and letting it stand for values and concepts.

(NOTE: Suggestions for topics requiring development by use of ANALOGY are on page 239, at the end of this section.)

Issues and Ideas

Discovering Patterns in Behavior and Relationships

Like most people, you have probably spent considerable time and effort trying to understand how people behave and how they maintain (or fail to maintain) relationships with each other. One way to do this is through careful observation of social interaction. Yet the complexity of human behavior often makes it difficult to isolate the patterns that can explain our relationships or predict our actions.

For this reason, scientists and other students of human behavior often look for explanatory patterns in studies of plants, animals, or natural processes. Historians sometimes discuss a civilization in terms of its germination, growth, flowering, and decay, for example. A sociologist may use a concept like "entropy" (from physics) to explain a society's decline into chaos, and an anthropologist (like Lauren Eiseley in "The Brown Wasps," pages 201–208 may turn to biology and natural history to explain our reluctance to abandon settings that once held meaning for us.

To borrow such explanatory patterns is to make use of analogy: explaining complex behaviors by those behaviors that seem simpler and easier to understand (though they may, in truth, be just as difficult and complicated). The risk in borrowing explanatory patterns is that they may oversimplify relationships (bees can represent hardworking groups, but bee societies are certainly less complex than human ones) or that they may be mostly inappropriate (we can talk of a friendship "blossoming" while we know that it has few other similarities to plants or plant life).

In reading the discussions of human behavior in Tom Wolfe's "O Rotten Gotham" and Barbara Kingsolver's "High Tide in Tucson," therefore, pay attention to how the writers use analogy as an effective expository strategy, and also to the ways they use it as a tool for understanding. Bear in mind that an explanation that is rhetorically successful may still take unfounded logical leaps or leave important questions unanswered.

TOM WOLFE

TOM WOLFE was born in 1931 and grew up in Richmond, Virginia, graduated from Washington and Lee University, and took
his doctorate at Yale. After working for several years as a
reporter for *The Washington Post,* he joined the staff of the *New
York Herald Tribune* in 1962. He has won two Washington Newspaper Guild Awards, one for humor and the other for foreign
news. Wolfe has been a regular contributor to *New York, Esquire,*
and other magazines. His books include *The Kandy-Kolored
Tangerine-Flake Streamline Baby* (1965), *The Electric Kool-Aid Acid
Test* (1968), *The Pump House Gang* (1968), *Radical Chic and Mau-
Mauing the Flak Catchers* (1970), *The New Journalism* (1973), *The
Painted Word* (1975), *The Right Stuff* (1977), *In Our Time* (1980),
Underneath the I-Beams: Inside the Compound (1981), *From Bauhaus
to Our House* (1981), *The Purple Decades: A Reader* (1984), and *The
Bonfire of the Vanities* (1986).

O Rotten Gotham—Sliding Down into the Behavioral Sink

"O Rotten Gotham—Sliding Down into the Behavioral Sink," as
used here, is excerpted from a longer selection by that title in
Wolfe's book *The Pump House Gang* (1968). Here, as he frequently
does, the author investigates an important aspect of modern life—
seriously, but in his characteristic and seemingly freewheeling
style. It is a style that is sometimes ridiculed by scholars but is far
more often admired. (Wolfe, as the serious student will discover, is
always in complete control of his materials and methods, using
them to create certain effects, to reinforce his ideas.) In this piece
his analogy is particularly noteworthy for the extensive usage he is
able to get from it.

I just spent two days with Edward T. Hall, an anthropologist, watching   1
thousands of my fellow New Yorkers short-circuiting themselves into
hot little twitching death balls with jolts of their own adrenalin. Dr.
Hall says it is overcrowding that does it. Overcrowding gets the

adrenalin going, and the adrenalin gets them hyped up. And here they are, hyped up, turning bilious, nephritic, a queer, autistic, sadistic, barren, batty, sloppy, hot-in-the-pants, chancred-on-the-flankers, leering, puling, numb—the usual in New York, in other words, and God knows what else. Dr. Hall has the theory that over-crowding has already thrown New York into a state of behavioral sink. Behavioral sink is a term from ethology, which is the study of how animals relate to their environment. Among animals, the sink winds up with a "population collapse" or "massive die-off." O Rot-ten Gotham.

It got to be easy to look at New Yorkers as animals, especially   2
looking down from some place like a balcony at Grand Central at the rush hour Friday afternoon. The floor was filled with the poor white humans, running around, dodging, blinking their eyes, making a sound like a pen full of starlings or rats or something.

"Listen to them skid," says Dr. Hall.   3

He was right. The poor old etiolate animals were out there skid-   4
ding on their rubber soles. You could hear it once he pointed it out. They stop short to keep from hitting somebody or because they are disoriented and they suddenly stop and look around, and they skid on their rubber-soled shoes, and a screech goes up. They pour out onto the floor down the escalators from the Pan-Am Building, from 42nd Street, from Lexington Avenue, up out of subways, down into subways, railroad trains, up into helicopters—

"You can also hear the helicopters all the way down here,"   5
says Dr. Hall. The sound of the helicopters using the roof of the Pan-Am Building nearly fifty stories up beats right through. "If it weren't for this ceiling"—he is referring to the very high ceiling in Grand Central—"this place would be unbearable with this kind of crowding. And yet they'll probably never 'waste' space like this again."

They screech! And the adrenal glands in all those poor white   6
animals enlarge, micrometer by micrometer, to the size of can-taloupes. Dr. Hall pulls a Minox camera out of a holster he has on his belt and stars shooting away at the human scurry. The Sink!

Dr. Hall has the Minox up to his eye—he is a slender man, calm,   7
52 years old, young-looking, an anthropologist who has worked with Navajos, Hopis, Spanish-Americans, Negroes, Trukese. He was the most important anthropologist in the government during the crucial years of the foreign aid program, the 1950s. He directed both the Point Four training program and the Human Relations Area

Files. He wrote *The Silent Language* and *The Hidden Dimension*, two books that are picking up the kind of "underground" following his friend Marshall McLuhan started picking up about five years ago. He teaches at the Illinois Institute of Technology, lives with his wife, Mildred, in a high-ceilinged town house on one of the last great residential streets in downtown Chicago, Astor Street; he has a grown son and daughter, loves good food, good wine, the relaxed, civilized life—but comes to New York with a Minox at his eye to record!—perfect—The Sink.

We really got down in there by walking down into the Lexing-   8
ton Avenue line subway stop under Grand Central. We inhaled those nice big fluffy fumes of human sweat, urine, effluvia, and sebaceous secretions. One old female human was already stroked out on the upper level, on a stretcher, with two policemen standing by. The other humans barely looked at her. They rushed into line. They bellied each other, haunch to paunch, down the stairs. Human heads shone through the gratings. The species North European tried to create bubbles of space around themselves, about a foot and a half in diameter—

"See, he's reacting against the line," says Dr. Hall.   9

—but the species Mediterranean presses on in. The hell with   10
bubbles of space. The species North European resents that, this male human behind him presses forward toward the booth . . . *breathing* on him, he's disgusted, he pulls out of the line entirely, the species Mediterranean resents him for resenting it, and neither of them realizes what the hell they are getting irritable about exactly. And in all of them the old adrenals grow another micrometer.

Dr. Hall whips out the Minox. Too perfect! The bottom of The   11
Sink.

It is the sheer overcrowding, such as occurs in the business sec-   12
tions of Manhattan five days a week and in Harlem, Bedford-Stuyvesant, southeast Bronx every day—sheer overcrowding is converting New Yorkers into animals in a sink pen. Dr. Hall's argument runs as follows: all animals, including birds, seem to have a built-in inherited requirement to have a certain amount of territory, space, to lead their lives in. Even if they have all the food they need, and there are no predatory animals threatening them, they cannot tolerate crowding beyond a certain point. No more than two hundred wild Norway rats can survive on a quarter acre of ground, for example, even when they are given all the food they can eat. They just die off.

But why? To find out, ethologists have run experiments on all   13
sorts of animals, from stickleback crabs to Sika deer. In one major
experiment, an ethologist named John Calhoun put some domesticated white Norway rats in a pen with four sections to it, connected
by ramps. Calhoun knew from previous experiments that the rats
tend to split up into groups of ten to twelve and that the pen, therefore, would hold forty to forty-eight rats comfortably, assuming they
formed four equal groups. He allowed them to reproduce until there
were eighty rats, balanced between male and female, but did not let
it get any more crowded. He kept them supplied with plenty of
food, water, and nesting materials. In other words, all their more
obvious needs were taken care of. A less obvious need—space—was
not. To the human eye, the pen did not even look especially
crowded. But to the rats, it was crowded beyond endurance.

The entire colony was soon plunged into a profound behavioral   14
sink. "The sink," said Calhoun, "is the outcome of any behavioral
process that collects animals together in unusually great numbers.
The unhealthy connotations of the term are not accidental: a behav
ioral sink does act to aggravate all forms of pathology that can be
found within a group."

For a start, long before the rat population reached eighty, a sta-   15
tus hierarchy had developed in the pen. Two dominant male rats
took over the two end sections, acquired harems of eight to ten
females each, and forced the rest of the rats into the two middle
pens. All the overcrowding took place in the middle pens. That was
where the "sink" hit. The aristocrat rats at the end grew bigger,
sleeker, healthier, and more secure the whole time.

In The Sink, meanwhile, nest building, courting, sex behavior,   16
reproduction, social organization, health—all of it went to pieces.
Normally, Norway rats have a mating ritual in which the male
chases the female, the female ducks down into a burrow and sticks
her head up to watch the male. He performs a little dance outside
the burrow, then she comes out, and he mounts her, usually for a
few seconds. When The Sink set in, however, no more than three
males—the dominant males in the middle sections—kept up the old
customs. The rest tried everything from satyrism to homosexuality
or else gave up on sex altogether. Some of the subordinate males
spent all their time chasing females. Three or four might chase one
female at the same time, and instead of stopping at the burrow
entrance for the ritual, they would charge right in. Once mounted,
they would hold on for minutes instead of the usual seconds.

Homosexuality rose sharply. So did bisexuality. Some males   17
would mount anything—males, females, babies, senescent rats, anything. Still other males dropped sexual activity altogether, wouldn't
fight and, in fact, would hardly move except when the other rats
slept. Occasionally, a female from the aristocrat rats' harems would
come over the ramps and into the middle sections to sample life in
The Sink. When she had had enough, she would run back up the
ramp. Sink males would give chase up to the top of the ramp, which
is to say, to the very edge of the aristocratic preserve. But one glance
from one of the king rats would stop them cold and they would
return to The Sink.

The slumming females from the harems had their adventures   18
and then returned to a placid, healthy life. Females in The Sink,
however, were ravaged, physically and psychologically. Pregnant
rats had trouble continuing pregnancy. The rate of miscarriages
increased significantly, and females started dying from tumors and
other disorders of the mammary glands, sex organs, uterus, ovaries,
and Fallopian tubes. Typically, their kidneys, livers, and adrenals
were also enlarged or diseased or showed other signs associated
with stress.

Child-rearing became totally disorganized. The females lost the   19
interest or the stamina to build nests and did not keep them up if
they did build them. In the general filth and confusion, they would
not put themselves out to save offspring they were momentarily
separated from. Frantic, even sadistic competition among the males
was going on all around them and rendering their lives chaotic. The
males began unprovoked and senseless assaults upon one another,
often in the form of tail-biting. Ordinarily, rats will suppress this
kind of behavior when it crops up. In The Sink, male rats gave up all
policing and just looked out for themselves. The "pecking order"
among males in The Sink was never stable. Normally, male rats set
up a three-class structure. Under the pressure of overcrowding,
however, they broke up into all sorts of unstable subclasses, cliques,
packs—and constantly pushed, probed, explored, tested one
another's power. Anyone was fair game, except for the aristocrats in
the end pens.

Calhoun kept the population down to eighty, so that the next   20
stage, "population collapse" or "massive die-off," did not occur. But
the autopsies showed that the pattern—as in the diseases among the
female rats—was already there.

The classic study of die-off was John J. Christian's study of Sika   21
deer on James Island in the Chesapeake Bay, west of Cambridge,
Maryland. Four or five of the deer had been released on the island,
which was 280 acres and uninhabited, in 1916. By 1955 they had
bred freely into a herd of 280 to 300. The population density was
only about one deer per acre at this point, but Christian knew that
this was already too high for the Sikas' inborn space requirements,
and something would give before long. For two years the number of
deer remained 280 to 300. But suddenly, in 1958, over half the deer
died; 161 carcasses were recovered. In 1959 more deer died and the
population steadied at about 80.

In two years, two-thirds of the herd had died. Why? It was not   22
starvation. In fact, all the deer collected were in excellent condition,
with well-developed muscles, shining coats, and fat deposits
between the muscles. In practically all the deer, however, the
adrenal glands had enlarged by 50 percent. Christian concluded that
the die-off was due to "shock following severe metabolic disturbance, probably as a result of prolonged adrenocortical hyperactivity. . . . There was no evidence of infection, starvation, or other
obvious cause to explain the mass mortality." In other words, the
constant stress of overpopulation, plus the normal stress of the cold
of the winter, had kept the adrenalin flowing so constantly in the
deer that their systems were depleted of blood sugar and they died
of shock.

Well, the white humans are still skidding and darting across the   23
floor of Grand Central. Dr. Hall listens a moment longer to the skidding and the darting noises, and then says, "You know, I've been on
commuter trains here after everyone has been through one of these
rushes, and I'll tell you, there is enough acid flowing in the stomachs
in every car to dissolve the rails underneath."

Just a little invisible acid bath for the linings to round off the   24
day. The ulcers the acids cause, of course, are the one disease people
have already been taught to associate with the stress of city life. But
over-crowding, as Dr. Hall sees it, raises a lot more hell with the
body than just ulcers. In everyday life in New York—just the usual,
getting to work, working in massively congested areas like 42nd
Street between Fifth Avenue and Lexington, especially now that the
Pam-Am Building is set in there, working in cubicles such as those
in the editorial offices at Time-Life, Inc., which Dr. Hall cites as typical of New York's poor handling of space, working in cubicles with

low ceilings and, often, no access to a window, while construction crews all over Manhattan drive everybody up the Masonite wall with air-pressure generators with noises up to the boil-a-brain decibel level, than rushing to get home, piling into subways and trains, fighting for time and for space, the usual day in New York—the whole now-normal thing keeps shooting jolts of adrenalin into the body, breaking down the body's defenses and winding up with the work-a-daddy human animal stroked out at the breakfast table with his head apoplexed like a cauliflower out of his $6.95 semi-spread Pima-cotton shirt, and nosed over into a plate of No-Kolresto egg substitute, signing off with the black thrombosis, cancer, kidney, liver, or stomach failure, and the adrenals ooze to a halt, the size of eggplants in July.

One of the people whose work Dr. Hall is interested in on this   25
score is Rene Dubos at the Rockefeller Institute. Dubos's work indicates that specific organisms, such as the tuberculosis bacillus or a pneumonia virus, can seldom be considered "the cause" of a disease. The germ or virus, apparently, has to work in combination with other things that have already broken the body down in some way— such as the old adrenal hyperactivity. Dr. Hall would like to see some autopsy studies made to record the size of adrenal glands in New York, especially of people crowded into slums and people who go through the full rush-hour-work-rush-hour cycle every day. He is afraid that until there is some clinical, statistical data on how over-crowding actually ravages the human body, no one will be willing to do anything about it. Even in so obvious a thing as air pollution, the pattern is familiar. Until people can actually see the smoke or smell the sulphur or feel the sting in their eyes, politicians will not get excited about it, even though it is well known that many of the lethal substances polluting the air are invisible and odorless. For one thing, most politicians are like the aristocrat rats. They are insulated from The Sink by practically sultanic buffers—limousines, chauffeurs, secretaries, aides-de-camp, doormen, shuttered houses, high-floor apartments. They almost never ride subways, fight rush hours, much less live in the slums or work in the Pam-Am Building.

Meanings and Values

1. Who are members of the "species Mediterranean"? The "species North European"? What could account for their differences in space requirements (pars. 8–10)?

2. Is this writing primarily objective or subjective? (See "Guide to Terms": *Objective/Subjective*.) Why?

3. Do you get the impression that the author is being unkind,"making fun"of the harried New Yorkers? How, if at all, does he prevent such an impression?

Expository Techniques

1. Is this analogy a success, or does the author work it *too* hard? Be prepared to defend your answer. (Guide: *Evaluation*.)

2. What are the benefits of the frequent return to what Dr. Hall is doing or saying (e.g., in pars. 3, 5, 7, 9, 11, and 23)?

3. Paragraph 12 has a useful function beyond the simple information it provides—a sort of organic relation to the coming development. Explain how this is accomplished.

4. The preceding two questions highlight the ways Wolfe deals with problems of transition in this essay. (Guide: *Transition*.) How are such issues also matters of coherence? (Guide: *Coherence*.)

5. Analyze stylistic differences, with resulting effects, between the following sections of the essay (Guide: *Style/Tone*):

   a. the description of chaos at Grand Central and the information about Dr. Hall in paragraph 7

   b. the Grand Central scene and the account of the laboratory experiment with rats in paragraphs 8–20

   c. the Grand Central scene and the final paragraph.

6. What is gained or lost by the unusual length and design of the last sentence of paragraph 24? (We can be sure that it did not "just happen" to Wolfe—and equally sure that a sentence of such length would be disastrous in most writing.) (Guide: *Syntax*.)

Diction and Vocabulary

1. What is the significance of the word "Gotham"?

2. Why do you think the author refers to "my fellow New Yorkers" in the first sentence? What would have been the effect had he not taken such a step?

3. Why does he consistently, after paragraph 2, refer to the people as "poor white humans," "poor human animals," etc.?

4. In paragraph 14 he refers to the connotations of the word "sink." What are its possible connotations? (Guide: *Connotations/Denotation*.)

5. Cite examples of verbal irony to be found in paragraphs 5, 8, and 24.

6. Consult your dictionary as needed for full understanding of the following words: autistic, puling (par.1); etiolate (4); effluvia, sebaceous (8); pathology (14); satyrism (16); senescent (17); decibel, thrombosis (24); lethal (25).

Read to Write

1. Wolfe considers population density to be a characteristic and challenging component of modern life. In her essay "High Tide in Tucson,"(pages 225–236), Barbara Kingsolver views the contemporary habit of moving far away from our childhood and family communities as a problematic behavior. Read Kingsolver's essay and then identify the ways you think her view of contemporary behavior differs from, and is similar to, Wolfe's view. Consider exploring these differences and similarities in an essay or developing your own perspective on a challenge created by modern behaviors or living conditions. You might also make a list of animals, natural events, or plants you can use as part of an analogy explaining the behaviors you discuss.

2. One especially effective technique Wolfe employs in "O Rotten Gotham" is observation—specifically the overall view afforded by a balcony high above the main hall of Grand Central Station. Adopt a similar perspective for an essay in which you observe, report on, and attempt to explain some kind of behavior. You might choose a tall vehicle (like a truck) that allows you to observe a traffic jam even while you are part of it. You might choose a bridge, a tall building, a playground slide, a Ferris wheel, or even a tree.

3. For his expository essay, Wolfe draws on theories from researchers, including Edward Hall, John Calhoun, John Christian, and Rene Dubos. Follow Wolfe's lead and do some research of your own into human and animal behavior.

4. Popular magazines can provide good summaries of contemporary research as can specialized encyclopedias and general interest books. Choose a theory or some research you think is insightful, and use it to help explain common behaviors, perhaps some that you have observed in the manner described in question 2. Consider building your essay around two or more explanatory theories as Wolfe does in his essay.

(NOTE: Suggestions for topics requiring development by use of ANALOGY are on page 239 at the end of this section.)

BARBARA KINGSOLVER

BARBARA KINGSOLVER was born in 1955 in Annapolis, Maryland,
and raised in eastern Kentucky. She studied biology at DePauw
University (B.A., 1977) and the University of Arizona (M.S., 1981)
and worked as a scientist and scientific writer before beginning
her career as a writer of fiction and essays. Her highly acclaimed
books include novels *The Bean Trees* (1988), *Animal Dreams* (1990),
Pigs in Heaven (1993), stories *Homeland and Other Stories* (1989),
poetry *Another America* (1992), and essays *High Tide in Tucson:
Essay from Now or Never* (1996).

High Tide in Tucson

This essay, from Kingsolver's book with the same title, is built
around a surprising and imaginative analogy. It offers a different
and more optimistic perspective on modern society and behavior
than Tom Wolfe does in the preceding essay ("O Rotten Gotham"),
yet, like Wolfe, the author draws heavily on scientific research for
her explanations.

A hermit crab lives in my house. Here in the desert he's hiding out   1
from local animal ordinances, at minimum, and maybe even the
international laws of native-species transport. For sure, he's an outlaw against nature. So be it

He arrived as a stowaway two Octobers ago. I had spent a week   2
in the Bahamas, and while I was there, wishing my daughter could
see those sparkling blue bays and sandy covers, I did exactly what
she would have done: I collected shells. Spiky murexes, smooth purple moon shells, ancient-looking whelks sand-blasted by the tide—I
tucked them in the pockets of my shirt and shorts until my lumpy,
suspect hemlines gave me away, like a refugee smuggling the family fortune. When it was time to go home, I rinsed my loot in the sink
and packed it carefully into a plastic carton, then nested it deep in
my suitcase for the journey to Arizona.

I got home in the middle of the night, but couldn't wait till morn-   3
ing to show my hand. I set the carton on the coffee table for my

daughter to open. In the dark living room her face glowed, in the way of antique stories about children and treasure. With perfect delicacy she laid the shells out on the table, counting, sorting, designating scientific categories like yellow-striped pinky, Barnacle Bill's pocketbook. . . Yeek! She let loose a sudden yelp, dropped her booty, and ran to the far end of the room. The largest, knottiest whelk had begun to move around. First it extended one long red talon of a leg, tap-tap-tapping like a blind man's cane. Then came half a dozen more red legs, plus a pair of eyes on stalks, and a purple claw that snapped open and shut in a way that could not mean We come in Friendship.

Who could blame this creature? It had fallen asleep to the sound   4
of the Caribbean tide and awakened on a coffee table in Tucson, Arizona, where the nearest standing water source of any real account was the municipal sewage-treatment plant.

With red stiletto legs splayed in all directions, it lunged and   5
jerked its huge shell this way and that, reminding me of the scene I make whenever I'm moved to rearrange the living-room sofa by myself. Then, while we watched in stunned reverence, the strange beast found its bearings and began to reveal a determined, crabby grace. It felt its way to the edge of the table and eased itself over, not falling bang to the floor but hanging suspended underneath within the long grasp of its ice-tong legs, lifting any two or three at a time while many others still held in place. In this remarkable fashion it scrambled around the underside of the table's rim, swift and sure and fearless like a rock climber's dream.

If you ask me, when something extraordinary shows up in your   6
life in the middle of the night, you give it a name and make it the best home you can.

The business of naming involved a grasp of hermit-crab gender   7
that was way out of our league. But our household had a deficit of males, so my daughter and I chose Buster, for balance. We gave him a terrarium with clean gravel and a small cactus plant dug out of the yard and a big cockleshell full of tap water. All this seemed to suit him fine. To my astonishment our local pet store carried a product called Vitaminized Hermit Crab Cakes. Tempting enough (till you read the ingredients) but we passed, since our household leans more toward the recycling ethic. We give him leftovers. Buster's rapture is the day I drag the unidentifiable things in cottage cheese containers out of the back of the fridge.

We've also learned to give him a continually changing assort-   8
ment of seashells, which he tries on and casts off like Cinderella's

stepsisters preening for the ball. He'll sometimes try to squeeze into ludicrous outfits too small to contain him (who can't relate?). In other moods, he will disappear into a conch the size of my two fists and sit for a day, immobilized by the weight of upward mobility. He is in every way the perfect housemate: quiet, entertaining, and willing to eat up the trash. He went to school for first-grade show-and-tell, and was such a hit the principal called up to congratulate me (I think) for being a broad-minded mother.

It was a long time, though, before we began to understand the 9
content of Buster's character. He required more patient observation than we were in the habit of giving to a small, cold-blooded life. As months went by, we would periodically notice with great disappointment that Buster seemed to be dead. Or not entirely dead, but ill, or maybe suffering the crab equivalent of the blues. He would burrow into a gravelly corner, shrink deep into his shell, and not move, for days and days. We'd take him out to play, dunk him in water, offer him a new frock—nothing. He wanted to be still.

Life being what it is, we'd eventually quit prodding our sick 10
friend to cheer up, and would move on to the next stage of a difficult friendship: neglect. We'd ignore him wholesale, only to realize at some point later on the he'd lapsed into hyperactivity. We'd find him ceaselessly patrolling the four corners of his world, turning over rocks, rooting out and dragging around truly disgusting pork-chop bones, digging up his cactus and replanting it on its head. At night when the household fell silent I would lie in bed listening to his methodical pebbly racket from the opposite end of the house. Buster was manic-depressive.

I wondered if he might be responding to the moon. I'm partial 11
to lunar cycles, ever since I learned as a teenager that human females in their natural state—which is to say, sleeping outdoors—arrive at menses in synchrony and ovulate with the full moon. My imagination remains captive to that primordial village: the comradely grumpiness of new-moon days, when the entire world at once would go on PMS alert. And the compensation that would turn up two weeks later on a wild wind, under that great round headlamp, driving both men and women to distraction with the overt prospect of conception. The surface of the land literally rises and falls—as much as fifty centimeters!—as the moon passes over, and we clay-footed mortals fall like dominoes before the swell. It's no surprise at all if a full moon inspires lyricists to corny love songs, or inmates to slamming themselves against barred windows. A hermit crab hardly seems this impetuous, but animals are notoriously responsive to the

full moon: wolves howl; roosters announce daybreak all night. Luna moths, Arctic loons, and lunatics have a sole inspiration in common. Buster's insomniac restlessness seemed likely to be a part of the worldwide full-moon fellowship.

But it wasn't, exactly. The full moon didn't shine on either end 12 of his cycle, the high or the low. We tried to keep track, but it soon became clear: Buster marched to his own drum. The cyclic force that moved him remained as mysterious to us as his true gender and the workings of his crustacean soul.

Buster's aquarium occupies a spot on our kitchen counter right 13 next to the coffeepot, and so it became my habit to begin mornings with chin in hands, pondering the oceanic mysteries while awaiting percolation. Finally, I remembered something. Years ago when I was a graduate student of animal behavior, I passed my days reading about the likes of animals' internal clocks. Temperature, photoperiod, the rise and fall of hormones—all these influences have been teased apart like so many threads from the rope that pulls every creature to its regulated destiny. But one story takes the cake. F. A. Brown, a researcher who is more or less the grandfather of the biological clock, set about in 1954 to track the cycles of intertidal oysters. He scooped his subjects from the clammy coast of Connecticut and moved them into the basement of a laboratory in landlocked Illinois. For the first fifteen days in their new aquariums, the oysters kept right up with their normal intertidal behavior: they spent time shut away in their shells, and time with their mouths wide open, siphoning their briny bath for the plankton that sustained them, as the tides ebbed and flowed on the distant Connecticut shore. In the next two weeks, they made a mystifying shift. They still carried out their cycles in unison, and were regular as the tides, but their high-tide behavior didn't coincide with high tide in Connecticut, or for that matter California, or any other tidal charts known to science. It dawned on the researchers after some calculations that the oysters were responding to high tide in Chicago. Never mind that the gentle mollusks lived in glass boxes in the basement of a steel-and-cement building. Nor that Chicago has no ocean. In the circumstances, the oysters were doing their best.

When Buster is running around for all he's worth, I can only 14 presume it's high tide in Tucson. With or without evidence, I'm romantic enough to believe it. This is the lesson of Buster, the poetry that camps outside the halls of science: Jump for joy, hallelujah. Even a desert has tides.

When I was twenty-two, I donned the shell of a tiny yellow   15
Renault and drove with all I owned from Kentucky to Tucson. I was
a typical young American, striking out. I had no earthly notion that
I was bringing on myself a calamity of the magnitude of the one that
befell poor Buster. I am the commonest kind of North American
refugee: I believe I like it here, far-flung from my original home. I've
come to love the desert that bristles and breathes and sleeps outside
my windows. In the course of seventeen years I've embedded
myself in a family here—neighbors, colleagues, friends I can't fore-
see living without, and a child who is native to this ground, with
loves of her own. I'm here for good, it seems.

And yet I never cease to long in my bones for what I left behind.   16
I open my eyes on every new day expecting that a creek will run
through my backyard under broad-leafed maples, and that my
mother will be whistling in the kitchen. Behind the howl of coyotes,
I'm listening for meadowlarks, I sometimes ache to be rocked in the
bosom of the blood relations and busybodies of my childhood. Particularly in my years as a mother without a mate, I have deeply
missed the safety net of extended family.

In a city of half a million I still really look at every face, antici-   17
pating recognition, because I grew up in a town where every face
meant something to me. I have trouble remembering to lock the
doors. Wariness of strangers I learned the hard way. When I was new
to the city, I let a man into my house one hot afternoon because he
seemed in dire need of a drink of water; when I turned from the
kitchen sink I found sharpened steel shoved against my belly. And so
I know, I know. But I cultivate suspicion with as much difficulty as I
force tomatoes to grow in the drought-stricken hardpan of my
strange backyard. No creek runs here, but I'm still listening to secret
tides, living as if I belonged to an earlier place: not Kentucky, necessarily, but a welcoming earth and a human family. A forest. A species.

In my life I've had frightening losses and unfathomable gifts: A   18
knife in my stomach. The death of an unborn child. Sunrise in a rain
forest. A stupendous column of blue butterflies rising from a Greek
monastery. A car that spontaneously caught fire while I was driving
it. The end of a marriage, followed by a year in which I could barely
understand how to keep living. The discovery, just weeks ago when
I rose from my desk and walked into the kitchen, of three strangers
industriously relieving my house of its contents.

I persuaded the strangers to put down the things they were   19
holding (what a bizarre tableau of anti-Magi they made, these three
unwise men, bearing a camera, an electric guitar, and a Singer

sewing machine), and to leave my home, pronto. My daughter asked excitedly when she got home from school, "Mom, did you say bad words?" (I told her this was the very occasion that bad words exist for.) The police said, variously, that I was lucky, foolhardy, and "a brave lady." But it's not good luck to be invaded, and neither foolish nor brave to stand your ground. It's only the way life goes, and I did it, just as years ago I fought off the knife; mourned the lost child; bore witness to the rain forest; claimed the blue butterflies as Holy Spirit in my private pantheon; got out of the burning car; survived the divorce by putting one foot in front of the other and taking good care of my child. On most important occasions, I cannot think how to respond, I simply do. What does it mean, anyway, to be an animal in human clothing? We carry around these big brains of ours like the crown jewels, but mostly I find that millions of years of evolution have prepared me for one thing only: to follow internal rhythms. To walk upright, to protect my loved ones, to cooperate with my family group—however broadly I care to define it—to do whatever will help us thrive. Obviously, some habits that saw us through the millennia are proving hazardous in a modern context: for example, the yen to consume carbohydrates and fat whenever they cross our path, or the proclivity for unchecked reproduction. But it's surely worth forgiving ourselves these tendencies a little, in light of the fact that they are what got us here. Like Buster, we are creatures of inexplicable cravings. Thinking isn't everything. The way I stock my refrigerator would amuse a level-headed interplanetary observer, who would see I'm responding not to real necessity but to the dread of famine honed in the African savannah. I can laugh at my Rhodesian Ridgeback as she furtively sniffs the houseplants for a place to bury bones, and circles to beat down the grass before lying on my kitchen floor. But she and I are exactly the same kind of hairpin.

　　We humans have to grant the presence of some past adapta-　20 tions, even in their unforgivable extremes, if only to admit they are permanent rocks in the steam we're obliged to navigate. It's easy to speculate and hard to prove, ever, that genes control our behaviors. Yet we are persistently, excruciatingly adept at many things that seem no more useful to modern life than the tracking of tides in a desert. At recognizing insider/outsider status, for example, starting with white vs. black and grading straight into distinctions so fine as to baffle the bystander—Serb and Bosnian, Hutu and Tutsi, Crip and Blood. We hold that children learn discrimination from their parents, but they learn if fiercely and well, world without end. Recite it by rote like a multiplication table. Take it to heart, though it's neither helpful nor appropriate, anymore than it is to hire the taller of two men applying for a position as bank clerk, though statistically we're likely to do that too. Deference to the physical superlative, a preference for the scent of our own clan: a thousand anachronisms dance down the strands of our DNA from a hidebound tribal past, guiding us toward the glories of survival, and some vainglories as well. If we resent being bound by these ropes, the best hope is to seize them out like snakes, by the throat, look them in the eye and own up to their venom.

But we rarely do, silly egghead of a species that we are. We   21
invent the most outlandish intellectual grounds to justify discrimination. We tap our toes to chaste love songs about the silvery moon without recognizing them as hymns to copulation. We can dress up our drives, put them in three-piece suits or ballet slippers, but still they drive us. The wonder of it is that our culture attaches almost unequivocal shame to our animal nature, believing brute urges must be hurtful, violent things. But it's no less an animal instinct that leads us to marry (species that benefit from monogamy tend to practice it); to organize a neighborhood cleanup campaign (rare and doomed is the creature that fouls its nest); to improvise and enforce morality (many primates socialize their young to be cooperative and ostracize adults who won't share food).

It's starting to look as if the most shameful tradition of Western   22
civilization is our need to deny we are animals. In just a few centuries of setting ourselves apart as landlords of the Garden of Eden, exempt from the natural order and entitled to hold dominion, we have managed to behave like so-called animals anyway, and on top of it to wreck most of what took three billion years to assemble. Air, water, earth, and fire—so much of our own element so vastly contaminated, we endanger our own future. Apparently we never owned the place after all. Like every other animal, we're locked into our niche: the mercury in the ocean, the pesticides on the soybean fields, all comes home to our breastfed babies. In the silent spring we are learning it's easier to escape from a chain gang than a food chain. Possibly we will have the sense to begin a new century by renewing our membership in the Animal Kingdom.

Not long ago I went backpacking in the Eagle Tail Mountains.   23
This range is a trackless wilderness in western Arizona that most people would call Godforsaken, taking for granted God's preference

for loamy topsoil and regular precipitation. Whoever created the Eagle Tails had dry heat on the agenda, and a thing for volcanic rock. Also cactus, twisted mesquites, and five-alarm sunsets. The hiker's program in a desert like this is dire and blunt: carry in enough water to keep you alive till you can find a water source: then fill your bottles and head for the next one, or straight back out. Experts warn adventurers in this region, without irony, to drink their water while they're still alive, as it won't help later.

Several canyons looked promising for springs on our topo-   24
graphical map, but turned up dry. Finally, at the top of a narrow, overgrown gorge we found a blessed tinaja, a deep, shaded hollow in the rock about the size of four or five claw-foot tubs, holding water. After we drank our fill, my friends struck out again, but I opted to stay and spend the day in the hospitable place that had slaked our thirst. On either side of the natural water tank, two shallow caves in the canyon wall faced each other, only a few dozen steps apart. By crossing from one to the other at noon, a person could spend the whole day here in shady comfort—or in colder weather, follow the winter sun. Anticipating a morning of reading, I pulled *Angle of Repose* out of my pack and looked for a place to settle on the flat, dusty floor of the west-facing shelter. Instead, my eyes were startled by a smooth corn-grinding stone. It sat in the exact center of its rock bowl, as if the Hohokam woman or man who used this mortar and pestle had walked off and left them there an hour ago. The Hohokam disappeared from the earth in A.D. 1450. It was inconceivable to me that no one had been here since then, but that may have been the case—that is the point of trackless wilderness. I picked up the grinding stone. The size and weight and smooth, balanced perfection of it in my hand filled me at once with a longing to possess it. In its time, this excellent stone was the most treasured thing in a life, a family, maybe the whole neighborhood. To whom it still belonged. I replaced it in the rock depression, which also felt smooth to my touch. Because my eyes now understood how to look at it, the ground under my feet came alive with worked flint chips and pottery shards. I walked across to the other cave and found its floor just as lively with historic debris. Hidden under brittlebush and catclaw I found another grinding stone, this one some distance from the depression in the cave floor that once answered its pressure daily, for the grinding of corn or mesquite beans.

For a whole day I marveled at this place, running my fingers 25
over the knife edges of dark flint chips, trying to fit together thick
red pieces of shattered clay jars, biting my lower lip like a child con-
centrating on a puzzle. I tried to guess the size of whole pots from
the curve of the broken pieces: some seemed as small as my two
cupped hands, and some maybe as big as a bucket. The sun scorched
my neck, reminding me to follow the shade across to the other shelter. Bees hummed at the edge of the water hole, nosing up to the
water, their abdomens pulsing like tiny hydraulic pumps; by late
afternoon they rimmed the pool completely, a collar of busy lace. Off
and on, the lazy hand of a hot breeze shuffled the white leaves of the
brittlebush. Once I looked up to see a screaming pair of red-tailed
hawks mating in midair, and once a clatter of hooves warned me to
hold still. A bighorn ram emerged through the brush, his head bent
low under his hefty cornice, and ambled by me with nothing on his
mind so much as a cool drink.

How long can a pestle stone lie still in the center of its mortar? 26
That long ago—that recently—people lived here. *Here,* exactly, and
not one valley over, or two, or twelve, because this place had all a
person needs: shelter, food, and permanent water. They organized
their lives around a catchment basin in a granite boulder, conform-
ing their desires to the earth's charities; they never expected the
opposite. The stories I grew up with lauded Moses for striking the
rock and bringing forth the bubbling stream. But the stories of the
Hohokam—oh, how they must have praised that good rock.

At dusk my friends returned with wonderful tales of the 27
ground they had covered. We camped for the night, refilled our can-
teens, and hiked back to the land of plumbing and a fair guarantee
of longevity. But I treasure my memory of the day I lingered near
water and covered no ground. I can't think of a day in my life in
which I've had such a clear fix on what it means to be human.

Want is a thing that unfurls unbidden like fungus, opening large 28
upon itself, stopless, filling the sky. But *needs,* from one day to the
next, are few enough to fit in a bucket, with room enough left to rattle like brittlebush in a dry wind.

For each of us—furred, feathered, or skinned alive—the whole 29
earth balances on the single precarious point of our own survival. In
the best of times, I hold in mind the need to care for things beyond
the self: poetry, humanity, grace. In other times, when it seems difficult merely to survive and be happy about it, the condition of my

thought tastes as simple as this: let me be a good animal today. I've spent months at a stretch, even years, with that taste in my mouth, and have found that it serves.

But it seems a wide gulf to cross, from the raw, green passion for   30
survival to the dispassionate, considered state of human grace. How does the animal mind construct a poetry for the modern artifice in which we now reside? Often I feel as disoriented as poor Buster, unprepared for the life that zooms headlong past my line of sight. This clutter of human paraphernalia and counterfeit necessities—what does it have to do with the genuine business of life on earth? It feels strange to me to be living in a box, hiding from the steadying influence of the moon; wearing the hide of a cow, which is supposed to be dyed to match God-knows-what, on my feet; making promises over the telephone about things I will do at a precise hour next *year*. (I always feel the urge to add, as my grandmother does, "Lord willing and the creeks don't rise!") I find it impossible to think, with a straight face, about what colors ought not to be worn after Labor Day. I can become hysterical over the fact that someone, somewhere, invented a thing called the mushroom scrubber, and that many other people undoubtedly feel they *need* to possess one. It's completely usual for me to get up in the morning, take a look around, and laugh out loud.

Strangest of all, I am carrying on with all of this in a desert, two   31
thousand miles from my verdant childhood home. I am disembodied. No one here remembers how I was before I grew to my present height. I'm called upon to reinvent my own childhood time and again; in the process, I wonder how I can ever know the truth about who I am. If someone had told me what I was headed for in that little Renault—that I was stowing away in a shell, bound to wake up to an alien life on a persistently foreign shore—I surely would not have done it. But no one warned me. My culture, as I understand it, values independence above all things—in part to ensure a mobile labor force, grease for the machine of a capitalist economy. Our fairy table commands: Little Pig, go out and seek your fortune! So I did.

Many years ago I read that the Tohono O'odham, who dwell in   32
the deserts near here, traditionally bury the umbilicus of a newborn son or daughter somewhere close to home and plant a tree over it, to hold the child in place. In a sentimental frame of mind, I did the same when my own baby's cord fell off. I'm staring at the tree right now, as I write—a lovely thing grown huge outside my window, home to woodpeckers, its boughs overarching the house, as dissimilar from the sapling I planted seven years ago as my present life is

from the tidy future I'd mapped out for us all when my baby was born. She will roam light-years from the base of that tree. I have no doubt of it. I can only hope she's growing as the tree is, absorbing strength and rhythms and a trust in the seasons, so she will always be able to listen for home.

I feel remorse about Buster's monumental relocation; it's a   33
weighty responsibility to have thrown someone else's life into permanent chaos. But as for my own, I can't be sorry I made the trip. Most of what I learned in the old place seems to suffice for the new: if the seasons like Chicago tides come at ridiculous times and I have to plant in September instead of May, and if I have to make up family from scratch, what matters is that I do have sisters and tomato plants, the essential things. Like Buster, I'm inclined to see the material backdrop of my life as mostly immaterial, compared with what moves inside of me. I hold on to my adopted shore, chanting private vows: wherever I am, let me never forget to distinguish *want* from *need*. Let me be a good animal today. Let me dance in the waves of my private tide, the habits of survival and love.

Every one of us is called upon, probably many times, to start a   34
new life. A frightening diagnosis, a marriage, a move, loss of a job or a limb or a loved one, a graduation, bringing a new baby home: it's impossible to think at first how this all will be possible. Eventually, what moves it all forward is the subterranean ebb and flow of being alive among the living.

In my own worst seasons I've come back from the colorless   35
world of despair by forcing myself to look hard, for a long time, at a single glorious thing: a flame of red geranium outside my bedroom window. And then another: my daughter in a yellow dress. And another: the perfect outline of a full, dark sphere behind the crescent moon. Until I learned to be in love with my life again. Like a stroke victim retraining new parts of the brain to grasp lost skills, I have taught myself joy, over and over again.

It's not such a wide gulf to cross, then, from survival to poetry.   36
We hold fast to the old passions of endurance that buckle and creak beneath us, dovetailed, tight as a good wooden boat to carry us onward. And onward full tilt we go, pitched and wrecked and absurdly resolute, driven in spite of everything to make good on a new shore. To be hopeful, to embrace one possibility after another— that is surely the basic instinct. Baser even than hate, the thing with teeth, which can be stilled with a tone of voice or stunned by beauty. If the whole world of the living has to turn on the single point of

remaining alive, that pointed endurance is the poetry of hope. The thing with feathers.

What a stroke of luck. What a singular brute feat of outrageous   37 fortune: to be born to citizenship in the Animal Kingdom. We love and we lose, go back to the start and do it right over again. For every heavy forebrain solemnly cataloging the facts of a harsh landscape, there's a rush of intuition behind it crying out: High tide! Time to move out into the glorious debris. Time to take this life for what it is.

Meanings and Values

1. In paragraph 22, Kingsolver says, "It's starting to look as if the most shameful tradition of Western civilization is our need to deny we are animals." In what ways, according to the essay, are we like other animals?

2. What are the superficial ways Buster resembles humans (see pars. 5, 8, 9, and 10)? What are the important (even profound) similarities (see pars. 11, 12, 15, 19, 30, and 33)?

3. Paragraphs 15–19 of this essay are devoted to some of the disruptions and problems created by contemporary ways of living. What answers or responses to these problems does the writer offer in paragraph 19? How do the problems and the responses help unify the essay? (See "Guide to Terms": *Unity*.)

Expository Techniques

1. At what point in the essay does Kingsolver first make an analogy between the hermit crab and herself?

2. For what purposes does the author raise, and then dismiss, the comparison of hermit crab behaviors and those of humans and other animals in terms of their correspondence to cycles of the moon? (In answering this question, consider both the scientific reasons and those related to the purpose and design of her essay.)

3. The writer divides this essay into four parts (pars. 1–14, 15–22, 23–28, and 29–37). Explain the content and purpose of each part, and tell why you think she chose to put them in this particular order. (Guide: *Purpose*.)

4. Discuss how the contrast between "wants" and "needs" at the end of paragraph 28 serves as a transition to the next paragraph and those that follow. (Guide: *Transition*.)

5. Discuss how the question "What does it mean, anyway, to be an animal in human clothing?" (par. 19) acts as a transition both within the paragraph and within the essay as a whole. (Guide: *Transition*.) Can

the passage be considered a rhetorical question? Why? (Guide: *Rhetorical Questions.*)

6. Kingsolver introduces some briefer analogies in paragraphs 32 and 36. What are they? Do they undermine or add to the effectiveness of the larger analogy around which the essay is constructed? In what ways? (Guide: *Evaluation.*)

Diction and Vocabulary

1. Discuss how the repetition of the word "tide" and related words helps to unify this essay. (Guide: *Unity.*)

2. In many places, Kingsolver mixes styles and kinds of vocabulary (diction) in imaginative ways. Examine paragraph 11 and note the instances in which she has chosen scientific terms and phrases rather than familiar, less formal wording. What seems to be the reason for her word choices. Do the same for instances of notably informal language. (Guide: *Diction; Colloquial Expressions.*) What effect does the mixed diction in the paragraph have on its overall style and tone? (Guide: *Style/Tone.*) How does the mixture serve, or fail to serve, the author's purposes?

3. If you do not know the meaning of any of the following words, look them up in a dictionary: murexes, whelks, (par. 2); deficit, terrarium, cockleshell (7); preening, ludicrous (8); hyperactivity (10); menses, synchrony, ovulate, lyricists, impetuous (11); crustacean (12); siphoning, briny, ebbed (13); tableau, pantheon, yen, proclivity, furtively (19); deference, anachronisms, vainglories (20); copulation, ostracize (21); topographical (24); lauded (26); longevity (27); dispassionate (30); verdant (31); umbilicus (32).

Read to Write

1. The following questions may help you discover topics for an expository essay: What behaviors, other than those discussed in "High Tide in Tucson," do you think are "natural" for humans? Are other people likely to agree, or would they point to social or cultural causes for the behaviors? Can you think of any animal behaviors that are similar and that suggest that the traits are inborn?

2. "High Tide in Tucson" begins with the story of a souvenir the writer brought back from vacation. By focusing on a souvenir or another object, you can introduce readers in an indirect or personal way to ideas and experiences you wish to discuss. Use this strategy to begin an expository essay of your own.

3. Comparing your behavior to that of a pet, as Kingsolver does, can have several advantages for you as a writer. You have probably observed a pet's behavior in detail over a long period of time—more

carefully than you have observed the activities of any other animal. You have seen the pet react to the same or similar situations that you have encountered. Follow Kingsolver's lead and prepare an essay on human and animal behavior based on your experiences with a pet.

(NOTE: Suggestions for topics requiring development by use of ANALOGY follow.)

Writing Suggestions for Section 6
Analogy

In any normal situation, the analogy is chosen to help explain a theme-idea that already exists—such as those in the first group below. But for classroom training, which is bound to be somewhat artificial, it is permissible to work from the other direction, to develop a theme that fits a preselected analogy-symbol.

1. State a central theme about one of the following general topics or a suitable one of your own, and develop it into a composition by use of an analogy of your own choosing.

   a. A well-organized school system.

   b. Starting a new business or other enterprise.

   c. The long-range value of programs for underprivileged children.

   d. Learning a new skill.

   e. The need for cooperation between management and labor.

   f. Today's intense competition for success.

   g. Dealing with stress.

   h. The results of ignorance.

2. Select an analogy-symbol from the list below and fashion a theme that it can illustrate. Develop your composition as instructed.

   a. A freeway at commuting time.

   b. Building a road through a wilderness.

   c. Building a bridge across a river.

   d. A merry-go-round.

   e. A wedding or a divorce.

   f. A car wash.

   g. Flood destruction of a levee.

   h. The tending of a young orchard.

   i. An animal predator stalking prey.

   j. A baseball game.

   k. A juggling act.

   l. An oasis.

   m. A duel.

   n. An airport.

239

7

Explaining Through *Process Analysis*

Process analysis explains how the steps of an operation lead to its completion. Although in one narrow sense it may be considered a kind of narration, process analysis has an important difference in purpose, and hence in approach. Other narration is mostly concerned with the story itself, or with a general concept illustrated by it, but process tells of methods that end in specified results. We might narrate a story about a rifle—its purchase, its role in colorful episodes, perhaps its eventual retirement from active service. (We could, for other purposes, *define* "rifle," or *classify* the types of rifles, and no doubt *compare* and *contrast* these types and *illustrate* by examples.) But showing how a rifle works, or how it is manufactured, or how it should be cared for—this is process, and it sometimes becomes the basic pattern of an exposition.

Most writers are especially concerned with two kinds of process, both of them apparent in the preceding example of rifles: the directional, which explains how to *do* something (how to shoot a gun or how to clean it); and the informational, which explains how something is or was *done* (how guns are manufactured). The directional process can range from the instructions on a shampoo bottle to a detailed plan showing how to make the United Nations more effective, and will often contain detailed justification for individual steps or for the process itself. The informational process, on the other hand, might explain the steps of a wide variety of operations or actions, of mental or evolutionary processes, with no how-to-do-it purpose at all—how someone went about choosing a college or how the planet Earth was formed. Informational process analysis has been seen in earlier selections: Staples explained how he keeps from frightening other people when he takes his evening walks, and Wolfe explained how the experiment with Norway rats was conducted.

Most process analyses are organized into simple, chronological steps. Indeed, the exact order is sometimes of greatest importance, as in a recipe. But occasionally there are problems in organization. The step-by-step format may need to be interrupted for descriptions, definitions, and other explanatory asides. If the process is a proposed solution, part of a problem-solution argument, then it may be necessary to justify each of the steps in turn and dismiss alternatives. And, still more of a problem, some processes defy a strict chronological treatment, because several things occur simultaneously. To explain the operating process of a gasoline engine, for example, the writer would be unable to convey at once everything that happens at the same time. Some way must be found to present the material in *general* stages, organized as subdivisions, so that the reader can see the step-by-step process through the confusion of interacting relationships.

Another difficulty in explaining by process analysis is estimating what knowledge the reader may already have. Presuming too little background may quickly lead to boredom or even irritation, with a resulting communication block; presuming too much will almost certainly leave the reader bewildered. Like a chain dependent on its weakest link for its strength, the entire process analysis can fail because of one unclear point that makes the rest incomprehensible.

Sample Paragraph (Annotated)

Process to be
analyzed.

Palmville has an unusual form of city government, at least compared with other cities in the state. Instead of an elected mayor, it has an appointed city manager responsible for all city operations and employees. This

Background on the
process.

arrangement is by no means unusual, yet Palmville also has no city council or board of supervisors. Instead, it has a Board of Proposers and a Town Meeting. How, then, are laws passed,

Reason for process
analysis.

budgets approved, and appointments made? Members of the Board of Proposers draw up proposals for new

Beginning of *informational* process. How the unusual procedure works. Begins chronologically then covers some of the key features of the process.

{ laws, regulations, hiring, and budgets, but they do not vote on the proposals. They send the proposals to the Town Meeting for a vote. Town Meetings are scheduled four times a year in the auditorium of the Civic Center. Only people who come to the meeting are eligible to vote on the proposals; they must be registered voters who live within the city limits. Upcoming Town Meetings are publicized through the local media. The system worked well when Palmville was a small town and there was little business to be done.

Problems and need for change in future.

{ Now the meetings last 8–10 hours; even so, important business often ends up being postponed until the next meeting. Although most Palmville residents enjoy the direct participation in government that the system allows, they have also begun to recognize the need for change.

Sample Paragraph (Process Analysis)

It's not the wind, though, that's the most dangerous part of a hurricane. It's the water, especially when something called the "storm surge" occurs. As the low-pressure eye of the hurricane sits over the ocean, the sea level literally rises into a dome of water. For every inch drop in barometric pressure, the ocean rises a foot higher. Now, out at sea, that means nothing. The rise is not even noticeable. But when that mound of water starts moving toward land, the situation becomes crucial. As the water approaches a shallow beach, the dome of water rises. It may rise ten to fifteen

feet in an hour and span fifty miles. Like
a marine bulldozer, the surge may rise
up twenty feet high, crash onto land,
and wash everything away. Then with
six- to eight-foot waves riding atop this
mound of water, the storm surge
destroys buildings, trees, cars, and
anything else in its path. It's this storm
surge that accounts for 90 percent of the
deaths during a hurricane.

JOE BUHLER, a professor of mathematics at Reed College, has published many scholarly articles as well as essays for more general audiences. Among the latter are essays on science, juggling, and the game Go. RON GRAHAM is associated with Bell Labs in Murray Hill, New Jersey, and has had a distinguished career as a mathematician. He has published many articles in his field of research and his work has been honored with membership in the National Academy of Sciences. He is a past president of the International Juggler's Association.

Give Juggling a Hand!

This instructional essay, a particularly compact explanation of an intriguing activity, was first published in *The Sciences*. It reflects the authors' enjoyment of juggling as well as their expertise. By providing some historical background, clear directions, and interesting explanations, the writers make the activity seem as enjoyable to readers as it is to them.

Nothing could be simpler than a game of catch. But just add another   1
ball or two and the game turns magical—the juggled balls take on a
life of their own. Suddenly, simple motions and common objects
blur into one stunning display after another.

In recent years, juggling has experienced a renaissance. Street   2
performers and skilled amateurs are practicing the ancient art in
parks, back yards, and on campuses around the globe. Membership
in the largely amateur International Jugglers' Association (IJA) has
more than doubled since 1979.

Juggling is actually 4000 years young. In Egypt, Asia, and the   3
Americas, it was once associated with religious ritual. In medieval
Europe, wandering minstrels often juggled; the term derives from
these *jongleurs*.

"Give Juggling a Hand" by Joe Buhler and Ron Graham from *The Sciences*, January/ February 1984. Reprinted by permission of THE SCIENCES. Individual Subscriptions are $21 per year in the U.S. Write to: The Sciences, 2 East 63rd Street, New York, NY 10021.

Amazing jugglers imported from the Orient—in particular the   4
"East Indian" Ramo Samee, who was said to string beads in his
mouth while turning rings with his fingers and toes, and the Japanese artist Takashima, who manipulated a cotton ball with a stick
held in his teeth—convinced 19th-century Europeans that juggling
could be extraordinary show business.

Perhaps the greatest juggler of all time was variety-show virtu-   5
oso Enrico Rastelli. By his death in 1931, he had taught himself to
juggle eight clubs, eight plates or ten balls; he could even bounce
three balls continuously on his head.

Most people assume that a skilled juggler can manage up to 20   6
objects. In fact, even five-ball juggling is very difficult and requires
about a year to master. Only a few jugglers worldwide have per-
fected seven-ball routines. At the 1986 IJA competition, one entrant
separately juggled nine rings, eight balls, and seven clubs.

Jugglers use a bewildering variety of objects, including bowling   7
balls, whips, plastic swimming pools, cube puzzles, fruit, flaming
torches, and playing cards. Performers trying for the largest number
of objects usually choose rings, which allow a tighter traffic pattern
and are stable when thrown to great heights. Several jugglers can
manage ten or 11 rings, and some are trying for 12 or 13.

Clubs are the most visually pleasing objects to juggle. They're   8
especially suited for passing back and forth between performers.
Because they take up a lot of space when they rotate and must be
caught at one end, juggling even five is tricky. Almost nobody can
manage seven, even for a few seconds.

Throughout history, all jugglers—from South Sea Islanders to   9
Aztec Indians—have used the same fundamental patterns:

The Cascade. Here, each ball travels from one hand to the other   10
and back again, following a looping path that looks like a figure
eight lying on its side. The juggler starts with two balls in his right
hand, using a scooping motion and releasing a ball when his throwing hand is level with his navel. As the first ball reaches its highest
point, the other hand scoops and releases a second ball, and as that
one reaches *its* apogee, he throws the third. Skilled jugglers can keep
three, five, or even seven balls going in a cascade, but never four or
six. With an even number, balls collide at the intersection of the figure eight.

The Shower. In this more difficult pattern, the balls follow a cir-   11
cular path as they are thrown upward by the right hand, caught by
the left and quickly passed back to the right. Since the right does all

the long-distance throwing, the shower is inherently asymmetrical and, therefore, inefficient; it is difficult with more than three objects.

The Fountain. This figure allows for a large number of balls. In a four-ball fountain, each hand juggles two balls independently in a circular motion. For symmetry, the number of balls is usually even. If the hands throw alternately and the two patterns interlock, it is surprisingly hard to discern that the fountain is made of two separate components and not one.   12

Because gravity causes objects to accelerate as they fall, a juggler has only a short time to catch and throw one ball before another drops into his hand—even if he throws high. A juggler who throws a ball eight feet in the air, for example, must catch it 1.4 seconds later, but throwing it four times that high only doubles the flight time.   13

The best way to understand juggling is to learn to do it yourself. Some people get the hang of the three-ball cascade in minutes, although most need at least a few days. Limit your sessions to ten minutes rather than frustrate yourself with a two-hour binge.   14

Step 1: One Ball. Practice throwing a ball from your right hand to your left and back, letting the ball rise to just above your head. Make the ball follow the path of a figure eight lying on its side, by "scooping" the ball and releasing it near the navel. Catch the ball at the side of your body, then repeat the sequence.   15

Step 2: Two Balls. Put one in each hand. Throw the ball in the left hand as in Step 1, and then, just as the ball passes its high point, throw the right-hand ball. Avoid releasing the second throw too early or tossing the balls to unequal heights.   16

At first it may be difficult to catch the balls. Don't worry. Focus instead on the accuracy and height of the throws. Catching will come naturally as soon as the throws are on target. If things seem hectic, try higher throws.   17

Step 3: Two Balls Reversed. Reverse the order of throws so that the sequence is right, then left.   18

Step 4: Three Balls. Now put two balls in your right hand and one in your left. Try to complete Step 2 while simply holding the extra ball. Pause, then do Step 3.   19

The third ball can make it difficult to catch the second throw. To solve this, throw the third ball just after the second reaches its high point. The sequence is thus right, left, right. At first it may be tough to persuade your right hand to make its second throw. Remember: catches are irrelevant in the beginning. Throw high,   20 accurately and slowly. Don't rush the tempo, and don't forget the figure-eight pattern.

Once you've mastered the three-ball cascade you'll want to try other patterns. A juggler is never finished: there is always one more ball.   21

Meanings and Values

1. Are readers in general likely to find the topic of this essay interesting? Why or why not? How do the authors encourage readers to consider juggling an amusing or worthwhile activity? Are these reasons presented directly or indirectly?

2. People often think juggling is difficult because it *looks* difficult. What do the writers say about the process to convince readers that they can master it?

3. What purposes are served by the historical background in paragraphs 3, 4, and 5? (See "Guide to Terms": *Purpose*.)

Expository Techniques

1. What technique do Buhler and Graham use to begin the essay? To conclude it? What makes these techniques successful (or unsuccessful) in this particular essay? (Guide: *Introductions; Closings*.)

2. Why do the authors describe different juggling patterns before they provide specific advice on beginning to juggle? Would the selection be more effective or less effective if the order were reversed? (Guide: *Evaluation*.)

3. Which expository patterns, other than process analysis, do the authors use to make juggling readily understandable and to help readers believe that they can master it?

Diction and Vocabulary

1. Tell how the diction and vocabulary choices in paragraphs 10–12 help make juggling seem simple. (Guide: *Diction*.)

2. How does the diction in paragraphs 14–20 contribute to the message that getting started with juggling is not as difficult as most readers might think?

3. If you do not know the meaning of some of the following terms, look them up in a dictionary: renaissance (par 2); virtuoso (5); cascade (10).

Read to Write

1. Physical activities can be difficult or challenging, but so can mental, social, or artistic activities. Think of activities you undertake with some success that others might find difficult, and list as many as you can. From the list, choose several that you are interested in writing about. Note which ones you might be able to explain in ways that will intrigue readers and teach them something useful. Choose one as the topic for an essay.

2. Near the beginning of their essay, Buhler and Graham offer historical background on the activity they are explaining. Do the same thing in an essay of your own. You may have to do some research to find appropriate information.

3. Many sports and hobbies can seem difficult or mystifying. Drawing on Buhler and Graham's essay as a model, create a set of instructions to simplify a seemingly challenging, dangerous, or mysterious sport or activity. Make the activity interesting and encourage readers to try it.

(NOTE: Suggestions for topics requiring developing by use of PROCESS ANALYSIS are on page 292 at the end of this section.)

ANN FARADAY studied at University College in London, where she received her Ph.D. in psychology. After additional research and training in the analysis of dreams, she developed her own method of interpretation. Much of her time is now spent lecturing on this approach to understanding dreams and on conducting research. She is the author of two books on analyzing and understanding dreams: *Dream Power* (1972) and *The Dream Game* (1974).

Unmasking Your Dream Images

Finding the right or best way to interpret dreams has been a concern of psychologists and other people for many years. In this excerpt from *The Dream Game*, Faraday uses process analysis along with examples to explain her approach.

There would not *be* a dream from the unconscious except as the person is confronting some issue in his conscious life—some conflict, anxiety, bafflement, fork in the road, puzzle or situation of compelling curiosity. That is, the incentive for dreaming—what cues off my particular dream on a particular night—is my need to "make something" of the world I am living in at the moment.

—Rollo May

[If you wish to understand and use your dreams, you can begin by 2 writing] down at least a few recent dreams along with notes of their *themes* (falling, being chased, meeting famous people, or whatever). . . . If you are able to relate your dreams to the events or thoughts of the day—without which any dream interpretation is incomplete—then several of your dreams should be clear to you. The majority of dreams, however, depict strange and even weird images and characters and usually do require further work before their meanings emerge. To tie the events and thoughts of the day to these dreams is particularly important because there are always several possible interpretations of each dream symbol, and only you can find the "correct" interpretation by relating it to something that was on your mind or in your heart as you fell asleep.

In deciding whether a dream image should be understood liter- 3 ally or symbolically, the rules are:

1. If the dream character—human, animal, vegetable, or min- 4 eral—is a *real* person or thing in your life or on your mind at the time of the dream, then it should be considered literally in the first instance and taken symbolically when and only when a literal interpretation makes no sense. (Even Jung, the archexponent of elaborate dream symbolism, was insistent that dreams of a husband, wife, child, neighbor, colleague, the dog, and anyone with whom we are in intimate contact at the time of the dream almost always refer to the individuals themselves rather than to anything more subtle.) I know from my own experience that it is a mistake to interpret a dream of your car failing as a symbol of failing *drive* in yourself until you have checked the car, since the dream may well be throwing up subliminal perceptions of something wrong with the engine which you have been too busy to notice during the course of the day.

2. If a dream character or image cannot be taken literally as a 5 real person or thing in your life, then it symbolizes either someone or something in your external life, or a part of your own personality which your heart is bringing to your attention. (Jung referred to the former as an *objective* interpretation, and to the latter as a *subjective* interpretation.)

In looking for the meaning of any symbolic dream image, 6 always check first to discover whether or not it symbolizes someone or something external to yourself at the time of the dream, for we dream about the world outside us just as much as we dream of our private inner world. For example, if you dream of Vincent Price, and the real Vincent Price does not figure personally in your life at the moment, then look around to see if anyone else would fit the name. Is there perhaps a Mr. or Mrs. Price or a Vincent in your present life to whom the dream could refer? If not, then you must ask yourself what Vincent Price means to you. It could be something like costliness (a pun on his name) or showmanship (an association based on his qualities), or whatever else he may mean to you personally. Is there someone in your present life—husband, wife, colleague, neighbor, and so on—who has behaved in an extravagant (or showy or entertaining) way during the previous day or two? If there is, then your dream is probably expressing concern about your relationship with this particular person.

If you can think of no such person, then you have to consider   7
the possibility that Vincent Price might be a part of yourself—which
is nice if you admire him, and not so good if you dislike him! Have
you behaved extravagantly or shown off during the past day or two?
Always remember that the dream exaggerates in order to bring its
point home to you; if you dream of a fascist and it turns out to represent part of your own personality, don't get too upset, for the
dream is merely saying that you *feel* you behaved a bit like a fascist
in the recent past, which may mean no more than some unpleasant
thought about your Jewish neighbor or a dictatorial attitude toward
your teenage son. If you continually dream of fascists and there are
none in your life, either literally or figuratively, then it is probably
fair to say that you have an inner conflict about this subject—but
once again, you must remember that the dream merely reflects *your
feeling* about yourself and your behavior, and your friends may not
see you in this light at all. As Erich Fromm writes in his book *The
Forgotten Language,* "Dreams are like a microscope through which
we look at the hidden occurrences in our soul."

    . . . I shall take several dreams from my collection to demon-   8
strate in a practical way the various techniques you can use to discover the identities of your dream characters and images. I have
chosen these few examples from thousands of dreams in order to
stress what I consider the most important points in dream interpretation, but they cannot be more than guidelines at this point in the
dream game. . . . I cannot interpret your dreams: you must do it for
yourself; my aim is to help you make a start. Even after applying all
the rules and suggestions given in this [essay], you will almost certainly find that some dreams still elude you. Don't worry about this
too much; it happens to all of us. But do continue to write down your
dreams, together with the events and thoughts of the day, for many
of them may become clearer to you as you get to know the meanings
of certain recurring symbols over a series of dreams. Very often you
will find that a certain elusive symbol in one dream reveals its meaning quite openly in another dream. When this starts happening, you
are ready to complete your dream glossary. . . .

    The other principles to be borne in mind at this stage in the   9
dream game are [as follows]:

    3. Even though dreams may take us back to childhood or con-   10
cern themselves with future possibilities, they are always triggered
by something on our minds or in our hearts at the time of the dream.
People or things that were once very intimate parts of our lives—

parents, siblings, childhood home, or friends—cannot be taken literally in our dreams if we are no longer directly involved with them. A dream does not indulge in reminiscence for its own sake. Such characters and images appear in our dreams either because they represent the voices of the past which still live on in us and influence our present behavior, or to tell us that something in our present situation reminds us of a similar situation in the past.

4. The feeling tone of a dream is always important and some-   11
times gives the clue to the meaning of a dream symbol. For example, if I dream of a dog passing me in the street wagging its tail and feel very dejected in the dream because it does not respond to my friendly call, the clue to the dream's meaning may come in remembering how upset I was at my husband's behavior the previous evening at a "cocktail" party—and my dream could be reflecting my heart's thought that he was so concerned with playing the "gay dog" that he failed to pay me any attention.

5. If you happen to know from reading books that some partic-   12
ular symbol occurs commonly in people's dreams and has been stated by experts to have a universal meaning, by all means take this as a *suggestion* of what the symbol *might* mean if it occurs in your own dream, for our dreams pick up and utilize symbols from anywhere in order to make their point. Never assume that it must have this particular meaning, however, for there might be other more personal associations that are more important to you which actually determine how your dreaming mind uses this particular symbol. Since the majority of people in the West were brought up in a house, for example, a dream house is likely to mean "living space"—a symbol of your personality itself—but even this symbol can have different meanings in different circumstances. Always check what the symbol means to you—and always check on a possible literal meaning in the first instance.

6. If the same dream image or character recurs frequently in   13
your dreams, then it is likely to have a similar meaning throughout a series of dreams, and for this reason it is helpful to compile a dream glossary of your own recurring symbols. You should not be surprised to discover, however, that on occasion this particular symbol has a different meaning, and can sometimes be merely part of the background with no great significance. Any symbol is influenced to a great extent by the symbols it is grouped with in any one dream, and we should always see it in the context of the dream as a whole.

7. Dreams do not come to tell us what we already know about   14
the people in our lives or about ourselves, so if at first sight a dream
seems to be doing no more than this, look deeper. At the very least,
it may be clarifying the thoughts of the heart by putting them in
vivid picture language or urging us to do something about a long-
standing problem—but the dream may have an altogether deeper
meaning which we can discover by looking again at its symbols.

8. A dream symbol is correctly interpreted when and only when   15
it makes sense to the dreamer in terms of his present life situation
and moves him to change his life constructively. Someone else may
see a different possible interpretation, but this is only what your
dream would mean to *him had he* dreamed it. Dreams do not arise
arbitrarily from some universal reservoir: they arise out of the
dreamer's present life experience and are meaningful to him alone.
While I cannot say that the *purpose* of dreams is to move us to change
our lives, I do insist that a "correct" interpretation—which means an
effective interpretation—shows the way. For this reason, I suggest
that anyone working on a dream successfully should conclude by
writing down *briefly* what the dream means and *what he is going to do
about it.* Jung made a habit of asking his patients, after they had
worked together on a dream, "Now, *in one sentence,* what is the
meaning of the dream?" [My colleagues and I] follow this rule in all
our dream work, though we allow two or three sentences if necessary. And we conclude by asking the dreamer what practical action
the dream message could lead him to take.

9. A dream is incorrectly (ineffectively) interpreted if the inter-   16
pretation leaves the dreamer disappointed or diminished. Many
psychotherapists still insist that they know the correct interpretation
of your dream and believe that the message which makes sense to
you may not be the one you need to see at any given moment in
time—apparently quite oblivious of the fact that their colleagues, on
the basis of the same dream, may be seeing quite different things for
you. You must learn to trust your *own* feelings and judgment.

Meanings and Values

1.   According to the quotation at the beginning of this selection, what is
     the purpose of dreaming? Why does Faraday think most people
     need to learn how to interpret their dreams?

2.   In your words, explain the distinction Faraday draws in paragraph
     4 between interpreting dreams literally and interpreting them

symbolically. (You may wish to look up the meaning of the terms *literally* and *symbolically*.)

3. Having read this selection, do you consider the procedure explained by the author to be useful and accurate, fanciful and unreliable, or somewhere in between? Is your evaluation based on the information presented in the essay? The way the essay is written? Your view of dreams and dream interpretation? Some combination? Explain. (See "Guide to Terms": *Evaluation*.)

Expository Techniques

1. Drawing on specific evidence from the essay for support, explain why you think this selection is a directional process, an informational process, or a mixture of the two. If you consider it a combination, identify those paragraphs that are primarily directional, primarily informational, and a mixture of the two.

2. Do the numbers indicate steps in the process? If not, what do they identify? Are the numbers used effectively? (Guide: *Evaluation*.)

3. Identify both the brief and extended examples in these paragraphs: 4, 6, 10, and 15. Choose two of these paragraphs and discuss whether the examples are intended as illustrations for explanatory statements or as a way of showing readers how to do something.

4. Where in the selection does the author mention other ways of interpreting dreams than the approach she thinks is correct? For what purpose does she mention these alternative approaches?

Diction and Vocabulary

1. Choose one of the longer paragraphs in this essay and explain why you think the diction is either abstract or concrete. (Guide: *Diction, Concrete/Abstract*.)

2. Consult the dictionary as needed for a full understanding of the following words, especially as they are used in this selection: subliminal (par. 4); objective, subjective (5); fascist, figuratively (7); elusive (8); arbitrarily (15).

Read to Write

1. Freewrite on what dreams mean to you and on how you interpret them. Extend your freewriting to consider what dreams mean to other people (especially friends) and to describe how others interpret them. Focus on potential topics for writing that you encountered in your freewriting and develop them further until you decide on one as a focus for a paper.

2. Faraday bases her interpretation of dreams on psychological theories and research. There are many other explanations of why dreams occur and what they mean, however. Do some research in recent articles and books and use the explanations and theories you find as the basis for a paper on dreaming, dreams, or the interpretation of dreams.

3. Follow Faraday's explanatory approach in this essay, and explain some other mental, emotional, or social phenomenon. You might consider topics such as dealing with various emotions, studying effectively, or forming deep and lasting friendships. Be sure your explanation includes specific instructions for dealing with the phenomenon or accomplishing a goal.

(NOTE: Suggestions for topics requiring development by use of PROCESS ANALYSIS are on page 292 at the end of this section.)

MIKE ROSE was born in Los Angeles in 1944. He studied at Loyola University of Los Angeles (B.A.) and at the University of Southern California (M.S.). He received an M.A. and a Ph.D. from the University of California at Los Angeles. He has been Director of Writing Programs at UCLA and currently teaches in the psychology department. Rose has written numerous articles on the cognitive processes that shape writing and on other topics related to writing and education. He is the author of *Writer's Block: The Cognitive Dimension* (1983), editor of *When a Writer Can't Write: Studies in Writer's Block and Other Composing Process Problems* (1984), and co-editor of *Perspectives on Literacy* (1989). Rose is an accomplished poet whose work has appeared in numerous magazines and collections. His award-winning book, *Lives on the Boundary* (1989), provides a moving account of his own education and the experiences of people struggling towards literacy. His most recent book, *Possible Lives: The Promise of Public Education in America* (1995) takes readers on a journey through effective classrooms across the United States.

Writing Around Rules

Originally written for the textbook *Patterns in Action* and addressed directly to composition students, this selection explores examples from the writing processes of several students and the author himself in order to explain how composing works (or fails to) and how to avoid barriers that can keep you from writing effectively.

I

Here's Liz, a junior English major, at work on a paper for a college   1
course: she has been given a two-page case study and must analyze
it using the ideas contained in a second, brief handout. She has
about one hour to complete her assignment. As she reads and
rereads the handouts, she scribbles notes to herself in the margins.
Liz is doing what most effective writers would do with such
materials: paraphrasing the main points in the passages, making
connections among them, recording associations to other pertinent

knowledge. But a closer look at these interpretive notes reveals something unusual: Liz seems to be editing them as she goes along, cleaning them up as though they were final copy. In one of her notes she jots down the phrase "is saying that not having creative work is the. . . ." She stops, thinks for a moment, and changes "is the" to "causes." (Later on, explaining this change, she'll comment that "you're not supposed to have passive verbs.") She then replaces "is saying" with "says," apparently following her directive about passive voice, but later changes it again, noting that "says" is "too colloquial." Liz pauses after this editing and looks up—she has forgotten what she initially was trying to capture in her writing. "That happens a lot," she says.

Liz was one of the many college students I studied over a two-   2
and-one-half-year period (*Writer's Block: The Cognitive Dimension*). The purpose of my study was to try to gain insight into what causes some young writers to compose with relative fluency and what leads others to experience more than their fair share of blocks, dead-ends, conflicts, and the frustrations of the blank page. What I uncovered was a whole array of problems that I would label as being primarily *cognitive* rather than primarily *emotional* in nature. That is, many students were engaging in self-defeating composing behaviors not because they had some deep-seated fear of revealing their thoughts or of being evaluated or because of some long-standing aversion to writing, but rather because they had somehow learned a number of rules, planning strategies, or assumptions about writing that limited rather than enhanced their composing. We saw Liz lose her train of thought by adhering too rigidly to stylistic rules when she should have been scribbling ideas freely in order to discover material for her essay. Let me offer two further vignettes that illustrate some of the other cognitive difficulties I uncovered.

Tyrrell, also a junior English major, says he doesn't like to   3
sketch out any sort of plan or draft of what he's going to write. He'll think about his topic, but his pen usually won't touch paper until he begins writing the one, and only, draft he'll produce. As he writes, he pauses frequently and at length to make all sorts of decisions about words, ideas, and rhetorical effects. In short, he plans his work as he goes along. There's nothing inherently wrong with writing this way, but where difficult assignments involving complex materials are concerned, it helps to sketch out a few ideas, some direction, a loose organizational structure before beginning to write. When a

coworker and I studied Tyrrell's composing, we noted the stylistic flourishes in his essay, but also its lack of direction. As my colleague noted, "[His] essay bogs down in description and in unexplained abstractions." Perhaps the essay would have had more direction if Tyrrell had roughed out a few ideas before composing his one and only draft. Why didn't he do so? Consider his comment on planning:

[Planning] is certainly not spontaneous and a lot of the times it's not even really what you feel because it becomes very mechanical. It's almost like— at least I feel—it's diabolical, you know, because . . . it'll sacrifice truth and real feelings that you have.

Tyrrell assumes that sketching out a plan before writing somehow violates the spontaneity of composing: to plan dooms one to write mechanical, unemotional prose. Yet, while too much planning may sometimes make the actual writing a joyless task, it is also true that most good writing is achieved through some kind of prefiguring, most often involving pen and paper. Such planning does not necessarily subvert spontaneity; in fact, since it reduces the load on the writer's immediate memory, it might actually free one to be more spontaneous, to follow the lead of new ideas as they emerge. Tyrrell's assumption, then, is inaccurate. By recognizing only this one path to spontaneity, he is probably limiting his effectiveness as a writer and, ironically, may be reducing his opportunities to be spontaneous.

Gary is an honors senior in biochemistry. When I observed 4 him, he spent over half of his writing time meticulously analyzing each sentence of the assignment's reading passage on one of the handouts. He understood the passage and the assignment well enough but wanted to make sure the passage was sufficiently broken down to be of use when he composed his essay. As Gary conducted this minute analysis, he wrote dozens and dozens of words and phrases across the handouts. He then summarized these words and phrases in a list of six items. He *then* tried to condense all six items into a thesis sentence:

I have concepts . . . and my task here is to say what is being said about all of those all at once.

Gary's method was, in this case, self-defeating. He worked in too precise a fashion, generating an unwieldy amount of preliminary material, which he didn't seem to be able to rank or thin out—and he was unable to focus his thinking in a single thesis sentence.

Gary's interpretive and planning strategies were inappropriately elaborate, and they were inflexible. It was not surprising that when Gary's hour was up, he had managed to write only three disconnected sentences. Not really an essay at all.

But what about the students who weren't stymied, who wrote   5 with relative fluency? They too talked of rules and assumptions and displayed planning strategies. The interesting thing, though, is that their rules were more flexible; that is, a rule seemed to include conditions under which it ought and ought not to be used. The rules weren't absolutes, but rather statements about what one might do in certain writing situations. Their assumptions, as well, were not absolute and they tended to enhance composing, opening up rather than restricting possibilities. And their planning strategies tended to be flexible and appropriate to the task. Fluent writers had their rules, strategies, and assumptions, but they were of a different kind from those of the blocked writers.

What to do? One is tempted to urge the blocked writers to clear   6 their minds of troubling rules, plans, and assumptions. In a few cases, that might not be such a bad idea. But what about Liz's preoccupation with passive constructions? Some degree of concern about casting one's language in the active voice is a good thing. And Gary's precise strategies? It would be hard to imagine good academic writing that isn't preceded by careful analysis of one's materials. Writers need the order and the guidance that rules, strategies, and assumptions provide. The answer to Liz's, Tyrrell's, and Gary's problems, then, lies in altering their approaches to make them more conditional, adaptive, and flexible. Let me explain further. For the sake of convenience, I'll focus on rules, though what I'll say has application to the assumptions we develop and the planning strategies we learn.

II

Writing is a phenomenally complex learned activity. To write in a   7 way that others can understand we must employ a large and complicated body of conventions. We learn from our parents or earliest teachers that script, in English, goes left to right straight across the page. We learn about letter formation, spelling, sentence structure, and so on. Some of this information we absorb more or less unconsciously through reading, and some of it we learn formally as guidelines, as directives . . . as rules.

And there are all kinds of rules. Some tell us how to format our   8
writing (for example, when to capitalize, how to paragraph, how to
footnote). There are grammar rules (for example, "Make a pronoun
agree in number with its antecedent"). There are preferences concerning style that are often stated as rules ("Avoid passive voice").
There are usage rules (*"That* always introduces restrictive clauses;
which can introduce both restrictive and nonrestrictive clauses").
There are rules that tell us how to compose ("Before you begin writing, decide on your thesis and write it down in a single declarative
sentence"). The list goes on and on. Some of these rules make sense;
others are confusing, questionable, or contradictory. Fortunately, we
assimilate a good deal of the information they contain gradually by
reading other writers, by writing ourselves, or by simply being
around print. Therefore, we can confirm or alter or reject them from
experience.

But all too often the rules are turned into absolutes. And that's   9
where the trouble begins. Most rules about writing should not be
expressed (in textbooks), stored (in our minds), or enacted (on the
page) as absolutes, as mathematical, unvarying directives. True, a
few rules apply in virtually all situations (for example, certain for-
matting rules or capitalization rules). But most rules do not. Writing
rules, like any rules about language, have a history and have a time
and place. They are highly context-bound.

Should you always, as some textbooks suggest, place your the-   10
sis sentence at the beginning of your first paragraph or, as others
suggest, work up to it and place it at the end of the paragraph?
Well, the answer is that both injunctions are right . . . and wrong.
Students writing essay exams would be well-advised to demonstrate their knowledge and direct the reader's attention as soon as
possible. But the writer who wants to evoke a mood might offer a
series of facts and events that gradually leads up to a thesis sentence. The writing situation, the rhetorical purpose, and the nature
of the material one is working with will provide the answer. A sin-
gle-edged rule cannot.

How about our use of language, usage rules? Certainly there's   11
a right and a wrong here? Again, not quite. First of all, there's a time
in one's writing to worry about such things. Concern yourself with
questions of usage too early in your composing and you'll end up
like Liz, worrying about the minutiae of language while your
thought fades to a wisp. Second, the social consequences of
following or ignoring such rules vary widely depending on whether

you're writing formal or informal prose. Third, usage rules themselves have an evolutionary history: we aren't obliged to follow some of the rules that turn-of-the-century writers had to deal with, and our rules will alter and even disappear as the English language moves on in time. No, there are no absolutes here either.

Well, how about some of the general, commonsense rules about   12
the very act of writing itself? Certainly, rules like "Think before you write" ought to be followed. Again, a qualification is in order. While it certainly is good advice to think through ideas before we record them for others to see, many people, in fact, use writing as a way of thinking. They make major decisions *as* they write. There are times when it's best to put a piece of writing aside and ponder, but there are also times when one ought to keep pen in hand and attempt to resolve a conceptual tangle by sketching out what comes to mind. Both approaches are legitimate.

I'll stop here. I hope I've shown that it's difficult to make hard   13
and fast statements about the structure, the language, or the composing of an essay. Unfortunately, there's a strong push in our culture to make absolute statements about writing, especially where issues of style and usage are concerned. But I hope by now the reader of this essay believes that most rules about writing—about how to do it, about how it should be structured, about what words to use—are not absolute, and should be taught and enacted in a flexible, context-dependent way. Given certain conditions, you follow them; given other conditions you modify or suspend them. A teacher may insist that a young writer follow a particular dictum in order to learn a pattern, but there must come a time when the teacher extends the lesson and explains when the dictum is and isn't appropriate.

Because I've relied on the writing of college students for my   14
illustrations, it might seem that my assertions—particularly about the connection between inflexible rules and blocking—apply only to young, developing writers. Not so. A professional writer's sense of self is intimately involved in his or her work, so, to be sure, the blocks and resistances such writers experience are often related to emotional factors. But the cognitive dimension we've seen with collegiate writers is present as well. The rules that trip up the professional writer may be different, but the fundamental processes and problems can be quite similar. Let me illustrate this point by coming closer to home and offering an illustration from my own writing, the composition of a poem.

III

Here's the background. My father has been dead for many years   15
now, but he is still very much present in my dreams. In one recent
dream, I was standing by his bedside; he was comatose. The dream
then shifted—as dreams often do—and I was outside watching him
tinker at a workbench. When I woke, I knew I had the central image
of a poem, a short elegy. Here is what finally emerged, five or so
revisions later:

> *The last we knew*
> *doctors were explaining "aneurysm."*
> *Father lay in the next room, asleep.*
> *We were surprised, then,*
> *to find him at his workbench,*
> *white oleander at his back*
> *rustling night music in direct sun.*
>
> *He set the vise*
> *on a bar of red metal*
> *and with thin flame*
> *pared it into petals.*
> *He cupped them, whispering.*
> *Slipping dowels through his fingers*
> *he made a fist, hard,*
> *opened it,*
> *and handed us two shining roses.*
>
> *We place them by him*
> *asleep in the next room.*

I was happy with the poem—with its images, its compression.   16
But I knew that the abrupt shifts in time and place could confuse
readers unless they knew that the poem is a dream vision. Now, I
didn't want to wreck the poem's compression or interrupt the
reader's movement through the events of the poem by intruding
into the lines themselves, by grabbing a reader by the collar and
yelling, "Hey! This is a dream. Get it?" I knew that I had to do whatever I was going to do in the title; the reader had to be clued in
before the poem began. At this point, I blocked. And for reasons not
unlike those that tripped up the students I had observed. Titles, to
my mind, did certain things, fit certain conventions that I had either
read or heard or somehow absorbed from years and years of reading other people's poems: Titles should add something to a poem,
not just state the obvious. Titles should be evocative. Titles take up
one line. Titles are direct and declarative. The words in a title should

be in one sentence. So went the list. Some of these rules I recall learning from mentors. Others I acquired somehow, somewhere. Some of the rules made sense. Others were nonsense. And some—like the injunctions to be evocative and to be direct—potentially conflicted. I tried titles like "The Dream Answer" and junked them quickly as cliches and as . . . well . . . just stupid. Days passed. And more days. I was stuck. I was working with a whole set of notions about titles that placed certain boundaries on what I could invent and what I would consider acceptable. All writers work within boundaries, but these were proving to be too restrictive.

One afternoon I was talking to my friend Bonnie Verburg—a   17
fine writer—about my dilemma. She thought for awhile and went to get a poem of her own: a dream poem. We made some comparisons and talked about the effects we were trying to get by keeping the dissociated structure of the dream. Then she asked why I didn't try a title that itself was dream-like, that is, that compressed disparate words or ideas or events together. Something clicked. I wasn't sure I was following exactly what Bonnie was asking of me, but I saw that I *could* have a title different from the kind dictated by my various directives and assumptions. The poem's title came quickly:

> Dream
> My Father's Flowers

Bonnie, in effect, had provided a new direction that I hadn't   18
seen as a possibility. My experience with her made it clear that some of my rules about titles were limiting rather than guiding my thinking. In solving the problem before me, I rejected some rules and recast others into more flexible directives, directives with some play in them that might now lead to the composing of effective titles for what I hope are reams of future poems.

Meanings and Values

1. What makes Liz's writing process ineffective? Tyrrell's? Gary's? What do they have in common with the difficulties Rose faces in his own work (as described in paragraphs 15–18)? Be specific.

2. What specific advice does Rose offer to students working to become more comfortable with writing and to become better writers?

3. What is the overall expository purpose of this essay? To what extent can it be considered informational? Directional? A combination of the two?

Expository Techniques

1. Why does Rose conclude the essay with an extended example from his own experience? In what ways does this strategy serve the purposes of the essay? In what ways, if any, does it detract from them? (See "Guide to Terms": *Purpose; Evaluation.*)

2. This essay has three separate sections. Can it be considered a unified essay? Why? (Guide: *Unity.*) What transitional devices does Rose employ to build coherence among the sections and among the paragraphs devoted to individual students in the first section? (Guide: *Coherence; Transition.*)

3. Where in the essay does Rose summarize the processes he has been explaining? For what reason(s) does he provide these summaries?

4. What role(s) do the rhetorical questions play in paragraphs 5 and 6? In paragraphs 10–12? (Guide: *Rhetorical Questions.*)

Diction and Vocabulary

1. How and why do the diction and style differ in Rose's description of his own writing process (pars. 15–18) and his descriptions of Liz's, Tyrrell's, and Gary's writing (pars. 2–4)? (Guide: *Diction; Style.*)

2. Describe the ways Rose varies sentence length and syntax in paragraph 16, and discuss his apparent purposes for doing so. (Guide: *Syntax.*)

3. If you do not know the meaning of some of the following terms, look them up in a dictionary: cognitive, vignettes (par. 2); rhetorical, flourishes, spontaneity, subvert (3); meticulously, unwieldy (4); fluency (5); passive, adaptive (6); antecedent (8); directives, context-bound (9); injunctions (10); minutiae (11); qualification, conceptual (12); dictum (13); comatose, aneurysm, dowels (15); evocative, declarative, mentors (16); disparate (17).

Read to Write

1. Freewrite about your own composing process, focusing, if possible, on the process by which you wrote a particular paper. Highlight your strengths as a writer and describe difficulties you often face or problems you find difficult to solve.

2. Rose concludes his essay with an example drawn from his own experience. Prepare an informational or directional analysis of a process in an essay of your own, and conclude with an extended explanation based upon your experience.

3. In an essay loosely modeled on "Writing Around Rules," analyze an activity, process, or situation containing a difficulty of some sort, and

suggest ways of getting around the difficulty or getting rid of it. Use extended examples similar to the way Rose uses them, and consider dividing your essay into sections.

(NOTE: Suggestions for topics requiring development by use of PROCESS ANALYSIS are on page 292 at the end of this section.)

Issues and Ideas

Advertising and Appearances—Shaping Realities

Do appearances count? When they come to us on television, in movies, or through advertisements, they do—at least that is what the authors of the essays that follow suggest.

James Twitchell explains how the images and strategies of advertising create and maintain a culture of which we are a part: a culture based on ever-present images and texts encouraging us to buy brand-name products, "adcult," as he refers to it. Adcult makes one product appear better or more desirable and helps shape our tastes, choices, environment, and values, a process Twitchell analyzes in detail.

Jean E. Kilbourne offers a sharply critical analysis of the images of physical appearance and of behavior which dominate various media and have influenced our attitudes towards our bodies, our values, and our behaviors in harmful ways. She focuses especially on the ways women participate in and are affected by this process, but her conclusions also apply to society at large.

Jessica Mitford's treatment of our fascination with appearances has an even harder edge. She offers a bitingly satiric and humorous view of our concern with the appearance of the dead, a form of manipulation that amounts almost to a denial of the reality of death. Though she puts primary blame on the funeral industry for creating and maintaining this obsession with false appearances, she includes in her indictment all of us who willingly tolerate the sham process.

Taken together, these essays demonstrate the importance of media images in contemporary life and suggest ways of interpreting and analyzing these images that can lead to further writing.

JAMES B. TWITCHELL was born in Burlington, Vermont, in 1943. He received his B.A. (1962), M.A. (1966), and Ph.D. (1969) from the University of North Carolina–Chapel Hill. He has taught at Duke University, California State University–Bakersfield, and the University of Florida, where he is currently Alumni Professor of English. Though much of Twitchell's writing has appeared in scholarly journals and in books issued by university presses, his work is nonetheless interesting and accessible to a wide audience of readers. Among his books are *Forbidden Partners: The Incest Taboo in Modern Culture* (1986); *Dreadful Pleasures: An Anatomy of Modern Horror* (1987); *Preposterous Violence: Fables of Aggression in Modern Culture* (1989); *Carnival Culture: The Trashing of Taste in America* (1992) (nominated for a National Book Award and a National Book Critics Circle Award); and *Adcult USA: The Triumph of Advertising in American Culture* (1996).

We Build Excitement

In this selection from *Adcult USA* (1966), James Twitchell talks about the process by which advertising became part of our culture and now serves as a primary force in shaping our culture, our perceptions, and our values. The selection is primarily informational and makes use of numerous examples in its analysis of the process. Twitchell is critical, at times, of the work of advertisers, but his criticism is much less harsh than that of many other writers, for, as he admits in the preface to *Adcult USA,* "I have always loved advertising."

The Hatter in the Strand of London, instead of making better felt-hats than   1
another, mounts a huge lath-and-plaster Hat, seven feet high, upon wheels; sends a man to drive it through the streets; hoping to be saved *thereby*. He has not attempted to *make* better hats, as he was appointed by the Universe to do, and as with this ingenuity of his he could very probably have done, but his whole industry is turned to *persuade* us that he has made such! He too knows that the Quack has become God.

THOMAS CARLYLE, *PAST AND PRESENT,* 1843

Thomas Carlyle just didn't get it. The Hatter in the Strand of Lon-   2
don was not in the business of making hats to make better hats. He made hats to make money. The Victorians may have commanded

the manufacturer to make the best of what he set out to do, but the culture of capitalism does not care so much about what he makes as about what he can sell. Hence the "best" hat becomes the most profitable hat. Ironically, perhaps he cannot make hats profitably unless he can market what he makes efficiently. The selling determines the making. And once he makes those best hats, especially if he has a machine to help him, heaven help him if he makes too many. If he has to spend some of his productive time acting like a nut in order to sell those hats, so be it.

The ingredients necessary to concoct an Adcult [culture of   3 advertising, eds.] are not complex. The Hatter in the Strand of London is crucial. Because the Hatter probably has enough hats for his own use, he makes something that has exchange value. Assuming that he can control the retail price, the more he manufactures, the more he takes advantage of the economies of mass production and the greater the profit. To control that retail price however, he needs some method to differentiate his hat or he will produce more than he can sell. After all, because the product is partially machine made, it is essentially interchangeable with a competitor's product made with the same machinery.

The process of differentiation, called branding, is the key ingre-   4 dient in all advertising. Make all the machine-made felt hats, biscuits, shoes, cigarettes, automobiles, or computer chips you want, but you cannot sell effectively until you can call it a Fedora, a Ritz, a Nike, a Marlboro, a Chevrolet, or an Intel 386. If everybody's biscuits are in the same barrel, and if they look pretty much the same, urging people to buy biscuits probably won't do the trick. Chances are, they won't buy your biscuit. As Thomas J. Barratt said at almost the same time that Carlyle was having at the Hatter, "Any fool can make soap. It takes a clever man to sell it." [1]Barratt was a clever man. He made a fortune by the end of the century by calling his soap Pears' Soap and making sure everyone knew about it by defacing miles of Anglo-American wall and newsprint space with "Have you had your Pears' today?" In many ways modern culture has been a battle between Carlyle and Barratt. If you aren't sure who won, look around you.

Adcult also requires purchasers with sufficient disposable   5 income to buy your product. And it doesn't hurt if your audience

[1]E. S. Tuner, *The Shocking History of Advertising* (New York: Dutton, 1953).

members have enough curiosity to listen to you tell them your biscuits are different when they know all biscuits are the same. But watch out: this process is not without risk. When money is tight, brands take flight. For reasons no one can understand, from time to time markets fall apart, advertising loses its grip, and the charade has to be reenacted. Procter & Gamble spent billions building its soap brands, Philip Morris did the same with premium cigarettes, as did IBM with the personal computer, only to have the demand for their brands suddenly plummet. Generics appear to eat up what advertising created. Brands can suddenly become just commodities again. The Hatter in the Strand soon responds by dropping his prices and by making a still larger lath-and-plaster hat.

 With those ingredients in the pot all an Adcult still needs is a   6
plasma, or conduit, between producer and consumer within which producers can, in the jargon of modern criticism, *inscribe* their message. The ever bigger lath-and-plaster hat is soon subject to diminishing returns. The brand may appear *on* his hat, but its name recognition is created *in* a medium. So along with his sign the Hatter may even decide to hire someone to advertise his product by voice. In the nineteenth century consumers still heard the cries of the costermonger (the coster is a kind of English apple) or other traders announcing their wares:

> *One-a-penny, two-a-penny, hot cross buns!*
> *One-a-penny, two for tup'ence, hot cross buns!*
>
> *Dust, O! Dust O! Bring it out today.*
> *Bring it out today! I shan't be here tomorrow!*
>
> *I sweep your Chimnies clean, O!*
> *I sweep your Chimney clean, O!*
>
> *Buy my Diddle Dumplings, hot! hot!*
> *Diddle, Diddle, Diddle, Dumplings, hot!*
>
> *Maids, I mend old Pans or Kettles,*
> *Mend old Pans or Kettles, O!*
>
> *Muffins, O! Crumpets! Muffins to-day!*
> *Crumpets, O! Muffins, O! Fresh to-day!*

 Street cries and moving hats "set upon wheels" are no longer   7
major conduits in modern Adcult. True, the urban bus has become a billboard. And the billboard plastered on a truck is making a

comeback in cluttered cities (the sides of such rolling billboards are lit fluorescently and can change panels every ten minutes), and the human voice can still be heard on street corners.[2] But they are no match for ink and electrons.

With the advent of print and paste, signs moved to walls. From the late seventeenth century to the middle of the nineteenth the great cities of western Europe were nightly plastered over—sometimes twice a night—with what became known as posters. Seventeenth-century London streets were so thick with signs that Charles II proclaimed that "no sign shall be hung across the streets shutting out the air and light of the heavens." Although it was against the law, even Fleet Street Prison was posted. As the "post no bills" regulations took hold, posters became free-standing billboards. The "boards" grew so thick in American that people could barely see Niagara Falls through the forest of Coca-Cola and Mennen's Toilet powder signs. N. W. Ayer Company executives bragged that if all the boards they had erected for Nabisco were painted on a fence, the fence would enclose the Panama Canal on either side, from sea to shining sea. 8

What distinguishes modern advertising is that it has jumped from the human voice and printed posters to anything that can carry it. Almost every physical object now carries advertising, almost every human environment is suffused with advertising, almost every moment of time is calibrated by advertising. 9

Start the day with breakfast. What's on the cereal box but the Ninja Turtles, Batman, or the Addams Family? Characters real or imagined once sold cereal; now they *are* the cereal. Once Wild Bill Hickock, Bob Mathias, Huckleberry Hound, and Yogi Bear touted Sugar Pops or Wheaties. Now the sugar gobs reappear every six months, renamed to cross-promote some event. When the most recent Robin Hood movie was released, a Prince of Thieves Cereal appeared on grocery shelves. Alas, the movie did not show Mr. Hood starting the day with his own brand. But Kellogg has tried for this brass ring of promotion anyway. It has marketed cereals with Jerry Seinfeld and Jay Leno on the boxes and then gone on to buy commercial time on 10

[2]In a sense, of course, advertising in various media is ancient. Commercial speech starts with the snake's spiel in the Garden of Eden, is heard in the cries of vendors in ancient Persia, is seen on walls of Pompeii as the marks listing prices of various prostitutes, is carried in our surnames (as with Smith, Weaver, Miller, Taylor, Baker . . .), and remains in the coats of arms over European hostelries with names like the Red Crown, the Gold Fox, and the Three Stars as well as in the symbolic images of the barber's pole or the golden balls of a pawn shop.

their network, NBC. It is of some comfort that while cereals sporting Barbie and Donkey Kong have gone stale on the shelves, the redoubtable Fred Flintstone and his Flintstones cereal survive.

Go to school. The classroom is the Valhalla of place-based media. Better than the doctor's office, the shopping mall, the health club, the hospital, and the airport, here you have the ideal—a captive audience with more disposable income than discretion. Advertising material is all over the place. For home economics classes Chef Boyardee supplies worksheets on how to use pasta; Prego counters with the Prego Science Challenge complete with an "instructional kit" to test the thickness of various spaghetti sauces. General Mills sends out samples of its candy along with a pamphlet, "Gushers: Wonders of the Earth," which encourages the kids to learn about geysers by biting the "fruit snack." Monsanto donates a video suggesting that the world cannot be fed without using pesticides; Union Carbide does the same, saying chemicals "add comfort to your lives." Exxon has an energy awareness game in which nonrenewable natural resources are not losers. K-Swiss sneakers provides shoes for participants in a video creation of an ad for . . . you guessed it. And Kodak, McDonald's, and Coca-Cola plaster a national essay contest about why kids should stay in school with corporate logos and concern. Clearly, one reason to stay in school is to consume more advertising.

Go shopping. The war, as they say, is in the store. Food shoppers make almost two-thirds of their buying decisions when they set foot in the aisle. Capitalizing on these last-minute decisions is why grocers don't alphabetize soup sections, why all the raisin bran cereals are not bunched together, and why high-profit toothbrushes are both nestled with toothpastes and stacked almost at random throughout the store. With more than fifteen hundred new items introduced to supermarkets each month, the need to inform and convince the querulous shopper of the new product is intense. The experience of food buying has become an advertising adventure.

A company called Ad-Tiles puts its ads on the floors in Pathmark stores, charging what amounts to 50 cents per thousand impressions. Flashing coupon dispensers are omnipresent, except near the upright freezers and open dairy case, because shoppers do not like to open doors to compare prices—too cold. They won't even open the door for coupons. The latest hot places for advertising are the checkout line and the shopping cart. The shopping cart, which revolutionized food shopping as much as self-service, because it determined the amount of food a shopper could buy, has come alive. VideOcart is here, almost. This shopping cart has a six-by-nine-inch screen affixed to what used to be the kiddie rumble seat, and infrared censors on the ceiling cause it to flash ads, messages, and recipes as you pass various products. The same technology that scans the Universal Product Code on your can of beans now scans the shopper. You are the can.

Go to a sporting event. It's football season. Let's go to a bowl game. Which one? Or which product? The Orange Bowl has become the Federal Express Orange Bowl, the Cotton Bowl has become the Mobil Cotton Bowl, the Sugar Bowl has become the USF&G Sugar Bowl, and the Sun Bowl has become the John Hancock Bowl. Not to mention the Sunkist Fiesta Bowl (now the IBM OS/2 Fiesta Bowl), the Mazda Gator Bowl (now the Outback Steakhouse Gator Bowl), the Sea World Holiday Bowl, the Domino's Pizza Copper Bowl, the California Raisin Bowl, and everyone's favorite, the Poulan/Weed Eater Independence Bowl. For a while even the Heisman Memorial Trophy was up for grabs. Merrill Lynch paid $1.5 million for promotional rights but not for a name change. Not yet. No matter: Merrill Lynch already has a golf tournament.

Take a trip. Get away from Adcult. Weren't we told in the famous Cunard advertisement that getting there is half the fun? Hop in a taxi. Some urban cabs have alphanumeric signs that scroll ten ads per minute across a panel on the back of the front seat. Gannett, the billboard-and-newspaper conglomerate, has been experimenting with installing these "electronic gutters" in subway cars and has contracted with the Transit Authority of New York to put them in six thousand cars. Nothing revolutionary here, just the electrifying of the advertising card, which has been a staple of public transportation since the first trolley. The company has also introduced what it calls the brand train and the brand bus in which a sponsor can buy all the ad space on a particular vehicle that runs a specific route. So Donna Karan's DKNY line has taken over an entire ten-car train that runs under Lexington Avenue on Manhattan's East Side, endlessly running beneath DKNY's superstore at Bloomingdale's. Gannett also installed radio equipment in bus shelters around midtown Manhattan for a news and business station. The New York City Department of Transportation ordered Gannett to pull the plug—too much noise.

No destination is safe. The Russian government has even sold   16
space inside Red Square. For something less than $1 million your
message can be part of the May Day celebration. Coca-Cola and
Pepsi are already in Pushkin Square. For $100,000 the side of GUM,
the largest department store in the world, is yours. Lenin's tomb is
off-limits, but above Lenin's tomb is OK. For about $30,000 you can
float a blimp. Who's itching to get onto Russian space? The usual
suspects: AT&T, Reebok, Sara Lee, and of course the ever-present
tobacco companies.[3]

Finally, no matter where you go in this world or beyond, when   17
you get home, your credit card bill for the trip will eventually
appear. When it does, it may have that tear-off tag on the envelope
upon which is printed yet another ad.

Almost as interesting as where advertising is, is where it might   18
be. Here are some of the more interesting venues contributed by
advertising men and women who make hundreds of thousands of
dollars thinking up and trying out some of these locations:

- Subway tokens.
- The backs of chairs in commuter trains.
- The Gateway Arch in St. Louis.
- Postage stamps and paper currency.
- In place of the telephone dial tone.
- Polo ponies.
- The bottom of golf holes, to be observed while putting and
  then while removing the ball.
- Self-serve gasoline pumps. Messages scroll along with the
  amount of gas pumped.
- Rural mailboxes. Although the Postal Service prohibits
  advertising on boxes, John Deere has produced a green and
  yellow version that retails for about $50.
- Astronauts' uniforms.
- Postcards. Laden with advertising, they are given to patrons
  by restaurants.

---

[3]Nor would you be ad free in outer space. For $500,000 NASA agreed that Columbia
Pictures could cover a rocket with an ad for Arnold Schwarzenegger's *Last Action
Hero* (the movie bombed before the missile flew). And Joel Babbit, an Atlanta ad exec,
almost succeeded in launching a billboard high in the heavens. The space billboard
was to be an unfolding screen set in geosynchronous orbit 250 miles above the equa-
tor; in the evening it would appear to be about the size of the moon—just right for a
logo. The usual suspects were interested, but the U.S. Department of Transportation
nixed the idea.

- School buses.
- Slot machines. Why should they come up cherries and oranges? Why not boxes of Tide?
- Catalogs. This has been done, most notably by *The Sharper Image*, but the reverse is almost as interesting—a recent *Lands' End* catalog included a story by David Mamet.
- Video games. "Cool Spot" is a game like "Pac Man," except it stars "Spot," the 7-Up mascot: "Yo! Noid" is a game centered around the Domino's Pizza character. "Mick and Mack: Global Gladiators" has a black hero who battles pollution. To get from level to level the player has to collect golden arches passed out by a gate-tending Ronald McDonald.

It may be of some comfort to critics of this use of the human 19 imagination that a new advertising medium has begun appearing *inside* advertising agencies. Called Media News, it appears on a never ending fifty-four-by-eight-inch alphanumeric display similar to the Dow Jones market ticker. Running across the board is information interspersed with thirty seconds of commercials. Advertisers pay $5,000 for thirteen weeks of ads in a medium described by its creators as "invasive without being aggravating." Poetic justice?

The rise of place-based (as it is known in the trade), in your face 20 (as it is experienced), or new media (as it is presented to the public) follows the principle that where blank space exists, there shall advertising be. The triumph of Adcult is attributable not so much to new products as to new media reaching new audiences. Each new invasion by commercialism is greeted with an outcry, followed by tentative acceptance, assumption, and expectation. And finally, of course, neglect.

Meanings and Values

1. What, according to the writer, did Thomas Carlyle fail to understand (see par. 1)? What key point about business and advertising does the writer make in rejecting Carlyle's point of view?

2. What are the ingredients of an adcult, and where does the writer discuss them? Is this definition satisfactory? In what ways, if any, might it be improved?

3. How does modern advertising differ from that of previous centuries? Be specific.

Expository Techniques

1. In what way are the italicized sentences beginning paragraphs 10, 11, 12, 14, and 15 linked to the second sentence in paragraph 9? Discuss how this linking provides coherence within the second half of the selection. (See "Guide to Terms": *Coherence*.) In what ways does paragraph 9, as a whole, help unify the selection? (Guide: *Unity*.)

2. In which paragraphs does the writer employ extended examples? In which does he use clusters of brief examples? Which paragraphs containing brief examples are especially effective? Why? Are any markedly less effective? Explain why.

3. How would you describe the overall tone of this selection? In what ways, if at all, does the tone add to or detract from the informational goals of the piece? Can the tone in paragraphs 10, 11, and 16 be considered either ironic or sarcastic? (Guide: *Irony*.) If so, does this tone undermine the writer's claim that "I have always loved advertising"? Explain. If not, what do you believe is the tone of these paragraphs?

Diction and Vocabulary

1. Would you characterize the diction in paragraphs 11–13 as *specific* or *general*? As *abstract* or *concrete*? (Guide: *Specific/General; Concrete/Abstract*.) Cite examples to support your conclusions. How does the diction contribute to the purpose and effect of these paragraphs? (Guide: *Purpose*.)

2. Compare the diction in paragraphs 5–6 and 15–16. Which makes greater use of formal diction, and why? Which makes greater use of colloquial language, and why? (Guide: *Colloquial Expressions*.) To what extent does the writer use the connotations of terms as well as their denotations to criticize advertisers? (Guide: *Connotation/Denotation*.) Is this criticism harsh or mild, direct or indirect? Explain.

3. If you do not know the meaning of some of the following terms, look them up in a dictionary: lath, quack (par. 1); differentiate (3); charade, plummet (5); conduit, inscribe, costermonger (6); suffused, calibrated (9); redoubtable (10); Valhalla (11); omnipresent (13); invasive (18); attributable, tentative, assumption (19).

Read to Write

1. Advertising is a good subject for expository writing. Make up a set of questions about advertising and then list details, ideas, and possible topics under each. When you are finished, look through the list to see if you can discover a focus for your writing. Here are several questions

to get you started: Other than manufacturers, who sponsors advertising? What different kinds of advertising do we encounter in a typical day? Do different kinds of advertising achieve their effects through different processes?

2. Twitchell uses paragraphs filled with detailed but short examples. Use a similar strategy in an essay of your own, perhaps exploring some other feature of contemporary life such as the attention paid to sports and sports heroes, popular magazines or novels, or the way television news programs operate.

3. Drawing on "We Build Excitement" as a model, create an essay of your own showing how the contemporary form of some activity or process (fishing, basketball, clothing design and manufacture, for example) differs from earlier forms. Also explain the special features of the contemporary process in detail.

(NOTE: Suggestions for topics requiring development by PROCESS ANALYSIS are on page 292 at the end of this section.)

JESSICA MITFORD was born in 1917, the daughter of an English peer. Her brother was sent to Eton, but she and her six sisters were educated at home by their mother. At the age of nineteen Mitford left home, eventually making her way to the United States in 1939. She made her home in San Francisco and she became an American citizen in 1944. She did not begin her writing career until she was thirty-eight. Her books are *Lifeitselfman-ship* (1956); her autobiography, *Daughters and Rebels* (1960); the bestseller *The American Way of Death* (1963); *The Trial of Dr. Spock* (1969); *Kind and Usual Punishment* (1973), a devastating study of the American penal system; *A Fine Old Conflict* (1977); and *Poison Penmanship* (1979). Mitford's articles have appeared in the *Atlantic, Harper's,* and *McCall's.*

To Dispel Fears of Live Burial

"To Dispel Fears of Live Burial" (editors' title) is a portion of *The American Way of Death,* a book described in *The New York Times* as a "savagely witty and well-documented exposé." The "savagely witty" style, evident in this selection, does not obscure the fact of its being a tightly organized, step-by-step process analysis.

Embalming is indeed a most extraordinary procedure, and one must   1
wonder at the docility of Americans who each year pay hundreds of millions of dollars for its perpetuation, blissfully ignorant of what it is all about, what is done, how it is done. Not one in ten thousand has any idea of what actually takes place. Books on the subject are extremely hard to come by. They are not to be found in most libraries or bookshops.

In an era when huge television audiences watch surgical opera-   2
tions in the comfort of their living rooms, when, thanks to the animated cartoon, the geography of the digestive system has become familiar territory even to the nursery school set, in a land where the satisfaction of curiosity about almost all matters is a national pastime,

the secrecy surrounding embalming can, surely, hardly be attributed to the inherent gruesomeness of the subject. Custom in this regard has within this century suffered a complete reversal. In the early days of American embalming, when it was performed in the home of the deceased, it was almost mandatory for some relative to stay by the embalmer's side and witness the procedure. Today, family members who might wish to be in attendance would certainly be dissuaded by the funeral director. All others, except apprentices, are excluded by law from the preparation room.

A close look at what does actually take place may explain in 3
large measure the undertaker's intractable reticence concerning a procedure that has become his major *raison d'être*. Is it possible he fears that public information about embalming might lead patrons to wonder if they really want this service? If the funeral men are loath to discuss the subject outside the trade, the reader may, understandably, be equally loath to go on reading at this point. For those who have the stomach for it, let us part the formaldehyde curtain. . . .

The body is first laid out in the undertaker's morgue—or rather, 4
Mr. Jones is reposing in the preparation room—to be readied to bid the world farewell.

The preparation room in any of the better funeral establishments 5
has the tiled and sterile look of a surgery, and indeed the embalmer-restorative artist who does his chores there is beginning to adopt the term "dermasurgeon" (appropriately corrupted by some mortician-writers as "demisurgeon") to describe his calling. His equipment, consisting of scalpels, scissors, augers, forceps, clamps, needles, pumps, tubes, bowls and basins, is crudely imitative of the surgeon's as is his technique, acquired in a nine- or twelve-month post-high-school course in an embalming school. He is supplied by an advanced chemical industry with a bewildering array of fluids, sprays, pastes, oils, powders, creams, to fix or soften tissue, shrink or distend it as needed, dry it here, restore the moisture there. There are cosmetics, waxes and paints, to fill and cover features, even plaster of Paris to replace entire limbs. There are ingenious aids to prop and stabilize the cadaver: A Vari-Pose Head Rest, the Edwards Arm and Hand Positioner, the Repose Block (to support the shoulders during the embalming), and the Throop Foot Positioner, which resembles an old-fashioned stocks.

Mr. John H. Eckels, president of the Eckels College of Mortuary 6
Science, thus describes the first part of the embalming procedure: "In the hands of a skilled practitioner, this work may be done in a

comparatively short time and without mutilating the body other than by slight incision—so slight that it scarcely would cause serious inconvenience if made upon a living person. It is necessary to remove the blood, and doing this not only helps in the disinfecting, but removes the principal cause of disfigurements due to discoloration."

Another textbook discusses the all-important time element: 7 "The earlier this is done, the better, for every hour that elapses between death and embalming will add to the problems and complications encountered. . . ." Just how soon should one get going on the embalming? The author tells us, "On the basis of such scanty information made available to this profession through its rudimentary and haphazard system of technical research, we must conclude that the best results are to be obtained if the subject is embalmed before life is completely extinct—that is, before cellular death has occurred. In the average case, this would mean within an hour after somatic death." For those who feel that there is something a little rudimentary, not to say haphazard, about this advice, a comforting thought is offered by another writer. Speaking of fears entertained in early days of premature burial, he points out, "One of the effects of embalming by chemical injection, however, has been to dispel fears of live burial." How true; once the blood is removed, chances of live burial are indeed remote.

To return to Mr. Jones, the blood is drained out through the 8 veins and replaced by embalming fluid pumped in through the arteries. As noted in *The Principles and Practices of Embalming*, "Every operator has a favorite injection and drainage point—a fact which becomes a handicap only if he fails or refuses to forsake his favorites when conditions demand it." Typical favorites are the carotid artery, femoral artery, jugular vein, subclavian vein. There are various choices of embalming fluid. If Flextone is used, it will produce a "mild, flexible rigidity. The skin retains a velvety softness, the tissues are rubbery and pliable. Ideal for women and children." It may be blended with B. and G. Products Company's Lyf-Lyk tint, which is guaranteed to reproduce "nature's own skin texture . . . the velvety appearance of living tissue." Suntone comes in three separate tints: Suntan; Special Cosmetic Tint, a pink shade "especially indicated for young female subjects"; and Regular Cosmetic Tint, moderately pink.

About three to six gallons of dyed and perfumed solution of 9 formaldehyde, glycerin, borax, phenol, alcohol, and water are soon circulating through Mr. Jones, whose mouth has been sewn together with a "needle directed upward between the upper lip and gum and brought out through the left nostril," with the corners raised slightly "for a more pleasant expression." If he should be bucktoothed, his teeth are cleaned with Bon Ami and coated with colorless nail polish. His eyes, meanwhile, are closed with flesh-tinted eye caps and eye cement.

The next step is to have at Mr. Jones with a thing called a trocar. 10 This is a long, hollow needle attached to a tube. It is jabbed into the abdomen, poked around the entrails and chest cavity, the contents of which are pumped out and replaced with "cavity fluid." This done, and the hole in the abdomen sewn up, Mr. Jones's face is heavily creamed (to protect the skin from burns which may be caused by leakage of the chemicals), and he is covered with a sheet and left unmolested for a while. But not for long—there is more, much more, in store for him. He has been embalmed, but not yet restored, and the best time to start the restorative work is eight to ten hours after embalming, when the tissues have become firm and dry.

The object of all this attention to the corpse, it must be remem- 11 bered, is to make it presentable for viewing in an attitude of healthy repose. "Our customs require the presentation of our dead in the semblance of normality . . . unmarred by the ravages of illness, disease or mutilation," says Mr. J. Sheridan Mayer in his *Restorative Art.* This is rather a large order since few people die in the full bloom of health, unravaged by illness and unmarked by some disfigurement. The funeral industry is equal to the challenge: "In some cases the gruesome appearance of a mutilated or disease-ridden subject may be quite discouraging. The task of restoration may seem impossible and shake the confidence of the embalmer. This is the time for intestinal fortitude and determination. Once the formative work is begun and affected tissues are cleaned or removed, all doubts of success vanish. It is surprising and gratifying to discover the results which may be obtained."

The embalmer, having allowed an appropriate interval to 12 elapse, returns to the attack, but now he brings into play the skill and equipment of sculptor and cosmetician. Is a hand missing? Casting one in plaster of Paris is a simple matter. "For replacement purposes, only a cast of the back of the hand is necessary; this is within the ability of the average operator and is quite adequate." If a lip or two, a nose or an ear should be missing, the embalmer has at hand a variety of restorative waxes with which to model replacements. Pores and skin texture are simulated by stippling with a little brush, and over this cosmetics are laid on. Head off? Decapitation cases are rather routinely handled. Ragged edges are trimmed, and head joined to torso with a series of splints, wires and sutures. It is a good idea to have a little something at the neck—a scarf or high collar—when time for viewing comes. Swollen mouth? Cut out tissue as needed from inside the lips. If too much is removed, the surface contour can easily be restored by padding with cotton. Swollen necks and cheeks are reduced by removing tissue through vertical incisions made down each side of the neck. "When the deceased is casketed, the pillow will hide the suture incisions . . . as an extra precaution against leakage, the suture may be painted with liquid sealer."

The opposite condition is more likely to present itself—that of   13
emaciation. His hypodermic syringe now loaded with massage cream, the embalmer seeks out and fills the hollowed and sunken areas by injection. In this procedure the backs of the hands and fingers and the under-chin area should not be neglected.

Positioning the lips is a problem that recurrently challenges the   14
ingenuity of the embalmer. Closed too tightly, they tend to give a stern, even disapproving expression. Ideally, embalmers feel, the lips should give the impression of being ever so slightly parted, the upper lip protruding slightly for a more youthful appearance. This takes some engineering, however, as the lips tend to drift apart. Lip drift can sometimes be remedied by pushing one or two straight pins through the inner margin of the lower lip and then inserting them between the two front upper teeth. If Mr. Jones happens to have no teeth, the pins can just as easily be anchored in his Armstrong Face Former and Denture Replacer. Another method to maintain lip closure is to dislocate the lower jaw, which is then held in its new position by a wire run through holes which have been drilled through the upper and lower jaws at the midline. As the French are fond of saying, *il faut souffrir pour être belle.*[1]

If Mr. Jones has died of jaundice, the embalming fluid will very   15
likely turn him green. Does this deter the embalmer? Not if he has intestinal fortitude. Masking pastes and cosmetics are heavily laid on, burial garments and casket interiors are color-correlated with particular care, and Jones is displayed beneath rose-colored lights. Friends will say, "How *well* he looks." Death by carbon monoxide, on the other hand, can be rather a good thing from the embalmer's viewpoint:

---

[1] You have to suffer if you want to be beautiful (Editor's note).

"One advantage is the fact that this type of discoloration is an exaggerated form of a natural pink coloration." This is nice because the healthy glow is already present and needs but little attention.

The patching and filling completed, Mr. Jones is now shaved, 16 washed and dressed. Cream-based cosmetic, available in pink, flesh, suntan, brunette and blond, is applied to his hands and face, his hair is shampooed and combed (and, in the case of Mrs. Jones, set), his hands manicured. For the horny-handed son of toil special care must be taken; cream should be applied to remove ingrained grime, and the nails cleaned. "If he were not in the habit of having them manicured in life, trimming and shaping is advised for better appearance—never questioned by kin."

Jones is now ready for casketing (this is the present participle of 17 the verb "to casket"). In this operation, his right shoulder should be depressed slightly "to turn the body a bit to the right and soften the appearance of lying flat on the back." Positioning the hands is a matter of importance, and special rubber positioning blocks may be used. The hands should be cupped slightly for a more lifelike, relaxed appearance. Proper placement of the body requires a delicate sense of balance. It should lie as high as possible in the casket, yet not so high that the lid, when lowered, will hit the nose. On the other hand, we are cautioned, placing the body too low "creates the impression that the body is in a box."

Jones is next wheeled into the appointed slumber room where a 18 few last touches may be added—his favorite pipe placed in his hand or, if he was a great reader, a book propped into position. (In the case of little Master Jones a Teddy bear may be clutched.) Here he will hold open house for a few days, visiting hours 10 A.M. to 9 P.M.

Meanings and Values

1. What is the author's tone? (See "Guide to Terms": *Style/Tone*.) What does the tone reveal about the writer's attitude towards the intense concern with the appearance of the dead exhibited by embalmers (and other people)?

2. Why was it formerly "almost mandatory" for some relative to witness the embalming procedure (par. 2)?

3. Do you believe that public information about this procedure would cost mortuaries much embalming business (par. 3)? Why, or why not? Why *do* people subject their dead to such a process?

4. Use the three-part system of evaluation found in the "Guide to Terms": *Evaluation* to judge the success of this process analysis.

Expository Techniques

1. What is the central theme? (Guide: *Unity*.) Which parts of the writing, if any, do not contribute to the theme, thus damaging unity? Which contribute to unity?

2. Beginning with paragraph 4, list or mark the transitional devices that help to bridge paragraphs. (Guide: *Transition*.) Briefly explain how coherence is aided by such interparagraph transitions.

3. In this selection, far more than in most, emphasis can best be studied in connection with style. In fact, the two are almost indistinguishable here, and few, if any, of the other methods of achieving emphasis are used at all. (Guide: *Emphasis; Style/Tone*.) Consider each of the following stylistic qualities (some may overlap; others are included in diction) and illustrate, by examples, how each creates emphasis.

   a. Number and selection of details—e.g., the equipment and "aids" (par. 5).

   b. Understatement—e.g., the "chances of live burial" (par. 7).

   c. Special use of quotations—e.g, "that the body is in a box" (par. 17).

   d. Sarcasm and/or other forms of irony—e.g., "How *well* he looks" (par. 15). (Guide: *Irony*.)

Diction and Vocabulary

1. Much of the essay's unique style (with resulting emphasis) comes from qualities of diction. Use examples to illustrate the following. (Some may be identical to those of the preceding answer, but they need not be.)

   a. Choice of common, low-key words to achieve sarcasm through understatement—e.g., "This is nice . . . " (par. 15).

   b. Terms of violence—e.g., "returns to the attack" (par. 12).

   c. Terms of the living—e.g., "will hold open house" (par. 18).

   d. The continuing use of "Mr. Jones."

2. Illustrate the meaning of "connotation" with examples of the quotations from morticians. (Guide: *Connotation/Denotation*.) Are these also examples of "euphemism"?

3. Use the dictionary as needed to understand the meanings of the following words: docility, perpetuation (par. 1); inherent, mandatory (2); intractable, reticence, *raison d'être* (3); ingenious (5); rudimentary, cellular, somatic (7); carotid artery, femoral artery, subclavian vein (8); semblance (11); simulated, stippling, sutures (12); emaciation (13); dispel (7, title).

Read to Write

1. Think of any other common practices in which we alter appearances to hide reality or create a new reality. Choose one practice you can analyze in detail as the subject for an essay.

2. Mitford presents an unpleasant subject—dead bodies—in such detail that it becomes intriguing (her humor helps here, too). Use a similar strategy in your own writing about a subject that readers might at first consider distasteful or boring.

3. Using Mitford's essay as a model—especially for tone and use of detail—create an essay of your own on the subject you chose in question 1.

(NOTE: Suggestions for topics requiring development by PROCESS ANALYSIS are on page 292 at the end of this section.)

JEAN E. KILBOURNE is a media critic whose award-winning films *Still Killing Us Softly* and *Calling the Shots* explore the relationships between media and advertising images and our values and behaviors. She lectures regularly on alcohol and cigarette advertising, images of women in advertising, and related issues.

Beauty . . . And the Beast of Advertising

In this essay, first published in *Media & Values* in 1989, Kilbourne analyzes the ways media images shape perceptions and values, particularly those of women. This essay blends a number of patterns, including definition, process analysis, and cause-and-effect analysis.

"You're a Halston woman from the very beginning," the advertise- 1
ment proclaims. The model stares provocatively at the viewer, her long blonde hair waving around her face, her bare chest partially covered by two curved bottles that give the illusion of breasts and a cleavage.

The average American is accustomed to blue-eyed blondes 2
seductively touting a variety of products. In this case, however, the blonde is about five years old.

Advertising is an over $100 billion a year industry and affects 3
all of us throughout our lives. We are each exposed to over 2,000 ads a day, constituting perhaps the most powerful educational force in society. The average adult will spend one and one-half years of his/her life watching television commercials. But the ads sell a great deal more than products. They sell values, images and concepts of success and worth, love and sexuality, popularity and normalcy. They tell us who we are and who we should be. Sometimes they sell addictions.

Advertising's foundation and economic lifeblood is the mass 4
media, and the primary purpose of the mass media is to deliver an audience to advertisers, just as the primary purpose of television programs is to deliver an audience for commercials.

Adolescents are particularly vulnerable, however, because they 5
are new and inexperienced consumers and are the prime targets of

many advertisements. They are in the process of learning their values and roles and developing their self-concepts. Most teenagers are sensitive to peer pressure and find it difficult to resist or even question the dominant cultural messages perpetuated and reinforced by the media. Mass communication has made possible a kind of nationally distributed peer pressure that erodes private and individual values and standards.

But what does society, and especially teenagers, learn from the   6
advertising messages that proliferate in the mass media? On the most obvious level they learn the stereotypes. Advertising creates a mythical, WASP-oriented world in which no one is ever ugly, overweight, poor, struggling or disabled either physically or mentally (unless you count the housewives who talk to little men in toilet bowls, animated germs in drains or muscle-bound giants clad in white clothing). And it is a world in which people talk only about products.

Housewives or Sex Objects

The aspect of advertising most in need of analysis and change is the   7
portrayal of women. Scientific studies and the most casual viewing yield the same conclusion: Women are shown almost exclusively as housewives or sex objects.

The housewife, pathologically obsessed by cleanliness and   8
lemon fresh scents, debates cleaning products with herself and worries about her husband's "ring around the collar."

The sex object is a mannequin, a shell. Conventional beauty is   9
her only attribute. She has no lines or wrinkles (which would indicate she had the bad taste and poor judgment to grow older), no scars or blemishes—indeed, she has no pores. She is thin, generally tall and long-legged, and, above all, she is young. All "beautiful" women in advertisements (including minority women), regardless of product or audience, conform to this norm. Women are constantly exhorted to emulate this ideal, to feel ashamed and guilty if they fail, and to feel that their desirability and lovability are contingent upon physical perfection.

Creating Artificiality

The image is artificial and can only be achieved artificially (even the   10
"natural look" requires much preparation and expense). Beauty is

something that comes from without; more than one million dollars is spent every hour on cosmetics. Desperate to conform to an ideal and impossible standard, many women go to great lengths to manipulate and change their faces and bodies. A woman is conditioned to view her face as a mask and her body as an object, as *things* separate from and more important than her real self, constantly in need of alteration, improvement, and disguise. She is made to feel dissatisfied with and ashamed of herself, whether she tries to achieve "the look" or not. Objectified constantly by others, she learns to objectify herself. (It is interesting to note that one in five college-age women have an eating disorder.)

"When *Glamour* magazine surveyed its readers in 1984, 75 per-   11
cent felt too heavy and only 15 percent felt just right. Nearly half of those who were actually underweight reported feeling too fat and wanting to diet. Among a sample of college women, 40 percent felt overweight when only 12 percent actually were too heavy," according to Rita Freedman in her book *Beauty Bound*.

There is evidence that this preoccupation with weight begins at   12
ever-earlier ages for women. According to a recent article in *New Age Journal*, "even grade-school girls are succumbing to sticklike standards of beauty enforced by a relentless parade of wasp-waisted fashion models, movie stars, and pop idols." A study by a University of California professor showed that nearly 80 percent of fourth-grade girls in the Bay Area are watching their weight.

A recent *Wall Street Journal* survey of students in four Chicago-   13
area schools found that more than half the fourth-grade girls were dieting and three-quarters felt they were overweight. One student said, "We don't expect boys to be that handsome. We take them as they are." Another added, "But boys expect girls to be perfect and beautiful. And skinny."

Dr. Steven Levenkron, author of *The Best Little Girl in the World*,   14
the story of an anorexic, says his blood pressure soars every time he opens a magazine and finds an ad for women's fashions. "If I had my way," he said, "every one of them would have to carry a line saying, 'Caution: This model may be hazardous to your health.'"

Women are also dismembered in commercials, their bodies sep-   15
arated into parts in need of change or improvement. If a woman has "acceptable" breasts, then she must also be sure that her legs are worth watching, her hips slim, her feet sexy, and that her buttocks look nude under her clothes ("like I'm not wearin' nothin'"). This image is difficult and costly to achieve and impossible to maintain

(unless you buy the product)—no one is flawless and everyone ages. Growing older is the great taboo. Women are encouraged to remain little girls ("because innocence is sexier than you think"), to be passive and dependent, never too mature. The contradictory message— "sensual, but not too far from innocence"—places women in a double bind; somehow we are supposed to be both sexy and virginal, experienced and naíve, seductive and chaste. The disparagement of maturity is, of course, insulting and frustrating to adult women, and the implication that little girls are seductive is dangerous to real children.

Influencing Sexual Attitudes

Young people also learn a great deal about sexual attitudes from the media and from advertising in particular. Advertising's approach to sex is pornographic; it reduces people to objects and de-emphasizes human contact and individuality. This reduction of sexuality to a dirty joke and of people to objects is the real obscenity of the culture. Although the sexual sell, overt and subliminal, is at a fevered pitch in most commercials, there is at the same time a notable absence of sex as an important and profound human activity. 16

There have been some changes in the images of women. Indeed, a "new woman" has emerged in commercials in recent years. She is generally presented as superwoman, who manages to do all the work at home and on the job (with the help of a product, of course, not of her husband or children or friends), or as the liberated woman, who owes her independence and self-esteem to the products she uses. These new images do not represent any real progress but rather create a myth of progress, an illusion that reduces complex sociopolitical problems to mundane personal ones. 17

Advertising images do not cause these problems, but they contribute to them by creating a climate in which the marketing of women's bodies—the sexual sell and dismemberment, distorted body image ideal and children as sex objects—is seen as acceptable. 18

This is the real tragedy, that many women internalize these stereotypes and learn their "limitations," thus establishing a self-fulfilling prophecy. If one accepts these mythical and degrading images, to some extent one actualizes them. By remaining unaware of the profound seriousness of the ubiquitous influence, the redundant message and the subliminal impact of advertisements, we ignore one of the most powerful "educational" forces in the 19 culture—one that greatly affects our self-images, our ability to relate to each other, and effectively destroys any awareness and action that might help to change that climate.

Meanings and Values

1. According to the writer, what does advertising tell women they should be, and by what process does it convey this message? Does the beginning of paragraph 18 accurately summarize the process the writer has been analyzing? If not, what is missing from the summary? Would the essay be stronger if the missing information were included? Why or why not? (See "Guide to Terms": *Evaluation.*)

2. Who or what is the "new woman" (par. 7)? Why does the writer believe that this image does "not represent any real progress"? Why would the absence of any discussion of the "new woman" weaken the expository purpose of the selection? (Guide: *Purpose.*)

3. At several places in the essay, Kilbourne discusses the consequences of advertising on teenagers while in much of the rest of the essay she focuses on women. Does the focus on teenagers undermine the unity of the essay? Why or why not? (Guide: *Unity.*)

Expository Techniques

1. What strategy does Kilbourne use to begin her essay (pars. 1–2)? (Guide: *Introductions.*) Can the opening of this essay be considered ironic? Why or why not? (Guide: *Irony.*) What strategy does she use to conclude the essay? (Guide: *Closings.*)

2. What kinds of evidence does the author provide to support her conclusions about the process of advertising and its consequences? Which kind of evidence do you consider most effective, and which least effective? Why? (Guide: *Evaluation.*)

3. Discuss how Kilbourne varies sentence length (and structure) to achieve emphasis in paragraphs 3, 9, and 15. (Guide: *Emphasis; Syntax.*)

Diction and Vocabulary

1. Where in the essay does the writer use numbers to present information? Be specific. Why can these numbers be considered a form of concrete diction? (Guide: *Concrete/Abstract; Diction.*) What do they contribute to the effects of the various passages in which they appear?

2. If you do not know the meaning of some of the following words, look them up in a dictionary: provocatively, cleavage (par. 1); touting (2);

stereotypes; WASP (6); pathologically (8); mannequin, attribute, exhorted, contingent (9); anorexic (14); sensual, disparagement (15); overt, subliminal (16); mundane (17); ubiquitous, redundant (19).

Read to Write

1. Spend some time observing advertisements on television or analyzing them in magazines. Take notes on the process by which they achieve their effects as well as the effects themselves. Look over your notes to find a focus and a thesis for an essay of your own.

2. Read (or reread) Brent Staples's essay, "Just Walk on By" (pages 57–63), for another example of an essay that begins with a reversal of expectations. Begin an essay of your own with a reversal of expectations similar to the ones created by Kilbourne and Staples.

3. Using Kilbourne's essay as a model, discuss the process of advertising as it affects a group or groups other than women in general. Feel free to take a positive view of advertising in contrast to Kilbourne's generally negative perspective.

(NOTE: Suggestions for topics requiring development by means of PROCESS ANALYSIS follow.)

Writing Suggestions for Section 7
Process Analysis

1. From one of the following topics develop a central theme into an *informational* process analysis, showing:

   a. How you selected a college.

   b. How you selected your future career or major field of study.

   c. How your family selected a home.

   d. How an unusual sport is played.

   e. How religious faith is achieved.

   f. How gasoline is made.

   g. How the air (or water) in _____ becomes polluted.

   h. How lightning kills.

   i. How foreign policy is made.

   j. How political campaigns are financed.

   k. How _____ Church was rebuilt.

   l. How fruit blossoms are pollinated.

   m. How a computer chip is designed or made.

2. Select a specific reader-audience and write a *directional* process analysis on one of the following topics, showing:

   a. How to *do* any of the processes suggested by topics 1a–e. (This treatment will require a different viewpoint, completely objective, and may require a different organization.)

   b. How to overcome shyness.

   c. How to overcome stage fright.

   d. How to make the best use of study time.

   e. How to write a college composition.

   f. How to sell an ugly house.

   g. How to prepare livestock or any other entry for a fair.

   h. How to start a club (or some other kind of recurring activity).

8

Analyzing *Cause-and-Effect* Relationships

Unlike process analysis, which merely tells *how*, causal analysis seeks to explain *why*. The two may be combined, but they need not be—many people have driven a car successfully after being told how to do it, never knowing or caring why the thing moved when they turned a key and worked a pedal or two.

Some causes and effects are not very complicated; at least their explanation requires only a simple statement. A car may sit in the garage for a while because its owner has no money for a license tag, and sometimes this is explanation enough. But frequently a much more thorough analysis is required, and this may even become the basic pattern of an exposition.

To explain fully the causes of a war or a depression or election results, the writer must seek not only *immediate* causes (the ones encountered first) but also *ultimate* causes (the basic, underlying factors that help to explain the more apparent ones). Business or professional people, as well as students, often have a pressing need for this type of analysis. How else could they fully understand or report on a failing sales campaign, diminishing church membership, a local increase in traffic accidents, or teenage use of drugs? The immediate cause of a disastrous warehouse fire could be faulty electrical wiring, but this might be attributed in turn to the company's unwise economy measures, which might be traced even further to undue pressures on the management to show large profits. The written analysis might logically stop at any point, of course, depending entirely on its purpose and the reader-audience for which it is intended.

Similarly, both the immediate and ultimate *effects* of an action or situation may, or may not, need to be fully explored. If a five percent pay raise is granted, what will be the immediate effect on the cost of production, leading to what ultimate effects on prices and, in some cases, on the economy of a business, a town, or perhaps the entire nation?

In earlier sections of this book we have seen several examples of causal analysis. In Section 3, for instance, Buckley gives some attention to both immediate and ultimate causes of American apathy, and in Section 6, Wolfe is concerned with both immediate and ultimate effects of overcrowding.

Causal analysis is one of the chief techniques of reasoning; and if the method is used at all, the reader must always have confidence in its thoroughness and logic. Here are some ways to avoid the most common faults in causal reasoning:

1. Never mistake the fact that something happens with or after another occurrence as evidence of a causal relationship—for example, that a black cat crossing the road caused the flat tire a few minutes later, or that a course in English composition caused a student's nervous breakdown that same semester.

2. Consider all possibly relevant factors before attributing causes. Perhaps studying English did result in a nervous breakdown, but the cause may also have been ill health, trouble at home, the stress of working while attending college, or the anguish of a love affair. (The composition course, by providing an "emotional" outlet, may even have helped postpone the breakdown!)

3. Support the analysis by more than mere assertions: offer evidence. It would not often be enough to *tell* why Shakespeare's wise Othello believed the villainous Iago—the dramatist's lines should be used as evidence, possibly supported by the opinions of at least one literary scholar. If you are explaining that capital punishment deters crime, do not expect the reader to take your word for it—give before-and-after statistics or the testimony of reliable authorities.

4. Be careful not to omit any links in the chain of causes or effects unless you are certain that the readers for whom the writing is intended will automatically make the right connections themselves—and this is frequently a dangerous assumption. To unwisely omit one or more of the links might leave the reader with only a vague, or even erroneous, impression of the causal connection, possibly invalidating all that follows and thus making the entire writing ineffective.

5. Be honest and objective. Writers (or thinkers) who bring their old prejudices to the task of causal analysis, or who fail to see the probability of *multiple* causes or effects, are almost certain to distort their analyses or to make them so superficial, so thin, as to be almost worthless.

Ordinarily the method of causal analysis is either to work logically from the immediate cause (or effect) down toward the most basic, or to start with the basic and work up toward the immediate. But after at least analyzing the subject and deciding what the purpose requires in the paragraph or entire composition, the writer will usually find that a satisfactory pattern suggests itself.

Sample Paragraph (Annotated)

A question introduces the phenomenon to be explained.

Why has Palmville grown so rapidly over the past decade? In response to a survey conducted last year by the Chamber of Commerce, most new residents said the reason they moved to Palmville was to escape from the living conditions in Valley City and its nearest suburbs, especially congestion, air pollution, and high housing costs.

An *ultimate cause,* though a negative one.

The ultimate cause does not provide a satisfactory explanation for the choice of Palmville.

Other towns nearby have not grown as rapidly as Palmville, however. On the survey, people also indicated why they chose to move here rather than to other towns in Nocatowie County, such as Lopestown, El Caton, or Fillmore Glen.

Immediate causes.

Use of the survey adds authority to the explanation.

People say they came to Palmville because of the location. Interstate 104 runs through the town on its way to Valley City, making commuting possible, though taxing. They came because M&T Realty spent a good deal on ads in the *Valley City Times* telling about affordable three-bedroom homes in the town. They came for the good schools and the nearby lakes and parks.

Taken together, the immediate causes provide a satisfactory explanation for the choice of Palmville.

{ Finally, almost all those surveyed said that they came in part because they were already familiar with the name of the town from the region's most famous agricultural product: The Palmville Onion.

Sample Paragraph (Cause/Effect)

Rap [music] started in discos, not the midtown glitter palaces like Studio 54 or New York, New York, but at Mel Quinn's on 42nd Street and Club 371 in the Bronx, where a young Harlemite who called himself D. J. Hollywood spun on the weekends. It wasn't unusual for black club jocks to talk to their audiences in the jive style of the old personality deejays. Two of the top black club spinners of the day, Pete (D. J.) Jones and Maboya, did so. Hollywood, just an adolescent when he started, created a more complicated, faster style, with more rhymes than his older mentors and call-and-response passages to encourage reaction from the dancers. At local bars, discos, and many illegal after-hours spots frequented by street people, Hollywood developed a huge word-of-mouth reputation. Tapes of his parties began appearing around the city on the then new and incredibly loud Japanese portable cassette players flooding into America. In Harlem, Kurtis Blow, Eddie Cheeba, and D. J. Lovebug Star-ski; in the Bronx, Junebug Star-ski, Grandmaster Flash, and Melle Mel; in Brooklyn, three kids from the projects called Whodini; and in Queens, Russell and Joey, the two youngest sons from the middle-class Simmons household—all shared a fascination with Hollywood's use of the rhythmic breaks in his club mixes and his verbal dexterity. These kids would all grow up to play a role in the local clubs and, later, a few would appear on the national scene to spread Hollywood's style. Back in the 1970s, while disco reigned in the media, the Black Main Streets of New York were listening to D. J. Hollywood, and learning.

Nelson George, *The Death of Rhythm and Blues* (1991).

SUSAN PERRY is a former staff writer for Time-Life, Inc., and now works full-time as a freelance writer specializing in health, business, and women's issues. Her articles have appeared in such publications as *Ms., The Washington Post,* and the *Minneapolis Star.* She is the author of *Nightmare* (1985) and *Natural Menopause* (1992). JAMES DAWSON is a science reporter who writes regularly for the *Minneapolis Star-Tribune.* Perry and Dawson co-authored *The Secrets Our Body Clocks Reveal* (1988).

What's Your Best Time of Day?

This essay, published as a magazine article, is drawn from *The Secrets Our Body Clocks Reveal.* The piece opens with examples of some puzzling behaviors, looks at their causes in the rhythms of our bodies, then examines some further effects of these rhythms. The authors make use of examples, classification, and process to support the cause-effect pattern and provide practical advice for taking advantage of the biological patterns that help govern our lives.

Every fall, Jane, a young mother and part-time librarian, begins to eat   1
more and often feels sleepy. Her mood is also darker, especially when
she awakens in the morning; it takes all her energy just to drag herself
out of bed. These symptoms persist until April, when warmer
weather and longer days seems to lighten her mood and alleviate her
cravings for food and sleep.

Joseph, a 48-year-old engineer for a Midwestern computer com-   2
pany, feels cranky early in the morning. But as the day progresses,
he becomes friendlier and more accommodating.

All living organisms, from mollusks to men and women, exhibit   3
biological rhythms. Some are short and can be measured in minutes
or hours. Others last days or months. The peaking of body

temperature, which occurs in most people every evening, is a daily rhythm. The menstrual cycle is a monthly rhythm. The increase in sexual drive in the autumn—not in the spring, as poets would have us believe—is a seasonal, or yearly, rhythm.

The idea that our bodies are in constant flux is fairly new—and   4
goes against traditional medical training. In the past, many doctors were taught to believe the body has a relatively stable, or homeostatic, internal environment. Any fluctuations were considered random and not meaningful enough to be studied.

As early as the 1940s, however, some scientists questioned the   5
homeostatic view of the body. Franz Halberg, a young European scientist working in the United States, noticed that the number of white blood cells in laboratory mice was dramatically higher and lower at different times of day. Gradually, such research spread to the study of other rhythms in other life forms, and the findings were sometimes startling. For example, the time of day when a person receives X-ray or drug treatment for cancer can affect treatment benefits and ultimately mean the difference between life and death.

This new science is called chronobiology, and the evidence sup-   6
porting it has become increasingly persuasive. Along the way, the scientific and medical communities are beginning to rethink their ideas about how the human body works, and gradually what had been considered a minor science just a few years ago is being studied in major universities and medical centers around the world. There are even chronobiologists working for the National Aeronautics and Space Administration, as well as for the National Institutes of Health and other government laboratories.

With their new findings, they are teaching us things that can   7
literally change our lives—by helping us organize ourselves so we can work *with* our natural rhythms rather than against them. This can enhance our outlook on life as well as our performance at work and play.

Because they are easy to detect and measure, more is known of   8
daily—or circadian (Latin for "about a day")—rhythms than other types. The most obvious daily rhythm is the sleep/wake cycle. But there are other daily cycles as well: temperature, blood pressure, hormone levels. Amid these and the body's other changing rhythms, you are simply a different person at 9 A.M. than you are at 3 P.M. How you feel, how well you work, your level of alertness, your sensitivity to taste and smell, the degree with which you enjoy food or take pleasure in music—all are changing throughout the day.

Most of us seem to reach our peak of alertness around noon. 9
Soon after that, alertness declines, and sleepiness may set in by
midafternoon.

Your short-term memory is best during the morning—in fact, 10
about 15 percent more efficient than at any other time of day. So,
students, take heed: when faced with a morning exam, it really does
pay to review your notes right before the test is given.

Long-term memory is different. Afternoon is the best time for 11
learning material that you want to recall days, weeks or months
later. Politicians, business executives or others who must learn
speeches would be smart to do their memorizing during that time of
day. If you are a student, you would be wise to schedule your more
difficult classes in the afternoon, rather than in the morning. You
should also try to do most of your studying in the afternoon, rather
than late at night. Many students believe they memorize better while
burning the midnight oil because their short-term recall is better
during the wee hours of the morning than in the afternoon. But
short-term memory won't help them much several days later, when
they face the exam.

By contrast, we tend to do best on cognitive tasks—things that 12
require the juggling of words and figures in one's head—during the
morning hours. This might be a good time, say, to balance a checkbook.

Your manual dexterity—the speed and coordination with 13
which you perform complicated tasks with your hands—peaks during the afternoon hours. Such work as carpentry, typing or sewing
will be a little easier at this time of day.

What about sports? During afternoon and early evening, your 14
coordination is at its peak, and you're able to react the quickest to an
outside stimulus—like a baseball speeding toward you at home
plate. Studies have also shown that late in the day, when your body
temperature is peaking, you will *perceive* a physical workout to be
easier and less fatiguing—whether it actually is or not. That means
you are more likely to work harder during a late-afternoon or early-
evening workout, and therefore benefit more from it. Studies involving swimmers, runners, shot-putters and rowing crews have shown
consistently that performance is better in the evening than in the
morning.

In fact, all of your senses—taste, sight, hearing, touch and 15
smell—may be at their keenest during late afternoon and early

evening. That could be why dinner usually tastes better to us than breakfast and why bright lights irritate us at night.

Even our perception of time changes from hour to hour. Not only does time seem to fly when you're having fun, but it also seems to fly even faster if you are having that fun in the late afternoon or early evening, when your body temperature is also peaking. 16

While all of us follow the same general pattern of ups and downs, the exact timing varies from person to person. It all depends on how your "biological" day is structured—how much of a morning or night person you are. The earlier your biological day gets going, the earlier you are likely to enter—and exit—the peak times for performing various tasks. An extreme morning person and an extreme night person may have circadian cycles that are a few hours apart. 17

Each of us can increase our knowledge about our individual rhythms. Learn how to listen to the inner beats of your body; let them set the pace of your day. You will live a healthier—and happier—life. As no less an authority than the Bible tells us, "To every thing there is a season, and a time to every purpose under heaven." 18

Meanings and Values

1. What cause(s) and effect(s) do the writers discuss in this selection?

2. According to the explanations in this essay, what are the best times to undertake the following activities, and why:

   a. play a sport

   b. balance a checkbook

   c. learn a speech

   d. prepare for an exam

Expository Techniques

1. What functions do the examples that open the essay perform for readers? (See "Guide to Terms": *Introductions*.)

2. Where in the essay do the authors use classification? Why? Where do the authors use process analysis? Why?

3. Would this essay be more effective if discussions of the causes and the effects were more clearly separated? Why, or why not? (Guide: *Evaluation*.)

4. Discuss the arrangement of paragraphs 9–12, paying special attention to parallel structures and transitions within and between paragraphs. (Guide: *Unity; Parallel Structure.*)

Diction and Vocabulary

1. In what ways does the diction in paragraphs 1 and 2 emphasize the contrasts being illustrated? (Guide: *Diction.*)

2. Discuss how the authors provide explanations of the following scientific or otherwise unfamiliar terms in the text so that readers will not have to pause to look them up: homeostatic (par. 4); circadian (8); cognitive tasks (12); manual dexterity (13).

3. Does the allusion that concludes the essay seem appropriate? Why, or why not? Try looking up the passage in the Bible (Ecclesiastes 3:1) to see if its original meaning is similar to the one it has in the context of this essay.

Read to Write

1. Assume for a moment that Perry and Dawson's view of the cause-effect relationship of body cycles and behavior is accurate. Think of how typical academic or work schedules might need to be altered to take into account the patterns described by the authors. What common practices seem particularly in need of change given the information provided here? Consider making such practical consequences the topic of an essay.

2. Perry and Dawson use numerous examples to explain and confirm the effects of body cycles. Do your experiences agree with what the authors say about the cycles that guide our behavior? In an essay of your own, provide examples that either support or contradict their conclusions, or that do the same for some other well-known explanation of behavior.

3. In a magazine like *Discover* or *Scientific American,* read an article that offers a physical explanation of human behavior. Or in a magazine like *Psychology Today,* read an article that offers a psychological or social explanation of behavior. Then, using "What's Your Best Time of Day?" as a model, create your own essay explaining both the cause and its effects on our daily lives.

(NOTE: Suggestions for topics requiring development by analysis of CAUSE AND EFFECT are on pages 343-344 at the end of this section.)

LINDA HASSELSTROM

LINDA HASSELSTROM is an essayist, poet, and environmental writer who is also a rancher in western South Dakota. Her books include *Caught by One Wing* **(1984) and** *Roadkill* **(1987) (poetry);** *Windbreak: A Woman Rancher on the Northern Plains* **(1987) and** *Going over East* **(1987) (journals and nonfiction); and** *Land Circle: Writings Collected from the Land* **(1991) (essays and poetry). Her essays have appeared in many magazines such as** *High Country News, Northern Lights, North American Review, Working Parents, Iowa Woman, Whole Earth Review,* **and** *Utne Reader* **as well as newspapers such as the** *Los Angeles Times* **and** *The Christian Science Monitor.*

A Peaceful Woman Explains Why She Carries a Pistol

This version of the essay "Why One Peaceful Woman Carries a Pistol" first appeared in the *Utne Reader*. In it, Hasselstrom takes a subject (gun ownership) usually dealt with in terms of general principles (the right to bear arms) or social trends and explores it in terms of a particular person in a particular setting. This focus on the individual leads to an analysis of cause and effect relationships that readers are likely to find either invigorating or disquieting, or both.

I am a peace-loving woman. But several events in the past 10 years 1 have convinced me I'm safer when I carry a pistol. This was a personal decision, but because handgun possession is a controversial subject, perhaps my reasoning will interest others.

I live in western South Dakota on a ranch 25 miles from the 2 nearest large town; for several years I spent winters alone here. As a free-lance writer, I travel alone a lot—more than 100,000 miles by car in the last four years. With women freer than ever before to travel alone, the odds of our encountering trouble seem to have risen. And help, in the West, can be hours away. Distances are great, roads are deserted, and the terrain is often too exposed to offer hiding places.

A woman who travels alone is advised, usually be men, to pro-   3
tect herself by avoiding bars and other "dangerous situations," by
approaching her car like an Indian scout, by locking doors and windows. But these precautions aren't always enough. I spent years following them and still found myself in dangerous situations. I began
to resent the idea that just because I am female, I have to be extra
careful.

A few years ago, with another woman, I camped for several   4
weeks in the West. We discussed self-defense, but neither of us had
taken a course in it. She was against firearms, and local police told
us Mace was illegal. So we armed ourselves with spray cans of
deodorant tucked into our sleeping bags. We never used our impro-
vised Mace because we were lucky enough to camp beside people
who came to our aid when men harassed us. But on one occasion we
visited a national park where our assigned space was less than 15
feet from other campers. When we returned from a walk, we found
our closest neighbors were two young men. As we gathered our
cooking gear, they drank beer and loudly discussed what they
would do to us after dark. Nearby campers, even families, ignored
them; rangers strolled past, unconcerned. When we asked the
rangers point-blank if they would protect us, one of them patted my
shoulder and said, "Don't worry, girls. They're just kidding." At
dusk we drove out of the park and hid our camp in the woods a few
miles away. The illegal spot was lovely, but our enjoyment of that
park was ruined. I returned from the trip determined to reconsider
the options available for protecting myself.

At that time, I lived alone on the ranch and taught night classes   5
in town. Along a city street I often traveled, a woman had a flat tire,
called for help on her CB radio, and got a rapist who left her beaten.
She was afraid to call for help again and stayed in her car until morning. For that reason, as well as because CBs work best along line-of-
sight, which wouldn't help much in the rolling hills where I live, I
ruled out a CB.

As I drove home one night, a car followed me. It passed me on   6
a narrow bridge while a passenger flashed a blinding spotlight in
my face. I braked sharply. The car stopped, angled across the bridge,
and four men jumped out. I realized the locked doors were useless
if they broke the windows of my pickup. I started forward, hoping
to knock their car aside so I could pass. Just then another car
appeared, and the men hastily got back in their car. They continued
to follow me, passing and repassing. I dared not go home because no

one else was there. I passed no lighted houses. Finally they pulled over to the roadside, and I decided to use their tactic: fear. Speeding, the pickup horn blaring, I swerved as close to them as I dared as I roared past. It worked; they turned off the highway. But I was frightened and angry. Even in my vehicle I was too vulnerable.

Other incidents occurred over the years. One day I glanced out   7
a field below my house and saw a man with a shotgun walking toward a pond full of ducks. I drove down and explained that the land was posted. I politely asked him to leave. He stared at me, and the muzzle of the shotgun began to rise. In a moment of utter clarity I realized that I was alone on the ranch, and that he could shoot me and simply drive away. The moment passed; the man left.

One night, I returned home from teaching a class to find deep   8
tire ruts in the wet ground of my yard, garbage in the driveway, and a large gas tank empty. A light shone in the house; I couldn't remember leaving it on. I was too embarrassed to drive to a neighboring ranch and wake someone up. An hour of cautious exploration convinced me the house was safe, but once inside, with the doors locked, I was still afraid. I kept thinking of how vulnerable I felt, prowling around my own house in the dark.

My first positive step was to take a kung fu class, which teaches   9
evasive or protective action when someone enters your space without permission. I learned to move confidently, scanning for possible attackers. I learned how to assess danger and techniques for avoiding it without combat.

I also learned that one must practice several hours every day to   10
be good at kung fu. By that time I had married George; when I practiced with him, I learned how *close* you must be to your attacker to use martial arts, and decided a 120-pound woman dare not let a six-foot, 220-pound attacker get that close unless she is very, very good at self-defense. I have since read articles by several women who were extremely well trained in the martial arts, but were raped and beaten anyway.

I thought back over the times in my life when I had been attacked   11
or threatened and tried to be realistic about my own behavior, searching for anything that had allowed me to become a victim. Overall, I was convinced that I had not been at fault. I don't believe myself to be either paranoid or a risk-taker, but I wanted more protection.

With some reluctance I decided to try carrying a pistol. George   12
had always carried one, despite his size and his training in martial arts. I practiced shooting until I was sure I could hit an attacker who

moved close enough to endanger me. Then I bought a license from the county sheriff, making it legal for me to carry the gun concealed.

But I was not yet ready to defend myself. George taught me that   13
the most important preparation was mental: convincing myself I could actually *shoot a person*. Few of us wish to hurt or kill another human being. But there is no point in having a gun—in fact, gun possession might increase your danger—unless you know you can use it. I got in the habit of rehearsing, as I drove or walked, the precise conditions that would be required before I would shoot someone.

People who have not grown up with the idea that they are   14
capable of protecting themselves—in other words, most women— might have to work hard to convince themselves of their ability, and of the necessity. Handgun ownership need not turn us into gunslingers, but it can be part of believing in, and relying on, *ourselves* for protection.

To be useful, a pistol had to be available. In my car, it's within   15
instant reach. When I enter a deserted rest stop at night, it's in my purse, with my hand on the grip. When I walk from a dark parking lot into a motel, it's in my hand, under a coat. At home, it's on the headboard. In short, I take it with me almost everywhere I go alone.

Just carrying a pistol is not protection; avoidance is still the best   16
approach to trouble. Subconsciously watching for signs of danger, I believe I've become more alert. Handgun use, not unlike driving, becomes instinctive. Each time I've drawn my gun—I have never fired it at another human being—I've simply found it in my hand.

I was driving the half-mile to the highway mailbox one day   17
when I saw a vehicle parked about midway down the road. Several men were standing in the ditch, relieving themselves. I have no objection to emergency urination, but I noticed they'd dumped several dozen beer cans in the road. Besides being ugly, cans can slash a cow's feet or stomach.

The men noticed me before they finished and made quite a per-   18
formance out of zipping their trousers while walking toward me. All four of them gathered around my small foreign car, and one of them demanded what the hell I wanted.

"This is private land. I'd appreciate it if you'd pick up the beer   19
cans."

"What beer cans?" said the belligerent one, putting both hands   20
on the car door and leaning in my window. His face was inches from mine, and the beer fumes were strong. The others laughed. One tried the passenger door, locked; another put his foot on the hood and

rocked the car. They circled, lightly thumping the roof, discussing my good fortune in meeting them and the benefits they were likely to bestow upon me. I felt very small and very trapped and they knew it.

"The ones you just threw out," I said politely.   21

"I don't see no beer cans. Why don't you get out here and show   22
them to me, honey?" said the belligerent one, reaching for the handle inside my door.

"Right over there," I said, still being polite, "—there, and over   23
there." I pointed with the pistol, which I'd slipped under my thigh. Within one minute the cans and the men were back in the car and headed down the road.

I believe this incident illustrates several important principles.   24
The men were trespassing and knew it; their judgment may have been impaired by alcohol. Their response to the polite request of a woman alone was to use their size, numbers, and sex to inspire fear. The pistol was a response in the same language. Politeness didn't work; I couldn't match them in size or number. Out of the car, I'd have been more vulnerable. The pistol just changed the balance of power. It worked again recently when I was driving in a desolate part of Wyoming. A man played cat-and-mouse with me for 30 miles, ultimately trying to run me off the road. When his car passed mine with only two inches to spare, I showed him my pistol, and he disappeared.

When I got my pistol, I told my husband, revising the old Colt   25
slogan, "God made men *and women*, but Sam Colt made them equal." Recently I have seen a gunmaker's ad with a similar sentiment. Perhaps this is an idea whose time has come, though the pacifist inside me will be saddened if the only way women can achieve equality is by carrying weapons.

We must treat a firearm's power with caution. "Power tends to   26
corrupt, and absolute power corrupts absolutely," as a man (Lord Acton) once said. A pistol is not the only way to avoid being raped or murdered in today's world, but, intelligently wielded, it can shift the balance of power and provide a measure of safety.

Meanings and Values

1.   State in your own words the phenomenon Hasselstrom analyzes in this essay. Does she explain causes, effects, or both? Identify specific portions of the essay to support your answer.

2.   What attitudes towards gun ownership does Hasselstrom probably anticipate her readers will bring to the essay? Be specific. Where in the essay, if at all, does she acknowledge likely attitudes?

3.   What point(s) of view towards gun ownership does the writer encourage readers to adopt? Where does she announce this outlook?

4.   How would you characterize the writer's purpose? Explanation? Argument? Self-justification? (See "Guide to Terms": *Purpose.*)

Expository Techniques

1.   Identify the main examples presented in this essay. Why, if at all, are we justified in considering this essay as primarily concerned with explaining causes and effects when so much of it is devoted to examples?

2.   In what ways does the writer use strategies of comparison and contrast in paragraphs 9–11 to consider and dismiss alternatives to gun owning (see Section 5)? Explain why her tactics in these paragraphs are successful or unsuccessful. (Guide: *Evaluation.*)

3.   What generalities concerning when and how to use a gun correctly does the writer present in paragraphs 12–26? Where in the paragraphs does she announce the generalities? For which does she provide supporting examples? Which of the examples, if any, also illustrate causes or effects of gun ownership?

Diction and Vocabulary

1.   Discuss the writer's use of connotation in paragraphs 4, 6–8, and 17–23 to create emotional emphasis that makes her reasons for owning a gun seem plausible and convincing. (Guide: *Connotation/Denotation.*)

2.   Tell how the writer's use of qualification and her word choice in the opening paragraph help keep the essay from becoming predominantly argumentative. (Guide: *Qualification; Diction.*)

3.   How might this essay have been different had the writer not made such frequent use of "I" in presenting examples and explanations?

Read to Write

1.   To identify possible topics for writing, think about how people's attitudes about issues like animal rights, gun control, approaches to education, and economic policies are likely to differ according to where they live or according to their economic and social status. Think about how you might identify such differences, their causes, and

their effects. You might also wish to identify other facts that affect people's outlooks in substantial ways.

2. Hasselstrom's essay is partly an "apology," that is, an attempt to explain and justify one's behavior, especially a behavior that seems unusual or unacceptable according to generally-accepted standards. An apology often looks at the causes of behaviors in order to justify them. If you behave in a way some people might consider strange (setting your alarm clock seventeen minutes ahead, for instance), prepare an essay in which you explain your behavior (and maybe even point out its positive effects).

3. Explore another issue over which there has been considerable public debate. Follow Hasselstrom's lead, and write about it from a personal perspective, exploring causes and effects and providing explanation rather than argument.

(NOTE: Suggestions for topics requiring development by analysis of CAUSE AND EFFECT are on pages 343-344 at the end of this section.)

CULLEN MURPHY grew up in Greenwich, Connecticut and attended school in both Greenwich and Dublin, Ireland. He received a B.A. from Amherst College in 1974 and soon after began working in the production department of *Change* magazine. In 1977 he was named editor of *The Wilson Quarterly*, and he has been managing editor of *The Atlantic Monthly* since 1985. In his parallel career, he has written the comic strip Prince Valiant since the middle 1970s (a comic strip which his father draws). Murphy is an essayist and nonfiction writer as well. His essays on many different topics have appeared in *The Atlantic Monthly* and other magazines, including *Harper's*. His first book, *Rubbish!* (with William Rathje), appeared in 1992, and a collection of his essays, *Just Curious*, was published in 1995.

Hello, Darkness

"Hello, Darkness" was first published in *The Atlantic Monthly* in 1996. With touches of humor, Murphy looks at a subject that troubles many people: lack of sleep. His explanations of a phenomenon that most of us view as a matter of personal behavior may at first seem surprising; nonetheless, they point convincingly to technology and social change as the culprits who have stolen sleep.

Americans today have plenty of reasons to be thankful that they were not Americans a hundred years ago, but they also have more than a few reasons to wish they had been. On the one hand, a hundred years ago there was no Voting Rights Act, no penicillin, and no zipper, and the first daily comic strip was still more than a decade away. On the other hand there was no income tax, no nuclear bomb, and no Maury Povich. Also on the plus side, the average American a hundred years ago was able to sleep 20 percent longer than the average American today. 1

That last figure, supported by various historical studies over the years, comes from a report released by the Better Sleep Council. Americans in the late 1800s are believed to have slept an average of 2 about nine and a half hours a night. The average today is about seven and a half hours. A survey by the Better Sleep Council reveals that on a typical weeknight almost 60 percent of Americans get *less* than seven hours of sleep. Other evidence seems to indicate that the rate of sleep loss is in fact accelerating.

Some may argue that the Better Sleep Council's news should be 3 discounted, on the grounds that the council has an interest in the story—it is supported (comfortably?) by the mattress industry.

I would counter that the data simply confirm what anecdotal 4 evidence already suggests is true. Independent experts at universities and hospitals speak as one on the subject, observing that as a nation we are laboring under a large and increasingly burdensome "sleep deficit," defined as the difference between how much sleep we need and how much we get.

Would that we could pass this particular deficit on to our chil- 5 dren! But the only way we can pay it back, the experts say, is by getting more sleep ourselves. Apparently, we're trying. A recent article in *The Wall Street Journal* took note of the growing phenomenon of employees napping at work, but I suspect that this barely covers the interest payments, which go right to Japan. (As you may have noticed, the Japanese are asleep most of the time that we're awake.)

Why, by degrees, are we banishing sleep? In a handful of 6 instances, arguably, the cause has been government over-regulation. I am thinking of the recent case of Sari Zayed, of Davis, California. Ms. Zayed, after being overheard by a neighbor, was awakened at 1:30 A.M. by a municipal "noise-abatement officer" who gave her a $50 citation for snoring too loudly. The amount of money that Ms. Zayed subsequently received in damages from the city of Davis would allow her to pay for nightly snoring citations from now to the end of the year.

America's sleep deficit, though, is surely a systemic phenome- 7 non. Many commentators would blame it on what might be called the AWOL factor—that is, the American Way of Life. We are by nature a busy and ambitious people whom tectonic social forces—declining average wage, high rate of divorce, two-paycheck families, instant telecommunications, jet travel across time zones, growing popularity of soccer for everyone older than four—have turned into a race of laboratory rats on a treadmill going nowhere ever faster. And there is obviously something to this explanation. It is noteworthy that television shows like *Seinfeld* and *Cheers,* on which nobody seems to have any real responsibilities (circumstances that accord more fully with most viewers' fantasies than with their actual lives), have come to constitute a distinct broadcast genre known as "time porn."

It is hard not to credit the importance of the AWOL factor, but I wonder if the driving force behind the sleep deficit is in fact more   8 pervasive, and indeed global in nature: the triumph of light. I am by no means a romantic or a Luddite when it comes to electricity (anyone who is should read Robert Caro's *The Years of Lyndon Johnson* for its haunting description of life in west Texas in the days before rural electrification), and I also don't subscribe to the fashionable opinion that electronic labor-saving devices (personal computers possibly excepted) end up consuming more labor than they save. Yet electricity's ubiquitous and seemingly most innocuous use—to power the common light bulb—could not help exacting a price in sleep. Electricity made it possible for the first time in history for masses of humanity to vanquish darkness.

I had never given much thought to the role of darkness in ordinary human affairs until I read a monograph prepared by John   9 Staudenmaier, a historian of technology and a Jesuit priest, for a recent conference at MIT. (The essay appears in a book called *Progress: Fact or Illusion,* edited by Leo Marx and Bruce Mazlish.) Staudenmaier makes the point—obvious when brought up, though we've mostly lost sight of it—that from the time of the hominid Lucy, in Hadar, Ethiopia, to the time of Thomas Edison, in West Orange, New Jersey, the onset of darkness sharply curtailed most kinds of activity for most of our ancestors. He writes,

Living with electric lights makes it difficult to retrieve the experience of a non-electrified society. For all but the very wealthy, who could afford exorbitant arrays of expensive artificial lights, nightfall brought the works of daytime to a definitive end. Activities that need good light—where sharp tools are wielded or sharply defined boundaries maintained; purposeful activities designed to achieve specific goals; in short, that which we call work—all this subsided in the dim light of evening. Absent the press of work, people typically took themselves safely to home and were left with time in the evening for less urgent and more sensual matters: storytelling, sex, prayer, sleep, dreaming.

Staudenmaier's comments on electric light occupy only a few   10 passages. His larger subject is Western intellectual history, and how metaphors of "enlightenment" came to be associated with orderliness, objectivity, and progress, even as metaphors of darkness came to signify the chaotic, the nonrational, the terrifying. He argues that we have lost, to our detriment, the medieval view that some aspects of life and understanding are not necessarily helped by clarity or harmed by ambiguity. Observing that Enlightenment ideals have "taken a fair beating" in the course of this century, Staudenmaier wonders if it is time to rediscover the metaphysical dark, that place "where visions are born and human purpose renewed."

I'll leave that thought where it is. But the implication of elec- 11 tricity in the sleep deficit seems hard to argue with. Whatever it is that we wish or are made to do—pursue leisure, earn a living—there are simply far more usable hours now in which to do it. Darkness was once an ocean into which our capacity to venture was greatly limited; now we are wresting vast areas of permanent lightness from the darkness, much the way the Dutch have wrested polders of dry land from the sea. So vast are these areas that in composite satellite photographs of the world at night the contours of civilization are clearly illuminated—the boundaries of continents, the metastases of cities. Even Wrigley Field, once a reliable pool of nocturnal darkness, would now show up seventeen nights during the baseball season. In the United States at midnight more than five million people are at work at full-time jobs. Supermarkets, gas stations, copy shops—many of these never close. I know of a dentist in Ohio who decided to open an all-night clinic, and has had the last laugh on friends who believed that he would never get patients. The supply-side theory may not have worked in economics, but it has certainly worked with regard to light: the more we get, the more we find ways to put it to use. And, of course, the more we get, the more we distance ourselves from the basic diurnal rhythm in which our evolution occurred.

Thomas Edison, famous for subsisting on catnaps, would have 12 wanted it this way. In contrast, Calvin Coolidge, a younger man with an older temperament, slept at least ten and often as much as eleven hours a day. Two world views collide here, and somewhere between them is a balance waiting to be struck. Where and how? The only useful contribution I can make is to recall life in Ireland in the mid-1960s. One of the elements that made it so congenial was a shared expertise among engineers at the Electricity Supply Board which resulted in regular but unpredictably occurring blackouts. The relentless march of time would suddenly be punctuated by a limbo of uncertain duration. Lights were extinguished. Clocks stopped. Television screens went black. Drivers became hesitant and generous at traffic signals. Society and all its components took a blessed time out.

There was also something in Ireland called "holy hour," a 13 period in the afternoon when all the pubs would close. Perhaps what Americans need is a holy hour in the form of a blackout—a brief

caesura in our way of life that might come every day at perhaps
nine-thirty or ten at night. Not the least of the holy hour's benefits, I
might add, would be an appealing new time slot for Maury Povich.

Meanings and Values

1. The writer mentions "anecdotal evidence" of a "'sleep deficit'" (par.
    4) but does not present it directly. Why do you think he chose not to
    offer it in detail? Is the essay weakened—or perhaps strengthened—
    by this omission? Explain. (See "Guide to Terms": *Evaluation*.)

2. Are we to take the example in paragraph 6 seriously? If not, what is
    its role in the essay? Is it an indication that we should not take other
    examples in the essay seriously? Why or why not?

3. Explain why the author might be justified in referring to certain tele-
    vision shows as "time porn." Do you think most readers will agree
    or disagree with his conclusion? Why?

4. According to this essay, what was lost when electricity made it pos-
    sible to "vanquish darkness" (8)?

Expository Techniques

1. Where does Murphy first announce the phenomenon he wishes to
    explain? Should this announcement be considered a thesis? Why or
    why not? (Guide: *Thesis*.)

2. What is the role of the rhetorical question that opens paragraph 6?
    (Guide: *Rhetorical Questions*.)

3. Which causes of the sleep deficit does the author consider most im-
    portant, and how does he signal their importance to readers? Which
    of the strategies for creating emphasis does he use with frequency in
    this essay? (Guide: *Emphasis*.)

4. Where in the essay does the author begin discussing the effects of
    electricity?

5. What is the role of the extended discussion of Staudenmaier's work
    in paragraphs 10 and 11? To what extent do these paragraphs contra-
    dict or complement Murphy's tone and approach in the rest of the
    essay? (Guide: *Style/Tone*.)

6. What strategy does the writer use to conclude the essay? (Guide:
    Closings.) How effective is the conclusion?

Diction and Vocabulary

1. To what does the title allude? (Guide: *Figures of Speech*.) How is the
    allusion related to the rest of the essay? Discuss how repetition of the

word "darkness," beginning with the title, serves to create unity and coherence in the essay. (Guide: *Unity; Coherence.*) Is the title effective even for readers who do not recognize the allusion? Why or why not?

2. What choices of words and phrases does the writer make in paragraph 8 to indicate the importance of electricity as one of the causes of the sleep deficit and the disappearance of "darkness" in our daily lives? (Guide: *Diction.*) Do you think the diction in this paragraph is appropriate to its purposes, or is it excessive? Explain. (Guide: *Evaluation.*)

3. If you do not know the meaning of some of the following terms, look them up in a dictionary: anecdotal (par. 4); systemic, tectonic (7); Luddite, innocuous, vanquish (8); hominid, curtailed (9); metastases, diurnal (11); subsisting, limbo, duration (12); caesura (13).

Read to Write

1. Try thinking of other modern inventions (airplanes, television, internet, credit cards) and the ways they have changed our society and shaped our lives. The inventions can be seemingly insignificant (cup holders in automobiles, telephone calling cards, zippers or velcro) and still be topics worth exploring because of their consequences, both good and bad.

2. This essay makes effective use of the concept of a "deficit," that is, the difference between what we have and what we ought to have. Use a similar strategy to begin an essay of your own by introducing some other kind of "deficit" whose causes and consequences are worth exploring.

3. Murphy looks at both the positive and negative sides of a particular kind of progress before focusing on some negative effects we rarely consider. Using his essay as a model, write about the unintended (and perhaps negative) consequences of some recent invention, change in attitude, or social custom.

(NOTE: Suggestions for topics requiring development by analysis of CAUSE AND EFFECT are on pages 343-344 at the end of this section.)

Issues and Ideas

Work, Success, and Failure

"What do you do (for a living)?" is a question people often ask when they meet someone for the first time. Clearly, we frequently define ourselves and others by our work. But is it appropriate to do this? Does our work shape our personalities and values? If so, how does this happen? Is it a good idea to build our lives around work?

In our society, moreover, work is usually a competitive enterprise: we succeed at work or we fail. Indeed, our entire economic system rests on a belief in the benefits of competition. No wonder, then, that success and failure should have such psychological importance for us, or that we should treat many other activities besides work as challenges at which we succeed and fail.

The links of cause and effect tying together concepts of work, success, failure, and challenge and leading to systems of value and behavior and complex, and certainly beyond the range of a single essay to unravel, if anyone can indeed do so. Nonetheless, the essays that follow address various elements in this complicated relationship. William Severini Kowinski, in "Kids in the Mall: Growing Up Controlled," explores the links between contemporary concepts of work and the self-images and values of teenagers. Randall Rothenberg in, "What Makes Sammy Walk?," asks why people have begun rejecting the importance of work in their lives, and addresses the effects of their following a different system of values. Peter Hillary, in "Everest is Mighty, We are Fragile," looks at the importance for individuals and society as a whole of taking on challenges, even those where failure can lead to disaster and death. Though they raise some serious questions about work, success, and failure, however, in the end, each of the writers affirms the importance of work and challenges in our lives.

WILLIAM SEVERINI KOWINSKI grew up in Greensburg, Pennsylvania. In 1964, the year before the first mall was built in Greensburg, he left to attend Knox College in Illinois. While attending Knox he spent a semester studying in the fiction and poetry workshops at the University of Iowa. Kowinski was a writer and editor for the Boston *Phoenix* and the Washington *Newsworks* and has written articles for a number of national newspapers and magazines including *Esquire, New Times,* and *The New York Times Magazine.* His book *The Malling of America: An Inside Look at the Great Consumer Paradise* (1985) is based on his travels to malls throughout the United States and Canada.

Kids in the Mall: Growing Up Controlled

Over the past thirty years, the number, size, and variety of suburban shopping malls have grown at astonishing rates, replacing, in many cases, both plazas and urban shopping districts. They are now important economic and cultural forces in American and Canadian society. In this chapter from *The Malling of America,* Kowinski looks at some of the ways malls have affected the teenagers who spend much of their time shopping, working, or just hanging around at the mall.

Butch heaved himself up and loomed over the group. "Like it was different 1 for me," he piped. "My folks used to drop me off at the shopping mall every morning and leave me all day. It was like a big free baby-sitter, you know? One night they never came back for me. Maybe they moved away. Maybe there's some kind of a Bureau of Missing Parents I could check with."

—Richard Peck
Secrets of the Shopping Mall, a
novel for teenagers

From his sister at Swarthmore, I'd heard about a kid in Florida 2 whose mother picked him up after school every day, drove him straight to the mall, and left him there until it closed—all at his insistence. I'd heard about a boy in Washington who, when his family

"Kids in the Mall: Growing up Controlled" from *"Kids in the Mall"* by William Severini Kowinski. Copyright © 1985 by William Severini Kowinski. Reprinted by permission of William Morrow & Company, Inc.

moved from one suburb to another, pedaled his bicycle five miles every day to get back to his old mall, where he once belonged.

Their stories aren't unusual. The mall is a common experience 3 for the majority of American youth; they have probably been going there all their lives. Some ran within their first large open space, saw their first fountain, bought their first toy, and read their first book in a mall. They may have smoked their first cigarette or first joint or turned them down, had their first kiss or lost their virginity in the mall parking lot. Teenagers in America now spend more time in the mall than anywhere else but home and school. Mostly it is their choice, but some of that mall time is put in as the result of two-paycheck and single-parent households, and the lack of other viable alternatives. But are these kids being harmed by the mall?

I wondered first of all what difference it makes for adolescents 4 to experience so many important moments in the mall. They are, after all, at play in the fields of its little world and they learn its ways; they adapt to it and make it adapt to them. It's here that these kids get their street sense, only it's mall sense. They are learning the ways of a large-scale artificial environment: its subtleties and flexibilities, its particular pleasures and resonances, and the attitudes it fosters.

The presence of so many teenagers for so much time was not 5 something mall developers planned on. In fact, it came as a big surprise. But kids became a fact of mall life very early, and the International Council of Shopping Centers found it necessary to commission a study, which they published along with a guide to mall managers on how to handle the teenage incursion.

The study found that "teenagers in suburban centers are bored 6 and come to the shopping centers mainly as a place to go. Teenagers in suburban centers spent more time fighting, drinking, littering and walking than did their urban counterparts, but presented fewer overall problems." The report observed that "adolescents congregated in groups of two to four and predominantly at locations selected by them rather than management." This probably had something to do with the decision to install game arcades, which allow management to channel these restless adolescents into naturally contained areas away from major traffic points of adult shoppers.

The guide concluded that mall management should tolerate 7 and even encourage the teenage presence because, in the words of the report, "The vast majority support the same set of values as does shopping center management." *The same set of values* means simply that mall kids are already preprogrammed to be consumers and that the mall can put the finishing touches to them as hard-core, lifelong shoppers just like everybody else. That, after all, is what the mall is about. So it shouldn't be surprising that in spending a lot of time there, adolescents find little that challenges the assumption that the goal of life is to make money and buy products, or that just about everything else in life is to be used to serve those ends.

Growing up in a high-consumption society already adds ines-   8
timable pressure to kids' lives. Clothes consciousness has invaded the grade schools, and popularity is linked with having the best, newest clothes in the currently acceptable styles. Even what they read has been affected. "Miss [Nancy] Drew wasn't obsessed with her wardrobe," noted *Wall Street Journal*. "But today the mystery in teen fiction for girls is what outfit the heroine will wear next." Shopping has become a survival skill and there is certainly no better place to learn it than the mall, where its importance is powerfully reinforced and certainly never questioned.

The mall as a university of suburban materialism, where Valley   9
Girls and Boys from coast to coast are educated in consumption, has its other lessons in this era of change in family life and sexual mores and their economic and social ramifications. The plethora of products in the mall, plus the pressure on teens to buy them, may contribute to the phenomenon that psychologist David Elkind calls "the hurried child": kids who are exposed to too much of the adult world too quickly, and must respond with a sophistication that belies their still-tender emotional development. Certainly the adult products marketed for children—form-fitting designer jeans, sexy tops for preteen girls—add to the social pressure to look like an adult, along with the home-grown need to understand adult finances (why mothers must work) and adult emotions (when parents divorce).

Kids spend so much time at the mall partly because their par-   10
ents allow it and even encourage it. The mall is safe, it doesn't seem to harbor any unsavory activities, and there is adult supervision; it is, after all, a controlled environment. So the temptation, especially for working parents, is to let the mall be their babysitter. At least the kids aren't watching TV. But the mall's role as a surrogate mother may be more extensive and more profound.

Karen Lansky, a writer living in Los Angeles, has looked into   11
the subject and she told me some of her conclusions about the effects on its teenaged denizens of the mall's controlled and controlling environment. "Structure is the dominant idea, since true 'mall rats'

lack just that in their homelives," she said, "and adolescents about to make the big leap into growing up crave more structure than our modern society cares to acknowledge." Karen pointed out some of the elements malls supply that kids used to get from their families, like warmth (Strawberry Shortcake dolls and similar cute and cuddly merchandise), old-fashioned mothering ("We do it all for you," the fast-food slogan), and even home cooking (the "homemade" treats at the food court).

The problem in all this, as Karen Lansky sees it, is that while   12
families nurture children by encouraging growth through the assumption of responsibility and then by letting them rest in the bosom of the family from the rigors of growing up, the mall as a structural mother encourages passivity and consumption, as long as the kid doesn't make trouble. Therefore all they learn about becoming adults is how to act and how to consume.

Kids are in the mall not only in the passive role of shoppers—   13
they also work there, especially as fast-food outlets infiltrate the mall's enclosure. There they learn how to hold a job and take responsibility, but still within the same value context. When *CBS Reports* went to Oak Park Mall in suburban Kansas City, Kansas, to tape part of their hour-long consideration of malls, "After the Dream Comes True," they interviewed a teenaged girl who worked in a fast-food outlet there. In a sequence that didn't make the final program, she described the major goal of her present life, which was to perfect the curl on top of the ice-cream cones that were her store's specialty. If she could do that, she would be moved from the lowly soft-drink dispenser to the more prestigious ice-cream division, the curl on top of the status ladder at her restaurant. These are the achievements that are important at the mall.

Other benefits of such jobs may also be overrated, according to   14
Laurence D. Steinberg of the University of California at Irvine's social ecology department, who did a study on teenage employment. Their jobs, he found, are generally simple, mindlessly repetitive and boring. They don't really learn anything, and the jobs don't lead anywhere. Teenagers also work primarily with other teenagers; even their supervisors are often just a little older than they are. "Kids need to spend time with adults," Steinberg told me. "Although they get benefits from peer relationships, without parents and other adults it's one-sided socialization. They hang out with each other, have age-segregated jobs, and watch TV."

Perhaps much of this is not so terrible or even so terribly differ- 15
ent. Now that they have so much more to contend with in their lives,
adolescents probably need more time to spend with other adolescents without adult impositions, just to sort things out. Though it is
more concentrated in the mall (and therefore perhaps a clearer target), the value system there is really the dominant one of the whole
society. Attitudes about curiosity, initiative, self-expression, empathy, and disinterested learning aren't necessarily made in the mall;
they are mirrored there, perhaps a bit more intensely—as through a
glass brightly.

Besides, the mall is not without its educational opportunities. 16
There are bookstores, where there is at least a short shelf of classics
at great prices, and other books from which it is possible to learn
more than how to do sit-ups. There are tools, from hammers to
VCRs, and products, from clothes to records, that can help the
young find and express themselves. There are older people with stories, and places to be alone or to talk one-on-one with a kindred
spirit. And there is always the passing show.

The mall itself may very well be an education about the 17
future. I was struck with the realization, as early as my first forays
into Greengate,[1] that the mall is only one of a number of enclosed
and controlled environments that are part of the lives of today's
young. The mall is just an extension, say, of those large suburban
schools—only there's Karmelkorn instead of chem lab, the ice rink
instead of the gym: It's high school without the impertinence of
classes.

Growing up, moving from home to school to the mall—from 18
enclosure to enclosure, transported in cars—is a curiously continu-
ous process, without much in the way of contrast or contract with
unenclosed reality. Places must tend to blur into one another. But
whatever differences and dangers there are in this, the skills these
adolescents are learning may turn out to be useful in their later
lives. For we seem to be moving inexorably into an age of pre-
planned and regulated environments, and this is the world they
will inherit.

Still, it might be better if they had more of a choice. One 19
teenaged girl confessed to *CBS Reports* that she sometimes felt she

[1]Greengate Mall in Greensburg, Pennsylvania, where Kowinski began his research on
malls (Editors' note).

was missing something by hanging out at the mall so much. "But I'm here," she said, "and this is what I have."

Meanings and Values

1. Do teenagers who spend their time in malls display any obviously unusual behavior? If so, in what ways do they behave? If not, how might one describe their behavior?

2. What question does this essay attempt to answer? Where in the essay is the question asked? Other than providing an answer to the question, what purpose or purposes does this selection have? (See "Guide to Terms": *Purpose.*)

3. What does Kowinski see as the major effects of malls on teenagers? What other, less important effects (if any) does he identify? Discuss whether or not the author presents enough evidence to convince most readers that he has correctly identified the effects.

4. Where in the essay does Kowinski consider causes other than the mall environment for the attitudes and behaviors of teenagers? Explain how the alternative explanation either undermines or adds to his view of the malls.

Expository Techniques

1. What strategies does the author employ in the introduction (pars. 1–3) to help convince readers of the importance of reading and thinking about what happens to teenagers as a result of the time they spend at malls? (Guide: *Introductions.*)

2. Discuss how the author uses examples, quotations from authorities, and various strategies of emphasis in paragraphs 8, 9, 11, 13, and 14 to indicate whether or not the effects of malls can be considered harmful. (Guide: *Emphasis.*)

3. Which sections of the essay are devoted *primarily* to exploring the effects of the mall environment? Which are devoted *primarily* to discussing whether or not the effects are harmful?

4. What use does the author make of qualification in presenting his conclusions in paragraphs 15 and 17–19? (Guide: *Qualification.*) Explain why this strategy adds to or weakens your confidence in his conclusions.

5. Explain how parallelism in paragraphs 17 and 18 helps emphasize similarities in the environments. (Guide: *Parallel Structure.*)

Diction and Vocabulary

1. Who is the Nancy Drew alluded to in paragraph 8? (Guide: *Figures of Speech*.) What is the purpose of this allusion?

2. What transitional devices are used to tie together paragraphs 7–9? (Guide: *Transition*.) Which are used to link paragraphs 10–13?

3. If you do not know the meaning of some of the following words, look them up in the dictionary: loomed, piped (par. 1); viable (3); resonances, fosters (4); incursion (5); inestimable (8); mores, ramifications, plethora (9); surrogate (10); denizens (11); nurture (12); socialization (14); impositions, empathy, disinterested (15); kindred (16); forays, impertinence (17); inexorably (18).

Read to Write

1. Use these questions to help develop a topic for an essay of your own: Were malls as important to you as they were to the people Kowinski describes in his essay? Based on your experience and observations, does Kowinski appear to be overstating the effects of malls on teenagers? What other influences on the lives of teenagers are as important or more important than malls (or than shopping in general)? Are malls important in people's lives because of the special experiences they offer, or simply because they bring together large numbers of people and offer work to many individuals?

2. Write an essay on the roles malls, electronic games, role-playing games, music concerts, or some other place/activity played in your social life. Like Kowinski, include numerous details to help illustrate and support your explanation.

3. What experiences and activities condition us for success or failure? Which ones give us important goals for work, personal relationships, and civic responsibility? Taking an approach similar to the one Kowinski employs in "Kids in the Mall," criticize the influence of the activities that characterize contemporary teenage life. Or, reverse Kowinski's approach and praise the effects of particular activities and experiences.

(NOTE: Suggestions for topics requiring development by analysis of CAUSE AND EFFECT are on pages 343-344 at the end of this section.)

PETER HILLARY is the son of Sir Edmund Hillary, the first man to
climb Mt. Everest successfully. A well-known mountain climber
in his own right, Peter Hillary made it to the top of Everest in
1990. He is also the author of *A Sunny Day in the Himalayas* (1980).

Everest Is Mighty, We Are Fragile

If so many people die trying to climb Mt. Everest, why do others
continue to challenge it? Why is it important for all of us that some
people continue to undertake the work of climbing Everest—even
if they fail? These are some of the questions Peter Hillary addresses
in his essay, published as an opinion piece in the *New York Times.*
Along the way, Hillary also manages to explore ways in which failure can be a kind of success, and success, in turn, can be a kind of
failure when it carries with it memories of others who did not succeed.

Over the past few years, I have watched the public perception of   1
Mount Everest drift from awe of the greatest mountain on earth and
respect for anyone who succeeds in scaling it to an assumption that
now things have changed.

Just as computer technology advances almost daily and our   2
back roads become highways and then freeways, people believe that
surely by now the tracks and camps on Everest are permanent fix-
tures that are improved each year. After all, in the Alps you can
climb to huts high above the snow line and sleep in a comfortable
bed and order food and wine from a concierge.

For Everest climbers, there has been progress, too, but it lies   3
only in the technology of our equipment and communications. The
mountain remains the same: huge, steep, cold and impassive toward
our human endeavor.

On the great mountains of the world there is constancy, and the   4
Everest that took the lives of George Leigh Mallory and Andrew
Irvine in the 1920's is the same Everest that was finally climbed by

my father, Sir Edmund Hillary, and Tenzing Norgay in 1953, the
same mountain climbed solo by Reinhold Messner in 1980, the same
summit I climbed on May 10, 1990, with Rob Hall and Gary Ball on
a brilliantly sunny day, and it is the same Everest that took the lives
of eight climbers, including Rob, in a terrible storm on May 10, 1996.

Some things never change. While having the right equipment   5
and clothing is essential, it is only 5 percent of the overall mountaineering equation, of what is needed to reach the top. The rest lies
with you. Do you have the drive, the psyche, the power?

Perhaps the greatest thing to change on Everest occurred on   6
May 29, 1953, when Dad and Tenzing reached the 29,028-foot summit for the first time.

It was like the breaking of the four-minute mile by Roger   7
Bannister. The way was clear for others to establish records, but now
not for humanity but for individuals. This is a new age in which
individual participation has usurped national spectatorship. Just
about everyone knows somebody who has jumped out of an airplane with a parachute on his back, rappelled down a cliff face,
rafted foaming white-water rapids or taken a motorcycle for a 100-
mile-per-hour blast around a race track.

And so it is no surprise to me that the 100-year-old profession   8
of guiding clients up mountains has extended to ascents of the
world's highest mountain—a mountain that has been climbed by
615 people in 43 years and has taken the lives of about 150. Many
clients are expert climbers without time to organize expeditions,
while others are more motivated than experienced. Nonetheless,
these professional expeditions have succeeded in getting many people to the summit safely.

Surely the time will come when the numbers of climbers on   9
Everest will have to be limited, just as Yosemite National Park has
been talking about doing. I would hate to see controls that were anything but first come, first served. The highly distasteful thought of a
panel of assessors scrutinizing your qualifications, commenting on
your objectives and counting the number of spare underpants in
your day pack is objectionable to me. It is anathema to the personal
right to challenge oneself.

What happened two weeks ago on Everest demonstrated the   10
unbridled might of the mountain, its furious high-altitude storms
and the fact that not even the experience and skill of two outstanding alpine leaders like Rob Hall and Scott Fischer is enough when
the Big E stirs.

I have heard people say they don't care about such climbers,   11
who, in their view, take pointless risks. It was suicidal; they knew
how dangerous it was. "They have satellite telephones, meteorolog-
ical reports, Gore-Tex jackets and good jobs. What are they doing?"

So should we discourage the risktakers by despising and shun-   12
ning them? Most of us want the people around us to be the same as
we are and to feel the same as we do—and yet intellectually most of
us will admit that variety is good. We admire people who try a little
harder and who push the envelope a little further. Every success by
an individual is an inspiration for his or her community—just as a
person's failure is a time for the community to take stock.

So while Rob lies stilled on the steep icy flanks of Everest, I take   13
stock both as a mountaineer and as a friend. I wonder about the
future of my own mountaineering. The fact that Rob and Gary, with
whom I climbed Everest in 1990, have died on 8,000-meter mountains scares me. This latest alpine horror makes me feel very vulnerable. Despite what some people try to tell themselves, we humans
are very fragile. We die easily.

The death of eight on Everest comes on the heels of my own   14
uncannily similar experience on K-2, the world's second highest
mountain, last year. On Aug. 13, eight climbers from three different
expeditions were ascending the steep ice gully called the Bottleneck,
just below the summit. I was becoming progressively concerned
about the bank of evil-looking clouds encroaching from the north,
from western China, and at midday, in a cloud and falling snow, I
decided to descend alone while the other seven continued on. (Other
climbers went back down earlier that day.) I imagined the seven
descending the following day and boasting of their sunset photographs from the summit, and asking, "Why didn't you come on up
with us?" None ever came back.

The weather deteriorated steadily, and I spent five hours of   15
lonely anguish, lost in cloud and wind on plunging flanks and
spurs between 26,500 and 24,000 feet. On finding the ledge where a
small tent was pitched, I clipped into the top of our fixed ropes and
began the 5,000-foot rappel down the Black Pyramid to the chim-
neys and couloirs of the lower Abruzzi Spur. As I leaned out over
the great void of the eastern flank of K-2, which was engulfed in a
cloud, the storm struck and I was blown about on the line like a
cork on a string. I knew I had entered a new phase of terrifying
uncertainty.

The storm raged into the night and early morning, blasting the   16
mountain with winds over 100 miles per hour. When I reached the
ledge at 22,000 feet where Camp 2 tents were lashed to the rock that
rose above, I joined two others who had turned back for a night of
fear that our tents would be shredded by the screaming storm, leaving us very vulnerable to the raging elements.

In my bones, I knew there was little hope for the seven on the   17
summit. They were no doubt blasted from the mountain by the jet-
stream winds, perhaps falling 12,000 feet to the twisting, turning
Godwin Austen glacier, which flows south through a corridor of
spires and summits.

Surviving is sometimes the most painful role to play in this life.   18
You get the opportunity to re-enact in your mind those closing
scenes again and again and again.

Even though he lived the high-profile life of an eminent adven-   19
turer and mountaineer, Rob Hall was a generous man, a good friend
to many. There are not too many who walk with the mantle of fame
and remain true to themselves.

So for those who wonder "Why do they do it?" I can only say   20
that through the haze of lament and loss that has swept across the
world of mountaineers and those who dream of mountains, I can
remember what I would have said before May 10: To climb the
great mountains is to leave the comfort of familiar places and to
challenge the very essence of oneself. Perhaps there is no greater
quest.

Meanings and Values

1. According to the writer, the recent, well-publicized deaths of expert
    climbers on Mt. Everest remind us of important lessons the moun-
    tain and the dangers of mountain climbing have to teach. What are
    these lessons?

2. Hillary seems to be saying that the deaths can be viewed as a good
    thing in some ways, despite the tragedy. In what ways does the es-
    say suggest that the deaths have some good consequences? How im-
    portant is the tone of the essay in getting readers to accept the propo-
    sition that good can come from tragedy? (See "Guide to Terms":
    Style/Tone.)

3. What answer does the writer offer to the familiar question, "Why
    climb Mt. Everest?" In what ways is his answer satisfactory or unsat-
    isfactory? Be specific in your answer.

Expository Techniques

1. How does Hillary establish himself as an authority on the subject of mountain climbing and on issues of success and failure? Where in the essay does he do these things? How does he manage to avoid the impression that he is gloating over the failures of other climbers?

2. Hillary is a mountaineer, not a professional writer. If he were a professional writer, do you think he would have organized this essay differently? Why or why not? (Guide: *Evaluation*.) What specific suggestions would you offer him, if any, for reorganizing the essay?

3. Where in the selection does Hillary provide an extended example? What is his purpose in employing this strategy? (Guide: *Purpose*.) What other expository patterns, if any, are used in the essay?

Diction and Vocabulary

1. Identify those places in the essay where the writer uses words like "constancy" to describe Everest and words like "fragile" to describe humans. What other words, or groups of words, does he associate with each? How does this pattern of diction reflect important ideas in the essay? In what way is it related to the discussion of causes and effects? (Guide: *Diction*.)

2. If you do not know the meaning of some of the following terms, look them up in a dictionary: concierge (par. 2); impassive (3); psyche (5); anathema (9); encroaching (14); rappel, couloirs (15); mantle (19).

Read to Write

1. It is easy to identify individual behaviors that are dangerous yet attractive to some people (skydiving, automobile racing, and the like). Societies as a whole can also undertake activities that threaten either individuals or the entire group. Make a list of such activities, and consider developing one of them into a topic for an essay analyzing causes and effects.

2. Hillary's essay is partly a response to a recent event. Write an essay of your own responding to some event of local or national interest. Consider its meaning and importance and bring to it the perspective of your own experience.

3. Many human behaviors seem unwise, wasteful, dangerous, or excessively selfish from one perspective, yet from another point of view they seem necessary, even beneficial. Prepare an essay of your own in which you, like Hillary, look at the causes and consequences of

such a behavior and demonstrate its necessity and benefits. (Or take the opposite approach and demonstrate how the causes and consequences of a behavior generally considered good can also be viewed in a negative light.)

(NOTE: Suggestions for topics requiring development by analysis of CAUSE AND EFFECT are on pages 343-344 at the end of this section.)

RANDALL ROTHENBERG is a writer whose essays have appeared in a wide variety of magazines. He has also published *The Neoliberals* (1984) and *Where the Suckers Moon* (1994), a chronicle of an advertising campaign.

What Makes Sammy Walk?

Why would people with good jobs stop working? What will happen to them? Why would people who lose their jobs not bother to find new ones? These are some of the questions Rothenberg addresses in this essay, first published in *Esquire* magazine in 1995. By altering the title of a novel from the 1950s, *What Makes Sammy Run*, Rothenberg makes plain his desire to look at the causes of a phenomenon that is a surprising reversal of the characteristic values and behaviors of modern society.

In Northgate, a Seattle neighborhood of sturdy homes and limitless   1
vistas, a support group meets twice a month to help its members through the emotionally wrenching, physically demanding withdrawal from addiction. Among them tonight are an accountant, a college administrator, a computer-company founder, and a state-government employee. They are not dependent on drugs, alcohol, sexual relationships, or the other themes of twelve-step programs. These thirteen men and women are seeking release from their reliance on jobs.

"My name is Darrel," says one. He is forty-two, a compact man   2
with neatly trimmed brown hair, dressed comfortably in a sweatshirt and jeans. "My interest is in getting out of the rat race and getting back to simplicity. I think it's a matter of time—not if but when I can do it." To prepare himself, he's deliberately stopped repairing or replacing broken household appliances. "The dryer pooped out, and we can do without the dryer," he says to approving nods.

A young woman follows. She is sitting on a couch, under a   3
bookshelf on which newsletters with names like *The Tightwad Gazette*

and *Simple Living* are neatly displayed. "My name is Laura," she says, twisting her fingers nervously. "I've decided to quit my job."

"Great!" barks the silver-haired man next to her.   4

Emboldened, she continues. "I'm gonna quit my job in June. It's   5
not really that hard." For months already, she and her boyfriend have been living on one income and banking the second. "So I'm gonna quit my job," Laura repeats, trying to convince herself. "I'll get all my time back."

Finally, eyes turn to David Heitmiller. He and his wife Jacque   6
Blix, forty-nine and forty-five, respectively, tall, calm, and articulate, are stalwarts and stars of this group.

"My name is Dave and I'm married to Jacque, and we've been   7
on a voluntary-simplicity track for close to four years now, and it worked out," he tells his confidants. "We went through a heavy-duty yuppie phase in the mid- to late-eighties, like many people did." But after realizing their folly, they went on a rigid program to control their spending and expand their savings. "We succeeded in reaching financial independence one year ago." At about the same time, U.S. West, where Dave had served in several executive jobs throughout seventeen years, offered him a buyout. Naturally, he took it.

"I haven't worked since. In a regular job, I should say. I have,   8
very voluntarily and simplistically, rebuilt my bicycle. I did all the work myself," he says proudly, "but I got the frame for free."

Do you have a Barnes & Noble superstore near you, one of those   9
giant book emporiums, replete with coffee shop, easy chairs, and browsable magazine stands? Skulk around one some afternoon and check out how many of its plush settees are occupied—and by whom. "A lot of people are reexamining," muses Jim Kirk, a Barnes & Noble vice-president. "A lot who were going a thousand miles an hour in the 1980s are now saying, 'Let's go thirty miles an hour.'"

Or perhaps you have a nouvelle coffee shop in your neighbor-   10
hood—not the modern move-'em-in-and-move-'em-out kind, but one of the Parisian set-a-spell variety popping up of late. Ever notice who's pausing over that steaming latte and the morning paper in the hours before noon?

Chances are that, dotted among the expected regulars—the   11
stroller-pushing moms, the aimless students, and the elderly—one third of the denizens are men, middle-class, middle-aged, and piddling around. Men who, in another life, were managers, financial planners, sales executives, attorneys, bankers, administrators, and

account executives. White-collar men, "the interchangeable parts of the big chains of authority that bind the society together," the late sociologist C. Wright Mills called them. Men like you.[1] Men who should be working. But aren't.

Every week, it seems, I run into an old friend, sometimes two or   12
three—Ivy Leaguers in their late thirties or forties, comfortable but far from rich—who have departed the fast track. Whether they were pushed or not, their reactions have been strikingly similar: After a lot of soul-searching, some agony, and perhaps a tiny bit of self-loathing, they have decided to remain in the slow lane. First it was Peter, Princeton B.A. and Harvard Law Review, who went on hourly wages and then went part-time at his West Coast firm in order to study botany. Then there was Rob, who, fired by his investment bank, decided to work part-time, on contract, so that he might dally with a paintbrush several mornings a week. Al, who'd spent the years after his M.B.A. and law degree planning international real estate ventures, forced his bank to fire him when it started withdrawing from the field. Before making any moves, he's taking at least a year off to spend time with his infant daughter, even as his wife begins her new life as a judicial clerk.

They may seem like cultural quirks—1990s versions of James   13
Dean's causeless heretic, who've substituted loafers for leather in their rebellion against America's Organization Man ethos—but it's not merely the economically and educationally resourceful who are joining the BarcaLounger brigade. Hundreds of thousands, perhaps millions, of otherwise normal men are banding together in a mass mystery that defies easy explanation. They are not turning on. They are not tuning in. But they are dropping out.

Last July, a Gallup poll found that some one third of all Americans   14
said they would take a 20 percent cut in income if they or their spouses could work fewer hours, an unprecedentedly high figure. Mere wishful thinking? When IBM offered employees a departure package in mid-1992, more than thirty-two thousand of the wing-tip warriors— 60 percent more than management had anticipated—took the buyout.

All around us are the unmistakable signs of a shift in the Amer-   15
ican character. Instead of working harder as times get tougher, men, including the salaried shock troops that sustain the corporate world, are working less.

---

[1]*Esquire* magazine, where the essay first appeared, is supposedly addressed to a male audience, though a huge proportion of its readers are women. (Editors' note)

For several years—even as their wives and sisters have contin-   16
ued on the trek toward more hours for higher pay—men have been
drifting away from work. At first, the departures were involuntary,
forced almost solely by the continuing disappearance of factory jobs
as microchips replaced muscle. In recent years, with corporate
downsizing decimating the one fourth of American workers classified as managers and professionals, some experts have begun to
notice a surge in deliberate departures.

"This has been going on among a core group of leading-edge   17
boomers, and some older than the boomers, probably since the early
seventies. The difference now is that it's going mainstream," says
Gerald Celente, director of the Trends Research Institute in
Rhinebeck, New York, "What's going on now in a lot of people's
minds is, Look, I'm working longer and harder, I'm falling back, I
hate my job, I don't know if I'm going to have a job—I don't want to
do this anymore!"

In the post–Timothy Leary world, this leave-taking lifestyle is no   18
longer referred to as dropping out. Some economists speak of "down-
shifting," the pursuit and acceptance of slower days and lower pay.
Others talk of a "voluntary-simplicity movement." Still others call it
a search for "exit strategies." Inferential Focus, a respected New York
trend-analysis company, says the desire "to take flight from current
employment predicaments has become pandemic."

It is evident in many varied phenomena. You can find a hint of   19
it in the Arts and Crafts–style armchairs, lamps, coffee tables, and
couches that the Rouse Company, the nation's premier shopping-
center developer, placed throughout the public spaces of Atlanta's
Perimeter Mall to make it more appealing to people with time on
their hands. It's in the baby-changing facilities Barnes & Noble has
placed in the men's restrooms of its superstores. And it's in the proliferation of newsletters—like *Living Cheap News* of San Jose, California; *Skinflint News* of Palm Harbor, Florida; and *Simple Living* of
Seattle—written for folks with empty schedules and shallow wallets.
(One such journal, *The Tightwad Gazette* of Leeds, Maine, has grown
to fifty thousand subscribers from a mere seventeen hundred in less
than five years.)

Data culled from government, industry, and think tanks point   20
to an astonishing transformation in the nature of work, which we
were raised to associate with eight-hour days at offices or factories.
The number of men in their traditional prime working years—early
twenties to early sixties—who worked full-time for at least eight out

of ten years fell nine percentage points from the 1970s to the 1980s. The recession that followed can only have added to their ranks, pulling the current number of "full-time full-timers" below 70 percent of American men. Of those employed, fully one fourth work on a temporary, contract, or part-time basis, according to the Economics Policy Institute in Washington, D.C. Link Resources Corporation, a technology-research company, says the total number of Americans who work at least part of the time at home, for themselves or for their employers, rose to 43.2 million in 1994 from fewer than 25 million just eight years ago.

Like it or not, man by man, modem by modem, we are becom-   21
ing a freelance nation. We are insecure, sure, but we are also, as the word implies, free.

"This whole simple-living phenomenon seems to be marginal,   22
but it's growing. It seems to be exploding," says Harvard economist Juliet B. Schor. The nation's leading critic of drudgery, Schor, in her 1992 book, *The Overworked American*, calculated that between 1969 and 1987, the average employed person put in an extra 163 hours a year on the job. It's a telling sign that her newest study, which began in February, is designed to establish how many Americans are laying back, and why they're doing so.

In pursuit of dropouts, Schor distributed a notice at a Massa-   23
chusetts unemployment center for white-collar workers established along the Route 128 high-tech corridor. The respondents told her similar tales. "Their jobs were too stressful. They were unsatisfied. They were searching for meaning," Schor recalls. "So they found other, lower-paying jobs, or they got themselves fired. They were no longer playing ball."

"Most had new jobs or situations that paid much less," she con-   24
tinues, "but they were much happier."

In that euphoria lies perhaps the most consequential and trou-   25
bling aspect of men's move to the sidelines. We were raised to labor—to honor sweat and revere the profit motive. For skilled, educated, and experienced people to find contentment in the absence of effort denotes a historical alteration in the meaning of work and a change in the importance of the work ethic in a nation whose willingness to toil distinguished it from the aristocracies from which our forebears fled. It also indicates an abandonment of the American dream by the people who have benefited from it the most. We are asking ourselves why we should work so hard, if forces beyond our

control are determining our fate; we are answering by earning little, consuming less, and opting out.

We are becoming, in short, a nation of middle-aged slackers. 26
. . . Its lure is ancient and tempting, the call to abjure work and 27
drop out. Even in "this bustling nineteenth century," Henry David Thoreau found a ready audience for his message that toil was enslaving the American mind. "Men labor under a mistake," he wrote in *Walden Pond*. "The better part of a man is soon plowed into the soil for compost. By a seeming fate, commonly called necessity, they are employed, as it says in an old book, laying up treasures which moth and rust will corrupt and thieves break through and steal. It is a fool's life, as they will find when they get to the end of it."

Thoreau notwithstanding, it would be a mistake to assume that 28
were it not for the drumbeat of commercialism and its appeals to our vanity, we would readily return to a state of nature. Thoreau exasperated his contemporaries: "To a healthy mind," James Russell Lowell wrote of him shortly after his death, "the world is a constant challenge." Such critics understood that, almost from the beginning, the character of Americans was distinguished from that of our European antecedents not by a search for leisure and contemplation but by our willingness to work and seek the rewards.

"The workman," wrote Tocqueville of his travels across this 29
new nation, "is filled with new ambition and new desires, he is harassed by new wants. Every instant he views with longing the profits of his employer; and in order to share them, he strives to dispose of his labor at a higher rate and he generally at length succeeds in the attempt."

As the decade wore on, Thoreau's message of self-reliance was 30
blended into this obsession with acquisition and fashioned into the American dream, which could be summarized in four words: Work and get rich.

The classic expression of this reverie sat prominently on my par- 31
ents' living-room bookshelf throughout my childhood. It was a thin volume titled *Acres of Diamonds*, a reprint of a motivational lecture that was delivered more than six thousand times in the late nineteenth and early twentieth centuries by Russell H. Conwell, a Baptist minister and the founder of Temple University in Philadelphia.

In the speech, Conwell recounted the apocryphal story of Ali 32
Hafed, a Persian farmer who was persuaded by a priest that fields of gemstones lay somewhere beyond the mountains of his domain. For

years, Ali Hafed roamed far and wide to find the treasure, eventually selling his farm to finance the expedition, exhausting himself
and dying a broke and broken man. Not long after Ali Hafed's
death, the farmer who had bought his land was leading a camel
across it when a gleam caught his eye. And there he discovered the
acres of diamonds, right in Ali Hafed's own backyard.

Conwell meant his lesson literally. The lecture is filled with   33
inspiring stories of entrepreneurs who searched their own environs
and found fabulous wealth: the man who made $52,000 inventing a
better hatpin; the fellow who made $90,000 developing rock candy.
"I say you ought to be rich; you have no right to be poor," Conwell
thundered to the multitudes. "You and I know there are some things
more valuable than money. . . . Nevertheless, the man of common
sense also knows that there is not any one of those things that is not
greatly enhanced by the use of money. Money is power." It's no
wonder that with such sentiments, *Acres of Diamonds* to this day
remains a favorite motivational reference, cited in life-insurance-
sales guides and at Amway conventions.

Luckily, this work ethic coincided with the needs of industrial   34
capitalism. Competitive success required firms continually to
increase their productivity—their ability to get fewer workers to
turn out more goods in less time, which makes products cheaper
and, therefore, more profitable. As large corporations took over the
management of the American economy, the workers who made this
nation the most productive the world had ever seen were rewarded
with an implied social contract: higher wages and lifetime job security for more and harder work. "What makes the economy function
well," Herbert Stein, the head of President Nixon's Council of Economic Advisers, once said, "is that a hundred million people get up
every morning and go to work, doing the best for themselves that
they can."

The bargain was a good one for America. In the fifteen years fol- 35
lowing the end of World War II, family income doubled. "Middle
class," a term that applied to only a third of the nation at the start of
the war, referred to two thirds by the mid–1970s.

As material comfort became a given, Americans found fulfill-   36
ment in the social esteem their professions and professional accou-
trements provided. "Satisfaction in work often rests upon status
satisfactions," C. Wright Mills wrote in the 1950s. "Status panic," he
believed, had become an essential motivation for people to work in
the white-collar world. The 1980s provided vigorous support for his

thesis. SUCCESS! shouted this magazine,[2] an avatar of the new work ethic, on its February 1985 cover, above a photo of a young man, his red tie flying, his briefcase clutched tightly to his chest. "It is the religion of the eighties. Everyone pursues it. Only the most driven and talented achieve it. Few know how to live with it. Or without it."

Today, it all seems so dated. Daniel Yankelovich's annual DYG   37
Scan trend-tracking study uncovered striking disaffection from work, with employees routinely expressing grave doubts about their futures, their employers' loyalty to them, the value of accrued professional experience, and even the bedrock tenet of the American work ethic—that work can set you free from want. In less than ten years, something has happened, either in our character or our economy, to upend the work ethic.

In large part, this development has arisen because work pro-   38
vides workers with fewer real rewards. Even though the economy, now in its third solid year of recovery, is booming, the benefits have been manifested almost entirely in the creation of new jobs, not in the improvement of existing ones. Real wages have declined in almost every sector of the economy since 1979, according to a McKinsey analysis of Labor Department data. Benefits, too, are disappearing. Defined-benefit pensions—retirement plans that guarantee fixed payments from departure to death—covered 84 percent of workers as recently as 1982. Today, slightly more than half of all workers have their futures thus secured.

"In the aftermath of the recession, we are witnessing a gradual   39
downward revision of expectations about accumulating material wealth to achieve success," says Yankelovich. "People are lowering their expectations about what they can get out of their jobs. They are putting their emotional investment into values and lifestyles that depend less on work and money."

Mark Baron changed his investment portfolio a few months   40
ago, joining the two million men who the U.S. Census Bureau says are now serving as full-time fathers. I came across his name in a newsletter called *At-Home Dad*, a publication filled with supportive assertions ("at-home dads have smarter kids") and practical advice ("pet-sitting for profit").

A thirty-seven-year-old former industrial-tool salesman from   41
Sharon, Massachusetts, Mark started talking two years ago with his wife, Andrea, about adding to their brood. They already had a three-

---

[2]*Esquire.* (Editors' note)

year-old son and part-time custody of Mark's twelve-year-old son from a previous marriage. They calculated the costs, psychic and physical. He and Andrea, a rising finance-company executive, hated what Mark called "the nuttiness in the morning—packing lunches, who's gonna stay home if the kid is sick. You walk in at 6:00 P.M. and you spend the whole night doing baths, packing kids up, making lunches for the next day. Nine o'clock at night, you collapse. And when you finish paying day-care expenses, incremental expenses, buying clothing for the road, lunches on the road, dry cleaning— was it worth it?" Out of Mark's salary, then in the mid-forties, they were left with $10,000 to $15,000 after taxes.

Instead of sacrificing the job of another baby, they decided to   42
jettison Marks' job. "We asked, 'Is it worth $10,000?' No. Forty, sure, but not for ten."

Implicit in the lesson of the work ethic was the idea of control—   43
that we create our own fate, that we are solely responsible for our destiny. If *Acres of Diamonds* retains an appeal, it is in the message that, inevitably, we *will* find our fortune if we search hard enough. But Americans no longer believe in that fervently. Many of those who did believe have had their dreams dashed by the onslaught of statistics, with names and faces attached, that have coursed through American business these past few years.

At first, we dismissed it as the curse of the blue-collar class.   44
When the five hundred largest U.S. manufacturing companies slashed payrolls by 4.7 million workers between 1980 and 1993, white-collar America sighed with relief. When the slashers came for the centurions of the "new economy"—when IBM began laying off 171,000 people between 1986 and 1994—the middle class worried a bit but blamed Big Blue's complacency and the recession that had sundered it. But when the recession ended, the assault continued. A week before Christmas, Mattel (a toy maker!) announced the elimination of one thousand jobs, despite record profits; a month later, on the same day it reported a 4 percent increase in fourth-quarter profits, American Home Products Corporation said it would cast off four thousand workers. It was clear the crash had come for everyone.

The villain is called downsizing, and it is demolishing the white-   45
collar world. For the first time since the Depression, middle-aged, middle-class, college-educated men are suffering a decline in their standard of living and their prospects for employment. During the last recession, for the first time in history, says Harvard economist

James Medoff, the percentage of unemployed white-collar workers grew. What's more, men aged thirty-five to fifty-four who are pitched from their jobs are increasingly unable to find full-time employment: The ranks of those classified as "permanently unemployed" rather than "temporarily unemployed" grew by 25 percent between the 1981 recession and the slump a decade later. Indeed, Medoff labels the 1990s "the era of middle-aged-male permanent-layoff unemployment."

The financial—not to mention emotional—impact on the   46
wealthier, and presumably more secure, part of this cohort has been crushing. Massachusetts Institute of Technology economist Frank Levy says that men aged forty-five to fifty-four with four years of college, middle managers who were "earning their age," saw their median earnings drop to $41,898 in 1992 from $48,189 just three years earlier. "This group has taken a pounding," Levy says.

Soon, they will be as dust, if the gurus of the new economy are   47
right. "I think there are a lot of people who will never find a job again," Michael Hammer, coauthor of the best-seller *Re-engineering the Corporation*, said recently. "If you can't design or sell a product, if you can't do real work, I'd get real nervous."

Middle-aged slacking is not a choice. It's a necessity.   48

"Pretty soon, we're all going to have to cut back anyway," says   49
Cecile Andrews [director of a Seattle-area workshop on voluntary simplicity], shrugging. "Are we going to be able to think of creative ways to live?"

At 6:45 on a Friday evening, I go with Cecile to the Phinney   50
Neighborhood Center, a massive brick schoolhouse in northwest Seattle, not far from the Honey Bear Bakery. Thirty-three men and women assemble in the basement auditorium for Cecile's latest voluntary-simplicity workshop, their first stab at exploring life played at 16 rpm. A bit nervously but soon with the unforced camaraderie of a platoon under fire, they introduce themselves to one another.

"Five months ago, I left my company," says a weary, heavyset   51
man in his early forties. "Sixty hours a week there is normal now. Charging forward, giving customers services they don't even want. And I survived four down sizings so far!"

"I'm going through one now," says the woman next to him, of   52
similar age, who's kept on her white anorak to ward off the chill. Her husband nods grimly.

A lithe, angular man introduces himself as a designer and a   53
builder. His eyes are narrow slits and his skin is sallow. "I work all
the time," he tells the woman next to him. "I've been trying to cut
back, save some money, so I can regain my time."

"I was in secretarial work for twenty-five years," his neighbor   54
responds. She doesn't give details, but somehow that career ended
abruptly. "For the last three, I've been driving vans back and forth
to the airport. It's heavy pressure. I don't like it. I've paid off my
credit cards. Now I want to do what I want to do."

"I just put in a proposal to cut my work back to thirty-two hours   55
a week and take a 20 percent pay cut," says a veterinary clinician.
"It's been accepted. I'm so happy."

Corporate downsizing and its requirements—longer hours for   56
less pay, a work environment with no security and little future—
have brought us to a crossroads. The social contract between
employees and their bosses has been broken. Without unions to
fight for them, and with the political and social environment turned
unsympathetically Darwinian, workers—especially managers and
professionals with a bit of a nest egg and a sense of emotional and
intellectual security—are starting to withhold the one bargaining
chip they have left: their time.

Dave Heitmiller and Jacque Blix know this well. They dropped   57
out before the economy dropped them. "Before, in the seventies, you
could still maybe get a job in a factory, buy a new car. Property values were appreciating everywhere. You could still count on doing
better than your folks did," Dave says. "That's all changed. We're
going through a dramatic change in the business world, and that's
affecting the worker bees. So some of us are saying, maybe there's a
better way."

So enamored is he of that "better way" that Dave has decided to   58
become a proselytizer, writing and perhaps speaking on behalf of the
downshifted life. Like new converts to any cause, he wants to surround himself with true believers, whose presence will support his
own decision to drop out. And, maybe, reassure himself that he's not
a quitter but the advance guard of the weary world order. "I'm thinking that part of my work—and I separate that in my mind from a job—
is promoting the concept of simple living," Dave says. "I've come to
believe in it as a philosophy and not merely an economic thing."

He remains defiant, though. This is not a career but a move-   59
ment. "I'm not doing it to earn my living," Dave wants me to know,

before he and Jacque take their '92 Nissan Sentra (bought used) over to their simplicity-circle meeting. "If I do make some extra money, fine, but that's not the goal."

No, the goal for him and his armchair army is to show the   60
nation that living simply is the best revenge.

Meanings and Values

1. In what ways do the people quoted in paragraphs 1–8 view work? What reactions are readers likely to have to these views? Be specific.

2. What questions about the new "drop out" phenomenon are readers likely to have after the first eight paragraphs of the essay, and which ones do paragraphs 9–26 attempt to answer? State in your own words the specific answers the writer provides.

3. In paragraphs 27–35, the writer traces changes over the last two hundred years in our view of work's importance. Briefly state the different ways we have regarded work.

Expository Techniques

1. In what ways does the writer present the speakers in paragraphs 1–8 as if they were members of a twelve-step program for addiction? What is his likely purpose for doing so? (Guide: *Purpose.*) Is there any irony in this portrayal? Why or why not? (Guide: *Irony.*)

2. During the course of the essay, the writer reviews many possible causes for the movement away from work. Often he lets others explain the possible causes rather than doing so himself. Where in the essay does he finally summarize his view of the causes? Why do you think he waits so long to do this?

3. Rothenberg begins and concludes this essay with a similar strategy. What is it? In what ways does this structure support, or fail to support, the purposes of the essay? (Guide: *Purpose.*)

4. How would you characterize the tone of this essay? In what ways is the choice of tone related to the expository purposes of the essay? If the essay were more argumentative, strongly endorsing or criticizing the trend, how would the tone be likely to change?

Diction and Vocabulary

1. Discuss the writer's use of diction and concrete detail to present the examples in paragraphs 2–4, 40–42, and 50–59. To what extent are the words and details chosen for expository purposes? What purposes

do they serve? To what extent do they reveal the writer's opinions and values? Be specific.

2. Identify the allusions in the last three sentences of paragraph 13 and in paragraph 60. (Guide: *Figures of Speech*.) In what ways does the author reverse the meaning of the original sayings to which they refer? How do the new phrases fit the ideas being explored in the essay?

3. If you do not know the meaning of some of the following words, look them up in a dictionary: articulate, stalwarts (par. 6); settees (9); nouvelle (10); denizens, piddling (11); heretic (13); involuntary (16); avatar (36); tenet (37); manifested (38); incremental (41); implicit, coursed (43); enamored, proselytizer (58).

Read to Write

1. Make a list of any other traditional values of work, leisure, health, well-being, fashion, art, or polite behavior that are currently being questioned or undermined by a significant number of people. Consider each set of values as a possible writing topic to which you can address these questions: Why are people questioning this value and in what ways? What are some of the possible consequences of this questioning?

2. Rothenberg uses specific examples of behavior to explain causes and consequences. In your own essay, explain a puzzling, unusual, or new form of behavior (including fashion, expression, or taste), by using similar kinds of examples, and employ concrete detail in presenting them.

3. Using "What Makes Sammy Walk?" as a model, address some other contemporary trend and explore causes and effects without turning your essay into an argument for or against the trend.

(NOTE: Suggestions for topics requiring development by analysis of CAUSE AND EFFECT follow.)

Writing Suggestions for Section 8
Cause and Effect

Analyze the immediate and ultimate causes and/or effects of one of the following subjects, or another suggested by them. (Be careful that your analysis does not develop into a mere listing of superficial "reasons.")

1. The ethnic makeup of a neighborhood.

2. Some *minor* discovery or invention.

3. The popularity of some modern singer or other celebrity.

4. The popularity of some fad of clothing or hair style.

5. The widespread fascination for antique cars (or guns, furniture, dishes, motorcycles, old bottles, etc.).

6. The widespread enjoyment of fishing or hunting.

7. Student cheating.

8. Too much pressure (on you or an acquaintance) for good school grades.

9. Your being a member of some minority, ethnic, or religious group.

10. Your association, as an outsider, with members of such a group.

11. The decision of some close acquaintance to enter the religious life.

12. Some unreasonable fear or anxiety that afflicts you or someone you know well.

13. The reluctance of many women today to enter what used to be primarily women's professions such as nursing.

14. Your tendency toward individualism.

15. The popularity of computer games.

16. The mainstreaming of handicapped children.

17. The appeal of careers that promise considerable financial rewards.

18. The appeal of a recent movie or current television series.

19. The willingness of some people to sacrifice personal relationships for professional success.

20. The disintegration of a marriage or family.

21. A family's move (or reluctance to move) to a new home.

22. A candidate's success in a local or national election.

23. A recent war or international conflict.
24. A trend in the national economy.
25. The concern with diet and physical fitness.
26. Worry about crime.
27. Attention to gender roles.
28. Personal stress or depression.
29. Desire for success.
30. Willingness to take risks, even extreme ones.

9

Using *Definition* to Help Explain

Few writing faults can cause a more serious communication block between writer and reader than using key terms that can have various meanings or shades of meaning. To be useful rather than detrimental, such terms must be adequately defined.

Of the two basic types of definition, only one is our special concern as a pattern of exposition. But the other, the simpler form, is often useful to clarify meanings of concrete or noncontroversial terms. This simple process is similar to that used most in dictionaries: either providing a synonym (for example, cinema: a motion picture), or placing the word in a class and then showing how it differs from others of the same class (for example, metheglin: an alcoholic liquor made of fermented honey—here the general class is "liquor," and the differences between metheglin and other liquors are that it is "alcoholic" and "made of fermented honey").

With many such abstract, unusual, or coined terms, typical readers are too limited by their own experiences and opinions (and no two sets are identical) for writers to expect understanding of the exact sense in which the terms are used. They have a right, of course, to use such abstract words any way they choose—as long as their readers know what that way is. The importance of making this meaning clear becomes crucial when the term is used as a key element of the overall explanation. And sometimes the term being defined is even more than a key element: it may be the subject itself, for purposes of either explanation or argument.

Extended definition, unlike the simple, dictionary type, follows no set and formal pattern. Often readers are not even aware of the process. Because it is an integral part of the overall subject, extended definition is written in the same tone as the rest of the exposition (or argument), usually with an attempt to interest the readers, as well as to inform or persuade them.

There are some expository techniques peculiar to definition alone. The purpose may be served by giving the *background* of the term. Or the definition may be clarified by *negation*, sometimes called "exclusion" or "differentiation," by showing what is *not* meant by the term. Still another way is to enumerate the *characteristics* of what is defined, sometimes isolating an essential one for special treatment.

To demonstrate the possibilities in these patterns, we can use the term *juvenile delinquency*, which might need defining in some contexts since it certainly means different things to different people. (Where do we draw the line, for instance, between "childish pranks" and antisocial behavior, or between delinquent and nondelinquent experimentation with sex or marijuana?) We might show how attitudes toward juvenile crime have changed: "youthful high spirits" was the label for some of our grandfathers' activities that would be called "delinquency" today. Or we could use negation, eliminating any classes of juvenile wrongdoing not considered delinquency in the current discussion. Or we could simply list characteristics of the juvenile delinquent or isolate one of these—disrespect for authority or lack of consideration for other people—as a universal.

But perhaps the most dependable techniques for defining are the basic expository patterns already studied. Writers could illustrate their meaning of *juvenile delinquency* by giving *examples* from their own experience, from newspaper accounts, or from other sources. (Every one of the introductions to the eleven sections of this book, each a definition, relies greatly on illustration by example.) They could analyze the subject by *classification* of types or degrees of delinquency. They could use the process of *comparison* and *contrast*, perhaps between delinquent and nondelinquent youth. Showing the *causes* and *effects* of juvenile crime could help explain their attitudes toward it, and hence its meaning for them. They might choose to use *analogy*, perhaps comparing the child to a young tree growing grotesque because of poor care and attention. Or a step-by-step analysis of the *process* by which a child becomes delinquent might, in some cases, help explain the intended meaning.

Few extended definitions would use all these methods, but the extent of their use must always depend on three factors: (1) the term itself, since some are more elusive and subject to misunderstanding than others; (2) the function the term is to serve in the writing, since it would be foolish to devote several pages to defining a term that serves only a casual or unimportant purpose; and (3) the prospective reader-audience, since writers want to avoid insulting the intelligence or background of their readers, yet want to go far enough to be sure of their understanding.

But this, of course, is a basic challenge in any good writing—analyzing the prospective readers and writing for the best effect on *them*.

Sample Paragraph (Annotated)

The subject to be defined is clearly announced. After all, few readers are likely to know what *Buhna* means, let alone *Buhna Bash*.

Some of the *characteristics*.

Every year on August 17, Palmville celebrates Buhna Bash, also known as Buhna Days or the Buhna Festival. Most of the day revolves around picnics, sports (including baseball, volleyball, and tennis tournaments), and the Palmville Onion Parade. The latter is presided over by the Onion of Ceremonies (winner of a costume contest). Where did the name Buhna come from? In part from Karl Buhler, the town's first settler, who helped incorporate the city in 1880. And in part from Salvador Nana, who was the first farmer in the region to cultivate the now-famous large, sweet onion called the Palmville Onion. The day may be a Bash, but it is a bash without alcohol and with plenty of laughter and exercise. For Palmville residents, Buhna Bash is like New Year's because it is a time of high spirits and hope for the coming year—often accompanied by optimistic resolutions.

Background of the term.

Negation or *exclusion* to indicate what the term does not mean.

Analogy with a brief example.

Sample Paragraph (Definition)

This is *orienteering*, a mixture of marathon, hike, and scavenger hunt, a cross-country race in which participants must locate a series of markers set in unfamiliar terrain by means of map and compass. The course, which may range from an acre of city park to twenty square miles of wilderness, is dotted with anywhere from four to fifteen "controls," red-and-white flags whose general locations are marked on the map by small circles. At each control there is a paper punch that produces a distinctive pattern on a card the racer carries. In most events the order in which the card must be punched is fixed; the route taken to reach each control, however, is up to the participant.

Excerpt from "Marathoning with Maps" by Linton Robinson from *Science,* published by The American Association for the Advancement of Science. Reprinted by permission.

ROGER WELSCH

ROGER WELSCH was a professor of English and anthropology at the University of Nebraska-Lincoln when he decided to move to a small tree farm in the central Plains. Since then he has made a living as a writer and television and radio columnist and has begun his "rural education." His essays on rural life have been collected in *It's Not the End of the Earth but You Can See It from Here: Tales of the Great Plains* (1990) and he writes a regular column for *Natural History* magazine. His other books include *Treasury of Nebraska Pioneer Folklore* (1966); *Shingling the Fog and Other Plains Lies* (1980); *Mister, You Got Yourself a Horse: Tales of Old-Time Horse Trading* (1981); *Omaha Tribal Myths and Trickster Tales* (1981); *Touching the Fire* (1992); and *Cather's Kitchens: Foodways in Literature and Life* (1987) and *Catfish at the Pump: Humor and the Frontier* (1987) (both with Linda K. Welsch).

Gypsies

As the title suggests, this essay offers a definition of a group of people rather than a term or concept. In addition, one of Welsch's tasks is to redefine a group whose reputation over the centuries has often been less than positive.

I was once talking with a Lakota wise man, Richard Fool Bull, wondering at his ability to sense what seemed to me to be mystic occurrences. Magic things seemed to happen to him fairly regularly. A hundred years ago they would have been called "visions" by the Indians. A thousand years ago they would have been called "miracles" even in our culture, but Mr. Fool Bull accepted them as a normal part of life. 1

"They *are* a normal part of life," he laughed when I expressed my amazement. "They happen all the time." 2

"To you maybe, Mr. Fool Bull, but not to me." 3

349

"Oh yes, to you too," he said, nodding seriously. "That is the   4
sad thing about white culture. You see, Roger, it is not a matter of me
being trained to see such things; *you* have been trained not to see
them."

That's not a new idea. In anthropology classes it is a common   5
teaching trick, for example, to tell students that there are still peoples of this world who do not know the connection between sexual
intercourse and pregnancy. That usually excites astonishment in
the class—how can anyone not understand a cause-and-effect that
obvious?

The professor lets the students throw around their obvious cul-   6
tural superiority for a few minutes and then asks, "What is the result
of eating asparagus?" It is rare that anyone responds with a serious
response. "Your urine smells to high heaven for a couple of hours,
that's what. Now, why is it you think these people are so stupid
because they have not realized an association that spans nine months
while you have never figured out a very obvious cause-and-effect
relationship that takes place over only a few minutes?" The fact of the
matter is, very obvious things, most not at all mystical, happen around
us all the time and we manage to remain totally oblivious to them.

I enjoy the regular—every few months or so—articles that   7
appear in the Omaha or Rising City newspapers that run pretty
much along these lines:

The Bleaker County Savings and Loan lost an estimated $900 in an unusual
fraud perpetrated against teller Judy Hockworthy last Thursday. According
to Ms. Hockworthy six or seven swarthy people—probably Indians or
Iranians—came in to the office at 48th and Caldwell Streets looking for
change for the parking meter and a fifty-dollar bill with an L in the serial
number.

Ms. Hockworthy reported that the men spoke broken English and the
women were dressed in loose, colorful clothing. The men had seventeen
one-hundred-dollar bills for which they wanted the change for the parking
meter and the fifty-dollar bills.

After several changes of the bills, the alleged defrauders left the office and
drove away in late-model pickup trucks, all with campers on the beds and
all with Illinois license plates.

The police have no suspects.

I love those stories. For one thing, I think it's wonderful that   8
these skilled con men get away with what they do in large part
because they have plenty of money in their hands when they enter
the bank. The thesis in our society, evidently, is, "Anyone who has

lots of money is obviously to be trusted" when every indication should tell us exactly the opposite.

But there is a deeper, philosophical reason for my affection for these enduring, widespread petty bilkers. You see, I like coyotes. I don't care if coyotes take 15 percent of the lambs and calves on western ranges. To me coyotes represent something very important—that creatures under the pressure of full warfare can survive. Out here coyotes are hunted with high-power rifles, traps, exploding baits, poison, airplanes, calls, chumming, and mobs. And yet survive. They *prosper!* That prospect gives coyotes like me a lot of hope, you see. 9

Well, newspaper stories like that are about human coyotes, I guess, Gypsies. That's who those "Indians or Iranians" are, Gypsies. Through a thousand years of resistance, through wars and contempt and murder and expulsion, the Gypsies survive. Before Hitler murdered the Jews, he murdered the Gypsies. 10

And yet here they are, still with us, and so skillfully concealed that most Americans haven't the foggiest notion they are still here. 11

Before I forget, let me tell you what happened in Germany. The Gypsies were almost totally eradicated in Germany, and do you know what happened after the Second World War? The Gypsies *swarmed* into Germany. Where would they be safer than where they had only a few years before been pariahs? They could still be hated in England or Sweden, but not in Germany. Gypsy caravans parked illegally under Autobahn overpasses and in department-store parking lots because the gypsies knew that here, where they had been most abused, now they would be most tolerated. 12

I admired especially the ones camped illegally under the overpasses. Can you imagine a better place to set up camp? Families sat at picnic tables and enjoyed supper even when it was raining like crazy or when the sun was blazing, peacefully watching the traffic whiz by. Overpass railings were festooned with wet laundry, a kind of Gypsy flag of resistance. 13

Gypsies are still visible throughout Europe, where their distinctive clothing and wagons and a long tradition make them easily recognized by the citizens of the countries they travel. In America Gypsies are almost invisible. Americans see them not as "Gypsies" but "slightly peculiar, dark people—maybe Iranians or Indians." The average American perceives their pickup trucks with inevitable camper toppers and "For Sale" signs as something strange—but almost never as "Gypsies"! 14

What I love about American Gypsies is that they are seen only   15
rarely, and then briefly, like comets. I, for one, feel graced when I
have the chance to see them, even if only in passing on the highway.

Fremont, Nebraska, used to be a popular place for Gypsies to   16
stop and for all I know may still be. It is on Highway 30, the Lincoln
Highway, and that was the main artery for cross-country travel for
many years. For the still nomadic Gypsies, the long, open stretches
of the Lincoln Highway must have been like a hometown. And Fremont is about halfway across America, so it was a logical meeting
and resting place for the eternal travelers.

As a boy I once read a newspaper report of a time when two   17
rival Gypsy bands wound up at a Gypsy cemetery in Fremont at the
same time—both paying respect, as I recall, to the hallowed memory
of the same patriarch of the tribe. The result was memorable. My rec-
ollection is that something like four hundred shots were fired, and
when the police finally sorted things out after the pitched battle,
they amassed a huge pile of knives, clubs, guns, brass knuckles, and
other weapons of choice.

Now, I am not a violent guy and you probably wonder what   18
possible saving grace I could deduce from a violent encounter like
that. Well, what I found *glorious* about it was that not a single person
was hurt. It was all posturing, maneuvering, threatening, and blus-
ter. Coyotes at play.

I've spoken with quite a few people in Fremont about the Gyp-   19
sies in the old days, and there are a lot of stories. The Gypsies often
asked to camp at farms and farmers would usually give them permission in order to avoid later retribution, but they made sure the
chickens and children were put to bed early and the mother and
father stayed up late to keep an eye on things.

Older farm women who remember when Gypsies would camp   20
near their farmsteads tell me that the Gypsy women and children
would often come to the house asking for eggs or milk and they
were usually given those simple things. Later inspection revealed
that the next day tools, cooking utensils, dogs, and even horses or
cows showed up missing—or perhaps I should say didn't show up
missing.

Today, savvy merchants close up the store the minute they hear   21
that the Gypsies are in town. For those too slow or inexperienced to
close up shop, the experience is usually that ten or twelve women
with voluminous clothing sweep into the store and scatter throughout the aisles. Merchandise disappears within the ample folds of the

clothing. The ensuing shouting, arguing, and linguistic confusion makes it impossible for the merchant, security, or even the police to sort out one woman from another, let alone retrieve pilfered goods, and the inventory is shot to hell for the rest of the year.

All except the new car and truck dealers. They love to see the Gypsies come to town. The Gypsies frequently buy new vehicles in Fremont, and their mode of operation is always the same. They come onto the lot, point to the vehicle they want, ask how much it is, and without any haggling whatsoever pay the price in cash.

Now, I know what's going to happen when folks read this. Latter-day Gypsies are going to say that I have slandered their people, that Gypsies never steal, that all the stories are fictions, that Gypsies actually travel around the world doing good deeds wherever they can. Well, anyone who tries to sell that sort of nonsense does the Gypsies a gross disservice. By lying about their people, they deny their heritage. I have no sympathy for people like that. Just as surely as Gypsies have leavened the cultural loaf of western civilization with their music, art, and food, they have enriched us all with their irrepressible resistance to change, their thousands of years of resistance to authority and order not their own.

There will be non-Gypsies who say I am real jerk for suggesting that common thievery is anything but common thievery and the Gypsies should learn to behave like Americans if they intend to live in this glorious land of the free, home of the brave. They should learn that nothing is more rewarding than money earned by the sweat of your brow—sort of like Ivan Boesky or Donald Trump or Don King, I guess. No, the Gypsies offer another alternative—survival by wit.

I don't condone cheating and thievery normally, but in the case of the Gypsies it is a cultural inheritance and its cleverness makes me glad to be a member of the same species as the Gypsies.

I used to think that one of the things I wanted to do in my life was to spend an afternoon or evening in a Gypsy camp. My fantasy was that I would spot a bunch of Gypsy pickup trucks in a small park some day, somewhere on the Plains—I know what to look for, after all. I imagined that what I would do on that occasion is walk into the camp with a couple of chickens and maybe a battered banjo I wouldn't mind losing over my shoulder. That way could trade the chickens for something to eat—something *Gypsy*—and play my banjo in exchange for some of their legendary music.

Unfortunately, the closest I have come to realizing that fantasy is one time when some friends and I stopped for a picnic lunch in a

22

23

24

25

26

27

public parking place at a large park in South Dakota. We were eating and I was eyeing ten or twelve pickup campers on the other side of the parking lot. I suspected they might be Gypsies.

As we were eating, two five- or six-year-old children approached   28
us from the direction of the trucks. They were beautiful children—dark-skinned with enormous, black eyes. Obviously they were Gypsies. "Would you like a cookie?" I asked them.

They nodded yes.   29

I held out the sack, but to my surprise they backed away a cou-   30
ple steps. No, they explained they would not take the cookies as a gift. They would accept them only if they could buy them from me.

Hummm. Maybe these weren't Gypsies. Gypsies steal, I   31
thought. They don't *buy*. I was put mentally off balance.

"How much you want for the cookies, Mister?" one of the chil-   32
dren asked.

These were great big chocolate chip cookies, and I had a big bag   33
of about sixty or seventy of them; they had cost me maybe eight dollars early that morning at the grocery store. "Tell you what, young man," I said. "How about a penny. Will you pay a penny for a cookie this big?"

He smiled and nodded yes, and I felt like a real prince for being   34
such a nice guy with these kids. And I felt like a real dope for all the things I had said in the past about Gypsies being—how shall I say it?—shrewd operators.

The little boy handed me a penny, and I gave him a cookie. His   35
little friend handed me a penny, and I gave him a cookie too. Gosh, what a pleasant little vignette, I thought.

Then suddenly, out of nowhere, I was surrounded by eighty lit-   36
tle children, all with pennies, all wanting cookies. So we wound up selling our entire supper, all of it—cookies, sandwiches, candy bars, chips, everything, for something like eighty-five cents!

These folks were Gypsies, all right—kids and all. I had been   37
had, but good. I had fallen for exactly the routine I had watched other people fall for for decades—my junior deceivers had confused me with their impressive wealth, they had let me believe that I was being the clever party to the exchange, they had come at me from a direction I would have never thought of looking into, and when it was all over, I still wasn't sure what had happened to me, how much I had lost, how it had ever developed, why I had been such a dope.

And I loved it. Every minute of it. I have savored the moment   38
over and over for these twenty years now. Outwitted by the Gypsies,
I was, and not just by Gypsies but by two five-year old Gypsies.

I still keep an old banjo around the house, and a few chickens,   39
just in case.

Meanings and Values

1. In your own words, summarize Welsch's attitudes towards Gypsies.

2. How would you characterize the tone of this essay? (See "Guide to Terms": *Style/Tone.*) How would you characterize its purpose? (Guide: *purpose.*)

3. Estimate the importance of tone in helping the essay achieve its purpose.

4. Welsch mentions other definitions of Gypsies as part of his attempt to redefine the group and change readers' attitudes. Where does he mention these other definitions and what are they?

Expository Techniques

1. Tell where the essay makes use of each of the following definition techniques.

    a. background

    b. negation

    c. enumeration

    d. analogy

2. At first, paragraphs 1–7 may appear to be only loosely related to the rest of the essay. Discuss whether they contribute to or undermine the unity of the selection. (Guide: *Unity.*) How, if at all, can these paragraphs be considered part of an effective introduction?

3. What is the central theme or thesis of this essay, and in what ways is it communicated to readers?

4. Which examples in the body of the essay are most successful in creating admiration (or at least respect) for Gypsies? Which are least successful? Why? (Guide: *Evaluation.*)

Diction and Vocabulary

1. Study the word choice in paragraphs 10 and 13 and explain how Welsch uses it to invite sympathy and admiration for his subjects.

Pay special attention to repetition and to the connotation of words. (Guide: *Connotation/Denotation.*)

2. What are the synonyms Welsch offers in paragraphs 1–6 for the phenomenon he refers to first as "mystic occurrences"? Offer a definition of the phenomenon yourself using any of the definition strategies discussed in the introduction to Section 9.

3. If you do not know the meaning of any of the following words, look them up in a dictionary: bilkers (par. 9); festooned (13); patriarch, amassed (17); posturing (18); retribution (19); vignette (35).

Read to Write

1. Try to think of any other group (or practices) that might be defended in a manner similar to the way Welsch defends Gypsies. List the kinds of things you might discuss in an essay on the topic.

2. Welsch introduces another speaker (parts 1–4) who provides him with important concepts for his definition. Employ a strategy like this in an essay of your own. You can introduce the speaker(s) at any point in the essay you consider appropriate.

3. Do question 1 above, then using "Gypsies" as a model, prepare the essay you have begun working on.

(NOTE: Suggestions for topics requiring development by use of DEFINITION are on page 392 at the end of this section.)

JOHN BERENDT

JOHN BERENDT was born in Syracuse, New York in 1939. He was a student at Harvard and received his B.A. in 1961. A journalist, essayist, and writer of nonfiction, he has also worked as an editor and columnist at *Esquire,* an editor at *Holiday* and *New York* magazines, and as an associate producer of *The David Frost Show* and the *Dick Cavett Show.* His essays and articles have appeared in numerous magazines, including *Forbes, Publisher's Weekly, Esquire, Architectural Digest,* and the *New Yorker.* His best-selling book, *Midnight in the Garden of Good and Evil* (1994) is a nonfiction account of unusual characters and scandalous goings on in Savannah, Georgia.

The Hoax

In this essay, first published in *Esquire,* Berendt takes a relatively straightforward approach to definition, yet through skillful writing and wit, he manages to offer a fresh and insightful understanding of a familiar term and the behavior it designates.

uses example to define a generality

When the humorist Robert Benchley was an undergraduate at Harvard eighty years ago, he and a couple of friends showed up one morning at the door of an elegant Beacon Hill mansion, dressed as furniture repairmen. They told the housekeeper they had come to pick up the sofa. Five minutes later they carried the sofa out the door, put it on a truck, and drove it three blocks away to another house, where, posing as deliverymen, they plunked it down in the parlor. That evening, as Benchley well knew, the couple living in house A were due to attend a party in house B. Whatever the outcome—and I'll get to that shortly—it was guaranteed to be a defining example of how proper Bostonians handle social crises. The wit inherent in Benchley's practical joke elevated it from the level of prank to the more respectable realm of hoax.

To qualify as a hoax, a prank must have magic in it—the word is derived from *hocus-pocus,* after all. Daring and irony are useful ingredients, too. A good example of a hoax is the ruse perpetrated by David Hampton, the young black man whose pretense of being Sidney Poitier's son inspired John Guare's *Six Degrees of Separation.*

Hampton managed to insinuate himself into two of New York's most sophisticated households—one headed by the president of the public-television station *WNET*, the other by the dean of the Columbia School of Journalism. Hampton's hoax touched a number of sensitive themes: snobbery, class, race, and sex, all of which playwright Guare deftly exploited.

Hampton is a member of an elite band of famous impostors that   3
includes a half-mad woman who for fifty years claimed to be Anastasia, the lost daughter of the assassinated czar Nicholas II; and a man named Harry Gerguson, who became a Hollywood restaurateur and darling of society in the 1930s and 1940s as the ersatz Russian prince Mike Romanoff.

daring Forgeries have been among the better hoaxes. Fake Vermeers   4
painted by an obscure Dutch artist, Hans van Meegeren, were so convincing that they fooled art dealers, collectors, and museums. The hoax came to light when Van Meegeren was arrested as a Nazi collaborator after the war. To prove he was not a Nazi, he admitted he had sold a fake Vermeer to Hermann Göring for $256,000. Then he owned up to having created other "Vermeers," and to prove he could do it, he painted *Jesus in the Temple* in the style of Vermeer while under guard in jail.

In a bizarre twist, a story much like Van Meegeren's became   5
the subject of the book *Fake!*, by Clifford Irving, who in 1972 attempted to pull of a spectacular hoax of his own: a wholly fraudulent "authorized" biography of Howard Hughes. Irving claimed to have conducted secret interviews with the reclusive Hughes, and McGraw-Hill gave him a big advance. Shortly before publication, Hughes surfaced by telephone and denied that he had ever spoken with Irving. Irving had already spent $100,000 of the advance; he was convicted of fraud and sent to jail.

As it happens, we are used to hoaxes where I come from. I grew   6
up just a few miles down the road from Cardiff, New York—a town made famous by the Cardiff Giant. As we learned in school, a farmer named Newell complained, back in 1889, that his well was running dry, and while he and his neighbors were digging a new one, they came upon what appeared to be the fossilized remains of a man twelve feet tall. Before the day was out, Newell had erected a tent and posted a sign charging a dollar for a glimpse of the "giant"— three dollars for a longer look. Throngs descended on Cardiff. It wasn't long before scientists determined that the giant had been carved from a block of gypsum. The hoax came undone fairly

quickly after that, but even so—as often happens with hoaxes—the giant became an even bigger attraction *because* it was a hoax. P. T. Barnum offered Newell a fortune for the giant, but Newell refused, and it was then that he got his comeuppance. Barnum simply made a replica and put it on display as the genuine Cardiff Giant. Newell's gig was ruined.

The consequences of hoaxes are what give them spice. Orson   7 Welles's lifelike 1938 radio broadcast of H. G. Well's *War of the Worlds* panicked millions of Americans, who were convinced that martians had landed in New Jersey. The forged diary of Adolf Hitler embarrassed historian Hugh Trevor-Roper, who had vouched for its authenticity, and *Newsweek* and *The Sunday Times* of London, both of which published excerpts in 1983 shortly before forensic tests proved that there were nylon fibers in the paper it was written on, which wouldn't have been possible had it originated before 1950. The five-hundred-thousand-year-old remains of Piltdown man, found in 1912, had anthropologists confused about human evolution until 1953, when fluoride tests exposed the bones as an elaborate modern hoax. And as for Robert Benchley's game on Beacon Hill, no one said a word about the sofa all evening, although there it sat in plain sight. One week later, however, couple A sent an anonymous package to couple B. It contained the sofa's slipcovers.

Meanings and Values

1. State Berendt's definition of a hoax in your own words, and indicate the difference between a hoax and a practical joke or prank. Look up *hoax* in a dictionary, and tell how Berendt's definition differs, if at all, from the one you encounter there.

2. Restate the meaning of this sentence, "The consequences of hoaxes are what give them spice" (par. 7), and discuss whether the examples that follow it provide satisfactory support for the writer's conclusion. (See "Guide to Terms": *Evaluation*.)

3. Other than defining the term *hoax*, what purposes do you think the writer had in mind for this essay? (Guide: *Purpose.*)

Expository Techniques

1. Discuss how the way Berendt presents the examples in paragraphs 2, 3, and 6 makes them seem imaginative (and somewhat harmless) escapades rather than criminal frauds or deceptions.

2. Determine what definition strategies Berendt uses in this essay. Which seem most effective, and why? (Guide: *Evaluation*.) *examples humor*

3. Evaluate the strategy Berendt uses to open and close the essay. What makes it successful or unsuccessful? *continuing a humorous example*

Diction and Vocabulary

1. To what extent does Berendt's presentation of the hoaxes described in paragraphs 2, 3, and 6 as escapades rather than crimes depend on the terms he uses to present them? (See Expository Techniques, question 1.) (Guide: *Diction*.)

2. If you do not know the meaning of some of the following terms, look them up in a dictionary: perpetrated (par. 2); ersatz (3); reclusive (5); gypsum, gig (6); vouched, forensic (7).

Read to Write

1. Pranks, jokes, humorous events, adventures, and absurd occurrences make enjoyable examples in essays, and they often reveal a good deal about human beings and their relationships. Make a list of possible examples of this sort, then freewrite about them as a way of discovering a possible topic and thesis.

2. Prepare an essay of your own offering a definition, and follow Berendt's lead by beginning it with an example that you leave incomplete until the last paragraph. *leaves reader hanging to know end*

3. Using Berendt's essay as a general pattern, create a definition of your own about a very different subject—such as the greatest loss, the most difficult task, or the biggest disappointment.

(NOTE: Suggestions for topics requiring development by DEFINITION are on page 392 at the end of this section.)

STEPHEN L. CARTER

STEPHEN L. CARTER is Professor of Law at Yale Law School, and
the author of several controversial but highly respected and
tightly-reasoned books that explore controversies in contemporary ethics, politics, and social relationships. After graduating
from Yale Law School, he had a variety of professional experiences, including clerking for Supreme Court Justice Thurgood
Marshall and working in a prestigious law firm. Carter's books
are *Reflections of an Affirmative Action Baby* (1992), *The Culture of
Disbelief: How American Law and Politics Trivialize Religious Devotion*
(1994), *The Confirmation Mess: Cleaning Up the Federal Appointments
Mess,* (1995), and *Integrity* (1997).

The Insufficiency of Honesty

Integrity is not simply a term or idea. It refers to a way of acting and
discerning the qualities of our actions. Integrity may be something
we all claim to admire and wish to have ourselves, but as Stephen
L. Carter points out in this essay first published in the *Atlantic
Monthly*, it can be very difficult to achieve.

A couple of years ago I began a university commencement address 1
by telling the audience that I was going to talk about integrity. The
crowd broke into applause. Applause! Just because they had heard
the word "integrity": that's how starved for it they were. They had
no idea how I was using the word, or what I was going to say about
integrity, or, indeed, whether I was for it or against it. But they knew
they liked the idea of talking about it.

Very well, let us consider this word "integrity." Integrity is like 2
the weather: every body talks about it but nobody knows what to do
about it. Integrity is that stuff that we always want more of. Some
say that we need to return to the good old days when we had a lot
more of it. Others say that we as a nation have never really had
enough of it. Hardly anybody stops to explain exactly what we mean
by it, or how we know it is a good thing, or why everybody needs to
have the same amount of it. Indeed, the only trouble with integrity
is that everybody who uses the word seems to mean something
slightly different.

For instance, when I refer to integrity, do I mean simply "hon-   3
esty"? The answer is no; although honesty is a virtue of importance,
it is a different virtue from integrity. Let us, for simplicity, think of
honesty as not lying; and let us further accept Sissela Bok's definition of a lie: "any intentionally deceptive message which is *stated.*"
Plainly, one cannot have integrity without being honest (although,
as we shall see, the matter gets complicated), but one can certainly
be honest and yet have little integrity.

When I refer to integrity, I have something very specific in   4
mind. Integrity, as I will use the term, requires three steps: discerning what is right and what is wrong; acting on what you have dis-
cerned, even at personal cost; and saying openly that you are acting
on your understanding of right and wrong. The first criterion cap-
tures the idea that integrity requires a degree of moral reflectiveness.
The second brings in the ideal of a person of integrity as steadfast, a
quality that includes keeping one's commitments. The third reminds
us that a person of integrity can be trusted.

The first point to understand about the difference between hon-   5
esty and integrity is that a person may be entirely honest without
ever engaging in the hard work of discernment that integrity
requires: she may tell us quite truthfully what she believes without
ever taking the time to figure out whether what she believes is good
and right and true. The problem may be as simple as someone's foolishly saying something that hurts a friend's feelings; a few moments
of thought would have revealed the likelihood of the hurt and the
lack of necessity for the comment. Or the problem may be more complex, as when a man who was raised from birth in a society that
preaches racism states his belief in one race's inferiority as a fact,
without ever really considering that perhaps this deeply held view
is wrong. Certainly the racist is being honest—he is telling us what
he actually thinks—but his honesty does not add up to integrity.

Telling Everything You Know

A wonderful epigram sometimes attributed to the filmmaker Sam   6
Goldwyn goes like this: "The most important thing in acting is
honesty; once you learn to fake that, you're in." The point is that
honesty can be something one *seems* to have. Without integrity, what
passes for honesty often is nothing of the kind; it is fake
honesty—or it is honest but irrelevant and perhaps even immoral.

Consider an example. A man who has been married for fifty   7
years confesses to his wife on his deathbed that he was unfaithful
thirty-five years earlier. The dishonesty was killing his spirit, he
says. Now he has cleared his conscience and is able to die in peace.

The husband has been honest—sort of. He has certainly unbur-   8
dened himself. And he has probably made his wife (soon to be his
widow) quite miserable in the process, because even if she forgives
him, she will not be able to remember him with quite the vivid
image of love and loyalty that she had hoped for. Arranging his own
emotional affairs to ease his transition to death, he has shifted to his
wife the burden of confusion and pain, perhaps for the rest of her
life. Moreover, he has attempted his honesty at the one time in his
life when it carries no risk; acting in accordance with what you think
is right and risking no loss in the process is a rather thin and unad-
mirable form of honesty.

Besides, even though the husband has been honest in a sense, he   9
has now twice been unfaithful to his wife: once thirty-five years ago,
when he had his affair, and again when, nearing death, he decided
that his own peace of mind was more important than hers. In trying
to be honest he has violated his marriage vow by acting toward his
wife not with love but with naked and perhaps even cruel self-
interest.

As my mother used to say, you don't have to tell people every-   10
thing you know. Lying and nondisclosure, as the law often recognizes, are not the same thing. Sometimes it is actually illegal to tell
what you know, as, for example, in the disclosure of certain financial
information by market insiders. Or it may be unethical, as when a
lawyer reveals a confidence entrusted to her by a client. It may be
simple bad manners, as in the case of a gratuitous comment to a colleague on his or her attire. And it may be subject to religious punishment, as when a Roman Catholic priest breaks the seal of the
confessional—an offense that carries automatic excommunication.

In all the cases just mentioned, the problem with telling every-   11
thing you know is that somebody else is harmed. Harm may not be
the intention, but it is certainly the effect. Honesty is most laudable
when we risk harm to ourselves; it becomes a good deal less so if we
instead risk harm to others when there is no gain to anyone other
than ourselves. Integrity may counsel keeping our secrets in order to
spare the feelings of others. Sometimes, as in the example of the
wayward husband, the reason we want to tell what we know is

precisely to shift our pain onto somebody else—a course of action dictated less by integrity than by self-interest. Fortunately, integrity and self-interest often coincide, as when a politician of integrity is rewarded with our votes. But often they do not, and it is at those moments that our integrity is truly tested.

Error

Another reason that honesty alone is no substitute for integrity is   12
that if forthrightness is not preceded by discernment, it may result in the expression of an incorrect moral judgment. In other words, I may be honest about what I believe, but if I have never tested my beliefs, I may be wrong. And here I mean "wrong" in a particular sense: the proposition in question is wrong if I would change my mind about it after hard moral reflection.

Consider this example. Having been taught all his life that   13
women are not as smart as men, a manager gives the women on his staff less-challenging assignments than he gives the men. He does this, he believes, for their own benefit: he does not want them to fail, and he believes that they will if he gives them tougher assignments. Moreover, when one of the women on his staff does poor work, he does not berate her as harshly as he would a man, because he expects nothing more. And he claims to be acting with integrity because he is acting according to his own deepest beliefs.

The manager fails the most basic test of integrity. The question   14
is not whether his actions are consistent with what he most deeply believes but whether he has done the hard work of discerning whether what he most deeply believes is right. The manager has not taken this harder step.

Moreover, even within the universe that the manager has con-   15
structed for himself, he is not acting with integrity. Although he is obviously wrong to think that the women on his staff are not as good as the men, even were he right, that would not justify applying different standards to their work. By so doing he betrays both his obligation to the institution that employs him and his duty as a manager to evaluate his employees.

The problem that the manager faces is an enormous one in our   16
practical politics, where having the dialogue that makes democracy work can seem impossible because of our tendency to cling to our views even when we have not examined them. As Jean Bethke

Elshtain has said, borrowing from John Courtney Murray, our politics are so fractured and contentious that we often cannot even reach *disagreement*. Our refusal to look closely at our own most cherished principles is surely a large part of the reason. Socrates thought the unexamined life not worth living. But the unhappy truth is that few of us actually have the time for constant reflection on our views—on public or private morality. Examine them we must, however, or we will never know whether we might be wrong.

None of this should be taken to mean that integrity as I have   17
described it presupposes a single correct truth. If, for example, your integrity-guided search tells you that affirmative action is wrong, and my integrity-guided search tells me that affirmative action is right, we need not conclude that one of us lacks integrity. As it happens, I believe—both as a Christian and as a secular citizen who struggles toward moral understanding—that we *can* find true and sound answers to our moral questions. But I do not pretend to have found very many of them, nor is an exposition of them my purpose here.

It is the case not that there aren't any right answers but that,   18
given human fallibility, we need to be careful in assuming that we have found them. However, today's political talk about how it is wrong for the government to impose one person's morality on somebody else is just mindless chatter. *Every* law imposes one person's morality on somebody else, because law has only two functions: to tell people to do what they would rather not or to forbid them to do what they would.

And if the surveys can be believed, there is far more moral   19
agreement in America than we sometimes allow ourselves to think. One of the reasons that character education for young people makes so much sense to so many people is precisely that there seems to be a core set of moral understandings—we might call them the American Core—that most of us accept. Some of the virtues in this American Core are, one hopes, relatively noncontroversial. About 500 American communities have signed on to Michael Josephson's program to emphasize the "six pillars" of good character: trustworthiness, respect, responsibility, caring, fairness, and citizenship. These virtues might lead to a similarly noncontroversial set of political values: having an honest regard for ourselves and others, protecting freedom of thought and religious belief, and refusing to steal or murder.

Honesty and Competing Responsibilities

A further problem with too great an exaltation of honesty is that it   20
may allow us to escape responsibilities that morality bids us bear. If
honesty is substituted for integrity, one might think that if I say I am
not planning to fulfill a duty, I need not fulfill it. But it would be a
peculiar morality indeed that granted us the right to avoid our
moral responsibilities simply by stating our intention to ignore
them. Integrity does not permit such an easy escape.

Consider an example. Before engaging in sex with a woman, her
lover tells her that if she gets pregnant, it is her problem, not his. She   21
says that she understands. In due course she does wind up pregnant.
If we believe, as I hope we do, that the man would ordinarily have a
moral responsibility toward both the child he will have helped to
bring into the world and the child's mother, then his honest statement of what he intends does not spare him that responsibility.

This vision of responsibility assumes that not all moral obligations stem from consent or from a stated intention. The linking of   22
obligations to promises is a rather modern and perhaps uniquely
Western way of looking at life, and perhaps a luxury that only the
well-to-do can afford. As Fred and Shulamit Korn (a philosopher
and an anthropologist) have pointed out, "If one looks at ethno-
graphic accounts of other societies, one finds that, while obligations
everywhere play a crucial role in social life, promising is not preem-
inent among the sources of obligation and is not even mentioned by
most anthropologists." The Korns have made a study of Tonga,
where promises are virtually unknown but the social order is
remarkably stable. If life without any promises seems extreme, we
Americans sometimes go too far the other way, parsing not only our
contracts but even our marriage vows in order to discover the
absolute minimum obligation that we have to others as a result of
our promises.

That some societies in the world have worked out evidently
functional structures of obligation without the need for promise or   23
consent does not tell us what *we* should do. But it serves as a
reminder of the basic proposition that our existence in civil society
creates a set of mutual responsibilities that philosophers used to capture in the fiction of the social contract. Nowadays, here in America,
people seem to spend their time thinking of even cleverer ways to
avoid their obligations, instead of doing what integrity commands
and fulfilling them. And all too often honesty is their excuse.

Meanings and Values

1. Most readers are likely to consider honesty a good trait. Why, therefore, do you think Carter created a definition that points out its shortcomings? What do you think was his overall purpose in writing the essay? Do you believe the essay has more than one purpose? If so, what are they? (See "Guide to Terms": *Purpose.*)

2. List the reasons the author gives for considering honesty insufficient. State in your own words why the author believes that the men in paragraphs 7–9 and 21 have honesty but lack integrity.

3. Does this essay have a thesis statement? If so, where is it? Does it adequately sum up the main idea of the entire essay? Why or why not? If it does not have a thesis statement, is the essay nonetheless organized around a main idea or theme? What is it? (Guide: *Thesis.*) Explain why you consider the essay unified or not unified. (Guide: *Unity.*)

Expository Techniques

1. If one of the main purposes of this essay is to define *integrity*, why does the writer spend so much time discussing the meaning of *honesty*? In formulating your answer, take into account various definition strategies and the likely responses of readers to concepts like *honesty*.

2. What is the main definition strategy Carter employs in this essay? How is the organization of the essay related to this strategy? Be specific in answering this question. What other definition patterns does the writer employ, and where in the essay does he use them?

3. Which paragraphs in the essay are devoted wholly, or mostly, to qualification? (Guide: *Qualification.*) What role(s) do they play in helping develop the definitions? Why would the essay be weaker without them?

4. Where in the essay does the writer use transitions at the beginnings of paragraphs to highlight the essay's organization and indicate the definition strategy he is employing? (Guide: *Transition.*)

Diction and Vocabulary

1. Throughout the essay, Carter uses contrasting words and concepts to explain the difference between honesty and integrity. Sometimes the contrasts involve the denotation of words and sometimes the connotations. (Guide: *Connotation/Denotation.*) Discuss the contrasts as they appear in paragraphs 6, 8, and 9, and explain the use Carter makes of them. (Guide: *Diction.*) Explain the extent to which Carter reinforces the contrasts through sentence structure. (Guide: *Syntax.*)

2. In the course of the essay, Carter repeats a small number of words quite frequently, often varying their form. What are the words? How are they related to the essay's thesis (or theme)? How do they contribute to the essay's coherence? (Guide: *Coherence.*)

3. If you do not know the meanings of some of the following terms, look them up in a dictionary: discerning, criterion, steadfast (par. 4); epigram (6); gratuitous, excommunication (10); laudable, counsel (11); forthrightness (12); contentious (16); presupposes (17); fallibility, impose (18); parsing (22).

Read and Write

1. Create a list of terms naming qualities that most people would agree are virtues (like *honesty* and *integrity*). Choose two and write three brief examples for each word that help define it. Choose examples that indicate what the term means and also some that indicate what it does not or should not mean. Include examples focusing on women as well as men. Choose one of the two terms as the focus of an expository essay.

2. Carter's title, "The Insufficiency of Honesty," suggests both a focus for the essay and an interesting approach, explaining why a particular quality is inadequate. Borrow this approach for an essay. Explain why your subject is inadequate, insufficient, or incomplete.

3. Rewrite Carter's essay substituting examples from women's experiences, or use the essay as a model for a discussion of moral concepts as they apply to both men and women.

(NOTE: Suggestions for topics requiring development by use of DEFINITION are on page 392 at the end of this section.)

Issues and Ideas

Redefining Relationships and Identities

Leave It to Beaver represents for many people a time and a culture whose values, relationships, and roles were simple, clear, and unchanging. Things were probably never that simple, though the television program certainly made them appear that way. Nonetheless, identities and relationships are certainly undergoing more changes and redefinition now than they were three decades ago. The changes involve not only the development of new identities but the recognition that all our identities are constructed from multiple—and sometimes seemingly incompatible—elements. The same is true for relationships, especially those within families.

Though we are always the children of our parents, sometimes we end up playing parental roles towards them, offering advice or counsel just as Veronica Chambers explains in her essay, "Mother's Day." Though we might like to think of ourselves as typically middle class, Middle Western, or business/labor minded in our values and outlooks, few, if any of us are so easily defined. As Kesaya Noda points out in her essay, "Growing Up Asian in America," to understand her identity she needs to view herself as American, Japanese, and a woman—all simultaneously. Something similar is probably true for all of us, whatever our primary ethnic, social, economic, religious, or gender identification.

Even such seemingly clear roles as "mother" and "father" can be filled by many different people and by more than one person, especially in this age of blended families. Michael Dorris, in "Father's Day," reminds us that even in the age of *Leave It to Beaver*, an allegiance to traditional values, such as fighting (and dying) for one's country, could alter traditional family roles and relationships.

Each of these essays reminds us that the need to understand our identities and our roles in relation to other people makes definition an important pattern of thought and analysis. Each essay also demonstrates many other expository patterns.

MICHAEL DORRIS

MICHAEL DORRIS (1945–1997) taught in the English Department at Dartmouth College. He was the parent of several adopted children afflicted with Fetal Alcohol Syndrome, an experience and a condition he wrote about movingly in the highly-praised book *The Broken Cord* (1990). Dorris also wrote about contemporary Native American culture (his own heritage) and the historical experience of Native Americans. Essays on these topics (as well as a wide range of other topics) have appeared in numerous magazines, and many are collected in the volume *Paper Trail* (1994). He was also the author of *Native Americans: Five Hundred Years After* and *A Guide to Research on North American Indians* (with Mary Lou Byler and Arlene Hirschfelder). Among his other books are *Working Men* (stories) (1994); *A Yellow Raft in Blue Water* (1989); and *Cloud Chamber* (1997); (novels) *Morning Girl* (young adult book) (1992); and *The Crown of Columbus* (novel, with Louise Erdrich) (1992).

Father's Day

The redefinition of fatherhood that Dorris offers in this essay, based on his own experiences growing up, calls into question conventional images of family roles and relationships. At the same time, however, it affirms many of the values that conventional definitions also embody. This double movement of redefinition and reaffirmation makes the essay particularly interesting.

My father, a career army officer, was twenty-seven when he was killed, and as a result, I can't help but take war personally. Over the years his image has coalesced for me as an amalgam of familiar anecdotes: a dashing mixed-blood man from the Northwest who, improbably, could do the rumba; a soldier who regularly had his uniform altered by a tailor so that it would fit better; a date, according to my mother, who "knew how to order" in a restaurant; the person whom, in certain lights and to some people, I resemble. He is a compromise of his quirkier qualities, indistinct, better remembered   1

370

for his death—my grandmother still wears a gold star on her best coat—than for his brief life.

From the perspective of the present, my father was a bit player 2 on the edges of the movie frame, the one who didn't make it back, whose fatality added anonymous atmosphere and a sense of mayhem to the plot. His grave, in a military cemetery near Tacoma, is located by graph paper like a small town on a map: E-9. He's frozen in age, a kid in a T-shirt, a pair of dog tags stored in a box in my closet. His willingness to die for his country may have contributed in some small part to the fall of the Nazis, but more in the way of a pawn exchanged for its counterpart, a pair of lives eliminated with the result that there were two fewer people to engage in combat. I was a few months old the last time he saw me, and a single photograph of me in his arms is the only hard evidence that we ever met.

The fact of my father's death exempted me, under the classifi- 3 cation "sole surviving son" (A-IV), from being drafted during the Vietnam War, but it also obliged me to empathize with the child of every serviceperson killed in an armed engagement. "Glory" is an inadequate substitute, a pale abstraction, compared to the enduring, baffling blankness of a missing parent.

There was a children's book in the 1950s—perhaps it still 4 exists—titled *The Happy Family*, and it was a piece of work. Dad toiled at the office, Mom baked in the kitchen, and brother and sister always had neighborhood friends sleeping over. The prototype of "Leave It to Beaver" and "Father Knows Best," this little text reflects a midcentury standard, a brightly illustrated reproach to my own unorthodox household, but luckily that wasn't the way I heard it. As read to me by my Aunt Marion—her acid delivery was laced with sarcasm and punctuated with many a sidelong glance—it turned into hilarious irony.

Compassionate and generous, irreverent, simultaneously opin- 5 ionated and open-minded, iron-willed and ever optimistic, my aunt was the one who pitched a baseball with me in the early summer evenings, who took me horseback riding, who sat by my bed when I was ill. A fierce, lifelong Democrat—a precinct captain even—she helped me find my first jobs and arranged among her friends at work for my escorts to the father-son dinners that closed each sports season. When the time came, she prevailed upon the elderly man next door to teach me how to shave.

"Daddy" Tingle, as he was known to his own children and 6 grandchildren, was a man of many talents. He could spit tobacco juice over the low roof of his garage, gum a sharpened mumbly-peg twig from the ground even without his false teeth, and produce, from the Bourbon Stockyards where he worked, the jewel-like cornea of a cow's eye—but he wasn't much of a shaver. After his instruction, neither am I.

Aunt Marion, on the other hand, was a font of information and influence. When I was fifteen, on a series of tempestuous Sunday mornings at a deserted River Road park, she gave me lessons in how to drive a stick shift. A great believer in the efficacy of the *World Book Encyclopedia*—the major literary purchase of my childhood—she insisted that I confirm any vague belief by looking it up. To the then-popular tune of "You, You, You," she counted my laps in the Crescent Hill pool while I practiced for a life-saving certificate. Operating on the assumption that anything out of the ordinary was probably good for me, she once offered to mortgage the house so that I could afford to go to Mali as a volunteer participant in Operation Crossroads Africa. She paid for my first Smith-Corona typewriter in thirty-six $4-a-week installments.   7

For over sixty years Aunt Marion was never without steady employment: telegraph operator for Western Union, budget officer for the city of Louisville, "new girl" at a small savings and loan (when, after twenty-five years in a patronage job, the Democrats lost the mayor's race), executive secretary for a nationally renowned attorney.   8

Being Aunt Marion, she didn't and doesn't give herself much credit. Unless dragged to center stage, she stands at the periphery in snapshots, minimizes her contributions. Every June for forty years I've sent her a Father's Day card.   9

Meanings and Values

1.   Dorris presents examples of three different men in the role of father. State in your own words the definitions of fatherhood, or of family roles, that each of these examples offers. In what sense can each of these images be viewed as symbolic? (See "Guide to Terms": *Symbol.*)

2.   In what sense are the pictures that represent traditional images of fatherhood and family roles inadequate? Why does the writer view Aunt Marion as a better father than the other father figures in the essay?

3.   What new definition (or re-definition) of fatherhood is Dorris offering in this essay? Try stating it in your own words. Why do you

think that Dorris does not offer his own concise definition of fatherhood in the essay? Is the essay more—or less—effective without it?
(Guide: *Evaluation*.)

Expository Techniques

1. Why do you think the writer offers two negative (or inadequate) ex-
    amples of fatherhood and family roles before beginning his positive
    example in paragraph 5? Why does he interrupt the positive exam-
    ple with another negative one in paragraph 6?

2. What strategy does Dorris use to move from the negative example in
    paragraph 4 to the positive one in paragraph 5? (Guide: *Transition*.)
    What transition strategies does he use to link the other paragraphs in
    the essay?

3. Part of the effectiveness of this essay lies in the variety, quantity, and
    vividness of the details the author provides in the examples. Identify
    the details in paragraph 2, and indicate whether they are specific or
    general. (Guide: *Specific/General*.) Look carefully at the sentence
    structure in paragraphs 2 and 5, and explain how Dorris shaped
    their syntax to allow for the inclusion of numerous details. (Guide:
    Syntax.)

4. Why does the writer wait until the last sentence to announce that he
    regards Aunt Marion as his "father"? Is this strategy effective? Why
    or why not? Does the last sentence serve to summarize the essay, or
    should we consider it a thesis statement of sorts? Explain. (Guide:
    Thesis.)

Diction and Vocabulary

1. Examine the language used to present details in paragraphs 1, 2, and
    4, and indicate where most of it seems to fall on a sliding scale from
    abstract to concrete. (Guide: *Concrete/Abstract*.) Indicate how the rela-
    tive concreteness or abstractness of the language aids in the effective
    presentation of the details. (Guide: *Evaluation*.)

2. If you do not know the meaning of some of the following terms, look
    them up in a dictionary: coalesced, amalgam, anecdotes, rumba (par.
    1); precinct (5); gum, mumbly-peg, cornea (6); tempestuous (7);
    periphery (9).

Read to Write

1. Think of the parenting roles various people have played in your life,
    and in the lives of people you know. Think of how people who are not
    blood relatives have acted like siblings, aunts, uncles, or grandparents.

Freewrite about different ways of viewing families and family relationships until you decide on a topic and direction for an essay.

2. Develop a definition of your own in which you give new meaning to a term but withhold either the term or the definition until the end of the essay, just as Dorris does.

3. Develop a definition of your own in a manner similar to "Father's Day," providing examples that indicate what the definition of the term, concept, or behavior is and what it is not.

(NOTE: Suggestions for topics requiring development by use of DEFINITION are on page 392 at the end of this section.)

KESAYA E. NODA was born in California and raised in rural New Hampshire. She did not learn Japanese until she graduated from high school, but she then spent two years living and studying in Japan. After college, she wrote *The Yamato Colony*, based on her research into the history of the California community to which her grandparents came as immigrants and in which her parents were raised. Following this, she worked and traveled in Japan for another year. Noda earned a master's degree from the Harvard Divinity School. She now teaches at Lesley College in Cambridge, Massachusetts.

Growing Up Asian in America

The act of definition in this essay is one of self-definition, both of an individual and, by implication, of a cultural group. This complex task is accomplished in an especially clear manner. In reading, pay attention to the different kinds of expository patterns Noda employs, including comparison and narration. Note, too, how clearly she makes the different pieces of the essay fit together.

Sometimes when I was growing up, my identity seemed to hurtle   1
toward me and paste itself right to my face. I felt that way, encountering the stereotypes of my race perpetuated by non-Japanese people (primarily white) who may or may not have had contact with other Japanese in America. "You don't like cheese, do you?" someone would ask. "I know your people don't like cheese." Sometimes questions came making allusions to history. That was another aspect of the identity. Events that had happened quite apart from the me who stood silent in that moment connected my face with an incomprehensible past. "Your parents were in California? Were they in those camps during the war?" And sometimes there were phrases or nicknames: "Lotus Blossom." I was sometimes addressed or referred

to as racially Japanese, sometimes as Japanese American, and sometimes as an Asian woman. Confusions and distortions abounded.

How is one to know and define oneself? From the inside—   2
within a context that is self defined, from a grounding in community
and a connection with culture and history that are comfortably
accepted? Or from the outside—in terms of messages received from
the media and people who are often ignorant? Even as an adult I can
still see two sides of my face and past. I can see from the inside out,
in freedom. And I can see from the outside in, driven by the old
voices of childhood and lost in anger and fear.

I Am Racially Japanese

A voice from my childhood says: "You are other. You are less than.   3
You are unalterably alien." This voice has its own history. We have
indeed been seen as other and alien since the early years of our
arrival in the United States. The very first immigrants were welcomed and sought as laborers to replace the dwindling numbers of
Chinese, whose influx had been cut off by the Chinese Exclusion Act
of 1882. The Japanese fell natural heir to the same anti-Asian prejudice that had arisen against the Chinese. As soon as they began striking for better wages, they were no longer welcomed.

I can see myself today as a person historically defined by law   4
and custom as being forever alien. Being neither "free white," nor
"African," our people in California were deemed "aliens, ineligible
for citizenship," no matter how long they intended to stay here.
Aliens ineligible for citizenship were prohibited from owning, buying, or leasing land. They did not and could not belong here. The
voice in me remembers that I am always a *Japanese* American in the
eyes of many. A third-generation German American is an American.
A third-generation Japanese American is a Japanese American.
Being Japanese means being a danger to the country during the war
and knowing how to use chopsticks. I wear this history on my face.

I move to the other side. I see a different light and claim a dif-   5
ferent context. My race is a line that stretches across ocean and time
to link me to the shrine where my grandmother was raised. Two
high, white banners lift in the wind at the top of the stone steps leading to the shrine. It is time for the summer festival. Black characters
are written against the sky as boldly as the clouds, as lightly as kites,
as sharply as the big black crows I used to see above the fields in New
Hampshire. At festival time there is liquor and food, ritual, discipline,

and abandonment. There is music and drunkenness and invocation. There is hope. Another season has come. Another season has gone.

I am racially Japanese. I have a certain claim to this crazy place 6 where the prayers intoned by a neighboring Shinto priest (standing in for my grandmother's nephew who is sick) are drowned out by the rehearsals for the pop singing contest in which most of the villagers will compete later that night. The village elders, the priest, and I stand respectfully upon the immaculate, shining wooden floor of the outer shrine, bowing our heads before the hidden powers. During the patchy intervals when I can hear him, I notice the priest has a stutter. His voice flutters up to my ears only occasionally because two men and a woman are singing gustily into a microphone in the compound, testing the sound system. A prerecorded tape of guitars, samisens, and drums accompanies them. Rock music and Shinto prayers. That night, to loud applause and cheers, a young man is given the award for the most *netsuretsu*—passionate, burning—rendition of a song. We roar our approval of the reward. Never mind that his voice had wandered and slid, now slightly above, now slightly below the given line of the melody. Netsuretsu. Netsuretsu.

In the morning, my grandmother's sister kneels at the foot of 7 the stone stairs to offer her morning prayers. She is too crippled to climb the stairs, so each morning she kneels here upon the path. She shuts her eyes for a few seconds, her motions as matter of fact as when she washes rice. I linger longer than she does, so reluctant to leave, savoring the connection I feel with my grandmother in America, the past, and the power that lives and shines in the morning sun.

Our family has served this shrine for generations. The family's 8 need to protect this claim to identity and place outweighs any individual claim to any individual hope. I am Japanese.

I Am a Japanese American

"Weak." I hear the voice from my childhood years. "Passive," I hear. 9 Our parents and grandparents were the one who were put into those camps. They went without resistance; they offered cooperation as proof of loyalty to America. "Victim," I hear. And, "Silent."

Our parents are painted as hard workers who were socially 10 uncomfortable and had difficulty expressing even the smallest opinion. Clean, quiet, motivated, and determined to match the American way; that is us, and that is the story of our time here.

"Why did you go into those camps," I raged at my parents,   11
frightened by my own inner silence and timidity. "Why didn't you
do anything to resist? Why didn't you name it the injustice it was?"
Couldn't our parents even think? Couldn't they? Why were we so
passive?

I shift my vision and my stance. I am in California. My uncle is   12
in the midst of the sweet potato harvest. He is pressed, trying to get
the harvesting crews onto the field as quickly as possible, worried
about the flow of equipment and people. His big pickup is pulled off
to the side, motor running, door ajar. I see two tractors in the yard in
front of an old shed; the flat bed harvesting platform on which the
workers will stand has already been brought over from the other
field. It's early morning. The workers stand loosely grouped and at
ease, but my uncle looks as harried and tense as a police officer trying to unsnarl a New York City traffic jam. Driving toward the shed,
I pull my car off the road to make way for an approaching tractor.
The front wheels of the car sink luxuriously into the soft, white sand
by the roadside and the car slides to a dreamy halt, tail still on the
road. I try to move forward. I try to move back. The front bites con-
tentedly into the sand, the back lifts itself at a jaunty angle. My uncle
sees me and storms down the road, running. He is shouting before
he is even near me.

"What's the matter with you," he screams. "What the hell are   13
you doing?" In his frenzy, he grabs his hat off his head and slashes
it through the air across his knee. He is beside himself. "Don't you
know how to drive in sand? What's the matter with you? You've
blocked the whole roadway. How am I supposed to get my tractors
out of here? Can't you use your head? You've cut off the whole
roadway, and we've got to get out of here."

I stand on the road before him helplessly thinking, "No, I don't   14
know how to drive in sand. I've never driven in sand."

"I'm sorry, uncle," I say, burying a smile beneath a look of sin-   15
cere apology. I notice my deep amusement and my affection for him
with great curiosity. I am usually devastated by anger. Not this time.

During the several years that follow I learn about the people   16
and the place, and much more about what has happened in this California village where my parents grew up. The issei, our grandparents, made this settlement in the desert. Their first crops were eaten
by rabbits and ravaged by insects. The land was so barren that men
walking from house to house sometimes got lost. Women came here
too. They bore children in 114 degree heat, then carried the babies

with them into the fields to nurse when they reached the end of each row of grapes or other truck farm crops.

I had had no idea what it meant to buy this kind of land and make it grow green. Or how, when the war came, there was no space at all for the subtlety of being who we were—Japanese Americans. Either/or was the way. I hadn't understood that people were literally afraid for their lives then, that their money had been frozen in banks; that there was a five-mile travel limit; that when the early evening curfew came and they were inside their houses, some of them watched helplessly as people they knew went into their barns to steal their belongings. The police were patrolling the road, interested only in violators of curfew. There was no help for them in the face of thievery. I had not been able to imagine before what it must have felt like to be an American—to know absolutely that one is an American—and yet to have almost everyone else deny it. Not only deny it, but challenge that identity with machine guns and troops of white American soldiers. In those circumstances it was difficult to say, "I'm a Japanese American." "American" had to do.

But now I can say that I am a Japanese American. It means I have a place here in this country, too. I have a place here on the East Coast, where our neighbor is so much a part of our family that my mother never passes her house at night without glancing at the lights to see if she is home and safe; where my parents have hauled hundreds of pounds of rocks from fields and arduously planted Christmas trees and blueberries, lilacs, asparagus, and crab apples; where my father still dreams of angling a stream to a new bed so that he can dig a pond in the field and fill it with water and fish. "The neighbors already came for their Christmas tree?" he asks in December. "Did they like it? Did they like it?"

I have a place on the West Coast where my relatives still farm, where I heard the stories of feuds and backbiting, and where I saw that people survived and flourished because fundamentally they trusted and relied upon one another. A death in the family is not just a death in a family; it is a death in the community. I saw people help each other with money, materials, labor, attention, and time. I saw men gather once a year, without fail, to clean the grounds of a ninety-year-old woman who had helped the community before, during, and after the war. I saw her remembering them with birthday cards sent to each of their children.

I come from a people with a long memory and a distinctive grace. We live our thanks. And we are Americans. Japanese Americans.

I Am a Japanese American Woman

Woman. The last piece of my identity. It has been easier by far for   21
me to know myself in Japan and to see my place in America than it
has been to accept my line of connection with my own mother. She
was my dark self, a figure in whom I thought I saw all that I feared
most in myself. Growing into womanhood and looking for some
model of strength, I turned away from her. Of course, I could not
find what I sought. I was looking for a black feminist or a white feminist. My mother is neither white nor black.

My mother is a woman who speaks with her life as much as   22
with her tongue. I think of her with her own mother. Grandmother
had Parkinson's disease and it had frozen her gait and set her fingers, tongue, and feet jerking and trembling in a terrible dance. My
aunts and uncles wanted her to be able to live in her own home.
They fed her, bathed her, dressed her, awoke at midnight to take her
for one last trip to the bathroom. My aunts (her daughters-in-law)
did most of the care, but my mother went from New Hampshire to
California each summer to spend a month living with grandmother,
because she wanted to and because she wanted to give my aunts at
least a small rest. During those hot summer days, mother lay on the
couch watching the television or reading, cooking foods that grandmother liked, and speaking little. Grandmother thrived under her
care.

The time finally came when it was too dangerous for grand-   23
mother to live alone. My relatives kept finding her on the floor
beside her bed when they went to wake her in the mornings. My
mother flew to California to help clean the house and make arrangements for grandmother to enter a local nursing home. On her last
day at home, while grandmother was sitting in her big, overstuffed
armchair, hair combed and wearing a green summer dress, my
mother went to her and knelt at her feet. "Here, Mamma," she said.
"I've polished your shoes." She lifted grandmother's legs and
helped her into the shiny black shoes. My grandmother looked
down and smiled slightly. She left her house walking, supported by
her children, carrying her pocket book, and wearing her polished
black shoes. "Look, Mamma," my mom had said, kneeling. "I've
polished your shoes."

Just the other day, my mother came to Boston to visit. She had   24
recently lost a lot of weight and was pleased with her new shape and
her feeling of good health. "Look at me, Kes," she exclaimed, turning

toward me, front and back, as naked as the day she was born. I saw her small breasts and the wide, brown scar, belly button to pubic hair, that marked her because my brother and I were both born by Caesarean section. Her hips were small. I was not a large baby, but there was so little room for me in her that when she was carrying me she could not even begin to bend over toward the floor. She hated it, she said.

"Don't I look good? Don't you think I look good?" 25

I looked at my mother, smiling and as happy as she, thinking of 26 all the times I have seen her naked. I have seen both my parents naked throughout my life, as they have seen me. From childhood through adulthood we've had our naked moments, sharing baths, idle conversations picked up as we moved between showers and closets, hurried moments at the beginning of days, quiet moments at the end of days.

I know this to be Japanese, this ease with the physical, and it 27 makes me think of an old, Japanese folk song. A young nursemaid, a fifteen-year-old girl, is singing a lullaby to a baby who is strapped to her back. The nursemaid has been sent as a servant to a place far from own home. "We're the beggars," she says, "and they are the nice people. Nice people wear fine sashes. Nice clothes."

> *If I should drop dead,*
> *bury me by the roadside!*
> *I'll give a flower*
> *to everyone who passes.*
>
> *What kind of flower?*
> *The cam-cam-camellia {tsun-tsun-tsubaki}*
> *watered by Heaven:*
> *alms water.*[1]

The nursemaid is the intersection of heaven and earth, the inter- 28 section of the human, the natural world, the body, and the soul. In this song, with clear eyes, she looks steadily at life, which is some- times so very terrible and sad. I think of her while looking at my mother, who is standing on the red and purple carpet before me, laughing, without any clothes.

I am my mother's daughter. And I am myself. 29

I am a Japanese American woman. 30

[1]Patia R. Isaku, *Mountain Storm, Pine Breeze: Folk Song in Japan* (Tucson: University of Arizona Press, 1981), 41.

Epilogue

I recently heard a man from West Africa share some memories of his   31
childhood. He was raised Muslim, but when he was a young man,
he found himself deeply drawn to Christianity. He struggled against
this inner impulse for years, trying to avoid the church yet feeling
pushed to return to it again and again. "I would have done *anything*
to avoid the change," he said. At last, he became Christian. Afterwards he was afraid to go home, fearing that he would not be
accepted. The fear was groundless, he discovered, when at last he
returned—he had separated himself, but his family and friends (all
Muslim) had not separated themselves from him.

The man, who is now a professor of religion, said that in the   32
Africa he knew as a child and a young man, pluralism was embraced
rather than feared. There was "a kind of tolerance that did not deny
your particularity," he said. He alluded to zestful, spontaneous
debates that would sometimes loudly erupt between Muslims and
Christians in the village's public spaces. His memories of an atheist
who harangued the villagers when he came to visit them once a
week moved me deeply. Perhaps the man was an agricultural advi-
sor or inspector. He harassed the women. He would say:

"Don't go to the fields! Don't even bother to go to the fields. Let God take
care of you. He'll send you the food. If you believe in God, why do you need
to work? You don't need to work! Let God put the seeds in the ground. Stay
home."

The professor said, "The women laughed, you know? They just   33
laughed. Their attitude was, 'Here is a child of God. When will he
come home?'"

The storyteller, the professor of religion, smiled the most fan-   34
tastic, tender smile as he told this story. "In my country, there is a
deep affirmation of the oneness of God," he said. "The atheist and
the women were having quite different experiences in their
encounter, though the atheist did not know this. He saw himself as
quite separate from the women. But the women did not see themselves as being separate from him. 'Here is a child of God,' they said.
'When will he come home?'"

Meanings and Values

1.   Define in your own words each of the identities Noda outlines for
     herself. How can the last section of the essay, "Epilogue" (pars.

31–34), be said to harmonize these identities or at least to suggest a way of building bridges among them?

2. Discuss how the opening section of this essay (pars. 1–2) explains the author's need to define herself and suggests indirectly that each of us needs to go through a similar process.

Expository Techniques

1. Apart from definition, what expository technique does Noda use to organize this essay as a whole? What expository pattern does she employ in paragraphs 3–8? In paragraphs 9–20? What pattern or patterns organize paragraphs 21–28? What pattern helps conclude the essay in paragraphs 31–34?

2. This essay makes use of a variety of expository patterns. Explain why it is accurate (or inaccurate) to refer to the overall pattern as one of definition. Be ready to defend your answer with evidence from the text.

3. Tell how paragraph 2 helps predict and justify the organization of the essay. Why is this kind of paragraph a useful part of the essay? For what kinds of essays might a paragraph like this be neither useful nor necessary?

4. Discuss the use of subtitles in organizing the essay. In what ways are they linked to the overall definition pattern? (See "Guide to Terms": *Unity.*)

Diction and Vocabulary

1. Each of the major sections in the body of the essay uses a different cluster of terms to explore and define a particular part of the author's identity. Tell what the clusters of terms are in each section.

2. Tell how the diction in paragraphs 22–28 contributes to their effectiveness. (Consider also the contribution made by the choice of details.) (Guide: *Diction.*)

3. If you do not know the meanings of some of the following terms, look them up in a dictionary: context (par. 2); influx (3); invocation (5); Shinto, samisens (6); issei (16); arduously (18); pluralism, spontaneous, harangued (32).

Read to Write

1. The closing example in the essay endorses "pluralism" (par. 32), tolerance for a variety of beliefs. Make a list of questions relating to pluralism that might lead to topics for an essay. Here are some to get you started: To what extent is our society already guided by such an

attitude? Give some examples. What might be some of the practical consequences (good and bad) of a thoroughgoing pluralism in our society? Is such an attitude really possible for a large society to adopt?

2. Use some of the concepts from Noda's essay in one of your own. If you believe that all people have multiple identities, try defining yours in an essay. If you can, try harmonizing them as well, or at least discuss the relationships among them.

3. Following Noda's example, build an essay of your own around a series of increasingly specific definitions such as her "I am racially Japanese," "I am a Japanese American," and "I am a Japanese American Woman."

(NOTE: Suggestions for topics requiring development by DEFINITION are on page 392 at the end of this section.)

VERONICA CHAMBERS **is a writer living in New York City. She is a contributing editor for** Glamour **magazine and has recently published a memoir,** Mama's Girl **(1996).**

Mother's Day

In this selection from her book *Mama's Girl*, published as an essay in *Glamour* magazine, Chambers uses a variety of expository patterns (comparison, example, narrative, cause-and-effect) to help understand why her Mother's Day gift received such a cool reception. As she considers the differences between her perspective as an African-American professional woman, a college-educated writer, and that of her mother, who struggled to raise her child on a maid's salary in the days when educational and occupational opportunities for African Americans were strictly limited, Chambers comes to a deeper appreciation of her mother's achievements.

A couple of years ago, I earned a good salary for the first time and I 1 wanted to do something special for my mother. So I sent her a gift certificate for a day at Elizabeth Arden. Included were a massage, facial, sauna and makeover—the works, plus tips. My mother wouldn't have to spend a dime, only the subway token it would take to get her there. I called here up on Mother's Day, all excited about the gift. She was excited, too, and described how it had come gift-wrapped with a big red bow. Then she asked me a question that broke my heart in two. "Vee?" she whispered. "Do they allow black people in those places?"

It was 1992 and my mother was asking whether Elizabeth 2 Arden would slam the red door in her black face. "Of course they allow black people!" I said, using an angry voice to conceal how hurt I felt. "I've paid for everything, including a tip for everyone who touches your body. So if anybody so much as looks at you funny, you tell me!"

Months went by and my mother did not use the gift certificate. 3
"You use it," she would tell me. "You work so hard. Burning the can-
dle at both ends. . . ." Finally, I got furious with her and made some
empty threat about refusing to talk to her until she went to Elizabeth
Arden. She wouldn't budge.

In my frustration I reimagined the situation as a Daliesque fan- 4
tasy in which I was an avenging angel pushing my mother through
the Red Door. When a friend suggested that perhaps my mother did
not want to go to Elizabeth Arden alone, I sent her neighbor a gift
certificate too, but it didn't help: She turned out to be just as afraid
to go as my mother.

Finally, almost a year later, my mother called and said, "Guess 5
where I've just been? Elizabeth Arden."

My heart almost stopped. "How was it?" I asked. 6

"Nice . . . but everyone there was just like you," she said coyly. 7

"Just like *me?*" I repeated disbelievingly, picturing the Fifth 8
Avenue crowd of older white women laid out on massage tables.

"Professionals. Upper-class women. You know," she replied. 9

While I was thrilled that she'd gone, that exchange made me 10
wonder what my mother saw when she looked at me. I wondered if
everything about me that she chose to see as being white—my education, my career, my social activities—obscured everything about
me that was black—my family, my community, my mother herself.
I always knew she saw me as different from her, but not until she
went to Elizabeth Arden did I realize how different.

I never stop feeling that I want to make things up to my 11
mother—make up for her difficulties with my father, from whom
she was eventually divorced, for my brother's failure to do well in
school or in a job, for the ways in which we all left her. So I buy her
things. If I'm shopping and I buy myself a suit, I'll get my mother a
blouse. I send her vases and candles and antique dolls. One of the
first questions I ask when I enter a store is: "Can you ship this somewhere for me?" I'd be a liar if I said my generosity was only about
bestowing kindnesses on my mother. It is also about easing my own
guilt.

I am more aware now of how my schooling and experiences 12
separate us, but I cannot get used to the distance. She is so much a
part of me that I half felt I graduated college for both of us. To me,
the newfound abundance of the money I can earn has meaning for
both of us. But my mother sees things differently. We are separated
by education and economics.

When I was in college, my mother once called me an Oreo— 13
black on the outside, white on the inside. The word, so cruel when it
comes from a black person's peers, was like a punch in the face coming from my mother—as if I were a total stranger and not her own
child. Later, when I told her how much it had hurt me, she said, "But
I was just joking!"

Now that I am working, she is fond of calling me a Buppie. I 14
hate it, I tell her, and ask her to stop. But if I talk about wanting to
see a certain play or deliberate over whether to buy a painting, she
can't help but let it slip: "You're such a Buppie." There is a texture
of affection and pride in her voice that suggests she's glad I'm not as
poor as she was when she was my age, but it is a pride I have trouble absorbing. Her voice says, "I am proud of you—but you are now
an entirely different being than I am."

Going from poor to middle class was both the longest and the 15
shortest transition I have ever made. Long, because every day that I
went without was just one of an unending stretch of days in which
I'd always done without. Once I'd craved things so deeply that I
kept myself away from malls and shops, so as not to preoccupy
myself with what I could not have. In college I collected mail-order
catalogs, marking them up with stars and circling the outfits I liked
in the colors and sizes I wanted. Desire became a game and playing
the game was satisfying in its own way. At the end of freshman year,
a friend asked, "Why do you always mark up those catalogs when
you never order anything?" I hadn't realized that anyone noticed
what had become a mindless habit, and I didn't know what to say.
Was he being cruel?

"I don't know," I said, feigning dumbness and vowing to keep 16
the catalogs out of sight.

But the jump from poverty to solvency seemed short and sud- 17
den because it was one I made alone. It was just me in an apartment,
staring at a paycheck that was bigger than any I'd ever seen. Who
could I call, without it sounding like I was bragging? Who wouldn't
immediately ask for a loan? Who would understand how a thousand dollars could feel so much like a million? I wanted my mother
there on the other end of the phone.

But I also felt guilty, because I felt she was much more deserv- 18
ing of that check than I was. I watched my mother work all her life
with no reward greater than a cost-of-living raise; she was always
just getting by. I knew that hard work was no guarantee of success.
Success was only a dream—the big payoff that never came from my

father's get-rich-quick schemes, or a winning lottery number that came to you in a vision. My life had been different. And even after going to college, even after years of hard work, I still felt deep inside that I was more lucky than successful. As if I had dreamed of a number and that number had come in.

My mother was neither lucky nor successful. She believed in the   19
promise of the civil rights movement, but never really thought what those rights would mean to her. She taught her children the importance of equality and pride, but never expected to live in equality herself.

I can see now that although she was affected by the benefits of   20
integration—no more sitting in the back of the bus, no more separate water fountains—most of the triumphs of the movement remained for my mother events that happened on TV. In 1970, my mother gave birth to me and worked as a secretary. In the 1990s, my mother is still a secretary. She's worked hard all her life, mostly for white people, and the civil rights movement did not change that. What it changed was me, and I wasn't some bright, young black woman that my mother saw on TV. I was her daughter. My success brought the benefits of integration through her front door, and that scared her. She could call me an Oreo and a Buppie and try to keep what I represented at a safe distance, but the things I bought her, the restaurants I took her to, forced her to consider life differently. Maybe it wouldn't take a winning lottery ticket for her to be able to lead a better life.

I called my mother recently and had a long talk about money.   21
My mother is only 45. She has so much life ahead of her. I was hoping that I could use some of what I've learned about saving and investing to make her life more comfortable, so I began to ask her questions: What do your retirement savings look like? What are your financial goals? She had to stop and think.

"You mean goals besides paying the rent and putting dinner on   22
the table?" She laughed nervously.

"Yes," I said. "What do you want to own? What trips do you   23
want to take?"

There wasn't much she wanted to own. What she really wanted   24
to do was travel. She wanted to go to Jamaica, Ghana, and Brazil. The tentativeness in her voice was so clear, as if just by speaking her wishes aloud, she might cause the genie to dive back into its bottle. My mother had never been able to see further ahead than the next day or next month. I knew then why it had scared her when, as a ten-

year-old, I started talking about college. She didn't know what we were going to eat for the next seven days, much less where she would find tuition in seven years.

Now as we discussed *her* money for the first time, I told my   25
mother that if she didn't dream, if she didn't think about what she wanted to have, then she was going to wake up and another 20 years would be gone. "There's nothing to save," she said, I asked if I could see her weekly budget. I told her I knew it was personal, but I needed to know exactly how much she and my stepfather made and where it was going. "What budget?" she said.

I wrote down all my mother's figures—how much she owed,   26
what little she had saved, how much she and my stepfather made. I did a budget and a savings plan and outlined a retirement plan that would give her some sort of nest egg.

"It's not a lot," I told her. "You'd probably still need to work.   27
But maybe you could save enough to open a business." I wrote out the plan and mailed it to her. When she called me back, I could tell she was impressed. She told me that she and my stepfather had gone over my plan and they thought they could stick to it.

My mother told me she had tried to save money when we were   28
little, but often she was too embarrassed to take a five dollar bill up to the teller's window and deposit it, so she would keep it in an envelope. By the next week, it would be gone.

"I feel like I can really be hopeful now," she said. "Like I have   29
something to look forward to besides bills." Then she paused and added, "I'm still going to play the lottery, and if I hit it, then to hell with your savings plan." I laughed and said that would be fine.

For the first time in my life, I hear in my mother's voice that she   30
is more than just coping, more than just figuring out how to get by. When I hear my mother talk, I can hear her dreaming and it's the sweetest sound in the world to me.

Meanings and Values

1. In what ways does the author's mother define her daughter? In what ways does the author define her mother? In what ways does the author define herself?

2. What social movements and changes in values and attitudes make necessary the redefinition of identity and roles the author undertakes in this essay? How many of these social movements are mentioned in the essay, and where are they mentioned?

3.   How are readers likely to react to the question at the end of para-
     graph 1? What might determine the ways different readers react?
     What proportion of readers do you think are likely to react as the
     writer does? Why?

Expository Techniques

1.   In what ways does the question at the end of paragraph 1 act as a jus-
     tification for the redefining of roles that Chambers undertakes in this
     essay? Does it provide justification for most readers as well as the
     writer? If not, how else does the writer justify the need for new defi-
     nitions?

2.   Can the sentence at the end of paragraph 1 be considered a thesis
     statement? Why or why not? If not, where else in the essay does the
     author make plain the purpose or thesis (main theme) of the piece?
     (See "Guide to Terms": *Thesis; Purpose.*)

3.   Which paragraphs in the essay use comparison as an expository pat-
     tern? What do they contribute to the process of definition?

Diction and Vocabulary

1.   Many of the paragraphs in this essay discuss conflicting definitions
     and misunderstandings. Discuss how the writer uses transitions in
     paragraphs 12–14 and 17–20 to emphasize such conflicts and con-
     trasting perspectives. (Guide: *Transition; Emphasis.*)

2.   To what does the word "Daliesque" in paragraph 4 allude? (Guide:
     Figures of Speech.) What does this reveal about the speaker's attitudes
     and perspective? What is a "Buppie"? Why would the writer be of-
     fended by the term?

3.   If you do not know the meaning of some of the following words,
     look them up in a dictionary: sauna (par. 1); disbelievingly (8); be-
     stowing (11); tentativeness (24).

Read to Write

1.   In what ways are college-educated children likely to view the world
     differently from their parents? Are there likely differences in per-
     spective between children who have attended graduate school and
     parents who attended college? Do differences in careers and kinds of
     work also lead to different perspectives? Consider exploring these
     and other contrasting outlooks (or definitions of values and identi-
     ties) in an expository essay.

2. Adopt Chamber's technique of drawing brief quotations from conversations as a way of conveying ideas and perspectives (especially contrasts) in an essay of your own.

3. Using "Mothers's Day" as a model, explore a relationship of your own that has involved shifting definitions and perspectives. Choose a relationship that reveals something about social relationships and values that other people might consider important in their own lives.

(NOTE: Suggestions for topics requiring development by DEFINITION follow.)

Writing Suggestions for Section 9
Definition

Develop a composition for a specified purpose and audience, using whatever methods and expository patterns will help convey a clear understanding of your meaning of one of the following terms:

1. Country music.
2. Conscience.
3. Religion.
4. Bigotry.
5. Success.
6. Empathy.
7. Family.
8. Hypocrisy.
9. Humor.
10. Sophistication.
11. Naiveté.
12. Cowardice.
13. Wisdom.
14. Integrity.
15. Morality.
16. Greed.
17. Social poise.
18. Intellectual (the person).
19. Pornography.
20. Courage.
21. Patriotism.
22. Equality (or equal opportunity).
23. Loyalty.
24. Stylishness (in clothing or behavior).
25. Fame.
26. Obesity.
27. Cheating.
28. Hero.
29. Feminine.
30. Masculine.

10

Explaining with the Help of *Description*

Exposition, as well as argument, can be made more vivid, and hence more understandable, with the support of description. Most exposition does contain some elements of description, and at times description carries almost the entire burden of the explanation, becoming a basic pattern for the expository purpose.

Description is most useful in painting a wordpicture of something concrete, such as a scene or a person. Its use is not restricted, however, to what we can perceive with our senses; we can also describe (or attempt to describe) an abstract concept, such as an emotion or a quality or a mood. But most attempts to describe fear, for instance, still resort to the physical—a "coldness around the heart," perhaps—and in such concrete ways communicate the abstract to the reader.

In its extreme forms, description is either *objective* or *impressionistic* (subjective), but most of its uses are somewhere between these extremes. Objective description is purely factual, uncolored by any feelings of the author; it is the type used for scientific papers and most business reports. But impressionistic description, as the term implies, at least tinges the purely factual with the author's personal impressions; instead of describing how something *is*, objectively, the author describes how it *seems*, subjectively. Such a description might refer to the "blazing heat" of an August day. Somewhat less impressionistic would be "extreme heat." But the scientist would describe it precisely as "64 degrees Celsius," and this would be purely objective reporting, unaffected by the impressions of the author. (No examples of the latter are included in this section, but many textbooks for other courses utilize the technique of pure objective description, as do encyclopedias. The McKibben essay in Further

Readings provides some good examples of objective description although not entirely unmixed with colorful impressionistic details.

The first and most important job in any descriptive endeavor is to select the details to be included. There are usually many from which to choose, and writers must constantly keep in mind the kind of picture they want to paint with words—for *their* purpose and *their* audience. Such a word-picture need not be entirely visual; in this respect writers have more freedom than artists, for writers can use strokes that will add the dimensions of sound, smell, and even touch. Such strokes, if made to seem natural enough, can help create a vivid and effective image in the reader's mind.

Most successful impressionistic description focuses on a single *dominant impression.* Of the many descriptive details ordinarily available for use, the author selects those that will help create a mood or atmosphere or emphasize a feature or quality. But more than the materials themselves are involved, for even diction can often assist in creating the desired dominant impression. Sometimes syntax is also an important factor, as in the use of short, hurried sentences to help convey a sense of urgency or excitement.

Actual structuring of passages is perhaps less troublesome in description than in most of the other patterns. But some kind of orderliness is needed for the sake of both readability and a realistic effect. (Neither objective nor impressionistic description can afford not to be realistic, in one manner or another.) In visual description, orderliness is usually achieved by presenting details as the eye would find them—that is, as arranged in space. We could describe a person from head to toe, or vice versa, or begin with the most noticeable feature and work from there. A scenic description might move from near to far or from far to near, from left to right or from right to left. It might also start with a broad, overall view, gradually narrowing to a focal point, probably the most significant feature of the scene. These are fairly standard kinds of description; but as the types and occasions for using description vary widely, so do the possibilities for interesting treatment. In many cases, writers are limited only by their own ingenuity.

But ingenuity should not be allowed to produce *excessive* description, an amazingly certain path to reader boredom. A few well-chosen details are better than profusion. Economy of words is desirable in any writing, and description is no exception. Appropriate use of figurative language and careful choice of strong nouns and verbs will help prevent the need for strings of modifiers, which are wasteful and can seem amateurish.

Even for the experienced writer, however, achieving good description remains a constant challenge; the beginner should not expect to attain this goal without working at it.

Sample Paragraph (Description)

Background.

Interpretation of the photograph.

Generally objective description of the photograph, though "almost smell" is certainly impressionistic.

The details of the photograph are presented objectively, but the description is filled with impressionistic observations about the dancer's moods and the emotional "temperature" of the scene.

The theme of this year's Amateur Photography Contest sponsored by the Palmville *Gazette* was "Snapshots of Palmville." There were two "Top Shot" award winners. Emily Grezibel looked to the past with a black-and-white photograph of Ericson's Feed Store. The peeling white paint on the front of the old clapboard building gleams in the hot midday sun and little puffs of dust follow the footsteps of the elderly farmer in dark bib overalls as he passes in front of the Blue Seal Feeds sign. One can almost smell the dust and the scents of feed, fertilizer, and oil hanging in the air. The title sums up the photograph's theme: "Fading." Brian Alonzo's color photograph "Saturday Night" is the other winner. Taken in the parking lot of the Palmville Mall, it shows a group of teenagers dancing to the music of a boom box sitting on the hood of a shiny, cherry-red convertible. Several of the couples dancing in the foreground appear to be singing along with the music and the dancers are frozen in the middle of joyous, athletic dance steps. Other teenagers sit on hoods of bright blue, turquoise, and yellow cars in a semicircle behind the dancers, clapping and smiling. The silent yet exciting sounds of the music seem to radiate

The central theme of the paragraph is the contrast between the generations and their outlooks.

from the entire picture. The whole scene is illuminated by the arc lights of the parking lot, making the picture seem a festival celebrating the energy and hopefulness of the next generation of Palmville citizens.

Sample Paragraph (Description)

It's no winter without an ice storm. When Robert Frost gazed at bowed-over birch trees and tried to think that boys had bent them playing, he knew better: "Ice-storms do that." They do that and a lot more, trimming disease and weakness out of the tree—the old tree's friend, as pneumonia used to be the old man's. Some of us provide life-support systems for our precious shrubs, boarding them over against the ice, for the ice storm takes the young or unlucky branch or birch as well as the rotten or feeble. One February morning we look out our windows over yards and fields littered with kindling, small twigs and great branches. We look out at a world turned into one diamond, ten thousand carats in the line of sight, twice as many facets. What a dazzle of spinning refracted light, spider webs of cold brilliance attacking our eyeballs! All winter we wear sunglasses to drive, more than we do in summer, and never so much as after an ice storm, with its painful glaze reflecting from maple and birch, granite boulder and stone wall, turning electric wires into bright silver filaments. The snow itself takes on a crust of ice, like the finish of a clay pot, that carries our weight and sends us

swooping and sliding. It's worth your
life to go for the mail. Until sand and
salt redeem the highway, Route 4 is
quiet. We cancel the appointment with
the dentist, stay home, and marvel at the
altered universe, knowing that midday
sun will strip ice from tree and roof and
restore our ordinary white winter
world.

SHARON CURTIN

SHARON CURTIN, a native of Douglas, Wyoming, was raised in a
family of ranchers and craftspeople. Curtin, a feminist and political leftist, has worked as a nurse in New York and California
but now devotes most of her time to writing and to operating a
small farm in Virginia.

Aging in the Land of the Young

"Aging in the Land of the Young" is the first part of Curtin's article by that title, as it appeared in the *Atlantic* in July 1972. It is
largely a carefully restructured composite of portions of her book
Nobody Ever Died of Old Age, also published in 1972. It illustrates the
subjective form of description, generally known as impressionistic
description.

Old men, old women, almost 20 million of them. They constitute 10   1
percent of the total population, and the percentage is steadily growing. Some of them, like conspirators, walk all bent over, as if hiding
some precious secret, filled with self-protection. The body seems to
gather itself around those vital parts, folding shoulders, arms, pelvis
like a fading rose. Watch and you see how fragile old people come
to think they are.

Aging paints every action gray, lies heavy on every movement,   2
imprisons every thought. It governs each decision with a ruthless
and single-minded perversity. To age is to learn the feeling of no
longer growing, of struggling to do old tasks, to remember familiar
actions. The cells of the brain are destroyed with thousands of unfelt
tiny strokes, little pockets of clotted blood wiping out memories and
abilities without warning. The body seems slowly to give up, randomly stopping, sometimes starting again as if to torture and tease

with the memory of lost strength. Hands become clumsy, frail transparencies, held together with knotted blue veins.

Sometimes it seems as if the distance between your feet and the 3 floor were constantly changing, as if you were walking on shifting and not quite solid ground. One foot down, slowly, carefully force the other foot forward. Sometimes you are a shuffler, not daring to lift your feet from the uncertain earth but forced to slide hesitantly forward in little whispering movements. Sometimes you are able to "step out," but this effort—in fact the pure exhilaration of easy movement—soon exhausts you.

The world becomes narrower as friends and family die or move 4 away. To climb stairs, to ride in a car, to walk to the corner, to talk on the telephone; each action seems to take away from the energy needed to stay alive. Everything is limited by the strength you hoard greedily. Your needs decrease, you require less food, less sleep, and finally less human contact; yet this little bit becomes more and more difficult. You fear that one day you will be reduced to the simple acts of breathing and taking nourishment. This is the ultimate stage you dread, the period of helplessness and hopelessness, when independence will be over.

There is nothing to prepare you for the experience of growing 5 old. Living is a process, an irreversible progression toward old age and eventual death. You see men of eighty still vital and straight as oaks; you see men of fifty reduced to gray shadows in the human landscape. The cellular clock differs for each one of us, and is profoundly affected by our own life experiences, our heredity, and perhaps most important, by the concepts of aging encountered in society and in oneself.

The aged live with enforced leisure, on fixed incomes, subject to 6 many chronic illnesses, and most of their money goes to keep a roof over their heads. They also live in a culture that worships youth.

A kind of cultural attitude makes me bigoted against old peo- 7 ple; it makes me think young is best; it makes me treat old people like outcasts.

Hate that gray? Wash it away!	8
Wrinkle cream.	9
Monkey glands.	10
Face-lifting.	11
Look like a bride again.	12
Don't trust anyone over thirty.	13
I fear growing old.	14
Feel Young Again!	15

I am afraid to grow old—we're all afraid. In fact, the fear of 16
growing old is so great that every aged person is an insult and a
threat to the society. They remind us of our own death, that our
body won't always remain smooth and responsive, but will someday betray us by aging, wrinkling, faltering, failing. The ideal way
to age would be to grow slowly invisible, gradually disappearing,
without causing worry or discomfort to the young. In some ways
that does happen. Sitting in a small park across from a nursing home
one day, I noticed that the young mothers and their children gathered on one side, and the old people from the home on the other.
Whenever a youngster would run over to the "wrong" side, chasing
a ball or just trying to cover all the available space, the old people
would lean forward and smile. But before any communication could
be established, the mother would come over, murmuring embarrassed apologies, and take her child back to the "young" side.

Now, it seemed to me that the children didn't feel any particu- 17
lar fear and the old people didn't seem to be threatened by the children. The division of space was drawn by the mothers. And the
mothers never looked at the old people who lined the other side of
the park like so many pigeons perched on the benches. These well-
dressed young matrons had a way of sliding their eyes over, around,
through the old people; they never looked at them directly. The old
people may as well have been invisible; they had no reality for the
youngsters, who were not permitted to speak to them, and they
offended the aesthetic eye of the mothers.

My early experiences were somewhat different; since I grew up 18
in a small town, my childhood had more of a nineteenth-century flavor. I knew a lot of old people, and considered some of them friends.
There was no culturally defined way for me to "relate" to old people, except the rules of courtesy which applied to all adults. My
grandparents were an integral and important part of the family and
of the community. I sometimes have a dreadful fear that mine will
be the last generation to know old people as friends, to have a sense
of what growing old means, to respect and understand man's mortality and his courage in the face of death. Mine may be the last generation to have a sense of living history, of stories passed from
generation to generation, of identity established by family history.

Meanings and Values

1. What is the general tone of this writing? (See "Guide to Terms":
    Style/Tone.)

2. If you find it depressing to read about aging, try to analyze why (especially in view of the fact that you are very likely many years from the stage of "a fading rose").

3. Why do you suppose it is more likely to be the mothers than the children who shun old people (pars. 16–17)?

4. Has this author avoided the excesses of sentimentality? Try to discover how. (Guide: *Sentimentality*.) If not, where does she fail?

Expository Techniques

1. Why should this writing be classed as primarily impressionistic, rather than objective? What is the dominant impression?

2. Analyze the role that selection of details plays in creating the dominant impression. Provide examples of the type of details that could have been included but were not. Are such omissions justifiable?

3. Paragraph 5 ends the almost pure description to begin another phase of the writing. What is it? How has the author provided for a smooth transition between the two? (Guide: *Transition*.)

4. Which previously studied patterns of exposition are also used in this writing? Cite paragraphs where each may be found.

Diction and Vocabulary

1. The author sometimes changes person—e.g., "they" to "you" after paragraph 2. Analyze where the changes occur. What justification, if any, can you find for each change?

2. Which two kinds of figures of speech do you find used liberally to achieve this description? (Guide: *Figures of Speech*.) Cite three or more examples of each. As nearly as you can tell, are any of them clichés? (Guide: *Clichés*.)

Read to Write

1. To identify and explore topics for writing, think about some of the consequences of current attitudes towards aging (as described by Curtin). Put your thoughts in the form of questions you could attempt to answer in an essay. Here are three questions to get you started. If Curtin is correct in her fears expressed in the last two sentences, what could be the consequences for society in general? If many people are still efficient at their jobs at age sixty-five, as is often argued, what practical reasons are there for forcing retirement at that age, and what are the negative consequences? If some very old people are not as affected by aging as the ones Curtin describes, what may account for this difference?

2. Curtin's selection begins with a description of old people and the process of aging. Use a similar strategy to begin an essay of your own. Start with a description of the people, relationships, or things you plan to explain, and in the course of the description introduce the main ideas, consequences, or issues you will take up in the rest of the essay.

3. A description is not a form of exposition unless it is used for expository purposes, as in "Aging in the Land of the Young." Follow Curtin's lead by using detailed description to explain a relationship, problem, or phenomenon whose importance and possible consequences may not be immediately apparent to readers, or to encourage readers to view critically actions and attitudes they take for granted.

(NOTE: Suggestions for topics requiring development by use of DESCRIPTION are on pages 433–434 at the end of this section.)

GEORGE SIMPSON

GEORGE SIMPSON, born in Virginia in 1950, received his B.A. in journalism from the University of North Carolina. He went to work for *Newsweek* in 1972 and in, 1978 became public affairs director for that magazine. Before joining *Newsweek,* Simpson worked for two years as a writer and editor for the *Carolina Financial Times* in Chapel Hill, North Carolina, and as a reporter for the *News-Gazette* in Lexington, Virginia. He received the Best Feature Writing award from Sigma Delta Chi in 1972 for a five-part investigative series on the University of North Carolina football program. He has written stories for *The New York Times, Sport, Glamour,* the *Winston-Salem Journal,* and *New York.*

The War Room at Bellevue

"The War Room at Bellevue" was first published in *New York* magazine. The author chose, for good reason, to stay strictly within a time sequence as he described the emergency ward. This essay is also noteworthy for the cumulative descriptive effect, which was accomplished almost entirely with objective details.

Bellevue. The name conjures up images of an indoor war zone: the 1
wounded and bleeding lining the halls, screaming for help while
harried doctors in blood-stained smocks rush from stretcher to
stretcher, fighting a losing battle against exhaustion and the crushing number of injured. "What's worse," says a longtime Bellevue
nurse, "is that we have this image of being a hospital only for ..."
She pauses, then lowers her voice, "for crazy people."

Though neither battlefield nor Bedlam is a valid image, there is 2
something extraordinary about the monstrous complex that spreads
for five blocks along First Avenue in Manhattan. It is said best by the
head nurse in Adult Emergency Service: "If you have any chance for
survival, you have it here." Survival—that is why they come. Why

do injured cops drive by a half-dozen other hospitals to be treated at Bellevue? They've seen the Bellevue emergency team in action.

9:00 P.M. It is a Friday night in the Bellevue emergency room.   3
The after-work crush is over (those who've suffered through the day, only to come for help after the five-o'clock whistle has blown) and it is nearly silent except for the mutter of voices at the admitting desk, where administrative personnel discuss who will go for coffee. Across the spotless white-walled lobby, ten people sit quietly, passively, in pastel plastic chairs, waiting for word of relatives or to see doctors. In the past 24 hours, 300 people have come to the Bellevue Adult Emergency Service. Fewer than 10 percent were true emergencies. One man sleeps fitfully in the emergency ward while his heartbeat, respiration, and blood pressure are monitored by control consoles mounted over his bed. Each heartbeat trips a tiny bleep in the monitor, which attending nurses can hear across the ward. A half hour ago, doctors in the trauma room withdrew a six-inch stiletto blade from his back. When he is stabilized, the patient will be moved upstairs to the twelve-bed Surgical Intensive Care Unit.

9:05 P.M. An ambulance backs into the receiving bay, its red and   4
yellow lights flashing in and out of the lobby. A split second later, the glass doors burst open as a nurse and an attendant roll a mobile stretcher into the lobby. When the nurse screams, "Emergency!" the lobby explodes with activity as the way is cleared to the trauma room. Doctors appear from nowhere and transfer the bloodied body of a black man to the treatment table. Within seconds his clothes are stripped away, revealing a tiny stab wound in his left side. Three doctors and three nurses rush around the victim, each performing a task necessary to begin treatment. Intravenous needles are inserted into his arms and groin. A doctor draws blood for the lab, in case surgery is necessary. A nurse begins inserting a catheter into the victim's penis and continues to feed in tubing until the catheter reaches the bladder. Urine flows through the tube into a plastic bag. Doctors are glad not to see blood in the urine. Another nurse records pulse and blood pressure.

The victim is in good shape. He shivers slightly, although the   5
trauma room is exceedingly warm. His face is bloodied, but shows no major lacerations. A third nurse, her elbow propped on the treatment table, asks the man a series of questions, trying to quickly outline his medical history. He answers abruptly. He is drunk. His left side is swabbed with yellow disinfectant and a doctor injects a local anesthetic. After a few seconds another doctor inserts his finger into

the wound. It sinks in all the way to the knuckle. He begins to rotate his finger like a child trying to get a marble out of a milk bottle. The patient screams bloody murder and tries to struggle free.

Meanwhile in the lobby, a security guard is ejecting a derelict 6 who has begun to drink from a bottle hidden in his coat pocket. "He's a regular, was in here just two days ago," says a nurse. "We checked him pretty good then, so he's probably okay now. Can you believe those were clean clothes we gave him?" The old man, blackened by filth, leaves quietly.

9:15 P.M. A young Hispanic man interrupts, saying his pregnant 7 girl friend, sitting outside in his car, is bleeding heavily from her vagina. She is rushed into an examination room, treated behind closed doors, and rolled into the observation ward, where, much later in the night, a gynecologist will treat her in a special room—the same one used to examine rape victims. Nearby, behind curtains, the neurologist examines an old white woman to determine if her headaches are due to head injury. They are not.

9:45 P.M. The trauma room has been cleared and cleaned merci- 8 lessly. The examination rooms are three-quarters full—another overdose, two asthmatics, a young woman with abdominal pains. In the hallway, a derelict who has been sleeping it off urinates all over the stretcher. He sleeps on while attendants change his clothes. An ambulance—one of four that patrol Manhattan for Bellevue from 42nd Street to Houston, river to river—delivers a middle-aged white woman and two cops, the three of them soaking wet. The woman has escaped from the psychiatric floor of a nearby hospital and tried to drown herself in the East River. The cops fished her out. She lies on a stretcher shivering beneath white blankets. Her eyes stare at the ceiling. She speaks clearly when an administrative worker begins routine questioning. The cops are given hospital gowns and wait to receive tetanus shots and gamma globulin—a hedge against infection from the befouled river water. They will hang around the E.R. for another two hours, telling their story to as many as six other policemen who show up to hear it. The woman is rolled into an examination room, where a male nurse speaks gently: "They tell me you fell into the river." "No," says the woman, "I jumped. I have to commit suicide." "Why?" asks the nurse. "Because I'm insane and I can't help [it]. I have to die." The nurse gradually discovers the woman has a history of psychological problems. She is given dry bedclothes and placed under guard in the hallway. She lies on her side, staring at the wall.

The pace continues of increase. Several more overdose victims   9
arrive by ambulance. One, a young black woman, had done a
striptease on the street just before passing out. A second black woman
is semiconscious and spends the better part of her time at Bellevue
alternately cursing at and pleading with the doctors. Attendants find
a plastic bottle coated with methadone in the pocket of a Hispanic
O.D. The treatment is routinely the same, and sooner or later involves
vomiting. Just after doctors begin to treat the O.D., he vomits great
quantities of wine and methadone in all directions. "Lovely business,
huh?" laments one of the doctors. A young nurse confides that if
there were other true emergencies, the overdose victims would be
given lower priority. "You can't help thinking they did it to themselves," she says, "while the others are accident victims."

10:30 P.M. A policeman who twisted his knee struggling with an   10
"alleged perpetrator" is examined and released. By 10:30, the lobby
is jammed with friends and relatives of patients in various stages of
treatment and recovery. The attendant who also functions as a trans-
lator for Hispanic patients adds chairs to accommodate the over-
flow. The medical walk-in rate stays steady—between eight and ten
patients waiting. A pair of derelicts, each with battered eyes, appear
at the admitting desk. One has a dramatically swollen face laced
with black stitches.

11:30 P.M. The husband of the attempted suicide arrives. He   11
thanks the police for saving his wife's life, then talks at length with
doctors about her condition. She continues to stare into the void and
does not react when her husband approaches her stretcher.

Meanwhile, patients arrive in the lobby at a steady pace. A   12
young G.I. on leave has lower-back pains; a Hispanic man complains
of pains in his side; occasionally parents hurry through the adult
E.R. carrying children to the pediatric E.R. A white woman of about
50 marches into the lobby from the walk-in entrance. Dried blood
covers her right eyebrow and upper lip. She begins to perform. "I
was assaulted on 28th and Lexington, I was," she says grandly, "and
I don't have to take it *anymore*. I was a bride 21 years ago and, God,
I was beautiful then." She has captured the attention of all present.
"I was there when the boys came home—on Memorial Day—and I
don't have to take this kind of treatment."

As midnight approaches, the nurses prepare for the shift   13
change. They must brief the incoming staff and make sure all reports
are up-to-date. One young brunet says, "Christ, I'm gonna go home
and take a shower—I smell like vomit."

11:50 P.M. The triage nurse is questioning an old black man   14
about chest pains, and a Hispanic woman is having an asthma
attack, when an ambulance, its sirens screaming full tilt, roars into
the receiving bay. There is a split-second pause as everyone drops
what he or she is doing and looks up. Then all hell breaks loose. Doctors and nurses are suddenly sprinting full-out toward the trauma
room. The glass doors burst open and the occupied stretcher is literally run past me. Cops follow. It is as if a comet has whooshed by. In
the trauma room it all becomes clear. A half-dozen doctors and
nurses surround the lifeless form of a Hispanic man with a shotgun
hole in his neck the size of your fist. Blood pours from a second gap-
ing wound in his chest. A respirator is slammed over his face, making his chest rise and fall as if he were breathing. "No pulse," reports
one doctor. A nurse jumps on a stool and, leaning over the man,
begins to pump his chest with her palms. "No blood pressure,"
screams another nurse. The ambulance driver appears shaken, "I
never thought I'd get here in time," he stutters. More doctors from
the trauma team upstairs arrive. Wrappings from syringes and
gauze pads fly through the air. The victim's eyes are open yet devoid
of life. His body takes on a yellow tinge. A male nurse winces at the
gunshot wound. "This guy really pissed off somebody," he says.
This is no ordinary shooting. It is an execution. IV's are jammed into
the body in the groin and arms. One doctor has been plugging in an
electrocardiograph and asks everyone to stop for a second so he can
get a reading. "Forget it," shouts the doctor in charge. "No time."
"Take it easy, Jimmy," someone yells at the head physician. It is
apparent by now that the man is dead, but the doctors keep trying
injections and finally they slit open the chest and reach inside almost
up to their elbows. They feel the extent of the damage and suddenly
it is all over. "I told 'em he was dead," says one nurse, withdrawing.
"They didn't listen." The room is very still. The doctors are momentarily disgusted, then go on about their business. The room clears
quickly. Finally there is only a male nurse and the still-warm body,
now waxy-yellow, with huge ribs exposed on both sides of the chest
and giant holes in both sides of the neck. The nurse speculates that
this is yet another murder in a Hispanic political struggle that has
brought many such victims to Bellevue. He marvels at the extent of
the wounds and repeats, "This guy was really blown away."

Midnight. A hysterical woman is hustled through the lobby into   15
an examination room. It is the dead man's wife, and she is nearly
delirious. "I know he's dead, I know he's dead," she screams over and

over. Within moments the lobby is filled with anxious relatives of the victim, waiting for word on his condition. The police are everywhere asking questions, but most people say they saw nothing. One young woman says she heard six shots, two louder than the other four. At some point, word is passed that the man is, in fact, dead. Another woman breaks down in hysterics; everywhere young Hispanics are crying and comforting each other. Plainclothes detectives make a quick examination of the body, check on the time of pronouncement of death, and begin to ask questions, but the bereaved are too stunned to talk. The rest of the uninvolved people in the lobby stare dumbly, their injuries suddenly paling in light of a death.

12:30 A.M. A black man appears at the admissions desk and says   16
he drank poison by mistake. He is told to have a seat. The ambulance brings in a young white woman, her head wrapped in white gauze. She is wailing terribly. A girl friend stands over her, crying, and a boyfriend clutches the injured woman's hands, saying, "I'm here, don't worry, I'm here." The victim has fallen downstairs at a friend's house. Attendants park her stretcher against the wall to wait for an examination room to clear. There are eight examination rooms and only three doctors. Unless you are truly an emergency, you will wait. One doctor is stitching up the eyebrow of a drunk who's been punched out. The friends of the woman who fell down the stairs glance up at the doctors anxiously, wondering why their friend isn't being treated faster.

1:10 A.M. A car pulls into the bay and a young Hispanic asks if   17
a shooting victim has been brought here. The security guard blurts out, "He's dead." The young man is stunned. He peels his tires leaving the bay.

1:20 A.M. The young woman of the stairs is getting stitches in a   18
small gash over her left eye when the same ambulance driver who brought in the gunshot victim delivers a man who has been stabbed in the back on East 3rd Street. Once again the trauma room goes from 0 to 60 in five seconds. The patient is drunk, which helps him endure the pain of having the catheter inserted through his penis into his bladder. Still he yells, "That hurts like a bastard," then adds sheepishly, "Excuse me, ladies." But he is not prepared for what comes next. An X-ray reveals a collapsed right lung. After just a shot of local anesthetic, the doctor slices open his side and inserts a long plastic tube. Internal bleeding had kept the lung pressed down and prevented it from reinflating. The tube releases the pressure. The ambulance driver says the cops grabbed the guy who ran the eight-

inch blade into the victim's back. "That's not the one," says the man. "They got the wrong guy." A nurse reports that there is not much of the victim's type blood available at the hospital. One of the doctors says that's okay, he won't need surgery. Meanwhile blood pours from the man's knife wound and the tube in his side. As the nurses work, they chat about personal matters, yet they respond immediately to orders from either doctor. "How ya doin'?" the doctor asks the patient. "Okay," he says. His blood spatters on the floor.

So it goes into the morning hours. A Valium overdose, a woman   19 who fainted, a man who went through the windshield of his car. More overdoses. More drunks with split eyebrows and chins. The doctors and nurses work without complaint. "This is nothing, about normal, I'd say," concludes the head nurse. "No big deal."

Meanings and Values

1. What is the author's point of view? (See "Guide to Terms": *Point of View*.) How is this reflected by the tone? (Guide: *Style/Tone*.)

2. Does Simpson ever slip into sentimentality—a common failing when describing the scenes of death and tragedy? (Guide: *Sentimentality*.) If so, where? If not, how does he avoid it?

3. Cite at least six facts learned from reading this piece that are told, not in general terms, but by specific, concrete details—e.g., that a high degree of cleanliness is maintained at Bellevue, illustrated by "the spotless white-walled lobby" (par. 3) and "the trauma room has been cleared and cleaned mercilessly" (par. 8). What are the advantages of having facts presented in this way?

Expository Techniques

1. Do you consider the writing to be primarily objective or impressionistic? What is the dominant impression, if any?

2. What is the value of using a timed sequence in such a description?

3. Does it seem to you that any of this description is excessive—i.e., unnecessary to the task at hand? If so, how might the piece be revised?

4. List, in skeletal form, the facts learned about the subject from reading the two-paragraph introduction. How well does it perform the three basic purposes of an introduction? (Guide: *Introductions*.)

5. What is the significance of the rhetorical question in paragraph 2? (Guide: *Rhetorical Questions*.) Why is it rhetorical?

6. Is the short closing effective? (Guide: *Closings*.) Why or why not?

Diction and Vocabulary

1. Cite the clichés in paragraphs 4, 5, 8, and 14. (Guide: *Clichés*.) What justification, if any, can you offer for their use?

2. Cite the allusion in paragraph 2, and explain its meaning and source. (Guide: *Figure of Speech*.)

3. Simpson uses some slang and other colloquialisms. (Cite as many of these as you can. (Guide: *Colloquial Expressions*.) Is their use justified? Why or why not?

Read to Write

1. If you have had a job or participated in an activity (sport, organization) that to an outsider might seem hectic or hazardous, consider describing it in an essay so that readers can come to understand it more clearly.

2. Consider arranging an expository essay of your own by using a time frame as Simpson does. Your purposes for using this device need not be the same, however, and you can use this strategy for expository patterns other than description.

3. Much of the power of Simpson's writing comes from the sensational nature of the subjects he describes and his careful selection of detail. If you have witnessed or participated in some other kind of "extreme" experience, help your readers understand it by describing and explaining it with the same mix of detail and commentary that Simpson offers.

(NOTE: Suggestions for topics requiring development by use of DESCRIPTION are on pages 433–434 at the end of this section.)

Issues and Ideas

Place and Person

Our environments shape us, but we in turn shape them, in large ways and small. This probably seems so obvious to you that you seldom stop to notice the many relationships between place and person. This, however, is exactly what the next three essays ask you to do. Joyce Maynard's "The Yellow Door House," Luis Rodriguez's "The Ice Cream Truck," and E. B. White's "Once More to the Lake" offer three rather different perspectives on the relationship of people and their surroundings.

Though a feeling of nostalgia—a sense of fond memories and loss—might seem most appropriate for journeys back to childhood settings, this is certainly far from the tone Luis Rodriguez takes in his description of gang life in a poor neighborhood. Joyce Maynard and E. B. White also ask readers to move beyond sentimental responses in their descriptions of places from the past. Indeed, when description is used as an expository strategy, it goes beyond simple re-creation of a setting to analysis and explanation.

An effective analysis of place and its relationship to character needs to focus not only on the details of the setting also but the extent to which they embody and enact social, cultural, and psychological influences. To grow up in a house with abundant artist's supplies (as Joyce Maynard did) is to encounter art not simply as an activity but as a set of values and as a way of living, as "The Yellow Door House" suggests. But while it can be insightful, this use of description is seldom objective, especially when the writer is describing scenes and events from his or her own experience. As a writer, therefore, you should try to remain aware of the extent to which your perspective shapes and reshapes the scenes you are presenting. As a reader, you also need to stay alert to this further dimension of the relationship between person and place.

JOYCE MAYNARD

JOYCE MAYNARD was born in 1953 and spent her childhood in Durham, New Hampshire, where her father taught at the nearby University of New Hampshire. At 19, while she was still a sophomore at Yale University, her first book appeared: *Looking Backward: A Chronicle of Growing Up Old in the Sixties* (1973). Maynard was a reporter for *The New York Times* and currently writes a syndicated newspaper column. She has also written monthly for *Parenting* magazine and has published three novels, *Baby Love* (1981), *To Die For* (1992), and *Where Love Goes* (1995). Many of her columns were reprinted in the collection *Domestic Affairs* (1987).

The Yellow Door House

Permanence, continuity, and change in place and personality are some of the ideas explored through description in this essay, originally published as one of the author's columns. Comparison plays an important part in the exposition as well, particularly in juxtaposing Maynard's memories of the house with its present reality.

I've known only two homes in my life: the one I live in now, with my husband and children, and another one, just sixty miles from here, where I grew up. My father's dead now, and even before that, my parents were divorced and my mother moved away from our old house. But though she rents the house out nine months of the year and hasn't spent a winter there for thirteen years, she hasn't sold our old house yet. It's still filled with our old belongings from our old life. And though my mother has another house now, and a good life, with another man, in a new place, she still comes back to the old house for a couple of months every summer. Every year I ask her, "Have you considered putting the house on the market?" And every summer the answer is "not yet."

1

412

My children call the place where I grew up the yellow door 2
house. They love the place, with its big, overgrown yard, the old
goldfish pond, the brick walkway, the white picket fence. On the
front door there's a heavy brass knocker my sons like to bang on to
announce their arrival for visits with their grandmother, and French
windows on either side that I was always cautioned against breaking as a child. (As now I caution my children.) There's a brass mail
slot I used to pass messages through to a friend waiting on the other
side. Now my daughter Audrey does the same.

It's a big house, a hip-roofed colonial, with ceilings higher than 3
anybody needs, and a sweeping staircase rising up from the front
hall, with a banister that children more adventurous than my sister
and I (mine, for instance) are always tempted to slide on. There are
plants everywhere, paintings my father made, Mexican pottery, and
a band of tin Mexican soldiers—one on horseback, one playing the
flute, one the tuba. We bought those soldiers on the first trip I ever
made to New York City. They cost way too much, but my mother
said we could get them if we took the bus home instead of flying. So
we did.

One room of the yellow door house is wood paneled and lined 4
with books. There used to be a big overstuffed armchair in it that I'd
settle into with my cookies and milk, when I came home from
school, to do my homework or watch "Leave It to Beaver." (That
chair is in my house now.) There's a porch with a swing out back,
and a sunny corner in the kitchen where I always ate my toast—
grilled in the oven, sometimes with cinnamon sugar and sometimes
jam, but always the way my mother made it, buttered on both sides.
My mother is a wonderful, natural cook, who would announce, on a
typical night, three different dessert possibilities, all homemade.
Now I wouldn't think of eating a third piece of blueberry pie. But the
old habits return when I walk into my mother's kitchen. The first
thing I do is go see what's in the refrigerator.

It's been fourteen years since I lived in the yellow door house, 5
but I could still make my way around it blindfolded. There are
places where the house could use some work now, and my mother
never was the best housekeeper. I open a drawer in the big Welsh
dresser in the dining room, looking for a safety pin, and so much
spills out (though not safety pins) that I can't close it again. A person
can choose from five different kinds of cookies in this house. There's
a whole closetful of fabric scraps and antique lace. Eight teapots. But
no yardstick, no light bulbs, no scissors.

My children's favorite place in the house is the attic. The front   6
half used to be the studio where my father painted, at night, when
he came home from his job as an English teacher. The paintings and
paints are long gone now; but my father was a lover of art supplies
and hopelessly extravagant when it came to acquiring them, so
every once in a while, even now, thirteen years since he's been here,
I'll come upon a box of unopened pastels, or watercolor pencils, or
the kind of art gum eraser he always used. I'll pick up a stub of an
oil pastel and hold it up to my nose, and a wave of feeling will wash
over me that almost makes my knees weak. Cadmium yellow light.
Cerulean blue. Suddenly I'm ten years old again, sitting on the grass
in a field a couple of miles down the road from here, with a sketch
pad on my lap and my father beside me, drawing a picture of Ski
Jump Hill.

Beyond the room that was my father's studio is the part of our   7
attic where my mother—a hoarder, like me—has stored away just
about every toy we ever owned, and most of our old dresses. A
ripped Chinese umbrella, a broken wicker rocker, a hooked rug she
started and never finished, an exercise roller, purchased around
1947, meant to undo the damage of all those blueberry pies. Songs I
wrote when I was nine. My sister's poems. My mother's notes from
college English class. My father's powerfully moving proclamations
of love to her, written when she was eighteen and he was thirty-
eight, when she was telling him she couldn't marry him and he was
telling her she must.

Every time we come to the yellow door house to visit, Audrey   8
and Charlie head for the attic—and though we have mostly cleaned
out my old Barbies now (and a Midge doll, whose turned-up nose
had been partly nibbled off by mice), we never seem to reach the end
of the treasures: My homemade dollhouse furniture (I packed it
away, room by room, with notes enclosed, to the daughter I knew I
would someday have, describing how I'd laid out the rooms.) An
old wooden recorder. A brass doll bed. Wonderfully detailed doll
clothes my mother made for us every Christmas (at the time, I
longed for store-bought). One year she knit a sweater, for a two-
inch-tall bear, using toothpicks for knitting needles. Another year
she sewed us matching skirts from an old patchwork quilt.

The little town where I grew up (and where I used to know just   9
about everyone) has been growing so fast that my mother hardly
knows anyone on our street anymore. A house like hers has become
so desirable that within days of her arrival this summer, my mother

got a call from a realtor asking if she'd be interested in selling. He named as a likely asking price a figure neither one of us could believe. My parents bought the house, thirty years ago, for a fifth of that amount, and still, they sometimes had to take out loans to meet the mortgage payments.

For years now, I have been telling my mother that it makes lit- 10
tle sense to hold on to the yellow door house (and to worry about tenants, make repairs, put away the Mexican tin soldiers every Labor Day and take them out again every Fourth of July). But I suddenly realized, hearing about this realtor's call, that when the day comes that my mother sells the house, I will be deeply shaken. I doubt if I will even want to drive down our old street after that, or even come back to the town, where I scarcely know anybody anymore. I don't much want to see some other family inventing new games, new rituals, in our house. Don't want to know where they put their Christmas tree, or what sort of paintings they hang on their walls. It would be crazy—impossible—to pack up and haul away all those dress-up clothes and bits of costume jewelry and boxes of old book reports and crumbs of pastels. But neither do I relish the thought of someday having to throw them out.

My mother's yellow door house is a perfect place to play hide- 11
and-seek, and last weekend, when I was there visiting with my three children, that's what my two sons and I did. I found a hiding place in the wood-paneled room, behind the couch. I scrunched myself up so small that several minutes passed without my sons' finding me, even though they passed through the room more than once.

Many families have rented the house since my mother ceased to 12
make it her full-time home, but the smell—I realized—hasn't changed. Listening to my children's voices calling out to me through the rooms, I studied a particular knothole in the paneling, and it came back to me that this knothole had always reminded me of an owl. I ran my finger over the wood floors and the upholstery on the side of the couch, and noted the dust my mother has always tended to leave in corners. I heard the sewing machine whirring upstairs: my mother, sewing doll clothes with Audrey. I smelled my mother's soup on the stove. And for a moment, I wanted time to freeze.

But then I let myself make a small noise. "We found you, we 13
found you," my boys sang out, falling into my arms. And then we all had lunch, with my mother's chocolate chip cookies for dessert— and headed back to the house I live in now. Whose door is green.

Meanings and Values

1. What connections between place and personality (her parents' or her own) does Maynard discuss directly or by implication in paragraphs 6, 7, 8, and 10?

2. Where in the opening paragraph does Maynard introduce the themes of change and continuity?

3. What does the author believe will be lost if her mother sells the house?

4. What is meant by the phrase "I wanted time to freeze" in paragraph 12? What actions does the author take in the next paragraph that undermine this wish and the values implied by it?

Expository Techniques

1. Identify the subjects Maynard describes in each of the paragraphs following the opening. Do these paragraphs generally focus on a single scene (or subject) or on several? Be ready to support your answer with examples from the text.

2. Can the descriptions in paragraphs 4 and 10 be considered unified? Why or why not? (See "Guide to Terms": *Unity*.)

3. What use does Maynard make of comparison in paragraphs 2, 12, and 13 to suggest ways that values and patterns of behavior are passed from generation to generation?

Diction and Vocabulary

1. Identify the concrete diction in paragraph 6 and discuss how it contributes to the effectiveness of the passage. (Guide: *Evaluation*.) What are the technical terms used in the passage, and how do they contribute to its effect? (Guide: *Diction*.)

2. Why does the author mention the television program "Leave It to Beaver" (par. 4)? In what ways did her home and family life resemble those depicted in the series? In what way did they differ?

Read to Write

1. Use the following questions and make up others like them in order to examine the relationship between place, personality, and values, and to discover possible topics for writing. Do many people today have a chance to return to the homes, apartments, or neighborhoods in which they grew up and which helped shape their values and personalities?

Is it likely that many spent their entire childhoods living in a single house or apartment? How are the childhood memories of people whose families often moved likely to differ from those of Maynard? Are their values likely to differ also?

2. Maynard moves from room to room in her description commenting on the meaning of the various scenes she encounters. Organize a descriptive essay of your own in a similar manner as a way of gradually building an understanding of your whole subject.

3. Prepare an essay describing one or more places where you lived as a child. In the course of the description, follow Maynard's lead and deal with questions of place, personality, change, loss, growth, continuity, and related matters, offering your insights, of course, and not Maynard's.

(NOTE: Suggestions for topics requiring development by use of DESCRIPTION are on pages 433–434 at the end of this section.)

LUIS J. RODRIGUEZ

LUIS J. RODRIGUEZ was born in El Paso, Texas in 1954 but spent his childhood and youth in Watts and East Los Angeles. While he was growing up, Rodriguez was both a gang member and an aspiring writer. At sixteen he began writing an account of his experiences with poverty and gang life in Los Angeles, an account which eventually became *Always Running—La Vida Loca: Gang Days in L.A.* (1993). His award-winning writing has also appeared in *Poems Across the Pavement* (1989), *The Concrete River* (1991), and articles in such magazines and newspapers as *The Chicago Review, TriQuarterly, Left Curve, Milestones, El Grito, The Los Angeles Times*, and *The National Catholic Reporter*. He currently lives in Chicago, where he runs the Tia Chucha Press, and he works with groups throughout the country seeking to reduce gang violence.

The Ice Cream Truck

In "The Ice Cream Truck,"[1] a selection from *Always Running*, Rodriguez links descriptions of several "ruins" (places, things, and people) with a loose narrative. Taken together, the descriptions help explain what it was like to grow up in a community shaped— or distorted—by poverty and careless violence.

"You *cholos* have great stories about climbing fences."   1

—a barrio boxing coach

The Hills blistered below a haze of sun and smog. Mothers   2
with wet strands of hair across their foreheads flung wash up to
dry on weathered lines. Sweat-drenched men lay on their backs
in the gravel of alleys, beneath broken-down cars propped up
on cinder blocks. *Charrangas* and *corridos* splashed out of open
windows.

Suddenly from over a hill, an ice cream truck raced by with   3
packs of children running beside it. A hurried version of "Old
McDonald Had A Farm" chimed through a speaker bolted on the

[1]Editors' title

truck's roof. The truck stopped long enough for somebody to toss out dozens of sidewalk sundaes, tootie-fruities and half-and-half bars to the children who gathered around, thrusting up small, dirt-caked hands that blossomed open as their shrieks blended with laughter.

Then the truck's transmission gears growled as it continued up 4 the slope, whipped around a corner and passed a few of us *vatos* assembled on a field off Toll Drive. We looked over toward the echoes of the burdensome chimes, the slip and boom of the clutch and rasp of gears as the ice cream truck entered the dead-end streets and curves of Las Lomas.

"*Orale, ése, ¿qué está pasando?*" a dude named Little Man asked 5 while passing a bottle of Tokay wine to Clavo.

"It's Toots and the *gaba*, you know, Axel," Clavo replied. "They 6 just stole an ice cream truck on Portrero Grande Drive."

"*¡Qué cábula!*" Little Man said. "They sure is crazy." 7

We continued to talk and drink until the day melted into night. 8

Little Man and one of the López brothers, Fernie, all Tribe, 9 were there in the field with me and my *camaradas* Clavo, Chicharrón, and Wilo. The four of us were so often together that the list of our names became a litany. We spray-painted our *placas* on the walls, followed by *AT* for Animal Tribe or *SSG* for South San Gabriel.

Everyone called me Chin because of my protruding jawbone. I 10 had it tattooed on my ankle.

We sat around a small roasting pit Chicharrón made from 11 branches and newspaper. Around us were ruins, remains of a home which had been condemned and later ravaged by fire. We assembled inside the old cement foundation with its scattered sections of brick and concrete walls splattered with markings and soot with rusted re-enforcing bars protruding from stone blocks.

We furnished the lot with beat-up couches and discarded sofas. 12 Somebody hung plastic from a remaining cinder-block wall to a low branch so homeboys could sleep there—and miss most of any rain— when there was nowhere else to go. It was really a vacant lot but we called all such lots "the fields."

Even as we talked, there was Noodles, a wino and old *tecato*, 13 crashed out on the sofa.

"Get up Noodles, time for some *refin*," Chicharrón exclaimed as 14 he placed stolen hot dogs and buns on the fire. Wilo threw a dirt clod at the sofa and Noodles mumbled some incoherent words.

"*Orale*, leave the *vato* alone, *ése*," Little Man said. 15
But Noodles got up, spittle dripping from his mouth. 16
"Hey *ése*, Noodles is awake, and man is he pissed," Wilo said. 17
"How can you tell?" Chicharrón asked. 18
"When he moves fast and you can't understand what he's say- 19
ing, then he's pissed," Wilo answered. "When he moves slow and
you still can't understand what he's saying, he's all right."
Noodles staggered toward us, his arms flailing, as if boxing— 20
huffing, puffing and dropping mucus from his nose.
"Get the hell out of here, *pinche*," Wilo said as he stood up and 21
pushed the wino aside.
"You thinks youse are tuss dues . . . you ain't so tuss," Noodles 22
said, throwing sloppy left hooks and uppercuts into the air.
Wilo placed his hand over Noodles' head, whose wiry body 23
looked like a strand from a dirty mop. Wilo was also thin and slip-
pery. The rest of us laughed and laughed at the two *flaquillos* goof-
ing around.
"Ah leave the *vato* alone, homeboy," Clavo suggested. "Let's 24
break out another bottle."
As we cooked, shared wine and told stories of *jainas* and the lit- 25
tle conquests, of fights for honor, homeys and the 'hood, a gray Mercury sedan with its headlights turned off crept up the road. Wilo was
the closest up the slope to the street. He looked over at the Mercury,
then frowned.
"Anybody recognize the *ranfla?*" Wilo inquired. 26
"*Chale*," Chicharrón responded. "It looks too funky to be gang- 27
bangers."
"Unless that's what they want it to look like." 28
Wilo moved up the slope from the field, followed by Clavo, 29
Chicharrón, and Little Man. Fernie stayed back with Noodles and
me. Wilo and Clavo were the first ones to hit the street as the Mercury delayed a turn around a curve.
Clavo moved to one side of the Mercury, its occupants covered 30
in darkness. He stretched out his arms and yelled out: "Here stand
The Animal Tribe—¡y qué!"
The Mercury stopped. A shadow stepped out of a bashed-in side 31
door, a sawed-off shotgun in his hands. Another shadow pushed an
automatic rifle out the side window.
"Sangra Diablos! ¡Qué rifa!" the dude with the shotgun yelled 32
out. Then a blast snapped at the night air.

Wilo and Chicharrón fell back down the slope. Automatic gun-   33
fire followed them as they rolled in the dirt. The bullets skimmed off
tree branches, knocked over trash cans and ricocheted off walls, Wilo
ended up face-down; Chicharrón landed on his butt. Noodles knelt
behind the sofa, whimpering. The cracking sounds stopped. The
Mercury sped off, its tires throwing up dirt and pebbles behind it.

I could see the car speeding down another hill. I ran up the   34
slope, slipping and sliding toward the road. On the street, Little Man
kneeled over Clavo, who lay sprawled on the ground and trembling.
Half of Clavo's face was shot full of pellets, countless black, stream-
ing round holes; his eye dripping into the dirt.

Wilo and the others climbed up and rushed up to Little Man.   35
Fernie began jumping up and down like he had been jolted with
lightning, letting out *gritos*. I kept looking at Clavo's face, thinking
something stupid like how he was such a dummy, always taking
chances, all the time being "the dude." Then I squatted on the
ground, closed my eyelid and let a tear stream down the side of my
face.

Windows flung upwards. Doors were pushed aside. People   36
bolted out of their homes. Mothers cursed in Spanish from behind
weather-beaten picket fences.

As Clavo was taken to the hospital, Fernie talked about getting   37
all the Tribe together, about meeting later that night, about guns and
warfare and "*ya estuvo*"—that's it. A war, fought for generations
between Lomas and Sangra, flared up again.

Later, as I walked down the hills on the way back home, sirens   38
tore across the sky and a sheriff's helicopter hovered nearby, beam-
ing a spotlight across shacks and brush, over every hole and crevice
of the neighborhood.

I mounted a fence which wound around a dirt embankment,   39
hoping to get out of the helicopter's sights. I looked over the other
side and there overturned at the bottom of the gully, to be ravaged
by scavengers for parts, to be another barrio monument, lay an ice
cream truck.

Meanings and Values

1.   In what way are the attitudes and behaviors of the groups of people
     in paragraphs 2 (adults), 3 (children), and 25 (youths) alike? In what
     ways do they differ? Does Rodriguez suggest that each group

responds to the environment in different ways? If so, how do the responses differ; if not, what do the responses have in common?

2. What commentary on the behavior and values of the young men is implied by the description of Noodles and his behavior?

3. Can the ice cream truck be considered a symbol, especially at the end of the selection? (See "Guide to Terms": *Symbol.*) If so, explain its meaning. If not, tell why the writer chose to have it appear at the beginning and again in paragraph 39.

4. In what ways can each of the following be considered ruined or decayed: the ice cream truck, the home where the youths gather, Noodles, the Animal Tribe after the confrontation, and the neighborhood as a whole? How is emphasis on decay and ruin in each of these cases related to the selection's central theme? (Guide: *Unity.*)

Expository Techniques

1. Identify the main subject or subjects being described in each of the following sections of the piece: paragraphs 2–4, 5–10, 11–12, 13–24, 25–33, 34–37, and 38–39. What indications are there in the text that the writer wants us to regard these as different units of the piece? (Hint: Look for shifts in time or place and for transitions.) (Guide: *Transition.*)

2. What aspects of the scene or the characters does Rodriguez focus on in paragraphs 2–4? 14–24? 33–35? 37–38? What might account for the differences (or similarities) in the descriptive techniques the writer employs in each of these sections?

3. Where in the essay does the author state or come close to stating the central theme? Should the central theme have been stated more (or less) directly? Why?

Diction and Vocabulary

1. This selection employs a number of Spanish words and phrases. Do you think that their presence will make the piece hard for most readers to understand? Why or why not? Explain your reasoning and support it with specific examples from the text. For what purpose might Rodriguez have included so many Spanish terms? (Guide: *Purpose.*)

2. Discuss the contribution of specific, concrete language to the descriptions in paragraphs 2–3 and 11–12. (Guide: *Concrete.*)

3. Identify two paragraphs from different parts of the selection in which Rodriguez uses slang and comment on the contributions of

the language to the portrait of the scene or person being described. (Guide: *Colloquial Expressions.*)

Read to Write

1. Compare Rodriguez's description of gang members and their community with those frequently presented on television and in films or newspapers. Think of any other familiar groups or communities and compare your knowledge of them with their representations in movies or on television. Consider turning your observations of accuracies and inaccuracies of media portrayals into an expository essay. Be ready to address the question of why films and television offer inaccurate portrayals (if you believe they do).

2. Prepare an essay of your own that includes slang or terms from another language in order to give readers an understanding of the people and relationships you are presenting. Take note of the places Rodriguez uses this strategy and his purposes for doing so, but don't feel that you need to be limited by his choices.

3. Write an essay about an adventure from your own childhood or high school years that reveals something about your community and its values. Include the way this setting shaped your relationships and activities.

(NOTE: Suggestions for topics requiring development by use of DESCRIPTION are on pages 433–434 at the end of this section.)

E. B. WHITE

E. B. WHITE, distinguished essayist, was born in Mount Vernon, New York, in 1899 and died in 1985 in North Brooklin, Maine. A graduate of Cornell University, White worked as a reporter and advertising copywriter, and in 1926 he joined the staff of the *New Yorker* magazine. After 1937 he did most of his writing at his farm in Maine, for many years contributing a regular column, "One Man's Meat," to *Harper's* magazine and freelance editorials for the "Notes and Comments" column of the *New Yorker*. White also wrote children's books, two volumes of verse, and, with James Thurber, *Is Sex Necessary?* (1929). With his wife, Katherine White, he compiled *A Subtreasury of American Humor* (1941). Collections of his own essays include *One Man's Meat* (1942), *The Second Tree from the Corner* (1953), *The Points of My Compass* (1962), and *Essays of E. B. White* (1977). In 1959 he revised and enlarged William Strunk's *The Elements of Style*, a textbook still widely used in college classrooms. White received many honors and writing awards for his crisp, highly individual style and his sturdy independence of thought.

Once More to the Lake

In this essay White relies primarily on description to convey his sense of the passage of time and the power of memory. The vivid scenes and the clear yet expressive prose in this essay are characteristic of his writing.

August 1941

One summer, along about 1904, my father rented a camp on a lake   1
in Maine and took us all there for the month of August. We all got
ringworm from some kittens and had to rub Pond's Extract on our
arms and legs night and morning, and my father rolled over in a
canoe with all his clothes on; but outside of that the vacation was a

success and from then on none of us ever thought there was any place in the world like that lake in Maine. We returned summer after summer—always on August 1 for one month. I have since become a salt-water man, but sometimes in summer there are days when the restlessness of the tides and the fearful cold of the sea water and the incessant wind that blows across the afternoon and into the evening make me wish for the placidity of a lake in the woods. A few weeks ago this feeling got so strong I bought myself a couple of bass hooks and a spinner and returned to the lake where we used to go, for a week's fishing and to revisit old haunts.

I took along my son, who had never had any fresh water up his   2 nose and who had seen lily pads only from train windows. On the journey over to the lake I began to wonder what it would be like. I wondered how time would have marred this unique, this holy spot—the coves and streams, the hills that the sun set behind, the camps and the paths behind the camps. I was sure that the tarred road would have found it out, and I wondered in what other ways it would be desolated. It is strange how much you can remember about places like that once you allow your mind to return into the grooves that lead back. You remember one thing, and that suddenly reminds you of another thing. I guess I remembered clearest of all the early mornings, when the lake was cool and motionless, remembered how the bedroom smelled of the lumber it was made of and of the wet woods whose scent entered through the screen. The partitions in the camp were thin and did not extend clear to the top of the rooms, and as I was always the first up I would dress softly so as not to wake the others, and sneak out into the sweet outdoors and start out in the canoe, keeping close along the shore in the long shadows of the pines. I remembered being very careful never to rub my paddle against the gunwale for fear of disturbing the stillness of the cathedral.

The lake had never been what you would call a wild lake. There   3 were cottages sprinkled around the shores, and it was in farming country although the shores of the lake were quite heavily wooded. Some of the cottages were owned by nearby farmers, and you would live at the shore and eat your meals at the farmhouse. That's what our family did. But although it wasn't wild, it was a fairly large and undisturbed lake and there were places in it that, to a child at least, seemed infinitely remote and primeval.

I was right about the tar: it led to within half a mile of the shore.   4 But when I got back there, with my boy, and we settled into a camp near a farmhouse and into the kind of summertime I had known, I could tell that it was going to be pretty much the same as it had been before—I knew it, lying in bed the first morning, smelling the bedroom and hearing the boy sneak quietly out and go off along the shore in a boat. I began to sustain the illusion that he was I, and therefore, by simple transposition, that I was my father. This sensation persisted, kept cropping up all the time we were there. It was not an entirely new feeling, but in this setting it grew much stronger. I seemed to be living a dual existence. I would be in the middle of some simple act, I would be picking up a bait box or laying down a table fork, or I would be saying something, and suddenly it would be not I but my father who was saying the words or making the gesture. It gave me a creepy sensation.

We went fishing the first morning. I felt the same damp moss   5 covering the worms in the bait can, and saw the dragonfly alight on the tip of my rod as it hovered a few inches from the surface of the water. It was the arrival of this fly that convinced me beyond any doubt that everything was as it always had been, that the years were a mirage and that there had been no years. The small waves were the same, chucking the rowboat under the chin as we fished at anchor, and the boat was the same boat, the same color green and the ribs broken in the same places, and under the floorboards the same freshwater leavings and débris—the dead helgramite, the wisps of moss, the rusty discarded fishhook, the dried blood from yesterday's catch. We stared silently at the tips of our rods, at the dragonflies that came and went. I lowered the tip of mine into the water, tentatively, pensively dislodging the fly, which darted two feet away, poised, darted two feet back, and came to rest again a little farther up the rod. There had been no years between the ducking of this dragonfly and the other one—the one that was part of memory. I looked at the boy, who was silently watching his fly, and it was my hands that held his rod, my eyes watching. I felt dizzy and didn't know which rod I was at the end of.

We caught two bass, hauling them in briskly as though they   6 were mackerel, pulling them over the side of the boat in a businesslike manner without any landing net, and stunning them with a blow on the back of the head. When we got back for a swim before lunch, the lake was exactly where we had left it, the same number of inches from the dock, and there was only the merest suggestion of a breeze. This seemed an utterly enchanted sea, this lake you could leave to its own devices for a few hours and come-back to, and find that it had not stirred, this constant and trustworthy body of water. In the shallows, the dark, water-soaked sticks and twigs, smooth and old, were undulating in clusters on the bottom against the clean ribbed sand, and the track of the mussel was plain. A school of minnows swam by, each minnow with its small individual shadow, doubling the attendance, so clear and sharp in the sunlight. Some of the other campers were in swimming, along the shore, one of them with a cake of soap, and the water felt thin and clear and unsubstantial. Over the years there had been this person with the cake of soap, this cultist, and here he was. There had been no years.

Up to the farmhouse to dinner through the teeming, dusty field, the road under our sneakers was only a two-track road. The middle track was missing, the one with the marks of the hooves and the splotches of dried, flaky manure. There had always been three tracks to choose from in choosing which track to walk in; now the choice was narrowed down to two. For a moment I missed terribly the middle alternative. But the way led past the tennis court, and something about the way it lay there in the sun reassured me; the tape had loosened along the backline, the alleys were green with plantains and other weeds, and the net (installed in June and removed in September) sagged in the dry noon, and the whole place steamed with midday heat and hunger and emptiness. There was a choice of pie for dessert, and one was blueberry and one was apple, and the waitresses were the same country girls, there having been no passage of time, only the illusion of it as in a dropped curtain—the waitresses were still fifteen; their hair had been washed, that was the only difference—they had been to the movies and seen the pretty girls with the clean hair. 7

Summertime, oh, summertime, pattern of life indelible, the fade-proof lake, the woods unshatterable, the pasture with the sweetfern and the juniper forever and ever, summer without end; this was the background, and the life along the shore was the design, their tiny docks with the flagpole and the American flag floating against the white clouds in the blue sky, the little paths over the roots of the trees leading from camp to camp and the paths leading back to the outhouses and the can of lime for sprinkling, and at the souvenir counters at the store the miniature birch-bark canoes and the postcards that showed things looking a little better than they looked. This was the American family at play, escaping the city heat, wondering whether the newcomers in the camp at the head of the 8 cove were "common" or "nice," wondering whether it was true that the people who drove up for Sunday dinner at the farmhouse were turned away because there wasn't enough chicken.

It seemed to me, as I kept remembering all this, that those times 9 and those summers had been infinitely precious and worth saving. There had been jollity and peace and goodness. The arriving (at the beginning of August) had been so big a business in itself, at the railway station the farm wagon drawn up, the first smell of the pine-laden air, the first glimpse of the smiling farmer, and the great importance of the trunks and your father's enormous authority in such matters, and the feel of the wagon under you for the long ten-mile haul, and at the top of the last long hill catching the first view of the lake after eleven months of not seeing this cherished body of water. The shouts and cries of the other campers when they saw you, and the trunks to be unpacked, to give up their rich burden. (Arriving was less exciting nowadays, when you sneaked up in your car and parked it under a tree near the camp and took out the bags and in five minutes it was all over, no fuss, no loud wonderful fuss about trunks.)

Peace and goodness and jollity. The only thing that was wrong 10 now, really, was the sound of the place, an unfamiliar nervous sound of the outboard motors. This was the note that jarred, the one thing that would sometimes break the illusion and set the years moving. In those other summertimes all motors were inboard; and when they were at a little distance, the noise they made was a sedative, an ingredient of summer sleep. They were one-cylinder and two-cylinder engines, and some were make-and-break and some were jump-spark, but they all made a sleepy sound across the lake. The one-lungers throbbed and fluttered, and the twin-cylinder ones purred and purred, and that was a quiet sound, too. But now the campers all had outboards. In the daytime, in the hot mornings, these motors made a petulant, irritable sound; at night, in the still evening when the afterglow lit the water, they whined about one's ears like mosquitoes. My boy loved our rented outboard, and his great desire was to achieve single-handed mastery over it, and authority, and he soon learned the trick of choking it a little (but not too much), and the adjustment of the needle valve. Watching him I would remember the things you could do with the old one-cylinder engine with the heavy flywheel, how you could have it eating out of your hand if you got really close to it spiritually. Motorboats in those days didn't have clutches, and you would make a landing by shutting off the motor at the proper time and coasting in with a dead rudder. But there was a way of reversing them, if you learned the trick, by cutting the switch and putting it on again exactly on the final dying revolution of the flywheel, so that it would kick back against compression and begin reversing. Approaching a dock in a strong following breeze, it was difficult to slow up sufficiently by the ordinary coasting method, and if a boy felt he had complete mastery over his motor, he was tempted to keep it running beyond its time and then reverse it a few feet from the dock. It took a cool nerve, because if you threw the switch a twentieth of a second too soon you would catch the flywheel when it still had speed enough to go up past center, and the boat would leap ahead, charging bull-fashion at the dock.

We had a good week at the camp. The bass were biting well and   11
the sun shone endlessly, day after day. We would be tired at night and lie down in the accumulated heat of the little bedrooms after the long hot day and the breeze would stir almost imperceptibly outside and the smell of the swamp drift in through the rusty screens. Sleep would come easily and in the morning the red squirrel would be on the roof, tapping out his gay routine. I kept remembering everything, lying in bed in the mornings—the small steamboat that had a long rounded stern like the lip of a Ubangi, and how quietly she ran on the moonlight sails, when the older boys played their mandolins and the girls sang and we ate doughnuts dipped in sugar, and how sweet the music was on the water in the shining night, and what it had felt like to think about girls then. After breakfast we would go up to the store and the things were in the same place—the minnows in a bottle, the plugs and spinners disarranged and pawed over by the youngsters from the boys' camp, the Fig Newtons and the Bee-man's gum. Outside, the road was tarred and cars stood in front of the store. Inside, all was just as it had always been, except there was more Coca-Cola and not so much Moxie and root beer and birch beer and sarsaparilla. We would walk out with the bottle of pop apiece and sometimes the pop would backfire up our noses and hurt. We explored the streams, quietly, where the turtles slid off the sunny logs and dug their way into the soft bottom; and we lay on the town wharf and fed worms to the tame bass. Everywhere we went I had trouble making out which was I, the one walking at my side, the one walking in my pants.

One afternoon while we were there at that lake a thunderstorm   12
came up. It was like the revival of an old melodrama that I had seen

long ago with childish awe. The second-act climax of the drama of the electrical disturbance over a lake in America had not changed in any important respect. This was the big scene, still the big scene. The whole thing was so familiar, the first feeling of oppression and heat and a general air around camp of not wanting to go very far away. In mid-afternoon (it was all the same) a curious darkening of the sky, and a lull in everything that had made life tick; and then the way the boats suddenly swung the other way at their moorings with the coming of a breeze out of the new quarter, and the premonitory rumble. Then the kettle drum, then the snare, then the bass drum and cymbals, then crackling light against the dark, and the gods grinning and licking their chops in the hills. Afterward the calm, the rain steadily rustling in the calm lake, the return of light and hope and spirits, and the campers running out in joy and relief to go swimming in the rain, their bright cries perpetuating the deathless joke about how they were getting simply drenched, and the children screaming with delight at the new sensation of bathing in the rain, and the joke about getting drenched linking the generations in a strong indestructible chain. And the comedian who waded in carrying an umbrella.

When the others went swimming, my son said he was going in, 13 too. He pulled his dripping trunks from the line where they had hung all through the shower and wrung them out. Languidly, and with no thought of going in, I watched him, his hard little body, skinny and bare, saw him wince slightly as he pulled up around his vitals the small, soggy, icy garment. As he buckled the swollen belt, suddenly my groin felt the chill of death.

Meanings and Values

1. In what ways have the lake and its surroundings remained the same since White's boyhood? Be specific. In what ways have they changed?

2. Can the lake be considered a personal symbol for White? (See "Guide to Terms": *Symbol*.) If so, what does it symbolize?

3. At one point in the essay White says, "I seemed to be living a dual existence" (par. 4). What is the meaning of this statement? How does this "dual existence" affect his point of view in the essay? (Guide: *Point of View*.) Is the "dual existence" emphasized more in the first half of the essay or the second half? Why?

4. Where in the essay does White link differences between the lake now and in his youth with a difference between his son's outlooks and his

own? Is this distance between father and son caused by changes in the world around them or merely the passage of time? Explain.

5. After spending a day on the lake, White remarks, "There had been no years" (par. 6). What other direct or indirect comments does he make about time and change? Be specific.

6. What is the tone of the essay? (Guide: *Style/Tone.*) Does the tone change or remain the same throughout the essay?

7. What is meant by the closing phrase of the essay, "suddenly my groin felt the chill of death" (par. 13)? Is this an appropriate way to end the essay? Why or why not?

Expository Techniques

1. In the first part of the essay White focuses on the unchanged aspects of the lake; in the second part he begins acknowledging the passage of time. Where does this shift in attitude take place? What strategies, including transitional devices, does White use to signal to the reader the shift in attitude? Be specific.

2. How does White use the discussion of outboard motors and inboard motors (par. 10) to summarize the differences between life at the lake in his youth and at the time of his return with his son?

3. Many of the descriptive passages in this essay convey a dominant impression, usually an emotion or mood. Discuss how the author's choice of details and author's suggest that the impression is more the observer's perspective than objective description of the lake. (Guide: *Syntax; Diction.*)

4. In many places the author combines description and comparison. Select a passage from the essay and discuss in detail how he combines the patterns. In what ways is the combination of description and comparison appropriate to the theme and the point of view of the essay?

Diction and Vocabulary

1. How much do the connotations of the words used in paragraph 8 contribute to the dominant impression the author is trying to create? (Guide: *Connotation/Denotation.*) In paragraph 10? What do these connotations suggest about the relation of person to place? Of observer to subject of observation?

2. Is the diction in this passage sentimental: "Summertime, oh, summertime, pattern of life indelible, the fade-proof lake, the woods unshatterable, the pasture with the sweetfern and the juniper forever and ever, summer without end . . . " (par. 8)? (Guide: *Sentimentality.*) If so, why would the author choose to use this style in the passage?

Does the passage contain an allusion? If so, what is alluded to and why? (Guide: *Figures of Speech.*)

3. In what sense can a tennis court steam "with midday heat and hunger and emptiness" (par. 7)?

4. What kind of paradox is presented in this passage: ". . . the waitresses were the same country girls, there having been no passage of time, only the illusion of it as in a dropped curtain—the waitresses were still fifteen; their hair had been washed, that was the only difference—they had been to the movies and seen the pretty girls with the clean hair" (par. 7)? (Guide: *Paradox.*)

5. Study the author's uses of the following words, consulting the dictionary as needed: incessant, placidity (par. 1); gunwale (2); primeval (3); transposition (4); helgramite, pensively (5); petulant (10); premonitory (12); languidly (13).

Read to Write

1. Following are possible subjects for essays that draw on ideas from "Once More to the Lake." If you have taken a summer vacation like the one recorded by White, consider writing an essay comparing your experiences and the setting to those in the essay. You might want to talk about how much our civilization—and our vacations—have changed since the time of the events in the essay. If you have read Marianna De Marco Torgovnick's "On Being White, Female, and Born in Bensonhurst," compare her account of returning to the neighborhood in which she grew up to White's account of the setting where he spent time as a youth. Exploring their different perspectives on the relationship of person and place could be the focus on an essay, or you could use their perspectives to develop one of your own. Discuss your relationship with your parents (or your children) insofar as that relationship includes experiences similar to the ones White describes in "Once More to the Lake."

2. In his descriptions, White creates symbols to convey his ideas about the passing of time. In an essay of your own, prepare a description of some object or place that symbolizes the passage of time. Try to control the tone of your description so it reflects your attitudes towards time and change.

3. Drawing on the strategies White employs in "Once More to the Lake," choose some place you remember from your childhood and have seen recently, and write a description of it comparing its present appearance with your memories of it. As you write, take into account the relationships of place and person, permanence and change, and the effect of experience on perception.

(NOTE: Suggestions for topics requiring development by use of DESCRIPTION follow.)

Writing Suggestions for Section 10
Description

1. Primarily by way of impressionistic description that focuses on a single dominant impression, show and explain the mood, or atmosphere, of one of the following:

   a. A country fair.

   b. A ball game.

   c. A rodeo.

   d. A wedding.

   e. A funeral.

   f. A busy store.

   g. A ghost town.

   h. A cave.

   i. A beach in summer (or winter).

   j. An antique shop.

   k. A party.

   l. A family dinner.

   m. A traffic jam.

   n. Reveille.

   o. An airport (or a bus depot).

   p. An automobile race (or a horse race).

   q. A home during one of its rush hours.

   r. The last night of holiday shopping.

   s. A natural scene at a certain time of day.

   t. The campus at examination time.

   u. A certain person at a time of great emotion—e.g., joy, anger, grief.

2. Using objective description as your basic pattern, explain the functional qualities or the significance of one of the following:

   a. A house for sale.

   b. A public building.

   c. A dairy barn.

   d. An ideal workshop (or hobby room).

e. An ideal garage.

f. A fast-food restaurant.

g. The layout of a town (or airport).

g. The layout of a farm.

i. A certain type of boat.

j. A sports complex.

11

Using *Narration* as an Expository Technique

Attempts to classify the functions of narration seem certain to develop difficulties and end in arbitrary and sometimes fuzzy distinctions. These need not distress us, however, if we remember that narration remains narration—a factual or fictional report of a sequence of events—and that our only reason for trying to divide it into categories is to find some means of studying its uses.

In a sense, as we have already seen in Section 7, exposition by process analysis makes one important, if rather narrow, use of narration, since it explains in sequence how specific steps lead to completion of some process. At the other extreme is narration that has very little to do with exposition: the story itself is the important thing, and instead of a series of steps leading obviously to a completed act, events *develop* out of each other and build suspense, however mild, through some kind of conflict. This use of narration includes the novel and the short story, as well as some news and sports reporting. Because we are studying exposition, however, we must avoid getting too involved with these uses of narration; they require special techniques, the study of which would require a whole course or, in fact, several courses.

Between the extremes of a very usable analysis of process and very intriguing narration for the story's sake—and often seeming to blur into one or the other—is narration for *explanation's* sake, to explain a concept that is more than process and that might have been explained by one of the other patterns of exposition. Here only the form is narrative; the function is expository.

Fortunately, the average student seldom needs to use narration for major explanatory purposes, as it has been used in each of the following selections. But to learn the handling of even minor or localized narration, the best procedure (short of taking several col-

435

lege courses, or at least one that concentrates on the narrative form) is simply to observe how successful writers use it to perform various functions. Localized narration can sometimes be helpful in developing any of the other major patterns of exposition—e.g., as in the Buckley essay (Section 3) or in Catton's (Section 5).

The most common problems can be summarized as follows:

1. *Selection of details.* As in writing description, the user of narration always has far more details available than can or should be used. Good unity demands the selection of only those details that are most relevant to the purpose and the desired effect.

2. *Time order.* The writer can use straight chronology, relating events as they happen (the usual method in minor uses of narration), or the flashback method, leaving the sequence temporarily in order to go back and relate some now-significant happening of a time prior to the main action. If flashback is used, it should be deliberate and for a valid reason—not merely because the episode was neglected at the beginning.

3. *Transitions.* The lazy writer of narration is apt to resort to the transitional style of a three-year-old: ". . . and then we . . . and then she . . . and then we. . . ." Avoiding this style may tax the ingenuity, but invariably the result is worth the extra investment of time and thought.

4. *Point of view.* This is a large and complex subject if dealt with fully, as a course in narration would do. Briefly, however, the writer should decide at the beginning whether the reader is to experience the action through a character's eyes (and ears and brain) or from an overall, objective view. This decision makes a difference in how much can be told, whose thoughts or secret actions can be included. The writer must be consistent throughout the narrative and include only information that could logically be known through the adopted point of view.

5. *Dialogue.* Presumably the writer already knows the mechanics of using quotations. Beyond these, the problems are to make conversation as natural-sounding as possible and yet to keep it from rambling through many useless details—to keep the narrative moving forward by *means* of dialogue.

As in most patterns of writing, the use of expository narration is most likely to be successful if the writer constantly keeps the purpose and audience in mind, remembering that the only reason for using the method in the first place—for doing *any* writing—is to communicate ideas. Soundness, clarity, and interest are the best means of attaining this goal.

Sample Paragraph (Annotated)

Central theme announced (reason for the narrative).

Narrative in generally chronological order.

Told from an "objective" point of view, not through the eyes of participants.

The story of Palmville's oil well is often told to newcomers in order to reveal the character of the town and, incidentally, to explain why city government policy is set by a Town Meeting rather than by a city council. In 1953, several successful oil wells were drilled in neighboring Yutawpa County, setting off an "Oil Rush" in this part of the state. The mayor at the time, Norbert Flax, was gripped by "Oil Fever" and devised a plan for city-funded drilling in what is now Anna May Wong Park. A citizen's group led by Herbert and Ellie Gomez opposed the plan, arguing that it would simply waste taxpayers' money. Recognizing that the mayor had the City Council on his side, Ellie and Herbert organized a campaign against the proposal, built around the theme of greater citizen participation in government and complete with marches, placards, and chants of "Par-Ti-Ci-Pa-Tion!" The wells were dry, the city had to triple the tax rate to pay off the debt, and growth in population and jobs was stunted for two decades. Since the debacle, citizen participation has been a key element in Palmville's government, the town has a city manager rather than a mayor, and all major policy decisions are made by the Town Meeting.

Sample Paragraph (Narration)

For anyone who has looked up from
the sullen South Georgia shore [island
near Antarctica] towards the soaring,
razor-edged peaks and the terrible chaos
of glaciers topped by swirling clouds
and scoured by mighty winds, the
knowledge of the crossing made by
these three men adds a wider dimension
to an already awe-inspiring sight. How
they did it, God only knows, but they
crossed the island in thirty-six hours.
They were fortunate that the weather
held, although many times great banks
of fog rolled in from the open sea,
creeping towards them over the snow
and threatening to obscure their way.
Confronted by precipices of ice and
walls of rock they had often to retrace
their steps adding many miles to the
journey. They walked almost without
rest. At one point they sat down in an
icy gully, the wind blowing the drift
around them, and so tired were they
that Worsely and Crean fell asleep
immediately. Shackleton, barely able to
keep himself awake, realized that to fall
asleep under such conditions would
prove fatal. After five minutes he woke
the other two, saying that they had slept
for half an hour.

Edwin Mickleburgh, *Beyond the Frozen Sea: Visions of Antarctica.* New York: St. Martin's
Press, 1987.

MARTIN GANSBERG

MARTIN GANSBERG, born in Brooklyn, New York, in 1920, received a Bachelor of Social Sciences degree from St. John's University. He has been an editor and reporter for *The New York Times* since 1942, including a three-year period as editor of its international edition in Paris. He also served on the faculty of Fairleigh Dickinson University. Gansberg has written for many magazines, including *Diplomat, Catholic Digest, Facts,* and *U.S. Lady.*

38 Who Saw Murder Didn't Call the Police

"38 Who Saw Murder. . ." was written for the New York Times in 1964, and for obvious reasons it has been anthologized frequently since then. Cast in a deceptively simple news style, it still provides material for serious thought, as well as a means of studying the use and technique of narration.

For more than half an hour 38 respectable, law-abiding citizens in   1
Queens watched a killer stalk and stab a woman in three separate attacks in Kew Gardens.

Twice their chatter and the sudden glow of their bedroom lights   2
interrupted him and frightened him off. Each time he returned, sought her out, and stabbed her again. Not one person telephoned the police during the assault; one witness called after the woman was dead.

That was two weeks ago today.   3

Still shocked is Assistant Chief Inspector Frederick M. Lussen,   4
in charge of the borough's detectives and a veteran of 25 years of homicide investigations. He can give a matter-of-fact recitation on many murders. But the Kew Gardens slaying baffles him—not because it is a murder, but because the "good people" failed to call the police.

"As we have reconstructed the crime," he said, "the assailant 5
had three chances to kill this woman during a 35-minute period. He
returned twice to complete the job. If we had been called when he
first attacked, the woman might not be dead now."

This is what the police say happened beginning at 3:20 A.M. in 6
the staid, middle-class, tree-lined Austin Street area:

Twenty-eight-year-old Catherine Genovese, who was called 7
Kitty by almost everyone in the neighborhood, was returning home
from her job as manager of a bar in Hollis. She parked her red Fiat
in a lot adjacent to the Kew Gardens Long Island Rail Road Station,
facing Mowbray Place. Like many residents of the neighborhood,
she had parked there day after day since her arrival from Connecticut a year ago, although the railroad frowns on the practice.

She turned off the lights of her car, locked the door, and started 8
to walk the 100 feet to the entrance of her apartment at 82–70 Austin
Street, which is in a Tudor building, with stores in the first floor and
apartments on the second.

The entrance to the apartment is in the rear of the building 9
because the front is rented to retail stores. At night the quiet neighborhood is shrouded in the slumbering darkness that marks most
residential areas.

Miss Genovese noticed a man at the far end of the lot, near a 10
seven-story apartment house at 82–40 Austin Street. She halted.
Then, nervously, she headed up Austin Street toward Lefferts Boulevard, where there is a call box to the 102nd Police Precinct in nearby
Richmond Hill.

She got as far as a street light in front of a bookstore before the 11
man grabbed her. She screamed. Lights went on in the 10-story apartment house at 82–67 Austin Street, which faces the bookstore. Windows slid open and voices punctuated the early-morning stillness.

Miss Genovese screamed: "Oh, my God, he stabbed me! Please 12
help me! Please help me!"

From one of the upper windows in the apartment house, a man 13
called down: "Let that girl alone!"

The assailant looked up at him, shrugged and walked down 14
Austin Street toward a white sedan parked a short distance away.
Miss Genovese struggled to her feet.

Lights went out. The killer returned to Miss Genovese, now try- 15
ing to make her way around the side of the building by the parking
lot to get to her apartment. The assailant stabbed her again.

"I'm dying!" she shrieked, "I'm dying!" 16

Windows were opened again, and lights went on in many   17
apartments. The assailant got into his car and drove away. Miss
Genovese staggered to her feet. A city bus, Q-10, the Lefferts
Boulevard line to Kennedy International Airport, passed. It was
3:35 A.M.

The assailant returned. By then, Miss Genovese had crawled to   18
the back of the building, where the freshly painted brown doors to
the apartment house held out hope for safety. The killer tried the
first door; she wasn't there. At the second door, 82–62 Austin Street,
he saw her slumped on the floor at the foot of the stairs. He stabbed
her a third time—fatally.

It was 3:50 by the time the police received their first call, from a   19
man who was a neighbor of Miss Genovese. In two minutes they were
at the scene. The neighbor, a 70-year-old woman, and another woman
were the only persons on the street. Nobody else came forward.

The man explained that he had called the police after much   20
deliberation. He had phoned a friend in Nassau County for advice
and then he had crossed the roof of the building to the apartment of
the elderly woman to get her to make the call.

"I didn't want to get involved," he sheepishly told the police.   21

Six days later, the police arrested Winston Moseley, a 29-year-   22
old business-machine operator, and charged him with homicide.
Moseley had no previous record. He is married, has two children
and owns a home at 133–19 Sutter Avenue, South Ozone Park,
Queens. On Wednesday, a court committed him to Kings County
Hospital for psychiatric observation.

When questioned by the police, Moseley also said that he had   23
slain Mrs. Annie May Johnson, 24, of 146–12 133rd Avenue, Jamaica,
on Feb. 29 and Barbara Kralik, 15, of 174–17 140th Avenue, Spring-
field Gardens, last July. In the Kralik case, the police are holding
Alvin L. Mitchell, who is said to have confessed to that slaying.

The police stressed how simple it would have been to have got-   24
ten in touch with them. "A phone call," said one of the detectives,
"would have done it." The police may be reached by dialing "O" for
operator or SPring 7-3100.

Today witnesses from the neighborhood, which is made up of   25
one-family homes in the $35,000 to $60,000 range with the exception
of the two apartment houses near the railroad station, find it difficult
to explain why they didn't call the police.

A housewife, knowingly if quite casually, said, "We thought it   26
was a lover's quarrel." A husband and wife both said, "Frankly, we

were afraid." They seemed aware of the fact that events might have been different. A distraught woman, wiping her hands on her apron, said, "I didn't want my husband to get involved."

One couple, now willing to talk about that night, said they   27
heard the first screams. The husband looked thoughtfully at the bookstore where the killer first grabbed Miss Genovese.

"We went to the window to see what was happening," he said,   28
"but the light from our bedroom made it difficult to see the street." The wife, still apprehensive, added: "I put out the light and we were able to see better."

Asked why they hadn't called the police, she shrugged and   29
replied: "I don't know."

A man peeked out from the slight opening in the doorway to his   30
apartment and rattled off an account of the killer's second attack. Why hadn't he called the police at the time? "I was tired," he said without emotion. "I went back to bed."

It was 4:25 A.M. when the ambulance arrived to take the body of   31
Miss Genovese. It drove off. "Then," a solemn police detective said, "the people came out."

Meanings and Values

1. What is Gansberg's central (expository) theme? How might he have developed this theme without using narration at all? Specify what patterns of exposition he could have used instead. Would any of them have been as effective as narration *for the purpose*? Why or why not?

2. Why has this narrative account of old news (the murder made its only headlines in 1964) retained its significance to this day? Are you able to see in this event a paradigm of any larger condition or situation? If so, explain, using examples as needed to illustrate your ideas.

Expository Techniques

1. What standard introductory technique is exemplified in the first paragraph? (Guide: *Introductions*.) How effective do you consider it? If you see anything ironic in the fact stated there, explain the irony. (Guide: *Irony*.)

2. Where does the main narration begin? What, then, is the function of the preceding paragraphs?

3. Study several of the paragraph transitions within the narration itself to determine Gansberg's method of advancing the time sequence (to

avoid overuse of "and then"). What is the technique? Is another needed? Why or why not?

4. What possible reasons do you see for the predominant use of short paragraphs in this piece? Does this selection lose any effectiveness because of the short paragraphs?

5. Undoubtedly, the author selected with care the few quotations from witnesses that he uses. What principle or principles do you think applied to his selection?

6. Explain why you think the quotation from the "solemn police detective" was, or was not, deliberately and carefully chosen to conclude the piece. (Guide: *Closings*.)

7. Briefly identify the point of view of the writing. (Guide: *Point of view*.) Is it consistent throughout? Show the relation, as you see it, between this point of view and the author's apparent attitude toward his subject matter.

8. Does he permit himself any sentimentality? If so, where? (Guide: *Sentimentality*.) If not, specifically what might he have included that would have slipped into melodrama or sentimentality?

Diction and Vocabulary

1. Why do you think the author used no difficult words in this narration? Do you find the writing at all belittling to college people because of this fact? Why or why not?

Read to Write

1. If you have read Tom Wolfe's "O Rotten Gotham" (Section 6) or Marianna De Marco Torgovnick's "On Being White, Female, and Born in Bensonhurst" (Section 5), apply and extend their views of how New Yorkers behave so that you can offer your own interpretation of the events in "38 Who Saw Murder Didn't Call the Police." Or draw on Gansberg's, Wolfe's, and Torgovnick's essays to help explain a more recent event of either local or national significance.

2. Gansberg uses numerous quotations from police and observers in his account. Use a similar technique in an expository essay of your own. Decide if your purposes for writing would be best served by your commenting on the significance and implications of the quotations or by letting them stand without extensive commentary.

3. Though he certainly has his own view of the events he reports on, Gansberg largely allows readers to question the motivations of the observers and make their own judgments on the lack of action. Prepare an account of some incident you witnessed and use a similar

approach. Call attention to the various motivations expressed by the participants, to the inconsistencies in their behavior, and to any other elements you wish readers to analyze and question. The event itself need not be of more than local significance (an account of a meeting or a sports event can offer interesting insights, for example), but your exposition should offer readers insights worth considering.

(NOTE: Suggestions for topics requiring development by NARRATION are on page 479 at the end of this section.)

CHANG-RAE LEE

CHANG-RAE LEE was born in South Korea in 1967. When he was
three years old, he and his family emigrated to the United States.
He is a graduate of Phillips Exeter Academy and Yale University.
He earned his M.F.A. degree from the University of Oregon
where he now teaches creative writing. Lee's novel, *Native Speaker*
(1996), was awarded the Ernest Hemingway Foundation/PEN
Award for First Fiction.

Uncle Chul Gets Rich

In "Uncle Chul Gets Rich," first published in 1996, Lee offers a
familiar narrative form—a story of success in business—set amid
contrasting values and cultures typical of immigrant experiences.
The issues Lee explores, however, will be familiar and important
for most readers.

My father's youngest brother, Uncle Chul, shared the Lees'   1
famously bad reaction to liquor, which was to turn beet-red in the
face, grow dizzy and finally get sick. In spite of this, he was always
happy to stay up late at family gatherings. After a few Scotches he
would really loosen up, and, with the notable exception of my
mother, we all appreciated his rough language and racy stories.
Only when Mother came in from the kitchen would his talk soften,
for he knew he had always fallen short in her eyes. If they were ever
alone together, say in the kitchen, after dinner, he would use the
most decorous voice in asking for a glass or a fresh bucket of ice, and
even offer to help load the dishwasher or run an errand to the store.

On one of those nights we sped off, both happy for a break in   2
the long evening. He asked me about school, what sports I was playing, but the conversation inevitably turned toward my parents, and
particularly my mother—how much she had invested in me, that I
was her great hope. I thought it was odd that he was speaking this
way, like my other relatives, and I answered with some criticism of

her—that she was too anxious and overbearing. He stared at me and, with a hard solemnity I had not heard from him before, said that my mother was one of the finest people one could ever know. He kept a grip on the wheel and in the ensuing quiet of the drive I could sense how he must have both admired and despised her. In many respects, my mother was an unrelenting woman. She tended to measure people by the mark of a few principles of conduct: ask no help from anyone, always plan for the long run and practice (her own variation of) the golden rule, which was to treat others much better than oneself.

In her mind, Uncle Chul sorely lacked on all these accounts. In   3
the weeks following our drive, my father would be deciding whether to lend him $10,000 to start a business. As always after dinner, my parents sat in the kitchen (the scent of sesame oil and pickled vegetables still in the air) and spoke in Korean, under the light of a fluorescent ring. My mother, in many ways the director of the family, questioned my uncle's character and will. Hadn't he performed poorly in school, failed to finish college? Hadn't he spent most of his youth perfecting his skills as a black belt in taekwondo and his billiards game? Wasn't he a gambler in spirit?

My father could defend him only weakly. Uncle Chul had a history of working hard only when reward was well within sight, like   4
cash piled high on the end of a pool table. His older brothers were all respected professionals and academics. My father was a doctor, a psychiatrist who had taught himself English in order to practice in America. Uncle Chul had left Korea after a series of failed ventures and odd jobs, and found himself broke with a wife and new baby. How valuable were his taekwondo trophies now? What could he possibly do in this country?

My parents argued fiercely and my father left the kitchen. But as   5
was my mother's way, she kept on pushing her side of the issue, thinking aloud. My father was throwing away his hard-earned money on the naïve wish that his little brother had magically changed. Uncle Chul was a poor risk and even now was complaining about his present job, hauling and cleaning produce for a greengrocer in Flushing. He would get to the store at 4. A.M. to prepare vegetables for the day's selling. While he shared a sofa bed with his nephew in his older brother's tiny apartment, his wife and infant daughter were still in Seoul, waiting for him to make enough money to send for them.

But his wages were only $250 a week for 70 hours of work and   6
he loathed the job, the brutal effort that went into clearing a few

cents a carrot, a quarter a soda, the niggling, daily accrual. The owners themselves would toil like slaves to see a till full of tattered ones and fives at day's end.

I knew Uncle Chul craved the big score, the quick hit, a rain of   7
cash. For the very reasons my mother had so little faith in him—his brashness, his flagrant ambitions—I admired him. Over Scotch and rice crackers, he would tell my father about the millions he was going to make by moving merchandise wholesale, in bigger-ticket items with decent margins. He would never touch another orange again. I remember my father absently nodding his head at each vague and grandiose idea, probably hearing my mothers' harangues.

The other men in my father's family were thick-lensed scrib-   8
blers who worked through their days from A to Z, assiduously removing uncertainty by paying close attention to the thousand details of each passing hour. My father worked long days at the hospital, and spent weekends pouring over volumes of Freud and Rank and Erickson in his second language, to "catch up" with the American doctors. When my father decided to lend Uncle Chul the $10,000, making it clear that no further discussion was needed, my mother transferred her worrying energy squarely onto me. It seemed no accident that her latest criticism was that I was "always looking for the easy way." I had, in fact, been feeling moody and rebellious, weary of being a good student and good boy. I was in the eighth grade, and my friends were beginning to drink beer and smoke pot. I secretly resolved to join them.

I was also taking solo train trips from Pleasantville, N.Y., down   9
to the city to visit my older cousins on the weekends, prompting questions from my mother about what kind of fun we were having. I didn't tell her that what thrilled me most was riding the elevated trains between Flushing and Grand Central, shuttling back and forth with the multitude. My new comer's heart was fearful and enthralled, and I naïvely thought Uncle Chul felt the same way. He had quit working for the greengrocer after getting the money, and brought over his wife and child. He was busy scouting out stores for his first business in America.

But Uncle Chul found that the leases for even the smallest stores   10
were $4,000 a month, and he seemed tense and even a little scared. I felt a strange pang of guilt because of the extra pressure on him—the $10,000 and the tenuous faith behind it. The only thing worse than losing the money was what my mother would never have to mention again: that he started working a little too late.

But he did find a store, in the Bronx, and we drove down one   11
Sunday to see it in all its new glory. It seemed as if half the tenement
buildings on the block were burned out or deserted, and the sidewalks were littered with garbage, broken glass and the rubble of
bricks and mortar. My father pulled up behind Uncle Chul's car and
we peered out to see if we had the right address. The shop couldn't
have been more than eight feet wide. A single foot-wide corridor
running its length was lined with accessories, odd-lot handbags and
tie clips and lighters; the stuff hung on plastic grids on the walls and
overhead. In the back, there was a hot plate on the floor, two stools
and a carton of instant ramen noodles.

Uncle Chul proudly showed us the merchandise and, from a   12
glass display box, gave me a watch; my sister got a faux-pearl neck-
lace. A customer peered in but waved her hand and scurried away.
My mother said that we were disturbing the business, and after a
rush of bows and goodbyes we were in the car, heading back to
Westchester.

Uncle Chul had no choice but to be in that neighborhood, in that   13
quarter-size store, with the risk of crime and no insurance. The
trade-off was the low rent, and it soon became clear that he had
made an excellent choice. With little competition on the block, the
money started coming in, and soon he moved to a larger store
nearby, and then moved again. His volume and cash flow surged,
and after selling each successive business, he staked his profit on the
next store.

We didn't see him much during this time, but when we did he   14
made sure to show off his success to my parents. My aunt wore
designer clothes, and Uncle Chul sported a fat gold Rolex. If we
were out somewhere, he would casually pull out a rolled wad of
$100's when a check arrived, proclaiming affably to his brothers that
it was his turn to pay.

But I noticed, too, that he and my aunt looked haggard and   15
pressed. They spoke hurriedly and ate as quickly as they could. My
mother would say something like, 'You've developed such expensive tastes,' and tell him that he was still frittering away his money
on useless luxuries.

When Uncle Chul amassed the war chest he needed to open the   16
wholesale business he had hoped for, he moved away from New
York. He had heard of opportunities in Texas, where goods could be
imported across the border and sold at big profits. Within a few years
he had more than 50 people working for him, selling, by containers

and truckloads, the same purses and belts he started with years before.

He bought a sprawling ranch house, brand-new and fitted with 17 jet-action bathtubs and wide-screen televisions. He hired a team of Mexican maids to keep the place running. He traded in his Cadillacs for BMW's and sent his daughters to private school. One summer he paid my sister outrageous wages to sit in his air-conditioned office and practice her Spanish with the retailers. The business was on automatic pilot—effortless. Uncle Chul was now a millionaire several times over, richer than all his brothers combined.

I spent time with him again years later, when my mother 18 became terminally ill. He visited regularly, always bearing gifts for the family. To me, he simply gave money. He knew I had quit my first job to become a writer, which meant little to him, except that I would be poor forever. Maybe, someday, my name would be famous, and he invested in that possibility, slipping me a couple of $100's when my mother wasn't looking. He did this naturally, with an ease and power in his grip full of cash. His money was like a weight outside his body, which he could press upon others, like me. But in my mother's presence, his swagger vanished, and he was just Uncle Chul again, prodigal and bereft.

He was especially solemn on the day of her funeral. Of the 19 many people who made their way to the cemetery and later to the house, I suspect Uncle Chul knew he was among those she would be most closely watching. My mother's friends had brought food and electric rice cookers and the men were in the living room, drinking companionably, speaking in low voices. My mother had been dying for nearly two years, and now that it was over waves of exhaustion and relief were washing over everyone in the house.

I remember Uncle Chul padding softly about the house, wary of 20 disturbing even the layer of dust on her furniture. He was speaking in a soft register, his voice faltering, like a nervous young minister on his first encounter with the bereaved. He was nodding and bowing, even helping the ladies gather cups and plates, exercising until the last visitor left a younger brother's respect and obedience to the family and the dead.

In the Korean tradition, mourners brought offerings of money, 21 all token amounts, except for Uncle Chul's fat envelope, which held thousands of dollars. He would have given more, he said, but his wholesale business wasn't doing so well anymore. I knew that wasn't the real reason. He must have known what my mother would have said, perhaps was telling him now—that he couldn't help but be the flashy one again.

Meanings and Values

1. How would you define an "All-American Success Story"? In what ways is Uncle Chul's story like an all-American success story? Be specific.

2. How do the values embodied by Uncle Chul and the narrative of his success differ from those embodied and expressed by the writer's mother?

3. Does the writer endorse either his mother's values or Uncle Chul's? If so, why and how? If not, why do you think he refrains from making his own opinion known?

Expository Techniques

1. What strategy does the writer use to begin this selection? To conclude it? (See "Guide to Terms": *Introductions; Closings.*) Are both strategies effective? Why or Why not? (Guide: *Evaluation.*)

2. What ideas does the writer highlight or emphasize by his choice of opening and closing strategies? Where else in the essay do these ideas receive emphasis, and through what means? (Guide: *Emphasis.*)

3. Where and for what purposes does this essay employ comparison/contrast as an expository pattern? (See Section 5.) Why should we consider narration, not comparison/contrast, as the dominant expository pattern in the selection?

Diction and Vocabulary

1. Choose a paragraph describing one of the characters and explain how the terms the writer has chosen reflect the values of the character. (Guide: *Diction.*)

2. If you do not know the meaning of some of the following terms, look them up in a dictionary: decorous (par. 1); taekwondo (3); niggling, accrual (6), tenuous (10).

Read to Write

1. Probe your own experiences of family, community, and work for people whose actions and words reflect differing values or cultural outlooks. Then write down a list of incidents in which these people

reflect the differences in their values. Consider using these incidents in an essay exploring the values and their implications.

2. Begin a narrative essay of your own with a vivid scene similar to the kind Lee uses in paragraph 1. Include some of the main ideas and themes you will explore in the essay.

3. Create a narrative essay using selected scenes from over a considerable period of time. Choose the scenes so that they reflect differing outlooks or perspectives, and arrange them, as Lee does, for an expository purpose.

(NOTE: Suggestions for topics requiring development by NARRATION are on page 479, at the end of this section.)

Issues and Ideas

Telling Stories about Ourselves and Our Values

Sometimes speaking directly about our values or perspectives does not clarify them or convey them effectively. The situation which gives rise to a particular moral judgment or leads to an ethical perspective can give someone else a better understanding than a detailed definition or even a careful comparison of differing perspectives. The more complex the idea or outlook, the more we may need to know about the events surrounding it. A detailed narrative can perhaps give readers a better understanding of causes and effects than an explanation that attempts to isolate them from the surrounding details.

The three essays that follow demonstrate the effectiveness of narration as an expository pattern for dealing with questions of value and personal outlook. Capital punishment has been the subject of many argumentative and expository essays, but few have offered the kind of insight into the minds of the prisoner and of those responsible for carrying out the sentence that George Orwell provides in "A Hanging." And few essays explore the moral ambiguities surrounding the practice as well as Orwell does.

Rita Williams's "The Quality of Mercy" likewise provides an insider's view, both of the relationship of victim and criminal and of the complex roles of race in both crime and law enforcement. Finally, Garrett Hongo uses narrative in "Kubota" to help explain the effect of World War II on Japanese Americans, to break a silence about the events, and to preserve memories that the participants were often unwilling to pass on themselves.

GEORGE ORWELL

GEORGE ORWELL (1903–1950), whose real name was Eric Blair, was a British novelist and essayist, well known for his satire. He was born in India and educated at Eton in England; he was wounded while fighting in the Spanish Civil War. Later he wrote the books *Animal Farm* (1945), a satire on Soviet history, and *1984* (1949), a vivid picture of life in a projected totalitarian society. He was, however, also sharply aware of injustices in democratic societies and was consistently socialistic in his views. Many of Orwell's essays are collected in *Critical Essays* (1946), *Shooting an Elephant and Other Essays* (1950), and *Such, Such Were the Joys* (1953).

A Hanging

"A Hanging" is typical of Orwell's essays in its setting—Burma— and in its subtle but biting commentary on colonialism, on capital punishment, even on one aspect of human nature itself. Although he is ostensibly giving a straightforward account of an execution, the author masterfully uses descriptive details and dialogue to create atmosphere and sharply drawn characterizations. The essay gives concrete form to a social message that is often delivered much less effectively in abstract generalities.

It was in Burma, a sodden morning of the rains. A sickly light, like 1 yellow tinfoil, was slanting over the high walls into the jail yard. We were waiting outside the condemned cells, a row of sheds fronted with double bars, like small animal cages. Each cell measured about ten feet by ten and was quite bare within except for a plank bed and a pot for drinking water. In some of them brown, silent men were squatting at the inner bars, with their blankets draped round them. These were the condemned men, due to be hanged within the next week or two.

One prisoner had been brought out of his cell. He was a Hindu,   2
a puny wisp of a man, with a shaven head and vague liquid eyes. He
had a thick, sprouting mustache, absurdly too big for his body, rather
like the mustache of a comic man on the films. Six tall Indian warders
were guarding him and getting him ready for the gallows. Two of
them stood by with rifles and fixed bayonets, while the others hand-
cuffed him, passed a chain through his handcuffs and fixed it to their
belts, and lashed his arms tight to his sides. They crowded very close
about him, with their hands always on him in a careful, caressing
grip, as though all the while feeling him to make sure he was there. It
was like men handling a fish which is still alive and may jump back
into the water. But he stood quite unresisting, yielding his arms
limply to the ropes, as though he hardly noticed what was happening.

Eight o'clock struck and a bugle call, desolately thin in the wet   3
air, floated from the distant barracks. The superintendent of the jail,
who was standing apart from the rest of us, moodily prodding the
gravel with his stick, raised his head at the sound. He was an army
doctor, with a grey toothbrush mustache and a gruff voice. "For
God's sake, hurry up, Francis," he said irritably. "The man ought to
have been dead by this time. Aren't you ready yet?"

Francis, the head jailer, a fat Dravidian in a white drill suit and   4
gold spectacles, waved his black hand. "Yes sir, yes sir," he bubbled.
"All iss satisfactorily prepared. The hangman iss waiting. We shall
proceed."

"Well, quick march, then. The prisoners can't get their breakfast   5
till this job's over."

We set out for the gallows. Two warders marched on either side   6
of the prisoner, with their rifles at the slope; two others marched
close against him, gripping him by arm and shoulder, as though at
once pushing and supporting him. The rest of us, magistrates and
the like, followed behind. Suddenly, when we had gone ten yards,
the procession stopped short without any order or warning. A dreadful thing had happened—a dog, come goodness knows whence, had
appeared in the yard. It came bounding among us with a loud vol-
ley of barks and leapt round us wagging its whole body, wild with
glee at finding so many human beings together. It was a large
woolly dog, half Airedale, half pariah. For moment it pranced
around us, and then, before anyone could stop it, it had made a dash
for the prisoner, and jumping up tried to lick his face. Everybody
stood aghast, too taken aback even to grab the dog.

"Who let that bloody brute in here?" said the superintendent   7
angrily. "Catch it, someone!"

A warder detached from the escort, charged clumsily after the   8
dog, but it danced and gambolled just out of his reach, taking everything as part of the game. A young Eurasian jailer picked up a handful of gravel and tried to stone the dog away, but it dodged the
stones and came after us again. Its yaps echoed from the jail walls.
The prisoner, in the grasp of the two warders, looked on incuriously,
as though this was another formality of the hanging. It was several
minutes before someone managed to catch the dog. Then we put my
handkerchief through its collar and moved off once more, with the
dog still straining and whimpering.

It was about forty yards to the gallows. I watched the bare   9
brown back of the prisoner marching in front of me. He walked
clumsily with his bound arms, but quite steadily, with that bobbing
gait of the Indian who never straightens his knees. At each step his
muscles slid neatly into place, the lock of hair on his scalp danced up
and down, his feet printed themselves on the wet gravel. And once,
in spite of the men who gripped him by each shoulder, he stepped
lightly aside to avoid a puddle on the path.

It is curious; but till that moment I had never realized what it   10
means to destroy a healthy, conscious man. When I saw the prisoner
step aside to avoid the puddle, I saw the mystery, the unspeakable
wrongness, of cutting a life short when it is in full tide. This man was
not dying, he was alive just as we are alive. All the organs of his
body were working—bowels digesting food, skin renewing itself,
nails growing, tissues forming—all toiling away in solemn foolery.
His nails would still be growing when he stood on the drop, when
he was falling through the air with a tenth-of-a-second to live. His
eyes saw the yellow gravel and the grey walls, and his brain still
remembered, foresaw, reasoned—even about puddles. He and we
were a party of men walking together, seeing, hearing, feeling,
understanding the same world; and in two minutes, with a sudden
snap, one of us would be gone—one mind less, one world less.

The gallows stood in a small yard, separate from the main   11
grounds of the prison, and overgrown with tall prickly weeds. It was
a brick erection like three sides of a shed, with planking on top, and
above that two beams and a crossbar with the rope dangling. The
hangman, a greyhaired convict in the white uniform of the prison,
was waiting beside his machine. He greeted us with a servile crouch
as we entered. At a word from Francis the two warders, gripping the
prisoner more closely than ever, half led, half pushed him to the gallows and helped him clumsily up the ladder. Then the hangman
climbed up and fixed the rope round the prisoner's neck.

We stood waiting, five yards away. The warders had formed in a   12
rough circle round the gallows. And then, when the noose was fixed,
the prisoner began crying out to his god. It was a high, reiterated cry
of "Ram! Ram! Ram! Ram!" not urgent and fearful like a prayer or cry
for help, but steady, rhythmical, almost like the tolling of a bell. The
dog answered the sound with a whine. The hangman, still standing
on the gallows, produced a small cotton bag like a flour bag and drew
it down over the prisoner's face. But the sound, muffled by the cloth,
still persisted, over and over again: "Ram! Ram! Ram! Ram! Ram!"

The hangman climbed down and stood ready, holding the   13
lever. Minutes seemed to pass. The steady, muffled crying from the
prisoner went on and on, "Ram! Ram! Ram!" never faltering for an
instant. The superintendent, his head on his chest, was slowly pok-
ing the ground with his stick; perhaps he was counting the cries,
allowing the prisoner a fixed number—fifty, perhaps, or a hundred.
Everyone had changed colour. The Indians had gone grey like bad
coffee, and one or two of the bayonets were wavering. We looked at
the lashed, hooded man on the drop, and listened to his cries—each
cry another second of life; the same thought was in all our minds; oh,
kill him quickly, get it over, stop that abominable noise!

Suddenly the superintendent made up his mind. Throwing up   14
his head he made a swift motion with his stick. "Chalo!" he shouted
almost fiercely.

There was a clanking noise, and then dead silence. The prisoner   15
had vanished, and the rope was twisting on itself. I let go of the dog,
and it galloped immediately to the back of the gallows; but when it
got there it stopped short, barked, and then retreated into a corner of
the yard, where it stood among the weeds, looking timorously out at
us. We went round the gallows to inspect the prisoners's body. He
was dangling with his toes pointed straight downwards, very
slowly revolving, as dead as a stone.

The superintendent reached out with his stick and poked the   16
bare brown body; it oscillated slightly. "*He's* all right," said the
superintendent. He backed out from under the gallows, and blew
out a deep breath. The moody look had gone out of his face quite
suddenly. He glanced at his wrist-watch. "Eight minutes past eight.
Well, that's all for this morning, thank God."

The warders unfixed bayonets and marched away. The dog,   17
sobered and conscious of having misbehaved itself, slipped after
them. We walked out of the gallows yard, past the condemned cells
with their waiting prisoners, into the big central yard of the prison.
The convicts, under the command of warders armed with lathis,

were already receiving their breakfast. They squatted in long rows, each man holding a tin pannikin, while two warders with buckets marched around ladling out rice; it seemed quite a homely, jolly scene, after the hanging. An enormous relief had come upon us now that the job was done. One felt an impulse to sing, to break into a run, to snigger. All at once everyone began chattering gaily.

The Eurasian boy walking beside me nodded towards the way   18
we had come, with a knowing smile. "Do you know, sir, our friend (he meant the dead man) when he heard his appeal had been dismissed, he pissed on the floor of his cell. From fright. Kindly take one of my cigarettes, sir. Do you not admire my new silver case, sir? From the boxwallah, two rupees eight annas. Classy European style."

Several people laughed—at what, nobody seemed certain.   19

Francis was walking by the superintendent, talking garrulously: 20
"Well, sir, all has passed off with the utmost satisfactoriness. It was all finished—flick! Like that. It iss not always so—oah, no! I have known cases where the doctor was obliged to go beneath the gallows and pull the prissoner's legs to ensure decease. Most disagreeable!"

"Wriggling about, eh? That's bad," said the superintendent.   21

"Ach, sir, it iss worse when they become refractory! One man, I   22
recall, clung to the bars of hiss cage when we went to take him out. You will scarcely credit, sir, that it took six warders to dislodge him, three pulling at each leg. We reasoned with him, 'My dear fellow,' we said, 'think of all the pain and trouble you are causing to us!' But no, he would not listen! Ach, he wass very troublesome!"

I found that I was laughing quite loudly. Everyone was laugh-   23
ing. Even the superintendent grinned in a tolerant way. "You'd better all come out and have a drink," he said quite genially. "I've got a bottle of whisky in the car. We could do with it."

We went through the big double gates of the prison into the   24
road. "Pulling at his legs!" exclaimed a Burmese magistrate suddenly, and burst into a loud chuckling. We all began laughing again. At that moment Francis' anecdote seemed extraordinarily funny. We all had a drink together, native and European alike, quite amicably. The dead man was a hundred yards away.

Meanings and Values

1.   What was the real reason for the superintendent's impatience?

2.   On first impression it may have seemed that the author gave undue attention to the dog's role in this narrative. Why was the episode such a "dreadful thing" (par. 6)? Why did the author think it worth

noting that the dog was excited at "finding so many human beings together"? Of what significance was the dog's trying to lick the prisoner's face?

3. Explain how the prisoner's stepping around a puddle could have given the author a new insight into what was about to happen (par. 10).

4. Why was there so much talking and laughing after the hanging was finished?

5. What is the broadest meaning of Orwell's last sentence?

Expository Techniques

1. Cite examples of both objective and impressionistic description in the first paragraph.

2. What is the primary time order used in this narrative? If there are any exceptions, state where.

3. Considering the relatively few words devoted to them, several of the characterizations in this essay are remarkably vivid—a result, obviously, of highly discriminating selection of details from the multitude of those that must have been available to the author. For each of the following people, list the character traits that we can observe, and state whether these impressions come to us through details of description, action, and/or dialogue.

   a. The prisoner.

   b. The superintendent.

   c. Francis.

   d. The Eurasian boy.

4. Why do you think the author included so many details of the preparation of the prisoner (par. 2)? Why did he include so many details about the dog and his actions? What is gained by the assortment of details in paragraph 10?

5. How would your characterize the tone of this selection? (Guide: *Style/Tone*)?

Diction and Vocabulary

1. A noteworthy element of Orwell's style is his occasional use of figurative language. Cite six metaphors and similes, and comment on their choice and effectiveness. (Guide: *Figures of Speech.*)

2. Orwell was always concerned with the precise effects that words could give to meaning and style. Cite at least six nonfigurative

words that seem to you particularly well chosen for their purpose. Show what their careful selection contributes to the description of atmosphere or to the subtle meanings of the author. (Guide: *Style/Tone*.)

Read to Write

1. Orwell's essay focuses on topics and issues that are often the subject of argumentative writing, but that lend themselves as well to writing with an expository purpose. Consider one of the following topics (or related issues) for an essay of your own: Select *one* of the points of controversy over capital punishment and present both sides with equal objectivity. Examine the moral right, or lack of it, of one country or one culture/ethnicity to impose their laws, customs, or beliefs on another country or group of people. Discuss one benefit of colonialism or economic and cultural dominance to those who are dominated *or* discuss the influence that a long suppressed or dominated group can have on a society or a culture.

2. Draw on Orwell's expository technique in an essay of your own by recounting a minor incident (like the actions of the dog in "A Hanging") that led to much deeper insight. Or use a minor incident to reveal and emphasize insights that readers probably have not considered before.

3. Using Orwell's essay as a general model, consider in your own writing the dilemma of a person whose "duty" seems to require one course of action and whose "conscience" requires the opposite course. Use concrete illustrations to show how serious such dilemmas can be.

(NOTE: Suggestions for topics requiring development by NARRATION are on page 479 at the end of this section.)

RITA WILLIAMS graduated from the California Institute of the Arts with a Master of Fine Arts degree. Her short stories have appeared in a variety of anthologies and magazines. She also writes op-ed articles, book reviews, and theater reviews for the *LA Weekly*. At present she is working on a book of essays, a novel about her family of African-American hunting guides in the Rocky Mountains, and a screenplay about an uncle who was a Civil War Veteran.

The Quality of Mercy

In this essay Williams looks at some of the complicated relationships between race and crime. Though her subject is one that lends itself easily to argument and anger, Williams keeps the essay's focus on exposition. She reports her anger and frustration as well as those of the young men who confront her; then she considers its meaning.

It's 10:30 on a Saturday night, and I am trying to drive up La 1 Cienega, but even at this hour, the turgid flow of traffic is maddening. I decide to cut over to Crescent Heights, which should move faster. As I swing right onto Airdrome, a pedestrian steps in front of my car. This strikes me as very wrong, but I stop.

When the guy moves around toward my side, I see why it feels 2 odd. He is a young, black kid, braced in a combat stance, and he is pointing a gun at me. Before the fear slams my senses shut, I register a baby face with dimples, a sensuous, pink mouth, and a Batman cap with the bill sideways of his head. His eyes are what make me lose hope. He looks bored.

Panic wrestles with paralysis as I contemplate flooring it and 3 running him down. But he would definitely shoot me, and I can tell from the size of the barrel that if he gets off even one round, it will be lethal.

He walks toward my door, and the closer he gets, the more I feel 4 my system become drowsy with fear.

But my thoughts surge through a list of protests so naive that it 5 surprises me. Having worked for years to transform my own black rage into something constructive, I had not realized I felt entitled to some kind of immunity. Instead, I am now staring down the cannon of this kid who is acting out *his* black rage.

Then two more guys appear, quiet as eels, a foot from the door. 6 I sense rather than see them, because I can't tear my eyes away from the escape route ahead. I struggle not to slide completely into shock. My unlocked car door swings open.

"Get out," the kid demands. His voice is close behind me to the 7 left. The muscles at the base of my head twitch as he gently rests the gun barrel at the base of my brainstem. I fantasize the trajectory of the bullet passing through the left rear of my skull and exploding out my right temple. I know I should do exactly as he says, but I'm too scared to move.

Then I remember something familiar about this kid's stance. His 8 teachers were probably cops. He has that same paramilitary detachment. Long ago, I was taught that when a jacked-up cop shakes you down, you keep your hands in plain sight and don't make any fast moves. that lesson was learned fighting for the civil rights of kids such as these. I hope now it will work to protect me from them.

Then another buried lesson surfaces. I was backpacking in 9 Wyoming and had fallen asleep in the afternoon. I awoke at dusk to find a young mountain lion on a ledge above me. Somehow I knew that I must not look it in the eye or give in to my panicky impulse to tear off down the mountain. So I acted as if I were unaware of any danger. Once the lion had satisfied itself that I was neither a threat nor a source of food, it vanished. My hope, now, is to maintain a posture of active passivity. So I continue staring ahead.

"I *said* get out of the car, bitch," the kid snaps. 10

The layers of contempt in the word *bitch* make me wonder 11 whether the plan is rape. I notice my legs cramp. I decide that exposing my entire body to his rage would be suicidal, so I don't move at all. But I have another problem. I'm angry. And that has to be contained.

I decide that I am not going to be punished for whatever it is 12 these kids hate women for. When I realize that such puny resistance as I will offer may be effective, it gives me courage. This is not the first group of bullies I have faced. At the WASP prep school I attended in rural Colorado, "nigger" was the nicest name they called me. It got so virulent I used to eat my meals on a tray in the lavatory. But one day I saw myself in the mirror, cowering on the can, scarfing down my lunch. And I realized this was the bottom. Nothing they could say to me could be worse than this, so I took my tray into the lunchroom.

From then on, it was open season. They went at me with a   13
renewed vengeance. Then one evening before study hall, I once
more lost my nerve. I just couldn't stand it, so I walked away from
school—which could have gotten me expelled. They loved it. And
that was it. I picked up a rock and decided to fight. And to my surprise, the chase ended, the name-calling stopped. Now, even though
these kids are black, it feels just like my old hometown.

The first kid drags a jagged fingernail across my throat as he   14
tries to yank me out of the car. But even though I haven't moved, I
am no longer immobile. My grip on the steering wheel tightens,
even as his pulling me slams my head against the roof of the car.
After a halfhearted go at it, he stops and moves away from the car.
There is whispering among the boys, and I pick up the phrase "Bitch
must be crazy." I pray that I won't slide into hysterical laughter.

This standoff has gone on far too long. The cars passing behind   15
me on brightly lit La Cienega sound so deliciously ordinary. I can
hear the clicking of the traffic signal as the lights cycle from green to
amber to red. Then I hear the guy who has been standing the farthest
away approach the car. He croons, "Ah, man. Man, this is a sister.
We can't be ripping off no sister."

I don't get it. Then I realize that, in the dark, they could not tell   16
that I was black. But in this epidemic of black-on-black violence, I
would never expect my race to protect me. If anything, it should
make them rip me off with impunity.

But the compassion flowing toward me from this young man is   17
unmistakable. He has interceded for me. And I'm sure that he is taking a tremendous risk by doing so. I also know that this delicate
dynamic could shift back in a breath. But I have to look at him anyway. "Thank you," I say, then floor it.

It's a good thing the car finds the way back home, because I   18
can't remember how to get there. When I am finally safe, I only want
to immerse myself in the mundane. I definitely do not want to call
the police. But somebody else might be in danger. So I have to do
something.

"Yes, Officer," I say to the policeman who comes on the line, "I   19
want to report an attempted, I don't know what, robbery or assault
or. . ."

"where did this happen, ma'am?"   20

"Over in Los Angeles, on Airdrome right off La Cienega."   21

"Sorry, ma'am. You'll have to call the Wilshire Division. We   22
don't handle L.A. stuff in this precinct. You need to call this number
and tell them what happened." The line goes dead.

Then the effort of holding myself together collapses, and I start 23
shivering.

While I make some tea, I chide myself to gain perspective. That 24
desk sergeant was not a therapist and my little incident which ended
well, will seem tame to him, given the calls he must field on a Saturday night in L.A. But I try the number he gave me.

"Wilshire District. Please hold." 25

I listen to a tape, which tells me to "Please hold during this 26
recording." Then a male voice answers.

"Wilshire Division." 27

"I want to report a holdup tonight." 28

"Where did it happen?" I fill in the details. "So why didn't you 29
just keep on driving?"

"Officer, he had this huge gun. I was certain he was going to 30
blow me away if I moved at all."

"Yeah, well, why did you stop in the first place?" 31

"I stop for pedestrians." Mine was clearly the stupidest phone 32
call he had received that evening.

"Well, what do you want to do?" he asks. "You want us to send 33
somebody out there to talk to you, or what?"

"Look, I just wanted to report what happened in case they 34
should try to hurt anyone else. I don't have any idea how the police
department handles these things, so you tell me."

"You weren't hurt, right?" 35

"No," I say, "unless you think having a gun held to your head 36
is hurtful."

He puts me on hold. When he comes back on five minutes later, 37
he says, "Call the dispatch commander and have them send out a
patrol car. I'm going to transfer you now."

"Wait," I say. "What's that number in case I get disconnected?" 38

He tells me the number, transfers me and I get disconnected. 39
When I call back, the recording I listened to earlier repeats itself
eight times. Now the voice is that of a woman, a black woman. Hope
for understanding, maybe even some empathy, comes back.

"You wish to make a report?" she asks. 40

"Please," I say. 41

"What was the location of the incident?" 42

I give her the information. Then I notice her tone shift when I 43
tell her that the one kid let me go because I was a "sister."

"These kids were black?" 44

"Yes," I reply, and before I can say anything else, she interrupts 45
me. " Will that be all?"

I can't quite let it go. So I ask her, "What do you think of how I 46
handled this situation?"

"Listen, lady, anybody who'd drive around in L.A. at night 47
without their door locked is crazy and, second, you ought to have
run those fools down. Then we could have sent a cruiser to take
them to the morgue. You can believe they would have done the
same to you. I don't understand you stopping in the first place."

I feel dumb. She does have a point. My door should have been 48
locked, but . . . I prepare to launch into a self defensive diatribe,
when it hits me that this black woman, and the cops I spoke to
before, and the kids who tried to hold me up would all concur that
I have been the fool this evening. And that she can't hear me any
more than they could have. So I decide to let it rest.

She tells me that she will send a cruiser out, but since I can't 49
identify any suspects, I shouldn't expect much.

Meanings and values

1. In your own words, tell what Williams is trying to *explain* through
    this narrative.

2. Is her purpose primarily to explain or to tell an involving story?
    What specific evidence of her purpose does the essay provide? (See
    "Guide to Terms": *Purpose.*)

3. In which paragraphs of the essay does she comment on the *expository*
    meaning of the narrative? According to these statements, what
    meaning or meanings does the narrative have?

Expository Techniques

1. Why do you think Williams waits until the fifth paragraph to reveal
    her own ethnic identity? What does she gain or lose by waiting so
    long to do so? (Guide: *Evaluation.*) Explain how the somewhat indi-
    rect phrase she uses to identify her ethnicity, "Having worked for
    years to transform my own black rage into something constructive,"
    helps her develop the central theme of the piece. (Guide: *Unity.*)

2. The subject Williams discusses could easily be the subject of an argu-
    mentative essay. Tell how her use of narrative in developing the es-
    say helps keep it from becoming an argumentative essay rather than
    an expository essay. (See Section 13: *Argument.*)

3. For what purpose(s) does Williams employ description in para-
    graph 2? What does her use of dialogue in paragraphs 17–24 add to
    the essay?

4. Discuss her use of repetition in the first sentence of paragraph 7 and the single sentence of paragraph 10 as a way of framing her thoughts at the time and introducing her explanations of the events. Discuss the use of a similar "framing" technique in paragraphs 10–15.

Diction and Vocabulary

1. Identify and explain the differences in style and tone between the language used by the young men (pars. 7, 10, and 13–15) and that used by the dispatch commander (pars. 40–47). (Guide: *Style/Tone.*) In what ways are either or both of these like or unlike the language Williams uses in the rest of the essay? Explain the extent to which these similarities or dissimilarities in language reflect differences in outlook.

2. Where in the essay does the writer make use of slang herself and for what purpose(s)? (Guide: *Colloquial Expressions.*)

3. Identify the simile in paragraph 6 and discuss its meaning. (Guide: *Figures of Speech.*)

4. If you do not know the meaning of some of the following words, look them up in a dictionary: sensuous (par. 2); trajectory (7); virulent, cowering (12); mundane (18); diatribe (48).

Read to Write

1. "The Quality of Mercy" suggests many possible topics for expository writing. You might discuss, for example, the extent to which crime within ethnic communities, or communities based on class, is a greater (or lesser) problem than crime which crosses such lines. You might address the question of whether crime within a group affects only that group or the society as a whole. Or you might turn to a newspaper or nightly newscast for stories that extend or complicate issues raised in Williams's essay.

2. Williams uses differences in her choice of words, in diction (see Guide: *Diction*), in formality (slang versus formal language), and in dialect to draw contrasts among the characters and points of view in her narrative. Use a similar strategy in your own writing to emphasize contrasting perspectives or ideas—or to reveal similarities that exist despite the differences in style or perspective.

3. Keeping "The Quality of Mercy" in mind, prepare a paper narrating your experience as a victim (or victimizer) and explain what the experience reveals about relationships, power, rage, and fear.

(NOTE: Suggestions for topics requiring development by NARRATION are on page 479 at the end of this section.)

GARRETT KAORU Hongo was born in 1951 and grew up in Hawaii in the village of Volcano, where he still spends much of his time. Hongo is both a poet and an essayist. His poems have appeared in a variety of magazines and in two volumes, *Yellow Light* (1982) and *River of Flowers* (1988), the latter receiving both a Lamont Poetry Prize and a Discover/ *The Nation* award. His most recent book is *Volcano: A Memoir of Hawai'i* (1995). Hongo is also known for his support and advocacy of multicultural (especially Asian-American) voices in contemporary writing. This support has taken the form of two highly-praised anthologies, *The Open Boat* (1993) (poetry) and *Under Western Eyes: Personal Essays from Asian American* (1995).

Kubota

"Kubota" was first published in the journal *Ploughshares* in 1990. In telling the story of his grandfather's experiences in World War II and the years following, Hongo also explains the situation in which Japanese Americans found themselves during the war. This use of the narrative of a single person to explore the experiences and perspectives of a group is a common role the pattern can play in expository writing.

On December 8, 1941, the day after the Japanese attack on Pearl Harbor in Hawaii, my grandfather barricaded himself with his family— my grandmother, my teenage mother, her two sisters and two brothers—inside of his home in La'ie, a sugar plantation village on Oahu's North Shore. This was my maternal grandfather, a man most villagers called by his last name, Kubota. It could mean either "Wayside Field" or else "Broken Dreams," depending on which ideograms he used. Kubota ran La'ie's general store, and the previous night, after a long day of bad news on the radio, some locals had come by, pounded on the front door, and made threats. One was said to have brandished a machete. They were angry and shocked, as the whole nation was in the aftermath of the surprise attack. Kubota was one of the few Japanese Americans in the village and president 1

"Kubota" by Garrett Hongo from *Under Western Eyes: Personal Essays from Asian America*. Reprinted by permission of Darhansoff & Verrill.

of the local Japanese language school. He had become a target for their rage and suspicion. A wise man, he locked all his doors and windows and did not open his store the next day, but stayed closed and waited for news from some official.

He was a *kibei*, a Japanese American born in Hawaii (a U.S. ter- 2 ritory then, so he was thus a citizen) but who was subsequently sent back by his father for formal education in Hiroshima, Japan, their home province. *Kibei* is written with two ideograms in Japanese: one is the world for "return" and the other is the world for "rice." Poetically, it means one who returns from America, known as the Land of Rice in Japanese (by contrast, Chinese immigrants called their new home Mountain of Gold).

Kubota was graduated from a Japanese high school and then 3 came back to Hawaii as a teenager. He spoke English—and a Hawaiian creole version of it at that—with a Japanese accent. But he was well liked and good at numbers, scrupulous and hard working like so many immigrants and children of immigrants. Castle & Cook, a grower's company that ran the sugarcane business along the North Shore, hired him on first as a stock boy and then appointed him to run one of its company stores. He did well, had the trust of management and labor—not an easy accomplishment in any day— married, had children, and had begun to exert himself in community affairs and excel in his own recreations. He put together a Japanese community organization that backed a Japanese language school for children and sponsored teachers from Japan. Kubota boarded many of them, in succession, in his own home. This made dinners a silent affair for his talkative, Hawaiian-bred children, as their stern *sensei*, or teacher, was nearly always at table and their own abilities in the Japanese language were as delinquent as their attendance. While Kubota and the *sensei* rattled on about things Japanese, speaking Japanese, his children hurried through their suppers and tried to run off early to listen to the radio shows.

After dinner, while the *sensei* graded exams seated in a wicker 4 chair in the spare room and his wife and children gathered around the radio in the front parlor, Kubota sat on the screened porch outside, reading the local Japanese newspapers. He finished reading about the same time as he finished the tea he drank for his digestion—a habit he'd learned in Japan—and then he'd get out his fishing gear and spread it out on the plank floors. The wraps on his rods needed to be redone, gears in his reels needed oil, and, once through with those tasks, he'd painstakingly wind on hundreds of yards of new line. Fishing was his hobby and his passion. He spent weekends camping along the North Shore beaches with his children, setting up umbrella tents, packing a rice pot and hibachi along for ·meals. And he caught fish. *Ulu'a* mostly, the huge surf-feeding fish known on the mainland as the jack crevalle, but he'd go after almost anything in its season. In Kawela, a plantation-owned bay nearby, he fished for mullet Hawaiian-style with a throw net, stalking the bottom-hugging, gray-backed schools as they gathered at the stream mouths and in the freshwater springs. In an outrigger out beyond the reef, he'd try for *aku*—the skipjack tuna prized for steaks and, sliced raw and mixed with fresh seaweed and cut onions, for *sashimi* salad. In Kahaluu and Ka'awa and on an offshore rock locals called Goat Island, he loved to go torching, stringing lanterns on bamboo poles stuck in the sand to attract *kumu'u*, the red goatfish, as they schooled at night just inside the reef. But in Lai'e on Laniloa Point near Kahuku, the northernmost tip of Oahu, he cast twelve-and fourteen-foot surf rods for the· huge, varicolored, and fast-running *ulu'a* as they ran for schools of squid and baitfish just beyond the biggest breakers and past the low sand flats wadable from the shore to nearly a half mile out. At sunset, against the western light, he looked as if he walked on water as he came back, fish and rods slung over his shoulders, stepping along the rock and coral path just inches under the surface of a running tide.

    When it was torching season, in December or January, he'd   5 drive out the afternoon before and stay with old friends, the Tanakas or Yoshikawas, shopkeepers like him who ran stores near the fishing grounds. They'd have been preparing for weeks, selecting and cutting their bamboo poles, cleaning the hurricane lanterns, tearing up burlap sacks for the cloths they'd soak with kerosene and tie onto sticks they'd poke into the soft sand of the shallows. Once lit, touched off with a Zippo lighter, these would be the torches they'd use as beacons to attract the schooling fish. In another time, they might have made up a dozen paper lanterns of the kind mostly used for decorating the summer folk dances outdoors on the grounds of the Buddhist church during O-Bon, the Festival for the Dead. But now, wealthy and modern and efficient killers of fish, Tanaka and Kubota used rag torches and Colemans and cast rods with tips made of Tonkin bamboo and butts of American-spun fiberglass. After just one good night, they might bring back a prize bounty of a dozen burlap bags filled with scores of bloody, rigid fish delicious to eat and even better to give away as gifts to friends, family, and special customers.

It was Monday night, the day after Pearl Harbor, and there was   6
a rattling knock at the front door. Two FBI agents presented themselves, showed identification, and took my grandfather in for questioning in Honolulu. He didn't return home for days. No one knew
what had happened or what was wrong. But there was a roundup
going on of all those in the Japanese-American community suspected
of sympathizing with the enemy and worse. My grandfather was suspected of espionage, and communicating with offshore Japanese sub-
marines launched from the attack fleet days before war began.
Torpedo planes and escort fighters, decorated with the insignia of
the Rising Sun, had taken an approach route from northwest of Oahu
directly across Kahuku Point and on toward Pearl. They had strafed
an auxiliary air station near the fishing grounds my grandfather
loved and destroyed a small gun battery there, killing three men.
Kubota was known to have sponsored and harbored Japanese
nationals in his own home. He had a radio. He had wholesale access
to firearms. Circumstances and an undertone of racial resentment
had combined with wartime hysteria in the aftermath of the tragic
naval battle to cast suspicion on the loyalties of my grandfather and
all other Japanese Americans. The FBI reached out and pulled hundreds of them in for questioning in dragnets cast throughout the
West Coast and Hawaii.

My grandfather was lucky; he'd somehow been let go after only   7
a few days. Others were not as fortunate. Hundreds, from small
communities in Washington, California, Oregon, and Hawaii, were
rounded up and, after what appeared to be routine questioning,
shipped off under Justice Department orders to holding centers in
Leuppe on the Navaho reservation in Arizona, in Fort Missoula in
Montana, and on Sand Island in Honolulu Harbor. There were other
special camps on Maui in Ha'iku and on Hawaii—the Big Island—
in my own home village of Volcano.

Many of these men—it was exclusively the Japanese-American   8
men suspected of ties to Japan who were initially rounded up—did
not see their families again for more than four years. Under a sus-
pension of due process that was only after the fact ruled as warranted by military necessity, they were, if only temporarily,
"disappeared" in Justice Department prison camps scattered in particularly desolate areas of the United States designated as militarily
"safe." These were grim forerunners of the assembly centers and
concentration camps for the 120,000 Japanese-American evacuees
that were to come later.

I am Kubota's eldest grandchild, and I remember him as a   9
lonely habitually silent old man who lived with us in our home near
Los Angeles for most of my childhood and adolescence. It was the
fifties, and my parents had emigrated from Hawaii to the mainland
in the hope of a better life away from the old sugar plantation. After
some success, they had sent back for my grandparents who did the
work of the household while my mother and father worked their
salaried city jobs. My grandmother cooked and sewed, washed our
clothes, and knitted in the front room under the light of a huge lamp
with a bright three-way bulb. Kubota raised a flower garden, read
up on soils and grasses in gardening books, and planted a zoysia
lawn in front and a dichondra one in back. He planted a small patch
near the rear block wall with green onions, eggplant, white Japanese
radishes, and cucumber. While he hoed and spaded the loamless,
clayey earth of Los Angeles, he sang particularly plangent songs in
Japanese about plum blossoms and bamboo groves.

Once, in the mid-sixties, after a dinner during which, as always,   10
he had been silent while he worked away at a meal of fish and rice
spiced with dabs of Chinese mustard and catsup thinned with soy
sauce, Kubota took his own dishes to the kitchen sink and washed
them up. He took a clean jelly jar out of the cupboard—the glass was
thick and its shape squatty like an old-fashioned. He reached around
to the hutch below where he kept his bourbon. He made himself a
drink and retired to the living room where I was expected to join
him for "talk story," the Hawaiian idiom for chewing the fat.

I was a teenager and, though I was bored listening to stories I'd   11
heard often enough before at holiday dinners, I was dutiful. I took
my spot on the couch next to Kubota and heard him out. Usually,
he'd tell me about his schooling in Japan where he learned judo
along with mathematics and literature. He'd learned the *soroban*
there—the abacus, which was the original pocket calculator of the
Far East—and that, along with his strong, judo-trained back, got him
his first job in Hawaii. This was the moral. "Study *ha-ahd*," he'd say
with pidgin emphasis. "Learn read good. Learn speak da kine *good*
English." The message is the familiar one taught to any children of
immigrants: success through education. And imitation. But this
time, Kubota reached down into his past and told me a different
story. I was thirteen by then, and I suppose he thought me ready for
it. He told me about Pearl Harbor, how the planes flew in wing after
wing of formations over his old house in La'ie in Hawaii, and how,
the next day, after Roosevelt had made his famous "Day of Infamy"

speech about the treachery of the Japanese, the FBI agents had come to his door and taken him in, hauled him off to Honolulu for questioning, and held him without charge for several days. I thought he was lying. I thought he was making up a kind of horror story to shock me and give his moral that much more starch. But it was true. I asked around. I brought it up during history class in junior high school, and my teacher, after silencing me and stepping me off to the back of the room, told me that it was indeed so. I asked my mother and she said it was true. I asked my schoolmates, who laughed and ridiculed me for being so ignorant. We lived in a Japanese-American community, and the parents of most of my classmates were the *nisei* who had been interned as teenagers all through the war. But there was a strange silence around all of this. There was a hush, as if one were invoking the ill powers of the dead when one brought it up. No one cared to speak about the evacuation and relocation for very long. It wasn't in our history books, though we were studying World War II at the time. It wasn't in the family albums of the people I knew and whom I'd visit staying over weekends with friends. And it wasn't anything that the family talked about or allowed me to keep bringing up either. I was given the facts, told sternly and pointedly that "it was war" and that "nothing could be done." "*Shikatta ga nai*" is the phrase in Japanese, a kind of resolute and determinist pronouncement on how to deal with inexplicable tragedy. I was to know it but not to dwell on it. Japanese Americans were busy trying to forget it ever happened and were having a hard enough time building their new lives after "camp." It was as if we had no history for four years and the relocation was something unspeakable.

But Kubota would not let it go. In session after session, for 12 months it seemed, he pounded away at his story. He wanted to tell me the names of the FBI agents. He went over their questions and his responses again and again. He'd tell me how one would try to act friendly toward him, offering him cigarettes while the other, who hounded him with accusations and threats, left the interrogation room. Good cop, bad cop, I thought to myself, already superficially streetwise from stories black classmates told of the Watts riots and from my having watched too many episodes of *Dragnet* and *The Mod Squad*. But Kubota was not interested with my experiences. I was not made yet, and he was determined that his stories be part of my making. He spoke quietly at first, mildly, but once into his narrative and after his drink was down, his voice would rise and quaver with resentment and he'd make his accusations. He gave his testimony to me and I held it at first cautiously in my conscience like it was an heirloom too delicate to expose to strangers and anyone outside of the world Kubota made with his words. "I give you story now," he once said, "and you learn speak good, eh?" It was my job, as the disciple of his preaching I had then become, Ananda to his Buddha, to reassure him with a promise. "You learn speak good like the Dillingham," he's say another time, referring to the wealthy scion of the grower family who had once run, unsuccessfully, for one of Hawaii's first senatorial seats. Or he'd then invoke a magical name, the name of one of his heroes, a man he thought particularly exemplary and righteous. "Learn speak dah good Ing-rish like *Mistah Inouye*," Kubota shouted. "He *lick* dah Dillingham even in debate. I saw on *terre-bision* myself." He was remembering the debates before the first senatorial election just before Hawaii was admitted to the Union as its fiftieth state. "You *tell* the story," Kubota would end. And I had my injunction.

The town we settled in after the move from Hawaii is called Gardena, the independently incorporated city south of Los Angeles and north of San Pedro harbor. At its northern limit, it borders on Watts and Compton, black towns. To the southwest are Torrance and Redondo Beach, white towns. To the rest of L.A., Gardena is primarily famous for having legalized five-card draw poker after the war. On Vermont Boulevard, its eastern border, there is a dingy little Vegas-like strip of card clubs with huge parking lots and flickering neon signs that spell out "The Rainbow" and "The Horseshoe" in timed sequences of varicolored lights. The town is only secondarily famous as the largest community of Japanese Americans in the United States outside of Honolulu, Hawaii. When I was in high school there, it seemed to me that every *sansei* kid I knew wanted to be a doctor, an engineer, or a pharmacist. Our fathers were gardeners or electricians or nurserymen or ran small businesses catering to other Japanese Americans. Our mothers worked in civil service for the city or as cashiers for Thrifty Drug. What the kids wanted was a good job, good pay, a fine home, and no troubles. No one wanted to mess with the law—from either side—and no one wanted to mess with language or art. They all talked about getting into the right clubs so that they could go to the right schools. There was a certain kind of sameness, an intensely enforced system of conformity. Style was all. Boys wore moccasin-sewn shoes from Flagg Brothers, black A-1 slacks, and Kensington shirts with high collars. Girls wore their hair up in stiff bouffants solidified in hairspray and knew all the latest

13

dances from the slauson to the funky chicken. We did well in chemistry and in math, no one who was Japanese but me spoke in English class or in history unless called upon, and no one talked about World War II. The day after Robert Kennedy was assassinated, after winning the California Democratic primary, we worked on calculus and elected class coordinators for the prom, featuring the 5th Dimension. We avoided grief. We avoided government. We avoided strong feelings and dangers of any kind. Once punished, we tried to maintain a concerted emotional and social discipline and would not willingly seek to fall out of the narrow margin of protective favor again.

But when I was thirteen, in junior high, I'd not understood why 14 it was so difficult for my classmates, those who were themselves Japanese-American, to talk about the relocation. They had cringed, too, when I tried to bring it up during our discussions of World War II. I was Hawaiian-born. They were mainland-born. Their parents had been in camp, had been the ones to suffer the complicated experience of having to distance themselves from their own history and all things Japanese in order to make their way back and into the American social and economic mainstream. It was out of this sense of shame and a fear of stigma I was only beginning to understand that the *nisei* had silenced themselves. And, for their children, among whom I grew up, they wanted no heritage, no culture, no contact with a defiled history. I recall the silence very well. The Japanese-American children around me were burdened in a way I was not. Their injunction was silence. Mine was to speak.

Away at college, in another protected world in its own way as 15 magical to me as the Hawaii of my childhood, I dreamed about my grandfather. Tired from studying languages, practicing German conjugations or scripting an army's worth of Chinese ideograms on a single sheet of paper, Kubota would come to me as I drifted off into sleep. Or I would walk across the newly mown ball field in back of my dormitory, cutting through a street-side phalanx of ancient eucalyptus trees on my way to visit friends off campus, and I would think of him, his anger, and his sadness.

I don't know myself what makes someone feel that kind of need 16 to have a story they've lived through be deposited somewhere, but I can guess. I think about *The Illiad, The Odyssey, The Peloponnesian Wars* of Thucydides, and a myraid of the works of literature I've studied. A character, almost a *topoi* he occurs so often, is frequently the witness who gives personal testimony about an event the rest of his community cannot even imagine. The sibyl is such a character. And Procne, the maid whose tongue is cut out so that she will not tell that she has been raped by her own brother-in-law, the king of Thebes. There are the dime novels, the epic blockbusters Hollywood makes into miniseries, and then there are the plain, relentless stories of witnesses who have suffered through horrors major and minor that have marked and changed their lives. I myself haven't talked to Holocaust victims. But I've read their survival stories and their stories of witness and been revolted and moved by them. My father-in-law, Al Thiessen, tells me his war stories again and again and I listen. A Mennonite who set aside the strictures of his own church in order to serve, he was a Marine codeman in the Pacific during World War II, in the Signal Corps on Guadalcanal, Morotai, and Bougainville. He was part of the island-hopping maneuver MacArthur had devised to win the war in the Pacific. He saw friends die from bombs which exploded not ten yards away. When he was with the 298th Signal Corps attached to the Thirteenth Air Force, he saw plane after plane come in and crash, just short of the runway, killing their crews, setting the jungle ablaze with oil and gas fires. Emergency wagons would scramble, bouncing over newly bulldozed land men used just the afternoon before for a football game. Every time we go fishing together, whether it's in a McKenzie boat drifting for salmon in Tillamook Bay or taking a lunch break from wading the riffles of a stream in the Cascades, he tells me about what happened to him and the young men in his unit. One was a Jewish boy from Brooklyn. One was a foul-mouthed kid from Kansas. They died. And he *has* to tell me. And I *have* to listen. It's a ritual payment the young owe their elders who have survived. The evacuation and relocation is something like that.

Kubota, my grandfather, had been ill with Alzheimer's disease   17 for some time before he died. At the house he'd built on Kamehameha Highway in Hau'ula, a seacoast village just down the road from La'ie where he had his store, he'd wander out from the garage or greenhouse where he'd set up a workbench, and trudge down to the beach or up toward the line of pines he'd planted while employed by the Work Projects Administration during the thirties. Kubota thought he was going fishing. Or he thought he was back at work for Roosevelt, planting pines as a windbreak or soilbreak on the windward flank of the Ko'olau Mountains, emerald monoliths rising out of sea and cane fields from Waialua to Kaneohe. When I visited, my grandmother would send me down to the beach to fetch him. Or I'd run down Kam Highway a quarter mile or so and find him hiding in the cane field by the roadside, counting stalks, measuring circumferences in the claw of his thumb and forefinger. The look on his face was confused or concentrated, I didn't know which. But I guessed he was going fishing again. I'd grab him and walk him back to his house on the highway. My grandmother would shut him in a room.

Within a few years, Kubota had a stroke and survived it, then 18 he had another one and was completely debilitated. The family decided to put him in a nursing home in Kahuku, just set back from the highway, within a mile or so of Kahuku Point and the Tanaka Store where he had his first job as a stock boy. He lived there three years, and I visited him once with my aunt. He was like a potato that had been worn down by cooking. Everything on him—his eyes, his teeth, his legs and torso—seemed like it had been sloughed away. What he had been was mostly gone now and I was looking at the nub of a man. In a wheelchair, he grasped my hands and tugged on them—violently. His hands were still thick and, I believed, strong enough to lift me out of my own seat into his lap. He murmured something in Japanese—he'd long ago ceased to speak any English. My aunt and I cried a little, and we left him.

I remember walking out on the black asphalt of the parking lot 19 of the nursing home. It was heat-cracked and eroded already, and grass had veined itself into the interstices. There were coconut trees around, a cane field I could see across the street, and the ocean I knew was pitching a surf just beyond it. The green Ko'olaus came up behind us. Somewhere nearby, alongside the beach, there was an abandoned airfield in the middle of the canes As a child, I'd come upon it playing one day, and my friends and I kept returning to it, day after day, playing war or sprinting games or coming to fly kites. I recognize it even now when I see it on TV—it's used as a site for action scenes in the detective shows Hollywood always sets in the islands: helicopter chasing the hero racing away in a Ferrari, or gun dealers making a clandestine rendezvous on the abandoned runway. It was the old airfield strafed by Japanese planes the day the major flight attacked Pearl Harbor. It was the airfield the FBI thought my grandfather had targeted in his night fishing and signaling with the long surf poles he'd stuck in the sandy bays near Kahuku Point.

Kubota died a short while after I visited him, but not, I thought, 20 without giving me a final message. I was on the mainland, in California studying for Ph.D. exams, when my grandmother called me with the news. It was a relief. He'd suffered from his debilitation a long time and I was grateful he'd gone. I went home for the funeral and gave the eulogy. My grandmother and I took his ashes home in a small, heavy metal box wrapped in a black *furoshiki*, a large silk scarf. She showed me the name the priest had given to him on his death, scripted with a calligraphy brush on a long, narrow talent of plain wood. Buddhist commoners, at death, are given priestly names, received symbolically into the clergy. The idea is that, in their next life, one of scholarship and leisure, they might meditate and attain the enlightenment the religion is aimed at. *"Shaku Shūchi,"* the ideograms read. It was Kubota's Buddhist name, incorporating characters from his family and given names. It meant "Shining Wisdom of the Law." He died on Pearl Harbor Day, December 7, 1983.

After years, after I'd finally come back to live in Hawaii again,   21
only once did I dream of Kubota, my grandfather. It was the same night I'd heard HR442, the redress bill for Japanese Americans, had been signed into law. In my dream that night Kabota was "torching," and he sang a Japanese song, a querulous and wavery folk ballad, as he hung paper lanterns on bamboo poles stuck into the sand in the shallow water of the lagoon behind the reef near Kahuku Point. Then he was at a work table, smoking a hand-rolled cigarette, letting it dangle from his lips Bogart-style as he drew, daintily and skillfully, with a narrow trim brush, ideogram after ideogram on a score of paper lanterns he had hung in a dark shed to dry. He had painted a talismanic mantra onto each lantern, the ideogram for the word "red" in Japanese, a bit of art blended with some superstition, a piece of sympathetic magic appealing to the magenta coloring on the rough skins of the schooling, night-feeding fish we wanted to attract to his baited hooks. He strung them from pole to pole in the dream then, hiking up his khaki worker's pants so his white ankles showed and wading through the shimmering black waters of the sand flats and then the reef. "The moon is leaving, leaving," he sang in Japanese. "Take me deeper in the savage sea." He turned and crouched like an ice racer then, leaning forward so that his unshaven face almost touched the light film of water. I could see the light stubble of beard like a fine, gray ash covering the lower half of his face. I could see his gold-rimmed spectacles. He held a small wooden boat in his cupped hands and placed it lightly on the sea and pushed it away. One of his lanterns was on it and, written in small neat rows like a sutra scroll, it had been decorated with the silverly names of all our dead.

Meanings and Values

1. Where in the essay does the writer provide information about Hawaiian society and culture during his grandfather's time? Where does he explore life in a Japanese-American community in Southern California? In addition to the events in own and Kubota's life, what other topics does the writer explore in the essay?

2. Why does the author spend so much time discussing witnesses and witnessing (par. 16)? How successful is he as a witness? (See "Guide to Terms": *Evaluation*.)

3. Analyze and explain in detail the meaning of the dream in the concluding paragraph. Make sure you interpret each part of the dream narrative.

Expository Techniques

1. What technique does the writer use to begin this essay? (Guide: *Introductions*.)

2. Why does the writer begin the narrative with Pearl Harbor Day and then move backwards in time to summarize the earlier stages of Kubota's life? In what ways does this strategy serve the expository purpose of the essay? (Guide: *Purpose*.) How does Hongo introduce the discussion of topics other than the specific events in his and Kubota's life? Does he manage to keep them from disrupting the unity of the narrative? (Guide: *Unity*.) If so, how does he accomplish this?

3. What is the function of the comparison in paragraph 19? Would the essay be changed in any significant way if this paragraph were dropped?

4. Identify the descriptive details in paragraphs 5, 9, 10, and 13. What ideas or qualities do they emphasize? In what other ways does the writer create emphasis in these paragraphs? (Guide: *Emphasis*.)

Diction and Vocabulary

1. Discuss the author's use of diction in paragraphs 4, 5, 13, 19, and 21 to create vivid, concrete details and to provide emphasis to key ideas. (Guide: *Diction; Emphasis*.)

2. If you do not know the meaning of some of the following words, look them up in a dictionary: ideograms (par. 1); scrupulous (3); zoysia, dichondra, loamless, plangent (9); quaver, injunction (12); phalanx (15).

Read to Write

1. Do some reading on the history and treatment of Japanese Americans during World War II, and choose one aspect of the subject to explore in an essay of your own. Or choose the fate of some other ethnic group whose loyalty became suspect during the course of a conflict, and explore the events and the consequences in an essay.

2. Hongo claims to have written this essay as an act of memory, to preserve experiences and knowledge that might otherwise be lost. Consider constructing an essay of your own for a similar purpose and use the patterns of remembered events to structure your narrative.

3. Patterning your essay after "Kubota," choose a person you know or have read about whose experiences are shared by a group of people or a segment of society. Prepare a story of that person's experiences that also tells the story of the group.

(NOTE: Topics for essays requiring development by NARRATION follow.)

Writing Suggestions for Section 11
Narration

Use narration as a primary partial pattern (e.g., in developed examples or in comparison) for one of the following expository themes or another suggested by them. Avoid the isolated personal account that has little broader significance. Remember, too, that development of the essay should itself make your point, without excessive moralizing.

1. People can still succeed without a college education.
2. The frontiers are not all gone.
3. When people succeed in communicating, they can learn to get along with each other.
4. Even with "careful" use of capital punishment, innocent people can be executed.
5. Sports don't always build character.
6. Physical danger can make us more aware of ourselves and our values.
7. Conditioning to the realities of the job is as important to the police officers as professional training.
8. It is possible for employees themselves to determine when they have reached their highest level of competence.
9. Wartime massacres are not a new development.
10. "Date rape" and sexual harassment on the job are devastating and generally unexpected.
11. Both heredity and environment shape personality.
12. Physical and mental handicaps can be overcome in some ways, but they are still a burden.
13. Toxic wastes pose a problem for many communities.
14. Hunting is a worthwhile and challenging sport.
15. Lack of money places considerable stress on a family or a marriage.
16. Exercise can become an obsession.
17. People who grow up in affluent surroundings don't understand what it is like to worry about money, to be hungry, or to live in a dangerous neighborhood.
18. Some jobs are simply degrading, either because of the work or because of the fellow workers.

12

Reasoning by Use of *Induction* and *Deduction*

Induction and Deduction, important as they are in argumentation, may also be useful methods of exposition. They are often used simply to explain a stand or conclusion, without any effort or need to win converts.

Induction is the process by which we accumulate evidence until, at some point, we can make the "inductive leap" and thus reach a useful *generalization*. The science laboratory employs this technique; hundreds of tests and experiments and analyses may be required before the scientist will generalize, for instance, that a disease is caused by a certain virus. It is also the primary technique of the prosecuting attorney who presents pieces of inductive evidence, asking the jury to make the inductive leap and conclude that the accused did indeed kill the victim.

Even the commonplace "process of elimination" also may be considered a form of induction. If it can be shown, for instance, that "A" does not have the strength to swing the murder weapon, that "B" was in a drunken sleep at the time of the crime, and that "C" had recently become blind and could not have found her way to the boathouse, then we may be ready for the inductive leap—that the foul deed must have been committed by "X," the only other person on the island. (The use of this kind of induction implies an added obligation, of course, to make certain that all the possibilities but *one* have been eliminated: if we fail to note that "Y," a visitor on a neighboring island, and his boat were unaccounted for that evening, then our conclusion is invalid.)

On a more personal level, of course, we all learned to use induction at a very early age. We may have disliked the taste of orange juice, winter squash, and carrots, and we were not too young to make a generalization: orange-colored food tastes bad.

Whereas induction is the method of reaching a potentially useful generalization (for example, Professor Melville always gives an "F" to students who cut his class three times), *deduction* is the method of *using* such a generality, now accepted as a fact (for example, if we cut this class again today, we will get an "F"). Working from a generalization already formulated—by ourselves, by someone else, or by tradition—we may deduce that a specific thing or circumstance that fits into the generality will act the same. Hence, if convinced that orange-colored food tastes bad, we will be reluctant to try pumpkin pie.

A personnel manager may have discovered over the years that electronics majors from Central College are invariably well trained in their field. His induction may have been based on the evidence of observations, records, and the opinions of fellow Rotary members; and, perhaps without realizing it, he has made the usable generalization about the training of Central College electronics majors. Later, when he has an application from Nancy Ortega, a graduate of Central College, his deductive process will probably work as follows: Central College turns out well-trained electronics majors; Ortega was trained at Central; therefore, Ortega must be well trained. Here he has used a generalization to apply to a specific case.

Put in this simplified form (which, in writing, it seldom is),[1] the deductive process is also called a "syllogism"—with the beginning generality known as the "major premise" and the specific that fits into the generality known as the "minor premise." For example:

Major premise—Orange-colored food is not fit to eat.
Minor premise—Pumpkin pie is orange-colored.
Conclusion—Pumpkin pie is not fit to eat.

Frequently, however, the validity of one or both of the premises may be questionable, and here is one of the functions of *in*duction: to give needed support—with evidence such as opinions of experts, and results of experiments or surveys—to the *de*ductive syllogism, whether stated or implied. Deductive reasoning, in whatever form

[1]Neither induction nor deduction is confined to a particular order of presentation. If we use specific evidence to *reach* a generalization, it is induction regardless of which part is stated first in a written or spoken account. (Very likely, both a prosecutor's opening remarks and a medical researcher's written reports first present their generalizations and then the inductive evidence by which they have been reached.) But if we use a generality in which to *place* a specific, it is still deduction, however stated. (Hence the reasoning of the personnel manager might be: "Ortega must be well trained because she was educated at C.C., and there's where they really know how to do it.")

presented, is only as sound as both its premises. The child's conviction that orange-colored food is not fit to eat was not necessarily true; therefore, the conclusion about pumpkin pie is not very trustworthy. The other conclusions, that we will automatically get an "F" by cutting Melville's class and that Ortega is well trained in electronics, can be only as reliable as the original generalizations that were used as deductive premises. If the generalizations themselves were based on flimsy or insufficient evidence, any future deduction using them is likely to be erroneous.

These two faults are common in induction: (1) the use of *flimsy* evidence—mere opinion, hearsay, or analogy, none of which can support a valid generalization—instead of verified facts or opinions of reliable authorities; and (2) the use of *too little* evidence, leading to a premature inductive leap.

The amount of evidence needed in any situation depends, of course, on purpose and audience. The success of two Central College graduates might be enough to convince some careless personnel director that all Central electronics graduates would be good employees, but two laboratory tests would not convince medical researchers that they had learned anything worthwhile about a disease-causing virus. The authors of the Declaration of Independence, in justifying their argument for rebellion to a wide variety of readers and listeners, explained why they considered the king tyrannical, by listing twenty-eight despotic acts of his government, each of which was a verifiable fact, a matter of public record.

Induction and deduction are highly logical processes, and any trace of weakness can seriously undermine an exposition that depends on their reasonableness. (Such weakness can, of course, be even more disastrous in argument.) Although no induction or deduction ever reaches absolute, 100 percent certainty, we should try to get from these methods as high a degree of *probability* as possible. (We can never positively prove, for instance, that the sun will rise in the east tomorrow, but thousands of years of inductive observation and theorizing make the fact extremely probable—and certainly sound enough for any working generalization.)

Students using induction and deduction in compositions, essay examinations, or term papers—showing that Stephen Crane was a naturalistic writer, or that our national policies are unfair to revolutionary movements—should always assume that they will have a skeptical audience that wants to know the logical basis for *all* generalizations and conclusions.

Sample Paragraph (Annotated)

The report to the committee follows an *inductive* pattern.

The evidence presented in the body of the paragraph becomes the basis for an *inductive generalization*.

Two *inductive generalizations*.

The generalizations become the basis for an informal *deductive* syllogism pointing toward an action that probably needs to be taken.

Having built four new elementary schools in the last five years, members of the Palmville School Board were convinced they had solved the problem with overcrowding that had plagued the public schools ever since the mid-1980s. As a result, they were disappointed when School Superintendent Marisa LaRoux made her mid-July Projected Enrollment Report. She pointed out that the town's population has expanded by several hundred more families than were projected because the good weather this year spurred home building and the low mortgage rates encouraged buyers. In addition, more families are deciding to have two or more children, bringing the average number of children per family to 1.9, much higher than the figure of 1.65 used in the past to calculate demands for school services. The superintendent also admitted that the decades-old policy of calculating a family of two as a family without children has proven to be a serious mistake because it ignored the many children growing up in single-parent families. Based on this information, the superintendent concluded that the overcrowding problem would continue this year and probably for many years in the future. Chairperson Clifton Washington summed up the school board's response this way: "The schools are overcrowded now, and if more students are going to be coming to us asking for instruction, then we'd better get back into the school-building business."

Sample Paragraph (Induction)

Roaming the site, I can't help noticing that when men start cooking, the hardware gets complicated. Custom-built cookers—massive contraptions of cast iron and stainless steel—may cost $15,000 or more; they incorporate the team's barbecue philosophy. "We burn straight hickory under a baffle," Jim Garts, coleader of the Hogaholics, points out as he gingerly opens a scorching firebox that vents smoke across a water tray beneath a 4-by-8-foot grill. It's built on a trailer the size of a mobile home. Other cookers have been fashioned from a marine diesel engine; from a '76 Datsun, with grilling racks instead of front seats, a chimney above the dash, and coals under the hood; and as a 15-foot version of Elvis Presley's guitar (by the Graceland Love Me Tenderloins). It's awesome ironmongery.

Daniel Cohen, "Cooking-off for Fame and Fortune," *Smithsonian*, September 1988, p. 132.

Sample Paragraph (Deduction)

It is an everyday fact of life that competitors producing similar products assert that their own goods or services are better than those of their rivals. Every product advertised—from pain relievers to fried chicken—is claimed to be better than its competitors. If all these companies sued for libel, the courts would be so overloaded with cases that they would grind to a halt. For years courts dismissed criticisms of businesses, products, and performances as expressions of opinion. When a restaurant owner sued a guidebook to New York restaurants for giving his establishment a bad review, he won a $20,000 verdict in compensatory damages and $5 in punitive damages. But this was overturned by the court of appeals. The court held that, with the exception of one item, the allegedly libelous statements were expressions of opinion, not fact. Among these statements were that the "dumplings, on our visit, resembled bad ravioli . . . chicken with chili was rubbery and the rice . . . totally insipid. . . ." Obviously, it would be impossible to prove the nature of the food served at that particular meal. What is tender to one palate may be rubbery to another. The one misstatement of fact, that the Peking duck was served in one dish instead of three, was in my opinion, a minor and insignificant part of the entire review. Had the review of the restaurant been considered as a whole . . . , this small misstatement of fact would have been treated as *de minimis.* That is a well-established doctrine requiring that minor matters not be considered by the courts. In this case, the court held that the restaurant was a public figure and had failed to prove actual malice.

BARBARA EHRENREICH

BARBARA EHRENREICH received a B.A. from Reed College and a Ph.D. from Rockefeller University in biology. She has been active in the women's movement and other movements for social change for a number of years and has taught women's issues at several universities, including New York University and the State University of New York—Old Westbury. She is a Fellow of the Institute for Policy Studies in Washington, D.C., and is active in the Democratic Socialists of America. A prolific author, Ehrenreich is a regular columnist for *Ms.* and *Mother Jones* and has published articles in a wide range of magazines, among them *Esquire,* the *Atlantic, Vogue, New Republic,* the *Wall Street Journal, TV Guide,* the *New York Times Magazine, Social Policy,* and *The Nation.* Her books include *For Her Own Good: 150 Years of the Experts' Advice to Women* (with Deirdre English) (1978); *The Hearts of Men: American Dreams and the Flight from Commitment* (1983); *Remarking Love: The Feminization of Sex* (with Elizabeth Hess and Gloria Jacobs) (1986); *Fear of Falling: The Inner Life of the Middle Class* (1989); and *The Worst Years of Our Lives: Irreverent Notes from a Decade of Greed* (1990).

Star Dreck

Ehrenreich's humorous example of inductive and deductive reasoning offers some pointed criticisms of our values. It also points out the ease with which logic can be twisted and misdirected. Thus the essay serves as a caution for both writers and readers.

When I was a kid, we knew very little about the stars, and much of   1
what we did know was imprecise and speculative in nature. But
such is the beauty of the human mind—forever reaching, forever
grasping—that we now know far more than we can possibly absorb
or usefully apply, and certainly far more than I ever expected to

know in my own lifetime: not only what they eat for breakfast and what their favorite colors are, but their secret self-doubts and worries, their hair-management problems, and the names and locations of their unclaimed progeny.

As in all expanding fields, we are faced with what the scholars 2 call an "information explosion," which is already taxing the resources of the available media. In the old days, there were only a few specialized journals, with titles like *Silver Screen* and *Swooning Starlets*. But today there are dozens of publications, such as *People* and *Us*, which make fast-breaking discoveries accessible even to the person of limited educational attainment. For the intellectual elite, we have such challenging sources as *Vanity Fair* and *Interview*, which provide the depth of analysis that is sadly lacking on *Entertainment Tonight*.

Of course there are still a few throwbacks who have failed to 3 appreciate our expanding knowledge of the stars. They point out that most Americans are profoundly ignorant—prone to believe that Botswana is in Florida or that the *Yellow Pages* is a "great book." But retro-pedants like Allan Bloom never bother to quiz us on Burt and Loni's baby problem, or the tribulations of Cher's unfortunately monikered "Bagel Boy." They forget that, as far as the majority of the world's population is concerned, star trivia *is* Western civilization.

I don't want to boast, but I do try to keep abreast. Once, for 4 example, I had the opportunity to shake the bejeweled hand of a very major star. But I didn't—not because I was shy; but because *I knew too much about her;* her former husband's megavitamin problem, her hairdresser's recent breakdown, her ill-concealed rivalry with Joan Collins. There was simply nothing left to say.

Theory, as usual, lags behind the frenetic accumulation of new 5 data, but already a few broad paradigmatic principles are beginning to emerge. There are three of them, just as there are three fundamental forces (not counting the fourth), three Stooges, and three Rambos. The first one is: all stars are related to each other.

It didn't used to be this way in the old days, when the average 6 star was the abused daughter of an alcoholic Mississippian. But in the last two decades, the stars have undergone a sudden and astonishing genetic convergence: there's Jamie Lee Curtis (daughter of Janet Leigh and Tony), Carrie Fisher (daughter of Debbie Reynolds and Eddie), Michael Douglas (son of Kirk), Jeff Bridges (son of Lloyd), Charlie Sheen (son of Martin), Emilio Estevez (brother of Charlie), and so on. Frankly, no one knows what this means, although the search is on for the "star gene," which could then be transferred, by familiar bioengineering techniques, to piglets, mice, and intestinal bacteria.

The second principle, which is again the result of very recent 7 research, is that *all stars work out.* Whether this is a response to the inevitable muscular weakening caused by inbreeding, or merely an attempt to fill in the empty hours between interviews for *Premiere*, no one knows, but it all began with Jane (daughter of Henry, sister of Peter).

The third and final principle, which we owe in part to the ded- 8 icated researchers at *Star* and similar journals, is that all stars—and especially those who do not work out—have had near-fatal encounters with cocaine (Richard Dreyfuss), alcohol (Don Johnson), food (Elizabeth Taylor), or the lack of it (Dolly Parton). Here again, inbreeding may be at work, but the net result is the unique life cycle of the star, which is not dissimilar to the classic saga of the hero as charted by Joseph Campbell: birth, abuse, the struggle against substances at Betty Ford—followed by redemption and inspiring appearances in "Just Say No" ads.

But as our knowledge increases, so does our frustration. Amer- 9 icans, after all, do not like knowing things (such as the location of Botswana) that they cannot do anything about. So, I say, give us some way of applying our ever-growing knowledge: let us *vote* on the lives of the stars!

After all, we're better informed about the lives of the stars than 10 we are about such dreary matters as deficit management and the balance of trade. In fact, we are probably in a better position to make star decisions than the stars themselves. Consider that tragic misstep: Bruce's marriage to Julianne—which led to the dullest album of his career and the temporary removal of his earring. One hundred million American women were prepared to say, "No, don't do it. Wait for a Jersey Girl. Or, better yet, wait for me to move to Jersey and become one!" But we couldn't do a thing.

Imagine if we could have a referendum on Barbara and Don (hold 11 out, Barb, he's just a bimbo!). Or a plebiscite on Michael Jackson's pigmentation (he'd be able to wear one of those "Black by Popular Demand" T-shirts!). Imagine the debates, the mass rallies and marches, the furious exchanges in the op-ed pages!

But of course the stars wouldn't accept that. They might rebel. 12 They'd go underground—get fat, go back to the substances of their youth, and hide out in unmarked mobile homes in Culver City. I guess there are some things that humankind just wasn't meant to tinker with—some things that will always fill our souls with helpless awe, and show us how insignificant and meaningless our own lives are in the grand scheme of things. And no matter how much we may learn about them, that is the function of the stars.

Meanings and Values

1. What two meanings does the word "stars" have in the opening paragraph?

2. What process of reasoning is illustrated (in fragmented form) in paragraph 9?

3. Try to identify as many targets of the author's ironic criticism as you can in paragraphs 9–12. (Hint: The most important targets are our own habits and values.)

4. Is it possible to identify a central theme for this essay? If so, what is it? If not, can the essay still be considered unified? (See "Guide to Terms": *Unity*.) What are some of its important themes?

Expository Techniques

1. In which paragraph does the author introduce the first of her generalizations, derived, she suggests, from a process of induction?

2. In which paragraphs does she announce and illustrate the rest of the deductive generalizations?

3. From what kinds of sources are most of the examples in the essay probably drawn? Be specific. Do you consider it likely that Ehrenreich means to poke fun at these sources? Why?

4. What reasons do we have for suspecting that the speaker in this essay is not the author? Describe the character and attitudes of the persona created for this essay. (Guide: *Persona*.)

Diction and Vocabulary

1. How does the pun in the opening paragraph (a play on the word "stars") serve to surprise readers and undermine their sense of what the essay is about?

2. In several passages in the essay, Ehrenreich uses scholarly and scientific language to discuss topics often found in gossip columns or popular magazines. Locate several examples of this use of language. For what purpose or purposes does the author employ this contrast between content and style? (Guide: *Style*.)

3.   There are numerous allusions in paragraphs 5, 7, and 8. Identify their sources. (Note: Some of the allusions refer to scholars and scientific theories.) What general purpose do these allusions serve?

4.   If you do not know the meaning of some of the following words, look them up in the dictionary: progeny (par. 1); pedants, tribulations (3); frenetic, paradigmatic (5); plebiscite (11).

Read to Write

1.   Brainstorm for a few minutes about magazines (other than those like *People*) that get a lot of interest from readers but whose subject matter can be viewed as not particularly important or perhaps even silly and trivial. Do the same for television programs. Next, cluster your ideas and see if their relationships suggest a focus for an essay.

2.   Ehrenreich uses two meanings of the word *star* so that she can speak of one meaning of the word, yet have her comments apply to a very different meaning. Choose another term with two distinct meanings and use it in a similar manner in an essay.

3.   Make Ehrenreich's essay a model as you use reasoning to reach absurd (and critical) conclusions about a subject. Try to retain the same kind of tone she uses and maintain the same kind of satiric approach.

(NOTE: Suggestions for topics requiring development by INDUCTION and DEDUCTION are on page 509 at the end of this section.)

PATRICIA KEAN is a writer living in New York City. She attended Georgetown University, receiving a B.A. in English, and the University of Wisconsin-Madison, earning an M.A. in English. After spending time teaching and working in publishing, she began her career as a free-lance writer specializing in education issues. Her articles and essays have appeared in magazines and newspapers like *Lingua Franca, The New York Times,* and *Newsday.*

Blowing Up the Tracks

Segregating students by ability ("tracking"), Kean explains, often means separating them on the basis of class, race, parental influence, or questionable testing procedures rather than real ability or potential. Though her explanations may not please everyone, she offers careful reasoning and detailed evidence to support her observations and she also reports on school districts that have abandoned tracking. This essay was first published in the *Washington Monthly.*

It's morning in New York, and some seventh graders are more equal 1 than others.

Class 7–16 files slowly into the room, prodded by hard-faced 2 men whose walkie-talkies crackle with static. A pleasant looking woman shouts over the din, "What's rule number one?" No reply. She writes on the board. "Rule One: Sit down."

Rule number two seems to be an unwritten law: Speak slowly. 3 Each of Mrs. H's syllables hangs in the air a second longer than necessary. In fact, the entire class seems to be conducted at 16 RPM. Books come out gradually. Kids wander about the room aimlessly. Twelve minutes into class, we settle down and begin to play "O. Henry Jeopardy," a game which requires students to supply one-word answers to questions like: "'O. Henry moved from North Carolina to what state—Andy? Find the word on the page."

The class takes out a vocabulary sheet. Some of the words they 4 are expected to find difficult include: popular, ranch, suitcase, arrested, recipe, tricky, ordinary, humorous, and grand jury.

Thirty minutes pass. Bells ring, doors slam. 5

Class 7–1 marches in unescorted, mindful of rule number one. 6
Paperbacks of Poe smack sharply on desks, notebooks rustle, and
kids lean forward expectantly, waiting for Mrs. H. to fire the first
question. What did we learn about the writer?

Hands shoot into the air. Though Edgar Allan Poe ends up 7
sounding a lot like Jerry Lee Lewis—a booze-hound who married
his 13-year-old cousin—these kids speak confidently, in paragraphs.
Absolutely no looking at the book allowed.

We also have a vocabulary sheet, drawn from "The Tell-Tale 8
Heart," containing words like: audacity, dissimulation, sagacity,
stealthy, anxiety, derision, agony, and supposition.

As I sit in the back of the classroom watching these two very dif- 9
ferent groups of seventh graders, my previous life as an English
teacher allows me to make an educated guess and a chilling predic-
tion. With the best of intentions, Mrs. H. is teaching the first group,
otherwise known as the "slow kids," as though they are fourth
graders, and the second, the honors group, as though they are high
school freshmen. Given the odds of finding a word like "ordinary"
on the SAT's, the children of 7–16 have a better chance of standing
before a "grand jury" than making it to college.

Tracking, the practice of placing students in "ability groups" 10
based on a host of ill-defined criteria—everything from test scores to
behavior to how much of a fuss a mother can be counted on to
make—encourages even well-meaning teachers and administrators
to turn out generation after generation of self-fulfilling prophecies.
"These kids know they're no Einsteins," Mrs. H. said of her low-
track class when we sat together in the teacher's lounge. "They know
they don't read well. This way I can go really slowly with them."

With his grades, however, young Albert would probably be 11
hanging right here with the rest of lunch table 7–16. That's where I
discover that while their school may think they're dumb, these kids
are anything but stupid. "That teacher," sniffs a pretty girl wearing
lots of purple lipstick. "She talks so slow. She thinks we're babies.
She takes a year to do anything." "What about that other one?" a girl
named Ingrid asks, referring to their once-a-week student teacher.
"He comes in and goes like this: Rail (pauses) road. Rail (pauses)
road. Like we don't know what railroad means!" The table breaks
up laughing.

Outside the walls of schools across the country, it's slowly 12
become an open secret that enforced homogeneity benefits no one.
The work of researchers like Jeannie Oakes of UCLA and Robert
Slavin of Johns Hopkins has proven that tracking does not merely

reflect differences—it causes them. Over time, slow kids get slower, while those in the middle and in the so-called "gifted and talented" top tracks fail to gain from isolation. Along the way, the practice resegregates the nation's schools, dividing the middle from the lower classes, white from black and brown. As the evidence piles up, everyone from the Carnegie Corporation to the National Governors Association has called for change.

Though some fashionably progressive schools have begun to   13
reform, tracking persists. Parent groups, school boards, teachers, and administrators who hold the power within schools cling to the myths and wax apocalyptic about the horrors of heterogeneity. On their side is the most potent force known to man: bureaucratic inertia. Because tracking puts kids in boxes, keeps the lid on, and shifts responsibility for mediocrity and failure away from the schools themselves, there is little incentive to change a nearly-century old tradition. "Research is research," the principal told me that day, "This is practice."

Back Track

Tracking has been around since just after the turn of the century. It   14
was then, as cities teemed with immigrants and industry, that education reformers like John Franklin Bobbitt began to argue that the school and the factory shared a common mission, to "work up the raw material into that finished product for which it was best adapted." By the twenties, the scientific principles that ruled the factory floor had been applied to the classroom. They believed the IQ test—which had just become popular—allowed pure science, not the whims of birth or class, to determine whether a child received the type of education appropriate for a future manager or a future laborer.

It hasn't quite worked out that way. Driven by standardized   15
tests, the descendants of the old IQ tests, tracking has evolved into a kind of educational triage premised on the notion that only the least wounded can be saved. Yet when the classroom operates like a battleground, society's casualties mount, and the results begin to seem absurd: Kids who enter school needing more get less, while the already enriched get, well, enricher. Then, too, the low-track graduates of 70 years ago held a distinct advantage over their modern counterparts: If tracking prepared them for mindless jobs, at least those jobs existed.

The sifting and winnowing starts as early as pre-K. Three-year   16
old Ebony and her classmates have won the highly prized "gifted
and talented" label after enduring a battery of IQ and psychological
tests. There's nothing wrong with the "regular" class in this Harlem
public school. But high expectations for Ebony and her new friends
bring tangible rewards like a weekly field trip and music and computer lessons.

Meanwhile, regular kids move on to regular kindergartens where   17
they too will be tested, and where it will be determined that some children need more help, perhaps a "pre-first grade" developmental year.
So by the time they're ready for first grade reading groups, certain six-
year-olds have already been marked as "sparrows"—the low performers in the class.

In the beginning, it doesn't seem to matter so much, because the   18
other reading groups—the robins and the eagles—are just a few feet
away and the class is together for most of the day. Trouble is, as they
toil over basic drill sheets, the sparrows are slipping farther behind.
The robins are gathering more challenging vocabulary words, and
the eagles soaring on to critical thinking skills.

Though policies vary, by fourth grade many of these groups   19
have flown into completely separate classrooms, turning an innocent three-tier reading system into three increasingly rigid academic
tracks—honors, regular, and remedial—by middle school.

Unless middle school principals take heroic measures like buying   20
expensive software or crafting daily schedules by hand, it often
becomes a lot easier to sort everybody by reading scores. So kids who
do well on reading tests can land in the high track for math, science,
social studies, even lunch, and move together as a self-contained unit
all day. Friendships form, attitudes harden. Kids on top study
together, kids in the middle console themselves by making fun of the
"nerds" above and the "dummies" below, and kids on the bottom
develop behavioral problems and get plenty of negative
reinforcement.

By high school, many low-track students are locked out of what   21
Jeannie Oakes calls "gatekeeper courses," the science, math, and foreign language classes that hold the key to life after twelfth grade.
Doors to college are slamming shut, though the kids themselves are
often the last to know. When researcher Anne Wheelock interviewed students in Boston's public schools, they'd all insist they
were going to become architects, teachers, and the like. What
courses were they taking? "Oh, Keyboarding II, Earth Science,

Consumer Math. This would be junior year and I'd ask, 'Are you taking Algebra?' and they'd say no."

Black Marks

A funny thing can happen to minority students on the way to being   22
tracked. Even when minority children score high, they often find
themselves placed in lower tracks where counselors and principals
assume they belong.

In Paula Hart's travels for The Achievement Council, a Los   23
Angeles-based educational advocacy group, she comes across district after district where black and Latino kids score in the 75th per-
centile for math, yet never quite make it into Algebra I, the classic
gatekeeper course. A strange phenomenon occurs in inner city areas
with large minority populations—high track classes shrink, and low
track classes expand to fit humble expectations for the entire school
population.

A few years ago, Dr. Norward Roussell's curiosity got the best   24
of him. As Selma, Alabama's first black school superintendent, he
couldn't help but notice that "gifted and talented" tracks were
nearly lily white in a district that was 70 percent black. When he
looked for answers in the files of high school students, he discovered
that a surprising number of low track minority kids had actually
scored higher than their white top track counterparts.

Parents of gifted and talented students staged a full-scale revolt   25
against Roussell's subsequent efforts to establish logical standards
for placement. In four days of public hearings, speaker after speaker
said the same thing: We're going to lose a lot of our students to other
schools. To Roussell, their meaning was clear: Put black kids in the
high tracks and we pull white kids out of the system. More blacks and
more low-income whites did make it to the top under the new criteria, but Roussell himself was left behind. The majority-white school
board chose not to renew his contract, and he's now superintendent
in Macon County, Alabama, a district that is overwhelmingly black.

Race and class divisions usually play themselves out in a more   26
subtle fashion. Talk to teachers about how their high track kids differ from their low track kids and most speak not of intelligence, but
of motivation and "family." It seems that being gifted and talented
is hereditary after all, largely a matter of having parents who read to
you, who take you to museums and concerts, and who know how to
work the system. Placement is often a matter of who's connected.
Jennifer P., a teacher in a Brooklyn elementary school saw a pattern

in her class. "The principal put all the kids whose parents were in the PTA in the top tracks no matter what their scores were. He figures that if his PTA's happy, he's happy."

Once the offspring of the brightest and the best connected have 27 been skimmed off in honors or regular tracks, low tracks begin to fill up with children whose parents are not likely to complain. These kids get less homework, spend less class time learning, and are often taught by the least experienced teachers, because avoiding them can become a reward for seniority in a profession where perks are few.

With the courts reluctant to get involved, even when tracking 28 leads to racial segregation and at least the appearance of civil rights violations, changing the system becomes an arduous local battle fought school by school. Those who undertake the delicate process of untracking need nerves of steel and should be prepared to find resistance from every quarter, since, as Slavin notes, parents of high-achieving kids will fight this to the death. One-time guidance counselor Hart learned this lesson more than a decade ago when she and two colleagues struggled to introduce a now-thriving college curriculum program at Los Angeles' Banning High. Their efforts to open top-track classes to all students prompted death threats from an unlikely source—their fellow teachers.

Off Track Betting

Anne Wheelock's new book, *Crossing the Tracks,* tells the stories of 29 schools that have successfully untracked or never tracked at all. Schools that make the transition often achieve dramatic results. True to its name, Pioneer Valley Regional school in Northfield, Massachusetts was one of the first in the nation to untrack. Since 1983, the number of Pioneer Valley seniors going on to higher education jumped from 37 to 80 percent. But, the author says, urban schools continue to lag behind. "We're talking about unequal distribution of reform," Wheelock declares. "Change is taking place in areas like Wellesley, Massachusetts and Jericho, Long Island. It's easier to untrack when kids are closer to one another to begin with."

It's also easier for educators to tinker with programs and make 30 cosmetic adjustments than it is to ask them to do what bureaucrats hate most: give up one method of doing things without having another to put in its place. Tracking is a system; untracking is a leap of faith. When difficult kids can no longer be dumped in low tracks, new ways must be found to deal with disruptive behavior: early intervention, intensive work with families, and lots of tutoring.

Untracking may also entail new instructional techniques like cooperative group learning and peer tutoring, but what it really demands is flexibility and improvisation.

It also demands that schools—and the rest of us—admit that   31
some kids will be so disruptive or violent that a solution for dealing with them must be found *outside* of the regular public school system. New York City seems close to such a conclusion. Schools Chancellor Joseph Fernandez is moving forward with a voluntary "academy" program, planning separate schools designed to meet the needs of chronic troublemakers. One of them, the Wildcat Academy, run by a non-profit group of the same name, plans to enroll 150 students by the end of the year. Wildcat kids will attend classes from nine to five, wear uniforms, hold part-time jobs, and be matched with mentors from professional fields. Districts in Florida and California are conducting similar experiments.

Moving away from tracking is not about taking away from the   32
gifted and talented and giving to the poor. That, as Wheelock notes, is "political suicide." It's not even about placing more black and Latino kids in their midst, a kind of pre-K affirmative action. Rather, it's about raising expectations for everyone. Or, as Slavin puts it: "You can maintain your tracking system. Just put everyone into the top track."

That's not as quixotic as it sounds. In fact, it's long been stan-   33
dard practice in the nation's Catholic schools, a system so backward it's actually progressive. When I taught in an untracked parochial high school, one size fit all—with the exception of the few we expelled for poor grades or behavior. My students, who differed widely in ability, interest, and background, nevertheless got Shakespeare, Thoreau, and Langston Hughes at the same pace, at the same time—and lived to tell the tale. Their survival came, in part, because my colleagues and I could decide if the cost of keeping a certain student around was too high and we had the option of sending him or her elsewhere if expulsion was warranted.

The result was that my honor students wrote elegant essays and   34
made it to Ivy League schools, right on schedule. And far from being held back by their "regular" and "irregular" counterparts, straight-A students were more likely to be challenged by questions they would never dream of asking. "Why are we studying this?" a big-haired girl snapping gum in the back of the room wondered aloud one day. Her question led to a discussion that turned into the best class I ever taught.

In four years, I never saw a single standardized test score. But 35
time after time I watched my students climb out of whatever mental
category I had put them in. Tracking sees to it that they never get
that chance. Flying directly in the face of Yogi Berra's rule Number
One, it tells kids it's over before it's even begun. For ultimately,
tracking stunts the opportunity for growth, the one area in which all
children are naturally gifted.

Meanings and Values

1. List the differences between class 7–16 and class 7–1 as they are described in paragraphs 2–8.

2. In what ways can paragraphs 9 and 12 be said to offer inductive generalizations? Can paragraph 1 be viewed as an inductive generalization even though it comes at the beginning of the essay, before the
   evidence on which it is based? Why or why not?

3. Discuss how the remainder of the essay can be said to follow deduc-
   tively from paragraphs 12 and 13.

4. Does this essay remain expository throughout, or are there portions
   that might be classified as argumentative? If so, what are they? (See
   "Guide to Terms": *Argument*.)

Expository Techniques

1. What relatively unusual strategy does the writer use to open this essay? Why do you think she chose it? (Guide: *Introductions*.)

2. Paragraph 12 announces topics taken up later in the essay. What are
   they, and where is each one discussed in the body of the essay?

3. Where in the essay does the writer use the following expository patterns: comparison, definition, and cause-effect? For what purposes
   are each of these patterns employed?

4. How does Kean create sympathy for students harmed by tracking in
   her discussion of them in paragraphs 11, 17–18, 20–21, and 23–24?
   Does she avoid sentimentality? (Guide: *Sentimentality*.) If not, does it
   undermine the effectiveness of the paragraphs? Why or why not?

Diction and Vocabulary

1. Explain how the contrasting vocabulary lists (pars. 4 and 8) serve to
   characterize the two groups. What does each set of words say about
   the kinds of careers and other situations teachers expect the students
   in a class to face in the future? (Hint: Pay attention to the words
   within quotation marks in paragraph 9.)

2. How does the writer use diction in paragraphs 3 and 6 to characterize the different groups of students? (Guide: *Diction.*)

3. In speaking of "a big-haired girl snapping gum" (par. 34), the author draws on a negative stereotype. What is the stereotype, and what use does she make of it in the paragraph?

4. If you do not know the meaning of some of the following words, look them up in a dictionary: audacity, dissimulation, sagacity, stealthy, derision, supposition (par. 8); apocalyptic, heterogeneity (13); perks (27); chronic (31).

Read to Write

1. Compare Kean's accounts with your experience of learning in a tracked or untracked program (or both). How accurate and trustworthy are her evidence and her conclusions? Develop your own ideas on the subject into an essay.

2. Develop part of Kean's subject matter by focusing on the testing procedure used to place students in different tracks and to test their fitness for college work. These tests have been the focus of controversy for many years. In your essay, report on one aspect of the controversy, such as racial bias, gender bias, or weakness in predicting actual performance.

3. Following Kean's example, focus on the experience of individuals and groups for an essay of your own about some aspect of secondary education.

(NOTE: Suggestions for topics requiring development by INDUCTION and DEDUCTION are on page 509 at the end of this section.)

Issues and Ideas

Digital Realities

To some people, computers may be simply one more appliance whose effects on daily life seem to be minimal. However, the number of people who can avoid working on computers seems to be shrinking, just as computer influence seems to be growing. Computers, the software they run, and their many networked connections, change the way we run our lives. They alter the time we need to spend at a task, the kind of tasks we can undertake, and our creative abilities. They alter our schedules, our places of work and play, and maybe even our friendships and personal relationships.

In very specific ways computers alter our concepts of time and space, of work and leisure, and of ourselves and others. We can say that computers create new realities for us, digital realities. The essays that follow use inductive and deductive reasoning to explore these digital realities. Maia Szalavitz in "A Virtual Life," considers her experiences as a computer user, sums them up, and then reviews her experiences to see if her perceptions and values have indeed changed as much as she suspects. Nicholas Negroponte, in "Place without Space," discusses some of the changes in thinking and relationships that computers make possible and considers some of their possible consequences. Both authors are a bit tentative in their conclusions because new digital realities may emerge in just a few years.

MAIA SZALAVITZ

MAIA SZALAVITZ, formerly a television producer, now spends her
time as a writer. She lives in New York City and is working on a
book about drug policy.

A Virtual Life

In this essay from *The New York Times Magazine,* Szalavitz uses
induction and deduction to explore digital reality and its consequences. Along the way, she compares the digital world to the
"real" world, acknowledging the attractions of the electronic
dimension.

After too long on the Net, even a phone call can be a shock. My   1
boyfriend's Liverpudlian accent suddenly becomes indecipherable
after the clarity of his words on screen; a secretary's clipped tonality
seems more rejecting than I'd imagined it would be. Time itself
becomes fluid—hours become minutes, and alternately seconds
stretch into days. Weekends, once a highlight of my week, are now
just two ordinary days.

For the last three years, since I stopped working as a producer   2
for Charlie Rose, I have done much of my work as a telecommuter.
I submit articles and edit them via E-mail and communicate with
colleagues on Internet mailing lists. My boyfriend lives in England,
so much of our relationship is also computer-mediated.

If I desired, I could stay inside for weeks without wanting any-   3
thing. I can order food, and manage my money, love and work. In
fact, at times I have spent as long as three weeks alone at home,
going out only to get mail and buy newspapers and groceries. I
watched most of the blizzard of '96 on TV.

But after a while, life itself begins to feel unreal. I start to feel as   4
though I've merged with my machines, taking data in, spitting them
back out, just another node on the Net. Others on line report the
same symptoms. We start to feel an aversion to outside forms of

socializing. It's like attending an A.A. meeting in a bar with everyone holding a half-sipped drink. We have become the Net naysayers' worst nightmare.

What first seemed like a luxury, crawling from bed to computer, 5 not worrying about hair, and clothes and face, has become an evasion, a lack of discipline. And once you start replacing real human contact with cyber-interaction, coming back out of the cave can be quite difficult.

I find myself shyer, more circumspect, more anxious. Or, con- 6 versely, when suddenly confronted with real live humans, I get manic, speak too much, interrupt. I constantly worry if I'm dressed appropriately, that perhaps I've actually forgotten to put on leggings and walked outside in the T-shirt and underwear I sleep and live in.

At times, I turn on the television and just leave it to chatter in 7 the background, something that I'd never done previously. The voices of the programs soothe me, but then I'm jarred by the commercials. I find myself sucked in by soap operas, or compulsively needing to keep up with the latest news and the weather. "Dateline," "Frontline," "Nightline," CNN, New York 1, every possible angle of every story over and over and over, even when they are of no possible use to me. Work moves from foreground to background. I decide to check my E-mail.

On line, I find myself attacking everyone in sight. I am irritable, 8 and easily angered. I find everyone on my mailing list insensitive, believing that they've forgotten that there are people actually reading their invective. I don't realize that I'm projecting until after I've been embarrassed by someone who politely points out that I've flamed her for agreeing with me.

When I'm in this state, I fight with my boyfriend as well, misin- 9 terpreting his intentions because of the lack of emotional cues given by our typed dialogue. The fight takes hours, because the system keeps crashing. I say a line, then he does, then crash! And yet we keep on, doggedly.

I'd never realized how important daily routine is: dressing for 10 work, sleeping normal hours. I'd never thought I relied so much on co-workers for company. I began to understand why long-term unemployment can be so insidious, why life without an externally supported daily plan can lead to higher rates of substance abuse, crime, suicide.

To counteract my life, I forced myself back into the real world. 11 I call people, set up social engagements with the few remaining friends who haven't fled New York City. I try to at least get to the gym, so as to differentiate the weekend from the rest of my week. I arrange interviews for stories, doctor's appointments—anything to get me out of the house and connected with others.

But sometimes, just one engagement is too much. I meet a friend 13 and her ripple of laughter is intolerable—the hum of conversation in the restaurant, overwhelming. I make my excuses and flee. I re-enter my apartment and run to the computer as though it were a sanctuary.

I click on the modem, the once-grating sound of the connection 14 now as pleasant as my favorite tune. I enter my password. The real world disappears.

Meanings and Values

1. What is the inductive generalization the author arrives at after spending "too long on the Net" (par. 1)? Where does she state it?

2. In which paragraphs does she apply this generalization in a deductive manner?

3. Explain the meaning of the following phrases: "I've flamed her for agreeing with me" (par. 8); "just another node on the Net" (4); and "The fight takes hours, because the system keeps crashing"(9).

Expository Techniques

1. How does the essay's conclusion re-enforce the inductive generalization arrived at earlier in the essay? What strategy does the writer employ to conclude the essay? (See "Guide to Terms": *Closings.*)

2. What do the beginning sentences of paragraphs 6–13 have in common in terms of wording or structure? (Guide: *Syntax.*) In what ways are these similarities related to the inductive generalization? Discuss how they help create coherence in the essay. (Guide: *Coherence.*)

3. Discuss the use of parallelism to provide emphasis in the sentences in paragraphs 3 and 11. (Guide: *Parallel Structure.*)

Diction and Vocabulary

1. Discuss the essay's use of computer terminology and slang used by people familiar with computers. Does this add to or detract from most readers' understanding of the essay? How would the essay be different if the terminology and slang were not used? (Guide: *Colloquial Expressions.*)

2. If you do not know the meaning of some of the following words, look them up in a dictionary: mediated (par. 2); aversion (4); evasion, cyber (5); circumspect, manic (6); invective (8); doggedly (9); insidious (10); counteract (11).

Read to Write

1. Freewrite about your computer experience or about typical behaviors of computer users that you have observed. Focus on one or two particularly interesting ideas, examples, or topics that deserve further development and write more about them, repeating the process as many times as you need to develop a topic and a focus for an essay.

2. Draw on Szalavitz's comparisons of the digital and the physical world in order to develop further comparisons in an essay of your own.

3. Using Szalavitz's essay as a model, use induction and deduction to explain your view of some of the consequences computers have (or may have) for our lives.

(NOTE: Suggestions for topics requiring development by INDUCTION and DEDUCTION are on page 509 at the end of this section.)

NICHOLAS NEGROPONTE

NICHOLAS NEGROPONTE teaches at the Massachusetts Institute of
Technology where he is Professor of Media Technology and
Founding Director of the Media Lab. He is the author of *Being
Digital* (1995).

Place Without Space

In this selection from *Being Digital*, Negroponte uses deductive
reasoning to speculate about the effects of electronic technology
on our lives. While we cannot predict the future with any certainty, by applying a deductive generalization to real and possible
circumstances, we can arrive at some idea of what *might be*, just as
Negroponte does in this selection.

In the same ways that hypertext removes the limitations of the 1
printed page, the post-information age will remove the limitations of
geography. Digital living will include less and less dependence
upon being in a specific place at a specific time, and the transmission
of place itself will start to become possible.

If I really could look out the electronic window of my living 2
room in Boston and see the Alps, hear the cowbells, and smell the
(digital) manure in summer, in a way I am very much in Switzer-
land. If instead of going to work by driving my atoms into town, I
log into my office and do my work electronically, exactly where is
my workplace?

In the future, we will have the telecommunications and virtual 3
reality technologies for a doctor in Houston to perform a delicate
operation on a patient in Alaska. In the nearer term, however, a
brain surgeon will need to be in the same operating theater at the
same time as the brain; many activities, like those of so-called
knowledge workers, are not as dependent on time and place and
will be decoupled from geography much sooner.

Today, writers and money managers find it practicable and far 4
more appealing to be in the Caribbean or South Pacific while preparing their manuscripts or managing their funds. However, in some
countries, like Japan, it will take longer to move away from space
and time dependence, because the native culture fights the trend.
(For example: one of the main reasons that Japan does not move to

506

daylight savings time in the summer is because going home "after dark" is considered necessary, and workers try not to arrive after or go home before their bosses.)

In the post-information age, since you may live and work at one 5 or many locations, the concept of an "address" now takes on new meaning.

When you have an account with America Online, CompuServe, 6 or Prodigy, you know your e-mail address, but you do not know where it physically exists. In the case of America Online, your Internet address is your ID followed by @aol.com—usable anywhere in the world. Not only do you not know where @aol.com is, whosoever sends a message to that address has no idea of where either it or you might be. The address becomes much more like a Social Security number than a street coordinate. It is a virtual address.

In my case, I happen to know where my address, @hq.media. 7 mit.edu, is physically located. It is a ten-year-old HP Unix machine in a closet near my office. But when people send me messages they are sending them to me, not to that closet. They might infer I am in Boston (which is usually not the case). In fact, I am usually in a different time zone, so not only space but time is shifted as well.

Meanings and Values

1. Where does Negroponte announce his deductive generalization, and what is it?

2. To what situations, real or imagined, does Negroponte apply the generalization? Be specific. What conclusions does he draw from the application of the generalization? Which of his predictions seem most probable to you, and why? Which seem less likely? Why?

3. Are there ways we can judge the quality of reasoning in an essay that looks toward the future? If so, what are they? (Use examples from this selection in answering this question.) If not, how can we evaluate an essay like this? (See "Guide to Terms": *Evaluation*.)

Expository Techniques

1. What patterns other than deduction does Negroponte use in this selection? Where does he employ them and for what purposes?

2. Is paragraph 5 simply a transition between other paragraphs, or does it constitute another deductive generalization? Why? (Guide: *Transition*.) If it is another generalization, does it disrupt the unity of the writing? (Guide: *Unity*.)

Diction and Vocabulary

1. Discuss how Negroponte uses pairs of terms like physical and virtual to designate different kinds of reality. Identify any other pairs of terms he uses in the essay and discuss their use.

2. If you do not know the meaning of some of the following terms, look them up in a dictionary: hypertext, digital (par. 1); narrowcasting (2); extrapolation, demographic (3); correlation (4); infinitesimal (5); idiosyncrasies (6); Chardonnay (7). (Note: you may have to consult a dictionary of computer terms for some of these words.)

Read to Write

1. Think of the different "places" you can go with a computer, and freewrite about the different kinds of reality you can encounter. Keep freewriting until you discover a focus for your own essay.

2. Use the uncoupling of places and times that Negroponte observes as a key idea for an essay of your own about future possibilities.

3. Using Negroponte's discussion as a model, try to predict some other future possibilities in the "post-information" or "digital" world.

(NOTE: Suggestions for topics requiring development by INDUCTION and DEDUCTION follow.)

Writing Suggestions for Section 12
Induction and Deduction

Choose one of the following unformed topics and shape your central theme from it. This could express the view you prefer or an opposing view. Develop your composition primarily by use of induction, alone or in combination with deduction. Unless otherwise directed by your instructor, be completely objective and limit yourself to exposition, rather than engaging in argumentation.

1. Little League baseball (or the activities of 4-H clubs, Boy Scouts, Girl Scouts, etc.) as a molder of character.
2. Conformity as an expression of insecurity.
3. Pop music as a mirror of contemporary values.
4. The status symbol as a motivator to success.
5. The liberal arts curriculum and its relevance to success in a career.
6. Student opinion as the guide to better educational institutions.
7. The role of public figures (including politicians, movie stars, and business people) in shaping attitudes and fashions.
8. The values of education, beyond dollars and cents.
9. Knowledge and its relation to wisdom.
10. The right of individuals to select the laws they obey.
11. Television commercials as a molder of morals.
12. The "other" side of one ecological problem.
13. The value of complete freedom from worry.
14. Homosexuality as in-born or as voluntary behavior.
15. Raising mentally challenged children at home.
16. Fashionable clothing as an expression of power (or a means of attaining status).

13

Using Patterns for *Argument*

Argument and exposition have many things in common. They both use the basic patterns of exposition; they share a concern for the audience; and they often deal with similar subjects, including social trends (changing relationships between men and women, the growth of the animal rights movement), recent developments (the creation of new strains of plants through genetic manipulation, medical treatment of the terminally ill), and issues of widespread concern (the quality of education, the effects of pollution). As a result, the study of argument is a logical companion to the study of exposition. Yet the two kinds of writing have very different purposes.

Expository writing shares information and ideas; it explores issues and explains problems. In exposition we select facts and ideas to give an accurate picture of a subject and arrange them as clearly as we can, emphasizing features likely to interest readers. To explain the importance of knowing how to use computers, for instance, an essay might provide examples of the roles of computers in business, industry, education, and research; it might describe the uses of computers for personal budgeting, recordkeeping, and entertainment; and it might emphasize that more everyday tasks than we realize are already heavily dependent on computers.

Argumentative writing, however, has a different motivation. It asks readers to choose one side of an issue or take a particular action, whether it is to buy a product, vote for a candidate, or build a new highway. In argument we select facts and ideas that provide strong support for our point of view and arrange this evidence in the most logical and persuasive order, taking care to provide appropriate background information and to acknowledge and refute opposing points of view. The evidence we choose is determined to a great extent by the attitudes and needs of the people we are trying to convince. For example, suppose we want to argue successfully that a high school or college ought to give all students advanced training in computer use. Our essay would need to provide examples of benefits to students that are great enough to justify the considerable expenses for equipment and staff. (Examples of greatly increased job opportunities and improved learning skills would make good evidence; discussions of how computers can be used for personal recordkeeping and managing household finances would not be likely to persuade school officials facing tight budgets.) And an effective essay would also answer possible objections to the proposal: Will only a limited number of students really benefit from advanced computer training? Are computers developing so rapidly that only large businesses and specialized institutes can afford to provide up-to-date training?

At the heart of an argumentative essay is the opinion we want readers to share or the action we want them to take. In argument this central theme is called the *thesis* or *proposition* and is often expressed concisely in a *thesis statement* designed to alert readers to the point of the argument. Some writers like to arrive at a sharply focused thesis early in the process of composing and use it to guide the selection and arrangement of evidence. Others settle on a tentative ("working") thesis, which they revise as the essay takes shape. In either case, checking frequently to see that factual evidence and supporting ideas or arguments are clearly linked to the thesis is a good way for writers to make sure their finished essays are coherent, unified arguments.

The purpose of a simple argumentative essay often falls into one of three categories. Some essays ask readers to agree with a value judgment ("The present city government is corrupt and ineffective"). Others propose a specific action ("Money from the student activity fee at this college should be used to establish and staff a fitness program available to all students"). And still others advance an opinion quite different from that held by most people ("Contrary to what many people believe, investing in stocks and bonds is not just for the wealthy—it is for people who want to become wealthy, too"). In situations calling for more complex arguments, however, writers should feel free to combine these purposes as long as the relationship among them is made clear to the reader. In a complex argument, for instance, we might *first* show that the city government is inefficient and corrupt and *then* argue that it is better to change the city charter to eliminate the opportunities for the abuse of power than it is to try to vote a new party into office or to support a reform faction within the existing political machine.

Another distinction is normally made between *logical argument* (usually called, simply, *argument*) and *persuasive argument* (usually termed *persuasion*). Whereas logical argument appeals to reason, persuasive argument appeals to the emotions. The aim of both, however, is to convince, and they are nearly always blended into whatever mixture seems most likely to do the convincing. After all, reason and emotion are both important human elements—and we may have to persuade someone even to listen to our logic. The emphasis on one or the other, of course, should depend on the subject and the audience.

Some authorities make a slightly different distinction: they say we argue merely to get people to change their minds, and we use persuasion to get them to *do* something about it—for example, to vote a Republican ticket, not just agree with the party platform. But this view is not entirely inconsistent with the other. We can hardly expect to change a *mind* by emotional appeal, but we can hope to get someone to *act* because of it.

The choice of supporting evidence for an argument depends in part on the subject and in part on the audience and situation. There is a good deal of evidence to support the argument that industry should turn to labor-saving machines and new work arrangements to increase its competitiveness. Company executives looking for ways to increase profits are likely to find almost all of this evidence persuasive, but workers and union leaders worried about loss of jobs and cuts in wages will probably be harder to persuade. Writers addressing the second group would need to choose evidence to show that industrial robots and work rules calling for fewer people would lead to increased sales, not lower wages and fewer jobs. And if the changes might actually cause layoffs, writers would have to show that without the changes a company might be forced to shut down entirely, throwing everyone out of work.

Variety in evidence gives the writer a chance to present an argument fully and at the same time helps persuade readers. Examples, facts and figures, statements from authorities, personal experience or the experience of other people—all these can be valuable sources of support. The basic patterns of exposition, too, can be viewed as ways to support arguments. For instance, to persuade people to take sailing (hang-gliding, skin-diving) lessons, we might tell the story of the inexperienced sailor who almost drowned even though she was sailing in a "safe" boat on a small lake. Or we might combine this narrative with a discussion of how lack of knowledge causes sailing accidents, with a classification of the dangers facing beginning sailors, or with examples of things that can go wrong while sailing. Most writers choose to combine patterns on the grounds that variety helps convince readers, just as three pieces of evidence are more convincing than one—as long as all three point to the same conclusion.

All the expository patterns can also be used to arrange factual evidence and supporting ideas or arguments, though some patterns are more useful than others. Entire arguments structured as narratives are rare, except for stories designed to show what the world will be like if we do not change our present environmental, military, or technological policies. But example, comparison and contrast, cause and effect, definition, and induction or deduction are frequently used to organize arguments. A series of *examples* can be an effective way of showing that a government social policy does not work and in fact hurts the people it is supposed to serve. *Cause and effect* can organize argument over who is to blame for a problem or over the possible consequences of a new program. *Comparison* and *contrast* can guide choices among competing products, among ways of disposing of toxic waste, or among directions for national economic policy. *Definition* is helpful when a controversy hinges on the interpretation of a key term or when the meaning of an important word is itself the subject of disagreement. *Induction* and *deduction* are useful in argument because they provide the kind of careful, logical reasoning necessary to convince many readers, especially those who may at first have little sympathy for the writer's opinion.

An argument need not be restricted to a single pattern. The choice of a pattern or a combination of patterns depends on the subject, the specific purpose, and the kinds of evidence needed to convince the audience to which the essay is directed. Some arguments about complicated, significant issues use so many patterns that they can be called *complex arguments.*

In addition to using the patterns of exposition, most argumentative essays also arrange evidence according to its potential impact on the audience. Three of the most common arrangements are ascending order, refutation-proof, and con-pro. In *ascending order,* the strongest, most complex, or most emotionally moving evidence comes last, where it can build on the rest of the evidence in the essay and is likely to have the greatest impact on the reader. *Refutation-proof* acknowledges opposing points of view early in the essay and then goes on to show why the author's outlook is superior. *Con-pro* presents an opposing point of view and then refutes it, continuing until all opposition has been dealt with and all positive arguments voiced; this strategy is particularly useful when there is strong opposition to the writer's thesis. The strategies can be combined, of course, as in a refutation-proof essay that builds up to its strongest evidence.

Accuracy and fairness in argument are not only morally correct, they can also be a means of persuasion. Accuracy in the use of facts, figures, quotations, and references can encourage readers to trust what an author has to say. And writers who are able to acknowledge and refute opposing arguments fairly and without hostility add strength to their own arguments and may even win the respect of those who disagree with them.

But the most important elements of effective argument are careful choice of evidence and clear, logical reasoning. It is never possible to arrive at absolute proof—argument, after all, assumes that there are at least two sides to the matter under discussion—yet a carefully constructed case will convince many readers. At the same time, a flaw in logic can undermine an otherwise reasonable argument and destroy a reader's confidence in its conclusions. The introduction to Section 12, "Reasoning by Use of *Induction* and *Deduction*," discusses some important errors to avoid in reasoning or in choosing evidence. Here are some others:

Post hoc ergo propter hoc ("After this therefore because of this")— Just because one thing happened *after* does not mean that the first event caused the second. In arguing without detailed supporting evidence that a recent drop in the crime rate is the result of a newly instituted anticrime policy, a writer might be committing this error, because there are other equally plausible explanations: a drop in the unemployment rate, for example, or a reduction in the number of people in the fifteen to twenty-five age bracket, the segment of the population that is responsible for a high proportion of all crimes.

Begging the question—A writer "begs the question" when he or she assumes the truth of something that is still to be proven. An argument that begins this way, "The recent, unjustified rise in utility rates should be reversed by the state legislature," assumes that the rise is "unjustified," though this important point needs to be proven.

Ignoring the question—A writer may "ignore the question" by shifting attention away from the issue at hand to some loosely related or even irrelevant matter: for example, "Senator Jones's plan for encouraging new industries cannot be any good because in the past he has opposed tax cuts for corporations" (this approach shifts attention away from the merits of Senator Jones's proposal). A related problem is the *ad hominem* (toward the person) argument, which substitutes personal attack for a discussion of the issue in question.

In composing argumentative essays, therefore, writers need to pay attention not only to what is necessary to convince an audience but also to the integrity of the evidence and arguments they advance in support of a thesis.

Sample Paragraph (Annotated)

The issue is outlined briefly.

{ The latest state proposal to divert more water from agricultural to residential uses might be expected to gain support from rapidly urbanizing Palmville. Speaking through their Town Meeting, however, the citizens of the town argue that the state should not meddle with arrangements that have contributed so much to the economic and social health of the region. The

Thesis statement.

Evidence and *supporting arguments.* (These five points will themselves need much more evidence, of course, in presenting the actual argument.)

report of the Town Meeting contained these arguments: (1) Farming in the Palmville area constitutes an important element in the state's food supply which would be expensive to replace. (2) Farms and support industries provide a large proportion of the jobs of Palmville residents. (3) The farms are an important part of the social fabric of the town and the region, providing, among other things, healthful summer employment for many of the town's youth. (4) Diverting water from the farms would cause many to be sold to real estate developers, thus increasing the population *and* the demand for water. (5) The town's zoning plan will limit growth over the next decade and should

l slow the increasing demand for water.
Whether state officials will be persuaded
by these arguments remains to be seen,
but Palmville residents hope to prevent
changes that might threaten the
community they have built so carefully.

Sample Paragraphs (Argument)

Still, the nearly two decades since
Congress created Earth Day have left no
doubt that our system of environmental
regulation badly needs an overhaul.
Overloaded with unrealistic deadlines
and sweeping legislation during the
1970s, battered by budget cuts during
the '80s, the Environmental Protection
Agency now needs to devise a
regulatory approach that's flexible and
effective, and that relies as much on
market-based incentives as rigid
penalties. As perverse as this may
sound, the EPA needs to stop trying to
ban pollution and start letting
companies pay for the privilege of
polluting.

The basic idea is to turn pollution into
a cost that, like any other expense, the
company will want to minimize. This
can be done directly by imposing a fee
or tax on the pollutants released into the
environment. It can be done indirectly
by making companies pay for pollution
permits. The government could even
auction off the permits (a nice "revenue
enhancer"). Alternatively, companies
with low pollution levels could sell
pollution rights to companies with
poorer controls—financially rewarding

the "clean" companies and penalizing
the laggards. All of these schemes
would force companies to pay for their
pollution, giving them an incentive to
find and use the most cost-effective
preventive technology.

From "Grime and Punishment," *The New Republic,* February 20, 1989. Reprinted by
permission.

Issues and Ideas

Current and Classic Controversies

An issue is a subject on which there is more than one point of view. Since arguments address differences and disagreements, they necessarily begin with an issue. When an issue disappears, however, so does the usefulness and relevance of an argument, unless, of course, the argument is expressed in language so moving and effective or with reasoning so precise and convincing that it remains admirable though the immediate concerns of the author and the audience may pass away.

An argument can become a classic for reasons other than style or logic, however. Martin Luther King, Jr.'s "Letter from Birmingham Jail" is on its way to being a classic, in expression and in content, because the issues it addresses live on (unfortunately) though in somewhat changed form. King's sentences from several decades ago still speak more or less directly to us and our lives. The same is true with Barbara Lawrence's essay, "Four-letter Words Can Hurt You," first published a little more than twenty years ago. The particular words we use may have changed somewhat, but the issues are still alive.

The other four essays in this section address contemporary questions, though the issues themselves have been around in some form for quite a while and are likely to remain with us in coming years. Christopher B. Daly's "How the Lawyers Stole Winter" focuses not only on concerns about children's safety and legal liability, but also on the much larger issue of personal responsibility. Richard Lynne's "Why Johnny Can't Read, but Yoshio Can," reflects continuing concerns about the failures of our educational system and worries that other countries are doing a better job. Alan Hirsch's "Don't Blame the Jury" takes its cue from sensational trials of the last few years, yet problems with guilt, innocence, and the jury system are a continuing issue in our legal system and in our society. Finally, John Davidson's "Menace to Society" puts the blame for violent behavior on children's cartoons, but social critics over the past few centuries have made similar accusations about many different media: comic books, broadside ballads, radio, even newspapers. The issue is a familiar and thorny one, but Davidson's evidence is new, his argument carefully worked out, and his perspective a fresh one.

ARGUMENT THROUGH COMPARISON AND CONTRAST

CHRISTOPHER B. DALY

> CHRISTOPHER DALY grew up in Medford, Massachusetts. He now
> lives with his family in Newton, Massachusetts and is a free-lance
> writer and contributor to magazines.

How the Lawyers Stole Winter

> In this essay, which appeared first in *Atlantic Monthly*, Daly uses
> comparison to make the case that in our attempts to prevent dan-
> gerous accidents, we (and in particular, the lawyers among us)
> have not only stolen some enjoyment from our lives but also less-
> ened responsibility for our own actions. He suggests that the result
> may be more danger, not less.

When I was a boy, my friends and I would come home from school   1
each day, change our clothes (because we were not allowed to wear
"play clothes" to school), and go outside until dinnertime. In the
early 1960s in Medford, a city on the outskirts of Boston, that was
pretty much what everybody did. Sometimes there might be flute
lessons, or an organized Little League game, but usually not. Usually we kids went out and played.

In winter, on our way home from the Gleason School, we would   2
go past Brooks Pond to check the ice. By throwing heavy stones onto
it, hammering it with downed branches, and, finally, jumping on it,
we could figure out if the ice was ready for skating. If it was, we would
hurry home to grab our skates, our sticks, and whatever other gear we
had, and then return to play hockey for the rest of the day. When the
streetlights came on, we knew it was time to jam our cold, stiff feet
back into our green rubber snow boots and get home for dinner.

I had these memories in mind recently when I moved, with my   3
wife and two young boys, into a house near a lake even closer to
Boston, in the city of Newton. As soon as Crystal Lake froze over, I

grabbed my skates and headed out. I was not the first one there, though: the lawyers had beaten me to the lake. They had warned the town recreation department to put it off limits. So I found a sign that said DANGER. THIN ICE. NO SKATING.

Knowing a thing or two about words myself, I put my own 4 gloss on the sign. I took it to mean *When the ice is thin, there is danger and there should be no skating.* Fair enough, I thought, but I knew that the obverse was also true: *When the ice is thick, it is safe and there should be skating.* Finding the ice plenty thick, I laced up my skates and glided out onto the miraculous glassy surface of the frozen lake. My wife, a native of Manhattan, would not let me take our two boys with me. But for as long as I could, I enjoyed the free, open-air delight of skating as it should be. After a few days others joined me, and we became an outlaw band of skaters.

What we were doing was once the heart of winter in New 5 England—and a lot of other places, too. It was clean, free exercise that needed no StairMasters, no health clubs, no appointments, and hardly any gear. Sadly, it is in danger of passing away. Nowadays it seems that every city and town and almost all property holders are so worried about liability and lawsuits that they simply throw up a sign or a fence and declare that henceforth there shall be no skating, and that's the end of it.

As a result, kids today live in a world of leagues, rinks, rules, 6 uniforms, adults, and rides—rides here, rides there, rides everywhere. It is not clear that they are better off; in some ways they are clearly *not* better off.

When I was a boy skating on Brooks Pond, there were no 7 grown-ups around. Once or twice a year, on a weekend day or a holiday, some parents might come by with a thermos of hot cocoa. Maybe they would build a fire (which we were forbidden to do), and we would gather round.

But for the most part the pond was the domain of children. In 8 the absence of adults, we made and enforced our own rules. We had hardly any gear—just some borrowed hockey gloves, some hand-me-down skates, maybe an elbow pad or two—so we played a clean form of hockey, with no high-sticking, no punching, and almost no checking. A single fight could ruin the whole afternoon. Indeed, as I remember it, thirty years later, it was the purest form of hockey I ever saw—until I got to see the Russian national team play the game.

But before we could play, we had to check the ice. We became 9 serious junior meteorologists, true connoisseurs of cold. We learned that the best weather for pond skating is plain, clear cold, with starry nights and no snow. (Snow not only mucks up the skating surface but also insulates the ice from the colder air above.) And we learned that moving water, even the gently flowing Mystic River, is a lot less likely to freeze than standing water. So we skated only on the pond. We learned all the weird whooping and cracking sounds that ice makes as it expands and contracts, and thus when to leave the ice.

Do kids learn these things today? I don't know. How would 10 they? We don't let them. Instead we post signs. Ruled by lawyers, cities and towns everywhere try to eliminate their legal liability. But try as they might, they cannot eliminate the underlying risk. Liability is a social construct; risk is a natural fact. When it is cold enough, ponds freeze. No sign or fence or ordinance can change that.

In fact, by focusing on liability and not teaching our kids how to 11 take risks, we are making their world more dangerous. When we were children, we had to learn to evaluate risks and handle them on our own. We had to learn, quite literally, to test the waters. As a result, we grew up to be savvier about ice and ponds than any kid could be who has skated only under adult supervision on a rink.

When I was a boy, despite the risks we took on the ice no one I 12 knew ever drowned. The only people I heard about who drowned were graduate students at Harvard or MIT who came from the tropics and were living through their first winters. Not knowing (after all, how could they?) about ice on moving water, they would innocently venture out onto the half-frozen Charles River, fall through, and die. They were literally out of their element.

Are we raising a generation of children who will be out of their 13 element? And if so, what can we do about it? We cannot just roll back the calendar. I cannot tell my six-year-old to head down to the lake by himself to play all afternoon—if for no other reason than that he would not find twenty or thirty other kids there, full of the collective wisdom about cold and ice that they had inherited, along with hockey equipment, from their older brothers and sisters. Somewhere along the line that link got broken.

The whole setting of childhood has changed. We cannot change 14 it again overnight. I cannot send my children out by themselves yet, but at least some of the time I can go out there with them. Maybe that is a start.

As for us, last winter was a very unusual one. We had ferocious 15 cold (near-zero temperatures on many nights) and tremendous snows (about a hundred inches in all). Eventually a strange thing happened. The town gave in—sort of. Sometime in January the recreation department "opened" a section of the lake, and even dispatched a snowplow truck to clear a good-sized patch of ice. The boys and I skated during the rest of winter. Ever vigilant, the town officials kept the THIN ICE signs up, even though their own truck could safely drive on the frozen surface. And they brought in "lifeguards" and all sorts of rules about the hours during which we could skate and where we had to stay.

But at least we were able to skate in the open air, on real ice.   16
And it was still free.   17

Meanings and Values

1. Summarize in your own words the issue the author is addressing in this essay. In what ways is this issue representative of similar issues in other settings and climates? Explain. Does this "representativeness" make the argument significant and interesting for people who are not worried about thin ice and have no interest in skating? Why or why not? (See "Guide to Terms": *Evaluation*.)

2. Daly presents his examples of growing up in the early 1960s as illustrations of a good way to teach children responsibility and to allow them to have healthy fun. Does he succeed in doing so? If so, what details in the examples or statements of interpretation are most convincing? If not, what keeps the examples from being successful?

3. What opposing points of view, if any, does Daly acknowledge? Would the essay be more (or less) effective if he spent more time dealing with possible objections to his argument? Make a list of possible objections to his argument and evidence that could be used to support them.

4. Does the writer offer possible answers to the problem he identifies? If so, what are they? Does the essay make a clear case that lawyers are to blame for the problem? If not, does this weaken the essay? Why or why not?

Argumentative Techniques

1. Why does the writer wait until paragraph 6 to offer an argumentative proposition (thesis)? What role(s) do the opening paragraphs play? Do they explain an issue or problem? Do they provide evidence that can be used to support the thesis? Be specific in your answer, and point to specific evidence to support your conclusions. (Guide: *Introductions*.)

2. Which sentence or sentences state the argumentative proposition (thesis)? (Guide: *Thesis*.) Restate it in your own words. Are all parts of

the essay clearly related to this thesis? If not, what are the functions of any parts not clearly related to the thesis? (Guide: *Unity*.) How is the comparison-contrast pattern related to the thesis? Explain. Would another arrangement of ideas and evidence be likely to provide more convincing development and support for the thesis? What arrangement, and why?

3. In what ways does the concluding sentence "echo" the beginning of the essay? Which paragraphs should be considered the conclusion of the essay? What functions do they perform? (Guide: *Closings*.)

Diction and Vocabulary

1. The effectiveness of this essay depends to a considerable extent on the writer's ability to make the account of his childhood experiences seem like a realistic ideal and not merely a sentimental, nostalgic excursion. How does the diction in paragraphs 1–2 and 7–9 aid him in staying away from too much sentimentality while at the same time making the experience seem attractive and worth reclaiming? If you think the examples are overly sentimental, explain why. (Guide: *Sentimentality*.)

2. What words with positive connotations does Daly associate with skating and playing hockey (see pars. 4 and 8)? (Guide: *Connotation/Denotation*). How do the connotations of these words help support his thesis?

3. If you do not know the meaning of some of the following words, look them up in a dictionary: gloss, obverse (par. 4); high-sticking, checking (8); meteorologists, connoisseurs (9); liability, construct (10); vigilant (15).

Read to Write

1. Make a list of other valuable childhood activities that have been curtailed, limited, or threatened by legal concerns. Should we ignore these concerns, find a way to accommodate them, or come up with different and less dangerous activities? Consider making an issue from this general subject area the focus of an argumentative essay.

2. Begin an argumentative essay of your own with examples of how things should be, then develop your argument by contrasting how they are with how they ought to be.

3. Using Daly's essay as a model, argue that in an attempt to deal with a problem, threat, or danger, we have taken steps that create more problems and dangers by taking away the need to be responsible for our actions.

(NOTE: Suggestions for topics requiring development by ARGUMENT are on page 573 at the end of this section.)

ARGUMENT THROUGH COMPARISON AND CONTRAST

RICHARD LYNN

> RICHARD LYNN was born in London, England, in 1930. He received a B.A. from King's College, Cambridge, in 1953 and was awarded a Ph.D. in 1956. He has taught at Exeter University and the Economic and Social Research Institute, Dublin, and is currently a professor of psychology at the University of Ulster. Among his books are *Personality and National Character* (1971), *An Introduction to the Study of Personality* (1971), *The Entrepreneur* (1974), and most recently, *Educational Achievement in Japan* (1988).

Why Johnny Can't Read, but Yoshio Can

> This essay was first published in the *National Review*, a magazine noted for its advocacy of conservative social, economic, and political policies. In the selection, Lynn compares the Japanese educational system to those of the United States and England in order to argue for changes in the latter two systems. Of particular interest in this essay is the way the comparison pattern lends itself to arguments urging the adoption of policies that have worked in another setting.

There can be no doubt that American schools compare poorly with Japanese schools. In the latter, there are no serious problems with poor discipline, violence, or truancy; Japanese children take school seriously and work hard. Japanese educational standards are high, and illiteracy is virtually unknown. 1

The evidence of Japan's high educational standards began to appear as long ago as the 1960s. In 1967 there was published the first of a series of studies of educational standards in a dozen or so economically developed nations, based on tests of carefully drawn representative samples of children. The first study was concerned with achievement in math on the part of 13- and 18-year-olds. In both age 2 groups the Japanese children came out well ahead of their coevals in other countries. The American 13-year-olds came out second to last for their age group; the American 18-year-olds, last. In both age groups, European children scored about halfway between the Japanese and the Americans.

Since then, further studies have appeared, covering science as   3
well as math. The pattern of results has always been the same: the Japanese have generally scored first, the Americans last or nearly last, and the Europeans have fallen somewhere in between. In early adolescence, when the first tests are taken, Japanese children are two or three years ahead of American children; by age 18, approximately 98 percent of Japanese children surpass their American counterparts.

Meanwhile, under the Reagan Administration, the United   4
States at least started to take notice of the problem. In 1983 the President's report, *A Nation at Risk,* described the state of American schools as a national disaster. A follow-up report issued by the then-secretary of education, Mr. William Bennett, earlier this year[1] claims that although some improvements have been made, these have been "disappointingly slow."

An examination of Japan's school system suggests that there are   5
three factors responsible for its success, which might be emulated by other countries: a strong national curriculum, stipulated by the government; strong incentives for students; and the stimulating effects of competition between schools.

The national curriculum in Japan is drawn up by the Depart-   6
ment of Education. It covers Japanese language and literature, math, science, social science, music, moral education, and physical education. From time to time, the Department of Education requests advice on the content of the curriculum from representatives of the teaching profession, industry, and the trade unions. Syllabi are then drawn up, setting out in detail the subject matter that has to be taught at each grade. These syllabi are issued to school principals, who are responsible for ensuring that the stipulated curriculum is taught in their schools. Inspectors periodically check that this is being done.

The Japanese national curriculum ensures such uniformly high   7
standards of teaching that almost all parents are happy to send their children to the local public school. There is no flight into private schools of the kind that has been taking place in America in recent years. Private schools do exist in Japan, but they are attended by less

[1] 1988, the year this essay was first published (Editors' note).

than 1 per cent of children in the age range of compulsory schooling (six to 15 years).

This tightly stipulated national curriculum provides a striking 8 contrast with the decentralized curriculum of schools in America. Officially, the curriculum in America is the responsibility of school principals with guidelines from state education officials. In practice, even school principals often have little idea of what is actually being taught in the classroom.

America and Britain have been unusual in leaving the curricu- 9 lum so largely in the hands of teachers. Some form of national curriculum is used throughout Continental Europe, although the syllabus is typically not specified in as much detail as in Japan. And now Britain is changing course: legislation currently going through Parliament will introduce a national curriculum for England and Wales, with the principal subjects being English, math, science, technology, a foreign language, history and geography, and art, music, and design. It is envisioned that the new curriculum will take up approximately 70 per cent of teaching time, leaving the remainder free for optional subjects such as a second foreign language, or extra science.

Under the terms of the new legislation, school children are 10 going to be given national tests at the ages of seven, 11, 14, and 16 to ensure that the curriculum has been taught and that children have learned it to a satisfactory standard. When the British national curriculum comes into effect, America will be left as the only major economically developed country without one.

To achieve high educational standards in schools it is necessary 11 to have motivated students as well as good teachers. A national curriculum acts as a discipline on teachers, causing them to teach efficiently, but it does nothing to provide incentives for students, an area in which American education is particularly weak.

One of the key factors in the Japanese education system is that 12 secondary schooling is split into two stages. At the age of 11 or 12, Japanese children enter junior high school. After three years there, they take competitive entrance examinations for senior high schools. In each locality there is a hierarchy of public esteem for these senior high schools, from the two or three that are regarded as the best in the area, through those considered to be good or average, down to those that (at least by Japanese standards) are considered to be poor.

The top schools enjoy national reputations, somewhat akin to 13 the famous English schools such as Eton and Harrow. But in England the high fees exacted by these schools mean that very few parents can afford them. Consequently there are few candidates for entry, and the entrance examinations offer little incentive to work for the great mass of children. By contrast, in Japan the elite senior high schools are open to everyone. While a good number of these schools are private (approximately 30 per cent nationwide, though in some major cities the figure is as high as 50 per cent), even these schools are enabled, by government subsidies, to keep their fees within the means of a large proportion of parents. The public schools also charge fees, but these are nominal, amounting to only a few hundred dollars a year, and loans are available to cover both fees and living expenses.

Thus children have every expectation of being able to attend the 14 best school they can qualify for; and, hence, the hierarchical rankings of senior high schools act as a powerful incentive for children preparing for the entrance examinations. There is no doubt that Japanese children work hard in response to these incentives. Starting as early as age ten, approximately half of them take extra tuition on weekends, in the evenings, and in the school holidays at supplementary coaching establishments known as *juku*, and even at that early age they do far more homework than American children. At about the age of 12, Japanese children enter the period of their lives known as *examination hell:* during this time, which lasts fully two years, it is said that those who sleep more than five hours a night have no hope of success, either in school or in life. For, in addition to conferring great social and intellectual status on their students, the elite senior high schools provide a first-rate academic education, which, in turn, normally enables the students to get into one of the elite universities and, eventually, to move into a good job in industry or government.

Although Japanese children are permitted to leave school at the 15 age of 15, 94 per cent of them proceed voluntarily to the senior high schools. Thus virtually all Japanese are exposed in early adolescence to the powerful incentive for academic work represented by the senior-high-school entrance examinations. There is nothing in the school systems of any of the Western countries resembling this powerful incentive.

The prestige of the elite senior high schools is sustained by the 16 extensive publicity they receive from the media. Each year the top hundred or so schools in Japan are ranked on the basis of the percentage of their pupils who obtain entry to the University of Tokyo,

Japan's most prestigious university. These rankings are widely reported in the print media, and the positions of the top twenty schools are announced on TV news programs, rather like the scores made by leading sports teams in the United States and Europe. At a local level, more detailed media coverage is devoted to the academic achievements of all the schools in the various localities, this time analyzed in terms of their pupils' success in obtaining entry to the lesser, but still highly regarded, local universities.

Thus, once Japanese 15-year-olds have been admitted to their   17
senior high schools, they are confronted with a fresh set of incentives in the form of entrance examinations to universities and colleges, which are likewise hierarchically ordered in public esteem. After the University of Tokyo, which stands at the apex of the status hierarchy, come the University of Kyoto and ten or so other highly prestigious universities, including the former Imperial Universities in the major provincial cities and the technological university of Hitosubashi, whose standing and reputation in Japan resembles that of the Massachusetts Institute of Technology in the United States.

Below these top dozen institutions stand some forty or so less   18
prestigious but still well-regarded universities. And after these come numerous smaller universities and colleges of varying degrees of standing and reputation.

To some extent the situation in Japan has parallels in the United   19
States and Europe, but there are two factors that make the importance of securing admission to an elite university substantially greater in Japan than in the West. In the first place, the entire Japanese system is geared toward providing lifelong employment, both in the private sector and in the civil service. It is practically unheard of for executives to switch from one corporation to another, or into public service and then back into the private sector, as in the United States and Europe. Employees are recruited directly out of college, and, needless to say, the major corporations and the civil service recruit virtually entirely from the top dozen universities. The smaller Japanese corporations operate along the same lines, although they widen their recruitment net to cover the next forty or so universities in the prestige hierarchy. Thus, obtaining entry to a prestigious university is a far more vital step for a successful career in Japan than it is in the United States or Europe.

Secondly, like the elite senior high schools, the elite universities   20
are meritocratic. The great majority of universities are public institutions, receiving substantial government subsidies. Again, as with

the senior high schools, fees are quite low, and loans are available to defray expenses. In principle and to a considerable extent in practice, any young Japanese can get into the University of Tokyo, or one of the other elite universities, provided only that he or she is talented enough and is prepared to do the work necessary to pass the entrance examinations. Knowing this, the public believes that *all* the most talented young Japanese go to one of these universities—and, conversely, that anyone who fails to get into one of these schools is necessarily less bright. Avoiding this stigma is, of course, a further incentive for the student to work hard to get in.

    The third significant factor responsible for the high educational standards in Japan is competition among schools. This operates principally among the senior high schools, and what they are competing for is academic reputation. The most prestigious senior high school in Japan is Kansei in Tokyo, and being a teacher at Kansei is something like being a professor at Harvard. The teachers' self-esteem is bound up with the academic reputation of their schools— a powerful motivator for teachers to teach well.   21

    In addition to this important factor of self-esteem, there is practical necessity. Since students are free to attend any school they can get into, if a school failed to provide good-quality teaching, it would no longer attract students. In business terms, its customers would fade away, and it would be forced to close. Thus the essential feature of the competition among the Japanese senior high schools is that it exposes the teachers to the discipline of the free-enterprise system. In the case of the public senior high schools, the system can be regarded as a form of market socialism in which the competing institutions are state-owned but nevertheless compete against each other for their customers. Here the Japanese have been successfully operating the kind of system that Mikhail Gorbachev may be feeling his way toward introducing in the Soviet Union. The Japanese private senior high schools add a further capitalist element to the system insofar as they offer their educational services more or less like firms operating in a conventional market.   22

    The problem of how market disciplines can be brought to bear on schools has been widely discussed in America and also in Britain ever since Milton Friedman raised it a quarter of a century or so ago, but solutions such as Friedman's voucher proposal seem as distant today as they did then. Although the proposal has been looked at sympathetically by Republicans in the United States and by Conservatives in Britain, politicians in both countries have fought shy of   23 introducing it. Probably they have concluded that the problems of getting vouchers into the hands of all parents, and dealing with losses, fraud, counterfeits, and so forth, are likely to be too great for the scheme to be feasible.

The Japanese have evolved a different method of exposing 24 schools to market forces. Subsidies are paid directly to the schools on a per-capita basis in accordance with the number of students they have. If a school's rolls decline, so do its incomes, both from subsidies and from fees. This applies to both the public and private senior high schools, although the public schools obviously receive a much greater proportion of their income as subsidies and a smaller proportion from fees.

A similar scheme is being introduced in Britain. The Thatcher 25 government is currently bringing in legislation that will permit public schools to opt out of local-authority control. Those that opt out will receive subsidies from the central government on the basis of the number of students they have. They will then be on their own, to sink or swim.

There is little doubt that this is the route that should be followed 26 in America. The exposure of American schools to the invigorating stimulus of competition, combined with the introduction of a national curriculum and the provision of stronger incentives for students, would work wonders. Rather than complaining about Japanese aggressiveness and instituting counterproductive protectionist measures, Americans ought to be looking to the source of Japan's power.

Meanings and Values

1. What is the issue or problem Lynn identifies in paragraphs 1–4?

2. Summarize briefly the main reasons Lynn offers for the success of the Japanese school system.

3. How does the curriculum in Japanese schools contrast with those in American and British schools, especially in motivating students to excel?

4. One possible weakness in this argument is that the author pays little attention to opposing points of view. Think of some reasonable objections a North American reader might have to the Japanese educational system. Try to identify some practical difficulties that stand in the way of the reforms the author proposes based on the Japanese model. Explain how you think the author might respond to these objections and possible problems.

Argumentative Techniques

1. What kinds of evidence does the author offer to demonstrate the seriousness of the problem he describes in the opening of the essay? (See "Guide to Terms": *Argument*.)

2. Why might the author have chosen to summarize his main supporting arguments in paragraph 5, early in the essay?

3. Discuss the strategies Lynn employs in paragraphs 11 and 21, which act as transitions between major segments of the essay. (Guide: *Transition*.) Tell how these two paragraphs, along with paragraphs 5 and 6, contribute to the overall coherence of the essay. (Guide: *Coherence*.)

4. How would you describe the tone of the essay? In what ways does the tone add to the persuasiveness of the argument? (Guide: *Style/Tone*.)

Diction and Vocabulary

1. Examine the diction in paragraphs 7, 14, and 22 to decide whether it is designed to appeal primarily to readers' emotions, reason, or both. (See the introduction to Section 13, p. 513, and Guide: *Diction*.) On the whole, would you characterize the writing in this selection as objective or subjective? Why? (Guide: *Objective/Subjective*.)

2. Identify the uses Lynn makes of parallel structures and contrasts in diction to emphasize the seriousness of the problem described in paragraphs 2 and 3. (Guide: *Parallel Structure*.)

3. Point out the transitional devices used in paragraphs to emphasize contrasts between the Japanese educational system and those of Britain and America. (Guide: *Transition*.)

Read to Write

1. Prepare a thesis for an essay in which you consider the recommendations in this essay and propose some educational reforms of your own that you believe would be just as effective—perhaps even more so.

2. Using comparison as a strategy, argue for some solutions to a local problem such as disposal of solid waste, improvement of the transportation system, better administration of school athletics, or control of drug and alcohol abuse.

3. In what other ways do you think North Americans can learn from the economic or social systems of other countries? Following Lynn's essay as a model, discuss this question as it applies to some specific issues. Pay particular attention to countries such as Japan that have been especially successful in recent decades.

(NOTE: Suggestions for topics requiring development by ARGUMENT are on page 573 at the end of this section.)

ARGUMENT THROUGH EXAMPLE

ALAN HIRSCH

ALAN HIRSCH works as an attorney and is also a free-lance writer. He is the co-author of a book on the constitution.

Don't Blame the Jury

Hirsch suggests that in focusing entirely on the jury when we disagree with a trial verdict, we may be missing the real culprit: the ways in which the legal system handicaps juries. He presents numerous examples from well-known and lesser-known trials to show how jury deliberations are often undermined. This essay was first published in *Troika* magazine.

Several recent high-trials, especially those of O.J. Simpson, the Menendez brothers, and the police officers who pummeled Rodney King, have spawned recognition that the criminal justice system doesn't work. Unfortunately, the precise problem has been misdiagnosed. 1

A growing chorus of commentators argues that the problem lies with ordinary people (jurors), who cannot be trusted to decide difficult cases. This gets things backwards. The professionals (judges, lawyers, and legislators) have created an irrational system that makes it impossible for ordinary citizens to play their proper role. 2

The problem begins with jury selection. The pool of prospective jurors is whittled down to a jury of twelve through two means: attorneys dismiss prospective jurors without giving any reason (the "peremptory challenge"), or the judge, with or without prompting from either side, dismisses prospective jurors "for cause." For better or worse, the peremptory challenge has deep roots in our criminal law and is here to stay. We must, however, give serious thought to sharply narrowing the basis of for-cause dismissals. 3

Clearly, some for-cause dismissals are necessary. At a minimum, the selection process should establish that no jurors are 4 acquainted with any of the parties, attorneys, or key witnesses. Beyond that, prospective jurors should be asked whether they have a predisposition in the matter and if they are capable of following the judge's instructions. Assuming satisfactory answers to these questions, it would seem that they should be eligible to serve on the case. Under current law, however, for-cause dismissals involve much more than rooting out conflicts of interest or bias. Whole categories of people are dismissed based on speculation that some circumstance could unconsciously compromise their impartiality. If the case deals with business fraud, the judge is apt to dismiss all business persons.

If the case involves a school, bid farewell to teachers, students,   5
and administrators. In child molestation cases, prospective jurors with young children are often dismissed. People with lawyers or police in their family are bounced from all kinds of cases. Anyone with stock investments may be tossed from an insider trading case.

Such people could swear under oath that they have no axes to   6
grind, but they will be dismissed on the ground that they may have axes to grind of which they are unaware. Increasingly, there is a sense that to be an impartial juror one must be a blank slate with respect to the facts and issues in the case.

This idea reflects a double standard. Judges often have knowl-   7
edge and opinions (and children and stocks), but only palpable conflicts of interest tend to be considered a basis for disqualification. Why do we trust judges so much more than jurors? Indeed, juror bias may be less problematic than judge bias, because a juror is only one of twelve decision makers, whereas a biased judge can single-handedly manipulate proceedings.

The dismissal of prospective jurors whose background suggests   8
any conceivable bias is bad enough. Even more disturbing, people who have heard anything about the charged crime or the defendant are likely to be excused. Even if these people have formed no opinions and have no discernible bias, they are viewed as contaminated by any awareness of the underlying facts or parties.

In high-profile cases, this leads to the search for jurors unat-   9
tuned to the world around them. In the McMartin child abuse case in California, a survey found that 97% of adults in the community had heard about the case. Seeking jurors from the remaining 3% invited an unqualified jury.

To capture the absurdity of this state of affairs, we cannot   10
improve on Mark Twain's characterization. In a highly-publicized

murder case of his time, the court kept off the jury anyone familiar with the facts. Twain described the result with characteristic panache:

"A minister, intelligent, esteemed, and greatly respected; a mer-   11
chant of high character and known probity; a mining superintendent of intelligence and unblemished reputation; a quartz-mill owner of excellent standing, were all questioned in the same way, and all set aside. Each said the public talk and the newspaper reports had not so biased his mind but that sworn testimony . . . would enable him to render a verdict without prejudice and in accordance with the facts. But of course such men could not be trusted with the case. Ignoramuses alone could mete out unsullied justice."

That Twain penned these words in 1871 suggests that the   12
foibles of jury selection are nothing new. However, it ought not be inferred that the Founding Fathers endorsed the equation of impartiality with ignorance. They valued "local" juries (the Sixth Amendment requires trial by a jury of "the State and district wherein the crime shall have been committed") in part so that jurors would be acquainted with the context of the case and grounded in the shared values and understanding of the community.

However, our criminal law increasingly moves in the opposite   13
direction, with the situation reaching comic proportions in some cases. Take the case of Oliver North. North testified before Congress in hearings televised nationwide and widely discussed. At his subsequent criminal trial, the judge decided to dismiss all jurors familiar with North's testimony before Congress. From a pool of 235 jurors, 212 were removed on this basis. Not surprisingly, the actual jury left something to be desired. The juror who became forewoman told the court, "I don't like the news. I don't like to watch it. It's depressing." Other jurors confessed to not reading newspapers or not understanding whatever they had heard about the case.

In the O.J. Simpson case, the task of finding a sufficiently igno-   14
rant jury was captured by a joke that made the rounds. "Knock knock. . . . Who's there? . . . O.J. . . . O.J. who? . . . Congratulations, you're on the jury!"

While these high-profile cases are particularly prone to produc-   15
ing an ignorant jury, the notion that jurors should lack even slight knowledge or tentative opinions relative to a case applies across the board. All too often, intelligent and well-informed jurors are dismissed precisely because they are intelligent and well-informed.

Obviously, jurors should base their decisions on the evidence   16
in the case, not on preconceived notions or outside information,

and should be emphatically instructed to this effect. But we do prospective jurors an injustice to assume that any familiarity with a case renders it impossible to render a fair verdict. And we do a larger injustice when we skew the jury toward the least informed members of the community.

Then too, the problem with the jury system transcends the   17 selection process. The wisest, best-informed members of the community could sit in the jury box and we'd still have no right to expect an accurate verdict, given the rules governing juror conduct. In some jurisdictions, jurors are not permitted to take notes. In most jurisdictions, they may not discuss the case among themselves prior to deliberations. And if, during deliberations, they request to see transcripts of testimony or the judge's instructions, in many jurisdictions the request is denied. Each of these practices is justified by assorted rationales, but they all come down to the fact that jurors are not trusted to behave like other decision makers.

These restrictions on juror conduct have come under attack in   18 recent years, and reform is underway. However, another practice that poses a more profound threat to jury decision making has gone largely unchallenged: a rule of evidence in all jurisdictions that deprives jurors of relevant evidence when judges fear they would misuse it.

The precise wording differs from jurisdiction to jurisdiction, but   19 typically provides that evidence, though relevant, must be excluded if its value is "outweighed by the danger of unfair prejudice." While taken for granted by most participants in the criminal justice system, this rule (the "prejudicial evidence" rule) interferes with a jury's ability to reach a sound verdict.

The parties in a trial obviously cannot be allowed to introduce   20 into evidence everything they believe will influence the jury. One reasonable limitation is that evidence must be relevant. For example, defense lawyers would love to introduce testimony that the defendant's family will suffer if he is convicted, or that the victim is a despicable character. But in a trial to determine whether the defendant committed a particular offense, such matters are clearly irrelevant.

So far, so good. The prejudicial evidence rule, however, permits   21 the exclusion of relevant evidence if the judge deems that its legitimate value or "weight" is outbalanced by its potential for unfair prejudice—that is, if the jury would likely attach too much or the wrong significance to it. Insofar as assigning the proper weight to evidence is central to the jury's role, it seems bizarre to deprive jurors of relevant material on the ground that they cannot weigh it properly.

That is not to say all relevant evidence must be admitted. A 22 party may wish to call a dozen witnesses to give identical testimony about a minor matter. The judge's authority to limit such repetitious, time-consuming material is necessary to ensure an orderly trial. Other rules excluding relevant material, such as that privy to lawyer/client or physician/patient privileges, derive from public policy. Legislatures have determined that, absent these privileges, people would be less willing to confide in lawyers and physicians, to the detriment of the public interest.

These rules reflect the fact that the jury's access to relevant evi- 23 dence must sometimes be tempered by other considerations. But the prejudicial evidence rule is different: it permits judges to exclude relevant material even absent a public policy reason, and even if the material does not violate any specific evidentiary taboo (such as "hearsay"). This is a rule of evidence designed to protect the jury from itself.

Traditionally, the prejudicial evidence rule was used sparingly, 24 primarily in cases of stark exhibits such as bloody photographs. Today, judges invoke this rule frequently, and exclude all kinds of material they believe would overwhelm jurors.

George Fletcher's recent book about high-profile criminal cases, 25 *With Justice for Some,* suggests the significance of this rule. In case after case, the rule played a role. In the 1st trial of Lyle and Erik Menendez, accused of murdering their parents for money, evidence was excluded that Erik wrote a play about a man who kills his parents for money. In the William Kennedy Smith rape case, evidence that Smith assaulted three other women was excluded. In the trial of police for beating Rodney King, the court excluded evidence that a defendant characterized a fight between blacks as "gorillas in the mist." And in the case of the subway vigilante Bernard Goetz, Goetz' statement that the way to clean up the street is to "get rid of spics and niggers" was excluded.

In each of these cases, the judge's doubts about the jury's ability 26 deprived the jury of relevant evidence. As it happens, in these cases the exclusions helped the defense. But the prejudicial evidence rule is an equal opportunity truth-defeater—it can harm as well as help a defendant. Thus, in the O.J. Simpson case, the rule led to the exclusion of potentially critical evidence showing Detective Mark Furhman's propensity to plant evidence.

In one sense, the defense got what it deserved. Throughout the   27
trial, defense counsel invoked the prejudicial evidence rule as a basis
for excluding prosecution evidence, including: photographs of the
victims' bodies; Simpson's history of spousal abuse; and a videotape
in which he joked about wife-beating. They were particularly outraged that Judge Ito allowed evidence of Simpson's abusive past.
This, they claimed, would sway the jury improperly.

Exploring the basis of their claim clarifies the problem with the   28
prejudicial evidence rule. The defense's concern was twofold. First,
the jury could improperly conclude that anyone who committed
past acts of violence must be guilty of the violent act with which he
is charged. Alternatively, the jury might decide to convict Simpson
because, whether or not he committed the murders, he'd shown
himself to be a bad man who deserves punishment. (Although the
latter might seem farfetched, it is often advanced as a basis for
excluding evidence of a defendant's prior bad acts.)

Both rationales rest on a painfully dim view of juries. It assumes   29
that the jury will either disregard its duty to decide the case before
it, or prove incapable of putting evidence in its proper perspective.

Are such notions justified? Actually, they are unproven. Fol-   30
lowing the verdict, the Simpson jurors said they were not overly
impressed with the evidence of abuse: just because Simpson battered his ex-wife didn't mean he killed her. Arguably, these jurors
gave too little weight to the evidence of spousal abuse. Certainly,
their elementary inference—not all abusers commit murder—is one
most jurors can draw.

Or, take the exercise video in which Simpson jokes about   31
wife-beating. His attorney, Robert Shapiro, argued that the prejudicial evidence rule required exclusion of this portion of the video,
insisting that it had hardly any evidentiary value since Simpson
was clearly joking. Shapiro protested too much; if Simpson's
remarks were patently meaningless jests, why did he care whether
the jury heard them? At the end of his lengthy statement about the
irrelevance of the jokes, Shapiro added that the video was "highly
prejudicial."

How can you have it both ways? How can material be mean-   32
ingless yet highly prejudicial? The only way these statements can be
reconciled is if we assume the jurors are dimwits. Simpson's jokes
were of limited significance, a miniscule piece in the prosecution
puzzle, but there was reason to fear that jurors would think them a
huge piece. While it is true that the flawed selection process produces

too many uninformed jurors, even the least educated know the difference between joking about violence and committing it.

Rather than arguing that the admission of evidence will create 33 unfair prejudice, lawyers should show the jury the weakness of the evidence and defuse the potential prejudice. In the marketplace of ideas, the proper response to weak arguments is not censorship but strong arguments. So too with weak evidence.

The various rules and practices discussed above inhibit the ability of jurors to reach an accurate verdict. Their task is then compounded by the fact that, unless they reach unanimity, they may not render a verdict at all—a hung jury results. While the Supreme Court has said the Constitution does not require a unanimous verdict, the federal courts and all but two states prohibit nonunanimous verdicts. As a result, juries are sometimes defined by their worst members: one or two obstinate or biased dissenters can hang the jury even in the face of clear evidence.

There are two primary rationales behind the unanimity requirement. First, it is said that if a nonunanimous verdict were permitted, juries would not bother to deliberate: they would essentially vote and disband. However, if this argument is accepted, it should lead not just to a unanimous jury requirement but a unanimity requirement in every multimember decision-making body (at least those that are expected to deliberate).

Deliberative bodies deliberate not because they must reach consensus, but because that is their job and they are committed to a decision that takes into account the concerns of all the members. Does the Supreme Court, for example, eschew argument in favor of mere nose-counting?

The risk of insufficient deliberations should be dealt with 37 directly, rather than by requiring unanimity. Jurors should be emphatically instructed to take the views of dissenting colleagues seriously and make every effort to persuade one another, ceasing deliberations only when they have exhausted such efforts. Moreover, when a jury announces that it has reached a verdict, the judge can poll the jurors to assure that deliberations were not cut off prematurely.

The second argument for requiring unanimity is that, as long as 38 any jurors vote to acquit, it cannot be said that the government proved guilt beyond a reasonable doubt. However, this argument fails to explain why unanimity is required not only for convictions but also for acquittals. More importantly, this argument defies common sense. Will the proposition that the earth is round not be proven beyond a reasonable doubt until the Flat Earth Society disbands? Does the existence of persons denying the Holocaust cast reasonable doubt that it took place? It is clearly a mistake to suggest that something cannot be proven beyond a reasonable doubt absent unanimity.

The various rules and practices discussed combine to create an   39
artificial environment obstructing the capacity of jurors to deliberate intelligently and reach an accurate verdict. A vicious cycle results. Whenever a jury renders a dubious verdict, critics call into question entrusting critical decisions to ordinary citizens. This distrust leads to more constraints that further impede the jury's ability to function well.

It's time to ask whether the fault is that of ordinary citizens   40
(jurors), or the elites who make and apply these rules. When jurors are selected in a way that eliminates informed members, are denied the most universal and time-tested means of obtaining and processing information, deprived of key evidence, and required to reach unanimity or else no verdict at all, why should we expect just decisions?

Meanings and Values

1. Hirsch claims that the "precise problem has been misdiagnosed" (par. 1). What problem does he address in the essay and what does he view as the proper diagnosis?

2. What is the argumentative thesis of this essay, and where is it introduced? (See "Guide to Terms": *Thesis.*) What solution to the problem (see question 1), if any, does Hirsch propose? If he offers a solution, is his proposal also the thesis of the essay? If not, can it be said that the essay has two theses? Why or why not?

Argumentative Techniques

1. Identify those paragraphs in the essay that begin with a topic sentence linked more or less directly to the essay's thesis. (Guide: *Unity.*) Next, indicate which of these topic sentences is supported by an example. How many, if any, of these paragraphs are developed by some argumentative strategy other than example, and what other patterns does the writer employ in these paragraphs?

2. Which paragraphs in the essay are not linked directly to the thesis but provide support and explanation to arguments advanced in the paragraphs that precede them?

3. What does the author gain by using Mark Twain's words from 1871 (par. 11)? He says that Twain's statement "suggests that the foibles of

jury selection are nothing new" (12); can Twain be considered an authority even though he was not a lawyer or a judge? Why or why not? (Guide: *Argument.*) In what ways does the touch of humor in the quotation from Twain add to the effectiveness of the argument?

4. Hirsch frequently varies sentence length to provide emphasis. Discuss his use of this strategy in paragraphs 2, 3, 7, 27, and 30. (Guide: *Emphasis.*) Explain the use of parallelism for emphasis in paragraphs 4, 5, and 16. (Guide: *Parallel Structure.*) Discuss how Hirsch uses the syntax of the sentences in paragraph 31 to emphasize the points he is making. (Guide: *Syntax.*)

Diction and Vocabulary

1. Where in this essay does Hirsch make marked use of legal language? Be specific in answering this question. In what ways might this language add to the force of his arguments? In what ways might they undermine the effectiveness of the essay? (Guide: *Evaluation.*) Has Hirsch avoided using technical terms in ways likely to irritate or confuse readers unfamiliar with them? Why or why not?

2. If you do not know the meaning of some of the following terms, look them up in a dictionary: pummeled (par. 1); peremptory (3); predisposition, compromise, impartiality (4); palpable, problematic (7); unsullied (11); rationales (17); absent (23); stark (24); propensity (26); minuscule (32); unanimity (34); eschew (36); dissenting (37).

Read to Write

1. News coverage of trials is often as controversial as the events of the trial or the crime. Think of issues surrounding news coverage of crimes and trials, and brainstorm some argumentative propositions you might wish to develop into the thesis for an essay.

2. Hirsch uses examples from trials likely to be familiar to most readers, and many of these trials have been featured on television news programs and in newspapers and magazines. For an essay of your own, make use of examples from similar sources.

3. Adopt Hirsch's strategy of arguing that a particular institution is not to blame for a problem because the real blame lies with people who have altered, restrained, or undermined the system. In the course of your argument, suggest (as he does) some ways to remedy the institution so that it can act effectively and properly.

(NOTE: Suggestions for topics requiring development by ARGUMENT are on page 573 at the end of this section.)

ARGUMENT THROUGH DEFINITION

BARBARA LAWRENCE

BARBARA LAWRENCE was born in Hanover, New Hampshire. After receiving a B.A. in French literature from Connecticut College, she worked as an editor on *McCall's, Redbook, Harper's Bazaar,* and the *New Yorker.* During this period she also took an M.A. in philosophy from New York University. Currently a professor of humanities at the State University of New York's College at Old Westbury, Lawrence has published criticism, poetry, and fiction in *Choice, Commonweal, Columbia Poetry, The New York Times,* and the *New Yorker.*

Four-Letter Words Can Hurt You

"Four-Letter Words Can Hurt You" first appeared in *The New York Times* and was later published in *Redbook.* In arguing against the "earthy, gut-honest" language often preferred by her students, Lawrence also provides a thoughtful, even scholarly, extended definition of *obscenity* itself. To accomplish her purpose, the author makes use of several other patterns as well.

Why should any words be called obscene? Don't they all describe 1 natural human functions? Am I trying to tell them, my students demand, that the "strong, earthy, gut-honest"—or, if they are fans of Norman Mailer, the "rich, liberating, existential"—language they use to describe sexual activity isn't preferable to "phony-sounding, middle-class words like 'intercourse' and 'copulate'?" "Cop You Late!" they say with fancy inflections and gagging grimaces. "Now, what is *that* supposed to mean?"

Well, what is it supposed to mean? And why indeed should one 2 group of words describing human functions and human organs be acceptable in ordinary conversation and another, describing presumably the same organs and functions, be tabooed—so much so, in fact, that some of these words still cannot appear in print in many parts of the English-speaking world?

The argument that these taboos exist only because of "sexual 3 hangups" (middle-class, middle-age, feminist), or even that they are a result of class oppression (the contempt of the Norman conquerors for the language of their Anglo-Saxon serfs), ignores a much more likely explanation, it seems to me, and that is the sources and functions of the words themselves.

The best known of the tabooed sexual words, for example, 4 comes from the German *ficken*, meaning "to strike"; combined, according to Partridge's etymological dictionary *Origins*, with the Latin sexual verb *futuere*: associated in turn with the Latin *fustis*, "a staff or cudgel"; the Celtic *buc*, "a point, hence to pierce"; the Irish *bot*, "the male member"; the Latin *battuere*, "to beat"; the Gaelic *batair*, "a cudgeller"; the Early Irish *bualaim*, "I strike"; and so forth. It is one of what etymologists sometimes called "the sadistic group of words for the man's part in copulation."

The brutality of this word, then, and its equivalents ("screw," 5 "bang," etc.) is not an illusion of the middle class or a crotchet of Women's Liberation. In their origins and imagery these words carry undeniably painful, if not sadistic, implications, the object of which is almost always female. Consider, for example, what a "screw" actually does to the wood it penetrates; what a painful, even mutilating, activity this kind of analogy suggests. "Screw" is particularly interesting in this context, since the noun, according to Partridge, comes from words meaning "groove," "nut," "ditch," "breeding sow," "scrofula" and "swelling," while the verb, besides its explicit imagery, has antecedent associations to "write on," "scratch," "scarify," and so forth—a revealing fusion of a mechanical or painful action with an obviously denigrated object.

Not all obscene words, of course, are as implicitly sadistic or 6 denigrating to women as these, but all that I know seem to serve a similar purpose: to reduce the human organism (especially the female organism) and human functions (especially sexual and procreative) to their least organic, most mechanical dimension; to substitute a trivializing or deforming resemblance for the complex human reality of what is being described.

Tabooed male descriptives, when they are not openly denigrat- 7 ing to women, often serve to divorce a male organ or function from any significant interaction with the female. Take the word *"testes,"* for example, suggesting "witnesses" (from the Latin *testis*) to the sexual and procreative strengths of the male organ; and the obscene counterpart of this word, which suggests little more than a mechanical shape. Or compare almost any of the "rich," "liberating" sexual verbs, so fashionable today among male writers, with that much-derived Latin word "copulate" ("to bind or join together") or even that Anglo-Saxon phrase (which seems to have had no trouble surviving the Norman Conquest) "make love."

How arrogantly self-involved the tabooed words seem in comparison to either of the other terms, and how contemptuous of the female partner. Understandably so, of course, if she is only a "skirt," a "broad," a "chick," a "pussycat" or a "piece." If she is, in other words no more than her skirt, or what her skirt conceals; no more than a breeder, or the broadest part of her; no more than a piece of a human being or a "piece of tail." 8

The most severely tabooed of all the female descriptives, incidentally, are those like a "piece of tail," which suggests (either explicitly or through antecedents) that there is no significant difference between the female channel through which we are all conceived and born and the anal outlet common to both sexes—a distinction that pornographers have always enjoyed obscuring. 9

This effort to deny women their biological identity, their individuality, their humanness, is such an important aspect of obscene language that one can only marvel at how seldom, in an era preoccupied with definitions of obscenity, this fact is brought to our attention. One problem, of course, is that many of the people in the best position to do this (critics, teachers, writers) are so reluctant today to admit that they are angered or shocked by obscenity. Bored, maybe, unimpressed, aesthetically displeased, but—no matter how brutal or denigrating the material—never angered, never shocked. 10

And yet how eloquently angered, how piously shocked many of these same people become if denigrating language is used about any minority group other than women; if the obscenities are racial or ethnic, that is, rather than sexual. Words like "coon," "kike," "spic," "wop," after all, deform identity, deny individuality and humanness in almost exactly the same way that sexual vulgarisms and obscenities do. 11

No one that I know, least of all my students, would fail to question the values of a society whose literature and entertainment rested heavily on racial or ethnic pejoratives. Are the values of a society whose literature and entertainment rest as heavily as ours on sexual pejoratives any less questionable? 12

Meanings and Values

1. Explain the meaning of *irony* by use of at least one illustration from the latter part of this essay. (See "Guide to Terms": *Irony*.)

2. Inasmuch as the selection itself includes many of the so-called "strong, earthy, gut-honest" words, could anyone logically call it obscene? Why or why not? To what extent, if at all, does the author's point of view help determine your answer? (Guide: *Point of View*.)

3. Compose, in your own words, a compact statement of Lawrence's thesis. (Guide: *Thesis*.) Are all parts of the essay completely relevant to this thesis? Justify your answer.

4. Evaluate this composition by use of our three-question system. (Guide: *Evaluation*.)

Argumentative Techniques

1. What is the purpose of this essay? (Guide: *Purpose*.)

2. What objection to her opinion does the author refute in paragraph 3, and how does she refute it? (Guide: *Refutation*.) Where else in the essay does she refute opposing arguments?

3. Are the evidence and supporting arguments in this essay arranged in a refutation-proof pattern? If not, describe the arrangement of the essay.

4. Which of the methods "peculiar to definition alone" (see the introduction to Section 9) does the author employ in developing this essay? What other patterns of exposition does she also use?

5. Which of the standard techniques of introduction are used? (Guide: *Introductions*.) Which methods are used to close the essay? (Guide: *Closing*.)

Diction and Vocabulary

1. How, if at all, is this discussion of words related to *connotation*? (Guide: *Connotation/Denotation*.) To what extent would connotations in this matter depend on the setting and circumstances in which the words are used? Cite illustrations to clarify your answer.

2. In view of the fact that the author uses frankly many of the "gut-honest" words, why do you suppose she plainly avoids others, such as in paragraphs 4 and 7?

3. The author says that a "kind of analogy" is suggested by some of the words discussed (par. 5). If you have studied Section 6 of this book, does her use of the term *analogy* seem in conflict with what you believed it to mean? Explain.

4. Study the author's uses of the following words, consulting the dictionary as needed: existential, grimaces (par. 1); etymological, cudgel (4); sadistic (4–6); crotchet, scrofula, explicit, antecedent, scarify (5); denigrated (5–7, 10–11); aesthetically (10); pejoratives (12).

Read to Write

1. Why do people use obscene language? Are these reasons satisfactory enough to keep from stigmatizing it or considering it impolite? Have our views of obscene language undergone any recent changes? Should we discourage the use of obscene language in more social situations than we currently do? Continue this list of questions until you have identified several possible topics for an essay.

2. Does the author make a justifiable comparison between obscene words and ethnic pejoratives? Using illustrations for specificity, carry the comparison further to show why it is sound, or explain why you consider it a weak comparison.

3. Following Lawrence's lead, discuss some other closely related group of terms and their significance, and suggest ways we should alter the way we use them.

(NOTE: Suggestions for topics requiring development by ARGUMENT are on page 573 at the end of this section.)

ARGUMENT THROUGH CAUSE AND EFFECT

JOHN DAVIDSON

JOHN DAVIDSON is a free-lance journalist living in Austin, Texas.

Menace to Society

This essay, from *Rolling Stone*, focuses on the much-discussed question of possible links between violent behavior and the depiction of violence on television, in movies, and in song lyrics. For Davidson, the blame lies squarely on the cartoons watched by children eight years old and younger.

With three-quarters of Americans surveyed convinced that movies, television and music spur young people to violence, and politicians on the left and right blasting the entertainment industry for irresponsibility, the debate over violence in popular culture is likely to be a key issue in the presidential campaign.[1]   1

Republican presidential front-runner Bob Dole, conservative guru William Bennett, black activist C. DeLores Tucker and liberal Democrat Sen. Paul Simon all have attacked portrayals of violence, treating the link between art and reality as gospel truth. They've found support for their claims from the American Psychological Association and the American Psychiatric Association, which have both issued reports stating that television violence causes aggression.   2

And a new controversy surrounding video games has been sparked by Lt. Col. Dave Grossman, a psychologist and Army Ranger. In his book *On Killing*, he claims that these games function like firing ranges, using the same type of conditioning employed to overcome soldiers' built-in inhibition to killing in the Vietnam War.   3

The research, however, is less clear. Most experts who have studied the issue believe there is *some* link—indirect, perhaps—   4

[1]This essay appeared before the 1996 presidential election, but it addresses issues that are still quite relevant (Editor's note).

between seeing violence and commiting it, but there is no agreement on how strong that link is or how to measure it. What's more, even those who argue most persuasively that there is a case to be made for connecting violence and culture agree that the biggest problem may not be teenagers seeing *Natural Born Killers* or listening to the Geto Boys but small children watching Saturday morning cartoons.

For the last 40 years, social scientists have attempted to measure   5
how media violence affects people, with the bulk of the research focused on television. One of the most influential studies was directed by George Gerbner. Beginning in 1967, Gerbner, who at that time was dean of the Annenberg School for Communication at the University of Pennsylvania, and his colleagues created a violence index that is still used to measure the percentage of network programs that have violence, the number of violent acts, the percentage of characters involved in violence and the percentage involved in killing. Their index doesn't reflect the increased amount of violent material made available through cable television and VCRs. (That count, according to the National Coalition on Television Violence, is that children in homes with cable TV and/or a VCR will see about 32,000 murders and 40,000 attempted murders by the time they're 18.)

Gerbner's group concluded that television acts as an electronic   6
melting pot, which creates a national culture. Part of that culture is "the mean-world syndrome," which leads people to believe that they are more likely to be victims of violence than they are in reality. "People who watch the most television are usually the ones who have fewer options, less money and less education," says Nancy Signorielli, a professor of communication at the University of Delaware who worked on the Gerbner study. "Their views of the world reflect what they see on television, and they overestimate their chances of being involved in violence." Like the man in Louisiana who in 1992 shot and killed a Japanese exchange student looking for a Halloween party, people overreact to perceived threats and act violently.

Remarkably, Gerbner found that the indexes have remained rel-   7
atively constant during the past two decades. Nonetheless, he's been accused of exaggerating the amount of violence by not taking context into consideration. A poke in the eye, as far as he's concerned, is basically a poke in the eye; his group counts *The Three Stooges* and Road Runner cartoons as violent programming.

A landmark study funded by the four major networks in   8
response to congressional pressure and released this past fall attem-

pted to correct that deficiency and qualify different types of violence by looking at time slot, parental advisory, duration, explicitness, relation to the story and consequences. Researchers at the Center for Communication Policy at the University of California at Los Angeles confirmed that context is crucial. In other words, a TV program that shows kids beating up a fellow student with impunity could have a more harmful effect than one that shows a couple of murderers who end up in jail. Even Signorielli acknowledges that context is important: "What we have in the U.S. is happy violence. In Japan, violence is much more graphic and much more realistic," she says. "There, television violence may actually work as a deterrent. But here, if someone's shot we don't see the wound. There's not much bleeding on U.S. television."

Leonard Eron, a research scientist at the University of Michigan, 9 has taken another approach. He began by studying how aggression develops in children, never considering television to be important. "I thought television was just another version of the sort of things children were exposed to in the past—fairy tales, stories and movies," says Eron. "But television is different, if in no other way than [that programs are] repeated over and over again."

Eron and his colleagues tested 875 third-graders in New York's 10 Columbia County and interviewed about 80 percent of their parents. To relieve tension in the interviews, Eron threw in a question about television viewing. What surprised him was the correlation between aggression and viewing habits. Children whose parents said they watched a lot of violent television turned out to be aggressive in school, and 10 years later, in the first of the follow-up studies, Eron discovered that what a child watched at 8 years old was "one of the best predictors" of adult aggression—more important than the parents' child-rearing habits or socioeconomic factors. "I could compare children over time," says Eron. "At 8, if the less aggressive of two children was watching more television violence, at 18, he would be the more aggressive of the two."

Eron's findings correspond with what psychologists believe 11 about child development: Children are most vulnerable to television from ages 2 to about 8, when they become more capable of distinguishing what they see on the screen from reality. The conclusions also conform to what we know about the development of a child's moral sense: It is developed by age 9 at the latest.

Just how children learn from the media is the subject of com- 12 peting theories. According to the simplest, the viewing of aggressive material triggers aggressive thoughts that influence subsequent actions. Kids imitate what they see, just as adults emulate styles of dress and behavior observed in movies and TV shows.

The theory is fine as far as it goes but doesn't take into account 13 the child's expectations and comprehension—nor does it explain the cumulative effects of watching violence. Educators theorize that a child's response depends upon five variables: the child's intellectual achievement, social popularity, identification with television characters, belief in the realism of the violence and the amount of fantasizing about aggression. If a child identifies with the characters, for instance, then he tends to internalize "scripts" for future aggressive behavior. As a child becomes more aggressive, he becomes less popular and more troublesome in school. The more trouble he has with teachers and friends, the more likely it is he will turn to aggressive television for affirmation, thus establishing a vicious cycle.

What turned out to be the most startling result of Eron's study, 14 however, was that a child's viewing beyond the age of 8 seems to have virtually *no* effect on his level of aggression: Once an 8-year-old's level of aggression is established, it tends to remain stable. If this is true, then most of the attacks on media are far off base. Children under the age of 8 are exposed to feature films but even with VCRs and cable, Hollywood movies are not staples in children's media diets in the same way that *Mighty Morphin Power Rangers* or *Teenage Mutant Ninja Turtles* are. In fact, the UCLA study singled out seven Saturday morning network shows including *Power Rangers* and *Ninja Turtles* for containing "sinister combat violence" or "violence for the sake of violence." The report warned that "the dark overtones and unrelenting combat in these shows constitute a fairly recent trend, which appears to be on the rise."

Of course, Eron's work is the subject of controversy. There are 15 experts who warn against linking culture and violence at all. Jonathan Freedman, a psychology professor at the University of Toronto, says that after thoroughly reviewing all the existing studies on television and violence, he had to conclude that there was no convincing evidence that the media have an influence on real violence. "You always hear that there are 3,000 studies that prove that television contributes to violence," says Freedman, "but that's absolutely false. There are maybe 200 pertinent studies, and almost no one has read the literature. It sounds plausible that television causes violence, and everyone takes the word of the so-called experts. I was amazed at how different the studies were from what was being said about them."

Of those 200 studies, Freedman says, about 160 are lab studies,   16
which he dismisses as "not totally irrelevant but not very meaningful." In typical lab studies, subjects are shown violent films, and then
an attempt is made to measure their response. In one study, increased
aggression was measured by showing children a balloon and asking
if it would be fun to break it. In others, children were given plastic
Bobo dolls that are designed to be hit. Freedman says that most
experimenters get positive results because violent programs are simply more arousing than neutral programs and because children
respond in the way they think the researchers expect them to. "All
that these experiments show is potential effect," says Freedman. "But
what is the real effect? In lab experiments they expose children to one
kind of media, but in the real world no one watches just violence. You
watch lots of different kinds of television. There's lots of different
mediating stimuli."

Freedman finds the field studies equally disappointing. He   17
thinks that Eron and his colleagues are true believers because
they've devoted their careers to and built their reputations on the
damaging effects of television violence. "Most people don't have
the statistical and methodological expertise to read and evaluate the
studies," Freedman explains. "Since [these study] committees all
base their conclusions on the words of these few experts, naturally
. . . they all conclude that television violence is harmful.

"People say that children are more aggressive," Freedman   18
continues. "More aggressive than when? Not more than 1880.
Somalia and Bosnia are worse than here, and Somalia doesn't have
television."

The research on video games and rap music is even more   19
inconclusive. A 1993 study of 357 seventh- and eighth-graders, for
instance, found that 32 percent said fantasy violence was their
favorite game category, while 17 percent chose human violence. But
the study is small and doesn't draw conclusions between the games
and aggression. As for rap, Peter Christiansen, a professor of communication at Lewis and Clark College, in Portland, Ore., says,
"Seventy-six percent of rap is purchased by middleclass kids. For
them, rap is a kind of cultural tourism. . . . They aren't turned on by
the explicit lyrics."

Poverty, the easy accessibility of guns, domestic abuse, social   20
instability and the like may all contribute more than the media do to
the level of violence. Even researchers like Signorielli warn against
drawing cause-and-effect conclusions. "You can't just blame TV for

the problems of society," she says. "Television contributes to children's aggressiveness, but it's only one of the factors."

Unfortunately, the political debate tends to ignore the nuances   21
and uncertainties contained in the research. In reaction to the wave of political pressure, Time Warner sold its interest in Interscope, which distributed some of rap's most inflammatory artists, and Time Warner Chairman Gerald Levin agreed to develop standards for the distribution and labeling of potentially objectionable music. Meanwhile, Jack Valenti, the president of the Motion Picture Association of America, has commented that the entertainment industry "must . . . act as if TV is indeed a factor in anti-social behavior," adding that the industry "has to be more responsible." Valenti, however, still questions the link between media and violence. A sociopath could be triggered by reading a Bible verse as easily as by watching a film. As Valenti says, "We can't create movies that are safe for deviants. Anything can set them off. We can't function at their level."

Fortunately, even the most fervent critics, like William Bennett,   22
still shy away from advocating legislative remedies; Bennett declares he hopes to "shame" the industry into taking a more responsible stand. Meanwhile, the Democrats are still pushing for a federal law that will create a ratings system for all programs and require new TVs to have a V chip, which gives parents the power to shut off certain pornographic or violent channels.

With the presidential race heating up, however, the rhetorical   23
battle isn't likely to cool down any time soon. Dole is demanding in his campaign ads that "Hollywood stop corrupting our children." He has said on the Senate floor: "Those who continue to deny that cultural messages can and do bore deep into the hearts and minds of our young people are deceiving themselves and ignoring reality."

Yet if Saturday morning cartoons are more a problem than Hol-   24
lywood blockbusters or rap music, who's ignoring reality?

Meanings and Values

1.   What is the argumentative proposition (thesis) in this essay, and where is it first stated? Is it repeated elsewhere in the essay? If so, where and why?

2.   Summarize briefly the conclusions of the research that Davidson describes in paragraphs 4–11. At what age, according to the research, are children most likely to be affected by television? At what age is a child's moral sense probably already developed? How does

the writer use these facts about child development to support his thesis?

3. What effect on children does the writer identify as a problem? What different possible causes does he identify in the course of the essay? Which possible causes does he reject? Which does he think is the likely cause? How does he suggest that we deal with the problem?

Argumentative Techniques

1. Why does the writer open the essay by citing people whose views he disagrees with? Does he do so for any purposes other than to refute their conclusions? If so, what are his other purposes? (See "Guide to Terms": *Refutation.*)

2. The writer makes considerable use of other people's research to introduce, develop, and support his argument. Where in the essay does he do so? Be specific. In what ways does this strategy add to, or detract from the persuasiveness of the essay?

3. This essay relies heavily on the research and conclusions of Leonard Eron. Where in the essay does the writer deal with possible objections to Eron's work? What are the possible weaknesses or qualifications in Eron's work that the writer identifies? Does he attempt to refute possible objections or qualify his own conclusions based on the limitations of Eron's research? (Guide: *Qualification.*) If so, does he do this effectively? Why or why not? If not, does this undermine the persuasiveness of the essay? Explain.

Diction and Vocabulary

1. Much of the diction in this essay is formal and scholarly. Identify examples of such diction in paragraphs 10–14, and explain how it adds to or detracts from the persuasiveness of the essay. (Guide: *Diction.*) Is the diction likely to limit the readership for this essay? In what ways?

2. Which paragraphs in the essay make use of numbers and statistics? What do these forms of language add to the essay? Does the author use them in ways that might make the paragraphs hard to read? Explain.

3. If you do not know the meaning of some of the following terms, look them up in a dictionary: inhibition (par. 3); syndrome (6); explicitness, impunity, deterrent (8); correlation (10); subsequent, emulate (12); nuances, sociopath, deviants (21).

Read to Write

1. The effects of television viewing on adults, as well as children, continue to be an area of considerable controversy. Freewrite on your television viewing habits as a child or now, and explore the possible effects. Then look up what psychologists and others have said about the possible effects. Finally, make a list of possible issues you might address in an essay of your own.

2. Follow Davidson's example and use research studies to support your argumentative thesis about an issue of current concern.

3. Television and films are not the only things that people point to as the causes of aggression or other negative effects in our lives. Choose some other thing that people often identify as a problem (air pollution, overcrowding, poor schooling, or the like) and construct an essay arguing for your view of its causes and effects. Use Davidson's strategies in "Menace to Society" as a model.

(NOTE: Suggestions for topics requiring development by ARGUMENT are on page 573 at the end of this section.)

COMPLEX ARGUMENT

MARTIN LUTHER KING, JR.

MARTIN LUTHER KING, JR. (1929–1968), was a Baptist minister, the president of the Southern Christian Leadership Conference, and a respected leader in the nationwide movement for equal rights for blacks. He was born in Atlanta, Georgia, and earned degrees from Morehouse College (A.B., 1948), Crozer Theological Seminary (B.D., 1951), Boston University (Ph.D., 1955), and Chicago Theological Seminary (D.D., 1957). He held honorary degrees from numerous other colleges and universities and was awarded the Nobel Peace Prize in 1964. Some of his books are *Stride Toward Freedom* (1958), *Strength to Love* (1963), and *Why We Can't Wait* (1964). King was assassinated April 4, 1968, in Memphis, Tennessee.

Letter from Birmingham Jail[1]

This letter, written to King's colleagues in the ministry, is a reasoned explanation for his actions during the civil rights protests in Birmingham. It is a good example of both persuasion and logical argument. Here the two are completely compatible, balancing each other in rather intricate but convincing and effective patterns.

My Dear Fellow Clergymen.

While confined here in the Birmingham city jail, I came across 1
your recent statement calling my present activities "unwise and

[1]This response to a published statement by eight fellow clergymen from Alabama (Bishop C. C. J. Carpenter, Bishop Joseph A. Durick, Rabbi Hilton L. Grafman, Bishop Paul Hardin, Bishop Holan B. Harmon, the Reverend George M. Murray, the Reverend Edward V. Ramage, and the Reverend Earl Stallings) was composed under somewhat constricting circumstances. Begun on the margins of the newspaper in which the statement appeared while I was in jail, the letter was continued on scraps of writing paper supplied by a friendly Negro trusty, and concluded on a pad my attorneys were eventually permitted to leave me. Although the text remains in substance unaltered, I have indulged in the author's prerogative of polishing it for publication.—King's note.

untimely." Seldom do I pause to answer criticism of my work and ideas. If I sought to answer all the criticisms that cross my desk, my secretaries would have little time for anything other than such correspondence in the course of the day, and I would have no time for constructive work. But since I feel that you are men of genuine good will and that your criticisms are sincerely set forth, I want to try to answer your statement in what I hope will be patient and reasonable terms.

I think I should indicate why I am here in Birmingham, since you   2
have been influenced by the view which argues against "outsiders coming in." I have the honor of serving as president of the Southern Christian Leadership Conference, an organization operating in every southern state, with headquarters in Atlanta, Georgia. We have some eighty-five affiliated organizations across the South, and one of them is the Alabama Christian Movement for Human Rights. Frequently we share staff, educational, and financial resources with our affiliates. Several months ago the affiliate here in Birmingham asked us to be on call to engage in a nonviolent direct-action program if such were deemed necessary. We readily consented, and when the hour came, we lived up to our promise. So I, along with several members of my staff, am here because I was invited here. I am here because I have organizational ties here.

But more basically, I am in Birmingham because injustice is   3
here. Just as the prophets of the eighth century B.C. left their villages and carried their "thus saith the Lord" far beyond the boundaries of their home towns, and just as the Apostle Paul left his village of Tarsus and carried the gospel of Jesus Christ to the far corners of the Greco-Roman world, so am I compelled to carry the gospel of freedom beyond my own home town. Like Paul, I must constantly respond to the Macedonian call for aid.

Moreover, I am cognizant of the interrelatedness of all commu-   4
nities and states. I cannot sit idly by in Atlanta and not be concerned about what happens in Birmingham. Injustice anywhere is a threat to justice everywhere. We are caught in an inescapable network of mutuality, tied in a single garment of destiny. Whatever affects one directly, affects all indirectly. Never again can we afford to live with the narrow, provincial "outside agitator" idea. Anyone who lives inside the United States can never be considered an outsider within its bounds.

You deplore the demonstrations taking place in Birmingham.   5
But your statement, I am sorry to say, fails to express a similar concern for the conditions that brought about the demonstrations. I am

sure that none of you would want to rest content with the superficial kind of social analysis that deals merely with effects and does not grapple with underlying causes. It is unfortunate that demonstrations are taking place in Birmingham, but it is even more unfortunate that the city's white power structure left the Negro community with no alternative.

In any nonviolent campaign there are four basic steps: collection   6
of the facts to determine whether injustices exist; negotiation; self-purification; and direct action. We have gone through all these steps in Birmingham. There can be no gainsaying the fact that racial injustice engulfs this community. Birmingham is probably the most thoroughly segregated city in the United States. Its ugly record of brutality is widely known. Negroes have experienced grossly unjust treatment in the courts. There have been more unsolved bombings of Negro homes and churches in Birmingham than in any other city in the nation. These are the hard, brutal facts of the case. On the basis of these conditions, Negro leaders sought to negotiate with the city fathers. But the latter consistently refused to engage in good-faith negotiation.

Then, last September, came the opportunity to talk with leaders   7
of Birmingham's economic community. In the course of the negotiations, certain promises were made by the merchants—for example, to remove the stores' humiliating racial signs. On the basis of these promises, the Reverend Fred Shuttlesworth and the leaders of the Alabama Christian Movement for Human Rights agreed to a moratorium on all demonstrations. As the weeks and months went by, we realized that we were the victims of a broken promise. A few signs, briefly removed, returned; the others remained.

As in so many past experiences, our hopes had been blasted,   8
and the shadow of deep disappointment settled upon us. We had no alternative except to prepare for direct action, whereby we would present our very bodies as a means of laying our case before the conscience of the local and the national community. Mindful of the difficulties involved, we decided to undertake a process of self-purification. We began a series of workshops on nonviolence, and we repeatedly asked ourselves: "Are you able to accept blows without retaliating?" "Are you able to endure the ordeal of jail?" We decided to schedule our direct-action program for the Easter season, realizing that except for Christmas, this is the main shopping period of the year. Knowing that a strong economic-withdrawal program would be the by-product of direct action, we felt that this would be

the best time to bring pressure to bear on the merchants for the needed change.

Then it occurred to us that Birmingham's mayoral election was   9
coming up in March, and we speedily decided to postpone action until after election day. When we discovered that the Commissioner of Public Safety, Eugene "Bull" Connor, had piled up enough votes to be in the run-off, we decided again to postpone action until the day after the run-off so that the demonstrations could not be used to cloud the issues. Like many others, we waited to see Mr. Connor defeated, and to this end we endured postponement after postponement. Having aided in this community need, we felt that our direct-action program could be delayed no longer.

You may well ask, "Why direct action? Why sit-ins, marches,   10
and so forth? Isn't negotiation a better path?" You are quite right in calling for negotiation. Indeed, this is the very purpose of direct action. Nonviolent direct action seeks to create such a crisis and foster such a tension that a community which has constantly refused to negotiate is forced to confront the issue. It seeks so to dramatize the issue that it can no longer be ignored. My citing the creation of tension as part of the work of the nonviolent-resister may sound rather shocking. But I must confess that I am not afraid of the word "tension." I have earnestly opposed violent tension, but there is a type of constructive, nonviolent tension which is necessary for growth. Just as Socrates felt that it was necessary to create a tension in the mind so that individuals could rise from the bondage of myths and half-truths to the unfettered realm of creative analysis and objective appraisal, so must we see the need for nonviolent gadflies to create the kind of tension in society that will help men rise from the dark depths of prejudice and racism to the majestic heights of understanding and brotherhood.

The purpose of our direct-action program is to create a situation   11
so crisis-packed that it will inevitably open the door to negotiation. I therefore concur with you in your call for negotiation. Too long has our beloved Southland been bogged down in a tragic effort to live in monologue rather than dialogue.

One of the basic points in your statement is that the action that I   12
and my associates have taken in Birmingham is untimely. Some have asked: "Why didn't you give the new city administration time to act?" The only answer that I can give to this query is that the new Birmingham administration must be prodded about as much as the outgoing one, before it will act. We are sadly mistaken if we feel that

the election of Albert Boutwell as mayor will bring the millennium to Birmingham. While Mr. Boutwell is a much more gentle person than Mr. Connor, they are both segregationists, dedicated to maintenance of the status quo. I have hoped that Mr. Boutwell will be reasonable enough to see the futility of massive resistance to desegregation. But he will not see this without pressure from devotees of civil rights. My friends, I must say to you that we have not made a single gain in civil rights without determined legal and nonviolent pressure. Lamentably, it is an historical fact that privileged groups seldom give up their privileges voluntarily. Individuals may see the moral light and voluntarily give up their unjust posture; but, as Reinhold Niebuhr has reminded us, groups tend to be more immoral than individuals.

We know through painful experience that freedom is never voluntarily given by the oppressor; it must be demanded by the oppressed. Frankly, I have yet to engage in a direct-action campaign that was "well timed" in the view of those who have not suffered unduly from the disease of segregation. For years now I have heard the word "Wait!" It rings in the ear of every Negro with piercing familiarity. This "Wait" has almost always meant "Never." We must come to see, with one of our distinguished jurists, that "justice too long delayed is justice denied."   13

We have waited for more than 340 years for our constitutional and God-given rights. The nations of Asia and Africa are moving with jetlike speed toward gaining political independence, but we still creep at horse-and-buggy pace toward gaining a cup of coffee at a lunch counter. Perhaps it is easy for those who have never felt the stinging darts of segregation to say, "Wait." But when you have seen vicious mobs lynch your mothers and fathers at will and drown your sisters and brothers at whim; when you have seen hate-filled policemen curse, kick, and even kill your black brothers and sisters; when you see the vast majority of your twenty million Negro brothers smothering in an airtight cage of poverty in the midst of an affluent society; when you suddenly find your tongue twisted and your speech stammering as you seek to explain to your six-year-old daughter why she can't go to the public amusement park that has just been advertised on television, and see tears welling up in her eyes when she is told that Funtown is closed to colored children, and see ominous clouds of inferiority beginning to form in her little mental sky, and see her beginning to distort her personality by developing an unconscious bitterness toward white people; when you have to concoct an answer for a five-year-old son who is asking, "Daddy,   14 why do white people treat colored people so mean?"; when you take a cross-country drive and find it necessary to sleep night after night in the uncomfortable corners of your automobile because no motel will accept you; when you are humiliated day in and day out by nagging signs reading "white" and "colored"; when your first name becomes "nigger," your middle name becomes "boy" (however old you are) and your last name becomes "John," and your wife and mother are never given the respected title "Mrs."; when you are harried by day and haunted by night by the fact that you are a Negro, living constantly at tiptoe stance, never quite knowing what to expect next, and are plagued with inner fears and outer resentments; when you are forever fighting a degenerating sense of "nobodiness"—then you will understand why we find it difficult to wait. There comes a time when the cup of endurance runs over, and men are no longer willing to be plunged into the abyss of despair. I hope, sirs, you can understand our legitimate and unavoidable impatience.

You express a great deal of anxiety over our willingness to   15
break laws. This is certainly a legitimate concern. Since we so diligently urge people to obey the Supreme Court's decision of 1954 outlawing segregation in the public schools, at first glance it may seem rather paradoxical for us consciously to break laws. One may well ask: "How can you advocate breaking some laws and obeying others?" The answer lies in the fact that there are two types of laws: just and unjust. I would be the first to advocate obeying just laws. One has not only a legal but a moral responsibility to obey just laws. Conversely, one has a moral responsibility to disobey unjust laws. I would agree with St. Augustine that "an unjust law is no law at all."

Now, what is the difference between the two? How does one   16
determine whether a law is just or unjust? A just law is a man-made code that squares with the moral law or the law of God. An unjust law is a code that is out of harmony with the moral law. To put it in the terms of St. Thomas Aquinas: An unjust law is a human law that is not rooted in eternal law and natural law. Any law that uplifts human personality is just. Any law that degrades human personality is unjust. All segregation statutes are unjust because segregation distorts the soul and damages the personality. It gives the segregator a false sense of superiority and the segregated a false sense of inferiority. Segregation, to use the terminology of the Jewish philosopher Martin Buber, substitutes an "I-it" relationship for an "I-thou" relationship and ends up relegating persons to the status of things.

Hence segregation is not only politically, economically, and socio-logically unsound, it is morally wrong and sinful. Paul Tillich has said that sin is separation. Is not segregation an existential expression of man's tragic separation, his awful estrangement, his terrible sinfulness? Thus it is that I can urge men to obey the 1954 decision of the Supreme Court, for it is morally right; and I can urge them to disobey segregation ordinances, for they are morally wrong.

Let us consider a more concrete example of just and unjust laws.   17
An unjust law is a code that a numerical or power majority group compels a minority group to obey but does not make binding on itself. This is *difference* made legal. By the same token, a just law is a code that a majority compels a minority to follow and that it is willing to follow itself. This is *sameness* made legal.

Let me give another explanation. A law is unjust if it is inflicted   18
on a minority that, as a result of being denied the right to vote, had no part in enacting or devising the law. Who can say that the legislature of Alabama which set up that state's segregation laws was democratically elected? Throughout Alabama all sorts of devious methods are used to prevent Negroes from becoming registered voters, and there are some counties in which, even though Negroes constitute a majority of the population, not a single Negro is registered. Can any law enacted under such circumstances be considered democratically structured?

Sometimes a law is just on its face and unjust in its application.   19
For instance, I have been arrested on a charge of parading without a permit. Now, there is nothing wrong in having an ordinance which requires a permit for a parade. But such an ordinance becomes unjust when it is used to maintain segregation and to deny citizens the First Amendment privilege of peaceful assembly and protest.

I hope you are able to see the distinction I am trying to point   20
out. In no sense do I advocate evading or defying the law, as would the rabid segregationist. That would lead to anarchy. One who breaks an unjust law must do so openly, lovingly, and with a willingness to accept the penalty. I submit that an individual who breaks a law that conscience tells him is unjust, and who willingly accepts the penalty of imprisonment in order to arouse the conscience of the community over its injustice, is in reality expressing the highest respect for the law.

Of course, there is nothing new about this kind of civil disobe-   21
dience. It was evidenced sublimely in the refusal of Shadrach, Meshach, and Abednego to obey the laws of Nebuchadnezzar, on

the ground that a higher moral law was at stake. It was practiced superbly by the early Christians, who were willing to face hungry lions and the excruciating pain of chopping blocks rather than submit to certain unjust laws of the Roman Empire. To a degree, academic freedom is a reality today because Socrates practiced civil disobedience. In our own nation, the Boston Tea Party represented a massive act of civil disobedience.

We should never forget that everything Adolf Hitler did in   22
Germany was "legal" and everything the Hungarian freedom fighters did in Hungary was "illegal." It was "illegal" to aid and comfort a Jew in Hitler's Germany. Even so, I am sure that, had I lived in Germany at the time, I would have aided and comforted my Jewish brothers. If today I lived in a Communist country where certain principles dear to the Christian faith are suppressed, I would openly advocate disobeying that country's anti-religious laws.

I must make two honest confessions to you, my Christian and   23
Jewish brothers. First, I must confess that over the past few years I have been gravely disappointed with the white moderate. I have almost reached the regrettable conclusion that the Negro's great stumbling block in his stride toward freedom is not the White Citizen's Counciler or the Ku Klux Klanner, but the white moderate, who is more devoted to "order" than to justice; who prefers a negative peace which is the absence of tension to a positive peace which is the presence of justice; who constantly says, "I agree with you in the goal you seek, but I cannot agree with your methods of direct action"; who paternalistically believes he can set the timetable for another man's freedom; who lives by a mythical concept of time and who constantly advises the Negro to wait for a "more convenient season." Shallow understanding from people of good will is more frustrating than absolute misunderstanding from people of ill will. Lukewarm acceptance is much more bewildering than outright rejection.

I had hoped that the white moderate would understand that   24
law and order exist for the purpose of establishing justice and that when they fail in this purpose they become the dangerously structured dams that block the flow of social progress. I had hoped that the white moderate would understand that the present tension in the South is a necessary phase of the transition from an obnoxious negative peace, in which the Negro passively accepted his unjust plight, to a substantive and positive peace, in which all men will respect the dignity and worth of human personality. Actually, we

who engage in nonviolent direct action are not the creators of tension. We merely bring to the surface the hidden tension that is already alive. We bring it out in the open, where it can be seen and dealt with. Like a boil that can never be cured so long as it is covered up but must be opened with all its ugliness to the natural medicines of air and light, injustice must be exposed, with all the tension its exposure creates, to the light of human conscience and the air of national opinion, before it can be cured.

In your statement you assert that our actions, even though   25
peaceful, must be condemned because they precipitate violence. But is this a logical assertion? Isn't this like condemning a robbed man because his possession of money precipitated the evil act of robbery? Isn't this like condemning Socrates because his unswerving commitment to truth and his philosophical inquiries precipitated the act by the misguided populace in which they made him drink hemlock? Isn't this like condemning Jesus because his unique God-consciousness and never-ceasing devotion to God's will precipitated the evil act of crucifixion? We must come to see that, as the federal courts have consistently affirmed, it is wrong to urge an individual to cease his efforts to gain his basic constitutional rights because the quest may precipitate violence. Society must protect the robbed and punish the robber.

I had also hoped that the white moderate would reject the myth   26
concerning time in relation to the struggle for freedom. I have just received a letter from a white brother in Texas. He writes: "All Christians know that the colored people will receive equal rights eventually, but it is possible that you are in too great a religious hurry. It has taken Christianity almost two thousand years to accomplish what it has. The teachings of Christ take time to come to earth." Such an attitude stems from a tragic misconception of time, from the strangely irrational notion that there is something in the very flow of time that will inevitably cure all ills. Actually, time itself is neutral; it can be used either destructively or constructively. More and more I feel that the people of ill will have used time much more effectively that have the people of good will. We will have to repent in this generation not merely for the hateful words and actions of the bad people, but for the appalling silence of the good people. Human progress never rolls in on wheels of inevitability; it comes through the tireless efforts of men willing to be co-workers with God, and without this hard work, time itself becomes an ally of the forces of social stagnation. We must use time creatively, in the knowledge

that the time is always ripe to do right. Now is the time to make real the promise of democracy and transform our pending national elegy into a creative psalm of brotherhood. Now is the time to lift our national policy from the quicksand of racial injustice to the solid rock of human dignity.

You speak of our activity in Birmingham as extreme. At first I   27
was rather disappointed that fellow clergymen would see my non-violent efforts as those of an extremist. I began thinking about the fact that I stand in the middle of two opposing forces in the Negro community. One is a force of complacency, made up in part of Negroes who, as a result of long years of oppression, are so drained of self-respect and a sense of "somebodiness" that they have adjusted to segregation; and in part of a few middle-class Negroes who, because of a degree of academic and economic security and because in some ways they profit by segregation, have become insensitive to the problems of the masses. The other force is one of bitterness and hatred, and it comes perilously close to advocating violence. It is expressed in the various black nationalist groups that are springing up across the nation, the largest and best-known being Elijah Muhammad's Muslim movement. Nourished by the Negro's frustration over the continued existence of racial discrimination, this movement is made up of people who have lost faith in America, who have absolutely repudiated Christianity, and who have concluded that the white man is an incorrigible "devil."

I have tried to stand between these two forces, saying that we   28
need emulate neither the "do-nothingism" of the complacent nor the hatred and despair of the black nationalist. For there is the more excellent way of love and nonviolent protest. I am grateful to God that, through the influence of the Negro church, the way of nonviolence became an integral part of our struggle.

If this philosophy had not emerged, by now many streets of the   29
South would, I am convinced, be flowing with blood. And I am further convinced that if our white brothers dismiss as "rabble-rousers" and "outside agitators" those of us who employ nonviolent direct action, and if they refuse to support our nonviolent efforts, millions of Negroes will, out of frustration and despair, seek solace and security in black-nationalist ideologies—a development that would inevitably lead to a frightening racial nightmare.

Oppressed people cannot remain oppressed forever. The yearn-   30
ing for freedom eventually manifests itself, and that is what has happened to the American Negro. Something within has reminded him of his birthright of freedom, and something without has reminded

him that it can be gained. Consciously or unconsciously, he has been caught up by the *Zeitgeist*, and with his black brothers of Africa and his brown and yellow brothers of Asia, South America, and the Caribbean, the United States Negro is moving with a sense of great urgency toward the promised land of racial justice. If one recognizes this vital urge that has engulfed the Negro community, one should readily understand why public demonstrations are taking place. The Negro has many pent-up resentments and latent frustrations, and he must release them. So let him march; let him make prayer pilgrimages to the city hall; let him go on freedom rides—and try to understand why he must do so. If his repressed emotions are not released in non-violent ways, they will seek expression through violence; this is not a threat but a fact of history. So I have not said to my people, "Get rid of your discontent." Rather, I have tried to say that this normal and healthy discontent can be channeled into the creative outlet of nonviolent direct action. And now this approach is being termed extremist.

But though I was initially disappointed at being categorized as   31
an extremist, as I continued to think about the matter I gradually gained a measure of satisfaction from the label. Was not Jesus an extremist for love: "Love your enemies, bless them that curse you, do good to them that hate you, and pray for them which despitefully use you, and persecute you." Was not Amos an extremist for justice: "Let justice roll down like waters and righteousness like an everflowing stream." Was not Paul an extremist for the Christian gospel: "I bear in my body the marks of the Lord Jesus." Was not Martin Luther an extremist: "Here I stand; I cannot do otherwise, so help me God." And John Bunyan: "I will stay in jail to the end of my days before I make a butchery of my conscience." And Abraham Lincoln: "This nation cannot survive half slave and half free." And Thomas Jefferson: "We hold these truths to be self-evident, that all men are created equal. . ." So the question is not whether we will be extremists, but what kind of extremists we will be. Will we be extremists for hate or for love? Will we be extremists for the preservation of injustice or for the extension of justice? In that dramatic scene on Calvary's hill three men were crucified. We must never forget that all three were crucified for the same crime—the crime of extremism. Two were extremists for immorality, and thus fell below their environment. The other, Jesus Christ, was an extremist for love, truth, and goodness, and thereby rose above his environment. Perhaps the South, the nation, and the world are in dire need of creative extremists.

I had hoped that the white moderate would see this need. Per-   32
haps I was too optimistic; perhaps I expected too much. I suppose I

should have realized that few members of the oppressor race can understand the deep groans and passionate yearnings of the oppressed race, and still fewer have the vision to see that injustice must be rooted out by strong, persistent, and determined action. I am thankful, however, that some of our white brothers in the South have grasped the meaning of this social revolution and committed themselves to it. They are still all too few in quantity, but they are big in quality. Some—such as Ralph McGill, Lillian Smith, Harry Golden, James McBride Dabbs, Anne Braden, and Sarah Patton Boyle—have written about our struggle in eloquent and prophetic terms. Others have marched with us down nameless streets of the South. They have languished in filthy, roach-infested jails, suffering the abuse and brutality of policemen who view them as "dirty nigger-lovers." Unlike so many of their moderate brothers and sisters, they have recognized the urgency of the moment and sensed the need for powerful "action" antidotes to combat the disease of segregation.

Let me take note of my other major disappointment. I have been   33
so greatly disappointed with the white church and its leadership. Of course, there are some notable exceptions. I am not unmindful of the fact that each of you has taken some significant stands on this issue. I commend you, Reverend Stallings, for your Christian stand on this past Sunday, in welcoming Negroes to your worship service on a nonsegregated basis. I commend the Catholic leaders of this state for integrating Spring Hill College several years ago.

But despite these notable exceptions, I must honestly reiterate   34
that I have been disappointed with the church. I do not say this as one of those negative critics who can always find something wrong with the church. I say this as a minister of the gospel, who loves the church; who has nurtured in its bosom; who has been sustained by its spiritual blessings and who will remain true to it as long as the cord of life shall lengthen.

When I was suddenly catapulted into the leadership of the bus   35
protest in Montgomery, Alabama, a few years ago, I felt we would be supported by the white church. I felt that the white ministers, priests, and rabbis of the South would be among our strongest allies. Instead, some have been outright opponents, refusing to understand the freedom movement and misrepresenting its leaders; all too many others have been more cautious than courageous and have remained silent behind the anesthetizing security of stained glass windows.

In spite of my shattered dreams, I came to Birmingham with the   36
hope that the white religious leadership of this community would
see the justice of our cause and, with deep moral concern, would
serve as the channel through which our just grievances could reach
the power structure. I had hoped that each of you would understand. But again I have been disappointed.

I have heard numerous southern religious leaders admonish   37
their worshipers to comply with a desegregation decision because it
is the law, but I have longed to hear white ministers declare: "Follow
this decree because integration is morally right and because the
Negro is your brother." In the midst of blatant injustices inflicted
upon the Negro, I have watched white churchmen stand on the side
line and mouth pious relevancies and sanctimonious trivialities. In
the midst of a mighty struggle to rid our nation of racial and economic injustice I have heard many ministers say: "Those are social
issues, with which the gospel has no real concern." And I have
watched many churches commit themselves to a completely other-
worldly religion which makes a strange, un-Biblical distinction
between body and soul, between the sacred and the secular.

I have traveled the length and breadth of Alabama, Mississippi,   38
and all the other southern states. On sweltering summer days and
crisp autumn mornings I have looked at the South's beautiful
churches with their lofty spires pointing heavenward. I have beheld
the impressive outlines of her massive religious-education buildings. Over and over I have found myself asking: "What kind of people worship here? Who is their God? Where were their voices when
the lips of Governor Barnett dripped with words of interposition
and nullification? Where were they when Governor Wallace gave a
clarion call for defiance and hatred? Where were their voices of support when bruised and weary Negro men and women decided to
rise from the dark dungeons of complacency to the bright hills of
creative protest?"

Yes, these questions are still in my mind. In deep disappoint-   39
ment I have wept over the laxity of the church. But be assured that
my tears have been tears of love. There can be no deep disappointment where there is not deep love. Yes, I love the church. How could
I do otherwise? I am in the rather unique position of being the son,
the grandson, and the great-grandson of preachers. Yes, I see the
church as the body of Christ. But, oh! How we have blemished and
scarred that body through social neglect and through fear of being
nonconformists.

There was a time when the church was very powerful—in the   40
time when the early Christians rejoiced at being deemed worthy to
suffer for what they believed. In those days the church was not merely
a thermometer that recorded the ideas and principles of popular
opinion; it was a thermostat that transformed the mores of society.
Whenever the early Christians entered a town, the people in power
became disturbed and immediately sought to convict the Christians
for being "disturbers of the peace" and "outside agitators." But the
Christians pressed on, in the conviction that they were "a colony of
heaven," called to obey God rather than man. Small in number, they
were big in commitment. They were too God-intoxicated to be "astro-
nomically intimidated." By their effort and example they brought an
end to such ancient evils as infanticide and gladiatorial contests.

Things are different now. So often the contemporary church is a   41
weak, ineffectual voice with an uncertain sound. So often it is an
archdefender of the status quo. Far from being disturbed by the presence of the church, the power structure of the average community is
consoled by the church's silent—and often even vocal—sanction of
things as they are.

But the judgment of God is upon the church as never before. If   42
today's church does not recapture the sacrificial spirit of the early
church, it will lose its authenticity, forfeit the loyalty of millions, and
be dismissed as an irrelevant social club with no meaning for the
twentieth century. Every day I meet young people whose disappointment with the church has turned into outright disgust.

Perhaps I have once again been too optimistic. Is organized reli-   43
gion too inextricably bound to the status quo to save our nation and
the world? Perhaps I must turn my faith to the inner spiritual
church, the church within the church, as the true *ekklesia*[2] and the
hope of the world. But again I am thankful to God that some noble
souls from the ranks of organized religion have broken loose from
the paralyzing chains of conformity and joined us as active partners
in the struggle for freedom. They have left their secure congrega-
tions and walked the streets of Albany, Georgia, with us. They have
gone down the highways of the South on tortuous rides for freedom.
Yes, they have gone to jail with us. Some have been dismissed from
their churches, have lost the support of their bishops and fellow
ministers. But they have acted in the faith that right defeated is
stronger than evil triumphant. Their witness has been the spiritual

[2]The Greek New Testament word for the early Christian church. (Editors' note.)

salt that has preserved the true meaning of the gospel in these troubled times. They have carved a tunnel of hope through the dark mountain of disappointment.

I hope the church as a whole will meet the challenge of this decisive hour. But even if the church does not come to the aid of justice, I have no despair about the future. I have no fear about the outcome of our struggle in Birmingham, even if our motives are at present misunderstood. We will reach the goal of freedom in Birmingham and all over the nation, because the goal of America is freedom. Abused and scorned though we may be, our destiny is tied up with America's destiny. Before the pilgrims landed at Plymouth, we were here. Before the pen of Jefferson etched the majestic words of the Declaration of Independence across the pages of history, we were here. For more than two centuries, our forebears labored in this country without wages; they made cotton king; they built the homes of their masters while suffering gross injustice and shameful humiliation—and yet out of a bottomless vitality they continued to thrive and develop. If the inexpressible cruelties of slavery could not stop us, the opposition we now face will surely fail. We will win our freedom because the sacred heritage of our nation and the eternal will of God are embodied in our echoing demands. 44

Before closing I feel impelled to mention one other point in your statement that has troubled me profoundly. You warmly commended the Birmingham police force for keeping "order" and "preventing violence." I doubt that you would have so warmly commended the police force if you had seen its dogs sinking their teeth into unarmed, nonviolent Negroes. I doubt that you would so quickly commend the policemen if you were to observe their ugly and inhumane treatment of Negroes here in the city jail; if you were to watch them push and curse old Negro women and young Negro girls; if you were to see them slap and kick old Negro men and young boys; if you were to observe them, as they did on two occasions, refuse to give us food because we wanted to sing our grace together. I cannot join you in your praise of the Birmingham police department. 45

It is true that the police have exercised a degree of discipline in handling the demonstrators. In this sense they have conducted themselves rather "nonviolently" in public. But for what purpose? To preserve the evil system of segregation. Over the past few years I have consistently preached that nonviolence demands that the means we use must be as pure as the ends we seek. I have tried to 46 make clear that it is wrong to use immoral means to attain moral ends. But now I must affirm that it is just as wrong, or perhaps even more so, to use moral means to preserve immoral ends. Perhaps Mr. Connor and his policemen have been rather nonviolent in public, as was Chief Pritchett in Albany, Georgia, but they have used the moral means of nonviolence to maintain the immoral end of racial injustice. As T.S. Eliot has said, "The last temptation is the greatest treason: To do the right deed for the wrong reason."

I wish you had commended the Negro sit-inners and demon-   47
strators of Birmingham for their sublime courage, their willingness to suffer, and their amazing discipline in the midst of great provocation. One day the South will recognize its real heroes. They will be the James Merediths, with the noble sense of purpose that enables them to face jeering and hostile mobs, and with the agonizing loneliness that characterizes the life of the pioneer. They will be old, oppressed, battered Negro women, symbolized in a seventy-two-year-old woman in Montgomery, Alabama, who rose up with a sense of dignity and with her people decided not to ride segregated buses, and who responded with ungrammatical profundity to one who inquired about her weariness: "My feets is tired, but my soul is at rest." They will be the young high school and college students, the young ministers of the gospel and a host of their elders, courageously and nonviolently sitting in at lunch counters and willingly going to jail for conscience' sake. One day the South will know that when these disinherited children of God sat down at lunch counters, they were in reality standing up for what is best in the American dream and for the most sacred values in our Judaeo-Christian heritage, thereby bringing our nation back to those great wells of democracy which were dug deep by the founding fathers in their formulation of the Constitution and the Declaration of Independence.

Never before have I written so long a letter. I'm afraid it is much   48
too long to take your precious time. I can assure you that it would have been much shorter if I had been writing from a comfortable desk, but what else can one do when he is alone in a narrow jail cell, other than write long letters, think long thoughts, and pray long prayers?

If I have said anything in this letter that overstates the truth and   49
indicates an unreasonable impatience, I beg you to forgive me. If I have said anything that understates the truth and indicates my having a patience that allows me to settle for anything less than brotherhood, I beg God to forgive me.

I hope this letter finds you strong in the faith. I also hope that 50 circumstances will soon make it possible for me to meet each of you, not as an integrationist or a civil-rights leader but as a fellow clergyman and a Christian brother. Let us all hope that the dark clouds of racial prejudice will soon pass away and the deep fog of misunderstanding will be lifted from our fear-drenched communities, and in some not too distant tomorrow the radiant stars of love and brotherhood will shine over our great nation with all their scintillating beauty.

Yours for the cause of Peace and Brotherhood,
MARTIN LUTHER KING, JR.

Meanings and Values

1. Does King's purpose in this essay go beyond responding to the criticism of the white clergymen? If so, what is his broader purpose?

2. Reconstruct as many of the arguments in the clergymen's letter as you can by studying King's refutation of their accusations.

3. What arguments are used in the essay to justify the demonstrations?

4. Summarize the distinction King makes between just and unjust laws.

5. What kind of behavior did King expect from the white moderates? Why was he disappointed?

6. How does King defend himself and his followers against the accusation that their actions lead to violence?

7. What is the thesis of this essay?

8. Like many other argumentative essays, this was written in response to a specific situation; yet it is widely regarded as a classic essay. What qualities give the essay its broad and lasting appeal?

Argumentative Techniques

1. How does King establish his reasonableness and fairness so that his audience will take the arguments in the essay seriously even if they are inclined at the start to reject his point of view?

2. Identify as many of the expository patterns as you can in this essay and explain what each contributes to the argument. (See "Guide to Terms": *Unity*.)

3. What standard techniques of refutation are used in this essay to deal with the accusations made by the clergymen? (Guide: *Refutation*.) Are any other strategies of refutation used in the essay?

4. State the argument in paragraph 6 as a syllogism. (See the introduction to Section 12, "Reasoning by Use of *Induction* and *Deduction*.") Do the same with the argument in paragraphs 15–22.

5. Identify several examples of inductive argument in this essay.

6. At what points in the argument does King use several examples, where one would do, in order to strengthen the argument through variety in evidence?

Diction and Vocabulary

1. Locate an example of each of the following figures of speech in the essay and explain what it contributes to the argument. (Guide: *Figures of Speech.*)

    a. Metaphor.

    b. Allusion.

    c. Simile.

    d. Paradox.

2. Discuss what resources of syntax King uses to construct a 28-line sentence in paragraph 14—without confusing the reader. (Guide: *Syntax.*)

3. Choose a paragraph that displays considerable variety in sentence length and structure and show how King uses variety in sentence style to convey his point. (Guide: *Style/Tone.*)

4. Choose two paragraphs, each with a different tone, and discuss how the diction of the passages differs and how the diction in each case contributes to the tone. (Guide: *Diction.*)

5. In many passages King uses the resources of diction and syntax to add emotional impact to logical argument. Choose such a passage and discuss how it mingles logic and emotion.

Read to Write

1. Use the following questions, and related questions, to probe possible topics for an essay: To what extent does the racism that King was protesting still exist in our society? Has it been replaced by other forms of discrimination?

2. In an essay of your own, discuss the practical consequences of King's distinction between just and unjust laws.

3. Use some of King's arguments to defend a more recent act of protest, or to encourage people to protest a policy you consider unjust. Or, if you wish, draw on his arguments to attack a recent protest on the grounds that it does not meet the high standards he sets.

(NOTE: Suggestions for topics requiring development by use of ARGUMENT follow.)

Writing Suggestions for Section 13
Argument

Choose one of the following topic areas, identify an issue (a conflict or problem) within it, and prepare an essay that tries to convince readers to share your opinion about the issue and to take any appropriate action. Use a variety of evidence in your essay, and choose any pattern of development you consider proper for the topic, for your thesis, and for the intended audience.

1. Gun control.
2. The quality of education in American elementary and secondary schools.
3. Treatment of critically ill newborn babies.
4. Hunting.
5. Euthanasia.
6. Censorship in public schools and libraries.
7. College athletics.
8. The problem of toxic waste or a similar environmental problem.
9. Careers versus family responsibilities.
10. The separation of church and state.
11. Law on the drinking age or on drunk driving.
12. Evolution versus creationism.
13. Medical ethics.
14. Government spending on social programs.
15. The quality of television programming.
16. The impact of divorce.
17. The effects of television viewing on children.
18. Professional sports.
19. Violence in service of an ideal or belief.
20. Scholarship and student loan policies.
21. Low pay for public service and the "helping" professions.
22. Cheating in college courses.
23. Drug and alcohol abuse.
24. Product safety and reliability.
25. Government economic or social policy.

Further Readings

MARGARET ATWOOD was born in Ottawa, Ontario, in 1939. After attending college in Canada, she went to graduate school at Harvard University. She has had a distinguished career as a novelist, poet, and essayist, and is generally considered to be one of the central figures in contemporary Canadian literature and culture. Atwood's international reputation as a writer rests on her novels, including *The Edible Woman* (1960), *Surfacing* (1972), *Life Before Man* (1979), *Bodily Harm* (1982), *The Handmaid's Tale* (1986), *Cat's Eye* (1989); *The Robber Bride* (1993) and her short stories, including *Bluebeard's Egg and Other Stories* (1986), though she has written poetry, television plays, and children's books as well. Her essays were collected in the volume *Second Words* (1982) and have continued to appear in magazines such as *Ms., Harper's, The Humanist, The New Republic,* and *Architectural Digest.* As an essayist, Atwood frequently writes about issues in contemporary culture and society, including the nature of Canadian culture and relationships between Canada and the United States.

Pornography

In the following essay, Atwood addresses the question of pornography with a directness and originality that are characteristic of her work. This essay originally appeared in *Chatelaine Magazine,* a mass-circulation women's magazine. As you read the selection, consider how well it addresses both the concerns of its original audience and the concerns about pornography a somewhat wider audience might have.

When I was in Finland a few years ago for an international writers' conference, I had occasion to say a few paragraphs in public on the subject of pornography. The context was a discussion of political repression, and I was suggesting the possibility of a link between the two. The immediate result was that a male journalist took several large bites out of me. Prudery and pornography are two halves of the 1 same coin, said he, and I was clearly a prude. What could you expect from an Anglo-Canadian? Afterward, a couple of pleasant Scandinavian men asked me what I had been so worked up about. All "pornography" means, they said, is graphic depictions of whores, and what was the harm in that?

Not until then did it strike me that the male journalist and I had 2 two entirely different things in mind. By "pornography," he meant naked bodies and sex. I, on the other hand, had recently been doing the research for my novel *Bodily Harm*, and was still in a state of shock from some of the material I had seen, including the Ontario Board of Film Censors' "outtakes." By "pornography," I meant women getting their nipples snipped off with garden shears, having meat hooks stuck into their vaginas, being disemboweled; little girls being raped; men (yes, there are some men) being smashed to a pulp and forcibly sodomized. The cutting edge of pornography, as far as I could see, was no longer simple old copulation, hanging from the chandelier or otherwise: it was death, messy, explicit and highly sadistic. I explained this to the nice Scandinavian men. "Oh, but that's just the United States," they said. "Everyone knows they're sick." In their country, they said, violent "pornography" of that kind was not permitted on television or in movies; indeed, excessive violence of any kind was not permitted. They had drawn a clear line between erotica, which earlier studies had shown did not incite men to more aggressive and brutal behavior toward women, and violence, which later studies indicated did.

Some time after that I was in Saskatchewan, where, because of 3 the scenes in *Bodily Harm,* I found myself on an open-line radio show answering questions about "pornography." Almost no one who phoned in was in favor of it, but again they weren't talking about the same stuff I was, because they hadn't seen it. Some of them were all set to stamp out bathing suits and negligees, and, if possible, any depictions of the female body whatsoever. God, it was implied, did not approve of female bodies, and sex of any kind, including that practised by bumblebees, should be shoved back into the dark, where it belonged. I had more than a suspicion that *Lady Chatterley's Lover*, Margaret Laurence's *The Diviners*, and indeed most books by most serious modern authors would have ended up as confetti if left in the hands of these callers.

For me, these two experiences illustrate the two poles of the 4 emotionally heated debate that is now thundering around this issue. They also underline the desirability and even the necessity of defining the terms. "Pornography" is now one of those catchalls, like "Marxism" and "feminism," that have become so broad they can mean almost anything, ranging from certain verses in the Bible, ads for skin lotion and sex tests for children to the contents of Penthouse, Naughty '90s postcards and films with titles containing the word *Nazi* that show vicious scenes of torture and killing. It's easy to say that sensible people can tell the difference. Unfortunately, opinions on what constitutes a sensible person vary.

But even sensible people tend to lose their cool when they start   5
talking about this subject. They soon stop talking and start yelling, and the name-calling begins. Those in favor of censorship (which may include groups not noticeably in agreement on other issues, such as some feminists and religious fundamentalists) accuse the others of exploiting women through the use of degrading images, contributing to the corruption of children, and adding to the general climate of violence and threat in which both women and children live in this society; or, though they may not give much of a hoot about actual women and children, they invoke moral standards and God's supposed aversion to "filth," "smut" and deviated *perversion*, which may mean ankles.

The camp in favor of total "freedom of expression" often   6
comes out howling as loud as the Romans would have if told they could no longer have innocent fun watching the lions eat up Christians. It too may include segments of the population who are not natural bedfellows: those who proclaim their God-given right to freedom, including the freedom to tote guns, drive when drunk, drool over chicken porn and get off on videotapes of women being raped and beaten, may be waving the same anticensorship banner as responsible liberals who fear the return of Mrs. Grundy, or gay groups for whom sexual emancipation involves the concept of "sexual theatre." *Whatever turns you on* is a handy motto, as is *A man's home is his castle* (and if it includes a dungeon with beautiful maidens strung up in chains and bleeding from every pore, that's his business).

Meanwhile, theoreticians theorize and speculators speculate. Is   7
today's pornography yet another indication of the hatred of the body, the deep mind-body split, which is supposed to pervade Western Christian society? Is it a backlash against the women's movement by men who are threatened by uppity female behavior in real life, so like to fantasize about women done up like outsize parcels, being turned into hamburger, kneeling at their feet in slave-like

adoration or sucking off guns? Is it a sign of collective impotence, of a generation of men who can't relate to real women at all but have to make do with bits of celluloid and paper? Is the current flood just a result of smart marketing and aggressive promotion by the money men in what has now become a multibillion-dollar industry? If they were selling movies about men getting their testicles stuck full of knitting needles by women with swastikas on their sleeves, would they do as well, or is this penchant somehow peculiarly male? If so, why? Is pornography a power trip rather than a sex one? Some say that those ropes, chains, muzzles and other restraining devices are an argument for the immense power female sexuality still wields in the male imagination: you don't put these things on dogs unless you're afraid of them. Others, more literary, wonder about the shift from the 19th-century Magic Woman or Femme Fatale image to the lollipop-licker, airhead or turkey-carcass treatment of women in porn today. The proporners don't care much about theory; they merely demand product. The antiporners don't care about it in the final analysis either; there's dirt on the street, and they want it cleaned up, now.

It seems to me that this conversation, with its *You're-a-prude/* 8 *You're-a-pervert* dialectic, will never get anywhere as long as we continue to think of this material as just "entertainment." Possibly we're deluded by the packaging, the format: magazine, book, movie, theatrical presentation. We're used to thinking of these things as part of the "entertainment industry," and we're used to thinking of ourselves as free adult people who ought to be able to see any kind of "entertainment" we want to. That was what the First Choice pay-TV debate was all about. After all, it's only entertainment, right? Entertainment means fun, and only a killjoy would be antifun. What's the harm?

This is obviously the central question: *What's the harm?* If there 9 isn't any real harm to any real people, then the antiporners can tsk-tsk and/or throw up as much as they like, but they can't rightfully expect more legal controls or sanctions. However, the no-harm position is far from being proven.

(For instance, there's a clear-cut case for banning—as the federal 10 government has proposed—movies, photos and videos that depict children engaging in sex with adults: real children are used to make the movies, and hardly anybody thinks this is ethical. The possibilities for coercion are too great.)

To shift the viewpoint, I'd like to suggest three other models for 11 looking at "pornography"—and here I mean the violent kind.

Those who find the idea of regulating pornographic materials repugnant because they think it's Fascist or Communist or otherwise not in accordance with the principles of an open democratic society should consider that Canada has made it illegal to disseminate material that may lead to hatred toward any group because of race or religion. I suggest that if pornography of the violent kind depicted these acts being done predominantly to Chinese, to blacks, to Catholics, it would be off the market immediately, under the present laws. Why is hate literature illegal? Because whoever made the law thought that such material might incite real people to do real awful things to other real people. The human brain is to a certain extent a computer: garbage in, garbage out. We only hear about the extreme cases (like that of American multimurderer Ted Bundy) in which pornography has contributed to the death and/or mutilation of women and/or men. Although pornography is not the only factor involved in the creation of such deviance, it certainly has upped the ante by suggesting both a variety of techniques and the social acceptability of such actions. Nobody knows yet what effect this stuff is having on the less psychotic.

Studies have shown that a large part of the market for all kinds   13
of porn, soft and hard, is drawn from the 16-to-21-year-old population of young men. Boys used to learn about sex on the street, or (in Italy, according to Fellini movies) from friendly whores, or, in more genteel surroundings, from girls, their parents, or, once upon a time, in school, more or less. Now porn has been added, and sex education in the schools is rapidly being phased out. The buck has been passed, and boys are being taught that all women secretly like to be raped and that real men get high on scooping out women's digestive tracts.

Boys learn their concept of masculinity from other men: is this   14
what most men want them to be learning? If word gets around that rapists are "normal" and even admirable men, will boys feel that in order to be normal, admirable and masculine they will have to be rapists? Human beings are enormously flexible, and how they turn out depends a lot on how they're educated, by the society in which they're immersed as well as by their teachers. In a society that advertises and glorifies rape or even implicitly condones it, more women get raped. It becomes socially acceptable. And at a time when men and the traditional male role have taken a lot of flak and men are confused and casting around for an acceptable way of being male (and, in some cases, not getting much comfort from women on that score), this must be at times a pleasing thought.

It would be naïve to think of violent pornography as just harm- 15
less entertainment. It's also an educational tool and a powerful pro-
paganda device. What happens when boy educated on porn meets
girl brought up on Harlequin romances? The clash of expectations
can be heard around the block. She wants him to get down on his
knees with a ring, he wants her to get down on all fours with a ring
in her nose. Can this marriage be saved?

Pornography has certain things in common with such addictive 16
substances as alcohol and drugs: for some, though by no means for
all, it induces chemical changes in the body, which the user finds
exciting and pleasurable. It also appears to attract a "hard core"of
habitual users and a penumbra of those who use it occasionally but
aren't dependent on it in any way. There are also significant numbers of men who aren't much interested in it, not because they're
undersexed but because real life is satisfying their needs, which may
not require as many appliances as those of users.

For the "hard core," pornography may function as alcohol does 17
for the alcoholic: tolerance develops, and a little is no longer enough.
This may account for the short viewing time and fast turnover in
porn theaters. Mary Brown, chairwoman of the Ontario Board of
Film Censors, estimates that for every one mainstream movie
requesting entrance to Ontario, there is one porno flick. Not only the
quantity consumed but the quality of explicitness must escalate,
which may account for the growing violence: once the big deal was
breasts, then it was genitals, then copulation, then that was no
longer enough and the hard users had to have more. The ultimate
kick is death, and after that, as the Marquis de Sade so boringly
demonstrated, multiple death.

The existence of alcoholism has not led us to ban social drink- 18
ing. On the other hand, we do have laws about drinking and driving, excessive drunkenness and other abuses of alcohol that may
result in injury or death to others.

This leads us back to the key question: what's the harm? 19
Nobody knows, but this society should find out fast, before the satu-
ration point is reached. The Scandinavian studies that showed a connection between depictions of sexual violence and increased impulse
toward it on the part of male viewers would be a starting point, but
many more questions remain to be raised as well as answered. What,
for instance, is the crucial difference between men who are users and
men who are not? Does using affect a man's relationship with actual
women, and, if so, adversely? Is there a clear line between erotica and

violent pornography, or are they on an escalating continuum? Is this
a "men versus women" issue, with all men secretly siding with the
proporners and all women secretly siding against? (I think not; there
are lots of men who don't think that running their true love through
the Cuisinart is the best way they can think of to spend a Saturday
night, and they're just as nauseated by films of someone else doing it
as women are.) Is pornography merely an expression of the sexual
confusion of this age or an active contributor to it?

Nobody wants to go back to the age of official repression, when   20
even piano legs were referred to as "limbs" and had to wear pan-
taloons to be decent. Neither do we want to end up in George
Orwell's *1984*, in which pornography is turned out by the State to
keep the proles in a state of torpor, sex itself is considered dirty and
the approved practise it only for reproduction. But Rome under the
emperors isn't such a good model either.

If all men and women respected each other, if sex were consid-   21
ered joyful and life-enhancing instead of a wallow in germ-filled
glop, if everyone were in love all the time, if, in other words, many
people's lives were more satisfactory for them than they appear to
be now, pornography might just go away on its own. But since this
is obviously not happening, we as a society are going to have to
make some informed and responsible decisions about how to deal
with it.

BILL MCKIBBEN

In his writing, Bill McKibben focuses on matters of the environment and on the relationship of nature to human activity. He examines the various media that surround and shape our lives, as well as the flood of information and ideas that has grown so rapidly in recent years. His essays and articles have appeared in a wide variety of magazines including *Vogue*, *Rolling Stone*, *Mother Jones*, *Buzzworm's Earth Journal*, *The New York Times Magazine*, *The New Yorker*, *Natural History*, *Good Housekeeping*, and *The New York Review of Books*. He has written three books: *The End of Nature* (1989), *The Age of Missing Information* (1992), and *Look at the Land; Aerial Reflections on America* (with Alex Maclean) (1993). McKibben lives in New York's Adirondack Mountains.

Late Afternoon

In his book, *The Age of Missing Information*, Bill McKibben tells of watching twenty-four hours of cable television and of spending twenty-four hours on a mountain in the Adirondack range. "Late Afternoon," a chapter from the book, offers two perspectives on our experience of time: time in the natural world and time in the modern, electronic world. Instead of presenting his thoughts in abstract prose, however, McKibben uses vivid, varied language to recreate the experience of time on the mountain and in front of the television set.

I can tell already there's not going to be much sunset tonight, just a   1
long, slow deepening. First the light will lose its crispness, begin to soften. The sun, already dropping toward the horizon, will stand on the ridge above the pond, turning the trees to fire, and then duck beneath it—but even at that point there will be hours of twilight. Depending on how you reckon its start and close, dusk lasts for hours, just like "day" and "night." The sky turns from blue to another blue to another blue still—faster at the dome than around the edges, but always imperceptibly. Watching the whole process is hard if you have anything else you could be doing—reading a book or making a fire. It seems from minute to minute the same, as if you were staring at a painting. But a star is out now—for a long time only one, and then suddenly ten. Blue, still blue—but black now?

It has been a perfect summer day, warm and airy and spacious.   2
The leaves are the deep matte green that imperceptibly replaces the
illuminated green of spring. But on a few trees—sick ones mainly,
though perhaps a few swamp maples too—a fringe of red has begun
to show. And the night air, on the lightest breeze, seems to carry a
small extra tang, a little more chill than the absence of the sun's heat
would account for. And the blueberries have ripened; some have
already withered. There is the sense of what is to come, that the slow
rotation through the stars is carrying the mountain forward to the
past, to yet another fall and winter and spring.

The question "What time is it?" draws a different answer on the   3
mountain and in front of the TV. And the answers, far from being
frivolous, have great environmental, social, personal meaning—the
mountain and the television aren't so much in different time zones as
in different dimensions. Human beings, of course, have perceived
time in two main ways: linearly and cyclically. Either history
advances forward through time or the world repeats endless cycles.
These different conceptions are rich; they've spawned religions and
philosophies for millennia. But, in truth, human beings were always
exposed to both—any honest Buddhist has a personal sense of the
course of his own current life, and even aggressively linear Christianity, with its sense of an approaching climax to history, is nonetheless soaked with the imagery of the seasons. In the last hundred
years, though—and more and more all the time—the linear view is
stomping out the other set of information, which is as old as man.

Take, just as one example, the length of the daylight hours. At   4
the latitude where I live, nightfall varies by three or four hours over
the course of a year. In December it's dark at four-thirty; at the end
of June the light lingers late into the evening. This is one of the ele-
mental pieces of information the world provides us—in other
species it triggers dormancy and hibernation, the coloring of leaves
and the gathering of food. Human beings always used to be sensitive to it—even after hours were invented, for millennia they were
seasonal hours. That is, daylight was divided into twelve hours, as
was dark—in the Northern Hemisphere, the period between, say,
1:00 and 2:00 P.M. was much longer during the summer than the winter. This piece of information proved too subtle for the mechanical
clock, which in the thirteenth century began to smooth out time. But
at least people still noticed the long, slow shift—felt it in their bones
like the ancient pagans who built their elaborate monuments to
mark the equinoxes and solstices. The spread of artificial light, and

the ability to continue all activity around the clock, eroded this sense much more radically than the clock. Now we hardly even recognize the change—if it's pitch-dark or sunny out, the evening news still comes on at seven and "prime time" starts at eight.

Our *bodies* still notice the changes. CNN, *Good Morning America*, 5 *CBS This Morning*, and the Discovery Channel all featured interviews with insomnia experts who prescribed fluorescent light therapy instead of Sominex. "Your body's internal functions respond to light, not to when you want to sleep," reported Dr. Charles Czeisler of the Circadian and Sleep Disorders Clinic. "People can work ten, twenty, thirty years on a night-shift schedule and their bodies never adjust." Despite the signals from our bodies, though, our heads, caught in the modern timelessness, win out—60 percent of Americans report "changing their sleeping habits so they can watch television." Prime time—the demarcation between the news/game show slot and the drama/comedy period—has almost certainly become the most significant line of the evening, replacing the evening star or the sun sinking beneath the horizon. TV doesn't even shut off for the night anymore: a few stations still carry "The Star-Spangled Banner" and a sermonette and then a test pattern, but most are eternal.

In much the same fashion, we ignore the progression of the sea- 6 sons, the shift not only in hours of light but in climate. This once-dominant cycle has everywhere been flattened by technology. In Egypt, where the three seasons were Inundation, Sufficiency, and Deficiency, the dams on the Nile have made it always the same time. In North America, our aggressive heating and air-conditioning serve the same function—make the seasons, at most, something to observe through the windows. True, there were plenty of ads this day reminding you that the period for wearing skimpy clothing was approaching ("Summer's right around the corner—you should really start getting in shape"; "Lean Cuisine makes under three hundred calories taste like a million, and summer is the time to look like a million"), but these serve only to underscore how lightly we take the change from one season to the next. Even the school calendar has more effect on most Americans than the calendar of the the seasons— no longer farmers, we do not find it strange that we would make our new beginnings (introduce our new TV shows!) just before harvest.

But does this really matter? Blessed with light bulbs and dams, 7 haven't we simply figured out a new, somewhat more efficient way to order our lives? We don't farm anymore, so why *should* we care much about the seasons or the length of the day? Because, I think, living in linear time means living with a different, and in many ways poorer, set of assumptions than living in cyclical time. On the mountain, feeling fall about to follow summer, I have a strong sense of what fall will be like—*fall*, not fall of 1991. The precise year, or the decade, matters little; it is a repeating pattern, and I know what it means for my life—that it's time to gather vegetables and can them, that it's time to put wood up for the winter. I know this fall won't be *precisely* the same as any other—a large part of rural conversation involves meticulous comparison of this year's snow or heat with the snow or heat of every other year. But I know they'll be *enough* alike, unless there is a storm so huge it changes the landscape. And even then how quickly the cycle reasserts itself.

A few economists, worried about the environment, have begun   8 to talk about "sustainable societies," which instead of using more and more all the time use the same amount each year, an amount they can comfortably produce. I said earlier that I think this debate is the essential one of the years ahead—that we must wean ourselves from constant and accelerating growth. But this could occur only in cyclical time, when the years repeat themselves through the seasons— when each year spring offers a fresh start from zero, and the winter an obvious end. In linear time the late summer ("the third quarter") of 1991 seems remarkably different from the third quarter of 1990. It is a year later, and woe to you if you haven't kept up with the times. The third quarter of 1990 is useful not as a *model* but only as a baseline to measure your progress into the intervening twelve months. And the only acceptable result is to have more, because you don't know what's coming. It's not winter the way it's been winter all the times of your life—it's the first quarter of 1992, and that may bring something altogether unprecedented, requiring you to have more. Not enough to say that if on the first of March you have "half your wood and your hay, you'll make it safely through to May." Because May is the second quarter of 1992, a time that's never been before.

In such a world, constant acceleration becomes only normal, only   9 reasonable. AT&T is running an ad where a boss demands that his subordinate call a client. He does, but because he is foolishly using the services of an AT&T competitor, it takes "as——long——as——this" to complete his call. It takes, to be exact, nine seconds, and he just misses the other party. These competing companies, the ads claim, are "up to forty percent slower"—that is, about three seconds. "This could add up to hundreds of wasted hours a year." (Actually it only adds up to an even two hundred hours if you make 240,000 calls annually, or 656 daily, or 82 an hour each day from nine to five.) Only a society obsessed with the linear passage of time would respond to an ad implying that going three seconds more slowly than technology permits might cost a guy his job. Viewed linearly, the rat race makes perfect sense—if there is a destination, you might as well get there first. But if, instead, you've internalized the seasons to the point where you realize you're on a wheel, you might slow down a little—might decide you're going nowhere impressively fast. If you're on a wheel, as mystics have long observed, speed is an illusion.

The most fascinating thing about dusk is the lack of demarca-   10
tion. It's one long smooth transition. Really, the whole day is one long transition—there are a dozen parts of morning, and the moment in the midafternoon when the sun reaches its height, but almost before you can decide that that was the height the blaze has turned to glow. By contrast, life, especially TV life, seems constantly to insist on more lines, more borders. TV expects you to shift entirely each half hour—a whole new set of characters has appeared, and probably they're demanding laughter instead of fear or sadness. It should be a remarkably unsettling rhythm, except that now we're used to it, and the slow sprawl of the sunset, if we tried to watch it with real attention, would seem unsettling. We complain incessantly about the "fast pace of modern life," and say that we have "no time." But of course most of us have lots of time, or else every study wouldn't show that we watch three or four or five hours of television a day. It's that time the way it really works has come to bore us. Or at least make us nervous, the way that silence does, and so we need to shut it out. We fill time, instead of letting it fill us.

All of those changes make it hard for time to ever ripen. "In   11
clock time," writes Kohak, "all times are uniform and arbitrary in their identity. Anything might be done at any of them with equal appropriateness or inappropriateness. There is no rightness, there are no seasons. Such patterns as life might have might well appear as no more than a convention, to be observed and violated at whim." That is to say, there is no rhythm—nothing like the image of summer following spring to help you orient yourself over the course of a lifetime. Which in turn makes it very strange to grow old and die. Almost no one talks about death on television, which is odd considering the number of corpses. (A rare exception was on one of the local public access channels where two agents demonstrated their sales pitches for viewers of *Insurance Corner*. "You've got to hit the hot button with the client, make them realize they *are* going to die,"

said one of the men. "That's right" said the other cheerfully. "The odds are one to one.")

People talk more about retirement on TV, but it clearly doesn't   12
reflect a necessary season in people's lives, only a law—a transition
as quick and brutal as *48 Hours* to *Falconcrest*. Its main consequence
is not philosophical but financial—the time when you go from earning money to living off accumulation. So on television, "coming to
terms" with aging inevitably means salting away cash, not wondering about death. The line between activity and retirement is as
devoid of information as the line between *Twin Peaks* and *Prime Time
Live*—there's no reason anyone even attempts to give you as to why
at sixty-five you should change your life. (One of the most interesting facts of the day came from a senior citizens' lobbyist who
claimed that Bismarck set the retirement age at sixty-five after his
actuaries told him almost all his bureaucrats would be dead by then,
reducing the need for pensions. Sixty-five in Bismarck's time, he
said, corresponds to one hundred and seventeen today.) The average American will spend two decades in "retirement," and since he
is still operating on linear time, what is he to do? Act young,
maybe—perhaps move into a "multiservice building" like the one
prepared by Fairfax County where college kids are hired to teach
you to dance to "Blame It on the Bossa Nova," or maybe buy cosmetics from Vikki LaMotta, the first over-fifty *Playboy* model, who
has her own infomercial. But there is no cadence to make the
approach of death less fearful. Maybe you'll just keep going, and
Willard Scott will be saying, "Hi to Besse Hamilton, of Shreveport,
who's two hundred sixty-two today—wotta pretty lady!" That must
be our hope, since we fail to prepare for death—indeed fight against
it with a strength that almost any other culture in almost any other
time would have considered bizarre.

On the mountain, of course, death surrounds you always. Dead   13
trees, the insects and the birds excavating their guts; dead leaves
under your feet beginning to disintegrate with a year of rain and
snow; dead bones in the woods where the coyotes hauled down a
deer; dead shrubs where the beavers revised the level of the pond
and flooded them out; the soil under your feet an enormous crypt
holding the death of all the years since the Ice Age ended. And there
is dying, too. Quick dying—the suddenly strangled cry of a rabbit in
the night when something takes him down. And slow, patient
dying: the maple sends out so few leaves this year that there is more
sun than shade beneath it, and moss spreads up its slowly rotting

trunk. And youth, of course shouldering up right next to age, vigor edging out gnarl—youth rooted in the death it will someday contribute to. You need not be an Eastern mystic anticipating physical rebirth to appreciate these cycles. This is the weary, austerely sublime wisdom of Ecclesiastes, too: "To everything there is a season, and a time for every purpose under heaven. A time to be born and a time to die." And that time to be born and to die is explicitly like the time to sow and to reap, to scatter and to gather. But we don't know those times anymore—it's harder and harder for us to imagine, as many people used to be able to divine, when our time has come.

What's worse, our culture won't lend us any dignity in those 14 moments. For television, the culture's great instrument, speaks to eighty-year-olds and eighteen-year-olds with the same voice. I think of my grandmother, spending her last years remote control in hand. She could watch what she felt like, of course, but almost all the choices had been created for those with desirable demographics. Television never grows old, never ceases that small talk that may be innocuous when you're thirty but should be monstrous by the end of your life. Right to the last day of my grandmother's life it continued to offer her the sight of Donahue discussing sex changes and Cosby making faces and Vanna spinning letters.

LESLIE MARMON SILKO was born in 1948 in Albuquerque, New Mexico. She was raised on the Laguna Pueblo Reservation and attended the University of New Mexico (B.A., 1969). Formerly on the English faculty of the University of Arizona, Silko now focuses full time on her writing, for which she has received many awards, including a MacArthur Foundation grant. Much of Silko's writing draws on Native American traditions and myths and on the interactions of Native American cultures and perspectives with the contemporary world. Her novels include the much-praised *Ceremony* (1977) and *Almanac of the Dead* (1991). She has also published a volume of poetry, *Laguna Woman* (1974); a collection of short stories, *Storyteller* (1981); an autobiography, *Sacred Water* (1993); and a collection of essays, *Yellow Woman and a Beauty of the Spirit* (1996).

Yellow Woman and a Beauty of the Spirit

"Yellow Woman and a Beauty of the Spirit," comes from the book with the same title. In this essay, Silko recalls her differences in appearance from other Laguna Pueblo children, the result of her mixed ancestry, and uses this memory as a springboard to an explanation of the traditional Pueblo disregard of physical appearance and emphasis instead on individual qualities of spirit as the basis of true beauty. She also discusses the Pueblo disregard of fixed gender, work, and family roles, but a correspondingly strong emphasis is on the quality of relationships among people, animals, and the land. As in much of her work, Silko's perspective lies at the center of the intersection between cultures.

From the time I was a small child, I was aware that I was different. I   1
looked different from my playmates. My two sisters looked different too. We didn't look quite like the other Laguna Pueblo children, but we didn't look quite white either. In the 1880s, my great-grandfather had followed his older brother west from Ohio to the New Mexico Territory to survey the land for the U.S. government. The two Marmon brothers came to the Laguna Pueblo reservation because they

had an Ohio cousin who already lived there. The Ohio cousin was involved in sending Indian children thousands of miles away from their families to the War Department's big Indian boarding school in Carlisle, Pennsylvania. Both brothers married full-blood Laguna Pueblo women. My great-grandfather had first married my great-grandmother's older sister, but she died in childbirth and left two small children. My great-grandmother was fifteen or twenty years younger than my great-grandfather. She had attended Carlisle Indian School and spoke and wrote English beautifully.

I called her Grandma A'mooh because that's what I heard her   2
say whenever she saw me. *A'mooh* means "granddaughter" in the Laguna language. I remember this word because her love and her acceptance of me as a small child were so important. I had sensed immediately that something about my appearance was not acceptable to some people, white and Indian. But I did not see any signs of that strain or anxiety in the face of my beloved Grandma A'mooh.

Younger people, people my parents' age, seemed to look at the   3
world in a more modern way. The modern way included racism. My physical appearance seemed not to matter to the old-time people. They looked at the world very differently; a person's appearance and possessions did not matter nearly as much as a person's behavior. For them, a person's value lies in how that person interacts with other people, how that person behaves toward the animals and the earth. That is what matters most to the old-time people. The Pueblo people believed this long before the Puritans arrived with their notions of sin and damnation, and racism. The old-time beliefs persist today; thus I will refer to the old-time people in the present tense as well as the past. Many worlds may coexist here.

I SPENT A great deal of time with my great-grandmother. Her   4
house was next to our house, and I used to wake up at dawn, hours before my parents or younger sisters, and I'd go wait on the porch swing or on the back steps by her kitchen door. She got up at dawn, but she was more than eighty years old, so she needed a little while to get dressed and to get the fire going in the cookstove. I had been carefully instructed by my parents not to bother her and to behave, and to try to help her any way I could. I always loved the early mornings when the air was so cool with a hint of rain smell in the breeze. In the dry New Mexico air, the least hint of dampness smells sweet.

My great-grandmother's yard was planted with lilac bushes   5
and iris; there were four o'clocks, cosmos, morning glories, and hollyhocks, and old-fashioned rosebushes that I helped her water. If the

garden hose got stuck on one of the big rocks that lined the path in the yard, I ran and pulled it free. That's what I came to do early every morning: to help Grandma water the plants before the heat of the day arrived.

Grandma A'mooh would tell about the old days, family stories   6 about relatives who had been killed by Apache raiders who stole the sheep our relatives had been herding near Swahnee. Sometimes she read Bible stories that we kids liked because of the illustrations of Jonah in the mouth of a whale and Daniel surrounded by lions. Grandma A'mooh would send me home when she took her nap, but when the sun got low and the afternoon began to cool off, I would be back on the porch swing, waiting for her to come out to water the plants and to haul in firewood for the evening. When Grandma was eighty-five, she still chopped her own kindling. She used to let me carry in the coal bucket for her, but she would not allow me to use the ax. I carried armloads of kindling too, and I learned to be proud of my strength.

I was allowed to listen quietly when Aunt Susie or Aunt Alice   7 came to visit Grandma. When I got old enough to cross the road alone, I went and visited them almost daily. They were vigorous women who valued books and writing. They were usually busy chopping wood or cooking but never hesitated to take time to answer my questions. Best of all they told me the *hummah-hah* stories, about an earlier time when animals and humans shared a common language. In the old days, the Pueblo people had educated their children in this manner; adults took time out to talk to and teach young people. Everyone was a teacher, and every activity had the potential to teach the child.

But as soon as I started kindergarten at the Bureau of Indian   8 Affairs day school, I began to learn more about the differences between the Laguna Pueblo world and the outside world. It was at school that I learned just how different I looked from my classmates. Sometimes tourists driving past on Route 66 would stop by Laguna Day School at recess time to take photographs of us kids. One day, when I was in the first grade, we all crowded around the smiling white tourists, who peered at our faces. We all wanted to be in the picture because afterward the tourists sometimes gave us each a penny. Just as we were all posed and ready to have our picture taken, the tourist man looked at me. "Not you," he said and motioned for me to step away from my classmates. I felt so embarrassed that I wanted to disappear. My classmates were puzzled by the tourists' behavior, but I knew the tourists didn't want me in their snapshot because I looked different, because I was part white. 9

IN THE VIEW of the old-time people, we are all sisters and brothers because the Mother Creator made all of us—all colors and all sizes. We are sisters and brothers, clanspeople of all the living beings around us. The plants, the birds, fish, clouds, water, even the clay— they all are related to us. The old-time people believe that all things, even rocks and water, have spirit and being. They understood that all things want only to continue being as they are; they need only to be left as they are. Thus the old folks used to tell us kids not to disturb the earth unnecessarily. All things as they were created exist already in harmony with one another as long as we do not disturb them.

As the old story tells us, Tse'itsi'nako, Thought Woman, the Spi- 10 der, thought of her three sisters, and as she thought of them, they came into being. Together with Thought Woman, they thought of the sun and the stars and the moon. The Mother Creators imagined the earth and the oceans, the animals and the people, and the ka'tsina spirits that reside in the mountains. The Mother Creators imagined all the plants that flower and the trees that bear fruit. As Thought Woman and her sisters thought of it, the whole universe came into being. In this universe, there is no absolute good or absolute bad; they are only balances and harmonies that ebb and flow. Some years the desert receives abundant rain, other years there is too little rain, and sometimes there is so much rain that floods cause destruction. But rain itself is neither innocent nor guilty. The rain is simply itself.

My great-grandmother was dark and handsome. Her expres- 11 sion in photographs is one of confidence and strength. I do not know if white people then or now would consider her beautiful. I do not know if the old-time Laguna Pueblo people considered her beautiful or if the old-time people even thought in those terms. To the Pueblo way of thinking, the act of comparing one living being with another was silly, because each being or thing is unique and therefore incomparably valuable because it is the only one of its kind. The old-time people thought it was crazy to attach such importance to a person's appearance. I understood very early that there were two distinct ways of interpreting the world. There was the white people's way and there was the Laguna way. In the Laguna way, it was bad manners to make comparisons that might hurt another person's feelings.

In everyday Pueblo life, not much attention was paid to one's 12 physical appearance or clothing. Ceremonial clothing was quite elaborate but was used only for the sacred dances. The traditional

Pueblo societies were communal and strictly egalitarian, which means that no matter how well or how poorly one might have dressed, there was no social ladder to fall from. All food and other resources were strictly shared so that no one person or group had more than another. I mention social status because it seems to me that most of the definitions of beauty in contemporary Western culture are really codes for determining social status. People no longer hide their face-lifts and they discuss their liposuctions because the point of the procedures isn't just cosmetic, it is social. It says to the world, "I have enough spare cash that I can afford surgery for cosmetic purposes."

In the old-time Pueblo world, beauty was manifested in behav- 13
ior and in one's relationships with other living beings. Beauty was as much a feeling of harmony as it was a visual, aural, or sensual effect. The whole person had to be beautiful, not just the face or the body; faces and bodies could not be separated from hearts and souls. Health was foremost in achieving this sense of well-being and harmony; in the old-time Pueblo world, a person who did not look healthy inspired feelings of worry and anxiety, not feelings of well-being. A healthy person, of course, is in harmony with the world around her; she is at peace with herself too. Thus an unhappy person or spiteful person would not be considered beautiful.

In the old days, strong, sturdy women were most admired. One 14
of my most vivid preschool memories is of the crew of Laguna women, in their forties and fifties, who came to cover our house with adobe plaster. They handled the ladders with great ease, and while two women ground the adobe mud on stones and added straw, another woman loaded the hod with mud and passed it up to the two women on ladders, who were smoothing the plaster on the wall with their hands. Since women owned the houses, they did the plastering. At Laguna, men did the basket making and the weaving of fine textiles; men helped a great deal with the child care too. Because the Creator is female, there is no stigma on being female; gender is not used to control behavior. No job was a man's job or a woman's job; the most able person did the work.

My Grandma Lily had been a Ford Model A mechanic when she 15
was a teenager. I remember when I was young, she was always fixing broken lamps and appliances. She was small and wiry, but she could lift her weight in rolled roofing or boxes of nails. When she was seventy-five, she was still repairing washing machines in my uncle's coin-operated laundry.

The old-time people paid no attention to birthdays. When a per-   16
son was ready to do something, she did it. When she no longer was
able, she stopped. Thus the traditional Pueblo people did not worry
about aging or about looking old because there were no social
boundaries drawn by the passage of years. It was not remarkable for
young men to marry women as old as their mothers. I never heard
anyone talk about "women's work" until after I left Laguna for college. Work was there to be done by any able-bodied person who
wanted to do it. At the same time, in the old-time Pueblo world, identity was acknowledged to be always in a flux; in the old stories, one
minute Spider Woman is a little spider under a yucca plant, and the
next instant she is a sprightly grandmother walking down the road.

When I was growing up, there was a young man from a nearby   17
village who wore nail polish and women's blouses and permed his
hair. People paid little attention to his appearance; he was always
part of a group of other young men from his village. No one ever
made fun of him. Pueblo communities were and still are very inter-
dependent, but they also have to be tolerant of individual eccentric-
ities because survival of the group means everyone has to cooperate.

In the old Pueblo world, differences were celebrated as signs of   18
the Mother Creator's grace. Persons born with exceptional physical
or sexual differences were highly respected and honored because
their physical differences gave them special positions as mediators
between this world and the spirit world. The great Navajo medicine
man of the 1920s, the Crawler, had a hunchback and could not walk
upright, but he was able to heal even the most difficult cases.

Before the arrival of Christian missionaries, a man could dress   19
as a woman and work with the women and even marry a man without any fanfare. Likewise, a woman was free to dress like a man, to
hunt and go to war with the men, and to marry a woman. In the old
Pueblo worldview, we are all a mixture of male and female, and this
sexual identity is changing constantly. Sexual inhibition did not
begin until the Christian missionaries arrived. For the old-time people, marriage was about teamwork and social relationships, not
about sexual excitement. In the days before the Puritans came, marriage did not mean an end to sex with people other than your
spouse. Women were just as likely as men to have a *si'ash,* or lover.

New life was so precious that pregnancy was always appro-   20
priate, and pregnancy before marriage was celebrated as a good
sign. Since the children belonged to the mother and her clan, and
women owned and bequeathed the houses and farmland, the exact

determination of paternity wasn't critical. Although fertility was prized, infertility was no problem because mothers with unplanned pregnancies gave their babies to childless couples within the clan in open adoption arrangements. Children called their mother's sisters "mother" as well, and a child became attached to a number of parent figures.

In the sacred kiva ceremonies, men mask and dress as women   21
to pay homage and to be possessed by the female energies of the spirit beings. Because differences in physical appearance were so highly valued, surgery to change one's face and body to resemble a model's face and body would be unimaginable. To be different, to be unique was blessed and was best of all.

THE TRADITIONAL CLOTHING of Pueblo women emphasized a   22
woman's sturdiness. Buckskin leggings wrapped around the legs protected her from scratches and injuries while she worked. The more layers of buckskin, the better. All those layers gave her legs the appearance of strength, like sturdy tree trunks. To demonstrate sisterhood and brotherhood with the plants and animals, the old-time people make masks and costumes that transform the human figures of the dancers into the animal beings they portray. Dancers paint their exposed skin; their postures and motions are adapted from their observations. But the motions are stylized. The observer sees not an actual eagle or actual deer dancing, but witnesses a human being, a dancer, gradually changing into a woman/buffalo or a man/deer. Every impulse is to reaffirm the urgent relationships that human beings have with the plant and animal world.

In the high desert plateau country, all vegetation, even weeds   23
and thorns, becomes special, and all life is precious and beautiful because without the plants, the insects, and the animals, human beings living here cannot survive. Perhaps human beings long ago noticed the devastating impact human activity can have on the plants and animals; maybe this is why tribal cultures devised the stories about humans and animals intermarrying, and the clans that bind humans to animals and plants through a whole complex of duties.

We children were always warned not to harm frogs or toads,   24
the beloved children of the rain clouds, because terrible floods would occur. I remember in the summer the old folks used to stick big bolls of cotton on the outside of their screen doors as bait to keep the flies from going in the house when the door was opened. The old folks staunchly resisted the killing of flies because once, long, long ago, when human beings were in a great deal of trouble, a Green

Bottle Fly carried the desperate messages of human beings to the Mother Creator in the Fourth World, below this one. Human beings had outraged the Mother Creator by neglecting the Mother Corn altar while they dabbled with sorcery and magic. The Mother Creator disappeared, and with her disappeared the rain clouds, and the plants and the animals too. The people began to starve, and they had no way of reaching the Mother Creator down below. Green Bottle Fly took the message to the Mother Creator, and the people were saved. To show their gratitude, the old folks refused to kill any flies.

THE OLD STORIES demonstrate the interrelationships that the   25 Pueblo people have maintained with their plant and animal clanspeople. Kochininako, Yellow Woman, represents all women in the old stories. Her deeds span the spectrum of human behavior and are mostly heroic acts, though in at least one story, she chooses to join the secret Destroyer Clan, which worships destruction and death. Because Laguna Pueblo cosmology features a female Creator, the status of women is equal with the status of men, and women appear as often as men in the old stories as hero figures. Yellow Woman is my favorite because she dares to cross traditional boundaries of ordinary behavior during times of crisis in order to save the Pueblo; her power lies in her courage and in her uninhibited sexuality, which the old-time Pueblo stories celebrate again and again because fertility was so highly valued.

The old stories always say that Yellow Woman was beautiful,   26 but remember that the old-time people were not so much thinking about physical appearances. In each story, the beauty that Yellow Woman possesses is the beauty of her passion, her daring, and her sheer strength to act when catastrophe is imminent.

In one story, the people are suffering during a great drought   27 and accompanying famine. Each day, Kochininako has to walk farther and farther from the village to find fresh water for her husband and children. One day she travels far, far to the east, to the plains, and she finally locates a freshwater spring. But when she reaches the pool, the water is churning violently as if something large had just gotten out of the pool. Kochininako does not want to see what huge creature had been at the pool, but just as she fills her water jar and turns to hurry away, a strong, sexy man in buffalo skin leggings appears by the pool. Little drops of water glisten on his chest. She cannot help but look at him because he is so strong and so good to look at. Able to transform himself from human to buffalo in the wink of an eye, Buffalo Man gallops away with her on his back.

Kochininako falls in love with Buffalo Man, and because of this liaison, the Buffalo People agree to give their bodies to the hunters to feed the starving Pueblo. Thus Kochininako's fearless sensuality results in the salvation of the people of her village, who are saved by the meat the Buffalo People "give" to them.

My father taught me and my sisters to shoot .22 rifles when we   28
were seven; I went hunting with my father when I was eight, and I killed my first mule deer buck when I was thirteen. The Kochininako stories were always my favorite because Yellow Woman had so many adventures. In one story, as she hunts rabbits to feed her family, a giant monster pursues her, but she has the courage and presence of mind to outwit it.

In another story, Kochininako has a fling with Whirlwind Man   29
and returns to her husband ten months later with twin baby boys. The twin boys grow up to be great heroes of the people. Once again, Kochininako's vibrant sexuality benefits her people.

The stories about Kochininako made me aware that sometimes   30
an individual must act despite disapproval, or concern for appearances or what others may say. From Yellow Woman's adventures, I learned to be comfortable with my differences. I even imagined that Yellow Woman had yellow skin, brown hair, and green eyes like mine, although her name does not refer to her color, but rather to the ritual color of the east.

There have been many other moments like the one with the   31
camera-toting tourist in the schoolyard. But the old-time people always say, remember the stories, the stories will help you be strong. So all these years I have depended on Kochininako and the stories of her adventures.

Kochininako is beautiful because she has the courage to act in   32
times of great peril, and her triumph is achieved by her sensuality, not through violence and destruction. For these qualities of the spirit, Yellow Woman and all women are beautiful.

A Guide to Terms

Abstract (See *Concrete/Abstract.*)

Allusion (See *Figures of Speech.*)

Analogy (See Section 6.)

Argument is writing that uses factual evidence and supporting ideas to convince readers to share the author's opinion on an issue or to take some action the writer considers appropriate or necessary. Like exposition, argument conveys information; however, it does so not to explain but to induce readers to favor one side in a conflict or to choose a particular course of action.

Some arguments appeal primarily to reason, others primarily to emotion. Most, however, mix reason and emotion in whatever way is appropriate for the issue and the audience. (See Section 13.)

Support for an argument can take a number of forms:

1. *Examples*—Real-life examples or hypothetical examples (used sparingly) can be convincing evidence if they are typical and if the author provides enough of them to illustrate all the major points in the argument or combines them with other kinds of evidence. (See Daly, Hirsch, Lynn.) Some examples are *specific*, referring to particular people or events. (See Daly.) Others are *general*, referring to kinds of events or people, usually corresponding in some way to the reader's experiences. (See Lynn.)

2. *Facts and figures*—Detailed information about a subject; particularly if presented in statistical form, can help convince readers by showing that the author's perspective on an issue is consistent with what is known about the subject. (See Lynn, Hirsch, Davidson.) But facts whose accuracy is questionable or statistics that are confusing can undermine an argument.

3. *Authority*—Supporting an argument with the ideas or the actual words of someone who is recognized as an expert can be an effective strategy as long as the author can show that the expert is a reliable witness and can combine the expert's opinion with other kinds of evidence that point in the same direction.

4. *Personal experience*—Examples drawn from personal experience or the experience of friends can be more detailed and vivid (and hence more convincing) than other kinds of evidence, but a writer should use this kind of evidence sparingly because readers may sometimes suspect that it represents no more than one person's way of looking at events. When combined with other kinds of evidence, however, examples drawn from personal experience can be an effective technique for persuasion. (See Daly.)

In addition, all the basic expository patterns can be used to support an argument. (See Section 13.)

Cause (See Section 8.)

Central Theme (See *Unity.*)

Classification (See Section 4.)

Clichés are tired expressions, perhaps once fresh and colorful, that have been overused until they have lost most of their effectiveness and become trite or hackneyed. The term is also applied, less commonly, to trite ideas or attitudes.

We may need to use clichés in conversation, of course, where the quick and economical phrase is an important and useful tool of expression—and where no one expects us to be constantly original. We are fortunate, in a way, to have a large accumulation of clichés from which to draw. To describe someone, without straining our originality very much, we can always declare that he is *as innocent as a lamb, as thin as a rail,* or *as fat as a pig;* that she is *as dumb as an ox, as sly as a fox,* or *as wise as an owl;* that he is *financially embarrassed* or *has a fly in the ointment* or *her ship has come in;* or that, *last but not least, in this day and age,* the *Grim Reaper* has taken him to *his eternal reward.* There is indeed *a large stockpile* from which we can draw for ordinary conversation. But the trite expression, written down on paper, is a permanent reminder that the writer is either lazy or not aware of the dullness of stereotypes—or, even more damaging, it is a clue that the ideas themselves may be threadbare, and therefore can be adequately expressed in threadbare language.

Occasionally, of course, a writer can use obvious clichés deliberately (see Lawrence, par. 1; Ehrenreich, "Star"; Stone). But usually to be fully effective, writing must be fresh, and should seem to have been written specifically for the occasion. Clichés, however fresh and appropriate at one time, have lost these qualities.

Closings are almost as much of a problem as introductions, and they are equally important. The function of a closing is simply "to close," of course, but this implies somehow tying the entire writing into a neat package, giving the final sense of unity to the whole endeavor, and thus leaving the reader with a sense of satisfaction instead of an uneasy feeling that there ought to be another page. There is no standard length for closings. A short composition may be effectively completed with one sentence— or even without any real closing at all, if the last point discussed is a strong or climactic one. A longer piece of writing, however, may end more slowly, perhaps through several paragraphs.

A few types of weak endings are so common that warnings are in order here. Careful writers will avoid these faults: (1) giving the effect of suddenly tiring and quitting; (2) ending on a minor detail or an apparent afterthought; (3) bringing up a new point in the closing; (4) using any new qualifying remark in the closing (if writers want their opinions to seem less dogmatic or generalized, they should go back to do their qualifying where the damage was done); (5) ending with an apology of any kind (authors who are not interested enough to become at least minor experts in their subject should not be wasting the reader's time).

Of the several acceptable ways of giving the sense of finality to a paper, the easiest is the *summary,* but it is also the least desirable for most short papers. Readers who have read and understood something only a page or two before probably do not need to have it reviewed for them. Such a review is apt to seem merely repetitious. Longer writings, of course, such as research or term papers, may require thorough summaries.

Several other closing techniques are available to writers. The following, which do not represent all the possibilities, are useful in many situations, and they can frequently be employed in combination:

1. *Using word signals*—e.g., *finally, at last, thus, and so, in conclusion,* as well as more original devices suggested by the subject itself. (See Simpson.)

2. *Changing the tempo*—usually a matter of sentence length or pace. This is a very subtle indication of finality, and it is difficult to achieve. (For examples of modified use, see Simpson, Walker, Dorris.)

3. *Restating the central idea of the writing*—sometimes a "statement" so fully developed that it practically becomes a summary itself. (See Catton, Carter, Buczynski.)

4. *Using climax*—a natural culmination of preceding points or, in some cases, the last major point itself. This is suitable, however, only if the materials have been so arranged that the last point is outstanding. (See Catton, Lawrence, Walker, Szalavitz.)

5. *Making suggestions,* perhaps mentioning a possible solution to the problem being discussed—a useful technique for exposition as well as for argument, and a natural signal of the end. (See Lynn.)

6. *Showing the topic's significance,* its effects, or the universality of its meaning—a commonly used technique that, if carefully handled, is an excellent indication of closing. (See Buckley, Lawrence, Noda, Kean.)

7. *Echoing the introduction*—a technique that has the virtue of improving the effect of unity by bringing the development around full circle, so to speak. The echo may be a reference to a problem posed or a significant expression, quotation, analogy, or symbol used in the introduction or elsewhere early in the composition. (See Buckley; Ehrenreich, "Men"; Berendt.)

8. *Using some rhetorical device*—a sort of catchall category, but a good supply source that includes several very effective techniques; pertinent quotations, anecdotes and brief dialogues, metaphors, allusions, ironic comments, and various kinds of witty or memorable remarks. All, however, run the risk of seeming forced and hence amateurish; but properly handled, they make for an effective closing. (See White, Lopate, Lawrence, Simpson, King.)

Coherence is a quality of good writing that results from the presentation of all parts in logical and clear relations.

Coherence and unity are usually studied together and, indeed, are almost inseparable. But whereas unity refers to the relation of parts to the central theme (see *Unity*), coherence refers to their relations with each other. In a coherent piece of writing, each sentence, each paragraph, each major division seems to grow out of those preceding it.

Several transitional devices (see *Transition*) help to make these relations clear, but far more fundamental to coherence is the sound organization of materials. From the first moment of visualizing the subject materials in pattern, the writer's goal must be clear and logical development. If it is, coherence is almost ensured.

Colloquial Expressions are characteristic of conversation and informal writing, and they are normally perfectly appropriate in those contexts. However, most writing done for college, business, or professional purposes is considered "formal" writing; and for such usage, colloquialisms are too informal, too *folksy* (itself a word most dictionaries would label "colloq.").

Some of the expressions appropriate only for informal usage are *kid* (for child), *boss* (for employer), *flunk, buddy, snooze, gym, a lot of, phone, skin flicks,* and *porn*. In addition, contractions such as *can't* and *I'd* are usually regarded as colloquialisms and are never permissible in, for instance, a research or term paper.

Slang is defined as a low level of colloquialism, but it is sometimes placed "below" colloquialism in respectability; even standard dictionaries differ as to just what the distinction is. (Some of the examples in the preceding paragraph, if included in dictionaries at all, are identified both ways.) At any rate, slang generally comprises words either coined or given novel meanings in an attempt at colorful or humorous expression. Slang often becomes limp with overuse, however, losing whatever vigor it first had. In time, slang expressions either disappear completely or graduate to more acceptable colloquial status and thence, possibly, into standard usage. (This is one way in which our language is constantly changing.) But until their "graduations," slang and colloquialism have an appropriate place in formal writing only if used sparingly and for special effect. Because dictionaries frequently differ in matters of usage, the student should be sure to use a standard edition approved by the instructor. (For further examples, see Viorst; Wolfe; Simpson, pars. 8, 16, 17; Williams, pars. 8, 11, 12.)

Comparison (See Section 5.)

Conclusions (See *Closings.*)

Concrete and **Abstract** words are both indispensable to the language, but a good rule in most writing is to use the concrete whenever possible. This policy also applies, of course, to sentences that express only abstract ideas, which concrete examples can often make clearer and more effective. Many expository and argumentative paragraphs are constructed with an abstract topic sentence and its concrete support. (See *Unity.*)

A concrete word names something that exists as an entity in itself, something that can be perceived by the human senses. We can see, tough, hear, and smell a horse—hence *horse* is a concrete word. But a horse's *strength* is not. We have no reason to doubt that strength exists, but it does not have an independent existence: something else must *be* strong or there is no strength. Hence *strength* is an abstract word.

Purely abstract reading is difficult for average readers; with no concrete images provided, they are constantly forced to make their own. Concrete writing helps readers to visualize and is therefore easier and faster to read. (See *Specific/General* for further discussion.)

Connotation and **Denotation** both refer to the meanings of words. Denotation is the direct, literal meaning as it would be found in a dictionary, whereas connotation refers to the response a word *really* arouses in the reader or listener. (See Wolfe, par. 14; Daly, Lawrence.)

There are two types of connotation: personal and general. Personal connotations vary widely, depending on the experiences and moods that an individual associates with the word. (This corresponds with personal symbolism; see *Symbol.*) *Waterfall* is not apt to have the same meaning for the happy young honeymooners at Yosemite as it has for the grieving mother whose child has just drowned in a waterfall. General connotations are those shared by many people. *Fireside,* far beyond its obvious dictionary definition, generally connotes warmth and security and good companionship. *Mother,* which denotatively means simply "female parent," means much more connotatively.

A word or phrase considered less distasteful or offensive than a more direct expression is called a *euphemism,* and this is also a matter of connotation. (See Mitford.) The various expressions used instead of the more direct "four-letter words" referring to daily bathroom events are examples of euphemisms. (See Wolfe's "mounting," pars. 16 and 17.) *Remains* is often used instead of *corpse,* and a few newspapers still have people *passing away* and being *laid to rest,* rather than *dying* and being *buried.*

But a serious respect for the importance of connotations goes far beyond euphemistic practices. Young writers can hardly expect to know all the different meanings of words for all their potential readers, but they can at least be aware that words do *have* different meanings. Of course, this is most important in persuasive writing—in political speeches, in advertising copywriting, and in any endeavor where some sort of public image is being created. When President Franklin Roosevelt began his series of informal radio talks, he called them "fireside chats," thus putting connotation to work. An advertising copywriter trying to evoke the feeling of love and tenderness associated with motherhood is not seriously tempted to use *female parent* instead of *mother.*

In exposition, where the primary purpose is to explain, the writer ordinarily tries to avoid words that may have emotional overtones, unless these can somehow be used to increase understanding. In argument, however, a writer may on occasion wish to appeal to the emotions.

Contrast (See Section 5.)

Deduction (See Section 12.)

Denotation (See *Connotation/Denotation.*)

Description (See Section 10.)

Diction refers simply to "choice of words," but, not so simply, it involves many problems of usage, some of which are explained under several other headings in this guide, e.g., *Clichés, Colloquial Expressions, Connotation/Denotation, Concrete/Abstract*—anything, in fact, that pertains primarily to word choices. But the characteristics of good diction may be more generally classified as follows:

1. *Accuracy*—the choice of words that mean exactly what the author intends.

2. *Economy*—the choice of the simplest and fewest words that will convey the exact meaning intended.

3. *Emphasis*—the choice of fresh, strong words, avoiding clichés and unnecessarily vague or general terms.

4. *Apporopriateness*—the choice of words that suit the subject matter, the prospective reader-audience, and the purpose of the writing.

(For contrasts of diction see Stone, Sanders, Welsch, Walker, Eiseley, King, Rodriguez, Twitchell, Murphy, Carter, Davidson.)

Division (See Section 4.)

Effect (See Section 8.)

Emphasis is almost certain to fall *somewhere,* and the author should be the one to decide where. A major point, not some minor detail, should be emphasized.

Following are the most common ways of achieving emphasis. Most of them apply to the sentence, the paragraph, or the overall writing—all of which can be seriously weakened by emphasis in the wrong places.

1. By *position*—The most emphatic position is usually at the end, the second most emphatic at the beginning. (There are a few exceptions, including news stories and certain kinds of scientific reports.) The middle, therefore, should be used for materials that do not deserve special emphasis. (See Buckley, for saving the most significant example unit last; Catton, par. 16; Raybon, for gradually increasing emphasis; and Dorris, for the long-withheld revelation of the real central theme.)

A sentence in which the main point is held until the last is called a *periodic sentence*, e.g., "After a long night of suspense and horror, the cavalry arrived." In a *loose sentence,* the main point is disposed of earlier and followed by dependencies, e.g., "The cavalry arrived after a long night of suspense and horror."

2. By *proportion*—Ordinarily, but not necessarily, important elements are given the most attention and thus automatically achieve a certain emphasis.

3. By *repetition*—Words and ideas may sometimes be given emphasis by reuse, usually in a different manner. If not cautiously handled, however, this method can seem merely repetitious, not emphatic. (See Atwood, who repeats words to give them varied meanings and highlight their importance; Ehrenreich, "Star," which provides an ironic example of the strategy.)

4. By *flat statement*—Although an obvious way to achieve emphasis is simply to *tell* the reader what is most important, it is often least effective, at least when used as the only method. Readers have a way of ignoring such pointers as "most important" and "especially true." (See Catton, par. 16.)

5. By *mechanical devices*—Emphasis can be achieved by using italics (underlining), capital letters, or exclamation points. But too often these devices are used, however unintentionally, to cover deficiencies of content or style. Their employment can quickly be overdone and their impact lost. (For a limited and therefore emphatic use of italics and capitalization, see Faraday.)

6. By *distinctiveness of style*—The author can emphasize subtly with fresh and concrete words or figures of speech, crisp or unusual structures, and careful control of paragraph or sentence lengths. (These methods are used in many essays in this book: see Buckley; Twain, who changes style radically for the second half of his essay; Catton; Stone, who uses numerous puns; Wolfe; Rodriguez, who draws on Spanish expressions; Curtin, pars. 7–15.) *Verbal irony* (see *Irony*), including *sarcasm* (see Buckley, Atwood.) and the rather specialized form known as *understatement,* is another valuable means of achieving distinctiveness of style and increasing emphasis. (See Wolfe; Mitford; Ehrenreich, "Star.")

Essay refers to a brief prose composition on a single topic, usually, but not always, communicating the author's personal ideas and impressions. Beyond this, because of the wide and loose application of the term, no satisfactory definition has been universally accepted.

Classifications of essay types have also been widely varied and sometimes not very meaningful. One basic and useful distinction, however, is between *formal* and *informal* essays, although many defy classification even in such broad categories as these. It is best to regard the two types as opposite ends of a continuum, along which most essays may be placed.

The formal essay usually develops an important theme through a logical progression of ideas, with full attention to unity and coherence, and in a serious tone. Although the style is seldom completely impersonal, it is literary rather than colloquial. (For examples of essays that are somewhere near the "formal" end of the continuum, see Buckley, Lynn, Eiseley, Catton, Kilbourne, Negroponte, Lawrence.)

The informal, or personal, essay is less elaborately organized and more chatty in style. First-person pronouns, contractions, and other colloquial or even slang expressions are often freely used. Informal essays are less serious in apparent purpose than formal essays. Although most do contian a worthwhile message or observation of some kind, an important purpose of many is to entertain. (See Stone, Wolf.)

The more personal and intimate informal essays may be classifiable as *familiar* essays, although, again, there is no well-established boundary. Familiar essays pertain to the author's own experience, ideas, or prejudices, frequently in a light and humorous style. (See Buczynski, Viorst, Curtin, White, Karn, Murphy.)

Evaluation of a literary piece, as for any other creative endeavor, is meaningful only when based on the answers to three questions: (1) What was the author's purpose? (2) How successfully was it fulfilled? (3) How worthwhile was it?

An architect could hardly be blamed for designing a poor gymnasium if the commission had been to design a library. Similarly, an author who is trying to explain for us why women are paid less than men cannot be faulted for failing to make the reader laugh. An author whose purpose is simply to amuse (a worthy goal) should not be condemned for teaching little about trichobothria. (Nothing prevents the author from trying to explain pornography through the use of humor, or trying to amuse by comparing two Civil War generals, but in these situations the purpose has changed—and grown almost unbearably harder to achieve.)

An architect who was commissioned to design a gymnasium, and who, in fact, designed one, however, could be justifiably criticized on whether the building is successful and attractive *as a gymnasium*. If an author is examining matters of cognition and personality (as is Rose), the reader has a right to expect sound reasoning and clear expository prose; and varied, detailed support ought to be expected in an essay that looks at the physical basis of human behavior (Perry and Dawson) or at the attitudes of people towards works and careers (Rothenberg).

Many things are written and published that succeed very well in carrying out the author's intent—but simply are not worthwhile. Although this is certainly justifiable grounds for unfavorable criticism, readers should first make full allowance for their own limitations and perhaps their narrow range of interests, evaluating the work as nearly as possible from the standpoint of the average reader for whom the writing was intended.

Figures of Speech are short, vivid comparisons, either stated or implied; but they are not literal comparisons (e.g., "Your car is like my car," which is presumably a plain statement of fact). Figures of speech are more imaginative. They imply analogy but, unlike analogy, are used less to inform than to make quick and forceful impressions. All figurative language is a comparison of unlikes, but the unlikes do have some interesting point of likeness, perhaps one never noticed before.

A *metaphor* merely suggests the comparison and is worded as if the two unlikes are the same thing—e.g., "the language of the river" and "was turned to blood" (Twain, par. 1) and "a great chapter in American life" (Catton, par. 1). (For some of the many other examples in this book, see Eiseley, King.)

A *simile* (which is sometimes classified as a special kind of metaphor) expresses a similarity directly, usually with the word *like* or *as* (Eiseley, par. 4, Lopate, par. 12).

A *personification*, which is actually a special type of either metaphor or simile, is usually classified as a "figure" in its own right. In personification, inanimate things are treated as if they had the qualities or powers of a person. Some people would also label as personification any characterization of inanimate objects as animals, or of animals as humans.

An *allusion* is literally any casual reference, any alluding, to something, but rhetorically it is limited to a figurative reference to a famous or literary person, event, or quotation, and it should be distinguished from the casual reference that has a literal function in the subject matter. Hence casual mention of Judas Iscariot's betrayal of Jesus is merely a reference, but calling a modern traitor a "Judas" is an allusion. A rooster might be referred to as "the Hitler of the barnyard," or a lover as a "Romeo." Many allusions refer to mythological or biblical persons or places. (See Buckley, par, 11; Wolfe, title and par. 1; and Simpson, par. 2, for a discussion of some commonly employed allusions.)

Irony and paradox (both discussed under their own headings) and analogy (see Section 6) are also frequently classed as figures of speech, and there are several other less common types that are really subclassifications of those already discussed.

General (See *Specific/General.*)

Illustration (See Section 3.)

Impressionistic Description (See Section 10.)

Induction (See Section 12.)

Introductions give readers their first impressions, which often turn out to be the lasting ones. In fact, unless an introduction succeeds in somehow attracting a reader's interest, he or she probably will read no further. The importance of the introduction is one reason that writing it is nearly always difficult.

When the writer remains at a loss for how to begin, it may be a good idea to forget about the introduction for a while and go ahead with the main body of the writing. Later the writer may find that a suitable introduction has suggested itself or even that the way the piece begins is actually introduction enough.

Introductions may vary in length from one sentence in a short composition to several paragraphs or even several pages in longer and more complex expositions and arguments, such as research papers and reports of various kinds.

Good introductions in expository writing have at least three and sometimes four functions.

1. *To identify the subject and set its limitations,* thus building as solid foundation for unity. This function usually includes some indication of the central theme, letting the reader know what point is to be made about the subject. Unlike the other forms of prose, which can often benefit by some degree of mystery, exposition has the primary purpose of explaining, so the reader has a right to know from the beginning just *what* is being explained.

2. *To interest the readers,* and thus ensure their attention. To be sure of doing this, writers must analyze their prospective readers and the readers' interest in their subject. The account of a new X-ray technique would need an entirely different kind of introduction if written for doctors than if written for the campus newspaper.

3. *To set the tone* of the rest of the writing. (See *Style/Tone.*) Tone varies greatly in writing, just as the tone of a person's voice varies with the person's mood. One function of the introduction is to let the reader know the author's attitude since it may have a subtle but important bearing on the communication.

4. *Frequently,* but not always, *to indicate the plan of organization.* Although seldom important in short, relatively simple compositions and essay examinations, this function of introductions can be especially valuable in more complex papers.

These are the necessary functions of an introduction. For best results, keep these guidelines in mind: (1) Avoid referring to the title, or even assuming that the reader has seen it. Make the introduction do all the introducing. (2) Avoid crude and uninteresting beginnings, such as "This paper is about. . . . " (3) Avoid going too abruptly into the main body—smooth transition is at least as important here as anywhere else. (4) Avoid overdoing the introduction, either in length or in extremes of style.

Fortunately, there are many good ways to introduce expository writing (and argumentative writing), and several of the most useful are illustrated by the selections in this book. Many writings, of course, combine two or more of the following techniques for interesting introductions.

1. *Stating the central theme,* which is sometimes fully enough explained in the introduction to become almost a preview summary of the exposition or argument to come. (See Tajima, Noda, Kean, Viorst.)

2. *Showing the significance of the subject,* or stressing its importance. (See Catton, Wolfe, Simpson.)

3. *Giving the background of the subject,* usually in brief form, in order to bring the reader up to date as early as possible for a better understanding of the matter at hand. (See Stone, Lynn.)

4. *"Focusing down"* to one aspect of the subject, a technique similar to that used in some movies, showing first a broad scope (of subject area, such as a landscape) and then progressively narrowing views until the focus is on one specific thing (perhaps the name "O'Grady O'Connor" on a mailbox by a gate— or the silent sufferers on Buckley's train). (See also Rooney.)

5. *Using a pertinent rhetorical device* that will attract interest as it leads into the main exposition—e.g., an anecdote, analogy, allusion, quotation, or paradox. (See Welsch, Simpson.)

6. *Using a short but vivid comparison or contrast* to emphasize the central idea. (See Lynn.)

7. *Posing a challenging question,* the answering of which the reader will assume to be the purpose of the writing. (See Lawrence, Buczynski.)

8. *Referring to the writer's experience with the subject,* perhaps even giving a detailed account of that experience. Some writings are simply continuations of experience so introduced, perhaps with the expository purpose of making the telling entirely evident only at the end or slowly unfolding it as the account progresses. (See White, Daly.)

9. *Presenting a startling statistic or other fact* that will indicate the nature of the subject to be discussed.

10. *Making an unusual statement* that can intrigue as well as introduce. (See Kean; Wolfe; Gansberg; Ehrenreich, "Star.")

11. *Making a commonplace remark* that can draw interest because of its very commonness in sound or meaning.

Irony, in its verbal form sometimes classed as a figure of speech, consists of saying one thing on the surface but meaning exactly (or nearly) the opposite—e.g., "this beautiful neighborhood of ours" may mean that it is a dump. (For other illustrations, see Stone, Wolfe, Mitford, Walker.)

Verbal irony has a wide range of tones, from the gentle, gay, or affectionate to the sharpness of outright *sarcasm* (see Buckley), which is always intended to cut. It may consist of only a word or phrase, it may be a simple *understatement* (see Mitford; Ehrenreich, "Star"), or it may be sustained as one of the major components of satire.

Irony can be an effective tool of exposition if its tone is consistent with the overall tone and if the writer is sure that the audience is bright enough to recognize it. In speech, a person usually indicates by voice or eye-expression that he is not to be taken literally; in writing, the words on the page have to speak for themselves. (See Stone for the use of parentheses to indicate ironic or humorous statements.)

In addition to verbal irony, there is also an *irony of situation*, in which there is a sharp contradiction between what is logically expected to happen and what does happen—e.g., a man sets a trap for an obnoxious neighbor and then gets caught in it himself. Or the ironic situation may simply be some discrepancy that an outsider can see while those involved cannot. (See Lawrence, pars. 11–12.)

Logical Argument (See Section 13.)

Loose Sentences (See *Emphasis.*)

Metaphor (See *Figures of Speech.*)

Narration (See Section 11.)

Objective writing and **Subjective** writing are distinguishable by the extent to which they reflect the author's personal attitudes or emotions. The difference is usually one of degree, as few writing endeavors can be completely objective or subjective.

Objective writing, seldom used in its pure form except in business or scientific reports, is impersonal and concerned almost entirely with straight narration, with logical analysis, or with the description of external appearances. (For somewhat objective writing, see Simpson; Staples, par. 1)

Subjective writing (in description called "impressionistic"— see Section 10) is more personalized, more expressive of the beliefs, ideals, or impressions of the author. Whereas in objective writing the emphasis is on the object being written about, in subjective writing the emphasis is on the way the author sees and interprets the object. (For some of the many examples in this book, see Twain; Lopate; Wolfe; Mitford; Welsch; Lawrence; Staples, after par. 1; Eiseley; Ehrenreich.)

Paradox is a statement or remark that, although seeming to be contradictory or absurd, actually contains some truth. Many paradoxical statements are also ironic.

Paragraph Unity (See *Unity.*)

Parallel Structure refers in principle to the same kind of "parallelism" that is studied in grammar: the principle that coordinate elements should have coordinate presentation, as in a pair or a series of verbs, prepositional phrases, gerunds. It is often as much a matter of "balance" as it is of parallelism.

But the principle of parallel structure, far from being just a negative "don't mix" set of rules, is also a positive rhetorical device. Many writers use it as an effective means of stressing variety of profusion in a group of nouns or modifiers, or of emphasizing parallel ideas in sentence parts, in two or more sentences, or even in two or more paragraphs. At times it can also be useful stylistically, to give a subtle poetic quality to the prose.

(For illustrations of parallel parts within a sentence, see Wolfe, pars. 1, 4; of parallel sentences themselves, see Catton, par. 14; of both parallel parts and parallel sentences, see Twain, Maynard, Viorst.)

Periodic Sentence (See *Emphasis.*)

Persona refers to a character created as the speaker in an essay or the narrator of a story. The attitudes and character of a persona often differ from those of the author, and their persona may be created as a way of submitting certain values or perspectives to examination and criticism. The speaker in Ehrenreich's "Star Dreck" is clearly a persona and advocates actions that the author would consider abhorrent if put into practice.

Personification (See *Figures of Speech.*)

Point of View in *argument* means the author's opinion on an issue or the thesis being advanced in an essay. In *exposition*, however, point of view is simply the position of the author in relation to the subject matter. Rhetorical point of view in exposition has little in common with the grammatical sort and differs somewhat from point of view in fiction.

A ranch in a mountain valley is seen differently by the ranch hand working at the corral, by the gardener deciding where to plant the petunias, by the artist or poet viewing the ranch from the mountainside, and by the geographer in a plane above, map-sketching the valley in relation to the entire range. It is the same ranch but the positions and attitudes of the viewers are different.

So it is with expository prose. The position and attitude of the author are the important lens through which the reader sees the subject. Consistency is important, because if the lens is changed without sufficient cause and explanation, the reader will become disconcerted, if not annoyed.

Obviously, since the point of view is partially a matter of attitude, the tone and often the style of writing are closely linked to it. (See *Style/Tone.*)

The expository selections in this book provide examples of numerous points of view. Rose's and Twain's are those of authority in their own fields of experience; Mitford's is as the debunking prober; Ehrenreich's is that of the angry observer of human behavior. In each of these (and the list could be extended to include all the selections in the book), the subject would seem vastly different if seen from some other point of view.

Process Analysis (See Section 7.)

Purpose that is clearly understood by the author before beginning to write is essential to both unity and coherence. A worthwhile practice, certainly in the training stages, is to write down the controlling purpose before even beginning to outline. Some instructors require both a statement of purpose and a statement of central theme or thesis. (See *Unity; Thesis.*)

The most basic element of a statement of purpose is the commitment to "explain" or, in some assignments, to "convince" (argument). But the statement of purpose, whether written down or only decided upon, goes further—e.g., "to argue that `dirty words' are logically offensive because of the sources and connotations of the words themselves" (Lawrence).

Qualification is the tempering of broad statements to make them more valid and acceptable, the authors themselves admitting the probability of exceptions. This qualifying can be done inconspicuously, to whatever degree needed, by the use of *possibly, nearly always* or *most often, usually* or *frequently, sometimes* or *occasionally.* Instead of saying, "Chemistry is the most valuable field of study," it would probably be more accurate and defensible to say that it is for *some* people, or that it *can* be the most valuable. (For examples of qualification, see Davidson.)

Refutation of opposing arguments is an important element in most argumentative essays, especially where the opposition is strong enough or reasonable enough to provide a real alternative to the author's opinion. A refutation consists of a brief summary of the opposing point of view along with a discussion of its inadequacies, a discussion which often helps support the author's own thesis.

Here are three commonly used strategies for refutation:

1. *Pointing out weaknesses in evidence*—If an opposing argument is based on inaccurate, incomplete, or misleading evidence, or if the argument does not take into account some new evidence that contradicts it, then the refutation should point out these weaknesses.

2. *Pointing out errors in logic*—If an opposing argument is loosely reasoned or contains major flaws in logic, then the refutation should point these problems out to the reader.

3. *Questioning the relevance of an argument*—If an opposing argument does not directly address the issue under consideration, then the refutation should point out that even though the argument may well be correct, it is not worth considering because it is not relevant.

Refutations should always be moderate in tone and accurate in representing opposing arguments; otherwise, readers may feel that the writer has treated the opposition unfairly and as a result judge the author's own argument more harshly.

Rhetorical Questions are posed with no expectation of receiving an answer; they are merely structural devices for launching or furthering a discussion or for achieving emphasis (See Lawrence; Ehrenreich, "Men," par. 1.)

Sarcasm (See *Irony.*)

Satire, sometimes called "extended irony," is a literary form that brings wit and humor to the serious task of pointing out frailties or evils of human institutions. It has thrived in Western literature since the time of the ancient Greeks, and English literature of the eighteenth century was particularly noteworthy for the extent and quality of its satire. Broadly, two types are recognized: *Horatian satire,* which is gentle, smiling, and aims to correct by invoking laughter and sympathy, and *Juvenalian satire,* which is sharper and points with anger, contempt, and/or moral indignation to corruption and evil.

Sentimentality, also called *sentimentalism,* is an exaggerated show of emotion, whether intentional or caused by lack of restraint. An author can sentimentalize almost any situation, but the trap is most dangerous when writing of timeworn emotional symbols or scenes—e.g., a broken heart, mother love, a lonely death, the conversion of a sinner. However sincere the author may be, if readers are not fully oriented to the worth and uniqueness of the situation described, they may be either resentful or amused at any attempt to play on their emotions. Sentimentality is, of course, one of the chief characteristics of melodrama. (For examples of writing that, less adeptly handled, could easily have slipped into sentimentality, see Buczynski, Twain, Catton, Raybon, Staples, Curtin, Simpson, Gansberg.)

Simile (See *Figures of Speech.*)

Slang (See *Colloquial Expressions.*)

Specific and **General** terms, and the distinctions between the two, are similar to concrete and abstract terms (as discussed under their own heading), and for our purpose there is no real need to keep the two sets of categories separated. Whether *corporation* is thought of as "abstract" and *Ajax Motor Company* as "concrete," or whether they are assigned to "general" and "specific" categories, the principle is the same: in most writing, *Ajax Motor Company* is better.

But "specific" and "general" are relative terms. For instance, the word *apple* is more specific than *fruit* but less so than *Winesap*. And *fruit*, as general as it certainly is in one respect, is still more specific than *food*. Such relationships are shown more clearly in a series, progressing from general to specific: *food, fruit, apple, Winesap;* or *vehicle, automobile, Ford, Mustang.* Modifiers and verbs can also have degrees of specificity: *bright, red, scarlet;* or *moved, sped, careened.* It is not difficult to see the advantages to the reader—and, of course, to the writer who needs to communicate an idea clearly—in "the scarlet Mustang careened through the pass," instead of "the bright-colored vehicle moved through the pass."

Obviously, however, there are times when the general or the abstract term or statement is essential—e.g., "A balanced diet includes some fruit," or "There was no vehicle in sight." But the use of specific language whenever possible is one of the best ways to improve diction and thus clarity and forcefulness in writing.

(Another important way of strengthening general, abstract writing is, of course, to use examples or other illustrations. See Section 3.)

Style and **Tone** are so closely linked and so often even elements of each other that it is best to consider them together.

But there is a difference. Think of two young men, each with his girlfriend on separate moonlit dates, whispering in nearly identical tender and loving tones of voice. One young man says, "Your eyes, dearest, reflect a thousand sparkling candles of heaven," and the other says, "Them eyes of yours—in this light—they sure do turn me on." Their *tones* were the same; their *styles* considerably different.

The same distinction exists in writing. But, naturally, with more complex subjects than the effect of moonlight on a lover's eyes, there are more complications in separating the two qualities, even for the purpose of study.

The tone is determined by the *attitude* of writers toward their subject and toward their audience. Writers, too, may be tender and loving, but they may be indignant, solemn, playful, enthusiastic, belligerent, contemptuous—the list could be as long as a list of the many "tones of voice." (In fact, wide ranges of tone may be illustrated by essays in this book. Compare, for example, those of the two parts of Twain; Eiseley and Mitford; Viorst and Lynn; Staples and Ehrenreich.)

Style, on the other hand, expresses the author's individuality through choices of words (see *Diction*), sentence patterns (see *Syntax*), and selection and arrangement of details and basic materials. (All these elements of style are illustrated in the contrasting statements of the moonstruck lads.) These matters of style are partially prescribed, of course, by the adopted tone, but they are still bound to reflect the writer's personality and mood, education and general background.

(Some of the more distinctive styles—partially affected by and affecting tone—represented by selections in this book are those of Viorst, Wolfe, Buckley, White, Noda, Stone, Silko, Eiseley, Murphy, Hongo, Staples, Walker, and Rodriguez.)

Subjective Writing (See *Objective/Subjective.*)

Symbol refers to anything that although real itself also suggests something broader or more significant—not just in greater numbers, however. A person would not symbolize a group or even humankind itself, although a person might be typical or representative in one or more abstract qualities. On the most elementary level, even words are symbols—e.g., *bear* brings to mind the furry beast itself. But more important is that things, persons, or even acts may also be symbolic, if they invoke abstract concepts, values, or qualities apart from themselves or their own kind. Such symbols, in everyday life as well as in literature and the other arts, are generally classifiable according to three types, which, although terminology differs, we may label *natural, personal,* and *conventional.*

In a natural symbol, the symbolic meaning is inherent in the thing itself. The sunrise naturally suggests new beginnings to most people, an island is almost synonymous with isolation, a cannon automatically suggests war; hence these are natural symbols. It does not matter that some things, by their nature, can suggest more than one concept. Although a valley may symbolize security to one person and captivity to another, both meanings, contradictory as they might seem, are inherent, and in both respects the valley is a natural symbol.

The personal symbol, depending as it does on private experience or perception, is meaningless to others unless they are
told about it or allowed to see its significance in context (as in
literature). Although the color green may symbolize the outdoor life to the farm boy trapped in the gray city (in this respect
perhaps a natural symbol), it can also symbolize romance to the
young woman proposed to while wearing her green blouse, or
dismal poverty to the woman who grew up in a weathered
green shanty; neither of these meanings is suggested by something *inherent* in the color green, so they are personal symbols.
Anything at all could take on private symbolic meaning, even
the odor of marigolds or the sound of a lawnmower. The sunrise itself could mean utter despair, instead of fresh opportunities, to the man who has long despised his daily job and cannot
find another.

Conventional symbols usually started as personal symbols,
but continued usage in life or art permits them to be generally
recognized for their broader meanings, which depend on custom rather than any inherent quality—e.g., the olive branch for
peace, the flag for love of country, the cross for Christianity, the
raised fist for revolutionary power.

Symbols are used less in expository and argumentative
writing than in fiction and poetry, but a few authors represented
in this book have either referred to the subtle symbolism of others or made use of it in developing their own ideas. Eiseley says
that the old men clung to their seats as if they were symbols.

Syntax is a very broad term—too broad, perhaps, to be very useful—
referring to the arrangement of words in a sentence. Good syntax
implies the use not only of correct grammar but also of effective
patterns. These patterns depend on sentences with good unity,
coherence, and emphasis, on the use of subordination and parallel construction as appropriate, on economy, and on a consistent
and interesting point of view. A pleasing variety of sentence patterns is also important in achieving effective syntax.

Theme (See *Unity.*)

Thesis In an argumentative essay, the central theme is often referred
to as the thesis, and to make sure that readers recognize it, the
thesis is often summed up briefly in a *thesis statement.* In a very

important sense, the thesis is the center of an argument because the whole essay is designed to make the reader agree with it and, hence, with the author's opinion. (See *Unity.*)

Tone (See *Style/Tone.*)

Transition is the relating of one topic to the next, and smooth transition is an important aid to the coherence of a sentence, a paragraph, or an entire piece of writing. (See *Coherence.*)

The most effective coherence, of course, comes about naturally with sound development of ideas, one growing logically into the next—and that depends on sound organization. But sometimes beneficial even in this situation, particularly in going from one paragraph to the next, is the use of appropriate transitional devices.

Readers are apt to be sensitive creatures, easy to lose. (And, of course, the writers are the real losers since they are the ones who presumably have something they want to communicate.) If the readers get into a new paragraph and the territory seems familiar, chances are that they will continue. But if there are no identifying landmarks, they will often begin to feel uneasy and will either start worrying about their slow comprehension or take a dislike to the author and the subject matter. Either way, a communication block arises, and very likely the author will soon have fewer readers.

A good policy, then, unless the progression of ideas is exceptionally smooth and obvious, is to provide some kind of familiar identification early in the new paragraph, to keep the reader feeling at ease with the different ideas. The effect is subtle but important. These familiar landmarks or transitional devices are sometimes applied deliberately but more often come naturally, especially when the prospective reader is kept constantly in mind at the time of writing.

An equally important reason for using some kinds of transitional devices, however, is a logical one: while functioning as bridges between ideas, they also assist the basic organization by pointing out the *relationship* of the ideas—and thus contributing still further to readability.

Transitional devices useful for bridging paragraph changes (and, some of them, to improve transitional flow within paragraphs) may be roughly classified as follows:

1. *Providing an "echo"* from the preceding paragraph. This may be the repetition of a key phrase or word, or a pronoun referring back to such a word, or a casual reference to an idea. (See Lopate, last two paragraphs; Wolfe, especially from pars. 1 to 2 and 4 to 5; Mitford.) Such an echo cannot be superimposed on new ideas, but must, by careful planning, be made an organic part of them.

2. *Devising a whole sentence or paragraph* to bridge other important paragraphs or major divisions. (See Lynn, pars. 11, 20, and 21.)

3. *Using parallel structure* in an important sentence of one paragraph and the first sentence of the next. This is a subtle means of making the reader feel at ease in the new surroundings, but it is seldom used because it is much more limited in its potential than the other methods of transition. (See Lawrence, pars. 1 to 2.)

4. *Using standard transitional expressions,* most of which have the additional advantage of indicating relationship of ideas. Only a few of those available are classified below, but nearly all the selections in this book amply illustrate such transitional expressions:

Time—soon, immediately, afterward, later, meanwhile, after a while.

Place—nearby, here, beyond, opposite.

Result—as a result, therefore, thus, consequently, hence.

Comparison—likewise, similarly, in such a manner.

Contrast—however, nevertheless, still, but, yet, on the other hand, after all, otherwise.

Addition—also, too, and, and then, furthermore, moreover, finally, first, second, third.

Miscellaneous—for example, for instance, in fact, indeed, on the whole, in other words.

Trite (See *Clichés.*)

Unity in writing is the same as unity in anything else—in a picture, a musical arrangement, a campus organization—and that is a *one*-ness, in which all parts contribute to an overall effect.

Many elements of good writing contribute in varying degrees to the effect of unity. Some of these are properly designed introductions and closings; consistency in point of view, tone, and style; sometimes the recurring use of analogy or thread of symbolism; occasionally the natural time boundaries of an experience or event, as in the selections of Mitford, Simpson, Gansberg, Orwell, and Williams.

But in most expository and argumentative writing the only dependable unifying force is the *central theme,* which every sentence, every word, must somehow help to support. (The central theme is also called the *central idea* or the *thesis* when pertaining to the entire writing and is almost always called the *thesis* in argument. In an expository or argumentative paragraph it is the same as the *topic sentence,* which may be implied or, if stated, may be located anywhere in the paragraph, but is usually placed first.) As soon as anything appears that is not related to the central idea, there are *two* units instead of one. Hence unity is basic to all other virtues of good writing, even to coherence and emphasis, the other two organic essentials. (See *Coherence; Emphasis.*)

An example of unity may be found in a single river system (for a practical use of analogy), with all its tributaries, big or little, meandering or straight, flowing into the main stream and making it bigger—or at least flowing into another tributary that finds its way to the main stream. This is *one* river system, an example of unity. Now picture another stream nearby that does not empty into the river but goes off in some other direction. There are now two systems, not one, and there is no longer unity.

It is the same way with writing. The central theme is the main river, flowing along from the first capital letter to the last period. Every drop of information or evidence must find its way into this theme-river, or it is not a part of the system. It matters not even slightly if the water is good, the idea-stream perhaps deeper and finer than any of the others: if it is not a tributary, it has no business pretending to be relevant to *this* theme of writing.

And that is why most students are required to state their central idea or thesis, usually in solid sentence form, before even starting to organize their ideas. If the writer can use only tributaries, it is very important to know from the start just what the river is.